SEÁN
LEMASS

THE ENIGMATIC PATRIOT

SEÁN LEMASS

THE ENIGMATIC PATRIOT

JOHN HORGAN

Gill & Macmillan

Gill & Macmillan Ltd
Goldenbridge
Dublin 8
with associated companies throughout the world
www.gillmacmillan.ie

First published in paperback 1999
© John Horgan 1997
0 7171 2939 X
Index compiled by Helen Litton
Design and print origination by Carole Lynch
Printed by ColourBooks Ltd, Dublin

This book is typeset in 11/13 pt Bembo

A catalogue record for this book is available from
the British Library.

1 3 5 4 2

For my children

Contents

List of Illustrations

Preface

Seán Lemass's life spanned almost three-quarters of this century, during which Ireland — or at least a substantial part of it — went from being a political and administrative unit within the United Kingdom to becoming a fully independent state. The paradox of patriotism, as Seán Lemass experienced it, and influenced it, during this period is that the same generation that achieved political and economic independence had to redefine patriotism itself. The attractiveness of Lemass for the biographer is partly this, that patriotism was one of his core values, and, even as he changed its content and articulated a new interpretation of what it meant in the contemporary world, he continued to refer to it in a way that some would today find old-fashioned. At the same time he was a man who lived and worked on the cusp of the new, forever prodding and chivvying his own followers, rather than following meekly in their wake. Coming after de Valera posed its own set of problems, but he did not make the mistake of trying to fill his predecessor's shoes: he was always his own man. And for a generation growing up in the nineteen-sixties, as I did, he also became — party allegiances notwithstanding — very much a symbol of a future that would be markedly different from our past.

Personal paths intersect in often curious ways, and this is why, as someone born four decades after Seán Lemass, I found myself sharing a committee (the Council of the Catholic Communications Institute of Ireland) with him in the late sixties. He was courtesy itself, and even though he rarely contributed to discussion, an occasional lift of his eyebrow bespoke a keen and exceptionally well-informed interest in the internal politics of that body. He would have been amused at the thought that the young trouble-maker who sat beside him then would have been reading his private governmental correspondence thirty years later. Part 1 of the book is a linear narrative; part 2 treats the Taoiseach years in a more appropriately thematic framework.

The genesis of this book was the discovery that Fergal Tobin of Gill & Macmillan shared my interest in Lemass, and he has done more than anyone else to bring it to completion across a sea of intervening vicissitudes. I owe a particular debt of gratitude also to Seán Lemass's family, in particular to his three daughters, Maureen Haughey, Peggy O'Brien, and Sheila O'Connor. All of them made me welcome in their homes in a special way that owes as much to the warmth and open-heartedness of their mother as it does to the unfailing courtesy and generosity of their father. Their husbands — Charles J. Haughey, Comdt Jack O'Brien, and John O'Connor — are also owed a debt of thanks. Sheila O'Connor's untimely death in March 1997 cruelly deprived her extended family of her marvellous personality, and it is a matter of particular regret that she did not live to see a book to which she contributed so much.

Mrs Doris Skinner, widow of the late Liam Skinner, who wrote an unpublished biography of Seán Lemass in 1961, was kind enough to allow me to see and quote from his extensive work and to use some of the exceptionally valuable photographs that he had assembled for use in that unfinished enterprise.

Of the published material about Lemass, particular mention must also be made of Brian Farrell's original biography; there were plenty of occasions when, hacking my way through the archival undergrowth, I found that Brian had been there before me, and I freely acknowledge my debt. I have been immensely helped also by the generosity of a number of fellow-academics, not least Professor J. J. Lee of University College, Cork, to whom part of this work was originally submitted as a doctoral study. Their willingness to share the fruits of their own research and to devote scarce time to reading and commenting on drafts has been of extraordinary assistance. Invaluable help was also supplied by Colm Barnes, who had done considerable work on a projected biography of Seán Lemass and who generously made all his material, including interviews with some of Lemass's contemporaries, available to me.

In the National Archives I found the Director, Dr David Craig, and his staff, particularly Tom Quinlan and Caitríona Crowe, essential guides through the exciting raw material in their care. In the Oireachtas Library the Director, Máire Corcoran, and Séamus Haughey helped me to trace innumerable references and to fill the gaps in my sometimes ragged notes. In both institutions special thanks are due to the paper-keepers, who put up with requests for more and more boxes of papers and bound volumes of newspapers with unfailing good humour, even as deadlines loomed. The access granted by the general secretary of Fianna Fáil, Pat Farrell, to that party's archives was invaluable, as was the expert help of his archivist colleague, Philip Hannon.

Above and beyond all this I owe an incalculable debt to my family, and in particular to my wife, Mary Jones, who not only preceded me into the byways of academic research and was generous with her own advice and encouragement but provided a support, particularly during the bouts of monomania that marked the final stages of the project, without which it would never have been completed.

Part 1

1

The Boy Soldier
1899–1916

'What the devil signifies right when your honour is concerned?'[1]

In the summer of 1915 a gang of boys set to work with rare energy and enthusiasm on a project on the beach at Skerries, County Dublin. Gathering some corrugated iron from a building site, they constructed a makeshift stockade. On top of the stockade they placed a Tricolour. Not far away — close enough to be in range — was a similar stockade, surmounted by a Union Jack. From behind these defences two equally determined gangs of boys exchanged volleys of stones, which made an altogether satisfying sound as they bounced off the corrugated iron.

The boys behind the Union Jack were Protestant orphans from an institution in the city, out in Skerries for the holidays. The boys behind the Tricolour were led by Noel and Seán Lemass, on holidays from their comfortable home in Capel Street.[1]

Seán Lemass had turned sixteen and had just completed his Intermediate Certificate examination at the O'Connell Schools, but he was hardly a mere schoolboy. He had been a member of the Irish Volunteers for about six months — lying about his age to secure enrolment — and there was an edge to this boisterous play that was the product of a historical process that had been gathering in intensity for more than three decades and that was also a portent of things to come. Within twelve months the rising tide of nationalism would leave a large part of Dublin, and Britain's Irish policy with it, in smoking ruins. That tide was itself the result of gravitational forces that stretched back, in the immediate sense, for a quarter of a century before Seán Lemass's birth and had their deeper origins in centuries of Irish history.

During the final three decades of the previous century, prompted in part by electoral reform and in part by a growing national self-awareness, the Irish members at Westminster had been increasingly expressing a separate identity and political consciousness. In 1873 they adopted the filibuster, which allowed them, despite their numerical insignificance, to distort and obstruct the proceedings of the House of Commons. By 1880 Parnell was in the ascendant, and by 1885 he had engineered a position in which the Liberals had undergone a Pauline conversion to the necessity for Home Rule. This was accentuated when, after the December 1885 election, the Irish MPs held the balance of power at Westminster.

The advent of Home Rule was therefore confidently expected in 1886. It failed to materialise, not only in that year but in any year. In 1893 Gladstone secured the agreement of the House of Commons to the second Home Rule Bill, but it was killed in the House of Lords. Two years later the Tories came to power, and the Irish members at Westminster lost the balance of power that they had successfully used to lever the Liberals into concessions. The Tories ruled for a decade; when the Liberals returned in 1906 they had enough seats to allow them to ignore the importunings of the Irish members, and the Irish Party did not hold the balance of power again until 1910.

If the Westminster log-jam could not be broken, there were at least eddies further upstream. The Local Government Act, 1898, provided, in effect for the first time, a political structure in the shape of elected county councils that gave nationalist politics a local habitation and a name. These councils were hardly models of public administration, but they helped to shape and give a purpose to nationalist political opinion in ways that had not been possible earlier. In a specifically urban context the foundation of the Irish Trades Union Congress in 1894 gave a focus to organised labour, particularly craft labour, that was to have its own political significance, and by 1910 it had recruited about seventy thousand workers.[2] And in 1905 the Sinn Féin movement was founded by Arthur Griffith.

In the period between 1895 and 1910, nonetheless, the so-called 'Irish question' had lost, at least temporarily, its power to inflame the English body politic. In 1899, when Seán Lemass was born, the Dublin newspapers gave little indication of the nature or extent of the growth of national feeling that was lapping closer to the foundations of this still largely self-satisfied world, although local authorities were sending in their subscriptions to the United Ireland League.[3] On the day of Lemass's birth a new branch of that organisation was in the process of being established by Michael Davitt at Ballyneety, County Limerick.[4] In time the continuing Fenian tradition in the shape of the Irish Republican Brotherhood would make such apparently decorous forms of protest largely redundant.

For the present, however, the political scene was generally quiescent, at least on the surface. In Dublin on that day it was business as usual. The columns of the *Freeman's Journal* were preoccupied with the proceedings of the Parliament at Westminster and the 'grave situation' in the Transvaal. The Public Health Committee for Dublin announced that the death rate in the city for the previous month had been 25.8 per cent, an increase on the figure for May. Sir Thomas Lipton's yacht, *Shamrock,* was taking the water against the American contender, *Columbia,* and a 250 lb sturgeon caught off the mouth of the Shannon was on display at the South City Market. The Dublin money market, such as it was, was quiet: consols were steady, the banks good, Guinness better. The Bank of Ireland announced a 12 per cent dividend (the *Freeman* itself managed a respectable interim 7 per cent), and terms were agreed in a boundary dispute between the city and Dublin County Council.

The developing political process was one the Lemass family had been associated with for a number of years. The family name is not Irish: it is probably a corruption of Le Maistre, and the family's oral history suggests that they were of Huguenot extraction and arrived in Ireland, by way of Scotland, in about 1827.[5] Seán Lemass himself once observed that the only unrelated person with the same surname that he met turned out to be a Pole who had changed his name.[6] One of his relations — as so often happened in the turbulent first decades of the century — was another Dublin man who was on the other side of the political divide and ended his career as a British colonial judge in Tangier. But Lemass was relatively uninterested in genealogy. After he became Taoiseach one researcher wrote to him to ask whether he would be interested in purchasing the results of his enquiries into the Lemass family. Lemass declined: he could not think of 'any purpose to which I could put the results of your researches.'[7]

The Lemasses had been firmly established in Dublin's north inner city — a much more salubrious neighbourhood then than it later became — for half a century or more. A Joseph Lemass kept a Singing Hall at 126–7 Capel Street up to the end of 1869, and ten years later another Lemass, first name unknown, was secretary of the Mechanics' Institute at 27 Lower Abbey Street, which had been used since 1848 for nationalist meetings and where Terence Bellew MacManus, the 1848 revolutionary, had lain in state in November 1861.[8] The Lemasses generally were active in nationalist enterprises of various kinds. William Lemass of 7 Grattan Bridge, a hatter, advertised regularly in the eighteen-eighties in the *Irishman.*

John Lemass, the future Taoiseach's grandfather, was a native of Armagh who had moved to Dublin, where he became a member of the Land League. Like William Lemass, he was a hatter and outfitter. When the league was suppressed he joined its successor, the Irish National League, becoming secretary for the Arran Quay ward. He was elected to Dublin City Council for this ward in 1885 and became part of the nationalist majority on that body. Up to 1835 the majority of members had been unionists; after the 1840 reform there was a gradual transfer of power to the Catholic middle class, but even then both the franchise and the eligibility for office were severely restricted. Candidates could not offer themselves for election unless they were worth at least £1,000 and occupied a house with a rateable valuation of £25. In 1898 there were fewer than 8,000 electors in the city, out of a population of 245,000.[9]

Lemass's grandfather formed part of the majority on the council that voted in 1885 to refuse a 'loyal address' to the Prince of Wales on the occasion of his visit to Dublin. This was no mere political gesture, as the atmosphere was becoming increasingly heated. Two years later, after the lord mayor, T. D. Sullivan, had been imprisoned for publishing the proceedings of the National League in the *Nation,* the council voted him the freedom of the city while he was still in custody.[10]

Parnell's death and the gradually changing external political environment, however, acted to soften these robust oppositional tactics. A majority on the city council voted to receive Queen Victoria in 1901, and in 1903 Lemass and his wife were among those presented in Dublin Castle to the new monarch, Edward VII. This development indicated less a change of political attitudes on the part of John Lemass than a change in political expectations: Edward was widely rumoured to favour some form of evolution in the constitutional relationship between Ireland and England, and nationalist policy at the time was to attend such functions in order to encourage him in this.

The business prospered, and John T. Lemass, son of the old nationalist, built it up further, preserving the past and building on it for the future in a careful, Edwardian way. In some ways he was a contrast to his own father — less politically involved, and quieter in manner. He was proud of the medals he won at a number of international exhibitions. When the shop was finally sold, in 1980, the effects that were auctioned included the wooden block used by the hatter as the mould for a hat made for Buck Whaley, the nineteenth-century Dublin rake.[11] The shop and family home was in Capel Street, where John T. Lemass owned number 3 and rented at least part of number 2. Number 2 is now, by a quirk of history, owned by the Cosgrave family and used as the offices of the family law firm.

In 1896 John T. Lemass married. His wife, Frances Phelan, was the daughter of a Kilkenny horticulturist who came to Dublin to work at the Botanic Gardens and also managed a florist's shop at 11 Wicklow Street. While her husband was, if anything, the strong, silent type, she was a tall, striking woman of enormous warmth of character, voluble and outgoing, a woman with 'an opinion on everything.'[12] She had strong political views, considerably more nationalist than her husband: one of her granddaughters described her affectionately as a 'Fenian'. She was the centrepiece of a lively, good-natured, closely knit and welcoming household.

The future Taoiseach, their second child, was born in the early hours of 15 July 1899.[13] Mrs Lemass, her husband and their first child, Noel, then almost eighteen months old, had moved from the probably slightly fetid atmosphere of quayside city life in Capel Street to Ballybrack for the summer and the confinement. They had rented Norwood Cottage, a pretty, whitewashed nineteenth-century lodge belonging to a local dairy farmer named Carter. It was not so small that it did not also have room for Mrs Lemass's nurse, a Holles Street midwife, Sarah Murphy, who had been brought along to ensure that everything would go smoothly. The infant was christened John Francis Lemass in the church of St Alphonsus and Columba on 21 July; his aunt Alicia Phelan was his only godparent. Subsequently he was dedicated to the Holy Family in a nearby convent.[14]

Capel Street was now a type of inner-city frontier. A century earlier the street had been close to the social centre of the capital and was described by a contemporary novelist as 'the fashionable promenade of Dublin.'[15] By 1909 this description was castigated as 'now laughable.'[16] Not only had the social centre of gravity crossed the river but the growth of Dublin during the Famine years and the conversion of so many of the formerly grand houses into tenements to accommodate the toiling masses of urban poor had created sharp demarcation lines between poverty and respectability. Inner-city blight was a reality; the city council, in thrall to powerful vested interests — notably publicans — rejected revaluation (which would have dramatically improved its tax base), while the prosperous suburbs of Pembroke and Rathmines developed and maintained a degree of local autonomy, which enabled them to turn their backs on their less prosperous neighbours.[17]

Capel Street itself now coincided almost exactly with one of these invisible frontiers. To the east lay the centres of business and commerce and the principal thoroughfares, although the view was often marred by the practice of hanging large letters spelling out public health messages (for example to epileptics) below the Wellington (Metal) Bridge.[18] To the west lay 'pockets of blight rivalling in frightfulness the worst slums of the Liberties,' as well as one of the city's two workhouses.[19] The mean life expectancy for a child born at the turn of the century was only forty-nine years.[20] TB, known by some English commentators as 'the Irish disease',[21] was rampant; Seán Lemass's sister Alice, a doctor, who may have contracted it from her work among the poor of Dublin, died from it in the early nineteen-forties.

Seán's younger brother, Patrick, more generally known as 'Pebby', was frail and died in his teens, apparently from asthma. There were seven children in all, born between 1897 and 1911: Alice, Noel, John (Seán), Claire, Mary Frances, Patrick, and Frank.

For all that it was touched by the contagion that was then rife in the city, the Lemass household was also a classically Edwardian ménage, socially if not politically. Sunday nights at 2 Capel Street were frequently the occasion for soirées reminiscent of a scene from an early Joyce story, as visitors arrived with musical instruments (there was already a piano in the house) for an evening of music and singing. The older Lemass boys listening in bed in their room on the top floor were presumably neither seen nor heard.[22] The relationship between father and sons was nonetheless a strong one. John T. Lemass took his boys on cycling holidays with him; many years later, when he was being made an honorary freeman of Sligo, Seán Lemass noted that this was one of the towns they had visited on their travels.[23]

Both Lemass parents were long-lived: John T. Lemass died aged seventy-nine in 1947, and his widow, known to everyone in the family as Granny Lemass, died in 1961, aged eighty-nine. She was as dominant a presence after her husband's death as she had been before it. Sometimes intimidating in her widow's weeds, she could still show a flash of spirit on occasion. One of her granddaughters still remembers the sense almost of shock when she was persuaded out on the floor for an impromptu dance at a house party to celebrate the granddaughter's engagement.[24]

The young John Lemass followed his older brother into the national school run by the Sisters of the Holy Faith at Haddington Road, where he was a studious child. Within the family his name rapidly became Jack and remained so for the rest of his life, even in the decades after 1916, when he himself changed it to Seán. For at least one of his teachers in Haddington Road, however, nothing changed. A nun who was plainly devoted to him, she followed his career with evident approbation for many years and always addressed him as 'John' when she wrote to him in the Department of Industry and Commerce, right up to the nineteen-forties.[25]

When he was almost nine and Noel almost eleven they transferred together to the O'Connell Schools in North Richmond Street, not far from the family home, where they were both admitted on 4 May 1908. His intellectual ability was not in doubt, and mathematics and history were two particular areas of aptitude. Problem-solving appealed to him in mathematics, but what is interesting about his involvement in history is that, although the Intermediate Certificate syllabus at that time ended for all effective purposes in 1660, he became particularly interested in the period from Elizabeth to the Georges.[26] It is not difficult to discern the influence of his teachers. Many years later he made his debt to them explicit when he specifically praised the Christian Brothers for their 'great work in sustaining and strengthening the spirit of Irish nationalism during a period when the youth of Ireland might have been easily induced to forgo such a spirit.'[27]

Notwithstanding his interest in these two critically important subjects, the countervailing attractions of a city that was seething with national sentiment and political controversy were at times difficult to resist. He was involved in the publication of a school magazine, in one issue of which in 1914 he brashly described a classmate and Capel Street neighbour, Jimmy O'Dea, as his intellectual inferior.[28] Among the other pupils in 1915 were Paddy Fanning, who was to become a friend of long standing; Dicky Gogan, another 1916 man and later Fianna Fáil TD; W. J. Coyne, later chief censor during the Second World War; and J. P. Beddy, who was to become head of the Industrial Development Authority when that body was set up by the first inter-party Government, despite Lemass's fierce initial opposition.

The school register records that he was a rapid learner, jumping from fourth to seventh standard between 1912 and 1913. This decision was obviously related to his examination results. The young Lemass sat twice for the Junior Grade (Intermediate) examination, in 1914 and 1915. He signed the examination entrance form as John Francis Lemass (twice misspelling his middle name as 'Frances' — his mother's name — and then correcting it). At his second attempt he achieved a first-class honours exhibition, with honours in arithmetic, history, geometry, experimental science, and French, and passes in English, Latin, and Irish. On the basis of his 1915 results he won a first-class exhibition in the mathematical group of subjects, worth £15. Three of his classmates did the same, affording the school a remarkable 40 per cent of the ten first-class exhibitions in the junior grade awarded in the country as a whole.[29]

He made his First Communion on 8 December 1909 but — unlike his brother Noel — appears not to have been confirmed: there is simply a succession of question marks in the space provided. Noel was confirmed on 9 March 1909 in the Pro-Cathedral in Marlborough Street at the age of twelve, which would indicate that Seán should have been confirmed in 1911, but this evidently did not happen. It may have happened somewhere else: when he married, the celebrant would have had to be satisfied that he had been both baptised and confirmed.

There are no special marks in the column in the school records headed *Character and conduct,* but this column seems to have been used exclusively for noting which boys won university scholarships. The register records the date of his leaving the school as 30 June 1915, but this has been crossed out in a later hand and *19 May 1916* substituted, together with the note in the same hand *Died 11.5.71, RIP.* The original date leaves an unexplained gap between then and Easter 1916: the effect of the alteration would be to suggest that he was still a registered pupil at the time of the Rising, but this act of retrospective *pietas* hardly seems necessary.

John T. Lemass had in the meantime broken the long-standing tradition of holidays in Killiney and had inaugurated a new one by taking a red-brick house beside the Pavilion cinema in Skerries for some weeks each summer. It was a tradition maintained by Seán Lemass for many years, until his own children left home; indeed he probably had a longer association with Skerries than with any other place. The venue also had a more political significance. His father had struck up an acquaintance with a permanent resident of the town, the journalist D. P. Moran, proprietor and editor of the *Leader,* a weekly newspaper that espoused the Irish-Ireland cause with a passionate if sometimes farouche dedication to the

doctrines of economic self-sufficiency in general and industrial development in particular.

Moran was a strong-minded and independent journalist who managed
to combine a dedication to Irish with the capacity to alienate many in the
language movement (often for entirely justifiable reasons). He was resolutely
opposed to the Irish Party and to the memory of Daniel O'Connell, whom
he regarded as its progenitor. The editorial in the first issue of the *Leader,*
published the year after Seán Lemass's birth, put it fairly and squarely: the
Irish nation meant a

> self-governing land, living, moving and having its own being in its own
> language, self-reliant, intellectually as well as politically independent,
> initiating its own reforms, developing its own manners and customs,
> creating its own literature out of its own distinctive consciousness,
> working to their fullest capacity the material resources of the country,
> inventing, criticizing, attempting, doing.[30]

This might have been a blueprint for the Lemass era, though that era was
still some years away. Certainly it evoked a strong chord in the nationalist
Lemass household, and the acquaintance between the two older men had an
economic as well as a personal basis. John T. advertised regularly in Moran's
paper.[31] As a contemporary and admirer of Moran's put it, 'the star of Irish
Ireland, when it first shone forth in our sky, was, and still is, a five-pointed
one: language, industries, music, dancing and games.'[32] For the Lemasses,
father and son, the industrial segment outshone all the rest.

Shortly after completing his Intermediate for the second time, Seán
became a student at Rosse College, which had been established in
St Stephen's Green in 1902 and had already achieved a substantial reputation
for providing vocational courses in areas such as law and accountancy, as
well as other commercial subjects. Its students would at that period have
included young university graduates as well as school-leavers.

Events, however, were moving at a pace that would shortly sever the
young Lemass's connection with the world of full-time education. In 1911
the Fenians Thomas Clarke, Seán Mac Diarmada and Bulmer Hobson
succeeded in taking over the moribund IRB, and by late 1913 their representatives had successfully secured key positions in the Volunteers. In 1914 the
Howth gun-running, and the fatalities that occurred when British
soldiers opened fire on a jeering crowd at Bachelor's Walk, prompted a
massive flow of new members to the Volunteers' ranks.

The Volunteers split when the leader of the Irish Party, John Redmond,
advocated support for the war. This reduced them to about ten thousand;
the remainder followed Redmond into the Irish National Volunteers and
were not to be associated with militant separatism thereafter. The Irish
Volunteers, however, became increasingly infiltrated by the secret IRB

and continued to attract the more nationally minded of the country's young men.

Economic and social conditions were also contributing to the rise of militancy. Unemployment in Dublin had been relatively stable after a spurt in the early eighteen-eighties, and the condition of the working class had to some extent improved during the nineties. But it began to grow rapidly again from 1904, and from 1907 onwards every year saw an increase in hardship.[33] The pressure on an already inadequate housing stock increased. By 1909 there were forty thousand people in the Pro-Cathedral parish, just across O'Connell Street from the Lemass household. In 1913 two tenement houses in North King Street, only a few hundred yards in the other direction, collapsed with the loss of thirteen lives.[34] In the same year the lock-out organised by the Dublin employers against the Irish Transport and General Workers' Union heightened tension in the capital.

In 1914 Home Rule had finally reached the British statute book, but it was immediately suspended indefinitely. The contrast with the Conscription Act, which was introduced, debated and passed in two weeks, was not lost on Irish opinion, which in some sectors was hardening perceptibly. One of the employees in the Lemass shop had in any case been urging Seán for some time to join the Volunteers, and when he demurred because of his age he was assured that he could pass muster because of his mature looks.[35] In January 1915, at the age of fifteen-and-a-half, he joined A Company of the 3rd Battalion of the Dublin City Regiment, together with his older brother, Noel. The battalion adjutant was Éamon de Valera, and Lemass was appointed de Valera's personal aide,[36] an accident of history that created a political and personal bond that, although tenuous at first, was to last for over half a century.

The two brothers had somewhat different temperaments, Noel's more carefree and happy-go-lucky, Seán's more focused and dedicated.[37] In the ensuing months, however, the seriousness of the enterprise they were engaged in impressed itself equally on both. Seán in particular applied himself to the part-time training with a sense of rigour and internal discipline that marked many aspects of his later career, and he was regarded as one of the most zealous Volunteers in the company. He was also observant. Pearse's personality made a particular impact on him, not least because he himself was at the time, as he later remarked, 'at a most impressionable age.'[38] Significantly, he also had a considerable regard for Connolly, 'because he was attempting to do what others hadn't done — to translate this emotional desire for freedom into a practical social policy.'[39] At that time, he was to explain later, 'even as a young fellow, I always had in my own mind the understanding that there was a great deal yet to be done. And in the various opportunities I had for studying, it was works which had a bearing on this problem that I found the most interesting.'[40]

John T. Lemass had been a stalwart supporter of the Irish Party who 'trusted John Redmond beyond argument, and indeed resented any questioning of his leadership.'[41] Evidently even this conviction was now weakening, for, according to Seán Lemass himself, their parents had approved of their action in joining the Volunteers,[42] though they had managed to arrange matters so that if there was an insurrection the two boys would not be mobilised.[43] An insurrection had in fact become increasingly likely. The IRB saw the war as a unique opportunity for action and had at least an arguable case for assuming that a rising, with the Howth weapons and those expected on the *Aud* by Easter, would have a reasonable chance of success. There were only about six thousand British troops and ten thousand armed police in Ireland at the time, compared with an estimated eighteen thousand Volunteers. The capture of the *Aud,* however, led to the last-minute cancellation of the manoeuvres planned for Easter Sunday, 23 April, which the IRB had planned to hijack and use as a vehicle for armed insurrection against British rule.

When the countermanding order was given by Eoin MacNeill, once he had heard of the plot, there was considerable confusion and dismay. By the morning of the following day the situation was still unclear, and the two Lemass boys, with their Capel Street friends Jimmy and Ken O'Dea, set off on an expedition to the Dublin Mountains.[44] They took the tram to Rathfarnham and walked from there to Glencree. On their way home, at about five o'clock, still some distance from Rathfarnham, they met Professor MacNeill and two of his sons on bicycles, riding towards the mountains. Noel and Seán spoke to the MacNeill boys, whom they knew slightly, and learned that the planned rising had in fact broken out. MacNeill himself was 'agitated and depressed' — a moderate enough response in all the circumstances — and made no secret of his belief that it was the end of everything he had been working for. For his young listeners, it was more of a beginning.[45]

The rising had resulted in the cancellation of most public transport, so Noel and Seán had to finish their journey home from Rathfarnham on foot. The only Volunteer post they passed on the way was in Jacob's factory in Bishop Street, but they could not establish contact with the garrison and so went home.

They got up early the next morning and left the house without telling their parents, determined to join the action. They tried the Four Courts first but were told there that A Company — de Valera's — was in Boland's Mills in Grand Canal Street. On their way across the city they first tried their luck at the GPO, where a Volunteer friend on sentry duty let them in, and they became part of the garrison. Noel Lemass was sent to another building across the street; Seán was equipped with a shotgun[46] and sent with others to the roof, where an arsenal of crude bombs with slow-burning fuses had been prepared in anticipation of an onslaught by British troops. He was to stay there for two days, taking the odd pot-shot but without ever having to hurl his bombs, or knowing whether he had hit anyone or not,[47] until they were ordered down into the building.

By Friday afternoon the GPO was in flames. Lemass was sent up to the roof to retrieve the Tricolour, but as soon as he reached the parapet British soldiers opened fire, and he beat a prudent retreat. At that stage a combined evacuation and offensive operation began, with Lemass one of a party under Oscar Traynor tunnelling through the houses along one side of Moore Street to get themselves into position to attack a British barricade at the end of the street. It was dangerous and dirty work. In one room the tunnelling party, covered by now in brick dust and plaster, happened across a terrified young woman and her children huddled in a corner, in another an old man astray in his wits. In a room above Hanlon's, the fish shop, they were confronted by a dog; Traynor patted it, and it decided not to bark.[48]

The offensive part of the operation was to involve a bayonet charge. Lemass wryly told an acquaintance many years later that when the rumour of this spread through the garrison 'there were bayonets everywhere.'[49] The less prudent, more impetuous Lemass not only exchanged his shotgun for a Martini rifle but also equipped himself with one of the discarded bayonets.[50] While waiting for obstacles to be removed, however, he fell asleep on a stairway. When he woke up it was to hear Seán Mac Diarmada announce that a decision had been taken to surrender. With the others he marched out into Moore Street, through Henry Street, and into O'Connell Street, where they surrendered their arms. They spent their first night in captivity in the open, in the gardens around the Rotunda. The next morning they were marched to Richmond Barracks in Inchicore.

There was little elation or even sense of achievement in this first, temporary prison for Lemass and his comrades. Most of them felt they were going to be shot and were fairly depressed.[51] Lemass was in a room crowded with about fifty men, including Thomas Ashe and Willie Pearse. At one point Ashe asked Lemass whether he was related to P. E. Lemass, the then secretary of the Board of Education, and was astounded to hear that the civil servant was Lemass's uncle. 'There are two types in the family' was Lemass's typically laconic explanation.[52]

The mass executions never materialised, but the deportations did, except for a handful of those involved. Lemass was one of the lucky ones, picked out by a DMP policeman who knew the family and who suggested to the British officer responsible for planning the deportation process that the lad was only a 'nipper' and should be sent home. 'He was old enough to handle a rifle,' the officer retorted, but he relented; Lemass was released.[53] He was not alone: the DMP records indicate that 749 of the 1,783 arrested were released without internment or trial.[54] He was, however, in a rare category in one respect, being one of only six students recorded by the *Irish Times* as having been among the 718 rank-and-file members of the Volunteers arrested immediately after the Rising.[55]

When he went back to Capel Street, it was with a certain sense of trepidation.

> I returned home after the Rising on a Saturday night — alone, because my brother who had been wounded in the fighting was still in hospital — wondering what family arguments our participation in it might involve, but on the following Sunday morning my father entered my bedroom with a large celluloid tri-colour button in the lapel of his coat. At first I thought this to be a demonstration of solidarity with his sons and perhaps an act of defiance of those of his own friends who were finding fault with us, but in the days following I found out how deeply he had been moved and how much the change in him reflected the change which had taken place amongst the Irish people as a whole. It was then I understood that the Easter Rising was not just an isolated incident in Irish history, but something much more profound.[56]

His parents were delighted that he had survived and had been released; in a sense, they were also proud. Like many Dubliners, however, Lemass senior was fairly sure that the rising had been an abject failure, and he made arrangements for his son's immediate return to Rosse College. Lemass was deeply chagrined at this decision, assuming that in the light of what had happened he would be given a large measure of control over his own destiny, and resumed his studies with bad grace.[57] His father urged him to complete his matriculation, which would have entitled him to study for the Bar, but this was a project that did not survive, undermined as it was by the increasing political temperature of the times and by Lemass's own somewhat jaundiced view of lawyers.[58] In later years he delighted in taking verbal aim at the profession.

One way or another his legal training, and his formal education in general, was rapidly drawing to a close. He had arrived, still a neophyte but battle-hardened, at man's estate.

During the winter of 1916/17 Lemass was frequently involved in skirmishes of one kind or another with the authorities and on one occasion was fired on by British soldiers when tearing down a recruiting poster. Although not yet at this stage a member of Sinn Féin,[59] he had already joined a makeshift organisation set up by Colonel Maurice Moore, which had virtually useless rifles — replacement ammunition was almost impossible to get — but was a useful training ground. In January 1917 he took his dud rifle and joined C Company of the 2nd Battalion, which had just been reorganised. In the climate of the time, with conscription threatened, people were flocking to the Volunteers, and adherents with Lemass's qualifications were especially welcome.[60] His father, accepting the inevitable, terminated Seán's increasingly external association with Rosse College and repatriated him to Capel Street to work in the family business, largely on the accounts. One young man who went into the shop to buy a hat at around that time remembered him as 'a young man in a stiff white collar, with a very much "take it or leave it" attitude.' The same customer was to become Lemass's private secretary in the Department of Industry and Commerce in 1944.[61]

For all that his mind was full of revolution and politics, figures maintained their early fascination for him. Going through the accounts, he noticed one particular trend that he brought to the attention of his father. The Lemass establishment, like many of its kind, frequently gave hats out on approval for a day or so. Young Seán noticed, however, that the return of unwanted hats, far from occurring randomly, appeared to occur in clusters. Equally significantly, he discovered that these cycles seemed to coincide with social events, particularly weddings. Putting two and two together, he scanned the newspapers for information about coming social events and put an instruction in the shop's diary that hats were not to be lent out on approval around these dates.[62] He was plainly absorbing the commercial realities of life at some speed, in spite of the fact that his mind was frequently elsewhere; this was the only commercial experience he was to have until he left ministerial office for the first time in 1948.

By this time young Lemass was already second lieutenant of his company, rapidly earning promotion to first lieutenant and enhanced responsibilities as the officer responsible for training and for arms procurement.[63] On occasion he would have his section out drilling all night in north Dublin, unable to return home because of the curfew. One of his tasks was to assure the spouses of his Volunteers that they had not been out on the tiles and sleeping off their over-indulgence in ditches.[64] Lemass was probably also a member of the Volunteer colour party that guarded Thomas Ashe's body during its lying in state in City Hall in 1918.[65] Increasingly, his work in the shop was taking second place to his military activities.

It was still, however, to all intents and purposes a phoney war. It was not until after the December 1918 election and the proclamation of the Republic by the Dáil on 21 January 1919 that open hostilities were seriously threatened. The British forces enjoyed harassing the parades of the Volunteers, who were armed only with hurleys, and Volunteer frustration rapidly increased. Later in 1919 Lemass was sent to the Dublin Brigade Convention charged with proposing a resolution to the effect that the Volunteers should no longer be 'cattle drovers, carrying sticks.'[66] When the convention failed to discuss this resolution Lemass's company threatened to resign *en masse,* and only the intervention of Liam Lynch and a change in headquarters policy on carrying arms at parades defused the situation.

As the tempo of the War of Independence quickened, Lemass began the intensive training of his men in street-fighting tactics. He was already thinking innovatively, not just on tactics but on organisation. Within the company he did not confine operations to a hard core of specially chosen Volunteers but gave them all a chance of involvement by dividing them into two equal groups, which alternated on different operations.[67] Company activities concentrated at first on raids for arms but then developed into other areas — including the tracking down and apprehension of a gang of robbers and the recovery of £500 worth of stolen jewellery, an operation personally commanded by Lemass.[68]

Some idea of his level of energy at the time can be gathered from the verve with which he threw himself into social and cultural as well as military and commercial activities. With Jimmy O'Dea he was a member of the Kilronan Players, an amateur dramatic society affiliated to the Irish Dramatic Union. Lemass trod the boards as a parish priest in the play *Maurice Hart* at the Father Mathew Hall and possibly in other productions as well.[69] The closest he came to fame, however, was in January 1920, when the group benefited from the Abbey's policy of allowing amateur groups to use the theatre on Sunday, the professional actors' night off. The play was Richard Brinsley Sheridan's *The Rivals*. O'Dea was Bob Acres, and Lemass was Sir Lucius O'Trigger. O'Trigger is an impoverished gallant who has lost his mansion, Blunderbuss Hall. He belongs to a clan of whom every male 'had killed his man,'[70] and he fights a duel with a brace of pistols which he habitually wears. In a telling passage, which Lemass would have delivered with considerable verve, O'Trigger rejects what he sees as sophistry and meaningless talk of 'rights' in favour of 'honour'.

> What the devil signifies right when your honour is concerned ? Do you think Achilles, or Alexander the Great, ever inquired where the right lay? No, by my soul, they drew their broad swords, and left the lazy sons of peace to settle the justice of it.[71]

Contemporary critiques of the play suggested that Sheridan, in drawing the character of O'Trigger, had been poking fun at his native country, a charge that Sheridan rebutted vigorously in later editions of the text.

> It is not without pleasure that I catch at an opportunity of justifying myself from the charge of intending any national reflection in the character of Sir Lucius O'Trigger ... If the condemnation of this comedy could have added one spark to the decaying flame of national attachment to the country supposed to be reflected on, I should have been happy in its fate.[72]

The self-identification of Lemass as the 'flame of national attachment' does not demand too great a leap of the imagination. The *Evening Mail* in its review of the play[73] managed to praise six members of the cast, including Jimmy O'Dea. The omission of Lemass's name suggests either that his thespian skills were below par or, more likely, that his growing revolutionary reputation did not go down well with the unionist *Mail*.[74]

Up to November 1920 Lemass remained a part-time member of the Volunteers. Even at that he was never very far from the action: further up Capel Street the Volunteer newspaper, *An tÓglach,* was regularly printed at a premises owned by an Englishman named Mitchell, where Oscar Traynor was employed.[75] On Sunday 21 November, however, in what was the climax of the Anglo-Irish struggle, a group of IRA men from the Dublin Brigade took part in a simultaneous attack on Englishmen living in different parts of Dublin who were — so Collins's intelligence had informed him — British agents. That attack, in which eleven men were killed and others wounded, prompted retaliation by the Black and Tans in Croke Park later that day, when twelve people died and sixty were wounded. Bloody Sunday, the name by which that day immediately became known, was in no sense a misnomer.

The names of those who carried out Collins's orders on that morning have never been disclosed *in toto*. In later years a number of the participants provided somewhat guarded accounts to British newspapers but did not identify many other participants. It was evidently one of the actions in the War of Independence that aroused such strong emotions that many Old IRA men, whether they had been involved or not, fell silently defensive about it. This was a mode to which Lemass himself often resorted, fending off one enquiry with the curt observation that 'firing squads don't have reunions.'

The circumstantial and hearsay evidence, however, suggests very strongly that Lemass was a member of Collins's squad on that day and that his policy of saying nothing about it, while never actually denying it, was as authentic an expression of his personality as his commitment to the original operation. There are no published records of his involvement, but there are three pieces of circumstantial evidence that point strongly to this conclusion.

The first is a letter from a British officer in Dublin to Lemass's father — after Lemass's arrest and internment in 1920 — which said that Lemass had been arrested because he was 'on Michael Collin's [sic] list.'[76] British intelligence is not of itself conclusive proof of anything, but here the second and third pieces of evidence can be brought into play. The second is in the papers left by C. S. ('Todd') Andrews to the UCD Archives, which include a series of notes Andrews made as part of his preparation for writing the first volume of his autobiography. One of these notes reads simply: 'Lemass and Bloody Sunday.'[77] There is no reference to this topic in the published work, an omission redolent of Conan Doyle's famous Sherlock Holmes story about the dog that didn't bark in the night.

The third piece of evidence, taken with the other two, is even more persuasive. It is the fact that in later years some of those close to Lemass personally seemed not only to have accepted it as a fact but to have been aware of significant details. One of them was Larry O'Brien, who became Lemass's private secretary in 1934. He had succeeded Alec Connolly in this position at the Department of Industry and Commerce and remained there for a decade. This was in itself an unusual length of time for any civil servant to hold such a post and cannot be explained simply by Fianna Fáil's well-documented suspicion of the civil service it had inherited from Cumann na nGaedheal. O'Brien's links with Lemass were, however, of a personal as well as an official nature, in that he was a brother of Paddy O'Brien, a close friend of Lemass who was shot during an engagement in Enniscorthy in which Lemass was also involved.

Larry O'Brien told the young man who was to succeed him in 1944, Kevin O'Doherty, that Lemass had not only taken part in the operation but had planned his part in it with unusual care. Lemass's target was on the south side of the Liffey, and the young IRA man, only just turned twenty-one, knew that all river crossings would be closely watched in the aftermath of the operation, as was indeed the case. He had also worked out, however, that there was one river crossing that would have escaped the attention of the British authorities: the south city ferry across the Liffey. Lemass and at least one companion took this route across the river before merging successfully into the throngs on the north side.[78]

The context in which this story was told is itself revealing. In later years Lemass would frequently be accused by political opponents of taking unnecessary risks; here there is evidence of an exceptionally cool young head. Lemass's gift for planning already included, not least in military matters, the careful mapping out of the line of retreat. Here was the hallmark not of a hot-headed guerrilla fighter but of a strategist and tactical thinker. There was even an echo of this many years later in an entirely different, even jocular, context. He was driving pell-mell down a narrow boreen while on holidays with his family and responded to his wife's apprehensiveness with the cheerful assertion, 'Anywhere I can drive down into I can back out of.'[79]

In November 1920, however, there was no backing out. Dick McKee and Peadar Clancy, who had planned the Bloody Sunday operation with Collins, were murdered in Dublin Castle. One source suggests that Lemass, who had a particularly high regard for McKee, was working in his father's shop the following morning when someone came to tell him of the deaths and that 'it was that deed which probably created within him the determin-ation never to rest until the objective for which McKee had given his life was attained.'[80] This somewhat heroic interpretation may have served discreetly to mask the fact that Lemass knew that it was now only a matter of time before he too became a marked man and that his decision to become a full-time soldier at this point was an entirely practical response to the danger that he might otherwise be easily picked up by the British military from behind the counter in Capel Street.

The life of a full-time Volunteer in 1920 was a difficult one. There was a curfew from midnight until five o'clock in Dublin, and the occasional military actions were punctuated by long hours during which the men would rest in safe houses, engaging in 'long acrimonious discussions, games of mental ping-pong in which ideas were clarified or hammered into shape, or became molten and fluid at our next meeting.'[81]

Other north-side operations in which Lemass's unit was involved were the capture and destruction of the RIC barracks at Raheny, a raid on the chief postal sorting office at the Rotunda, and an arms raid at the King's Inns. Ironically, given the events of half a century later, Lemass was appointed to oversee the boycott of Belfast goods in Dublin, as an indirect reprisal for the concurrent attacks on nationalists in that city, and discharged his task with such characteristic efficiency and ruthlessness that recalcitrant shops quickly decided that 'compliance with his orders would stave off quite an amount of really troublesome complications.'[82]

Despite his youth he was occasionally called upon for relatively senior tasks. At a Dublin Brigade meeting in 1919 or the following year the Brigadier, Leo Henderson, had to leave, and Lemass took the chair. According to one participant, he did not open his mouth for the remainder of the meeting.[83]

Lemass did not remain at liberty for long. While visiting his home in December 1920 he was seized by British forces and sent to Ballykinlar, County Down, as an internee, where the republican prisoners' commanding officer was Joseph McGrath.[84]

Ballykinlar was like many of the internment camps for Volunteers during the War of Independence: a combination of seriousness of purpose, self-improvement, and cultural activities. Music and Irish classes were common. Lemass used the opportunity to resume his education, in particular reading everything about economics that came his way.[85] For all that, it was not as intense an educational experience as the later internment in the Curragh. For most of the internees, and perhaps especially the southerners, Ballykinlar often had a light-hearted atmosphere. There were amateur dramatics and a camp céilí band, no doubt largely stimulated by the presence of Martin Walton, of the Dublin musical family, who taught some of his companions to play the fiddle.

One of the camp customs was keeping autograph books, in which fellow-internees wrote their names, accompanied by a motto or a stanza of verse. In one of them, kept by Thomas O'Rourke, who taught the internees Irish, Lemass chose this stanza to express his own nationalist emotions:

It's easy to cry when you're beaten — and die.
It's easy to crawfish and crawl;
But to fight and to fight when hope's out of sight
Why that's the best game of them all.[86]

In another such book, kept by a northerner named Frank Carney, Lemass's robust and self-confident words stand out among the more traditionally pious or sentimental offerings by many of the other inmates. Inscribed 'Hut 26', it ran:

I'd like to bet
That I'll come home yet
With a brass band
Playing before.[87]

Although they had been locked up for a common cause, there was an undercurrent of differences between northern and southern republicans even at that time. Some northerners disliked Lemass, or were at least suspicious of him, because he would not go to Mass while in the camp. Some of the more pious internees also used to recite the Rosary each evening. Lemass was not among them. Standing a little apart, he would utter, like a liturgical response at the end of the prayer: 'Oh God, if there is a God, save my soul, if I have a soul.'[88]

2

The Democratic Option
1921–32
'The gunmen and the communists are voting for Fianna Fáil'

I n December 1921 the signing of the Treaty precipitated a general release of internees. Seán Lemass, along with many others, was put on a special train from Belfast to Dublin. At Dundalk, bottles of a clear liquid with the typed label *Whiskey* were supplied by well-wishers on the platform, and Lemass, uncharacteristically, overindulged. In Dublin, where popular sentiment wrongly assumed that the internees had been maltreated and would be in need of medical attention, an ambulance had been sent to welcome the train; Lemass, *hors de combat* because of the poitín, was the only passenger who needed assistance.[1] For the remainder of his life he drank very little, explaining to friends: 'It's not virtue; it just doesn't agree with my stomach.'[2]

The political situation in Dublin and within the republican movement generally was still inchoate and confused, and the deep political divisions that were emerging had not yet become case-hardened. There is indeed evidence that Lemass was not at first to be found among the ranks of the more zealous republicans, for whom the Treaty was unacceptable in any shape or form. Like many other undecided Volunteers, he must have watched the series of discussions that took place in the Dáil over the Christmas period with a sense of the historic choice that was facing them all.

He was already friendly with Jim Ryan from Wexford, whose family exemplified the way in which an initially fluid political situation eventually hardened into the divisions of the Civil War. Two of Ryan's sisters, Kate and Phyllis, favoured the Treaty, but Seán T. O'Kelly (who was to marry first Kate and, after her death, Phyllis) returned from Paris and argued the opposite case with such effect that they changed their minds. Another Ryan sister, Mary Josephine (generally known as 'Min'), was to marry Richard Mulcahy, Chief of Staff of the IRA during the War of Independence and commander-in-chief of the Free State forces after 1922. In taped reminiscences later she noted that Jim Ryan had expressed his belief that the

Treaty would be passed, even though he personally would vote against it; he subsequently did not take an active part in the Civil War. She also spoke to her family on a number of occasions in later years of her conviction that both Ryan and Lemass were at first inclined to accept the Treaty as a workable option.[3]

They were not alone. After the signing but before the return of the delegates from London de Valera himself supported, or at least was prepared to accept, the Treaty, before a decisive intervention by Austin Stack changed his mind; and even Rory O'Connor, although temperamentally inclined to oppose it, was prepared to 'work it for all it's worth', hoping that the number of those prepared to oppose it would reach critical mass.[4]

Lemass was certainly enthusiastic enough to accept an initial appointment as a training officer to what was intended to be the Garda Síochána when the rudiments of the new force were established in January. It was an action that marked him off, at the very least, from those republicans who were opposed to the Treaty root and branch. Events, however, were to achieve a momentum of their own, as the middle ground became increasingly untenable.

What was at stake was the authority of the Provisional Government, established after the Dáil vote on 7 January, which revealed that de Valera had only minority support for his position. On 12 January four army officers, including Oscar Traynor and Rory O'Connor, issued a statement demanding the holding of an army convention to declare the army's allegiance to the Republic — an implicit rejection of the authority of the new Dáil. This challenge was finessed by the government, but others followed in its wake. De Valera and his TDs stayed away from the session of the Dáil called to ratify the Treaty on 14 January, thus adding substantially to the growing crisis of legitimacy.

When Lemass's first pay cheque arrived it had been drawn not on the Dáil, as he had apparently expected, but on the controversial Provisional Government, which had been set up as a direct result of the British government's Government of Ireland Act, 1920, and which was to be the recipient of the powers being transferred under the Treaty. Angered by what he saw as a step further away from the realisation of the Republic, he resigned. His next move, however, was into Beggar's Bush barracks, also as a training officer.

It is difficult to explain this move other than by reference to the power struggle then in progress in the army, which was an altogether more important entity than the Garda Síochána. It was vitally important at that stage, and still legally possible, for Volunteers who opposed the Treaty to join or remain in the army in substantial numbers, in order to influence the outcome of the internal debate to the greatest possible extent. The unresolved tensions created by the evolving situation finally became unbearable, however, after a confrontation between Free State forces and Liam Lynch's Volunteers in Limerick in late February and early March, and Lemass and others left the barracks to report to the now openly dissident Rory O'Connor.[5]

In March the political and military situation began to come to a head. O'Connor and others called a special convention of the army, which was attended by and large only by those opposed to the Treaty and which repudiated the authority of the Dáil. Within a few weeks these forces, now known to the political establishment as the 'Irregulars', seized the Four Courts and other prominent buildings in Dublin and fortified them. Throughout the country, although there were no serious outbreaks of violence, government and irregular forces jockeyed for position. The stalemate continued until 30 June, when Collins's forces went into action against the Four Courts garrison.

Lemass's decision to throw in his lot with O'Connor and Traynor was significant. Traynor had been commandant of the Dublin Brigade and therefore Lemass's commanding officer during the War of Independence. He commanded considerable moral authority among republicans generally and remained a *bête noire* of the Free State authorities right up to the early nineteen-thirties, when he was described by Eoin O'Duffy, then Commissioner of the Garda Síochána, as 'the embodiment of subterranean crime.'[6] Rory O'Connor was just as ardent — so much so that not even Traynor, who believed that it was military folly to have two hundred of the best fighting men available to them confined inside a walled fortress, was able to convince him of the dangers involved. There can be little doubt that Lemass's indecision, such as it had been, was by now firmly eradicated. By siding with O'Connor and by joining him in that hopeless occupation, Lemass in effect chose what was, of all the options available, one of the most daring, even quixotic.

His commitment was rewarded by O'Connor, who made him adjutant and in effect second in command. In his own contribution to the conduct of the defence, Lemass, in a way that was to become characteristic of his conduct in later life, insisted on the supreme importance of morale and — appropriately enough for the son of an outfitter — on the role of dress in enhancing and maintaining morale. 'The poorer you are, the better you have to dress,' he was to say many years later. Throughout the fighting he would insist that the men turn out for inspection with their uniforms and kit clean and polished, or as clean and polished as was possible in the circumstances, in order to bolster morale. He was, one of his comrades-in-arms recalled, extremely smartly dressed by any guerrilla standards and 'reserved in manner, a characteristic which helped him to maintain strict discipline on Army barrack lines.'[7]

He had, as it happened, plenty of time to impose his discipline. For some weeks there were no overt hostilities, and the Four Courts garrison was organised like a regular army camp. One of Lemass's functions was to give passes authorising men to leave the building; as he did so he flamboyantly affixed to the passes the seal of the Lord Chief Justice of Ireland.[8]

It was a lost cause from the beginning; and when the garrison surrendered, on 30 June 1921, Lemass was captured with the others. Fortunately for him he was one of a group of prisoners that was temporarily incarcerated in a nearby distillery building. There were bars on the internal window, but the men forced them, and Lemass and five of his companions, including Ernie O'Malley, Joe Griffin, and Paddy Rigney, succeeded in making their way to the street door and escaping.[9] Women in the street outside raised the alarm, and the Free State troops prevented the others from following them.[10]

The experience of the Four Courts garrison became a powerful political cement for those who had been involved in it. Lemass forged a close friendship here with the Flemings — there were at least two brothers — who were such dedicated republicans that one of the cells in Port Laoise prison became known as 'Fleming's cell' because it was almost permanently occupied by one of them.[11] Equally, many of the men who had been involved formed the core of Lemass's constituency and organisational machine in Dublin for many years. Some of the old loyalties never quite died. There was an annual Mass in Dublin Castle for the Four Courts garrison, and one year, when Lemass was Taoiseach and was unable to attend, he sent his son, Noel, to represent him. When Noel introduced himself to the secretary of the organisation, a man known as 'Skinner' Reilly, as the representative of the Taoiseach, Reilly replied fiercely: 'You're not here to represent the Taoiseach. You're here to represent your father. There's no-one here representing the Taoiseach.'[12]

In the first phase of the Civil War, Lemass headed south from Dublin with Paddy O'Brien, another member of the Four Courts garrison, who had escaped from hospital after the surrender, and both made contact with the remnants of the republican forces. Lemass was appointed to the Headquarters Staff of the Eastern Command of the IRA, serving in Wexford, Carlow, and the adjoining counties. It was not a negligible force. The divisional commander, Pat Fleming, assembled some three hundred men to besiege Enniscorthy in July 1922: the party included Lemass, Tom Derrig (later Minister for Education), Francis Carty (later editor of the *Irish Press*), Ernie O'Malley, and Paddy O'Brien.

One of the first operations was to send a scouting party into the town to reconnoitre for a possible attack on the castle, where the Free State troops were based. There are two versions of the skirmish that followed. Younger does not include Lemass in this party,[13] whereas Skinner does.[14] Younger suggests that the party was five strong; Skinner says it comprised 'seven or eight men,' including Lemass, Fleming, O'Malley, and Derrig. The only names common to both accounts are O'Brien, Spillane (both of whom sustained fatal wounds), and Carty. What is generally agreed is that the IRA party was successfully ambushed by Free State troops, that Spillane died on the spot, and that Paddy O'Brien died later. The IRA regrouped and made a successful attack a few days later. The National Army officers who surrendered were given their side arms back and allowed to leave the area.

Reconciliation of the two versions is difficult. If neither Lemass nor Fleming was involved in the reconnaissance party, both were certainly involved in the second assault. Alternatively, the bitterness with which Lemass subsequently referred to the shooting of O'Brien may have been related to a sense of regret that he had not been at his side to help him when he fell during the ambush of the scouting party. There is a folk memory in Pat Fleming's family that Fleming had 'pulled Lemass out of the firing line in Enniscorthy'[15] and that this contributed to the exceptional closeness between Lemass and the Flemings in later years.

It is impossible to confirm this anecdote, especially as Pat Fleming, like many of his generation, talked little about this bitter period, even to his immediate family. What is unmistakable is the closeness of the relationship between the two men. Lemass became a director of Fleming's Fireclay Ltd almost immediately after leaving office in 1948[16] and made representations on behalf of the company to Bord na Móna many years later when tiles for the new cooling-towers of the turf-fired generating stations were being purchased.[17]

After the failure of the Enniscorthy operation a number of the Volunteers returned towards Dublin and were almost surrounded near Baltinglass. Lemass evaded capture and, with Tom Derrig, walked the thirty-seven miles from there to Dublin, arriving finally 'with very sore feet.'[18] It was a period of declining fortunes for the anti-Treaty forces: they were to decline still further as the Free State military and security forces got on top of the situation and the more active Irregulars were rounded up and interned. Lemass, now technically an employee in his father's shop again, was appointed Director of Intelligence for the Dublin Brigade of the IRA. The shop was conveniently located as a sort of entrepôt for information, and informants could readily pass themselves off as customers if the need arose.

Lemass's focus was sharp to the point of excluding all extraneous considerations. During one intelligence meeting at a safe house in Ranelagh the conversation turned to literature. George Moore, W. B. Yeats and the Abbey Theatre supplanted questions of communications, intelligence, and subversion. Lemass was 'so obviously bored by the talk that he finally left the group, standing up ostentatiously to gaze gloomily out of the window. It was the first indication I had of Lemass's contempt for what he regarded as intellectuals.'[19] This was carried through into later life. As Director of

Organisation for Fianna Fáil in 1954–57 he delighted in sending out aspiring young graduate applicants for party membership to scale lamp-posts with election posters.

His period as Director of Intelligence was not prolonged. He was arrested on the quays near O'Connell Bridge in November 1922 and sent to Hare Park Camp in the Curragh on 28 November.[20] In the camp his by now evident qualities ensured his nomination as 'line leader' (leader of one of the three or four lines of huts in that section of the camp). In the confined circumstances of the camp, marked by physical hardship and a certain amount of maltreatment,[21] he was not noted for gregariousness. He had a natural reserve, which was intensified by his sharply focused sense of self-improvement. His personal fastidiousness was also much in evidence: the toothbrush moustache he sported earned him among his comrades the sobriquet of 'Charlie Chaplin'. He was also known, perhaps because of his somewhat Mediterranean appearance, as 'the Jewman' by contemporaries who recalled him spending considerable time sitting in a corner mulling over books on economics. When the soldiers guarding them were paid, Lemass would emerge from his monastic labours in the sphere of economics and politics and relieve them of substantial amounts of money in a poker school.[22]

This fraternisation did not imply acquiescence. Lemass was involved with another prisoner, Alf Mac Lochlainn, in drafting an affidavit on prison conditions, which no longer survives. Lemass, Mac Lochlainn and others were simultaneously organising an escape tunnel,[23] but this was discovered, and he and the others were sent to the 'glasshouse' or military prison, where they were handcuffed for hours at a stretch to a rack on the wall, their feet barely touching the ground. They might even have been shot (attempting to escape was punishable by death under the regulations governing the camps) but for de Valera's ceasefire order, which brought about a general reduction in tension and the eventual transfer of the prisoners concerned to Mountjoy.[24]

It was during this period that one of the most formative events in Lemass's life occurred: the death of his brother Noel. After 1916 Noel had become an apprentice engineer in the Great Southern Railway and remained a covert member of the Volunteers, but not on active service. When he finished his apprenticeship he went to work in Cork and did not return to Dublin to take an active part in the War of Independence until later, when he was also (when not in prison) in the employment of Dublin Corporation.[25] He was promoted to captain and was reputedly one of those whom the British forces had been authorised to shoot on sight.[26] This suggests, at the very least, a considered official view of his lethal potential.

There are conflicting rumours about his part in the Civil War. His mother told a Dublin newspaper that he 'refused to fight his own' after the Treaty split, but there were other reports that Collins was suspicious of him.[27] Certainly the British view of his activities, even if exaggerated, suggests that his mother's defence was inspired by loyalty rather than any detailed knowledge of what he was up to. He was captured at Kilmainham on 14 August 1922 and taken to Gormanston Camp but escaped on 14 September. He was found on the beach at Skerries by a member of the Fox family from the town, with whom he had been friendly as a child, and sheltered by them until it was safe for him to move on.[28] After the ceasefire of May 1923 he ignored a demand that he sign a declaration of allegiance to the new Free State government.[29]

In June 1923 he was abducted in broad daylight in Dublin by a number of men in plain clothes. It was generally assumed, though never proved, that they were members of, or connected with, the Free State forces. At that time there were no fewer than three secret service elements in the these forces. One of them, the Criminal Investigation Division, operated from Oriel House in Westland Row, and its function was to investigate or interrogate suspected members of the Irregulars. It gained a reputation for 'ruthlessness, and, at times, for savagery.'[30] This was the organisation with which Joe McGrath, Lemass's former OC in Ballykinlar and now Minister for Industry and Commerce in the Free State government, had an established connection.

Noel Lemass was held in secret until the end of September or early October, when he was shot twice in the head and his body dumped in the Dublin Mountains. It was discovered there on 12 October. O'Higgins — possibly coincidentally, although the close connection between the events suggests strongly that this was not the case — persuaded the government to disband all three secret forces later in the same month, despite vigorous protests by McGrath. Noel Lemass had possibly been tortured before his death, but an inquest ended inconclusively.

Given that the Civil War had in effect ended with the ceasefire on 24 May, the date of Noel Lemass's abduction and murder suggests strongly that another agenda was in operation that has never been disclosed. Although this is little more than speculation, it may have had something to do with Noel Lemass's role during the period of overt hostilities. Although his mother maintained that he did not take part in military activities during the Civil War, some of his actions then may have given rise to a vendetta.

Seán Lemass was released on compassionate grounds when his brother's body was found. There was little enough compassion elsewhere. The boys' mother was driven to write to the press at one point to complain that the authorities had refused to return to her his rosary beads, a gold tie-pin, and 'one or two other little things that could be of no value to anyone except his parents' and that they had sent only a formal acknowledgment of her letter.[31]

Burying the memories of the Civil War was not always an easy task, but Lemass succeeded to a greater extent than many of his contemporaries. The only visible sign of the past for many years was the picture of his brother in uniform that had a permanent place of honour in his study at home. Nevertheless the memories were not buried so deep that they did not occasionally surface, sometimes with near-volcanic intensity. Lemass's composure in the Dáil in the face of political taunts and jibes was legendary, but there were occasions when even his iron self-discipline slipped. In 1948, freshly in opposition, he nailed his colours to the mast with deeply felt eloquence, rejecting the suggestion that the Republic of Ireland Bill, which the Dáil was then discussing, was a natural extension of the Treaty.

> On behalf of those who fought with me, those friends who died or who were broken or exiled in opposition to the Treaty, I am going to deny that assertion with all the vehemence I can ... I am not going to support the Bill in silence if by doing so I am to be taken as accepting now the very contention I fought against all my life ... Sergeant O'Brien, my friend and comrade in 1916 and 1922, was shot down from behind a hedge.[32]

Almost two decades later, as Taoiseach, he was unexpectedly provoked by a sally from James Dillon and warned the Fine Gael leader, 'white-faced with anger,' that he would never succeed in getting him to debate the Civil War.[33] As Taoiseach he responded with considerable reserve to a suggestion by de Valera in 1963 that historical papers on the 1921–22 Treaty negotiations be released, arguing that it might lead to the 'revival of old controversies.'[34] When he was being interviewed by Michael Mills for the series of biographical articles published in the *Irish Press* early in 1969, the question of the Civil War came up. When Mills pressed for further details Lemass's eyes suddenly filled with tears, and he had to pause for some moments to compose himself before making it clear that he preferred not to talk about that period in modern Irish history. 'Terrible things were done by both sides,' he told Mills. 'I'd prefer not to talk about it.'[35]

Dr Paddy Fanning, who had been a contemporary of Lemass in the O'Connell Schools and was for many years a medical officer in the Department of Health, told acquaintances in private on a number of occasions that he had been responsible for getting Lemass to shake the hand of at least one of the people who may have been implicated in his brother's murder — Joe McGrath. The significance of the handshake, which took place at a race meeting in the early years of Fianna Fáil's first period in government, would not have been lost on many of those present on that occasion. And Paddy McGrath, Joe's son, was appointed to the Seanad by Jack Lynch in 1969 (where he was an infrequent attender and even more infrequent speaker).

Lemass obviously considered the hatchet to have been well and truly buried. He told his first ardfheis as Taoiseach in 1959: 'The old antagonisms have no place in the Ireland of tomorrow. We have never abandoned the hope that some day, somehow, that would be brought about as a prelude to another great era of national accomplishment.'[36]

As far as the McGraths were concerned, the burial of the old antagonisms had been long signalled, in the most unambiguous way possible, by the scale of donations from that source to Fianna Fáil. Some time after McGrath's resignation in controversial circumstances from his position as Minister for Industry and Commerce in March 1924, the government entrusted to his private company, Irish Hospitals' Trust, the running of the hospital sweepstakes, which became the foundation of a substantial private fortune. The political munificence that followed was not confined to the party to which McGrath had originally belonged: in the 1954 general election Irish Hospitals' Trust contributed £2,500 (£40,400 in 1996 values) of the £20,000 (£323,400 in 1996 values) collected by Fianna Fáil, one of the largest donations to the party on that occasion. In the 1957 election it contributed £5,000 (£72,600 in 1996 values) of the total of £17,500 (£254,000 in 1996 values); and in the 1961 election a McGrath contribution of £10,000 (£134,000 in 1996 values) amounted to almost a third of the £31,600 total (£425,000 in 1996 values). It can be assumed that the family probably also made donations to other parties, although records are not available.[37] When McGrath died in 1966, just before the fiftieth anniversary of the Rising, a photograph in the *Irish Times* showed a deeply pensive Lemass at his graveside.

Lemass's release gave him new scope for political activity. He resumed his role as Director of Intelligence, but it is not clear when he first joined Sinn Féin. A pristine membership card in his personal papers, possibly the first one he ever received, is dated 8 February 1924 and records that he paid seven shillings and sixpence in advance for a whole year's subscription. He was then attached to the 'Cumann Ardchraobh' or headquarters branch and to the Stephen's Green Comhairle Ceantair.

It is quite possible that in the hectic circumstances of the time the formalities of membership came some time after the spontaneous political commitment. Lemass was elected to the Standing Committee of Sinn Féin at the 1923 ardfheis as part of an emotional response to the discovery of Noel Lemass's body and was not aware of his election until after the event. This supports the theory that his election may have been a popular gesture by the rank and file and that his formal adhesion to the organisation represented a ratification of the new status quo. He threw himself wholeheartedly into the work: military activity was in any case a rapidly diminishing option. He was Director of Elections for Pat Nash, the Sinn Féin candidate in the Belfast by-election in 1924, but Nash was beaten by Joe Devlin and the old nationalist vote.[38]

REPRESENTATIVE POLITICS: THE FIRST STEPS

By this time Lemass was already cutting his teeth on democratic politics. There were to be two by-elections in the same year in which he was to figure, both in the Dublin South constituency. Sinn Féin was fiercely abstentionist, and the political atmosphere was raw, confrontational, and often bitter: the events and the atrocities of the Civil War were a recent memory.

The first by-election, in March 1924, was caused by the death of a Cumann na nGaedheal deputy, Philip Cosgrave. Lemass was chosen as a candidate without his knowledge, which was less a reflection of what the organisation thought of him than of its view of the political process generally: 'in those days, there was no rush among Republicans to become politicians.'[39] The campaign was organised in the old Sinn Féin style, with an emphasis on the personation of dead electors and a multiplicity of public meetings at different places, to which orators and audiences often moved in unison. This increasingly struck Lemass as an inefficient use of human resources, but it was to be some time before he could refashion political campaigning in his own style. At a meeting of the Sinn Féin Standing Committee in June 1924 he even secured agreement on a motion condemning personation at elections and urging the government to do something about it.[40]

Anti-Treaty politics in the twenties also called for a share of courage, and Lemass, for all his reputed command of rhetoric when addressing rural republican audiences, was at first diffident when it came to speaking on his own behalf in front of the traditionally caustic Dublin crowds. Tommy Davy, who ran for the city council for Sinn Féin in 1924, was with Lemass at what may have been his first public meeting as a candidate in Dublin, at the fountain in James's Street in the heart of his constituency. It was a wet evening, and Lemass was speaking, as was the custom, from a horse-drawn dray. As he began his speech, somewhat hesitantly, the horse moved, Lemass's hat fell off, and the wheels of the dray rolled over it. 'I can truthfully say I'm not speaking through my hat any more,' he observed, before continuing more confidently.[41] An account by another contemporary of him delivering another early speech, from the back of a wagonette at Power's Court, off Mount Street, noted that he stood his ground even as missiles rained down around him. At the end of his speech one of his more battle-hardened companions, Constance Markievicz, congratulated him quietly: 'You'll go far, Seán.'[42]

Even at this stage Lemass was developing what was to become a sure touch with the Dublin working-class voter, his speeches a heady mixture of socialist and republican rhetoric. On one of several platforms he shared with Markievicz he declared that the coming republican government would be ruled by the worker, and its first function would be to ensure that the hungry would be fed.[43] From the earliest years he had a reputation within the party for having a horizon that extended beyond narrow constitutional issues.

He had always what could at times be construed as socialism. He was thinking very much ahead of a whole lot of people who were thinking merely in terms of the national entity and what went with the national entity. He was thinking always more of the conditions of the people — he was a real republican in that sense … and he didn't leave out the bigger national question either, but ultimately he realised, like Pearse did in my opinion and Rooney and many of the leaders, that you must base whatever fight you're going to make on that—not so much on equality as equality of opportunity for the masses; and that was his policy in quintessence.[44]

The republican ingredient of his campaign was stark and uncompromising: it was against England they were fighting, he told one enthusiastic crowd at College Green.[45] And the coincidence of the army mutiny and the election count encouraged him to have a bitter side-swipe at the victors of the Civil War. If the army had wanted to mutiny, he suggested, it should have mutinied when Liam Mellows and his comrades were shot.[46] Lemass's affection for Mellows was more than transitory; in spite of his almost total suppression of Civil War animosities in later years he would on occasion — particularly in opposition — take members of his family on drives into County Wexford on a quasi-pilgrimage to the graveyard at Castletown where Mellows was buried.[47]

Lemass secured 13,639 votes, just under two thousand less than the government candidate, James O'Mara, but two thousand more than the previous anti-Treaty candidate in the same constituency, a teacher named Michael O'Mullane. O'Mara was elected on transfers from a candidate standing on a purely protectionist trade platform. Interestingly, in the light of Fianna Fáil's future policy, the Cumann na nGaedheal candidate got four protectionist transfers for every one that went to Lemass, indicating at the very least that Sinn Féin's economic policy, such as it was at the time, was either not very clearly understood or completely discounted in the light of the party's abstentionism. It was a significant achievement from a standing start.

Lemass's speeches in this period, evidently fuelled not only by orthodox nationalist sentiment but also by the memory of his brother's recent murder, continued to reflect the aftermath of the Civil War and the issues underlying that conflict. Their tone is hard-line and uncompromising, indicating that he had no doubts about abstentionism or any other aspects of Sinn Féin's current policies. He told the men of the Dublin Brigade of the IRA, after a commemorative Mass, that they had 'beaten the flower of the British Army' in 1916, which was at the least something of an overstatement.[48]

England was still the enemy, he told a meeting in Tuam, and it was against it they must strike, and against those traitors who stood for it in Ireland. They demanded that the 'rebel Parliament and Seanad' should clear out of Ireland.[49] Again, in March, he warned that Sinn Féin would boycott the forthcoming Tailteann Games if the internees were not released.[50] Rousing speeches like this made a popular choice for venues outside Dublin. A letter from the Kerry Brigade of the IRA to GHQ in 1924, intercepted by Free State intelligence, noted that the brigade had asked Lemass to come down to Kerry for three meetings and that 'he is a great man to give an oration, so we are told.'[51]

In spite of all this gadding about, Lemass's personal life was flowering. The Lemasses had for many years been friendly with the Hughes family, not least because the two families tended to holiday in Skerries at the same time. This was where Seán met one of the daughters of Thomas Hughes, a buyer at Arnott's in Henry Street. Kathleen Hughes was the same age as Seán, had been educated at the Dominican College in Muckross Park, and worked as a shorthand typist in an engineer's office.[52] Tall and striking in appearance, she had a good soprano voice and had been trained by the noted teacher Vincent O'Brien. As friendship evolved into affection and commitment, the Hughes family's doubts about the appropriateness of the relationship were in no way diminished. 'That boy is always on the run. He'll never make a home for you' was the prospective father-in-law's comment,[53] and it was to be another three years before the couple married, during which time Lemass's attractions as a prospective son-in-law must have diminished still further. They were certainly not enhanced when, on one trip up the Dublin Mountains on his motorcycle with Kathleen in the sidecar, he turned around to speak to her to discover that the sidecar had become detached and that he was now riding solo.

Electoral failure and lack of prospects notwithstanding, Seán Lemass and Kathleen Hughes eventually decided to marry, despite the disapproval of Kathleen's parents. The motorcycle was sold to subsidise the event, and the ceremony took place in the Church of the Holy Name, Beechwood Avenue, Ranelagh, on 24 August 1924.[54] Jimmy O'Dea, Lemass's old school friend, dramatic collaborator and Capel Street neighbour, in later years to become one of Ireland's best-loved comedians for his inimitable Dublin working-class humour, was best man. Mary Flanagan was bridesmaid, and only a handful of close friends were in attendance. It looked like an inauspicious beginning, but the relationship was plainly central to both the young people and became for Lemass in later years a source of extraordinary stability, serenity and good humour in his private life.

When they returned from their honeymoon in London, Lemass continued his organisational work for Sinn Féin. He was active at the 1924 ardfheis, and it was not long before another electoral opportunity presented itself, again in the South Dublin constituency. This time the vacancy was caused by the appointment of the Cumann na nGaedheal attorney-general, Hugh Kennedy, as Chief Justice, and Lemass's nomination for the by-election was ratified at the Sinn Féin Standing Committee meeting of 22 September 1924.

The Lemass election machine, revivified by its candidate's conviction that organisation was a better use of personnel than personation, swung into high gear. Kennedy's appointment in particular handed Lemass a ready-made election issue: jobbery and corruption. Séamus Hughes, the government candidate, was handicapped by his reputed association with the government's intelligence services. Lemass's election literature did not put a tooth in it:

— Vote for Lemass and put an end to the reign of the jobber
— Hughes of Oriel House
— Hughes the Foreman Spy
— Hughes of the Notorious Civilian Defence Force.[55]

On the positive side, he stressed social and economic issues in a hand-bill that, although it gave priority to traditional Sinn Féin constitutional objectives, went into unusual detail on other issues. Lemass, it proclaimed, stood for

— The protection of our industries by the imposition of adequate tariffs, with proper safeguards against profiteering
— The rebuilding of Ireland, not from the top down but from the bottom up.
— Free education including free books and luncheon, for children, and a proper system of scholarships, not only enabling the child of the poorest Irishman to reach the University if sufficiently brilliant, but recouping his poor parents for the loss of his services to them during the period of his education for the State.
— Vote for Lemass and social justice.[56]

Lemass's speeches followed the same pattern as those of the earlier election. A republican government would set little store by the 'rights of property and the sacredness of interests,' he told one enthusiastic meeting, but would legislate 'in the interests of the whole Irish people and not in the interests of a privileged class.'[57]

Despite a modest increase in the government vote, Lemass won the seat on 18 November 1924, in a two-horse race, by 17,297 votes to 16,340 for Hughes. He was to remain a public representative for the next forty-five years, and his nomination to the party's Organisation Committee in December 1924 was proof of his high standing in the Executive Committee.

The former candidate, Michael O'Mullane, was not prepared to retire into obscurity, and a bout of tough constituency infighting ensued. Lemass had to fight his corner, and he applied his customary skills to outwitting and outmanoeuvring a potentially dangerous rival. Contemporary photographs show O'Mullane helping to chair a victorious Lemass away from the election count in November 1924; but yet another by-election was necessitated in the same constituency in March 1925, and this gave the former candidate another opportunity to come back into the fray.

On 29 December 1924 a constituency convention, properly constituted, nominated O'Mullane as the candidate. The Standing Committee on 5 January 1925 heard an astonishing letter read in which O'Mullane withdrew his candidacy in what was plainly a fit of pique. Following the convention on 29 December, he explained, a meeting had been organised and posters printed by head office with his name on them, but at the last minute he had been asked by head office not to speak, because his selection had not been ratified. He was now resigning, he told the committee, because his failure to speak at the meeting was being misunderstood. The executive postponed a decision until its meeting on 12 January 1925, when presumably his pique had been overcome; his ratification was proposed by Lemass and seconded by Markievicz.

This apparent mending of the fences between the two constituency rivals did not last for long. After the declaration of the result of the election on 12 March, O'Mullane, whose vote had declined dramatically, decided to apportion blame for his failure on some opponents within the organisation. He made an incautious attack on Father Michael O'Flanagan, a redoubtable republican cleric and member of the Standing Committee (who was also, with Lemass, a member of the Economic Committee), who had been campaigning elsewhere in the country. O'Mullane regarded O'Flanagan's criticism of the episcopacy as a factor in his defeat and said that although the priest had been inspired by unselfish motives 'his words could not but injure the deep religious feelings of the Irish people.'[58] O'Mullane's position, however, was already tenuous. He was increasingly becoming known as someone who was sceptical about the policy of abstentionism: in the words of a contemporary, 'he was the first to say, "Come on and capture the Dáil".'[59]

Lemass had now been given an opportunity, which he grasped with his customary despatch, to move against his constituency rival. In public he issued a statement defending Father O'Flanagan. In private he raised O'Mullane's remarks at the Standing Committee meeting of 16 March, and he subsequently orchestrated a campaign through his own branch and the constituency organisation to undermine O'Mullane's position at the Standing Committee meetings of 6 April and 20 April. Garda intelligence notes for the period observe accurately that Lemass 'spoke for the Irregular Cabinet' in defending Father O'Flanagan in the newspapers, and O'Mullane was eventually expelled from Sinn Féin.[60] There was a double irony in this: not only was Lemass himself shortly to become a convert to parliamentary politics but his view of O'Flanagan was substantially modified in later years, when he spoke caustically of him as someone who had been 'under the impression that he was a kind of spiritual chaplain, and Pope to the Sinn Féin organisation.'[61]

There is even evidence that de Valera's conversion dates from around this time. The South City by-election had been one of nine held simultaneously; the republicans had won only two of the seats, and these with an indifferent showing. De Valera confided to Joe McGarrity a year later:

> Since the nine Bye-elections I have been convinced that the programme on which we were working would not win the people in the present conditions. It was too high, and too sweeping. The oath, on the other hand, is a definite objective, within reasonable striking distance.[62]

Electoral activity was becoming Lemass's all-consuming priority. He was appointed to chair a new organisation committee for Dublin on 4 May 1925.[63] He subsequently resigned from the Economic Committee, though not before it had produced a wide-ranging set of resolutions. These called for a system of protection and bounties for industry, 'especially agriculture,' but also advocated that cumainn 'should give special attention to the development of electricity from native sources' and that 'every section in Ireland should adopt the spirit of co-operation and service rather than that of supremacy and individual gain.'[64] Farrell suggests that his economic ideas were 'not acceptable,'[65] but this seems unlikely in a general sense: one of the few proposals from the Economic Committee that failed to get the executive's approval was for the party to protest against the importing of steel girders, because Ireland could 'produce as good material at home.' This was regarded as 'not feasible.'

Lemass's special electoral responsibility in relation to Dublin became evident in May 1925 when it was acknowledged that he would work with the Standing Committee's organisation subcommittee only when available. He proposed the creation of a reorganisation committee for the capital and 'one body to unite and control all the activities of Sinn Féin in Dublin City and County.'[66]

His interest in economics had not gone entirely underground. At the 1925 Sinn Féin ardfheis the Rathmines Cumann, from Lemass's constituency, passed a resolution requiring the executive to formulate, within three months, a 'national economic and cultural programme'. Lemass's influence can be seen in the demand that this programme include a comprehensive tariff package; its other notable feature was its call for the abolition of the standing army, an opinion that was canvassed particularly strongly by Mary MacSwiney. He continued to advance it later in the Dáil, but it evaporated rapidly as a policy after Fianna Fáil assumed office in 1932.

Almost immediately he was given yet another opportunity to test the electoral waters. Local elections were held in the midsummer of 1925 — the first for five years and the first under the new Free State government. Lemass suddenly appeared in the lists for Rathmines Urban District

Council.[67] He now lived in the area — in Terenure—but notwithstanding his change of address, his decision to contest Rathmines was a risky enough one.

It would have been even riskier had all his potential electors been aware of his continuing involvement with the IRA. On 2 July he and Aiken were writing secretly to Seán T. O'Kelly with news of their project 'to induce into the Army young men who have grown to manhood since the termination of the Civil War' and giving notice of their intention 'to maintain the Army as an effective force, capable of being brought into immediate action should the occasion arise that would justify or necessitate its use.'[68] At the same time he was closely involved in the organisation of an IRA mission to Russia involving Gerry Boland and Seán Russell. Lemass's constituents might have been even more alarmed had they known that one of the objectives of this particular mission — reflecting a theme that was to become one of Lemass's life-long passions — was to study the use of aeroplanes in warfare.[69] (The Free State forces had in fact used military aircraft both for bombing and strafing during the early part of 1923.)

The Rathmines area was predominantly middle-class and unionist. It had almost no indigenous working class and was less volatile politically than almost any other ward in the city at the time, with the possible exception of Clontarf. There were only nine candidates in the seven-seat ward Lemass contested, and the quota was only 210 votes, so the contest was hardly an exacting one, and the entire election was marked by considerable apathy. Lemass was elected to the fifth seat without having reached even this modest quota. Those who polled ahead of him included such luminaries as Mary Kettle and — ironically, in view of future events — William Norton, who, like Mrs Kettle, stood for the Labour Party and was briefly Lemass's ally in attempts to embarrass the Free State majority on the council. Another member was Constance Markievicz; and although the political balance of the newly elected council was still effectively unionist, the election of Lemass and the others was at least a straw in the wind.

A promising career in local politics rapidly ground to a halt, however, when the council's majority showed plainly what it thought of the disruptive tactics Lemass and a group of supporters, including Markievicz, developed. The majority group steamrolled Lemass and his allies into the ground, and on 3 March 1926 he gave up local politics as a bad job. His letter of resignation was read to the council and accepted. The burghers of Rathmines simultaneously agreed, no doubt with mixed emotions, to remit the fine of £1 due by the recalcitrant councillor. The councillor himself hardly gave it a backward glance: he had other fish to fry.

COMHAIRLE NA DTEACHTAÍ

Lemass's election to the Dáil, more significant than his brief episode with Rathmines Urban District Council, now entitled him to membership of Comhairle na dTeachtaí. This was an unusual creation of Éamon de Valera's, its membership comprising the Sinn Féin members of the Second Dáil and other Sinn Féin members who had been elected subsequently but who had not taken their seats in the post-Treaty Dáil. From 1923 to 1926 it functioned fitfully in a political context in which reality and fantasy were increasingly uncomfortable bed-fellows. It operated at arm's length from the Ardchomhairle of Sinn Féin, although some people were inevitably members of both, and the debate between tactical and theological abstention-ists about the political path to be followed was replicated in both bodies.

Comhairle na dTeachtaí attempted to underline its constitutional claims by creating a number of portfolios and by discussing policy matters at some length. Its initial proceedings, however, were handicapped by the absence of a number of key participants; it was inevitably strongly influenced by those who were outside prison, and these included a number of strong-minded women, not least Constance Markievicz, Kathleen Lynn, and Mary MacSwiney (whose ideas on social and economic organisation were communicated in frequent and lengthy epistles to the Comhairle's acting president, P. J. Ruttledge). Markievicz was head of Cumann na mBan, and this organisation's fierce republicanism, echoing the stand taken during the Treaty debates by, among others, Erskine Childers, led contemporary wits to dub Sinn Féin the 'women and Childers party'.[70]

Little love was lost between women like these and those — generally male — republicans who emerged from prison to try to resume control of the movement; but Kevin Boland, at least, recalls his father telling him that Lemass got on better with the radical women than many of his comrades, seeing them less as nuisances to be sidelined and more as fellow-workers in the political struggle. Boland recalled that Markievicz was given to referring to Lemass occasionally at this time as Mephistopheles — presumably because of his penchant for a pencil moustache and his sleek back hair. And he added:

> Actually Lemass was one of the first people in FF to recognise the valuable role of women. Up to then the prevailing ethos in the organi-sation had been 'those bloody women' — a reference to the fact that while the leaders were in jail, people like Markievicz and MacSwiney were outside, taking all sorts of decisions which had the effect of influencing Sinn Féin away from the constitutional movement.[71]

The fact that Lemass was markedly younger than many of the other leaders was probably a factor. His mother, of course, was a politically radical woman. His closeness to Markievicz in particular — they shared a political stamping-ground in Rathmines — is also evidenced to some extent by documents on which they would have collaborated at around this time. She was to die in 1927, already a legend to the poor of Dublin, an icon undimmed by the subsequent bitter split in the movement to which she had devoted all her energy.

The first recorded contribution by Lemass to the proceedings of Comhairle na dTeachtaí came in the following year, just before his election in Rathmines and during one of a number of discussions on the management of *An Phoblacht*. The paper was at that time under the stewardship of a Newspaper Committee, and various members of the Comhairle, unhappy with the direction the paper was taking, proposed a strengthening of the committee. One member, J. O'Doherty, wanted to subsume the efforts of the publication into a full-blooded Department of Propaganda.[72] Lemass plainly had little time for top-heavy committees when there was important propaganda work to be done. Supported by Kathleen Clarke, Tom Clarke's widow, he proposed that 'the Organising Director, the Manager and the Editor get a free hand and that the other Committee be abolished.' He was defeated on this and then seconded the president's successful compromise proposal that a committee be appointed to advise the Cabinet on the management of the paper and to report back to the Comhairle.[73]

It is probable that Lemass also contributed to a draft policy statement on the North in 1925 that proposed committing Comhairle na dTeachtaí to 'recognising, as all people of this country do recognise, the many costly and uneconomic results [of partition] that are now in evidence' and proposing 'to endeavour to effect a basis of unity through the Medium of a Senate or a Council of all-Ireland. Our purpose would be to secure Free Trade with the Thirty-Two counties, concerted action on all matters of mutual Economic and Cultural Interest.'[74]

It is at this point that the sparse evidence available suggests that Lemass was seriously beginning to question the wisdom of abstention. While the minutes of the meeting of 22 June 1925 suffer unduly from compression, they indicate quite clearly that while he did not feel himself to be in a position to call for an end to the abstentionist policy, he was in the process of trying to work out whether there could be a way around it. The minutes record that, on the question of participation in the Dáil, 'Seán Lemass mentioned some alternative policies, yet he believed that as a minority we could go in there, attack legality of the Parliament but recognise only that it is the Parliamentary machinery of the government of this country. He was not certain that this would be the best policy.'[75] There was no way of going 'in there' without confronting the question of the oath.

His indecision, such as it was, failed to reach the notice of the Free State intelligence service. Garda informants, who reported regularly throughout 1925 and the early part of 1926 on the progress of the debate about abstention within Sinn Féin, unfailingly allocated Lemass (and frequently de Valera himself) to the more hard-line group. One agent reported in October 1925 that 'a number of leaders in the Sinn Féin organisation, headed by Éamonn Donnelly, want a change in policy and entry into the Dáil; De Valera, supported by Lemass and a majority of the military section, opposes this and the opposition are endeavouring to remove him from office as a result.'[76] In November another agent reported that 'the Army are dead against this course [entry into the Dáil] and have on their side three women TDs, Lemass and O. Traynor.'[77] The following January this opinion was reinforced by an agent who reported that 'the extreme element of the political group, headed by Seán Lemass and Miss McSwiney, are opposed to entry into the Dáil. The moderates support de Valera's policy of entry on condition that the oath is withdrawn.'[78]

The relationship between the military and political wings of the movement was in a state of flux. In contrast to the views of the intelligence service, a number of leading IRA figures suspected that Aiken and Lemass in particular were prepared, as early as 1925, to jettison the opposition to the oath, or at least to enter the Dáil if it were abolished. One embittered member of the Army Council, A. Cooney, said eight years later that both Aiken and Lemass had disingenuously supported at the convention a proposal to dissociate the IRA from political control because they were 'heartily glad to be rid of the Governmental position to which the allegiance of the Army would tend to bind them.'[79]

The public events that Lemass was undoubtedly associated with at this time, however, suggest that he was slow to abandon his political role as Minister for Defence, even if the activities he retained influence over smacked more of vigilantism than of military might. The 1925 Sinn Féin ardfheis, for example, had passed a resolution instructing all delegates to take action against British propaganda in cinemas. Lemass, speaking to the motion, echoed strongly held current views about the effectiveness of the new medium as a political and ideological weapon when he warned that 'the principles of Irish nationalism were in danger of extinction amongst a large section of people as a result of this propaganda.'[80]

There was more to this than met the eye. Some days previously armed men had held up the management of the Masterpiece cinema in Talbot Street, Dublin, and disrupted the showing of the British war film *Ypres*. On 30 November a similar escapade took place in Galway, where IRA men seized a copy of the film *Zeebrugge*. The ardfheis resolution had the dual function of providing a retrospective justification for the earlier military action (presumably carried out on Lemass's orders as Minister for Defence, or at least with his approval) and a mandate for the subsequent one.

It was an exceptionally busy period for Lemass. Even as the ardfheis was meeting he and his able secretary, George Gilmore, were planning a successful rescue attempt of republican prisoners in Mountjoy. Gilmore considered Lemass to be exceptionally cool in emergencies and provided some evidence of Lemass's single-minded attention to detail — and his ability to sideline possibly dangerous distractions—when he observed that Lemass had one prisoner with strong socialist convictions, Mick Price, transferred to another section of Mountjoy prison in October 1923 'in case he might affect the other prisoners with Larkinism.'[81] The escape took place on 27 November and involved nineteen prisoners in all. Lemass regarded it as one of the most successful operations he had been involved in.

The political reality of Lemass's position within the movement, however, was undoubtedly more complex. Éamon de Valera's success in veiling his true intentions from his own followers evidently posed an even more insuperable barrier to intelligence agents. Where Lemass's role is concerned, the evidence suggests that his close involvement with the IRA, accurately flagged by the intelligence service, had a number of different objectives, none of which excluded the possibility that a realignment was taking place on the question of shifting the focus of republican attack from the supposed illegitimacy of the Dáil itself to the political inconvenience of the oath.

One simple objective was the maintenance of his increasingly nominal role as Minister for Defence. A second was his evident desire to head off a split by associating the power centres in the IRA for as long as possible with the process of political evolution that was taking place. Finally there was the fact that Lemass was plainly using younger elements in the IRA to assist him in what he saw as the vital task of revitalising Sinn Féin organisationally. It would not have been surprising if some of the younger elements in the IRA that he counted on were more in sympathy both with his organisational initiatives and with his attempt to widen the political options. One Free State police informant noted:

> Lemass is on the reorganisation Committee, and he is endeavouring to supplant the present committee of the Sinn Féin Cumann on the North side by members of the military section or, as he puts it, by infusing young and new blood into the organisation. This is the reason for the ill feeling against Lemass in the North side, as the 'old bloods' refuse to be supplanted, and new and rival Cumanns are springing up … There are now two Erskine Childers Cumanns in the North side.[82]

By early 1926 the government's intelligence service, by now catching up with political reality, had discerned that the moderates within Sinn Féin were now led by Boland and Lemass.[83]

The strains were already beginning to show. At a meeting of Comhairle na dTeachtaí in early 1926, when members were getting bogged down in a semi-theological discussion about the relationship between the Comhairle and the Second Dáil, it was suggested that actions of the Comhairle needed to be ratified by the anti-Treaty minority in order to acquire constitutional validity. Lemass exploded:

> I was never a member of the Second Dáil but I was a member of this body and I held a position on the executive as the Head of the department of defence. In that position I sanctioned certain military acts, for example, the raid on Mountjoy prison in November last. I think it is a most astounding suggestion that my action needs any ratification from this Body. I think that we should resent that very much. These acts were just as valid then as they are now. I, as one of this body in giving my approval to this act gave it all the justification needed.[84]

In time the tensions led irrevocably to the split. Already in November 1925 there had been a meeting of the Army Council in Dalkey at which the IRA in effect renounced the last remnants of democratic control and accountability. It was evident to at least some of the participants that the game was entering a new and decisive phase. De Valera told the meeting that the army's decision to revert to its former status as a volunteer body had removed 'the last shred of authority from the [Republican] Government.'[85]

Lemass, who had been nominated in late February 1925 to succeed Aiken as Minister for Defence 'on a temporary basis,'[86] blamed some unnamed members of the Comhairle, at a meeting of that body held around the same time, for stirring up dissension in the ranks. He believed, he said, that

> certain deputies here present discussed with members outside this body certain matters, whether that affected or created a feeling of suspicion … In fact I have definite information that certain suspicions were aroused amongst different sections of the army through the indiscreet utterances of people whose names I am aware of.[87]

Deputy Frank Fahy of Galway challenged Lemass to say whether or not he was one of the deputies Lemass had in mind, observing defiantly that he had been 'discussing matters with people who were not republicans at their request from several counties in Ireland.' His tone of outraged innocence was not entirely convincing, and Lemass declined to take the bait. The now ex-Minister for Defence told the same meeting that 'certain proposals for securing Army-Sinn Féin co-ordination were placed before the Army convention by himself' but that 'since 6 o'clock he had no further responsibility and was not even now a member of the army.'[88] Both he and Aiken had in fact been expelled from the IRA, although Aiken later said that he had not been formally notified of his expulsion until the day after he entered the Dáil.[89]

This abrupt end to a shadow ministerial career appears not to have been fully followed through, for Lemass still plainly regarded himself as Minister for Defence on behalf of Comhairle na dTeachtaí when overseeing the

Mountjoy escape twelve days later. He was also making plain his flexibility on the central political issue, and the question of Dáil participation was increasingly on the agenda. By June 1926 he was telling a meeting of the Comhairle that he

> did not see that principle was involved at all and thought that the matter was certainly open for discussion: that is, the proposal to go into the FSP [Free State parliament] if the oath was removed altogether. We had used the elections as a means for getting republican deputies elected, but without admitting the legality of the F.SP by doing so. We are admitting nothing except the fact of their existence — the fact that they control the machinery. Therefore, he held that, altogether apart from the question as to whether it is good policy or not, in fact, if we are free to consider it, it is our duty to do it.[90]

Lemass was rapidly establishing himself as a force to be reckoned with through the medium of the republican press. A series of five articles he wrote for *An Phoblacht* between September 1925 and January 1926 was notable for his critical evaluation of Sinn Féin's organisation and policies. In one of them, which probably caused the greatest political controversy within the organisation, he suggested that Sinn Féin should concentrate on a limited political objective: the abolition of the oath of allegiance. That this was now also becoming de Valera's policy and the policy issue on which the organisation was to suffer its major split less than six months later was hardly coincidental.

Lemass attacked what he saw as the 'signs of decay' in Sinn Féin: members spending time squabbling 'like old women' about trivial points of rules and procedure, and an organisation as a whole that had become calcified from the top down. The timing of the articles was significant, for elections to the officerships were due, and Lemass in effect declared 'no confidence' in the existing officers by calling for the election of men and women who were young and active and not afraid of change.[91] He did not have it all his own way: one of his opponents pointed to his initial electoral failure as evidence of his lack of organisational skill[92] and accused him of being prepared to give conditional acceptance to the oath.

By now Lemass, according to Farrell, was 'virtually inviting schism.'[93] External events, in addition, notably the failure of the Boundary Commission at the end of 1925 to make any significant difference to the map of partition, were adding considerably to the tensions in the party. With the covert help of P. J. Ruttledge, the editor, Lemass managed to eke out the controversy. On 29 January 1926 he was arguing passionately that the oath was 'the most obvious' of a number of immediately realisable objectives that were necessary staging posts on the way to 'the reality we want.' His contributions continued until the end of February 1926, by which time they would undoubtedly have had a substantial — but, as it turned out, not substantial enough — impact on the mind of delegates gathering for the ardfheis.

Farrell suggests that the articles 'seemed designed to drive de Valera from debate to decision.'[94] Lemass's call for members to move away from debating abstruse points and towards action, whether it amounted to a call for schism or not, was evidently a demand for more radical change than some of the party's hierarchy were yet willing to contemplate. It was also, however, given de Valera's private reaction to the 1925 by-elections, far less likely to have been an attempt to influence de Valera himself and much more likely to have been an attempt to influence others on de Valera's behalf. 'Lemass said all that de Valera wished to say, and he said it well.'[95] Not for the first or last time, the respect felt by the younger man for de Valera's intuition found vigorous political expression.

In the early months of 1926 the tensions within Sinn Féin came inexorably to a head. At the ardfheis, which took place in March in Rathmines Town Hall, de Valera's motion to the effect that the removal of the oath — if this were possible — would make parliamentary politics a matter of policy rather than of principle was defeated. Apparently resigned to permanent defeat, de Valera walked out of the hall with Lemass and confided to him that he would now be leaving public life. Lemass, astonished, pulled his mentor back from a potentially momentous decision, although the process apparently necessitated more than one argument. De Valera's son Vivion later told Charles Haughey that Lemass went out to de Valera's home in Cross Avenue in Blackrock and told him: 'We have to form a political party. We have to get into politics.'[96]

Lemass had been elected to the Sinn Féin Standing Committee for 1926, and he moved swiftly and decisively into action. On 19 March he wrote to all members of the committee saying that it had been decided unanimously 'to proceed with the advocacy of the President's [de Valera's] policy, and, if necessary, to form an organisation for the purpose, subject to the approval of the President.'[97]

The name for the new organisation was still undecided. De Valera wanted Fianna Fáil; Lemass favoured the Republican Party. The hurriedly printed letter-heading provided evidence of the continuing disagreement. On 24 March it was *The Republican Party,* of which Lemass alone was acting secretary. De Valera formally resigned from Sinn Féin on 28 March, together with Lemass, Austin Stack, and Art O'Connor. By 6 April a General Organisation Committee had been formed for an organisation that was now described as 'Fianna Fáil (Irish Republican Party)'. By 14 April, when Lemass wrote out to invite support for 'a progressive republican party based on the actual conditions of the moment,' it had reverted to 'Republican Party', but de Valera's choice was, neither for the first nor the last time, to prevail over Lemass's less romantic proposal, albeit in a compromise formula in which both titles were used. Lemass and Gerry Boland were appointed to the new party's Policy Committee,[98] and in their message to the party's first ardfheis, in November of that year, they argued that the name had been chosen 'to convey ... the idea of an association of selected citizens, banded together for the purpose of rendering voluntary service to the Irish nation.'[99]

A contemporary photograph of the members striding into the Everyman Theatre (now the Gate) to attend the first Fianna Fáil ardfheis on 24 November 1924 shows Lemass just behind de Valera, in an immaculately tailored double-breasted suit with knife-edge creases in the trousers and a bowler hat at a slight but unmistakably jaunty angle.[100] The generation gap between the two men is evidenced by their sartorial styles. De Valera's appears positively dowdy, while Lemass's dress sense was carried through into everyday life: walking to work in the mornings he was still every inch the military man, with a belted coat, a peaked cap at a tilt, and a seviceable ashplant tucked under his arm 'in the style of an officer leading a regiment.'[101]

For the next fifty years Lemass's name was to be increasingly associated with de Valera's in this 'association of selected citizens'. And his special gifts in organisation were rapidly deployed in the service of the new party.

For all the bravura displays at the previous year's ardfheis, serious under-lying political and organisational difficulties had been emerging within the old Sinn Féin. Despite the best efforts of Lemass and others on the party's various committees, organisation in particular was in a critical state. The private organisational report to the ardfheis — subsequently leaked to the press by government sources — noted that the number of branches had fallen from 1,500 in 1923 to 797 in 1924. Of the latter only 178 had paid their affiliation fees in full, and a further 202 were represented by partial payments. The party's financial deficit for the year was £1,321.

Within the new party the task of organisation fell jointly on the shoulders of Lemass and Boland. Lemass bought five old Ford cars for £5, to be driven by himself and four other party organisers. A fast and impatient driver, he cared little for the comfort of his passengers in his desire to maximise the party membership and its electoral base at this critical stage of its existence. On one occasion when his car had broken down, Lemass telephoned de Valera to explain his predicament, to be astonished by de Valera's accurate surmise that he had broken down just outside Port Laoise. 'How on earth did you know?' Lemass asked. 'I happen to know', de Valera replied, 'that there's a long, straight, wide piece of road there, and that before that point it is very winding. I also know you and your impatience — and I know you could not resist slogging the old car.' On another occasion he arrived at an after-Mass meeting in Clara with one of his passengers, the future minister Paddy Little, pouring blood from his nose after the car had hit a bad bump on its trajectory from Tullamore.[102]

At public meetings Lemass had no time for false heroics or rhetoric. At one of them a party worthy was telling a hungry Dublin crowd about a tour he had once returned from when Lemass, waiting his turn to speak, whispered to his neighbour with barely concealed impatience: 'Why doesn't he just talk about bread and butter?'[103]

The modus operandi of the new organisation was simplicity itself: to identify the key republican activists in each area, especially if they were undecided about the political course to be adopted in the wake of the split between Sinn Féin and Fianna Fáil, and bring them into the new party in the certain knowledge that each would be followed by a strong cohort of supporters. They were to find out, encouragingly, that the opinion of the ardfheis had not been an accurate reflection of the feelings of the organisation in the country as a whole.

Some of Lemass's efforts were more successful than others. In Donegal he once found his way to a farmhouse and asked a small boy where his father was working, to be given directions to a nearby hayfield. The man he was looking for was Neil Blaney, the political patriarch who would have stayed with Peadar O'Donnell and the old Sinn Féin were it not for Lemass's persuasiveness.[104] The youngster, astonished at the apparition from the metropolis, was the young Neil Blaney, later to be a minister in Lemass's first Government.

Elsewhere in Donegal, probably in the southern part of the then united constituency, and often enough in other parts of the country, the very impetuousness and decision-driven praxis that made him such a force to be reckoned with had its negative side, especially among more conservative republicans, who didn't like being rushed into commitments, however much they might sympathise with the cause. Kevin Boland remembered:

> My father was joint honorary secretary of Fianna Fáil with Lemass, and they worked very closely together. As it developed, however, Lemass became the headquarters man, my father the field man. Lemass had an abrupt manner: he didn't have the balance that was required for country people. He came to realise himself that he couldn't deal with the rural mind: it was too lackadaisical. My father had the patience for it — it took him three years to get Moylan to join. The thing was that if you identified a key IRA man in any one locality and got him to join, then you had a ready-made organisation that came along with him. The first time I ever heard really bad language it was about Lemass, and it was from Éamonn Donnelly, a Newry man who was involved in organisation. On a trip back from Donegal once he used really bad language — he detested Lemass! It must have been something to do with what he found in Donegal.[105]

The strong feeling between Lemass and Gerry Boland would emerge in other arguments that were to recur in future years. In the meantime they worked in harness, organising Fianna Fáil's access to democratic power through the cumainn and the ballot box. One of Fianna Fáil's founding members described Lemass many years later: 'I always considered he brought military methods into politics — kindly military methods, if you like: but everything was in the nature of a disciplinary task which had to be done and not to be complained about.'[106]

One of the first fruits of success was in the two 1927 general elections. Fianna Fáil was still outside the Dáil but growing exponentially in the country. One astute political scientist has argued both that Fianna Fáil's abstentionist period helped positively to build up its grass-roots organisation and that the proportionately greater electoral advances made as a result of this organisational drive were within the urban centres, rather than on the western periphery of the country.[107] This was the drive that Lemass, as the chief urban genius, was most closely associated with.

The Cosgrave Cumann na nGaedheal government's desire to force Fianna Fáil to make the hard choice between coming into the Dáil and going into the electoral oblivion of permanent abstentionism eventually succeeded. Its chief weapon was a new law that required all Dáil candidates to affirm that if elected they would take the oath. This put it up to Sinn Féin in no uncertain fashion: if they declined to make the necessary preliminary declaration their names would not even appear on the ballot paper; if they took it, their moral armour in relation to the oath would be severely dented. This Cosgrave tactic added considerably to the pressure on Fianna Fáil and was aided no doubt by increasing unease within the new party, as it added to its number of TDs, about the prospect of shouldering more and more responsibility without being allowed to taste even a morsel of power.

Cumann na nGaedheal was to remain in government for another five years. The ultimate price of its success in forcing Fianna Fáil to make the unpalatable choice, however, was high: the party, and its successor, Fine Gael, was never again to form a single-party administration, and Fianna Fáil was to occupy the cabinet room for sixteen unbroken years from 1932.

The first of the 1927 elections, in June, saw Lemass heavily involved in the national campaign. With Boland he wrote the party's election address, which harped on a major Fianna Fáil theme: the need for all those who had split from it in the past to come back into the fold.[108] He topped the poll in his own constituency and was easily elected. The party achieved a remarkable degree of success for one that had been in existence for just over a year, securing only 1 per cent less of the national vote than the united Sinn Féin organisation had secured four years earlier and the same number of seats. The party even went so far as to appoint three whips — Lemass, Gerry Boland, and Frank Aiken[109]— and to endorse further feelers being put out by de Valera towards the Labour Party. Lemass seconded a motion endorsing a proposed pledge by de Valera to Labour.[110]

But Fianna Fáil was still outside the Dáil. On 23 June de Valera got the National Executive to agree to support a legal action by Lemass and Seán T. O'Kelly to challenge the constitutionality of the oath.[111] Lemass, who was evidently sceptical about the potential of such a move, said it would be 'like arraigning the devil in the court of Hell,'[112] but events were already over-taking them. Kevin O'Higgins, the Minister for Justice, was assassinated on 10 July, and the Electoral Amendment Bill published the following month meant that deputies who failed to take the oath would be unseated. The gun had not yet been taken out of politics but in an electoral sense it was now aimed at the heads of de Valera and his followers.

Lemass, who had already said in July that 'we have been urged to take [the oath] and break it; we will not do that because political morality should not sink so low,'[113] was now centrally involved in the party's reconsideration of its position. A lengthy meeting heard both Lemass and de Valera, among others, report that their own constituency organisations would favour enter-ing the Dáil. Only six of the TDs present were doubtful or voted against. At the end of the meeting Lemass was appointed to a smaller committee of party members to consider their position in relation to the oath,[114] and in that committee he argued strongly for the 'empty formula' approach.[115] On Friday 12 August 1927 de Valera, Lemass and the other Fianna Fáil deputies finally declared the oath to be an empty formula and took their seats in the Dáil.

Lemass's shift against abstention was not, it appears, accompanied by any belief in the necessity of doing business with other parties—at least not initially. Before the second 1927 election Thomas Johnson made an over-ture to Fianna Fáil about possible collaboration,[116] which Eoin Duffy and others on the Fianna Fáil National Executive thought deserved a positive response. According to Duffy, Lemass, possibly spiky at the failure of the earlier pledge to Labour on which he had co-operated with de Valera, 'killed it.'[117] Once inside the gates of Leinster House, however, co-operation became easier. Fianna Fáil and Labour's attempt to unseat the government failed but precipitated another general election, in which Fianna Fáil increased its Dáil representation from 44 to 57 seats and Lemass increased his personal margin over his closest constituency rival by 1,500 votes.

Returned again to the Dáil, Lemass threw himself into parliamentary politics with the energy of one released from long confinement. From then until the Fianna Fáil government took office in 1932 he fulfilled three critical roles: as party organiser on a national scale, as an office-holder and tactician within the parliamentary party, and as a vigorous debater and controversialist in the Dáil itself, whose contributions, with one or two notable exceptions, helped to push the Civil War further into the background of politics than most contemporary participants or observers would have thought possible.

His work as a party organiser has largely been unrecorded and will perforce remain so: the infant organisation's documentary records are functional and sparse. During this period, he told one colleague, he 'had not seen Dublin on a Sunday for three years,'[118] and during the hectic pre-electoral July–August period of 1932 he was, unusually for him, rarely present at parliamentary party meetings.[119]

The reports that Lemass and Boland, the two honorary secretaries, made to the annual ardfheiseanna provide vivid evidence of the nature of the organisational drive and of the energy that went into it. The report to the 1927 ardfheis, as well as issuing the customary warning that many of the 1,307 cumainn were in need of reorganisation, embodied a vision of the party as a two-way information system. It was not simply that the cumainn were expected to carry out orders from head office: they also had to 'pay special attention to the work of supplying the Teachtaí with reliable information concerning matters of local importance.'[120] This was to remain at the core of Lemass's understanding of the role of the party until he ceased to hold public office. There was an important distinction, however, between organisation and information, on the one hand, and policy. Supplying the first two was the responsibility of the party as such: the third was the exclusive preserve of those who had secured electoral mandates and, *a fortiori,* of Fianna Fáil governments.

It is hardly coincidental that the same ardfheis passed a resolution from a cumann in Lemass's constituency that pointedly indicated what 'matters of local importance' might be. It called for a propaganda campaign throughout the cumainn in support of Irish industries, and specifically instructed local units of the party to make reports to head office on all factories closed in their area, detailing the date of closure, the reason for closure, the identity of the owners, the state of the machinery, the possibilities of reopening, and 'any other useful information.'

Lemass was not above applying pressure through the ardfheis to make his task as a party whip easier. Some TDs were apparently reluctant attenders even then, and even in Fianna Fáil; the Fintan Lalor Cumann in Rathmines, also in his constituency, secured ardfheis approval in 1928 for a resolution that any TD who missed more than a third of the Dáil divisions in which he or she should have voted should be reported to all cumainn in the constituency concerned and should be ineligible for reselection as a candidate.[121] It is difficult, in retrospect, to see how the certainty — rather than the threat — of deselection could encourage errant TDs to mend their ways.

The same ardfheis instructed TDs, also on the basis of a motion from Rathmines, to visit every cumann in their constituencies at least once every six months. This may be thought a counsel of perfection, but for Lemass in particular it was evidently not an unwelcome burden, even though this was a year in which he visited both Northern Ireland and London as part of the organisation drive. Throughout his public life he was a conscientious attender at Comhairle Dáilcheantair meetings in particular and regarded it as an essential way of keeping in touch with grass-roots sentiment. He generally went to listen, not to give an oration.

The records of the Fianna Fáil parliamentary party, while scarcely expansive, provide an intriguing picture of Lemass as a man who took to his responsibilities as whip with some relish, or at the very least a marked sense of dedication, who lost internal party votes as well as winning them, and who was rapidly establishing himself as virtually the only person, apart from de Valera himself, entitled to speak with full authority on economic matters.

As whip Lemass made it a priority to fashion the somewhat hetero-geneous parliamentary party into the disciplined political organisation it later became. It was not always an easy task, and the documents of the period are redolent of the latent hostility between the Civil War opponents, leading to a de facto cold war in which even the ordinary social courtesies were harsh-ly proscribed. It was only four years, after all, since these parliamentarians, now on opposite sides of a democratically constituted parliament, had been lying in wait for each other, guns in their hands, behind ditches. That they could talk to each other at all was some kind of a political miracle, but the thawing process was necessarily long and difficult.

The party as a whole was, if anything, even more hostile. The 1929 ardfheis in November passed a resolution objecting to the attendance of Fianna Fáil parliamentarians at social functions promoted by Free State ministers. Such expressions of opinion were in a sense the tip of the iceberg of the remaining anti-constitutional feeling within Fianna Fáil; and it was Lemass's job to manage this collective emotion in such a way as to keep it under control, without allowing its adherents to feel that they were being treated in a cavalier fashion by their political leaders. The Civil War was still a fresh and, for some, a bitter memory. This undoubtedly explains his recom-mending that 'members should not conduct any business with Cumann na nGaedheal ministers in the bar or restaurant, and that fraternisation under any circumstances be not permitted.'[122]

What appears to have been a failure in this policy area is reflected in the subsequent even more draconian Lemass-driven decision that the bar in Leinster House 'be definitely out of bounds for members of the party.'[123] A number of parliamentary party meetings in 1929 in fact had to deal with the vexed question of a small number of members who were observed to be drunk in the precincts of the Dáil. Another, probably more common failing was a reluctance to pay parliamentary party subscriptions. Lemass also won support for his proposals that nobody be excused from participation in a Dáil vote without a medical certificate,[124] for a declaration on the need for secrecy about party meetings,[125] and for a decision that nobody speak in the Dáil without the permission of the whips.[126]

Throughout this period there was a high degree of co-ordination between the parliamentary party and the Central Committee (later known as the National Executive). The minutes of both organisations reveal that Lemass's pre-eminence in the economic sphere was rapidly securing acceptance. He was also on occasion to be found in a minority position, most noticeably where de Valera's passion for austerity seemed to him to be counterproductive. The parliamentary party's decision on 10 October 1927 that no government minister be paid more than £1,000 a year was passed by a majority only after a long discussion.[127] When the General Committee agreed in addition to oppose pensions for former ministers, Lemass was not present, and at the following meeting he raised an objection to the fact that the question had been decided in his absence, but without pushing for the matter to be reopened.[128]

Some time later he found himself with Seán MacEntee in a minority of two when the committee took a decision that a maximum of £1,000 a year should also apply to civil service salaries;[129] and the same alliance found themselves outvoted on a proposal that would have made the appointment of county managers a function of central government.[130] It should be remembered that £1,000 was a very substantial amount of money at this time: in 1997 it would be equivalent to close on £34,000, without making any additional correction for growth in gross national product in the interim. This evidently represented a personal change of policy on Lemass's part. During the second 1927 campaign he had promised, with evident relish, that Fianna Fáil in office would reduce the number of 'the more highly paid officials ... and the reduction of salaries which are out of all proportion to the worth of those receiving them.'[131] He also found himself on the losing side in an argument about whether public houses should be allowed to open on St Patrick's Day: the narrow 6-5 vote against the proposal saw him and de Valera on opposite sides.[132] The committee subsequently relented to the extent that it agreed not to oppose railway bars opening 'for five minutes before and after trains on St Patrick's Day.'[133]

Although he was actively engaged in most aspects of policy formulation — an activity to which parties in opposition generally devote unusual amounts of energy — Lemass maintained his preoccupation with economic policy. He had been appointed chairman of the parliamentary party's Industry and Commerce Committee immediately after the second 1927 election.[134] Within a week the party was discussing the question of unemployment, the remedy for which was seen (at least in part) as increased protection for domestically produced buses, locomotives, furniture, and house-building materials.[135] By December Lemass was working on an anti-trust Bill and led a lengthy discussion on price fixing and 'rings'. Criticism of the 1928 budget, he argued strongly, 'should be directed against the government's failure to impose any additional Protective Tariffs.'[136]

His activity inside the Dáil was matched by energy outside and an extraordinary appetite for work. In February 1928 he was despatched to London to investigate the possibility of setting up Fianna Fáil cumainn there.[137] One contemporary commentator contrasted Lemass's work rate with that of his leader's and suggested that he gave six speeches to every one by the Chief: 'Such a marked contrast between a leader and a lieu-tenant is most unusual.'[138] Another described him bluntly as 'the brains of the Fianna Fáil Party.'[139]

Lemass was the first party spokesman to submit a typed memorandum to any committee of the party[140]— a practice that de Valera urged should be widely emulated — and thereafter documents arrived at one or other committee with bewildering rapidity: on industrial protection, the Industrial Trust Company, boots, woollens, coaches, hosiery, paper, the Department of Posts and Telegraphs, and other economic matters. Unfortunately only one of these memorandums survives. It is a lengthy document summarising Lemass's views on economic policy, prepared for the Central Committee and sent to Frank Gallagher on 26 July 1929 with a covering letter noting that it was not for publication.[141] In the breadth of its approach it is a remarkable document of more than thirty pages, covering the whole spectrum of economic development as it was then understood and tackling forthrightly, if not always successfully, some of the thorny issues that Fianna Fáil, and indeed Ireland, was beginning to grapple with.

Lemass plainly senses a difficulty in that his economic and his political instincts are tugging him in different directions. In economics he is close to being a free-trader and speaks with some admiration of the concept of a 'United States of Europe', which had recently been advanced by Aristide Briand. Briand, who was born in 1862, was a lawyer and journalist as well as a politician of the left who had already been twice Prime Minister of France when he became Minister for Foreign Affairs in 1925. The follow-ing year he successfully established the Kellogg-Briand pact with the United States, which precluded war between the two countries, and then 'hit on the notion of solving the German problem by making it irrelevant.'[142] His grand design, announced at the League of Nations in 1929, just before Lemass submitted his memorandum to Fianna Fáil, was for a European federal union that would not impair national sovereignties. Even more to the point, the object was to achieve a general lowering of tariffs in the interest of world trade and to establish in Europe a 'common market'.[143]

Lemass found the internal logic difficult to resist: 'if the only factor to be taken into account is the welfare of mankind as a whole, irrespective of local or national interests, the case of unlimited freedom of trade is unanswerable.' De Valera himself was another convert, but whereas he was to turn away from the idea in disillusion later, it had a permanent influence on Lemass's philosophy, which was not to flower fully for another four decades. For the time being, however, the welfare of mankind as a whole had to take second place to the establishment of the Irish Republic. In the real world, Lemass argued, there are separate nations and there is a 'spirit of nationality' which is 'sometimes disasterous [sic]' but 'on the whole beneficial.' In this context, while 'possibly in the far future the spirit of nationality will die out and the project of a world state may take practical shape … the agitation for protection of industries is identical with the struggle for the preservation of our nation.' In other words, in any conflict between the economic and the political, the political has to be the victor.

Lemass here was not only providing a political and cultural rationale for the new and growing international belief in protectionism but was elaborating a praxis that was to provide a much-needed justification for many of de Valera's most cherished visions of the future. It was to be the guiding part of his economic philosophy for the best part of a quarter of a century, but it would also, by and large, fail to secure the objectives that Lemass and Fianna Fáil consistently set for themselves: a consistent and even dramatic reduction in unemployment and emigration. In fifteen years, Lemass pointed out, half a million people — a figure equivalent to the entire population of Connacht — had left. Many more were to leave in the years that followed, whether Fianna Fáil was in power or not. The spirit of nationality might die out in 'the far future'; in the here and now it was the engine that drove everything.

Lemass could hardly have expected that his instinctive hankering after free trade would have to be sidelined, or suppressed, for another thirty years. Some of the weaker points in his 1929 document too are more readily perceived with the benefit of hindsight. One of its key — and most questionable — assumptions is of relative stability in domestic and international economic activity. 'Our object', he wrote, 'is to secure the highest possible standard of living for the greatest number of human beings in Ireland … The goal of our efforts should be to keep the Irish people in Ireland and provide prosperity for them here. Everything else, even cheap living and accepted notions about efficiency, must be sacrificed to that end.'

Advocating a policy of tariffs and customs duties to protect industries and the creation of a central bank, he compared Irish and Danish agriculture to buttress his belief that with the existing agricultural work force productivity could be vastly increased, so that agriculture, the engine of economic growth, would be able to play its full part in the creation of national prosperity.

None of this would have been exceptional, and much of it would have been possible, in a world whose other governments and citizens were prepared to facilitate such a plan. In practice, however, the analysis was deficient in a number of important areas. It failed to identify, much less address, the likely consequences for economic policy of economic retaliation by other countries (although Lemass would doubtless have replied to this that in 1929 our first objective was self-sufficiency and that exports would come later). By comparing Irish and Danish agricultural productivity on the basis of a single year's figures, instead of studying trends over time, he allowed himself to envisage a dramatic increase in agricultural productivity rather than realising that the more likely consequence was a dramatic increase in rural depopulation, migration, and emigration. And there was certainly an element of optimism in his belief that Irish people — or at least those who had a choice — would willingly exchange the advantages of 'cheap living' elsewhere (notably in Britain and still to some extent in the United States) for the somewhat less tangible benefits of remaining in Ireland. It was certainly inconsistent with his clear understanding that such altruism could not be expected from farmers, who would have to be wooed with tariffs, subsidies and prohibitions of various kinds, because 'it is obviously unfair, and probably impossible, to make agriculturalists change their form of production for another of a less profitable nature'!

Elsewhere in the document too there is a sense of facts being somewhat brutally treated to fit into an argument, and of inconsistencies. While Irish industries should never be handed over to foreign interests, who seldom developed an export trade and tended to appoint non-nationals to senior management positions, 'there is no-one who will suggest that any action should be taken to interfere with such concerns as Messrs Guinness of Dublin and Messrs Ford of Cork.'

All this was accompanied by a brief, and prophetic, analysis of the economic consequences of partition, in which he warned that the longer partition existed the less easy it would be to solve, as there would be 'in each area a tendency towards economic self-sufficiency which will take no account of the resources or needs of the other part, and vested interests in the maintenance of the Border will grow up.' In the future, he warned, the inevitable awakening of the national conscience created a 'prospect of future strife, which is inherent in the situation [and] will act as a deterrent to progress on both sides of the Border.'

In the Dáil he displayed a degree of moral courage in the debate in 1929 on the Censorship of Publications Bill, which was taking place in an atmosphere dominated by the rhetoric and tactics of Father R. S. Devane's Irish Vigilance Association. This Bill was brought forward by the government in the wake of the publication in 1926 of the report of the Committee on Evil Literature. Within Fianna Fáil the initial discussion was withdrawn from the full parliamentary party to a special committee, of which both Lemass and de Valera were members.[144] This was almost certainly a device to prevent a rump developing within the party in favour of even more extreme forms of censorship than were then proposed.

Lemass — whose welcome for the Bill was characterised by some measured reservations — warned that it was easy to go too far in matters of censorship and criticised in particular the vagueness of the phrase that condemned literature 'calculated to excite' sexual passion. 'It is obvious of course to everybody', he said, 'that sexual passion in itself is neither indecent nor immoral.'[145] But arguably it was not so obvious to many of his contemporaries, both inside Fianna Fáil and outside it. Lemass also played unusually sophisticated politics with a disingenuous plea that the government should not include the concept of 'public morality' in the Bill, because the government newspapers had consistently declared opposition to land annuities to be 'contrary to public morality.' Patrick Hogan, the Minister for Agriculture, took up the challenge and replied spiritedly that if this were the case, then questions of public morality could readily be extended to other matters, 'whether commandeering is a proper word for robbery or theft, and I suppose the next time we are taking an oath we will call it an empty formula and push the Bible two feet away.'[146] Lemass was not so easily provoked on this occasion, although Hogan evidently did his best. (This was one of the very few occasions in a Dáil debate, then or since, in which the word 'morality' was used in a context that did not imply sexual morality.)

Despite his having to mark a number of ministers in the Dáil, as well as reorganising and strengthening the party outside it, Lemass allowed private life to claim at least some of his time. His young family was growing. His daughter Maureen, who later married Charles Haughey, was born in 1925. His daughter Peggy, whose husband, Jack O'Brien, was an army officer later chosen as Lemass's aide-de-camp when he was Taoiseach, was born in 1927. His only son, Noel, was born in 1929; and Sheila, his youngest child, was the only one born after he went into government, in 1934. She married a businessman, John O'Connor.

Lemass managed to improve the family situation, moving from his first marital home in a flat in Terenure to a more substantial house at 33 Villiers Road, Rathgar. The holidays in Skerries were resumed, and the friendship with Jimmy O'Dea was continued; one of Kathleen's sisters was to marry one of O'Dea's brothers.

Despite his acting ambitions having been side-tracked, Lemass still loved treading the boards. Before ministerial gravitas intervened, he, O'Dea and others used to put on plays and sketches in a hall in Skerries during the holidays. Lemass's already extraordinary memory could now be devoted to light-hearted pursuits; his recitation of 'The Green Eye of the Little Yellow God' was a favourite Skerries party piece. Recitations like 'Dangerous Dan McGrew' and songs like 'Wrap the Green Flag Round Me' were also staples of his repertoire.[147]

It was to be expected that a politician as energetic as Lemass would occasionally give hostages to fortune. One such, given in public, was when he advocated the establishment of a 'national economic council such as exists in Germany and France and such as is suggested by one of the big English parties for that nation,' which would decide the entire economic policy of the country.[148] This early willingness to hand over the levers of power to non-elected organisations was not long-lived. De Valera was to retreat from it rapidly after assuming office in 1932, and many years later Lemass's own considered position was briefly stated:

> I have not much faith in Councils or Commissions which are set up to advise, or prepare programmes for Governments, in the sphere of major policy. It has always seemed to me to be undesirable to attempt to divorce responsibility for framing policy from responsibility for its execution.[149]

Even more surprisingly, given his later differences of opinion with de Valera on the question of the usefulness of international organisations, he is to be found submitting a memorandum to the party's General Committee in 1931 advocating that the Free State not remain a member of the League of Nations and suggesting that the party make a commitment to withdraw from it if they came to power. The committee declined to accept his arguments on withdrawal, taking the softer option of deciding that the TDs should vote against the estimate for the Department of External Affairs when it came up in the Dáil.[150]

A 'SLIGHTLY CONSTITUTIONAL PARTY'

One of the important themes of these early years has been explored in rela-tion to the much-quoted Dáil exchange in 1928 in which Lemass described Fianna Fáil as a 'slightly constitutional party'.[151] It was certainly a remark made in the heat of the moment, and Lemass, while not unusual among Fianna Fáil politicians of the era in beating a republican drum, rapidly sought to cover his tracks. His outburst was gladly seized on by some of his opponents. Patrick McGilligan, the Minister for Industry and Commerce, was particularly happy to have been handed a weapon by his tormentor and saw it as an effort by Lemass to restore his standing within the IRA or as an example of the Jekyll and Hyde contrast between the serious politician and the unreformable gunman.[152]

Farrell argues that Lemass's remarks 'certainly suggest a less than whole-hearted commitment to democratic processes and reflect a pragmatic willingness to "go on the offensive" and use force to achieve political aims.'[153] His case, however, is not a strong one. In the first place, as Farrell also points out, Lemass, within a month, went to considerable lengths to repeat the phrase in a completely different context. This was when he suggested that Cumann na nGaedheal's creative attitude to amending the 1922 Constitution entitled that party also to the 'slightly constitutional' epithet: what was sauce for the goose could be sauce for the gander, and in a hot and steamy kitchen nobody could be quite sure who was wielding the ladle.

Secondly, the burden of the speech in which Lemass made this interjection was a sophisticated argument in favour of releasing political prisoners, which hinged on the undoubted fact that Lemass himself, and other Fianna Fáil members of the Dáil, had been up to their necks in similar activities. Lemass referred to the 1925 Mountjoy jail escape and to a speech in which Cosgrave alleged that at that time Lemass had been Minister for Defence and Frank Aiken Chief of Staff of the IRA. In a passage that glossed over his and Aiken's expulsion from the IRA and delicately finessed the issue of his own involvement, he posed the question:

> I do not know where President Cosgrave got his information. A number of these sensational disclosures which were made here were wrong and were founded on false information and, *possibly*, this information was of the same kind. But, if the information was correct, then Deputy Aiken and myself must have had knowledge of the Mountjoy incident and have sanctioned it, and, if the incident was of such a nature that three years after the event everyone connected with it must be punished to save the prestige of the State, it is strange that Deputy Aiken and I are here *if we had anything to do with it,* while those who actually engaged in it are prisoners in Mountjoy. [Emphasis added.][154]

Thirdly, there is a great deal of additional evidence to suggest that the intensity of Lemass's utterances on this issue, on the question of political prisoners generally and on the need to repeal repressive legislation was related primarily to his main political objective. This was to reassure those members of the party who were unhappy about the decision to enter the Dáil that Fianna Fáil's new-found willingness to operate the hated Cosgrave system did not mean that its republican teeth had been drawn. To this end, many Fianna Fáil speeches in 1928 and 1929, Lemass's among them, were vibrant, often dramatic reiterations of republican themes. One such speech by Lemass in 1928 managed to question the political credentials of the government on almost every count, alleging, among other things, that it had no policy on partition, that its policing policy was 'going to include in the definition of crime the desire to achieve the full political independence of Ireland,' and that the British were still in effective control of the armed forces.[155]

In a rare comment made after his retirement, Lemass elaborated on his motivation of more than four decades earlier:

> Our political problem of that time was to take a group of people who had fought in the Civil War and were still bitter in their defeat to make

them feel that political action would help them to achieve what they had not achieved during the Civil War. So all that time we had to appear to be — not to be reactionary — to constantly move these people away from the idea that the political objectives could be achieved only by physical force.[156]

During the September 1927 election campaign Lemass warned that Cosgrave's insistence that republicans should 'do penance' for their misdeeds was a recipe for disturbance, political instability, and industrial decay.[157]

During the same campaign he had to deal with an even more difficult problem when he took it on himself to reply directly to opponents who implied—as part of one of the main issues of the campaign — that Fianna Fáil's commitment to democracy had to be seen in the light of the fact that the IRA had not surrendered their dumped arms. The issue of the dumps was first raised by a Cumann na nGaedheal election advertisement, which trumpeted, *Why Fianna Fáil is Afraid — Because Fianna Fáil has got the Dumps and Dev. in the Dumps,*[158] and then in speeches by Cosgrave[159] and by Lemass's Cumann na nGaedheal rival in the Dublin South City constituency, Vincent Price SC.[160]

Lemass's riposte, when it came, was expressed in language that echoed some of the rhetoric of the 1995–97 controversy over the decommissioning of IRA weapons in Northern Ireland and that could legitimately be considered as positive, given the circumstances of the time. He had, he said, lately spoken in Athlone, with 'barracks to the right of him, barracks to the left of him, and barracks in front of him, all full of armed soldiers,' but

> the dumps are harmless if no-one goes near them; they are dangerous only if there is hate between Irishmen ... All danger from the dumps will be removed when the causes of ill-feeling between Irishmen are removed ... I believe that the arms in the Free State barracks are a greater threat to the peace of Ireland than are the guns rusting in the holes in the mountains. If Mr. Cosgrave is afraid of the dumps he also knows that Fianna Fáil does not control them. My offer ... is that we will promise to use our influence with those who control the dumps if Mr. Cosgrave will use his influence with those in control of the arms in the barracks, to put the whole lot together to be bartered for steam engines, and so do away with the possibility of another Civil War in Ireland.[161]

When his Dáil speeches were aimed primarily at disaffected republicans outside the Dáil, Lemass wanted to give the impression that his heart was in the right place. At other times he was capable of more eirenic noises, which attracted favourable notice on the government side of the house, not least from W. T. Cosgrave.[162] Indeed it would probably not be going too far to say that the McGilligan depiction of the two Lemasses was soon supplanted by a generalised Cumann na nGaedheal view that there were two Fianna Fáils: the de Valera Fianna Fáil, led by the arch-villain himself, and the Lemass Fianna Fáil, with whom honest men could perhaps do business.

It may have been a stance partly dictated by a forlorn hope of driving a wedge between de Valera and his most able lieutenant (if it was, it almost certainly had the effect of reinforcing the bond between them), but there was also a genuine air of wistfulness about it, a sense that had Lemass been on their side, many things might have been different. It was an attitude that was to find intermittent expression in subsequent years, outside the Dáil as well as inside. Alexis FitzGerald, for many years a senior figure in post-war Fine Gael, once confided to a friend his belief that Lemass was 'temperamentally and intellectually a Fine Gael type.'[163] Interestingly, it was mirrored in the attitude of many of the British politicians and senior civil servants the two Fianna Fáil leaders were to come in contact with later, although it is more difficult in the latter case not to suspect a more conscious attempt to secure political advantage by the tried and trusted policy of divide and rule.

On economic and national matters, however, the differences between Lemass and Cumann na nGaedheal were sharp. They were embodied in a formal way in the workings of the Economic Committee appointed by the government in 1928 under the chairmanship of Ernest Blythe. The committee had a huge remit but in effect tackled only one problem: wheat-growing. The minority Fianna Fáil membership on the committee put politics in the driving seat and economics between the shafts: growing wheat, whatever the economic implications of doing so, should be 'the first function of the Saorstát,'[164] because wheat was the primary component of bread, and bread was the staple diet of the population, and because the population was in decline.

The committee had no other significance except for two things. One was its composition: this was unusual in that it combined members of the Oireachtas and outside experts in a relatively tightly knit group. Lemass, for one, retained an affection for this formula: he was to propose it — unsuccessfully — many years later as a model for what eventually became the 1966 all-party committee on the Constitution. The second was the government's decision to appoint John Leydon, a civil servant in the Department of Finance, to act as secretary to the committee. They were in little doubt that they were appointing a safe pair of hands: Leydon was, and remained throughout his career, sceptical about the value of protectionism. But the calibre of his mind evidently impressed Lemass.

Lemass, however, was still in opposition, and the fiery young TD had little doubt but that executive political power should be used to coerce vested interests in society — notably those represented by the 'capitalist class' and the 'financial institutions' — to do the government's bidding in the interests of the 'plain, honest-to-goodness working men' who had built up the worth of the country.[165] He could be withering when he felt the occasion demanded it. Increasingly frustrated by the dilatoriness of the government's Tariff Commission and by what he saw as its failure to institute a full-blooded regime of industrial protection, he suggested that its members 'never appeared to be able to contemplate the possibilities of Irishmen fulfilling any other function than that of tinkers and handymen, pandering to the comforts of foreign tourists or acting as hewers of wood and drawers of water to such foreign industrialists as think fit to avail of such resources as are to be had here.'[166]

His speech on the estimate for the Department of Industry and Commerce in 1928 was to all intents and purposes a personal manifesto. He argued passionately for decasualisation of labour, the creation of a state investment trust and the introduction of state schemes of work, and national-isation of the railways. He uttered the heresy that 'our agricultural industry is overstaffed,' but capped it with the ringing declaration that 'it is the direct responsibility of the State to provide employment for those for whom private enterprise in agriculture or business is unable to provide.'[167]

But neither was he a dour ideologue. In the same year he enlivened an angry debate about the government's plan to alter the age limit for eligi-bility for the Seanad — an institution for which he never professed much regard, then or later — with the suggestion that it would be better to confine membership to citizens who were either under the age of six or over the age of sixty. 'One considerable advantage about having young people in the Seanad would be ... that they would not be influenced by the *Irish Times* because they would not be able to read it ... People over sixty would have found the *Irish Times* out by this.'[168]

His speaking style was originally forceful almost to the point of offensiveness: he was once accused of having given 'a corner-boy speech' — which, in the circumstances, might have been a compliment. The leader regarded him as a fluent speaker but suggested that 'he has yet to prove himself as an efficient politician.'[169] The *Irish Times* suggested later in the same year that he 'would be good if he were not so aggressively histrionic.'[170] Evidently taking some of these criticisms to heart, he modulated his deliv-ery to one that remained clipped and direct, without long, rambling sentences. Peadar McMahon, who had been Chief of Staff of the army and was Secretary of the Department of Defence for many years after 1927, once told Liam Cosgrave that Lemass had modelled his speaking style on that of Liam's father, W. T. Cosgrave. McMahon's source for this opinion was J. J. Parkinson, a senator and race-horse trainer with whom Lemass was sometimes pictured at race meetings and who was an occasional visitor to Lemass's offices in Industry and Commerce towards the end of the war.[171] McMahon was Parkinson's son-in-law, and his conversation with Cosgrave took place in Parkinson's house.[172]

The occasionally benign Cumann na nGaedheal view of Lemass would have been enhanced by a statement he made in January 1930 in explanation of Fianna Fáil's decision not to attend the official function of welcome for the new Papal Nuncio, Archbishop Paschal Robinson.[173] Lemass, while making it clear that the 1929 ardfheis decision 'binds our hands' and that 'there is no intention that we are going to depart from that policy,' said that he wanted to make it clear 'that we are not just trying to maintain an attitude of hostility to Free State Ministers as a result of incidents arising out of the Civil War' and that 'we have frequently met and co-operated with Ministers on Committees of the Dáil and in the house, where our views agreed as to the proper action to be taken.' The policy, he made clear, was not based on actions or statements of members of the government but adopted because 'recent actions by the Civic Guards, which presumably have been sanctioned by the Executive Council, have made it impossible for us to create the atmosphere that we would like to create in this country.'

This was patently a broad hint at the nature of the relatively limited steps that he expected the government to take in order to establish government with the consent of the governed, given at a time when de Valera was out of the country and without any consultation with the party organisation. These remarks led immediately to an undoubtedly acrimonious discussion at a special meeting of the Central Committee. This meeting decided unanimously that 'no statement of Fianna Fáil policy be issued in the name of the Party or Organisation except with the authorisation of the General Committee or with the authorisation of the acting chairman [Seán T. O'Kelly].'[174] The stable door had been banged shut, but the latch had been seriously damaged. All in all, and especially in the light of subsequent events, it is probably more accurate to assume that Lemass's more controversial statements in the Dáil two years earlier represented more of a farewell to arms than any sort of considered threat to resume hostilities.

The Cosgrave government's approach to the 1932 election was marked by an extraordinary tendency to embrace policies guaranteed to bring about defeat. When Ernest Blythe, as Minister for Finance, reduced the old age pension it was only the latest in a series of own-goals that had virtually every interest group in the country ranged against them. Their final *auto-da-fé* was to haul the editor of the *Irish Press*, Frank Gallagher, before a military tribunal on a charge of seditious libel.

External factors were equally unfavourable to the government. The Wall Street crash of 1929 had dramatically affected industrial employment in the United States, and thousands of Irish people who would otherwise have used the safety valve of emigration were now still in Ireland, unemployed and angry. The British general election of 1931 had put into office a coalition government that set out on a highly protectionist policy, and Irish industries faced the threat of dumping on an unprecedented scale.[175]

Cumann na nGaedheal now reached in vain for every weapon in its armoury, introducing a budget that increased the tempo of nascent protectionism and was warmly welcomed as such by manufacturers. As far as the electorate as a whole was concerned, however, such gestures were by now irrelevant. Shortly before polling day Cumann na nGaedheal warned the voters in a front-page advertisement in the *Irish Times:* 'The Gunmen are Voting for Fianna Fáil — The Communists are voting for Fianna Fáil.'[176] Both statements had the merit of being largely true, although to some extent beside the point, as the total number of gunmen and communists would scarcely have been enough to elect one TD.

The government's alarm, however, would have been intensified had they been aware of a conversation between Lemass and Peadar O'Donnell during the election campaign, in which Lemass told the still militant O'Donnell: 'Don't you see that we stand to gain from your organisation so long as we cannot be accused of starting the turmoil?'[177] This, however, can legitimately be interpreted as a measure of Lemass's willingness to ruthlessly exploit every opportunity for electoral advantage, rather than as evidence of any substantial degree of ambiguity on the issue of physical force. His campaign speeches, in contrast, were strongly designed to reassure doubtful or wavering voters by impressing on them the solidity, reliability and even conservatism of Fianna Fáil. His tactic was to combine attacks on the Cumann na nGaedheal economic policy for running 'like melted wax in the moulds of British diplomacy' with reassurances that Fianna Fáil 'would take no action consistent with the development of home industries which would endanger [trade with Britain] in any way.'[178]

Nor were his assurances aimed solely at businessmen. Evidently responding to government allegations about the totalitarian tendencies of Fianna Fáil, he twice promised the electorate that the referendum would be reintroduced into the Free State Constitution[179] so that the people could exercise a degree of supervision over the government if they were worried about what it was doing. The popular initiative for constitutional change, in which the process of amending the constitution could be initiated by securing the signatures of 90,000 voters for an amendment, had been abolished by the Cosgrave government in 1928 after de Valera succeeded in securing 96,000 signatures in May to force a plebiscite on the oath. Once in government, de Valera (and no doubt Lemass himself) was quick to see the unwisdom of reintroducing it. The government's increasing willingness to amend the 1922 Constitution to suit its own purposes, coming as it did only a few months after Lemass's 'slightly constitutional' remark, helps to place his comments in a historically relevant context.

More significantly, Lemass went to considerable lengths to indicate the orthodoxy of the parentage of Fianna Fáil policies. The party's social programme, he said, was 'along the lines laid down in the Pope's encyclicals.'[180] Not only that, but

> Fianna Fáil's policy was being misrepresented as being related to Communism. We stand for permanent peace between Irishmen, between Ireland and its neighbours, and in economic terms we stand not for Communism but for a constructive alternative to Communism. A Fianna Fáil government will endeavour to manage the affairs of the nation in the spirit of Cardinal McRory.[181]

Underlying many of his speeches was a constant refrain: conflict was to be avoided as counterproductive and corrosive; Fianna Fáil's policy was one of unity among all classes, because when all were working together the common good was served,[182] and unless they got the co-operation of all parties in an effort to solve their difficulties, things were likely to get worse.[183] Lemass was as conscious of the risks of alienating significant sections of opinion in private as he was in public. On one occasion, being driven to an election rally by his fellow-candidate Aodhagán O'Rahilly, he expressed anxiety at the rate at which they were proceeding through Mount Brown, a populous working-class estate with narrow streets unsuited to motor traffic. 'If you knocked down a child here,' he said to O'Rahilly with a sense of priorities that seemed inappropriate to the younger man, 'you'd lose a thousand votes.'[184] These were not the utterances of a young man storming the barricades but of an already seasoned campaigner who knew that the middle ground was the decisive territory to be fought over and who was developing a strategy to conquer it. More than this, however, he was also engaged in the process of elaborating his own personal ideology, a combination of de Valera-style populism and a conviction that Ireland's political and economic development could proceed along unique and Christian-inspired lines, which he maintained throughout his political career with relatively little change.

Others were slower to be convinced that Fianna Fáil had changed its spots. The *Irish Times* warned that now was the time for 'all unionists and imperialists to do their duty,' and added: 'The Marxian evangel cannot prevail. Its prophets and their few dupes in Ireland can draw a lesson from the study of Soviet land laws.'[185]

It was not enough. As the votes rolled in it became rapidly evident that Fianna Fáil, with Labour's support, would form the next government. The same newspaper that disclosed that *The Puritan* by Liam O'Flaherty had just been banned by the new Censorship Board recorded that Seán Lemass had received 10,426 votes in the South Dublin constituency.[186] He would at last be given an opportunity to put his policies to the test.

Even before the new government was announced, Lemass's name was to the fore. He and Gerry Boland were among the few tipped for ministries.

In the first photograph of the new government, de Valera had Lemass and P. J. Ruttledge — who as editor of *An Phoblacht* six years previously had defied the party bureaucracy by continuing to publish Lemass's pungent critique of the organisation—sitting on either side of him.[187] The following day de Valera was pictured making a 'talkie' on the Leinster House lawn, Lemass attentively at his elbow.[188] De Valera's body language revealed his affection for the younger man more clearly than any political title could convey.

3

Reconstruction
1932–38
The House that Jack Built

W hen Fianna Fáil members entered the Dáil in 1927 some of them, according to popular legend, had guns in their pockets. When they went into government five years later their accession to power was accompanied by almost as great a sense of apprehension. The outgoing government's policies had, under the Local Government Act, 1925, discriminated actively against Fianna Fáil activists or supporters in the critical area of public employment. The established civil service were presumed to be, in the unvarnished words of one of Lemass's contemporaries, 'a gang of Free Staters,' who simply could not be trusted; equally, many in the civil service saw their incoming political masters as 'ogres' who would in time devour them.[1]

Not everyone saw quite as black a picture, particularly where Lemass was concerned. Joseph Brennan, who as a Dublin Castle civil servant in 1921 had done invaluable and dangerous work for Michael Collins and who had been Secretary of the Department of Finance from 1923 to 1927, noted in 1932 that Lemass seemed a bit dour in manner but that this wore off on acquaintance. 'He is the shrewdest of the Ministers and I doubt if he will continue indefinitely to be an obedient servant to Dev, as he has a mind of his own. His chief defect as a Minister seems to be an exaggerated belief in the efficacy of state action and if he retains this he may do a lot of harm.'[2]

The outgoing Secretary of the Department of Industry and Commerce was Gordon Campbell. His son, the journalist Patrick Campbell, recalled his father speaking of the new Fianna Fáil government in the nineteen-thirties, his Anglo-Irish hauteur mingled with an irreducible element of loyalty to his old department: 'This present Government simply hasn't got the faintest idea of what it's doing. Lemass is all right but the rest of them couldn't run a village shop ... in Ballyslumgullion. The trade figures are appalling. They're recklessly importing every kind of trivial foreign luxury at prohibitive prices and all they can do in exchange is send a few flea-bitten cows to England.'[3]

Campbell's successor, John Leydon, was the civil servant who had already attracted Lemass's notice in 1928 in the Dáil committee on the economy, of which he had been secretary. Leydon was born on a small farm in Arigna, County Roscommon, in 1895, a relative, though a distant one, of the wealthier mine-owning family of the region. He had been a clerical student at Maynooth before joining the civil service and, like many other civil servants, had been posted to London, where he was an active member of the Gaelic League and of the League for Irish Self-Determination.[4] He successfully applied for permission to return to Ireland in 1923,[5] was appointed to the staff of the Department of Finance, and worked on the administration of compensation claims for damage suffered during the hostilities — a task in which his probity, executive skills and concern for standards were rapidly discerned by the first Free State government.

W. T. Cosgrave approached Leydon, following the 1932 election but before the change of government, with the proposal that he should become Secretary of the Department of Industry and Commerce. Leydon informed him that as there was a new government coming in he would prefer to leave the choice of Secretary to that government. When Lemass became minister he sent for Leydon and offered him the post. Leydon was 'very flattered,' and he said to Lemass that he had read many of his speeches — perhaps all his speeches — and that there were a number of points with which he was in disagreement. He wished to make this clear in order that Lemass could, if he so wished, reconsider his offer. Lemass, however, said, 'What I want is a man who will show me where I am wrong — the last thing I want is a yes-man.'[6]

In the sixteen years between then and 1948 the Leydon-Lemass partnership was critical, and Leydon — like Lemass, an intensely private man — provided the essential foundation for many of Lemass's achievements. One of his few weaknesses was for large cars, in which, because of his small stature, he was virtually invisible. Dublin wags used to say that if you saw a large American car going around Dublin with nobody driving it, that was Leydon.[7]

Leydon repaid Lemass's confidence by maintaining a strict loyalty to his political master, even when he disagreed with his policies. Nor did Lemass fail to recognise Leydon's gifts, appointing him chairman of Aer Lingus and Aer Rianta (1937–49) and of Irish Shipping (1941–49). According to C. S. Andrews, Leydon's influence waned to some extent after 1948, although he served as economic adviser to William Norton, Lemass's successor in the second inter-party Government, in 1955–56. Thereafter his public role was exercised largely in organisations such as the Institute of Public Administration and the Irish Management Institute. He remained a loyal admirer of Lemass until his own death in 1979. A visitor who interviewed him in 1974 in Our Lady's Manor, Dalkey, noted that a framed photograph of Lemass was placed prominently, and to a degree incongruously, among the pictures of the Sacred Heart and other religious motifs that were the only other decorations in the room.[8]

When Lemass assumed office he found himself in charge of one of the largest departments and one that was spread over no fewer than fourteen different buildings. If he wanted to see any senior officer in the department that officer had to be given twenty-four hours' notice so that he could arrange to leave someone else in charge of the building he was working in and travel over to meet the minister at a convenient time.[9] Lemass quickly organised the building of the new offices of the department in Kildare Street, on the site of the old Maples Hotel, although it took the Department of Finance two years to agree to his plans. His political opponents in later years were not slow to see this as early evidence of the empire-building tendencies they often reproached him with. In fact the department was already an empire in embryo, its responsibilities covering a huge range of economic and social activities, many of them eventually hived off into separate departments.

If the changeover in personnel was in some respects abrupt and fraught with suspicion and mistrust, the change in the direction of national policy in the economic field was less traumatic, and slightly more organic, than sometimes appeared to be the case. The Cosgrave government, particularly in the person of its Minister for Agriculture, Patrick Hogan,[10] had espoused a policy of free trade, not least because it was the conventional wisdom of the age, but even before Fianna Fáil had entered the Dáil there were signs that this commitment was wavering.

Some imports were restricted from 1924 onwards, and in 1926 the Tariff Commission was established to assist the government in framing a policy of selective protection. To some extent, therefore, Lemass and Fianna Fáil could claim — as Lemass had already done in November 1931 — that this was 'a further indication of the conversion of the Cumann na nGaedheal party to the policy of Fianna Fáil.'[11] But where Cumann na nGaedheal had acted hesitantly and fitfully, Lemass went into action like a whirlwind.

It was in some respects more a change of pace than a change of policy. William Peters, the British trade official in Dublin, wrote to his superiors that 'it is, I think, quite wrong to suppose that the present policy of extreme protectionism would not have been adopted by the Cosgrave government had it remained in office.'[12] The main difference, he suggested, was that what the Cosgrave government would have done in a period of between five and ten years de Valera had attempted in two. He also signalled the remarkable degree to which the new Fianna Fáil government was winning business confidence, contrasting the 'unity of direction and co-operation' that he discerned between the government and manufacturers during this period with the 'lack of unity and absence of co-operation' that he perceived in Britain. Given the traditional, almost neurotic British suspicion of Fianna Fáil, this was praise indeed for Lemass's strategy.

Between its accession to power in 1932 and the outbreak of the Second World War in 1939, Fianna Fáil had to cope not only with the high levels of unemployment and emigration that faced them at the outset but with the effects of the economic war with Britain over the land annuities (which they of course initiated) and the challenge of securing electoral dominance. There were no fewer than four general elections in the six years from 1932 to 1938.

For all its self-confidence, the new Executive Council (as the government was still called) was also to some extent 'pre-political', in Tom Garvin's phrase. In other words, they had to explore the nature and tensions of ideological differences after, rather than before, assuming office. They were agreed on protectionism and self-sufficiency, but these were inadequate enough signposts to the complex world of economic management and political decision-making. Their impressive public unity in the face of the emerging ideological differences they were to experience, especially on key economic issues, was battle-hardened both by their resistance to the moral siren song of Sinn Féin and by their determination to keep Cumann na nGaedheal at bay.

It was also a reflection of de Valera's political skills. Within the government itself he was pre-eminent and maintained his dominance almost effortlessly. Nonetheless his interests were, as Lemass himself pointed out, 'primarily political: he was not greatly interested in the details of economic policies. He applied simple tests to economic problems.'[13] It is also worth remembering that governments of the nineteen-thirties were small: ten was the maximum number until after the adoption of the Constitution of 1937, which set the limit at fifteen, and there were never more than five parliamentary secretaries. This increased the likelihood that public unity would be maintained, just as it must have, on occasion, magnified the internal disagreements.

Seán T. O'Kelly and Frank Aiken were particularly close to de Valera. O'Kelly was appointed Vice-President (Tánaiste after 1937) and maintained this significant role until elected to the Presidency in 1945. Aiken's relationship with de Valera, however, was in the long run more significant, because he was a much younger man — he was only a year older than Lemass — and remained a power within the party right up to Lemass's retirement. He also had, in contrast to Lemass, a significant range of ministerial appointments and up to Lemass's appointment as Tánaiste in 1945 might have been regarded as the better bet for the succession.

Aiken had a quirky approach to economic and financial matters and leaned towards distributism. He was also a part-time inventor and took out a number of patents — one for an electric cooker in the nineteen-fifties and another, for a sprung heel for a shoe, while he was a Government minister in 1961. He had a substantial farm in County Dublin, where he experimented with plants and agricultural processes. More significantly, he was part of a powerful axis involving C. S. Andrews and de Valera; he had an access to de Valera that was possibly even more significant than that enjoyed by Lemass, and he and Andrews had taken part in a legendary 'long march' together during the Civil War. Andrews could therefore short-circuit opposition or foot-dragging from within Lemass's department — on turf or on anything else — by going directly to Lemass through Aiken. There were undoubtedly times in the Lemass-Andrews relationship when each thought the other was a cross he was required to bear.

Seán MacEntee was the unknown factor. Closer in age to de Valera than to Aiken or Lemass, he would have been an obvious candidate for the succession had de Valera retired earlier. He cut his political teeth in his home town of Belfast as a member of Connolly's Socialist Party of Ireland and in his early years in national politics favoured measures such as the compulsory repatriation of capital, the taxing of wealth, and increases in social welfare payments. De Valera appointed him his first Minister for Finance, but he had by no means an unhampered run in that post, being supplanted on various occasions by Seán T. O'Kelly and Frank Aiken. His last spell in Finance ended in 1954; and although Lemass is generally credited with preventing his reappointment in 1957, it is likely that de Valera himself would have thought MacEntee's policies partly responsible for the 1954 election defeat.

The age factor was significant from the start. Lemass was the youngest minister and maintained this record for over thirty years, until Desmond O'Malley's appointment to the Government in 1969; at a function after his retirement, Lemass checked with O'Malley on exactly what age he had been when he was first appointed and regretfully conceded that his own record had been beaten. Aiken was only a year older than Lemass, but MacEntee was his senior by ten years.

One useful contemporary indicator of their standing is the election to the Fianna Fáil National Executive. In 1933 Aiken polled extremely well, with 521 votes, ahead of Lemass, who was elected second with 421.[14] This suggests a well-established pecking order, with Aiken seen as the natural second-in-command to the Chief, at least at this stage. They were united, however, in a number of important ways. They accepted de Valera's leadership unquestioningly; they never aired government disagreements in any external forum; and they never allowed political disagreements to colour the close personal relationships that had been forged during the War of Independence and the Civil War. In all probability Lemass and Aiken had one other thing in common: each would have had a view of himself as a potential successor to the Chief. De Valera was only fifty and still at the peak of his political and creative potential, but he was seventeen years older than Lemass and sixteen years older than Aiken. It was almost inevitable that one of them would succeed him.

Lemass and the government moved swiftly in some areas, less swiftly in others. The ministers had barely settled in behind their desks on 9 March 1932 when moves were begun to redeem some of the campaign promises. Lemass saw his first delegation — of woollen manufacturers looking for an increase in the 20 per cent tariff — on 23 March and was 'attentive' to their suggestions,[15] but the first executive action came shortly after 26 March, when the new Minister for Agriculture, Dr James Ryan, received a deputation of workers in the agricultural machinery industry, a centre of which was his own Wexford constituency. The following day Lemass imposed an emergency duty of $33\frac{1}{3}$ per cent on all imported agricultural machinery (with 25 per cent duty for Commonwealth imports), and the *Irish Times* suggested knowingly that Wexford was 'expected to derive great benefit from the tariff.'[16] Dr Ryan, although much more cautious in economic policy matters than the younger man, remained a rare source of friendship, steadiness and advice to Lemass throughout his public life.

Lemass spent his first five weeks in office almost submerged in consultations aimed at assessing the strength of the economy and meeting four delegations a day.[17] The *Irish Press* triumphantly announced, almost immediately, that Lemass's new economic policy would be announced within a matter of days,[18] but, interestingly, it never appeared. What happened instead was that over a month later the government appointed an economic policy committee: there were to be no solo runs in de Valera's first government. The new committee comprised de Valera, Lemass, Ryan (Agriculture) and Senator Joseph Connolly (Posts and Telegraphs).

The initial exclusion of the Minister for Finance, Seán MacEntee, has been widely commented on. He was added to the committee at its meeting of 22 September 1932, bringing its strength up to half the total membership of the government. Equally puzzling is the inclusion of Connolly, an 'adversary' of Lemass.[19] It may have been an attempt by de Valera to balance the ticket, given what he knew of the views of the people concerned. It is certainly true that Connolly differed with Lemass on some aspects of industrial policy,[20] but the differences appear to have been low-level ones, based on a differing set of geographical priorities rather than differences in principle. It is notable that a lengthy political memoir by Connolly contains not a single reference either to Lemass or to his fellow-northerner MacEntee.[21] On the other hand, Lemass's private secretary for his first two years in office was Connolly's brother, Alec, a choice that would hardly have been apposite had the two ministers been permanently at daggers drawn.

It was only after this committee had been appointed that, on 27 May, the government agreed to the establishment of an Industrial Development Branch within the Department of Industry and Commerce, to be charged with the examination of proposals for the establishment of new industries and the development of existing ones and with the administration of the Trade Loans (Guarantee) Acts.[22]

CRISIS? WHAT CRISIS?

Lemass resigned as joint honorary secretary of Fianna Fáil on his appointment to the government, being replaced by Oscar Traynor,[23] who was not to become a minister until 1936. As his ministerial responsibilities became increasingly demanding, he found little time to attend even the meetings of the Fianna Fáil parliamentary party. The party's Central Executive Committee had by now virtually been replaced by the government,[24] and in this forum Lemass was to find that his sense of urgency, and indeed of impending crisis, was not necessarily widely shared.

During the summer Lemass was extremely busy. He attended the Commonwealth Conference in Ottawa, where he failed to secure Commonwealth preferences for Irish exports but found the Canadians as friendly as the British were hostile.[25] Attending such a conference was, to say the least of it, an unusual experience for the senior Fianna Fáil personnel involved — Seán T. O'Kelly, Vice-President of the Executive Council, Lemass, Minister for Industry and Commerce, and James Ryan, Minister for Agriculture. The Irish delegation, perhaps unwilling to jettison any potential friends at the conference by indulging in heroics or gesture politics, subscribed to a number of statements implying that no formal rupture with the Commonwealth was in sight. The 'Statement of the Free State Delegation' included the statement that 'the Free State is, unlike most of the other States of the Commonwealth, relatively small,' as well as references to 'other members of the Commonwealth.' Nor did the three Irish ministers dissent from the conference's unanimous adoption of a resolution of 'devotion and affection' to 'His Majesty the King-Emperor.'[26]

British hostility was of course conditioned by the outbreak of the economic war between the two countries, initiated when the Irish government suspended payment to the British exchequer of land annuities paid by Irish farmers as part of the nineteenth-century settlement of the land question. The British had imposed retaliatory tariffs on Irish exports, and relations between the two countries had deteriorated steadily. Its effects on Irish economic life were intensified daily, as Lemass continued with his survey of the needs and capacity of industry. By the autumn he had become convinced that the situation called for drastic action. Interestingly, his first important *démarche* was not in connection with industry but with agriculture, and it was one from which he was forced to beat a strategic retreat. His proposal that agricultural output be handled by a special Board for External Trade, over which he would presumably exercise power, fell before the combined opposition of Ryan and MacEntee. By November, however, he was back in the fray, with two lengthy memorandums that set out his ideas in a form guaranteed to attract attention.

The first, on 7 November, dramatically evoked the spectre of 1847, warning that Ireland had reached the point 'where a collapse of our economic system is in sight' and predicting a return to 'famine conditions for a large number of our people.' Accepting that not even the termination of the economic war would improve Ireland's condition (there was a global slump in agricultural prices), he put a stark set of alternatives to the government: they had to choose between a 'national reorganisation' of economic activity and a new trade treaty with Britain. The former would involve a number of ideas that might have seemed like common sense to their author but some of which were undoubtedly heretical in the eyes of many of his colleagues. They included cuts in expenditure ('including education'), the virtual nationalisation of essential imports under a 'wholesale organisation which would purchase supplies and sell them at reduced prices,' a decision to take all surplus farmers off the land, the creation of a state bank and a state industrial credit organisation, and a massive public works programme.

All these radical proposals, or even a selection of them, would have been a heavy undertaking for a country such as Ireland even if external circumstances were beneficial or neutral. But the onset of the economic war had created a new situation in which the political decision to withhold the land annuities had evoked retaliatory measures aimed at Ireland's most basic industry and the source of most of its wealth, such as it was: agriculture. In effect, embarking simultaneously on a programme of self-sufficiency and the economic war was fraught with danger. Lemass recognised this, and his memorandum urged 'postponing the annuities war until we are in a better position to fight it.' By then, however, economic sense was political heresy, and politics was in the driving seat.

A week later he fired two final shots, proposing that landlords (including local authorities) be prohibited from evicting tenants who were *bona fide* unemployed and suggesting the creation of an unemployment assistance scheme along British lines.

The Executive Council meeting on 18 November 1932 brusquely disposed of his proposals on eviction, despite his (probably disingenuous) plea that they had already been favourably considered by a British Conservative government in the mid-twenties. His proposals for an unemployment assistance scheme were delivered into the jaws of the Secretary of the Department of Finance, J. J. McElligott, who set about masticating them with his customary vigour. He expressed horror in particular at the thought that workers should be paid for doing nothing. Nor did the government accept Lemass's stark set of options as set out in his first memo. In a process familiar to most students of democratic political systems, its members rejected measures they believed to be politically suicidal, postponed matters on which they were divided, and accepted suggestions it would have been churlish to oppose. At their meeting on 5 December they asked Lemass to prepare a more detailed scheme for marketing exports but shot down his plans for a quantitative restriction on imports and deferred his proposals for an industrial credit organisation.

Lemass was forced to withdraw his suggestions in relation to emergency import duties and land annuities; but not even these sacrifices were enough to save the remainder of his grand scheme. If Ryan's opposition to Lemass's plans for the future of agriculture had not been enough, McElligott's withering comments to MacEntee would have provided the *coup de grâce*. 'To withdraw [farmers] from such production in which they have experience', he wrote, 'and to maintain them in idleness pending their absorption at some distant date in industry is, in my opinion, a wholly indefensible policy.'[27] There was a central difficulty here for Lemass's policy: agriculture was to remain, for the indefinite future, Ireland's largest industry and the bedrock of its export trade. Lemass's failure to gain an input into agricultural policy, then and later, was to hamstring many of his efforts in other fields. It was noticeable that none of the state-sponsored organisations he was to establish as minister was to operate other than on the margins of agriculture, with the exception of the industrial alcohol plants, which were spectacularly unsuccessful, and the sugar company.

There was to be no quick fix. But Lemass, blocked on some lines of advance, had no shortage of other avenues open to him. Within the next five years he was to address sequentially the task of creating the building-blocks for industrial development. The foundations were represented by the Control of Manufactures Acts, 1932–34, and the related establishment of the Industrial Credit Corporation in 1933. The new tariff regime provided the scaffolding for the structure; the ground floor and upper storey were, respectively, the social legislation (including legislation on social welfare and on workers' rights) and a new tier of state-sponsored companies to fill the gaps left by private enterprise or remedy the deficiencies that a suspicious Fianna Fáil administration thought existed in the departments of state.

The stiffening of the tariff regime and the preparation of the Control of Manufactures Acts, combined with the establishment of the Industrial Credit Corporation, addressed two problems simultaneously: the need to give a rapid boost to employment and the need to wean industrialists and manufacturers away from their political and class-based associations with Cumann na nGaedheal. They were to be buttressed by three other projects of more direct relevance to the burgeoning Fianna Fáil electorate: agricultural price support, new social legislation (including legislation on unemployment assistance and conditions of employment), and a housing drive. By virtue of his specific ministerial responsibilities, Lemass controlled the organisation and direction of most of the key elements in this quiverful of new policies.

The Control of Manufactures Act, which had its first reading on 8 June 1932 and became law on 29 October the same year, was clearly intended to be the foundation of Lemass's broad economic policy. The initial government decision on the proposal records agreement on a policy designed 'to build up the industries of the country with native capital and organisation and to permit outside control of industries only when the possibility of developing the industries concerned under home control had been exhausted.'[28]

Translating these admirably clear sentiments into a workable policy proved a little more difficult. The earliest draft, as presented to the Executive Council, included powers over native industry that were plainly not to the liking of the majority of Lemass's colleagues, however much they may have appealed to its author's sense of urgency. Lemass's proposed system of licensing for all enterprises was too much for them to swallow, and they instructed him to redraft it in such a way as to ensure that existing businesses, businesses owned by people born in Ireland or resident here for a specific period or companies controlled by Irish people should not need to secure a licence from the department.[29] The lines of disagreement were already becoming clear. Lemass plainly believed that while there should be special protection for Irish industry it should have no special exemption from the demands of his industrial policy. Equally, the more conservative elements in the government had a more optimistic view than he had of the way in which native entrepreneurs would react to this undoubted stimulus.

After it had been redrafted by a committee from which he had been excluded,[30] Lemass was finally entrusted with an Act that he described as 'the barest minimum which any Government starting on a protective policy in a country like this would have to undertake.'[31] His barely concealed frustration hardly mollified the opposition, who accused him of erecting barriers to foreign investment, threatening the link with sterling, and generally putting the future of the country at risk.

The Act in practice invited circumvention or evasion, and British companies, conscious of the size of the Irish market in certain basic commodities — notably flour, cement, and clothing — adapted themselves rapidly to the new situation. William Peters was sanguine: 'Any commercial lawyer could suggest legal means of enabling firms to comply with the requirements of the Act, and the Act simply prescribes the cloak which capital other than Irish Free State native capital will have to wear in the Irish Free State.'[32]

The opposition in the Dáil was to some extent wrong-footed, but this did not prevent them from attempting to extract such political capital as they could from the situation. Some of it carried quite unsavoury implications. One of his most persistent critics, Richard Mulcahy, quizzed Lemass whether businessmen who rejoiced in the names of Matz, Gaw, Lucks and Silverstein were 'Irish nationals within the meaning of the Act.'

Lemass threw it back in his face: they were 'names associated with industry in this country for a long number of years, some of whom are a lot better Irishmen than the Deputy.'[33]

In general Lemass rode with the punches, or at least discriminated between various levels of evasion or defiance in the light of an overall strategy that was not yet entirely clear. One of his problems was, quite simply, the dawning realisation that the policy he had adopted might in certain circumstances operate against his declared objectives. For example, how would Irish businessmen and industrialists react to the protection so generously offered? Would they actually become less competitive, rather than more innovative and energetic? For political reasons the policy could not be changed, much less dropped; but the fine-tuning that could be carried out by a minister and civil servants who were developing a penchant for centralisation and attention to detail was virtually unlimited.

A close study of the initial implementation of the Control of Manu-factures Act suggests that even at this early stage the needs of the economy as Lemass perceived them, and not any rigid adherence to Sinn Féin doctrine, were rapidly becoming the touchstone of Industry and Commerce's practice.[34] One company engaged in food-processing incurred ministerial displeasure for adopting a scheme that gave nominal control of its operations to Irish shareholders while diverting 93 per cent of its profits to English investors. Another, involved in textiles, which devised an almost identical arrangement received official encouragement, including financial guarantees from the Industrial Credit Company. It is difficult to quarrel with Daly's conclusion that the critical difference between the two enterprises was that the former was operating in an area thickly populated by Irish businesses, while the latter offered the capital-intensive, high-technology development that Lemass and Leydon welcomed.[35] Cement (which was exempt from the Act) became in effect a foreign monopoly, although an efficient one, after all prospects of native investment of the magnitude required evaporated.

Of the loopholes that appeared in the operation of the 1932 Act, some were remedied more quickly than others. What rapidly became clear was that the welcome extended by manufacturers to the tariffs and the Control of Manufactures Acts rapidly developed into demands that the government improve on even these exceptionally generous measures. A deputation of manufacturers, which no doubt for good reasons included the managing director of Urney Chocolates in Tallaght, R. Gallagher, a founding director of the *Irish Press,* met Lemass in March 1933 to make two substantive points. In the first place, the share threshold for Irish ownership was too low (although they were unwilling or unable to suggest a more appropriate figure), and secondly, the Act should be amended to give the minister power to prevent the entry of any company, whether native or foreign-controlled, into an industry where production had reached saturation point.[36]

Their representations were accompanied by detailed accounts of the misdeeds of their competitors, suggesting a fondness for industrial espionage that must have absorbed a considerable amount of managerial time and energy. Lemass introduced an amending Act in 1934 that met some of the manufacturers' complaints, but by no means all of them. There would have been legal difficulties in quashing competition to the degree they desired; but even if there had not been, one can sense Lemass's patience already wearing a little thin.

The tone of one of the explanatory memorandums for the government on the draft of the 1934 Bill implied that Lemass's action in establishing new industrial undertakings on his own account was a cause of considerable anxiety among his colleagues. Both the industrial alcohol companies and the Sugar Company, he assured them, were the products of unusual circum-stances and not blueprints to be followed. The lineaments of an unresolved tussle between the minister and Leydon in particular can be discerned in the careful statement that the 'development of an industry by a State department is impracticable and undesirable except in peculiar cases' and that 'investment by the State in the shares of an industrial Company is also undesirable.'[37]

These developments, as might be expected, were being closely watched by British diplomatic and commercial interests. William Peters kept his superiors in the Dominions Office closely informed about developments. In January 1934, in a lengthy analysis of a speech on industrial policy that Lemass had just made to the Convention of National Manufacturers,[38] he noted Lemass's unwillingness to provide information about the proposed location of new factories, even to the Dáil, and described the forthcoming Act as one that would be designed to shut out undesirable (as opposed, no doubt, to desirable) 'alien' industrialists. Percipiently, he noted that although 'the government believes in decentralisation of industry and not in large scale production ... little has been done to check the natural tendency of new industries to establish themselves in Dublin.'[39] Whether he knew it or not, this was one of the main points of departure for Lemass's critics within the government, not least Connolly and Boland.

Case histories from three key areas — flour milling, the motor industry, and textiles — provide graphic examples of Lemass's techniques in action during this period. The question of flour milling had been a touchstone for Fianna Fáil since the 1928–29 Economic Committee, and it was complicated by the fact that the giant British firm of Ranks had since 1930 controlled a third of the milling capacity of the Free State. Lemass banned flour imports except under licence in 1933, and by 1936 the Irish mills had virtually gained a monopoly of the domestic market. Lemass saw off further foreign competition in rough and ready terms when, in 1936, Hovis revealed their intention to set up a new milling business — fully within the terms of the Control of Manufactures Acts — to make Hovis bread in Dublin. They immediately received an 'intimation' from the minister that he would prefer that they would not go on with the manufacture of Hovis flour.

> The Minister was interviewed, and, although admitting that what was proposed to be done was perfectly legal, stated that there were powerful objections raised by another Milling Company and therefore he could not see his way to permit the manufacture of Hovis flour in the Irish Free State, and that if we persisted an excise duty of 2d. a pound on the flour would be imposed.[40]

Hovis had to retreat, licking their wounds, their discomfiture accentuated by the fact that an Irish milling company was cheerfully making and selling bootleg 'Hovis' bread.

The chief mechanism available to Lemass under the 1932 Act was to promise exclusivity — in effect a monopoly — to foreign manufacturers who might otherwise have been deterred by the financial provisions of the Act. This was notably operated in the case of Dunlop, which was being actively courted by Lemass but which was anxious about investing heavily in a situation in which Irish manufacturers might be encouraged to pirate their ideas and muscle in on their territory. Lemass agreed, confidentially, that if he asked Dunlop to manufacture any particular item he would countenance domestic competition only to the degree to which Dunlop was unable to meet demand.[41] Although Lemass was keen to get Dunlop into Ireland, it was not at any price, and he let the company know that a French firm was also in contention. Dunlop wanted its exclusivity rights written into an Act of the Oireachtas, but Lemass refused, agreeing instead to an exchange of letters.

The case was also notable for a game of bluff involving the site of Dunlop's proposed new factory. Government policy favoured decentralisation, and it is clear from the documents that its motive was in this case openly political as well as social. Sir George Beharrel of Dunlop told the Dominions Office that Lemass wanted him to set up in Tralee, because the town was 'one of the centres of trouble and disaffection,'[42] but he was sharply critical of Tralee because of distribution costs and because the quality of the labour available was 'quite unsuitable'. He would, he averred, break with the Irish government rather than establish anywhere other than in Dublin. This hard line eventually succumbed to Lemass's blandishments: Cork emerged as the honourable compromise; and Charles Tennyson, the Dunlop company secretary, noted that the minister had 'met us on the whole very fairly.'[43]

It is clear that Lemass did not, in this and in other cases, simply sit back and wait for proposals from foreign manufacturers but frequently — in actions that ran counter to at least the spirit of the Act and perhaps some of his government colleagues' more narrowly focused concerns — actively solicited them. As one Board of Trade official noted,

> a Lancashire cotton man tells me that he has been asked by someone acting on behalf of the Irish government whether he would be prepared to consider a proposal for the establishment in the Irish Free State of cotton spinning and weaving mills sufficient to meet at least the full domestic requirements there.[44]

The unnamed manufacturer, the Colonial Office was assured, would resist these overtures as a matter of patriotism. The big spinning firm of Salts was not so choosy, and it became another of Lemass's later acquisitions for the Irish industrial infrastructure.

There is some evidence that Lemass's brusque approach to the problems of industrial development gave rise to intermittent jitters, not just in the government but in the Fianna Fáil parliamentary party. A meeting of that body early in 1933 'accepted the need for prior consultation' on policies that might 'materially alter the National and Economic outlook of Fianna Fáil.'[45] Reading between the lines of this carefully worded minute it is easy to discern members' concern at the speed and direction of policy development under Lemass.

Equally, his own vision of the way forward sometimes led him to brush aside interests that he regarded as merely sectional. On several occasions he successfully resisted appeals by Col. Maurice Moore TD for a grant from his department for the National Industrial and Development Association.[46] And in the autumn de Valera, in a set piece clearly designed to rally the troops, told the parliamentary party that 'the more he examined the policy of self-sufficiency for the Nation, the more he was satisfied it was the right policy. He also pointed out our intention to decentralise industries as far as possible.'[47] If Lemass, who was present, made a contribution to the discussion it was not recorded.

The same meeting set up a special committee of the party's Executive Council to deal with economic matters. This may have been a fig-leaf. As already noted, the Central Executive Committee had already been superseded, to all practical purposes, by the new government, and this move may have been designed to reassure parliamentary party members that the party, as such, still had the controlling voice in economic policy matters. Possibly as a result of this development the parliamentary party's own committee on industry and commerce, headed by Lemass's constituency colleague Joe Briscoe, which had been appointed together with other committees on 25 April, ran into the sand. Subsequent minutes showed that members were not assiduous in attending, and volunteers were called for, but without conspicuous success.

What was evident above all was the sense of confidence engendered in Lemass by his first few months in office. Nowhere was this more marked than during the snap election of 1933, called by de Valera when it appeared likely that the Labour Party would withdraw its support in the light of projected pay cuts in the public service. Lemass, as director of elections, put in a barnstorming personal performance. There was a marked contrast with 1932. The appeals to the cautious middle ground of the electorate, which had formed such a strong motif in the earlier campaign, gave way to speeches that were strong on traditional nationalism and designed to further isolate and weaken Cumann na nGaedheal.

Lemass raised the political temperature calculatedly with an allegation that, in the circumstances of the time, was little short of sensational. J. H. Thomas, the British Dominions Secretary, he said, had told him in Ottawa that the British confidently expected civil war to break out again in Ireland before the Commonwealth Conference was over. Thomas had even shown him reports received from Ireland to this effect, garnered by the 'extensive secret service' that they maintained there. When the Irish delegation had been in sight of a settlement,

> some report came from Ireland of a speech by the leader of Cumann na nGaedheal giving the impression that British policy was succeeding. At this the British drew back again in the hope that their friends would settle the problem for them in Ireland, because they felt that the Army Comrades [Association] would bring civil war.

He added:

> Speaking with full recognition of my responsibilities, I say that the economic war would never have been started if members of the Cumann na nGaedheal party had not suggested to England in the months preceding it the adoption of such tactics ... It would not last a fortnight if Cumann na nGaedheal had the horse sense to keep their mouths shut at the time.[48]

Accusing Thomas of 'economic Black-and-Tannery',[49] Lemass succeeded in dragging the British politician directly into the campaign. Thomas issued a statement in London denying that intelligence reports from Ireland had been the operative factor in the failure to reach agreement but without denying the substance of the reports themselves.[50] Lemass mended his hand to some extent,[51] but the mud had been well and truly thrown, with obvious effect.

If Lemass pulled no punches in his inferences about the alleged anti-national activities of his principal opponents, he cannily continued with his related strategy aimed at securing the continued allegiance of former Cumann na nGaedheal supporters in the business and industrial sector. He assured them that protection would not be disturbed and that what Fianna Fáil was implementing was in reality 'the old National Policy.'[52]

Towards the end of the campaign Lemass broached the Northern question. As far as policy was concerned it was a strong dose of the old-time religion, a hymn to 'triumphant nationalism' in which the achievements of Fianna Fáil in its brief period in office were the key to the future. Categorising Stormont as a puppet parliament, he claimed that 'the greatest achievement of Fianna Fáil was that they had brought from the Six Counties the Nationalist members of the Northern parliament onto their platforms. Not only the divisions of 1922 but those of 1918 had been healed.'[53] Three days later he told the party's final rally in College Green, Dublin, that on a recent tour of the border counties of Louth, Cavan and Monaghan he had been deeply impressed by his experiences.

> I heard at first hand the views of those who have been the victims of that great wrong against Ireland — our separated kinsmen in the Six Counties — and they told me that they are waiting and praying … in the hope that the triumphant nationalism of the people in the South, combined with their determination, will secure for us again the unity of our historic country.[54]

The significance of this broadside is that Lemass rarely spoke on Northern policy again in these terms, and for most of the succeeding two decades his references to the North were infrequent and for the most part perfunctory. The territory was to be left to de Valera.

As was so often the case, however, the political attitudes enunciated on Fianna Fáil platforms were to be undermined, or at least overshadowed, by the effects of the economic policies adopted by the party in government. Nationalists generally had at the time a belief that partition could not last for ever and that the Northern statelet would collapse under a combination of political and economic pressure from the South. This would certainly explain — although it would not necessarily excuse — the vigour with which de Valera and Lemass pursued policies that had the side-effect of pushing many unionist suspicions about the South past the point of no return, or at the very least providing unionists with powerful circumstantial evidence that Dublin would cheerfully and rapidly destroy their economy in the interests of bringing about unity. These policies were a logical extension of the Belfast boycott that Lemass had been closely involved with during the War of Independence.

Northern political and commercial interests were acutely aware of the post-Treaty implications for their economy of Dublin's policies but did not evince any real concern until after Fianna Fáil came to power.[55] The passage of the Control of Manufactures Acts and the Control of Imports Act by 1934 converted mild concern into overt alarm, and the Northern government was unavailingly pressing London to bring about trade talks between North and South. One Northern civil servant commented:

> It must be patently obvious to anyone studying the question that it is the policy of that State to use any means at its disposal either to force or to persuade Northern Ireland, or a part thereof, to come into an Irish Republic, or at least to come under whatever form of government may prevail in Dublin ... This campaign is not merely the outcome of recent political events, but is the putting into force of a plan carefully considered years ago, and consistent with the views of the late Arthur Griffiths [sic], whose political doctrine was that a united Ireland could produce internally practically all of its needs, with a consequently disastrous effect upon the trade of Great Britain, while any surplus requirements could be purchased from foreign countries.[56]

Subsequent events did little to alleviate these and similar fears on the part of Northern interests. The economic game, such as it was, was being played out essentially between Ireland and England, with Northern Ireland being regarded as little better than a cipher. The principal reasons for this were the overriding importance of the strategic issue (Britain's control of the ports), the economic war over the annuities, and the fact that Ireland's agricultural surplus was linked inextricably with the British market.

A related problem concerned exports generally. While it could be argued that the government's tariff policy favoured national industrial development, it had two inescapably negative effects on exports. The first was the tendency for a non-competitive environment to develop for firms producing behind tariff walls, leading to higher prices than might otherwise be necessary, and a consequent weakening of the position of Irish products in competitive markets overseas. Lemass and the government attacked this problem largely through an extensive and detailed system of price control, although this proved to be — as will be seen — less successful than had been envisaged.

The second was the inevitable tendency of other governments, in an era characterised by a worldwide trend towards protection, to retaliate against Irish tariff policy by putting up their own barriers to Irish goods. Lemass was conscious of the problem, arguing in one of his 1932 memorandums to the government that 'on the basis of present consumption in the Saorstát, the fullest possible industrial development here could not absorb 100,000 unemployed without an export market.'[57]

Even at this early stage, Industry and Commerce was looking with some urgency at the prospects of securing alternatives to the British market for Irish goods. In September 1933 a departmental conference, headed by Leydon, agreed that

> it is clear that a stage has now been reached where efforts must be directed along the lines of procuring the removal of these obstacles

which impede the sale of Saorstát Éireann products in European markets by the negotiation of fresh commercial agreements. In this connection the Government's tariff policy on imports would require to be considered in relation to the restrictions ... which other countries impose on Irish products; in particular the question of maintaining most-favoured nation treatment and Commonwealth preference will arise.[58]

Lemass was equally frank in public.

International trade must be on a reciprocal basis, and in the long run we must endeavour to trade with those countries which are prepared to take our commodities in return.[59]

Soon afterwards the Department of External Affairs recommended that a new section be set up within the department to increase exports, noting that the Free State 'has no trade representatives except in France, Germany and the USA.'[60] The record from then on, however, is conspicuously bereft of any evidence that Lemass's concern about exports was shared to any substantial degree by his government colleagues. This suggests in turn that for the majority of them the goal of self-sufficiency could be achieved without the need to pay any serious attention to exports. Indeed the economic history of the nineteen-thirties, at least up to the conclusion of the 1938 agreement with Britain, is a picture of erratic development, fuelled by external as much as by internal factors. Fianna Fáil was able to claim the credit for the advances that were made, without any detailed analysis of the degree to which these had been brought about by external factors or any examination of the long-term costs of domestic policies. The satisfaction of the domestic market by domestic industry — the prime objective of the tariff policy — had in many respects been achieved before the outbreak of the Second World War; but that war, and the electoral volatility after it, prevented a smooth transition to a new phase of development for another two decades.

On the positive side, output and employment increased dramatically during the 1930–39 period. The trend was enhanced not only by government policies but by the increasing unattractiveness or unavailability of emigration as a safety valve. The volume of industrial production grew by nearly 50 per cent between 1931 and 1938; total industrial employment rose from 110,600 to 166,100 in the same period, an annual average growth rate of over 6 per cent; the population rose by some 50,000 between 1930 and 1935; and a massive housing drive, which had the dual effect of creating substantial additional employment and delivering on Fianna Fáil social policy promises, ensured that almost three-quarters of all new house construction in the 1923–38 period was actually undertaken in the period 1932–38. The policy was not of course cost-free, but even though 'the taxpayer might be uncertain how great a bill, in tariffs, subsidies and guarantees, he might be called upon to meet ... he could not deny that he got something for his money.'[61]

The greater costs were to be found in the export field and in the area of balance of payments. In an era of increasing international protectionism Lemass's ideas about reciprocal trading arrangements were a chimera. The idea that Ireland should develop export markets in countries whose goods we had no need of was even further in the future, and, in general, export promotion was relegated to the status of a pious aspiration.

Even more seriously, the export of agricultural products — the traditional banker for the economy — was disastrously affected by the Economic War. Between 1924 and 1934 alone exports declined from £50 million to £16 million,[62] and between 1931 and 1936 exports suffered a 'catastrophic' drop,[63] not least in the agricultural area, hardest hit by the economic war. The volume of merchandise exports fell by 29 per cent between 1931 and 1933, and indeed it was to be another three decades before the 1930 volume of merchandise exports was reached again. When in August 1934 Guinness was reported to be planning the construction of a brewery in London to escape the effects of the tariff wall, the news was greeted by the Belfast *News Letter* as compelling evidence of the 'economic ruin of the Free State.'[64]

LABOUR POLICY

Although the numbers at work improved substantially, unemployment remained high, and despite the resumption of emigration on a substantial scale after 1935 the true rate of unemployment again reached traditional levels. While the farmers suffered, however, the general air of optimism and buoyancy encouraged the Minister for Industry and Commerce to embark, with characteristic vigour, on the more visible sections of his industrial edifice. If the tariff policy had provided the scaffolding (scaffolding that was to remain rustily in place long after its usefulness had become questionable) and the Control of Manufactures Acts the foundations, labour policy was to raise the building at least to the point where the potential height of the finished construction could be anticipated.

More than thirty years later, on the verge of his own retirement from public life, Lemass agreed that Fianna Fáil's 1932 plan looked 'very unsophisticated' but defended it trenchantly because it had 'helped to shift the centre of emphasis in Irish politics from arguments about the Treaty to social and economic development.'[65] After his retirement he was to observe:

> The big events of our first year in Government were the industrial policy, which was applied in a ruthless way without any clear picture of its merits, and the social developments, of which the first was the

unemployment assistance scheme ... The idea at that time was to set up industries which would produce the type of goods we had formerly been importing. The aim was to supply the home market with these goods where the scale of activity would be economic. This of course limited the scope of industrial development but it did produce a tremendous upsurge of new industries.[66]

Cosgrave himself, who in 1926 had described Irish businessmen as 'antique furniture',[67] could not have been unalterably opposed to what Lemass was trying to do, however much he might have quibbled with its pace and precise sense of direction. But the unresolved tensions within the government, and between some of its stated objectives, were to affect the development of policy as de Valera steered his evidently argumentative colleagues towards intermittent agreement, in a climate in which government confidentiality was a key factor.

There is no shortage of supporting evidence for Lemass's own self-description as 'ruthless'. T. K. Whitaker, later a key figure in economic development before and during Lemass's period as Taoiseach, put it more urbanely: 'On several occasions during the 1932–38 period the desirability of a more scientific basis for the tariffs was suggested to Lemass by the Secretary of his Department, only to receive an Augustinian reply: the advice was appropriate but premature.'[68] By January 1936 more than half of the two thousand items on the official imports list were subject to tariffs, while other non-tariff barriers, such as quotas, duties, and import licences, were added as and when Lemass thought necessary. The peak of tariff activity was already in sight, however, and was achieved later the same year. Although tariffs were to remain an essential feature of industrial policy for another three decades or more, Lemass increasingly saw them as an instrument to be adapted flexibly to the needs of a core industrial policy rather than as a permanent part of that policy. In any event they were normally reviewed after they had been in place for only six months.

In relation to social policies Lemass was at least as much a man of his time as a man of the future. As an urban politician he had witnessed, and indeed helped significantly to engineer, growing electoral support for Fianna Fáil among the working class. He was also no stranger to the social deprivation rampant in the Dublin tenements, where as late as 1936 some 65,000 people, or 14 per cent of the city's population, still lived at densities of four or more to a room.[69] This suggested a two-strand policy, one strand to create new statutory rights for workers, the other to provide forms of income support that would help to consolidate electoral support for Fianna Fáil not only among the urban poor but among the dwindling, but still substantial, rural proletariat.

These social conditions of themselves suggested the need for new legislation, but there were other factors. One was the anxiety of employers about the growth of sweatshops, outside the state's regulatory framework, which was threatening their dominance of the indigenous market. Another was the anxiety of male trade unionists about the growing use of female and child labour and the degree to which this trend — particularly the use of female labour — was perceived as threatening male jobs.

The trade union movement in the thirties was also in the process of confronting a number of highly intractable problems, some organisational, others political. The organisational problems related to the vexed question whether unions should be organised on a bloc basis within particular industries or whether horizontal forms of organisation were more appropriate. The political problems related to the fact that a substantial proportion of trade unionists were members of British unions. The problems frequently overlapped; even where they did not, personal rivalries and leadership ambitions added to the turbulence of what was already a volatile situation. And 'waiting in the wings', as one authority put it succinctly, 'was a government, separatist, nationalist and impatient for order.'[70]

Lemass himself suggested that as far as he knew it was the first time that such measures had been introduced by a government that was 'still a democratic government dependent entirely upon a parliamentary institution for its power.'[71] This was gilding the lily in some respects. Although the package was radical in a number of ways, Lemass was in the happy situation of knowing that it would be welcomed by both sides of industry. Viewed in this context, the legislation embodied in his chosen instruments — the Conditions of Employment Act, 1936, and the 1939 law providing for a week's paid holiday for all workers — could also be interpreted as a canny and hugely successful attempt to commandeer the middle ground of industrial organisation and to consolidate Fianna Fáil's electoral support at a relatively modest cost — a cost, moreover, that would be borne by employers rather than by the state.

The adult working week was set at forty-eight hours, overtime was restricted, wage agreements could be registered and made legally enforceable, the employment of women and of young people was closely controlled, and the working day, with some exceptions, was set to end at 8 p.m. Lemass's own view was clearly outlined in his introductory speech: the employment of workers and their remuneration 'cannot be left to be determined by the laws of supply and demand'; the reduction in the maximum working week was being proposed 'not primarily because of its effect on unemployment, but because it is desirable'; the working hours of young people aged between fourteen and eighteen should be controlled to avoid exploitation, but 'it is not contrary either to Christian civilisation or to good economic organisation that such persons should be employed'; and the registration of agreements between unions and employers for the purpose of making them enforceable, far from making trade unions redundant, should be welcomed by every trade unionist.[72] Nor was external praise far behind: the *Economist* praised the government for having enacted 'an industrial code far ahead of that in force in any other country.'[73]

Not all the costs of this legislation were borne by the employers. Many of them were borne by women, and there were increasing signs that Fianna Fáil generally, and Lemass in particular, had an absolutely mainstream attitude to women's place in society, an attitude that found its most substantial contemporary expression in the Constitution of 1937. Here there was a sharp divergence between Lemass's political sense and his strategy for economic management. In the nineteen-twenties, as already noted, he was unusual among his contemporaries in seeing the value of women as political allies. In the early thirties he ridiculed Eoin O'Duffy's Irish version of Italian fascism, which he suggested had been acquired 'during a fortnight's cruise in the Mediterranean,' and in particular O'Duffy's suggestion that for political purposes women should be attached to the vocational groupings of their husbands or fathers. 'I think on that alone any man could be certified,' he observed tartly.[74]

Lemass's own home life was of course middle-class and orthodox in the deepest sense. Kathleen regarded her family responsibilities as paramount, and Lemass's life as a government minister did not leave much room for relaxation. Off duty, however, he was at least as attentive a father as many other men of his generation and probably more so than many. Family picnic outings, often in company with family friends, to Brittas Bay and Portmarnock were common, although Lemass himself rarely ventured into the water. When they were on summer holidays in Skerries, where Ernie O'Malley and his family sometimes took a house at the same time, there were outings to Newgrange and to Laytown races. As the children grew up some of them developed a passion for riding: their father would accompany them to gymkhanas, and the Dublin Horse Show was an essential fixture in the calendar every year.

He took a keen interest too in his children's reading and, although he never actually censored their choices, once indicated, in the most oblique way, that one of his daughters might postpone her plan to read *All Quiet on the Western Front*. He remained himself a compulsive reader; from time to time Kathleen upbraided him affectionately for spending money on books that she thought might have been better spent elsewhere in the household.

C. S. Andrews's wife thought the early Sinn Féin leaders were sexist. 'Had she known Seán Lemass,' Andrews commented many years later, 'her misgivings about the attitude of the Fianna Fáil leadership to women's status would have been reinforced.'[75] De Valera, three years before drafting the Constitution, left his parliamentary party in no doubt where he stood. While he argued strongly against child labour, he also maintained that 'as far as possible there should be no woman labour — that if doles were to be given it would be far more advantageous and less deteriorating to give the dole to women and to give all the work possible to men.'[76] Six months later Lemass publicly endorsed the same thesis, with only one difference. Whereas de Valera seemed to envisage a permanent domestic role for all women, Lemass at least limited his observations to those women who were married with children. He also made his comments in the context of arguing for increased provision for social welfare, in effect another element of his policy.

> If we are to solve our social problems and take full advantage of increased productivity, we must at some stage make it possible for a large number of people to get a livelihood without being obliged to work for it. We can do that by taking out of industry those who are too young or too old, the physically unfit, and the mothers of families, who should be at home tending their children, instead of tending the machine.[77]

In restricting the areas in which women were allowed to work, Lemass could claim to be supporting the policy of the International Labour Organisation, arguing that the Act's provisions for restricting night work had been incorporated specifically 'so that the International Labour Convention prohibiting the employment of women married workers at night may be fulfilled.'[78] He had plenty of industrial support, as the male-dominated unions could also see the writing on the wall and were moving to protect the interests of the majority of their members.[79] Even some prominent female trade unionists gave hostages to fortune. In a speech in 1932 the president of the Irish Women Workers' Union, Louie Bennett, suggested that increased female employment had been detrimental to family life and a possible cause of male unemployment and hence of increased poverty.[80] In 1933 the Department of Industry and Commerce told the Irish Trades Union Congress, in response to its representations, that the minister was 'convinced of the necessity of statutory prohibition [of certain types of female employment] for without it, women may rapidly be recruited for most classes of industry that are likely to be developed here.'[81]

At one stage Lemass contemplated taking even more draconian steps.

> The Minister's attention has been drawn to the efficiency of female labour in the new industrial undertakings in the country. In many cases the employment of women has been facilitated by the introduction of machinery. The Minister had under consideration the question of the prohibition of the use of machinery, which in all cases is manufactured outside the Saorstát, but owing to the advanced organisation of the industries now in operation in the Saorstát the Minister is of the opinion that he would not be justified in introducing such restrictions. In order to reserve certain avenues of employment for adult men, the

Minister is of the opinion that it will be necessary for him to limit by Order the employment of women either in certain industries or in certain operations.[82]

Defending his proposals on the employment of women in the Bill, Lemass denied that he was opposed to female labour as such, arguing that his intention was to create machinery that would 'arrest any tendency which may develop in future to substitute female for male labour in consequence of alterations in the mechanical methods of production in any industry.' He raised the spectre of Derry, where 'there is very little work for the men except to mind the children and look after the households,' and cannily quoted Louie Bennett, who had suggested only three days earlier that 'there are ... many mechanical processes so monotonous that men find them intolerable ... Women endure such monotony with less evil effect upon their nervous system.'[83]

As a strategy it was at least partly successful. In the protected industries that were established after 1932, male employment between 1934 and 1947 increased by 38 per cent, whereas female employment increased by only 28 per cent.[84]

THE STATE COMPANIES

The final policy tier of the nineteen-thirties was the extension of the system of state companies, which came under the aegis of Lemass's department and were inaugurated in line with his declared policy of providing state investment to generate employment and economic growth in areas where private enterprise — possibly because of the scale of the investment and the risks involved — had been slow to embark on initiatives. Each of the companies concerned, however, had its own genesis; and not all of them attracted Lemass's personal involvement or encouragement to the same degree. The Cumann na nGaedheal government had created three such enterprises in 1927: the ESB, the Dairy Disposal Company Ltd, and the Agricultural Credit Company. Of these three the creation of the ESB was the most significant, given that the amount of money involved was very substantial, as was the degree of trust the Dáil was prepared to accord to the minister, and the relative freedom given to the ESB board.

Under Lemass, key sectors were identified. In 1933 both Comhlucht Siúicre Éireann and the Industrial Credit Corporation were established; Aer Lingus was established in 1936 and Aer Rianta the following year; and 1939 saw the establishment of Ceimicí Tta, the Irish Tourist Board, and the Irish Life Assurance Company. Because each of the companies concerned had a different genesis, no single management model applied to them all. The only constant, at least as far as Lemass was concerned, was his preference for the term 'state-sponsored' as opposed to 'semi-state' as a descriptive term.[85]

Not all the companies were successful. The Sugar Company, at least, harnessed an important agricultural resource and contributed significantly to the alleviation of shortages of this commodity during the war years. Lemass's attempts to create a bridgehead between Ireland and a major oil company ended in fairly ignominious failure.[86] An unsuccessful attempt to generate the raw material for industrial alcohol from indigenous products such as potatoes was equally unsuccessful: although alcohol was successfully produced — the capital funds for the factories engendered a dramatic increase in the estimates for Lemass's department, which financed them directly — the economics of the operation were shaky from the start.

The industrial alcohol episode indeed has been described as 'the most ineffective self-sufficiency and decentralisation operation undertaken, an unsavoury example of Lemass's empire building, and a classic illustration of the problem of investment absolved from conventional economic criteria.'[87] Leydon, robustly independent as ever, told Lemass it would be cheaper to distribute potatoes free and to employ a large labour force on public works than to persist with this particular experiment.

A broader view might be more sympathetic to the experiment, or at least introduce some mitigating factors. The actual business of setting up the state company — including drafting the articles and memorandum of association — fell to a gifted young civil servant in the Department of Finance, T. K. Whitaker, whose first important responsibility it was. Many years later Whitaker noted that the best that could be predicted for the enterprise was a somewhat erratic performance and that its viability was considerably impaired when — as frequently happened — farmers broke their contracts to supply the factories with potatoes when the open market price soared above the contract price.[88]

Aer Lingus was just as close to Lemass's heart as industrial alcohol and tourism but considerably more successful. His enthusiasm had deep roots. As a young man he used to go and watch the 'flivvers', the shaky early aeroplanes, taking off from Leopardstown racecourse and 'travelling a few yards amidst great cheering.'[89] McElligott was doubtful about the project, arguing that a highly successful airline was being run in Sweden on the basis of private enterprise.[90] Lemass and Leydon, however, saw it as a potential national asset; Lemass in particular believed it vitally necessary for the country to have national control of its external communications and envisaged the airline as a second line of defence in any emergency.

The new company's policy, according to Lemass himself early in 1937, was anything but modest. It would aim 'among other things, at making the Saorstát the international junction for air traffic between Europe and North America, not only by direct services by air, but also by providing air connections at Saorstát ports with transatlantic shipping. It should, we think, be feasible in time to establish air services connecting the Saorstát directly with all the principal countries' — all this at a time when Aer Lingus was operating two small aircraft on two routes out of three temporary structures at a military aerodrome.

There was an almost Promethean aspect to Lemass's passion for the air and aeroplanes. After the war he and Leydon wheedled dollars out of a reluctant Department of Finance to pay for a small fleet of Douglas DC3 aircraft, prepared for war but never used in hostilities. He was one of the party when a DC3 took its inaugural flight from Dublin to a function in Shannon. In the course of the flight in the still stripped-out plane he enthusiastically accepted the American pilot's invitation to take the controls and subjected his terrified fellow-passengers to a series of heart-stopping manoeuvres before resuming his seat.[91] Much later, just before his election as Taoiseach, he was to describe the aeroplane as 'the real instrument of liberation for this country and, from that aspect ... perhaps the single most important development of this century.'[92] And after he retired he told Rex Cathcart, who entertained him in Belfast on the occasion of a UTV interview, that the creation of Aer Lingus was the decision for which he would most like to be remembered: it was the act that best symbolised for him Ireland's ability to break free of its island restrictions and create meaningful links with the world outside.[93]

The tone of the latter part of the decade, as far as Lemass was concerned, was — in spite of the economic war — almost continuously upbeat. He set about his multifarious tasks with enthusiasm, chivvying and admonishing where necessary. His waking hours were almost entirely devoted to work, in which he revelled.

He occasionally allowed himself to indulge in a display of Victorian moral values. This is evident above all in the exchange of letters he had with de Valera about the drafting of the 1937 Constitution.[94] Neither Lemass nor his department offered any observations on the first draft, but he evidently went through the penultimate draft carefully. Two sections in particular attracted his attention. In article 45 ('Directive principles of social policy') Lemass suggested the phrase 'Justice and charity shall determine the relations between classes.' De Valera, however, was chary of introducing the dangerous terminology of social class into the Constitution; accordingly he accepted only half of the Lemass formula, and the final version (article 45.1) declares that the state shall strive to create a social order in which 'justice and charity shall inform all the institutions of the national life.'

The second was in relation to article 45.2.1, which declares that citizens 'may through their occupations find the means of making reasonable provision for their domestic needs.' Lemass's preferred formulation embodied a considerable value judgment: 'Citizens who are willing may find the means through their occupations and citizens who are not willing may find the means otherwise.' If 'willing' were replaced by 'able and willing', he added, it would read even better. This suggested change, redolent of the Victorian distinction between the 'deserving' and the 'undeserving' poor, was not made. De Valera was more sensitive to another of Lemass's suggestions for the same section, which focused on a phrase suggesting that workers' wages should provide adequately for their needs. 'I suggest that the use of the word "adequately" is dangerous. When the State pays rural workers 24/– [24 shillings] a week it enables them to provide for their needs but not adequately. I suggest the substitution of "adequately meeting" by "providing for".' The final version of the article, with its reference to citizens finding through their occupations 'the means of making reasonable provision for their domestic needs,' was a classic de Valera compromise.

Lemass was already becoming impatient with some of the foreseeable but inevitable by-products of his own policies, not least in relation to the Control of Manufactures Acts. What had happened in effect was that behind the tariff walls, and supported by the Control of Manufactures Acts, manufacturers had discovered a new-found sense of unity and purpose, and the two organisations chiefly concerned, the National Industrial and Development Association and the Federation of Saorstát Industries, were moving towards a joint position. The FSI saw its principal role as promoting native capital for native industries and had developed a 'federation national mark' to identify goods produced by wholly Irish firms.[95] The fusion of the two organisations was announced at the NIDA annual dinner in Dublin on 19 January 1937, and contemporary reports indicate that the policy thrust of the united organisation would be aggressive. More, it revealed quite openly a strong sense of dissatisfaction with the operation of the Acts that were supposed to protect Irish industry. In their view,

> the continuance of the penetration of external interests into Irish industry and its harmful influence, which has been stressed again and again by the Council, must be brought home to the country as a whole … Any measure of political freedom which we may achieve is weakened and in many cases nullified by the hold which foreign capital and credit has in controlling the future of industrial enterprise.[96]

The FSI was plainly critical of government policy in this regard and in particular of what they perceived as its failure to give greater protection to Irish capital. Lemass, however, although he was the guest of honour at the function, not only chose to ignore the criticism but embarked on a counter-offensive, which was to become a recurring theme of his speeches up to the outbreak of war and throughout the forties. The real problem, he implied, was not foreign capital as such but native inefficiency; the government's industrial policy had by now been 'generally accepted', and if greater levels of efficiency were not forthcoming 'more direct methods would have to be adopted.'[97]

Lemass's belief in the efficacy of the Control of Manufactures Acts as an instrument of industrial policy was already wearing thin, and rather earlier than has generally been supposed. He had the open support of the *Irish Press,* which not only sidelined his critics' speeches and emphasised his offensive but explained editorially that 'Mr. Lemass, while agreeing that the aim should be to make Irish industry as Irish in every sense of the word as possible, does not think that the complaints in this respect which have been made are quite justified.'[98]

Lemass's public profile was expanding internationally as well as nationally, and in June 1937, with significant American support, he was elected president of the International Labour Organisation at its meeting in Geneva. His presidential interventions were notable for a number of reasons. The first was his ringing assertion that whereas 'we believe in nationalism as an economic as well as a political policy ... good nationalism economically and socially is inescapable [*sic*] from good internationalism.'[99] What 'good internationalism' actually involved was, perhaps deliberately, left undefined: the context suggests that his own internationalism was confined, for reasons of political necessity, to occasions such as this on which rhetoric could safely be employed.

A second was the degree to which, reversing the economic model that he and all traditional economists generally followed, he argued that social policy and social investment should help to determine the shape and thrust of a government's economic policies: that social progress was not an optional extra to be tacked on to economic growth but should be integral to government policies from the outset. He told the conference:

> No longer is social policy regarded as subsidiary to economics ... no longer are social aims whittled down to fit the requirements of economics but rather is economic policy modified to facilitate the attainment of the social objectives of governments ... In all countries there is growing in the minds of men a deep conviction that destitution or poverty, arising from unemployment or any other cause, are not inevitable phenomena, but capable of being remedied by sound national planning, supported by international economic co-operation.[100]

The third element was a development that was gratuitous and unexpected. A number of Irish delegates to the session, including Lemass himself and Fred Summerfield of the Federation of Saorstát Industries, concluded their remarks by invoking the blessing of God on the work of the conference. The Reuter correspondent at the conference — unaware of Lemass's private scepticism on religious matters — observed: 'This is the first time that any delegation, whether of Governments, employers or workers, has brought in the Almighty's name to bless the work, and the practice of the Irish government and employers' representatives has aroused much comment.'[101]

Lemass was still in Geneva when the Dáil was dissolved by de Valera and a general election called for 1 July; the referendum on the new constitution was held on the same date. Lemass had already circulated the Control of Prices Bill,[102] which the government evidently hoped would help to soften up the electorate. His contributions to the election campaign, after a 'tumultuous' welcome in his South Dublin constituency,[103] were relatively low-key. The divisive rhetoric of 1933 had given way to appeals to the middle ground again. The new Constitution, Lemass declared, was 'possibly the first attempt made to translate into practical law the principles of social justice as laid down by Pope Leo XIII,'[104] and both he and his leader increasingly promoted what was by now becoming a kind of leitmotif of Fianna Fáil populism: the idea of a classless society in which, perhaps paradoxically, trade unions were especially valued. De Valera wanted 'every Irishman, whether workers, employers or employees, to regard themselves as brothers in the nation.'[105] Lemass told his urban audiences that the forty-hour week would 'win out in the end,'[106] that social services would be further extended as the national resources grew,[107] and that there would be 'no more vigorous opponent to any attempt, to any plan, for Hitlerising the Irish trade union movement than I will be.'[108]

In an election characterised by a low poll he nevertheless pushed his share of the vote up to 2.24 quotas, the second-best result he ever achieved. Fianna Fáil, however, had lost its absolute majority and was returned to government only with Labour Party support. A new election would not be long delayed, and de Valera seized the opportunity in July 1938, when defeated on a technical vote in the Dáil on a matter connected with the arbitration process for civil service salaries. His judgment was vindicated, and he retrieved his overall majority. Lemass, who as usual was actively involved as director of elections, had to exercise his powers to the full to revive the flagging enthusiasm of local organisations, not least in the light of their 'strong disinclination to organise collections.'[109] Although his own vote slipped, he still secured 2.06 quotas, evidence — if such were needed — of his continuing personal popularity. Fianna Fáil, however, saw its total vote go up by more than 6 per cent to 51.9 per cent (a figure never exceeded thereafter) and formed a government that was to last for a full five-year term.

De Valera was now well placed to negotiate with the British government as the chill wind of impending international hostilities made itself felt. The fruitless attempt to secure enforceable commitments from the British on partition in return for concessions on defence and trade matters have been well documented.[110] On the purely trade side, however, Lemass's role was significant. He was instrumental in securing British acceptance of the proposition that when it came to assessing the case of infant Irish industries for continuing protection, the Irish government would be 'the final judge'.[111] Leydon appears to have been successful in establishing the essential link between the agreements that were eventually concluded, suggesting that they be treated on an all-or-nothing basis. Lemass himself, while loyally supporting the Taoiseach's hard line against concessions to Northern industry, appeared to a number of British negotiators to be more flexible than de Valera, even seeming at one stage to offer himself as a mediator between the opposing positions.

> Mr. Lemass seemed far more prepared to discuss our plan in a reasonable way, and to see whether there was any means of reaching some agreement which was mutually satisfactory. But whenever he began to develop at any length an argument which might have led to some compromise, one or other of his colleagues intervened with a fresh uncompromising statement of their views.[112]

There was undoubtedly an element of wishful thinking in all of this; but it is unwise to assume that the experienced British negotiators were insensitive to slight but significant differences of opinion between the members of the Irish team, if only for the purpose of attempting to exploit them. It was not to be the last time that British government representatives were keen to discern differences between the two men.

Only minor concessions were made to Northern Ireland in the Anglo-Irish Agreement, which came into force on 19 May 1938. The immediate effect of this agreement, as far as trade between North and South was concerned, was evidently beneficial to the South; between May 1938 and February 1939 exports from Northern Ireland to the Republic had increased by only 4 per cent, while those from the South to the North had gone up by 25 per cent.[113]

In the aftermath of the 1938 agreement Lemass, strengthened by the outcome of the negotiations, felt the need to put out feelers towards the North. A series of discussions took place between Leydon and his British and Northern counterparts in June 1938, which aroused optimism on both sides. Although tariffs as such were not on the negotiating table, this marked a development from the position adopted by both Lemass and de Valera in the London negotiations earlier in the same year, when British requests for special treatment for Northern Ireland goods were rejected emphatically by the Taoiseach and Lemass alike.[114] Lemass now wrote to de Valera to suggest that in order to enhance the collaboration with the British 'imposed by our national interests' there was a need for greater co-ordination between North and South. 'It will probably be realised by the Government of Northern Ireland after these discussions that the community of interests between us is sufficiently great to warrant discussions of wider scope.'[115]

This tentative step towards acknowledging that political friendship needed a better foundation than economic hostility was, however, torpedoed by two developments. The first was the probably coincidental publication of an interview with de Valera in the London *Evening Standard* in which he detailed his proposals for a federal solution of the Northern problem but made what would have been in any case a bitter pill more unpalatable to the unionists by using the language of 'concessions'. This slightly modified but still traditional expression of aspiration towards unity had the effect of throwing a lighted match into the tinder-dry undergrowth of unionist fears.[116] The interview, a well-disposed British civil servant told Leydon, 'has aroused quite as much uneasiness and ill-feeling as I thought it would when I first saw it, and has been, and still is, the main subject of every speech at every Orange Lodge. This is a problem completely out of our control and Civil Servants can do nothing more than shed a silent tear about it.'[117]

It is nonetheless significant that this particular articulation of the possible structure of a future united Ireland — in effect a non-unitary state — was adopted wholeheartedly by Lemass and remained his guiding concept right up to his retirement, even though his strategy towards its achievement, as will be seen, differed markedly from that of his predecessor.

The second problem was caused by the changing patterns of trade in the wake of the Anglo-Irish Agreement. In the five months from June, imports into the Republic from Britain had gone down by 9.6 per cent and imports from Northern Ireland had gone down by 14 per cent, whereas Irish exports to Britain had gone up by 12 per cent and to the North by no less than 24 per cent.

With a panoply of other legislation in place, including new laws on prices, and the good will of the trade unions, Lemass might well have been in a good position to develop industrial policy from a position of strength. September 1939, however, and the outbreak of war created a scenario so radically different from what had gone before that Lemass not only had to put many of his cherished schemes on the back burner, including any ideas he might have had of undoing, or at least ameliorating, the effects of Fianna Fáil's full-blown economic policies on the economic welfare of their compatriots north of the border, but also had to devise a whole new range of policies for dealing with the emergency of the war years.

From one point of view, the balance sheet of the previous seven years had been an encouraging one. In 1933 there were twenty-four publicly quoted Irish companies with an aggregate capital of £5 million; by 1939 the number had more than trebled, to seventy-eight, and aggregate capital employed had doubled.[118] As the two ratios show, the companies were on average smaller, but the level of economic activity involved cannot be gain-said. The population outflow, if not halted, at least had been partially staunched; but even this brought problems in its train, particularly in rural areas, where the ratio of population to land discouraged marriage. In that decade some 25 per cent of women in their late forties as well as 30 per cent of men had never married. Many of the new jobs were in fact not in the protected industries but in the government-generated activities of social housing and other infrastructure developments. As Lemass reflected ruefully in opposition a decade later, the fact that the unemployment register had not shown any marked improvement during the period, despite the creation of thousands of new jobs, was because many of the new jobs had been taken not by the unemployed but by the marginal self-employed, who had not been entitled to appear on the unemployment register.[119]

Some of the forms of protection and subsidy can be said, admittedly with the benefit of hindsight, to have been disastrously scattergun in nature. Some of the improvement was due to external circumstances and some of it to Lemass's energy and drive. If the fortuitous combination of circumstances worked to favour his policies, however, the support he was getting from his own party was rarely better than lukewarm, and it is difficult to quarrel with one writer's conclusion that he was 'thwarted by his cabinet colleagues more often than he succeeded during the 1930s.'[120] Gerry Boland, according to his son,

> had a very sarcastic tongue. Above all he didn't agree with Lemass's industrial policy, setting up all these little factories everywhere making inferior goods and huge profits. Later it became personal. He believed more in industry based on fish, food and farming. He was particularly opposed to the CKD[121] car assembly business as a fake 'industry' producing an inferior article for which you paid double the price. He used to refer scornfully to 'back-lane factories'. He didn't see why we should, for instance, attempt to beat places like Sheffield at their own game — although ironically Newbridge Cutlery was one of the successes. I remember that we paid for it during the war, trying to shave with the razor blades that were made here. He could never see the huge packing cases containing the 'raw material' for the car assembly 'industry' being unloaded at the docks without rumbling about 'bloody madness' and I heard the 'back lane factories' from him long before it became the stock in trade of Labour and Fine Gael deputies … He was probably not alone in maintaining that it would be better if Lemass's undoubted drive was directed towards establishing really major industries based on native resources, for example, that we should, at that early stage, get into the food processing business which was going to expand.[122]

Even his actual and potential allies were from time to time to be found among his critics. C. S. Andrews, who believed that Lemass had to be pushed into turf development because he thought that turf had negative connotations in the race consciousness of the Irish people, also suggested that Lemass in his early years as a minister was too blinkered, worked too hard in his office, and didn't broaden his mind enough. 'The only relaxation in his life was card playing and you don't enlighten your mind or broaden your vision among card players or horsy men.'[123]

Lemass was in fact playing golf in Skerries just before the outbreak of the Second World War on the morning of 1 September 1939, when two British flying-boats landed in the bay. The distraught local sergeant telephoned Lemass at the golf club to ask him what to do. 'Tell them to get away,' was the terse rejoinder.[124] Not all problems over the next five years were to be solved so easily, but the advent of war, and his elevation to Minister for Supplies, was to affect Lemass in two ways. Positively, it was to give him the opportunity to shrug off his critics, inside and outside the party, and give him a degree of power and freedom of action he had never hitherto experienced and was not to experience again until the late nineteen-fifties. Negatively, it was to postpone serious consideration of the wisdom of the economic policies Fianna Fáil had pursued unrelentingly for the previous seven years and of the willingness or ability of industry to respond to these policies in the way Lemass had expected it would. The maintenance of supplies during the war that was engulfing Europe now had to take precedence over everything else.

4

War, Peace, and the Cock-Sparrow in Merrion Street

1939–48

By the outbreak of war Lemass's life as a politician had become virtually all-consuming. He had the newspapers delivered to the house and had generally filleted them over breakfast, mentally taking a number of important political decisions even before he left for the office. Once in the office the late Dáil sessions and other work meant that he often came home after the children had gone to bed. He rarely took holidays. His wife recalled:

> Sometimes Dáil business would keep him away until after midnight. Then there were at least five or six functions a week which he felt we had to attend. He used to say to me that our lives were not our own in politics. Even when we used to take a house in Skerries for the summer months, Seán never joined us until night time and even then he carried a briefcase full of business with him ... He was always emotionally upset by a crisis in the home, but if there was a crisis in Government at the same time he had no doubt where his duty lay. And that was in Leinster House.[1]

Kathleen Lemass enjoyed socialising and, even though she could rarely persuade her husband to venture onto a dance floor, enjoyed the entertaining that went with Lemass's ministerial functions. She usually joined the holiday poker sessions in Skerries Golf Club too, although she would generally retire before the men rolled up their sleeves and got down to the early morning session. During the war Skerries became even more central to the family than before. Lemass had originally thought of sending Kathleen and the children to somewhere down the country, as there was always the possibility that Dublin might be bombed. The eventual compromise was Skerries, where they were sent for long periods during the summer months. This did not, as it happened, shield them completely from the war, and the children recalled seeing and hearing gunfire between ships and planes in the Irish Sea.

Under these circumstances it was in effect Kathleen who provided the still centre, the locus of warmth, affection and continuity for her husband and children. For all his absences Lemass reciprocated with equal warmth and with intense loyalty and support. It probably helped that Kathleen had no political agenda of her own and indeed was in some respects an innocent abroad in the world of power and controversy in which her husband was daily immersed. On one occasion when Lemass was Taoiseach she opened the front door to some people she did not recognise and then ushered them into another room, informing her husband that some ministers were waiting to see him. Puzzled, because he wasn't expecting any of his Government colleagues, Lemass went in to greet them, only to discover that the 'ministers' (as they had described themselves to Kathleen) were Jehovah's Witnesses.[2]

The young TD and minister and his young family led a peripatetic life. As a newly married man in 1925 he lived in a flat in a house called Rokeby in Terenure Road, moving later to a flat in Albany Road and from there to one in Villiers Road, Rathgar, where he lived when he first became a minister in 1932. From there the family moved to Churchtown Park House. All these homes were rented; the perceived insecurity of his political career, and probably the relative inadequacy of his income, did not encourage ideas of house purchase. De Valera's first working majority in 1933 was wafer-thin, and this too would have engendered caution.

At the end of the thirties Seán and Kathleen bought the family home at 53 Palmerston Road from John T. and Frances Lemass. Neighbours in Palmerston Road at that time included Lombard Murphy, the son of William Martin Murphy; Alfie Byrne; Joseph Griffin, who occasionally came up to discuss old times with him over a cup of tea;[3] and the young accountant Russell Murphy. Although the move marked a definite improvement in the degree of comfort for the family, it did not mean that all worries had been banished. One of the principal worries in 1943–44 was health. Kathleen Lemass described it in 1968:

> My three daughters all got TB at the same time. My eldest, who was eighteen or nineteen, was very bad and she had to spend two years in hospital. It was before they had discovered the drugs to cure TB easily and people were dying from it in their thousands from it in this country at the time. It was a real killer and I was worried to death.[4]

Kathleen kept her two younger daughters at home and nursed them herself. 'I wouldn't let anybody else look after them. It was really such a terrible disease at that time, I was really down and out for a year or two.'[5] In the big house in Palmerston Road the children's bedrooms were on the top floor, and her daughters in particular have an abiding memory of their mother journeying ceaselessly with meals on trays for them from the kitchen on the ground floor.[6]

It was a large house, plentifully stocked with books, with room for the children to entertain their friends. It would have been the custom at that time for the children, especially in their early teens, to have their contemporaries in the house for social evenings, which were under decorous parental supervision and at which a 'cup' would be the strongest form of stimulant allowed. It is a measure of the closeness of the political families involved that the MacEntees and the Lemasses socialised easily on this basis, despite their fathers' frequent political battles.[7] The family lived there until the fifties, when they moved to 26 Hillside Drive, Rathfarnham.

There was a table-tennis table in the basement of 53 Palmerston Road, and Seán would join in family tournaments there. At certain key points in their lives, notably when their secondary school careers came to an end, each of the children would be summoned to the paternal presence for a little speech about his or her future. Lemass encouraged his daughters in the direction of further education. Maureen did a BComm in UCD, and Peggy did a BSc in the same college. Sheila, the youngest, had little interest in the prospect of higher education, and Lemass, although he respected her wishes, did not attempt to conceal his disappointment.

Nor did Lemass's only son, Noel, go to university. He was educated first at CUS in Leeson Street but, possibly because a firmer hand was thought to be necessary, was later sent to boarding school, at Newbridge College in County Kildare. After leaving school he undertook business training and became an executive member and branch secretary of the Irish Commercial Travellers' Association. He eventually followed his father into politics, somewhat to Lemass's discomfiture or at any rate at an age that his father thought was too young. He was elected to Dublin City Council in 1955 and won a Dáil seat for Fianna Fáil in a by-election in the Dublin South-West constituency the following year.

Noel had to wait until his father retired from politics for political preferment, becoming Parliamentary Secretary to the Minister for Finance from 1969 to 1973. He would not have been led to expect otherwise: although his father was director of elections for the two by-elections that were held simultaneously in 1956, in one of which Noel was the successful Fianna Fáil candidate, Lemass did not make a single speech in the constituency in which his son was standing. At first, indeed, Lemass believed that his son would not make a good TD, but 'before he died he told him that he was improving, and to dedicate himself to politics.'[8]

Nonetheless, Noel Lemass's political career was ill-starred, and the effort of attempting to live up to his father's massive reputation must have been a source of considerable personal pressure. He would, on occasion, attempt unsuccessfully to impress his father with impractical schemes. The arrival on the political scene of Charles Haughey, his brother-in-law, whose ambition was supported by considerable ability, must have seemed to Noel like a bad hand dealt by fate. On occasion the strain showed in his social life. When this happened, his father's gruff fondness for him never tempted him to seek or endorse special treatment for his sometimes wayward son. Lemass was once, as Taoiseach, at an IMI conference in Killarney when he was contacted by the authorities in Liverpool, into whose clutches Noel had fallen as the result of some social misdemeanour and who wanted to know what should be done. 'Haven't you got procedures?' Lemass growled. And that was the end of the affair.[9]

All Lemass's children remember the care, even fastidiousness, with which their father kept his public and private lives separate, sometimes to their intense annoyance, as in relation to his unwavering policy that his official car should not be used to transport his children to or from social engagements. Even when her husband was Taoiseach, Kathleen used to make her daily journey to Mass on a bicycle. When well-wishers sent the family gifts of tea during the war — a commodity in extraordinarily short supply — the gifts were always repacked and returned to the donors. As a minister on trips abroad he never claimed his daily allowance — to which he would have been automatically entitled without producing any vouchers or receipts — unless he had actually spent the money.[10] When he was given fees for writing articles he invariably (following a practice established by de Valera[11]) turned the money over to the Irish Red Cross.[12]

He attempted — unsuccessfully — to persuade his younger brother Frank not to leave his promising but poorly paid job as an accountant with Craig Gardner for a position as secretary to the Dublin United Tramway Company, on the grounds that as minister he would have to negotiate with the company. Later, when Frank moved to CIE, a special job title had to be created for him to avoid any semblance of a potential conflict of interest with his older brother.[13]

The war period was to provide several notable examples of Lemass's personal incorruptibility, even as it made new and substantial demands on his organisational and political talents. At first his significance in Government was recognised by the creation of the new post of Minister for Supplies, to which he was appointed on 8 September 1939. In de Valera's version of what happened Lemass himself suggested the creation of the department, and 'the penalty for suggesting it was that it was given to him.'[14]

His pivotal role in the management of the war economy was indicated by de Valera's choice of Lemass, together with the new Minister for Finance, James Ryan, to take part in secret trade negotiations with London in April 1940. These negotiations eventually foundered in November on a British insistence that Irish ports be made available for transhipment and repair facilities, which the Government plainly felt would irretrievably compromise Irish neutrality. They were notable, however, for one unusual gesture. While in London both Lemass and Ryan, partially prompted by the

British representative in Dublin, Sir John Maffey, who had seen them before they went,[15] called at Buckingham Palace on 2 May 1940 and signed the visitors' book there.[16] It is highly unlikely that the two ministers would have made such a gesture without de Valera's explicit approval, although the Taoiseach some seven years later had apparently no recollection of it. At the same time the signing of the visitors' book was essentially a social courtesy and did not imply that the visitors had met the monarch.

The upper reaches of the British administration believed that Lemass was 'genuinely anxious' to improve North-South relations, in contrast to de Valera.[17] In June of the same year, when de Valera, Aiken and Lemass had abortive discussions with British ministers about the possibility of engineering a solution to the partition question if Ireland abandoned its neutrality, Malcolm MacDonald, the British Dominions Secretary, noted that Lemass 'seemed to be prepared to discuss our plan in a more reasonable way, but his contributions to discussion were usually cut short by fresh uncompromising interventions from one or other of his colleagues.'[18]

When Lemass resigned from his position as Minister for Industry and Commerce in September 1939 he was succeeded by Seán MacEntee. Leydon went with him to Supplies; the relationship which had begun in such an unusual fashion had been case-hardened by seven years of working closely together. As contemporaries noted, they complemented each other admirably. Leydon saved Lemass from the untoward effects of decisions that had been made, as Lemass himself later acknowledged, in an occasionally slapdash fashion. Leydon would get decisions from Lemass; Lemass would get action from Leydon. Together they fashioned a plan for the duration of the war that was, with some modifications, to earn the minister a reputation for fairness and impartiality.[19] It also involved a certain degree of cannibalism. Leydon's eagle eye noticed, shortly after the establishment of the new department, that there was a section on transport and maritime affairs in the Department of Industry and Commerce, which did not seem to have woken up to the great urgency of the shipping question. He discussed it with Lemass, who went straight to the Government and got permission to absorb the section into Supplies; within two days of the Government decision Leydon had drafted a scheme for the establishment of Irish Shipping Ltd and was bidding for ships in the London market before registration.[20]

It was also during this period, no doubt partly because of the tough and unpopular decisions Lemass had to take, that rumours about the extent and significance of personal problems, principally recurrent whispers about gambling, gained some currency both within and outside Lemass's own party. Among the more extravagant were rumours that he had become politically compromised by the extent of his gambling debts; that he had been bailed out either by a consortium of bookmakers or by some of his wealthier friends (one version of this story had Joe McGrath organising a betting coup against Lemass's Dublin bookmaker that bankrupted the unfortunate bookie and let Lemass off the hook); and that he kept a string of racehorses at the Curragh in the name of A. P. Reynolds.[21] The rumours surfaced even in British and American confidential briefing documents, although unaccompanied by anything remotely resembling evidence. One such summary, prepared for John F. Kennedy by the CIA, suggested that 'there were rumours that he was engaged in black market operations during World War II' and that 'he is an inveterate gambler and as a result has at times been involved in serious financial difficulties.'[22] These stories gave rise to numerous political innuendoes closer to home, notably from James Dillon and the *Irish Times.*

When looking at these allegations today there is a risk of failing to take the social habits of the time fully into account, of succumbing to a distorting and ahistorical kind of hindsight. Seán Lemass's youth was not only pre-television but in effect pre-radio. Card-playing in particular was probably one of the most popular leisure activities in the country, apart from going to the pub — something that Lemass rarely did. In Lemass's case there was the additional factor of the best part of a couple of years in prison, during the War of Independence and during the Civil War. In Ballykinlar and the Curragh alike, card-playing was an essential antidote to unutterable boredom.

There is no available evidence to support any of the allegations of impropriety, and a great deal of circumstantial evidence that suggests the opposite. Lemass's son-in-law Charles Haughey suggests that he was 'far too disciplined a person to get into trouble. He was very careful about money and would never owe money. When we went on holidays — to Laragh or to Donegal — he'd be very prudent about money.'[23] Lemass's wife put it equally simply. 'Seán was not a wealthy man, although he could have been if he had wanted. He would just ask for all the bills each month and write out the cheques. We never owed a penny to anyone and Seán didn't care about money as long as there was enough to meet the bills.'[24]

Lemass participated in a number of regular poker schools. The most regular of all was at Skerries Golf Club, where occasionally the blinds were drawn and play would go on until dawn.[25] The club was a sort of no-man's-land to which Lemass could retreat from the hurly-burly of politics — even though on occasion, particularly during the war when he was Minister for Supplies, he would be surrounded by business people anxious to get shipping space for goods they wanted to import. Both at the card table and on the golf course, in fact, many of Lemass's companions were very definitely of a different political persuasion. When one of them, Leo Flanagan, once asked Lemass why so many of his social companions were Fine Gaelers, Lemass sucked briefly on his pipe before grunting in reply: 'I have the others!'

In his social relations generally, Lemass eschewed politics. At the card table, in the fishing-boat or on the golf course this particular topic was in effect not on the agenda. His manner was always unpretentious. On one occasion Flanagan found Lemass — then a minister — queuing with his wife for admission to Flanagan's cinema in Skerries. Lemass was with difficulty persuaded to accept a free season ticket, inscribed *Without prejudice.* 'You should have left out the "out",' Lemass remarked to the donor.[26]

Poker companions in the school included Donncha O'Dea, regarded virtually as a professional, who was once told by his companions that they would refuse to play with him any longer if he didn't take off the eye-shade he habitually wore. Others included Ben Fagan, the City Analyst; Dr Paddy Fanning, who had been at the O'Connell Schools at the same time as Lemass; Sammy Lyons, the architect; the McIlvenna brothers, who owned the hotel in Skerries where the school passed many nights; and the Mulcahy brothers. Lemass 'burned his fingers at times' but, as a player, 'could handle himself.' At the other end of the scale, and perhaps in a different school, were players like Stephen O'Flaherty, the Volkswagen concessionaire, who not only lost heavily but boasted about his losses.[27] Estimates of what was lost are hard to come by, but a big loser in the fifties might on occasion have lost a thousand pounds, which was a very considerable sum indeed (£14,000 in 1996 values). Lemass described himself as a 'not very good' poker player. 'I'd always be looking for the miracle.'[28]

During the war years there was frequently a poker school involving Lemass and Jim Ryan in the young Eoin Ryan's flat close to Leinster House, not least because it obviated the need for the players (who would have included Noel Griffin, Bob Flood of Terenure, and Bob Briscoe) to decamp to Jim Ryan's house in Greystones; but stakes were modest.[29] With Lemass the playing was the thing, rather than the money.

While politics may generally have been left outside the door, it occasionally obtruded. In May 1941, when the North Strand in Dublin was bombed by German aircraft, Lemass was taking part in a poker school at Peter McCarthy's house in Dublin. One of Lemass's officials stuck his head around the door to tell him the news but was chased away before he could open his mouth. Taking his courage in both hands about half an hour later, the official reappeared and insisted on telling his story. Hardly surprisingly, Lemass began to take his leave of the company, when his host intervened in an attempt to forestall him. There were two reasons why Lemass couldn't leave, he argued. In the first place, he was winning, and in the second, it would leave only six players, and he — McCarthy — always preferred to play with seven. On this occasion affairs of state triumphed.

When Lemass visited Ottawa as Tánaiste in 1953 he came down to breakfast one morning in his hotel and put $100 on the table — his winnings from the previous night's poker school with J. D. Kearney, the former

Canadian High Commissioner in Dublin and a long-time friend.[30] The money was spent for the benefit of the delegation generally.

The elements of risk, bluff and chance involved evidently appealed at a deep and important psychological level to a man whose entire political career was based on attempts — not always successful by any means but determined and highly planned and co-ordinated — to control all the variables, to predict the outcomes, and to direct the action. In a sense, away from the political arena Lemass enjoyed the psychological games involved to a degree that made some of his social companions wary. Although his golf handicap varied between 18 and 14, he was never too bothered about getting it down, as this would adversely affect his ability to win money from his companions. Equally, he was known for his ability to put his rivals off their tee shots or critical putts by distracting them at the crucial moment.[31] He was always ready to chance his arm; on one famous occasion when he hooked a bird by accident on a sea-fishing expedition he argued with a straight face — but unavailingly — for it to be included in the weight of his total catch.

He had a passionate attachment to horse-racing, and studied form intently every weekend. He loved frequenting race meetings but abandoned the practice completely as Taoiseach, as he felt that — apart from the few formal occasions when his presence as Taoiseach was expected — race meetings were beneath the dignity of the office. Nor did he bet as Taoiseach, with very rare exceptions. On one such occasion he was given a tip by Joe McGrath for a horse running at an English meeting. The bet was put on by proxy, and the horse duly obliged at 100 to 1.

One possible pointer to his general attitude to gambling is provided by his decision during his last period as Minister for Industry and Commerce in 1957–59 to turn down a plan for the establishment of a casino in Ireland, despite the fact that the plan had the enthusiastic backing at the time of all the principal tourism interests, including the tourist board.[32] Among Lemass's own circle, C. S. Andrews was certainly in favour; so was the hotelier Ken Besson, then proprietor of the famous Russell Hotel in St Stephen's Green. The proposal, however, was successfully opposed by two other substantial interests, the Catholic Church and Irish Hospitals' Trust; and a delegation from the tourist board was told flatly of Lemass's decision, although the reasons were never publicly stated.

His sensitivity to questions of conflict of interest was of particular significance during his period in the Department of Supplies. Despite the rumours, there has been no evidence of any kind that he ever abused his position there and some significant evidence to the contrary, as for example his 'grim satisfaction in the fact that acquaintances of his own were prosecuted in the special court set up to deal with offences under the rationing legislation.'[33] Lemass's office was, as might be expected, the recipient of representations of every kind, for the power he wielded was immense. In the circumstances, straight dealing was not only advisable but essential.

On one occasion, etched in the memory of at least one of the participants, de Valera's private secretary, Kathleen O'Connell, rang Lemass's private secretary, Kevin O'Doherty, to enquire what the position was in relation to a particular trader whose quota for a particular class of goods had been withdrawn. It was in fact a personal enquiry by O'Connell, but O'Doherty, assuming that the request had originated with de Valera, rang Tom Murray in the department and asked him to send up the file, telling him that the Taoiseach's office was interested. Nothing happened for some two hours, and then, to O'Doherty's astonishment — and indeed alarm — he picked up his telephone to hear de Valera's voice telling him: 'I never interfere in the affairs of my ministers.' Murray, it transpired, had gone to Leydon about it, Leydon had gone to Lemass, and Lemass had raised it directly with de Valera.[34] The matter was never mentioned again.

The occasions on which, even momentarily, the Lemass line wavered were so few as to be memorable in themselves. On one of them, he was faced with a request from Dan Breen for permission to export a case of whiskey to lubricate some business deal he was negotiating in Britain — not a serious problem in itself but the third such application from the same source. Lemass drew on his pipe for a moment before giving his verdict: 'Tell Breen I'll do it — but it's the last time.'

The general mode, however, was irreproachable. On one occasion towards the end of the war P. J. Little, then Minister for Posts and Telegraphs, asked Lemass if there was any chance that a fine levied on a constituent for trading in the black market could be remitted. The response was swift: 'I have restrained myself from investigating the case, as I believe it would lead to me doubling the fine.'[35]

Master and servant could both bend on occasion, but it was very rare. Leydon once unilaterally rescinded the obligatory resignation of a clerk-typist who had left the service to get married, after her fiancé died just before the wedding.[36] And Lemass himself was not impervious to special circumstances, which were addressed with a mixture of sensitivity and despatch.

> Lemass had a human streak but I only really saw it once. A letter came in to him written on pages torn out of a school exercise book, by a boy at school at Westland Row. It was written at the request of the boy's mother, on behalf of his father, a taxi driver whose petrol allocation had been revoked after he had been caught taking a party of golfers home from the Hermitage Golf Club. The father had gone to England to try and get work. The boy was trying to get a job as a messenger but his teacher had said that if he stayed at the school he

would get a scholarship. The letter had come in that morning's mail, and as Lemass was passing through my office I showed it to him. His response was quite unprecedented. He asked for the file, and asked for a typist to come into his private office with him, and dictated a reply to the lad there and then. He told the lad to tell his father that he would restore his petrol allocation there and then. He was also to tell his mother that he was to remain at school. And he was to tell his father, also, that if he offended further, Lemass would have no mercy on him.[37]

The Government minister who had left school at fifteen to pick up a rifle in the GPO had, in a small way, completed the circle.

Lemass's own political instincts were becoming sharply honed during this period. When his new private secretary let it be known informally that he proposed to go out and canvass for Fianna Fáil in the evenings during the 1944 election the word came back from the minister's office, equally informally: 'He can do what he likes, but if he's found out he'll be sacked from the civil service, and I won't defend him.'

And Lemass's humour, the more underrated for its frequently deadpan delivery, showed itself from time to time like the smile on the face of the tiger. During the 1944 election campaign he and his private secretary were lunching at a provincial hotel when they noticed on the other side of the dining-room a party of senior Fine Gael politicians, including Richard Mulcahy and T.F. O'Higgins. At the end of the lunch Lemass told his secretary:

> Go over to General Mulcahy and tell him that I am approving an additional allocation of petrol for the Fine Gael election campaign — and tell him from me that I hope that there will not be a repeat of what happened during the last election, when a Dublin taxi arrived at Listowel races full of members of the Fine Gael party, but festooned with banners urging people to vote for Fianna Fáil![38]

In January 1945 Lemass found himself in Waterford, where he had arrived in the depths of winter an hour early for a meeting with the Chamber of Commerce and had been despatched to a clammy waiting-room heated by a small fire of damp turf. The only diversion supplied was a copy of the local newspaper, and he studied this intently for some time. 'It says here', he remarked to his secretary, 'that the local boxing club has just elected its officers. The president is a priest, the treasurer is a doctor, and the secretary is an undertaker. I'd say they've got things about right — wouldn't you?'[39]

The war encouraged Lemass to develop new administrative methods. In the Department of Supplies all the officials concerned with decision-making were enabled to attend the departmental conferences at which decisions were taken, short-circuiting the paperwork and bureaucratic procedures. All the officials concerned were required to attend meetings at eleven each day, bringing their files, without notice of any agenda or waiting for records to be produced; everyone was free to speak on all matters under discussion, whether it was within their area of responsibility or not. 'At departmental conferences, Lemass loved being the district justice; it was a court of summary jurisdiction.'[40] The personal risk to Lemass was that there would be no records to justify decisions or illuminate the transactions.[41] It is a measure of the increasing capacity of his legendary memory for departmental minutiae, as well as for the intuitive quality of his decision-making, that this unprecedented process functioned with apparent smoothness throughout the period of existence of the department. Indeed a more orthodox version of it was subsequently imported into the Department of Industry and Commerce.

Lemass always took personal responsibility for his department's actions, which was why he evoked such strong loyalty among his staff. He also gave his civil servants, even relatively junior ones, the kind of implicit support that gave them the right to pursue and even to castigate superior officials. On the morning of one summer Government meeting towards the end of the war, when Lemass was staying with his family in Skerries, his car broke down twice on the way into Dublin, making him late for the meeting. Without disguising his annoyance, he told his private secretary, Kevin O'Doherty, to take the matter up with the Garda authorities, who were responsible for the maintenance of the car. O'Doherty set off in pursuit of his quarry in the full knowledge that his minister would back him to the hilt, and eventually, after penetrating the best smokescreens that the Garda HQ in the Phoenix Park could lay down, tracked down the Commissioner to Woodbrook, where he was playing golf. He insisted that the Commissioner be summoned in from the course, and informed him tersely of his minister's opinion that if Garda cars could convey the Commissioner to Woodbrook without mishap they should convey ministers to Government meetings with equal reliability. Lemass's car never broke down again.[42]

Later in the war, in another innovation, Lemass held weekly press briefings every Monday morning on the supply situation with political journalists from each of the national newspapers, for which officials were required to prepare one-page summaries for each commodity. Only a small fraction of what he told the journalists was ever published: the rest was for background, and Lemass was frank in disclosing information about supplies, his world-ranging efforts to secure them, and his attempts to improvise transport arrangements in wartime.

This combination of openness and efficiency did much to offset the inevitable unpopularity that attached to some of the minister's decisions, even those over which he had little direct control. The derisive sobriquet 'Half-Ounce Lemass', which was hung around his neck during this period, referred to the progressive reduction in the allowance of tea that had been necessitated when the British government unilaterally abrogated earlier agreements on which the Government had been relying. Sugar, however, was one of his success stories. Thanks to the sugarbeet industry, Ireland had plenty of this commodity, and Lemass played to his strength. When the British began to short-change him on tea, he began to tighten up on exports of sugar, at the same time letting it be known that extra rations were available domestically for certain specified purposes, such as preserving soft fruit and feeding bees during the winter. The additional quantities were administered in generous measure. Not long after the war Lemass explained wryly to William Sweetman, the editor of the *Irish Press*, that if anyone had added up the acreage under soft fruit that had been notified to the Department of Industry and Commerce as part of a successful application for additional sugar it would have exceeded all the arable land in Ireland.[43]

One subject on which he was notably silent was the Government's attitude towards the IRA. The war period saw not only internment but the execution of a number of republicans whose crimes — including the murder of gardaí — sprang from a passionate belief that England's difficulty was Ireland's opportunity: Paddy McGrath and Thomas Harte in Mountjoy in September 1940, Richard Goss in Port Laoise in August 1941, George Plant in Port Laoise in March 1942, and Charlie Kerins in Mountjoy in February 1944. This aspect of Government policy was controversial, to say the least, and provoked among other things the resignation of Kathleen Clarke, Tom Clarke's widow, from Fianna Fáil in May 1943.[44]

Lemass was certainly among those Government ministers with direct experience of revolutionary warfare whose credentials for defending such a policy would have been impeccable. In sharp contrast to some of his colleagues, however — notably Gerald Boland, who as Minister for Justice signed the execution warrants, and Seán MacEntee — he made no speeches on the issue, and some members of his family felt that he was on occasion close to breaking with the Government. His mother's attitude may well have been a factor: her analysis was a simple one, and she told him forcefully during this period, according to one account, that the Government was locking up young men whose only crime was to take up arms in the same way that he and his brother had done a quarter of a century earlier.[45] The pressures were so great that silence was the only way out. Kathleen Lemass recalled after her husband's death: 'I know how it pained him. He never spoke about it but he seemed to fall very quiet and look into the fire thinking. At times like that I always stayed quiet and left him alone with his thoughts.'[46]

The war also encouraged, occasionally dramatically, the *dirigiste* tendencies that had already begun to manifest themselves in Lemass's approach to industrial development. Although he appears not to have lost faith in his essential belief both in self-sufficiency and in the role of private enterprise, his views on the need for private enterprise to be state-supported and occasionally state-directed were reinforced.[47] The apparent inconsistency in these two positions is at first sight difficult to explain. If, however, he was moving away from the idea that tariffs and quotas would produce the desired result, the likelihood is that he was simply exploring the possibility of using other instruments of economic management that might succeed where tariffs and quotas were failing, among them state investment, controlled monopoly production, efficiency audits, and tax breaks. The last of these never surmounted the hurdles erected by the Department of Finance; the others were gelded by a shortage of capital funds, a lack of enthusiasm on the part of colleagues, and the electoral unpredictability that marked the years between 1949 and 1957.

The war forced Lemass to mark time on two important fronts. One was his relationship with the trade union movement, which went noticeably off the boil under the stress of wartime conditions, despite his best attempts to continue building bridges to this important constituency. The other was the kind of industrial development that might have taken place had the war not intervened. Some industries, notably cement and rubber, were kept going during the war only by Lemass's acumen in bargaining Ireland's surplus productive capacity against Britain's control of the raw materials: supplies would be shipped to Ireland and processed here in some secrecy, the bargain being that Ireland was permitted to retain a certain proportion of the finished product.

The numbers employed in the protected industries contracted substantially in the early years of the war, and the first increase, in September 1944, amounted only to two thousand over the figure for the previous year. There was continuing emigration to Britain, not only of men prepared to take up the labour slack in British factories caused by large-scale mobilisation but of women — whom Lemass insisted should be deloused on their way to the boat because if they were found to have head-louse infestation on arrival 'the country would be held up to opprobrium.'[48]

Lemass's appointment as Minister for Supplies had to some extent taken him out of the loop of industrial development generally. But once the management system in Supplies had been set up and was running smoothly, he went to de Valera and persuaded him — probably without much difficulty — to restore him to his suzerainty of Industry and Commerce, on the grounds that 'he was bored because there wasn't enough work for him to do.'[49] As far as the public was concerned, this announcement 'came as a surprise ... as he was thought to be fully occupied in the Department of Supplies.'[50] John Leydon remained secretary of both departments, and the physical arrangement of the offices indicated the power structure with some clarity: Leydon's office had direct access to Lemass's, while R. C. Ferguson, who had been deputising for Leydon in Industry and Commerce during Lemass's initial translation to supplies, had access to Lemass only through the office of the minister's private secretary.[51]

Planning for the Future

As far as economic and industrial development was concerned, the nineteen-forties were marked — not least because of the experience of the war itself but also because of the widespread favourable (even uncritical) international publicity that had attended the fledgling Soviet Union's attempts in this field in the twenties and thirties — by an increasing international appreciation of the value of planning and by the development and increasing sophistication of employment and social policies, foreshadowed by the work of Beveridge and Keynes. Keynes died in 1946, but by then his ideas had been generally accepted by a wide range of contemporary political leaders, including such an unlikely convert as Averell Harriman[52] and the entire post-war French political elite. In a sense it is not remarkable that Lemass was part of this international growth of consciousness; what was to cause him difficulty was that his colleagues, by and large, were so wary of it. Beveridge's *Full Employment in a Free Society* (1944) remained in Lemass's library until his death, even after several weedings occasioned by moving house from Palmerston Road to Rathfarnham. The remaining books contain plenty of evidence of his preoccupations during this period: well-thumbed volumes include Barbara Wotton's *Freedom under Planning* (1945) and F. E. Lawley's *The Growth of Collective Economy* (1938).

Under the influence of these books, among others, and also impressed by — and possibly envious of — the observable effects of the degree to which Britain became a command economy during the war, Lemass pressed ahead. The period between 1942 and 1945 in particular established a high-water mark for his own interventionist ideas that was never to be surpassed and that witnessed the launch of a national debate on economic planning.

In one sense the war and the inevitable constraints that accompanied it prevented any organic development of the economic policies that Lemass had hitherto followed. In another sense it seemed, if anything, to intensify his frustration at the slowness with which industry had responded to the stimulus of protection, the incoherence of labour policy, and the inflexibility of the agricultural sector. If protection hadn't worked, what would? Could the unions be enlisted as partners in a new national sense of enterprise? Could the dead hand of aged and unproductive farmers be lifted from the land?

In February 1942 Lemass invoked the concept of a national plan as something that would banish 'the five Beveridge giants: Want, Disease, Ignorance, Squalor and Idleness.'[53] Throughout this period Beveridge loomed large in his thoughts. Some writers have suggested that Keynes's lecture in Dublin in 1933, with its implications for deficit budgeting, would have come as a welcome support to the new Fianna Fáil Government and to Lemass in particular. However, it not only ran counter to the received economic wisdom of the capital and its intelligentsia at the time but was sharply qualified by Keynes's bluntly expressed belief that Ireland was not large enough for more than 'a very modest measure of self-sufficiency'[54] and that pushing it to extremes would involve a 'disastrous reduction' in living standards.[55] Not surprisingly, Keynesian doctrine was virtually buried for another quarter of a century.

Four months after his pro-Beveridge speech Lemass sent de Valera a lengthy memorandum on labour policy.[56] It was a decade since his first passionate attempt to take control of economic policy; but although this attempt was less prescriptive it was not attended by much more success. It addressed the problem of formulating a labour policy both for the war years and the post-war period and charged that the Government had not yet taken sufficient powers to deal with the situation. Suggesting the creation of a new Department of Labour, the memorandum called for close management of the agricultural labour force, the creation of a pool system of labour for urban industrial employment, and a ban on emigration for all pool workers.

> A general scheme of control of labour, introduced to cope with the circumstances of the Emergency, should be retained after the Emergency has passed and become a permanent feature of the State's labour organisation. The idea of amalgamating the social services in one Ministry might be implemented after the Emergency through the Ministry of Labour.

Like many of the suggestions Lemass bombarded the Government with during the war years, his proposal for a Department of Labour was not taken up. He followed it therefore with a suggestion to de Valera in September 1942 that an economic planning committee be established, staffed by the secretaries of the departments most closely involved.[57] This indicates at the very least a belief that many of his colleagues did not share his ideas and that he expected to find greater support among the upper echelons of the civil service. De Valera countered by establishing instead a Government committee, set up on 24 November 1942, whose membership comprised himself, Seán T. O'Kelly (who was both Tánaiste and Minister for Finance), and Lemass. The committee held forty-nine meetings between December 1942 and April 1945, when it was enlarged, and held a further nine meetings up to July 1945.[58] In the proceedings of the committee, however, de Valera's agenda seemed to be at least as prominent as Lemass's. Although it agreed to give further study to a proposal from Lemass for 'setting up a small aircraft factory' (7 January 1943), an inordinate amount of time seems to have been spent discussing minor or peripheral issues, such as the development of Westport harbour (21 February 1944), the production of educational films (25 October 1943), the Dún Laoghaire dump (3 March 1943), and even athletics (21 February 1944).

In a sense, the subtext of much of the argument during 1943 and 1944 was the concept, the practicality and the extent of planning. Not all Lemass's colleagues were enamoured of the concept. De Valera, although he supported it at meetings of the Government, tended to allow it to get bogged down in minutiae, believing that planning was 'a very interesting but very seductive occupation,' and warned against the dangers of 'daydreaming and building castles in the air.'[59] MacEntee, less inhibitedly, attacked the planned economy vigorously, both in private and in public.[60] During the 1944 election campaign he invoked the spectre of Trotsky in the aphorism 'He who does not obey, neither shall he eat.'[61] He could have defended his views by arguing that he was attacking the Labour Party and assorted 'fellow-travellers'; but some of his targets may well have been closer to home.

In the absence of any dramatic successes on the economic planning front, Lemass turned to elements of industrial and economic policy, in which he had a greater say. He was already at this stage, rather earlier than has generally been supposed, moving away from uncritical support for both the Control of Manufactures Acts and the tariff and quota system. In the circumstances of the war, however, his tentative suggestions in these areas fell on stony ground, and they were not revived in any formal way until the nineteen-fifties.

His doubts about the Control of Manufactures Acts were embodied in a lengthy memorandum prepared by R. C. Ferguson in Industry and Commerce in December 1942, which Ferguson recorded as being specifically in line with a directive from Lemass. De Valera had written to Lemass to raise a number of points about post-war development, and Ferguson replied on Lemass's behalf:

> So far as the participation of foreign firms in industrial production in this country is concerned, the Control of Manufactures Acts represent Government policy hitherto. While it is not possible to anticipate changes in the post war period to the extent of being able to forecast what changes, either in the direction of tightening up or loosening the terms of these Acts in respect of foreign participation in industry, [might be made,] it is very necessary to reconsider, as a matter of general policy, the principles contained in these Acts.[62]

The context in which this initiative was taken bears some consideration. The Federation of Irish Manufacturers was continually making representations to Industry and Commerce — and continued to do so right up to 1959 — about the unfair advantages they believe accrued to foreign firms under Government policy and may well have been concerned, even at this stage, about rumours that foreign investment would be more encouraged in the future. Ferguson's reference to 'principles', on the other hand, certainly implies a loosening of the Acts, as it would have made little sense to tighten them further.

Lemass's impatience was bubbling to the surface. In his speech to the Federation of Irish Manufacturers in 1944, for instance, he advocated the introduction of a credit-based export system along Swiss lines for firms interested in developing exports. More significantly, he coupled his traditional statements on the need for protection with a warning. In theory the Government could withdraw protection, but in practice it was not always easy. This meant, logically, that 'we must have ways of eliminating inefficient units and the intention to apply them ruthlessly when the need arises if the whole programme of industrial development is to be carried through.' It also meant that 'many industries can only be established as single units,' without any effective competition in the market — which led to the need for new statutory powers to protect the public.[63] The paradox was that while Lemass was implying that efficiency was the price industry had to pay for protection, there was increasing evidence that inefficiency and protection went hand in hand.

His doubts about the wisdom of the decentralisation policy, which had been for some two decades a keystone of Fianna Fáil thinking, were to persist.

> The establishment of industries in smaller towns has had an unsettling effect on agricultural labour and on local general labourer wage rates, which is not conducive to the increased efficiency of the agricultural industry. It is for consideration whether, in future, new industries should not be directed to urban centres (excluding Dublin, if desired) such as Cork, Limerick and Waterford, except where the exploitation of a local mineral deposit, or the processing of agricultural products is involved.[64]

The logic of establishing important new industries as single-unit monopolies, had it ever been followed through, would have had significant implications both for industrial development generally and for the traditional Fianna Fáil policy based on the concept of a multiplicity of highly decentralised small or medium-sized production units.

When the British government published its White Paper on full employment in 1944, Lemass went back on the offensive. He generated a 45-page memorandum in the form of a commentary on the British White Paper, which was sent to the secretary of the Government, Maurice Moynihan, on 21 November 1944, submitted to the Government's economic policy committee on 17 January 1945, and in effect drove the subsequent discussion.[65]

His most controversial proposals were aimed at agriculture. Quoting both Beveridge and Keynes to support his case, Lemass argued vigorously for the compulsory consolidation of smallholdings where the output of the smaller units fell below desirable levels.

> By one method or another, it is necessary to ensure that the Nation's resources of agricultural land are fully utilised. The rights of owners should not include the right to allow land to go derelict or to be utilised below its reasonable productive capacity. Only a limited number of families can be settled on the land, on economic holdings, and policy must be directed to ensuring that ownership will be confined to persons willing and capable of working them adequately.[66]

Just in case his audience had missed the point, Lemass went on to describe his objective as 'the elimination of incompetent or lazy farmers'[67] and to argue for a high degree of state centralisation in the marketing and price support systems, because 'a community of small farmers cannot organise themselves for these purposes and only the State has the power and the resources to do the job thoroughly.'[68]

This proposal attracted partial support from one unexpected quarter: the Department of Finance. Finance did not go as far in urging compulsory consolidation of holdings but, in a recommendation that went directly counter to de Valera's established policy, suggested that at least 'the question should be examined whether the continuance of the policy of land division is compatible with the effort to secure higher efficiency in production and increased employment on the land.'

This muted support, as might have been expected, was not enough to salvage any element of Lemass's extremely radical proposal, and the *coup de grâce* was provided by the Minister for Agriculture, Jim Ryan. While acknowledging that there might be certain circumstances in which 'there would be a good case for the State taking over and making arrangements to have the lands put to proper use through new ownership,' he enunciated the party's gospel in terms that embodied a not so subliminal warning about the possible electoral effects of what he clearly saw as a disastrous policy proposal.

> There are a number of holdings in every parish falling below a reasonable productive capacity due to some failing on the part of the present owner but who probably has a young family growing up, one member of which would in time pull the place together and become in due course a first class farmer. In the meantime the family somehow or other are reared and set out in life as useful citizens. Indeed the lessons which the poverty of the home teach them very often make them good workers wherever they go. It would be unthinkable to disturb

the family in such cases no matter how much below the desired standard the farm might presently be. If displacement were done on a small scale only it would have little or no effect on output and if it were done to such an extent as to have a substantial effect on output there would be danger of serious agitation and public disturbance.

Ryan's fatalism is, in retrospect, deeply disturbing. His praise of the virtues of poverty and his apparent disregard for, or assumptions about, the future welfare of the family members other than the one who 'would in time pull the place together' amount to cold comfort. But they reflected Fianna Fáil and bureaucratic orthodoxy, and this was more than enough to scuttle Lemass's attempt to improve productivity in agriculture.

Two years after his Government defeat on this issue Lemass rounded brusquely on those who were keening for a vanishing way of life that he plainly saw had little real value or prospect for the future.

> There is no such thing as a flight from the land. It is a normal and healthy feature of a national economy based on Agriculture that there is a steady flow of manpower from rural areas to employment in non-agricultural pursuits. The term 'flight from the land' must mean the land being left derelict for want of people to work it. The very opposite tendency is in evidence here, where the demand for land is very strong. In fact, our problem is very largely one of attracting from the land and providing with alternative means of livelihood a substantial number of those now under-employed on it ... The abolition of unemployment, poverty and squalor cannot be accomplished by Government decree, or by wishful thinking, but only by increasing the national production of wealth through hard, competent work, in which every individual must pull his full weight.[69]

It was to be the last substantial effort the Minister for Industry and Commerce would make in this contentious area. Thereafter his references to agriculture were increasingly perfunctory and — with the exception of a number of speeches praising the co-operative ideal in 1964 — lacking depth.

In relation to industrial development generally, Lemass to some extent took both sides of the road. Although he argued that 'conditions in other industries [i.e. other than agriculture] do not require State regulation in similar degree,'[70] he also sketched out what was, at least in potential, a major programme of expansion for state industry, while at the same time qualifying his proposals with the observation that in certain circumstances they might not need to be implemented fully, or at all.

> It may, however, be necessary for the State to take the initiative in the establishment of many large-scale industrial enterprises which are

required to enable full use to be made of natural resources, or which because of their nature can only be established on a monopoly basis.[71]

Foreseeing the effect that his plans might have on the unions, Lemass advocated a reorganisation and rationalisation of the trade union movement generally as a preliminary to acknowledging a new role for them in industrial management. At the same time,

> the conclusion is inescapable that a full employment policy is incompatible with the old practice of settling wage rates by direct negotiations between employers and Trade Unions, or by strikes and lock-outs, and that in return for the removal of the fear of unemployment, the workers must be willing to accept the supervision of wage rates by a public authority charged with the responsibility of protecting the real value of wages.[72]

The idea that trade unionists would accept the supervision of wage rates by statute in the post-war period, conditioned though it may have been by the success of wages policy during the war years, was plainly consigned to that special limbo reserved for most of Lemass's more impatient or (as his colleagues would have seen it) impracticable proposals.

The memorandum contained further evidence that Lemass was rethinking the two pillars of Fianna Fáil economic policy, protective tariffs and the Control of Manufactures Acts. Hindsight suggests that the twin policies were pulling in opposite directions when it came to creating jobs and that saturation of the home market had been achieved as early as 1936 or 1937 by companies that were not even remotely interested in developing an export trade.[73] He now placed another question mark against the Control of Manufactures Acts, at least in relation to industries that might be established specifically for export. Equally significantly, he stressed the need for a new system of budgeting. Quoting Beveridge (again) and Nicholas Kaldor, Lemass argued that the state

> should accept the responsibility of ensuring that total outlay is always sufficient to result in the full employment of output capacity, by whatever methods may be considered most suitable in the circumstances prevailing at any time, but in the last resort by increasing its own expenditure and financing this increased expenditure by borrowing.[74]

Government debate on the more practical of Lemass's suggestions was possibly clouded by the reaction to some of his more *outré* proposals. In the event, almost nothing was salvaged from the wreckage, with the exception of the proposal to establish an industrial credit organisation.

Lemass had not, however, finished with the matter, especially where private industry was concerned. If the carrot of tariffs and quotas had not

1. Lemass's parents

2. Noel (left) *and Seán as toddlers*

3. Seán (left) *with his mother, Alice, and Noel*

4. The junior and middle grade exhibitioners at O'Connell Schools, 1915. Lemass is in the third row, extreme left.

THE RIVALS

A Comedy in Five Acts, by Richard Brinsley Sheridan

Presented by

THE KILRONAN PLAYERS'

Dramatis Personæ :

THOMAS (a Coachmen)	Harry O'Driscoll
FAG	Arthur Kearns
LYDIA LANGUISH	Eileen Browne
LUCY (a Maid)	Gertrude Hughes
JULIA MELVILLE	Kathleen Walshe
MRS. MALAPROP	Rhona Fanning
SIR ANTHONY ABSOLUTE	Tom J. Powell
CAPTAIN ABSOLUTE	Laurence O'Dea
FAULKLAND	Francis Purcell
BOB ACRES	James A. O'Dea
SIR LUCIUS O'TRIGGER	Sean F. Lemass
DAVID (Acre's servant)	Tom Meldon

A Maid, Boy, Servants, etc.

5. *A playbill from a 1920s amateur production of Sheridan's* The Rivals *in which Lemass played Sir Lucius O'Trigger to Jimmy O'Dea's Bob Acres*

6. *Prisoners in Ballykinlar Camp, 1921. Lemass is in the third row, third from the right.*

7. *Lemass outside the Dáil in 1927 following his refusal to take the oath*

8. *Addressing a meeting at Charles Kickham's monument in Main Street, Tipperary, in the 1920s*

9. *Lemass being shouldered by his supporters following his victory in the 1924 election*

10. Lemass and James Ryan, shortly after their appointments to the 1932 government

Mr. Lemass opens a New Factory for making keys for opening New Factories.

11. *This* Dublin Opinion *cartoon wittily captures the public image of Lemass in his early years as Minister for Industry and Commerce.*

12. *Relaxing with friends at Kelly's Hotel in Rosslare, 1935.* Left to right: *unknown; Seamus Moore (Old IRA friend); Dr Paddy Fanning, Department of Health; Lemass; Joe Griffin, Secretary of the Sugar Company; Fintan Carroll, an old friend of Lemass and brother-in-law of Paddy Fanning.*

13. *Lemass at Baldonnell Aerodrome in the 1930s. He said many years later that Aer Lingus was his proudest achievement.*

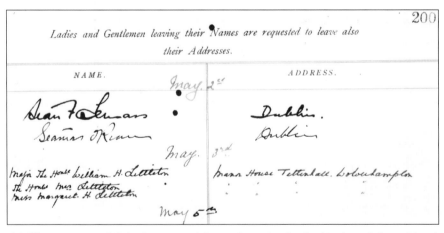

14. *The signature of Seán Lemass and James Ryan in the Buckingham Palace visitors' book, at the time of their London visit in 1940 to negotiate a supplies system with the British*

15. *Lemass, James Ryan and Seán T. O'Kelly in France as part of an Irish government delegation in the 1930s*

16. *A party of TDs on a trip to Shannon Airport in 1947. The distinctive figure of Éamon de Valera stands near the centre of the photograph. To his left is William Norton, leader of the Labour Party, who is flanked on the other side by Lemass. The young J.F. Dempsey, already a senior figure in the airline, stands on the extreme right. The future Taoiseach Liam Cosgrave is seventh from the right.*

17. *Lemass on a ministerial visit to Shannon Airport in 1947*

succeeded, perhaps the stick of compulsion would be more effective. He prepared the ground with a ringing declaration that 'the commercial organisation of this State is based firmly on the principle of private competitive enterprise' and registered the Government's 'conviction that better conditions would return all the quicker once private enterprise were allowed free play again.'[75] He then went on, within five months, to make it abundantly clear that the 'free play' he envisaged giving to private enterprise would be within a framework of rules established by himself. In a speech to the Cork Chamber of Commerce laced with references to Beveridge, he declared that although 'education, and discussion leading to agreement' were his preferred instruments for securing public acceptance of his policies, they would be replaced by tougher measures if they failed. In the post-war situation the Government would seek powers to supervise efficiency and regulate prices; it would introduce sanctions, possibly even including a restriction of dividends; there would be a state organisation to build up exports and another to control agricultural exports. If the banks did not voluntarily co-operate with Government policy, stock and share transactions would be controlled. And a new kind of budgetary policy would have to be followed, relying on budgets 'made with reference to available manpower, not to money.'[76]

The stage was being set for Lemass's controversial industrial efficiency and prices legislation, signalled by him in June 1945 in his introductory speech on the estimates for his department, when he confidently expressed the hope that it would be before the Dáil 'in the course of the next few months.'[77] It did not finally appear until 1947, and died with the Fianna Fáil Government the following year; the delay in formulating it and getting Government approval speaks for itself.

In the meantime, however, times were still hard, and rationing for some commodities was to remain in force for another three years. Lemass's weekly briefings with the political correspondents continued, and what was most remarkable about these sessions, according to T. P. Kilfeather, who attended them on behalf of the *Irish Independent,* was Lemass's delight in the informality of the exchanges and in the

> uninhibited comments he got on the post-war scene from our rather cynical group. The boyish flashes may have been a reaction to the removal of wartime tension and anxiety. It was a side of his character he was never to reveal to newspapermen again, for after his briefing sessions were discontinued he returned to a brusque and aloof manner.[78]

The enthusiasm he displayed in his meetings with journalists in the years immediately after the war was plainly born of his determination, fostered by the enforced hiatus caused by the hostilities, to hit the ground running. Already in 1944 he had been talking frankly about the failure of more than a decade of Fianna Fáil government to abolish social evils, of the extent to which the standard of living depended on international trade, and on the danger of relying on exports to one market of a limited range of perishable products.[79] The immediate post-war period provided further evidence of his full agenda.

His path, however, was littered with a fair number of obstacles. One of them was the continuing opposition, by an effective majority of his Government colleagues, to the more interventionist elements of his strategy. Although his tillage programme had been supported by his ministerial colleagues, his proposals about the need to tackle the problem of agricultural productivity generally by taking less efficient farmers off the land were not. In 1941 his ideas about an interventionist and managerialist Central Bank were, after a long struggle, neutered by MacEntee and his dedicated officials in the Department of Finance.[80] His passionate belief in planning inevitably involved him in actual or potential turf wars with other ministers — wars that de Valera defused, characteristically, by letting the protagonists talk themselves into a state of exhaustion.

He also had a problem with the vexed question of tariffs. At first there was no problem: the operation of the tariff system had been suspended during the war, and its reintroduction was being delayed by the anomalous situation in which it was easier to import manufactured products than the raw material required to manufacture them.[81] Lemass was not only having second thoughts about the effectiveness of tariffs, and the Control of Manufactures Acts, but was coming under pressure from the Department of Finance, which was looking for a comprehensive review of all existing controls. His decision not to mount a blanket defence of the status quo spoke for itself, but he was plainly looking for more sophisticated and subtle instruments that might achieve the desired objectives more efficiently.

Even before the war, as has been seen, he had been urging manufacturers to increase their general levels of efficiency and productivity. By October 1945 he had begun to take the anti-tariff argument more explicitly into account.

> In the early years of the industrial programme a policy of protection was necessary in order to enable new industries to establish themselves on a secure basis. While it will be the government's aim to maintain *adequate* protection for *new* industries against *unfair* competition, it is no part of its policy to continue protection where it is clear that a particular industry is not striving and progressive towards maximum efficiency ... The industrial structure of this country has been erected on a basis of private enterprise and, subject to any control and regulation which the public interest may from time to time dictate, the Government feels that in general the continued expansion and development of industry may be safely entrusted to private individuals

and groups operating under the democratic constitution which this State provides. [Emphasis added.][82]

He warned in the same document that private industry had 'special responsibilities to the public' and that if it failed to discharge them it would have to answer to 'the people, who are the final arbiters of public policy.' Given that the people had no mechanism for calling industrialists to account, this was, in the circumstances, no more than a lightly coded threat, backed by an assertion of democratic legitimacy for whatever action he proposed to take.

He could not have failed to notice the inefficiency and profiteering that the tariffs policy had encouraged in some quarters. James Dillon attacked this with brio in his response to Lemass's 1945 estimates speech, pointing out that Guinness and Jacob's had flourished in an era when free trade was a byword. Now, he thundered, warming to his theme:

> This is the first generation in over a century when tariff racketeers have been able to impose themselves on our people as the only method of industrial expansion in Ireland ... You remember, Sir, the day when the doctrine of Fianna Fáil was economic self-sufficiency, but hardened old politicians like yourself and myself have watched them beat a strategic retreat from that fraud. The *Irish Press* has been working overtime to cover it with a smoke screen and to explain that the proud galleon of self-sufficiency that went into the smoke-screen is the same as the rowing boat that has come out again.[83]

Lemass's main problem was that removing the tariffs without substituting other policies would, by exposing all manufacturers to the harsh blast of foreign competition, impinge on employment and also on those industrialists — many of whom had become personal friends — who had taken him at his word and had done their best to build up a genuine industrial base behind the protective tariff wall. Despite his quite exceptional measures to encourage industrial growth, nascent Irish industry was precisely that: overwhelmingly small in scale and correspondingly vulnerable. Three-quarters of the firms listed by his department in 1948 had fewer than twenty employees, and among the remaining 25 per cent the average number of employees was only eighty-two.[84] If dismantling the tariff regime threatened to seriously erode these companies' share of the domestic market, this could be portrayed as a failure of nerve on his part, or even a breach of faith.

There was another problem too. Three years earlier, Ferguson's memorandum to de Valera, written at Lemass's direction, had attacked the 'commissions and profits of middlemen', particularly those involved in distributing products in which one firm had a virtual monopoly. Given what he had been saying in private, Lemass must have bitten his tongue at Dillon's charges, which contained a sufficiently large grain of truth to be unpalatable. Unusually, he made no reference to them in his reply to the debate.

In all the circumstances, he behaved in a most un-Lemassian way: talking frequently about the need to expose industry to effective competition but never doing anything to bring it about, and indeed on occasion defending the policy against the attacks from the Department of Finance and other quarters. It is difficult to avoid the conclusion that his uncharacteristic indecisiveness stemmed from two factors. One was the difficulty in getting political agreement for the policies he felt should replace protection; the other was a genuine inability to reconcile his personal sense of loyalty to those businessmen and industrialists who had taken him at his word, with his increasingly urgent recognition that the cocoon he had created had to be ruptured before any major industrial development could take place. Indeed any assessment of Lemass's character and motivation, on this or on other issues, has to recognise that loyalty was for him a core value and one that could override even economic imperatives that were becoming increasingly obvious.

His increasing preoccupation with private enterprise reached the antennae of one of his former admirers — if that is not too strong a word for Jim Larkin junior, who at one stage was a fellow-TD in the South Dublin constituency. Larkin suggested that 'for a long period Deputy Lemass had a rather socialistic outlook but at a certain point about 1945 he began to deviate to some extent from that and he seemed to pay more regard to the interests of private ownership and private control.'[85] Larkin's pessimism was to some degree misplaced. As late as 1947 Lemass was proposing, in the teeth of vigorous opposition from the Department of Finance, the establishment of a permanent company, financed out of public funds, to buy Irish Steel.[86] In itself this proposal was less an expression of undue statism on Lemass's part than of a concern — born of wartime conditions that prompted a number of similar decisions, not least on fertiliser — to prevent the country ever again becoming dependent on external suppliers for strategic commodities as far as this was possible.

THE TRADE UNIONS

If Lemass and Jim Larkin had a certain mutual regard, Lemass's relationship with the trade union movement as a whole inevitably suffered during the war. The social legislation of the nineteen-thirties was forgotten fairly rapidly in an atmosphere of privation, shortages and wage controls that had even the most loyal Fianna Fáil trade unionists chafing at the bit.

Lemass's attitude to the unions was conditioned by a number of factors. In the first place, he believed that the multiplicity of unions, and inter-union rivalries, militated directly against proper industrial organisation, not least because it meant that he, as Minister for Industry and Commerce, was dealing with a hydra rather than with a single, coherent organisation, as was rapidly coming into existence on the employers' side of industry. He was also — if intermittently — opposed to restrictive practices that undercut efficiency and competitiveness. And his opposition to British unions, which organised a significant number of Irish workers, sprang from political as well as industrial motives.

A special conference of the Irish Trades Union Congress in 1936 had created a commission to explore the general situation of trade unions. William O'Brien, general secretary of the ITGWU, whose thinking dominated the work of the commission, was a strong proponent of the idea that all union members should be grouped in ten or so industrial unions. O'Brien's arguments carried the commission but were defeated at a special conference in 1939. The Government moved in swiftly. Seán MacEntee, who had replaced Lemass as Minister for Industry and Commerce, claimed not only that the Government had instigated the 1936 commission but that the proposals in the 1941 Bill (modelled largely on the commission's defeated proposals) were necessary to cure 'the evils which ... curse and plague Irish industry.'[87]

In popular perception, and to a large degree also in reality, these proposals substantially supported the views of the main Irish unions and therefore would hardly have evoked disagreement from Lemass. Indeed, even before he passed this particular chalice on to MacEntee, Lemass had gone on record with his view that the trade union movement as a whole had been 'indifferent to the problem of unemployment.'[88] In effect, just as the employers had failed to respond as he had hoped to the cocoon of protection, so also the unions were turning to bite the hand that had fed them with the Conditions of Employment Act, paid holidays, and a basketful of other social legislation. Ingratitude, on all industrial fronts, was prompting the replacement of the carrot with the stick.

The passage of the Bill, however, and not merely because of MacEntee's notoriously pugnacious manner, actively contributed to something that made a bad situation worse: the organisational split in the trade union movement, which had been festering since 1939 and was to flower in its full malignancy some six years later.

Popular opinion during this period, especially on the left, credited Fianna Fáil in general and Lemass in particular with the desire to split, and therefore politically neutralise, the trade union movement. A more considered analysis suggests that Lemass had a number of different objectives, which were occasionally in conflict. He was concerned to maximise union support for Fianna Fáil; and he was temperamentally and politically opposed to the fact that so many Irish workers were organised in British unions. These two objectives inevitably encouraged fissiparous tendencies among trade unionists. On the other hand, his desire to incorporate the trade union movement as a whole into the business of national planning and wages policy-making demanded, of its essence, a united trade union movement that could deliver its members in support of negotiated and agreed national policies; this pulled in the opposite direction.

The unions were, as it happened, already suspicious of the Government's intentions. The announcement of a wages standstill in 1941,[89] in the wake of MacEntee's controversial trade union legislation, added fuel to the flames. When Lemass resumed control at Industry and Commerce in August 1941 he took stock of the situation, which at that time involved a widespread but poorly organised national campaign of resistance, and set about organising a type of pincer movement that would, he hoped, defuse opposition to those elements of the Act he considered central, while making such accommodations as were politic in the circumstances. He set 1 May 1942, 'with a somewhat exquisite — if unconscious — irony,'[90] as the date for the coming into force of the section of the Act that required unions to take out negotiating licences from the state. Shortly afterwards he announced that he would be prepared to consider changes in the wages standstill order, but only for unions that had taken out negotiating licences under the Act.

Simultaneously, having sucked the leadership of the trade union movement into semi-formal negotiations about their objections to the Act, he rapidly ensured the passing of the amending Trade Union Act, 1942, which met many union objectives without modifying the central thrust of the original legislation. Subsequent amending orders issued by Lemass under the legislation had the effect of cooling the temperature considerably; but whereas his own standing with the movement and with workers generally had improved to some extent, it was not enough to prevent the slide into disunity. A controversial invitation to a trade union congress in wartime Britain provided the excuse, but the die had already been cast, and the movement as a whole split in April 1945 into two mutually suspicious parts: the Congress of Irish Unions, opposed to foreign control, and the Irish Trades Union Congress, which proclaimed the need for trade union unity, not least between North and South.

Lemass's views about the value of sectorally based unions received a setback at this time with the decision of the Supreme Court in the National Union of Railwaymen case. This case, brought by the NUR against the constitutionality of the 1941 Act, had in fact opened in July 1945. When part III of the Act, which created a tribunal to determine the right of unions to be given the sole power of organising workers of a particular class, was struck down by the court as being in conflict with article 40.6.1 of the Constitution, Lemass felt a keen sense of disappointment, to which he was to return in later years. It also added to his distrust of lawyers. The reorganisation of the trade union movement was an object he never lost sight of; he was to return to it as Taoiseach, although with no conspicuous success.

One of his major initiatives, the Labour Court, was in effect his fourth bite at the cherry of structural reform in the area of labour relations after the contentious Trade Union Act of 1941. The first was his amending legislation that softened the impact of the MacEntee Act. In 1942, as has been noted, he was unsuccessful with his proposal for the establishment of a Department of Labour. In 1944 he failed to get Government support for a wide-ranging commission of inquiry on a wages policy for economic development in the post-war era.

The Labour Court was more successful. It was devised to create a statutory framework for the wage negotiations that would follow the ending of wage control in September 1946. It was certainly necessary: because of isolation and the six years of statutory control, unions did not know where to pitch their wage claims, and some general unions were pressing for increases of more than 70 per cent.[91] Lemass drafted the preliminary memorandum for the legislation to establish the Labour Court at home in a child's exercise-book in December 1946. When he brought it into the office it was typed at top speed and sent out to the employers and trade union organisations, with a request for their immediate comments. After Christmas, the drafting of a Bill went ahead, despite the fact that the employers had not submitted their comments. When Lemass enquired about the reason for the delay he discovered that the memorandum had been kept in a safe in the employers' office over Christmas, and had then been forgotten!

The Act, and the structure it created, went a certain distance towards creating a positive atmosphere for industrial negotiations, not least because recourse to the Labour Court was limited to licensed unions, and at first to the private sector. This of itself contributed substantially to the unions' sense of organisation and purpose in the post-war period and gave rise to the system of national pay bargaining to which the public service unions were to contribute, with marked effect, during Lemass's tenure as Taoiseach. The effectiveness of the Labour Court, on the other hand, was always in danger of being undermined by the inevitable tendency to have recourse to ministerial intervention, especially where strategic industries, such as the ESB, were concerned.

Lemass's equally strong views about the value of Irish rather than British unions were only barely concealed, and within the Labour Party and the trade union movement itself storm cones were being hoisted. T. J. Murphy TD, a member of the ITGWU, gave vent to a barbed comment in private that made the most serious allegations about William O'Brien, general secretary of the ITGWU, in the wake of his appointment as a director of the Central Bank on its establishment in 1942.

> O'Brien has moved very near the FF Govt. £50,000 of Union funds were given [to] the Govt. free of Interest. Shortly after O'B became a

bank director £500 p.a. ... There are other signs that he would like to help a minority Govt ... He controls nearly ¼ million of money. He is now as always a menace to the growth of a Labour Party as Larkin also is ... I do earnestly [?] hope there may yet be in Ireland a Labour Party freed from all the Old Men of the Sea who have ... prevented it from developing as it should.[92]

Lemass's attitude was evident in a number of important decisions in 1945–46, notably his appointment of CIU nominees to the board of the Road Transport Authority in August 1945, excluding the possibility of ITUC representation, and his decision to allocate both trade union seats at the ILO conference in Paris in October 1945 to the CIU.[93] In all of this Lemass, as McCarthy observes, 'managed to combine a warm, co-operative approach to the trade union movement with a steely approach to the Labour Party on the general grounds that his party, Fianna Fáil, was more representative politically of the bulk of trade union members than was the Labour Party, which on a head count was manifestly true.'[94]

While this observation accurately describes Lemass's tactics, it falls somewhat short of a full assessment. The growth of electoral support for the Labour Party during the war years was in fact quite striking: its share nationally rose from 10 per cent in 1938 to 15 per cent in 1943, and its 1943 total of seventeen Dáil seats was not to be exceeded until 1954. Its sharp slump between the elections of 1943 and 1944 was due not only to its inherent divisions and the consequent creation of the National Labour Party but to the fact that some of these divisions — notably those fomented by conservative trade unions concerned about largely imaginary dangers of communist infiltration — were actively encouraged by some sections within Fianna Fáil.

In this process Seán MacEntee was as important a factor as Lemass. The two ministers interacted successfully, although not necessarily in a co-ordinated way. Lemass habitually claimed Fianna Fáil's moral legitimacy as the most politically effective arm of labour, while MacEntee stoked the fears about alien influences. In the 1943 election Lemass proclaimed that 'the era of Fianna Fáil government was the era of trade union progress,'[95] while the following day his Government colleague warned, typically, that the Labour Party was 'honeycombed with agents of the Comintern.'[96]

Not all Lemass's colleagues were enamoured of the way in which he courted the trade union movement. As one of them put it many years later, 'in his dealings with the unions, there seemed to be a lacuna in his mind; he displays a sentimentality and naïveté that seemed to deny reason and ignore the public good. This was surprising because he never appeared either sentimental or naïve.'[97]

There was, however, nothing sentimental or naïve about Lemass's appeal to his own electorate. In the 1943 and 1944 elections he received 2.47 and

2.5 quotas, respectively. He was never to exceed the latter figure, which may be partly explained by the fact that it was a lack-lustre election with a particularly low turn-out (the quota was almost five hundred votes, or 8 per cent, lower than in the previous election). Even though in the 1947 election the Labour Party — in the form of Jim Larkin junior — won a seat from an independent in the South Dublin constituency, it was plain that even at a time of increased Labour support, Lemass was more than holding his own.

South Dublin, as it happened, was home to one of the few concentrations of Jewish working-class and lower middle-class voters in the country, but a sense of realism about the employment situation persuaded Lemass against one policy initiative that would have won him favour in this quarter (though it might also have disadvantaged him in others). He objected to an extremely modest proposal from the Department of External Affairs that Ireland should take about 250 Jewish refugees from the Continent, giving high unemployment as his reason.[98] De Valera, on this issue, was considerably more forceful, urging that Ireland might eventually find homes for up to ten thousand, although in the event no more than 925 were admitted in the five years to 1950, half of these already having connections of some sort with Ireland. It is difficult, however, to infer hard-heartedness on Lemass's part, as he evidently thought that the more practical approach was to tackle the problem of food supplies to Europe's starving refugees, a problem that he approached with his customary vigour after the war ended and at a time when shortages were still common in Ireland. He was to receive a papal decoration for this work, the Cross of St Gregory the Great, in 1950, after going into opposition. Ironically in view of all this, some at least of his critics were not convinced that he had done the right thing. 'You let the Jews in,' one political opponent charged in 1950 in the course of a bitter Dáil exchange.[99] And many years later an anonymous British Foreign Office official, drawing up a profile of Lemass in advance of trade negotiations, remarked that he was rumoured to be of Jewish origin and that 'his appearance does not belie this fact.'[100]

TÁNAISTE

By now, of course, Lemass had already moved up a significant notch within the party. The election of Seán T. O'Kelly as President in June 1945 had left de Valera with an important vacancy to fill, that of Tánaiste. Lemass's wartime reputation was substantial. In the benign words of a contemporary,

> he kept the bit and the sup in our mouths, he kept our fires burning and our lamps lighting, he kept our lorries and buses and cars (some of our cars, anyway) on the road, he kept, almost by a miracle, our trains

running a couple of times a week, he kept up a supply of food and necessaries between town and town and between town and country.'[101]

The *Cork Examiner* thought the race was an open one but that the likely successor to O'Kelly would be MacEntee, while 'the names of Mr. Lemass and Mr. Ryan are also mentioned in this connection.'[102] The *Irish Times,* however, predicted the appointment of Lemass, pointing out that the votes for the two opposition candidates in Dublin had exceeded the Fianna Fáil vote in the capital by twenty thousand.[103] This supposed motivation for de Valera's choice does not really hold water and was probably influenced by the Dublin-centredness of that paper's readership and editorial policies. MacEntee was also, of course, a Dublin TD, although he was not a Dubliner; he was a decade older than Lemass; and his confrontational style had a limited appeal outside his own constituency. In any event de Valera's decision to nominate Lemass was in all probability taken before the election. The same paper incorrectly predicted that MacEntee would be restored to Finance; in the event it was Frank Aiken who claimed, and got, the prize[104] and was to retain it until the 1948 election.

Aiken's interest in the development of natural resources made him a natural ally for Lemass in at least one area. Lemass had long been personally convinced that Ireland had more in the way of natural resources than had been generally supposed — or that, at the very least, we should spend some time and energy looking for them. In his 1933 submission to the Government on the establishment of an industrial research council almost half the voted funds were destined for 'special investigations directed to the development of the State's resources [and to] specialised study of the more intensive use of native materials in the home industries.'[105] In February 1941 this developed into a new proposal for a national institute for industrial research. This was finally created by statute in 1946 as the Institute for Industrial Research and Standards.

If there were divided opinions about mineral development, the situation regarding turf could hardly have been more different. C. S. Andrews, whose name is permanently associated with turf development, is somewhat dismissive of Lemass's involvement in, and commitment to, this industry. 'He asked me to take on the development of the bogs to get Frank Aiken off his back.'[106] In fact there had been a turf development section within the Department of Industry and Commerce since 1936, though Bord na Móna was not set up until 1946. According to Andrews,[107] it is certainly true that Aiken was in effect the progenitor and political patron of turf development right from the start. Lemass, in Andrews's opinion, had no interest in turf as such. He had financed the development of a briquette factory and thought this was a sufficient discharge of election promises. Aiken, however, was pressing for more, and in particular for the development of turf as a source of wax and motor oil. Lemass then asked Andrews to come into Industry and Commerce to oversee the development, and Andrews set out to establish a turf industry on the basis of his experience with the ESB, which he had left in 1932.

A. J. Woods, who was closely involved in the natural resource development during this period as a director of Mianraí Tta and Bord na Móna, noted that

> I never met any of the Cabinet or the Fianna Fáil people who would ever discuss Avoca, whereas they would discuss Bord na Móna, and would be interested in it ... When inspectors came to Mianraí from the department they would come down almost as school inspectors — in a very critical, analytical way. In other places, i.e. Bord na Móna, they would be more interested to know, and they were listening to you and quite expansive. There was quite a restraining thing on Mianraí Teo. ... In Bord na Móna we always had the entrée above the heads of the civil service. In Mianraí we operated always through the civil service.[108]

Bord na Móna itself was different from the boards of many other state companies, in that its members met practically every evening in each other's houses as friends, often with Aiken present. Andrews, for his part, had enough seniority, and technical knowledge, to be able to tell Aiken, as the occasion demanded, to forget his less practical schemes. In this sense, although Bord na Móna came within Lemass's remit and was indeed an area to which he gave strong if intermittent personal attention, it remained essentially an empire within an empire.

Another natural resources area was the development of phosphates for fertiliser. This issue was to rumble on through the years, right up to Lemass's period as Taoiseach. During the war it was virtually impossible to obtain supplies from abroad; local supplies were of poor quality and quantity. This problem had become deeply inscribed on Lemass's consciousness, with the effect that after the war he and a number of civil servants in his department, notably J. B. Hynes, actively pursued the issue of a national phosphates industry, despite the fact that by then phosphates had become, and were to remain, a glut on the world market.

Senior civil servants in Finance, not least Whitaker, remained stoutly opposed to a policy that would, as they saw it, have Ireland voluntarily increase farmers' input costs instead of taking advantage of a dumping policy that would not have displaced or threatened native industrial employment, because there was none.[109] Lemass's general opposition to dumping, however, was by now so ingrained that he supported Hynes's efforts until, many years later, they eventually succeeded.

If turf and phosphate development represented the acceptable face of self-sufficiency, the world outside was not going to stand idly by and allow

Ireland chart its own course to prosperity. This was particularly true of post-war Britain, whose leaders had hungry mouths to feed. This induced a permanent level of concern about, and opposition to, de Valera's economic policy, one official memorandum commenting: 'It is unlikely … that we shall succeed in persuading the Éire Government to abandon entirely her self-sufficiency policy.'[110] The British representative in Ireland, Lord Rugby, in his preparatory reports for the late 1947 round of trade negotiations, expressed surprise at de Valera's unwillingness to see this scenario from the British point of view.

> What I described to him as a heaven-sent market for their agricultural production he regarded as a scheme for putting a chain around their necks. No doubt the self-sufficiency motif will be dutifully played up by the delegation as a whole, but there are hard-headed men in the party and the country who know that Mr. de Valera's Gaelic sanctuary is not viable and who, while rendering lip service to Sinn Féin doctrine, will take a realistic view of the concessions proposed.[111]

There is strong circumstantial evidence that Lemass was one of the 'hard-headed men' Rugby had in mind. The briefing notes for the British delegation to the 1947 talks comment that Lemass (described incorrectly as a former Chief of Staff of the IRA) was 'a lucid speaker and probably the ablest member of the Éire government.' Rugby's own assessment, also included, was that he was 'a man of sound practical sense, not swayed by political emotions [and] on present showing the obvious man to succeed Mr. de Valera as Prime Minister.'

It is difficult to know how much Rugby's views were conditioned by wishful thinking. Other assessments of the post-war Government were more jaundiced: C. S. Andrews suggested in 1983, long after the events concerned, that after the war Lemass was feeling the strain and had lost much of his fire, whereas some members of de Valera's Government were less than energetic and the public was becoming bored with them. As against that, the energy with which Lemass now set out to tackle the problem of industrial inefficiency belies Andrews's later verdict.

The drive for efficiency

Lemass now proposed to visit industry with a regime resembling that which he had unsuccessfully proposed for farmers in 1942. The Industrial Efficiency and Prices Bill, 1947, which had been in gestation since 1945, embodied these and related insights but was never to pass into law, being overtaken by the 1948 election. It was a powerful legislative expression of Lemass's developmental creed at a critical point in Irish polit-ical and economic history; it was also plainly his best guess at reconciling the dilemma hinted at earlier:

how to improve efficiency and productivity as a necessary prelude to re-examining the tariff policy.

One part of the Bill proposed setting up industrial councils to involve workers in the development of various private enterprises. The more contentious sections, however — notably section V — were designed to institute a regime that would have made wartime forms of price control resemble the voice of sweet reasonableness.

Lemass had come to the conclusion that the protected industries — or at least a substantial number of them — had utterly failed to deliver their part of the bargain and were profit-taking rather than developing or providing additional employment. As he put it in his speech on the second reading (which can be read, in another perspective, as a discreet confession of failure), 'in times such as those through which we are now passing, and in regard to goods which are scarce, we have to impose limitations and checks of one kind or another which may even operate to penalise efficiency by giving it no greater financial rewards than incompetence can secure.'[112]

He was precluded from making radical alterations to the tariff structure in the short term by the predictable political consequences of the unemployment that would ensue, a problem he was more prepared to acknowledge in opposition than in government. Equally, he was precluded — by personal conviction, by his cultural context, and by the political hazards involved — from being seen to increase the level of direct governmental intervention in job creation. Private industry still had to do the job, and if the controls he had first introduced in 1932, strengthened in 1937 and reinforced again in 1938 and 1939 were ineffective, then bigger and better controls had to take their place.

> The Government does not believe that the economic development of this country can be advanced by any system of State socialism. We do not want to extend the area of State control of business activity, or to interfere unduly in the operation of private commercial enterprise. We believe that at the present stage of our development private enterprise will give speedier and more satisfactory expansion of our economy than would be possible by any system of State trading or Governmental direction of industry and commerce.[113]

The Bill was to introduce a prices commission, with draconian powers. In Lemass's defence it must be said that these powers were to be exercised only in relation to the protected industries. Indeed he went so far as to indicate that the writing was on the wall and that it was 'at least problematical whether we will ever again require the assistance of tariffs and other import restrictions on the scale in which they were in operation before the war.'[114] Nonetheless the Bill would have allowed the Minister for Industry and Commerce a greater power of personal intervention than any previous legislation, without reference to the commission or any other body and to an extent that raised an important question about his commitment to avoiding interfering 'unduly' with private enterprise.

Lemass's frustration with the existing legislation, and particularly with the role of the District Court, was patent. In one case, he told the Dáil, a man in Kerry built a cinema without a licence, using timber and cement for which he had not got a permit. After being fined £5 in the District Court for these offences he 'decided that this was a reasonable charge [and] built another cinema, again without a licence and again without any permit for cement or for timber ... Again he was fined £5.'[115]

The Bill, which Lemass acknowledged might 'perturb' some deputies, provided instead for a range of penalties up to a maximum of ten years' penal servitude, a fine of £5,000 (£105,000 in 1996 terms), and continuing fines of £50 a day (£1,050 in 1996 terms) on businesses that failed to comply with directions issued by the commission.

James Dillon led the attack on the Bill. He had been involved in the retail trade for a quarter of a century, he told the Dáil, and had made his money out of 'pins and needles, bacon and calico.' The situation the minister was creating, he warned, was one in which 'Harland and Wolff's, if we had the blessings of a united Ireland, would be told how to build transatlantic liners by a cock-sparrow in Merrion Street.'[116]

The grand design, however, was still-born. The growing success of the newly formed Clann na Poblachta in two by-elections, giving rise to a fear that any undue postponement of the election would only make things worse, led to de Valera's decision to call a general election early in 1948. It was one of the longest campaigns ever held. Evidently convinced that a lengthy campaign would be needed to demonstrate the dangers to national stability posed by an alternative Government, and despite the fact that unduly long campaigns had in the past tended to diminish rather than increase the Fianna Fáil vote, the Government announced on 1 January that polling day would be 4 February.

The election of 1948 was one in which electoral weariness and post-war dissatisfactions were significant factors. The years since the war had also seen the number of attacks on Lemass increase. Two of the three tribunals established during the last phase of Fianna Fáil's period of office to deal with allegations of corruption were in areas that were directly or indirectly under Lemass's control. One involved suggestions of the manipulation of railway shares, the other a charge that Lemass had 'improperly authorised dubious foreign financiers to purchase the moribund Locke's distillery.'[117] Lemass was cleared of all charges and insinuations, but in some cases the iron went deep. This was particularly true of the Locke's distillery controversy, where his chief tormentors were Oliver Flanagan and James Dillon. Both paid an unusual price for their persistent (and unfounded) insinuations. It was the normal custom for ministers to sign letters of reply to all representations from TDs, regardless of whether they were members of the Government party or not. In the case of these two Fine Gael deputies Lemass gave explicit instructions to his office that replies to their correspondence were not to be prepared for his signature but should be issued instead only from civil servants.[118]

On occasion Lemass went to some lengths to signal a potential conflict of interest. After his return to office in 1951 he was asked by the captain of Skerries Golf Club to assist the club in seeking a subvention from Bord Fáilte. Lemass gave Flanagan a letter of introduction to T. J. O'Driscoll, the director-general of Bord Fáilte, to which he appended a not-so-cryptic PS: 'My only interest in the matter is that I am president of the Club.' A grant for £11,500 ensued.[119]

The election of 1948 was also a 'red scare' election. The onset of labour problems, caused partly by the trade union split and partly by the fact that the end of the war did not produce a rapid improvement in living standards for people generally, led in turn to a growing political disenchantment with Fianna Fáil, notably among national teachers. It also saw the emergence of Clann na Poblachta as an electoral force that capitalised skilfully on a growing belief among more radical Fianna Fáil voters that, on the North and on economic issues alike, their party had gone soft and flabby. The red scare tactics had been used against Fianna Fáil in 1932 by the Cosgrave government, and Seán MacEntee had warmed up the theme to a limited extent against the Labour Party in the 1943 and 1944 elections. In 1948, however, the gloves came off completely.

The main Fianna Fáil protagonist was again MacEntee, who went closer and closer to the bone as he exercised the scalpel of his tongue on the Labour Party, Clann na Poblachta, Saor Éire, and anyone else within range. Lemass, for all that he was more general in his warnings, was no less forceful. The constant theme, as expressed in a speech at Arklow on 4 January, was that Ireland was 'on the list for attack in the campaign now being waged to destroy Christian democracy in Europe,' that although France or Germany might be first in the firing line the same organisation was at work to 'undermine and overcome every democratic government in western Europe,' and that the organisation of international communism was 'directed by skilled experts who have already on many occasions indicated their hostility to this country.'[120]

The campaign had a number of other unusual features. Notable among them was the fact that Lemass was frequently heckled, which was noted even by the *Irish Press*. In response, Fianna Fáil pulled out all the stops. Lemass was greeted by 'two brigades of torchbearers' for a meeting in Smithfield, Dublin, and in Cork by a hundred torchbearers, three-quarters of whom were UCC students.[121]

His Cork visit was notable for another, less publicised event: his first meeting with Jack Lynch, who was to become his successor. Lynch, a star of the Cork hurling team and a rising young barrister who was making his name in the courts (he had been the first person in Ireland to defend a cattle rustler), had been adopted as a Fianna Fáil candidate for the Cork City constituency. He was invited to meet Lemass on his visit and to sit in on negotiations that Lemass was conducting with the city's butchers about meat prices. Lynch was astonished at Lemass's ability to negotiate across the table without notes or officials and with a photographic recall of the tiniest details of negotiations that had taken place twelve months previously. The nitty-gritty of the discussions, indeed, was so intense that the tyro candidate privately wondered whether, if this was what politics involved, he hadn't made the wrong decision.[122]

De Valera himself plainly regarded Lemass as one of his trump cards — possibly his only one. Workers, he said, could not have 'a greater friend in government than the present Minister for Industry and Commerce. If I were getting off the political stage and leaving a wish behind for our people, I could wish for nothing better than to have such a type of Minister to be always here for our people. Seán Lemass always watched the interests of the weaker sections of the community' and was 'always for the workers.'[123]

Lemass did his best to provide evidence for de Valera's assertion. Whatever happened, he urged, Fianna Fáil was the workers' party, and 'houses for the workers must come first.'[124] More significantly, he averred, no trade union representative had ever had difficulty of access to him or in bringing to him any problems affecting their members; and 'it would be bad for Ireland if it should happen that they should ever have in office a government with which any section of the trade union movement felt they could not discuss their problems. We believe in national government, not class government.'[125]

But although Lemass and de Valera operated in tandem in this crucial appeal to the working-class electorate, there was a dramatic difference in emphasis between them on another important issue, that of partition, which indicates that Lemass's thinking on this issue had been evolving and that the traditional pieties, in his view, needed to be put into a new framework. Speaking at Clones on 28 January, he attacked a speech by William Warnock, the Stormont government minister, that had compared living standards north and south of the border; Lemass argued that 'whatever differences there might now be, the ending of partition would raise both.' Fianna Fáil wanted 'to end Partition by good will, because without a united Ireland, their relations with their nearest neighbour could never be on a purely friendly basis, [and] because reunion would contribute to the wealth and development of the whole island.'[126]

The following day de Valera, from a vantage point even further north and in language that could not have been used unblushingly by a spokesman for unreconstructed republicanism in the late nineteen-nineties, declared in Letterkenny that 'the territory of the O'Donnells is free, and, please God, we will soon stand in the territory of O'Neill, and it will be free.'[127] The contrast with Lemass's more measured and rationally argued irredentism is marked.

De Valera was now sixty-six and suffering increasing problems with his eyesight. Despite his extravagant benediction of Lemass he was to remain centre-stage for more than another decade. Fianna Fáil, indeed, was confidently, but mistakenly, anticipating the assistance of the National Labour Party — formed at least in part because of the successful anti-communist scare-mongering of MacEntee and Lemass — in the formation of the next Government. But Fianna Fáil's departure to the opposition benches in all probability convinced de Valera, if convincing were needed, that his helmsmanship was needed more than ever to restore the party to power.

Lemass's private views on being relegated to the opposition benches have not been recorded. His public farewell to office was an au revoir rather than an adieu: 'We are leaving you this country in good shape. There are problems to be faced. Some will be difficult of solution and some will tax the ingenuity and ability of the government to the limits; but intrinsically the country is all right. That is the way you are getting it. Make sure that you hand it back that way.'[128] The cold print of this exchange does not do justice to Lemass's body language. The other former Fianna Fáil ministers preserved a studied attitude of indifference as the vote in the Dáil ushered them out of office, but Lemass was too angry to attempt to conceal his emotions. His voice was shaking with rage and his face was contorted with disappointment as he 'shouted across the floor' of the chamber.[129]

His anger and frustration had complex roots. While some was un-doubtedly directed at the opportunism that he felt had deprived Fianna Fáil of office after the difficult and dangerous years of the war, some of the targets of his anger were plainly to be found beside or behind him on the Fianna Fáil benches. His experience of managing supplies during the war had given him a sense of near-omnipotence, but this had been pared away and undermined by the unwillingness of his Government colleagues to engage in post-war planning on the serious level he felt was needed. His belief that the sort of tax reliefs that were being made available to British industry to stimulate development should also be applied in Ireland had fallen at the Department of Finance fence in 1945.[130] The ranks of Irish industry had failed to deliver growth and jobs in spite of having been handed almost every form of protection they had asked for. The country appeared to be settling down to business as usual just at the time when he felt the need for a great leap forward.

The Prices and Industrial Efficiency Bill, 1947, a legislative statement of his determination to compel industry where he could not cajole it into doing what he wanted, would die with the Fianna Fáil Government. If he felt betrayed, cheated and let down it was because it looked as if all his expectations were doomed to be dashed to the ground.

Some people were glad to see him go. Not long after the change of Government the Secretary of the Department of Finance, J. J. McElligott, told the new Taoiseach, John A Costello, that the country had been a dictatorship under Fianna Fáil. It was not de Valera who had been the dictator, he added: it had been Lemass.[131]

Lemass himself was not above offering light-hearted reassurance to his former nemesis. 'You're safe,' he told McElligott. 'Anyone who can get economics into Frank Aiken's head will be all right.'[132]

5

Out of the Doldrums
1948–59

'Has Ireland a future?'

The 1948 general election ushered in a nine-year period of political instability and inconsistent approaches to economic policy, exacerbated by the poor performance of agriculture. For this and other reasons the economy was slow to come back on stream — if indeed it had ever been on stream. Among organised workers the memory of statutory wage controls and other limitations was strong enough to obscure the statistics and the Government research that indicated that, all things considered, workers had actually not done too badly. It also interrupted the hitherto smooth progress Lemass had been making towards the leadership of his party, in that de Valera's undoubted personal sense of mission was enhanced rather than undermined by electoral failure.

The result of Fianna Fáil's loss of office in 1948 has been interpreted as a defining moment in modern Irish politics — the creation of a 'Fianna Fáil v. the Rest' scenario, which was to persist until the unheralded and in many ways unprecedented alliance between Charles Haughey's Fianna Fáil and Desmond O'Malley's Progressive Democrats in 1989. The analysis of this phenomenon, however, has concentrated on the unlikely and often fragile alliances that have ranged themselves against Fianna Fáil in the intervening decades. Less examined, but possibly even more important for the purposes of this study, was the effect it had on Fianna Fáil.

In the first place it fuelled a belief that Fianna Fáil's loss of office was a temporary blip in Ireland's political progress towards national maturity and self-fulfilment. The inter-party Government was seen, in Lemass's unusually cutting words, as 'nothing except a post-election interval' in this progress.[1] Secondly, and for Seán Lemass more significantly, it put paid to any prospect, however slight, that de Valera might shortly relinquish the reins as leader of his party.

As early as 1946, British diplomats were suggesting that Lemass was 'expected to succeed the long man,'[2] but de Valera was to remain leader for another decade. It was increasingly a different kind of leadership. For a time after the election de Valera virtually disappeared from view and Lemass took his place at Government meetings and in the Dáil. This was partly because de Valera chose to absent himself on a number of tours abroad — to the United States, Australia, New Zealand, and India — to publicise Ireland's case on partition. It was a decision that in any case spared him the undoubted difficulty of having to continue to make an impact on national politics from the seat of the leader of the opposition, without notes and civil service support and afflicted by deteriorating eyesight.

In strictly party terms, however, it was at best a fallow period for the former Tánaiste. Despite the fact that he was unanimously elected vice-chairman of the parliamentary party, on Jim Ryan's nomination,[3] morale was low after the election defeat, and the response to his initiatives was unenthusiastic or even hostile. The parliamentary party agendas were dull and uninspiring. There was a contentious series of discussions on proposals from Lemass and Ryan for the creation of a levy on Oireachtas members of the party, which the sponsors had to withdraw after opposition from rank-and-file TDs.[4]

Although party meetings were sometimes fractious and discontented, Lemass was rapidly acquiring an aura of authority. Jack Lynch recalls that at his first parliamentary party meeting after the 1948 election there was considerable discussion and argument about some topic on the agenda, which was quelled only when Lemass intervened.

Party discipline was wavering in opposition. Lemass (with Aiken) was much preoccupied with riding herd on absentee deputies[5] or reaffirming the rule — evidently because it needed reaffirming — forbidding Fianna Fáil deputies to approach Government ministers or parliamentary secretaries 'except in the case of deputations or with the consent of the Chief Whip.'[6] Lemass and Ryan also experienced defeat on another proposal, on the face of it less controversial, to establish a series of committees within the parliamentary party to sharpen the political attacks on ministers. After two lengthy discussions they were forced to withdraw it.[7]

For Lemass the period between the 1948 election and his own election by Fianna Fáil as de Valera's successor in 1959 was marked by a series of changes, both personal and political, that was eventually to accelerate the development of his thinking on economic, social and political issues.

On a personal level the change in his circumstances was dramatic. Under de Valera ministerial salaries had never been extravagant and indeed had been reduced when the party first took office in 1932; but they allowed at least for a measure of comfort and security.[8] Lemass was now in opposition and financially unprepared for it, despite an unostentatious life-style. His apparent extravagance in buying suits — he would order up to ten a year from F. X. Kelly's in Grafton Street — was certainly less personal vanity than the expression of a belief that the people deserved public representatives who would maintain certain standards, both political and sartorial. The turnover of suits was probably accelerated by Lemass's generosity to his old comrades, particularly those who had fallen on hard times.[9] He was a careful money manager,[10] but the sudden decline in income involved in his transfer to the other side of the Dáil within weeks of the election on 4 February was accentuated by the illness of one of his daughters, Sheila, which necessitated expensive hospital treatment.[11]

There were rumours that the former minister had been offered a lucrative appointment with a large business enterprise, and indeed it would be surprising if such an offer had not been made. There was certainly an immediate, if temporary, financial embarrassment, which was tackled in a reassuringly orthodox manner by the arrangement of an overdraft of £1,000 (some £20,300 in 1997 terms) from the National City Bank in Dame Street, against which the bank held the deeds of his house as security.[12] The significance of this amount can also be assessed in another way: it was the same sum that was voted by the parliamentary party to de Valera — half of which was to be treated as expenses — as a special allowance in opposition.

THE IRISH PRESS

Three days after securing this loan, Lemass's financial worries were to all intents and purposes solved by the decision — in which de Valera as controlling director must have played the main role — to invite him to join the *Irish Press* as managing director.[13] Within a month he had also begun to acquire a small number of other directorships, notably of Fleming's Fireclay Ltd[14] and another as a director of the car importers Lincoln and Nolan Ltd, despite the fact that he was unable to afford one of their new cars.[15] These directorships and his Dáil salary combined probably gave him more disposable income than he had had as a minister.

These modest developments provide in themselves a revealing commentary on Lemass's probity. He had been Minister for Industry and Commerce almost continuously since 1932; for most of the war years he had also been Minister for Supplies. In both positions he would have been uniquely placed to convert public office to private profit had he been so minded, and indeed the rumours on this score, both during and after the war, were a constant source of annoyance. 'There is probably no member of this house', he remarked acidly after losing office, 'against whom more allegations have been made than against me.'[16]

Opposition was a good time for the family too. There would be holiday expeditions to the country in Lemass's Rover or Ford V8; at times there would be more than one car. Portnablagh was a favourite destination; on one trip to Donegal he pointed out to them the hayfield in which the

Fianna Fáil organisation for the constituency had been inaugurated by himself and Neil Blaney senior in the nineteen-twenties.

He took to his new role as managing director of the *Irish Press* with characteristic vigour. The management style of the paper had not been such as to inspire much confidence. Its first editor, Frank Gallagher, had resigned after failing to secure de Valera's support in a battle with the board over the importing of an American expert to sort out the newspaper's finances; another editor lasted only a matter of weeks; and yet another, who had been appointed during one of de Valera's absences in America, was dismissed when de Valera returned. Before Lemass's appointment the management structure was curiously inadequate: there was, for instance, no management layer between de Valera and the general manager. It was a gap that Lemass was ideally suited to fill.

His agenda was strongly political rather than cultural in tone — although he once acted to remove the 'Superman' cartoon strip from one of the group's papers because it offended him deeply.[17] He had little interest in the literary side of the paper, although he could on occasion be generous to others who were struggling to keep the ship of culture afloat. His family had a link with the *Capuchin Annual,* which was edited by Father Senan from an office above the Lemass shop in Capel Street, and Lemass not only gave money himself to support the venture but persuaded others, including Joe McGrath, to do likewise. Father Senan once introduced Benedict Kiely to Lemass, who told the young writer: 'There's not enough money going into the arts in Ireland, but if the country doesn't run and prosper there'll be no money for the arts or for anything else either.'[18]

Although Lemass's role in the *Irish Press* was strictly speaking only a managerial one, it quickly became an open secret that many of the more pungent unsigned contributions also came from his pen, notably the anonymous 'political commentary', which betrayed a familiarity with the workings of the Dáil that few journalists could match. Some of them were joint efforts with Brendan Malin, the political correspondent,[19] but on many occasions the robust Lemass prose evidently needed little editing.

A typical example, dealing with political jobbery, discoursed knowledge-ably on Lemass's favourite objects of obloquy, the 'lawyer-deputies', and the allocation of state briefs to barristers who were members of the Oireachtas.[20] Before he returned to office, and before the ranks of Fianna Fáil deputies were themselves swollen by accessions from the Law Library, he was to declare that he was 'proud of being a member of a Government which did not contain a single lawyer.'[21] The training of a lawyer, he once advised Seán Flanagan, a young colleague for whom he had a high regard, was the worst kind for a political career. This training was to get the facts and consider how they could be used so as to induce others to arrive at a predetermined conclusion: the duty of a politician was to arrive at conclusions based on the facts.[22]

William Norton, his onetime ally in the unlikely setting of Rathmines Urban District Council[23] and now the inter-party Government's Minister for Social Welfare, referred scathingly to 'the deputy's leading articles in the *Irish Press*,'[24] secure in the knowledge that the allegation would not be denied, as indeed it was not. Lemass never claimed authorship, but, if challenged, he stood over anything he wrote.[25]

In the Dáil in 1948 Lemass had publicly questioned Norton's fitness to hold office as a minister in the light of his other role as 'a committee man of a trade union having business with Government departments.'[26] The following year in the *Irish Press* he went one better — but without the protection of parliamentary privilege. In a week in which the Dáil had to be adjourned because there was no business for it to do he gave Brendan Malin a note about Norton, suggesting that he spent most of his time on party matters and left his department to run itself. It was a moderate enough criticism, but Norton, despite being advised strongly against this course of action by his solicitors, immediately sued for libel.

Lemass spent a lengthy period in the witness box, arguing that the article was fair comment and making it clear that he was enjoying his new job. William O'Brien FitzGerald, Norton's counsel, tried to trip Lemass up by quoting from one of his earlier unsigned articles.[27] Lemass was prepared, and unrepentant.

> *Mr. Lemass:* That referred to news given by Radio Éireann, not in a newspaper.
>
> *Mr. FitzGerald:* Do you suggest you ought to draw the distinction that news given by Radio Éireann should be given in that way and that news given in the *Irish Press* should be in another form?
>
> *Mr. Lemass:* I think news given by Radio Éireann, which is a public service, should be given without regard for its political effect. To lay down the same standard for a newspaper is ridiculous ... We try to give it objectively with due regard for its importance, and we have a close regard for its political effect.

He disingenuously suggested that he had really been trying to help Norton, by offering him the support of the *Irish Press* in his battles with Government colleagues. And he added:

> I do not regard it as a criticism of any Minister to say that he gives a large part of his time to political or party matters. I did it myself when I was a Minister.[28]

The jury found for Norton after ten minutes' deliberation but awarded him only £1 in damages.[29] The result prompted Seán MacEntee's famous description of the Labour leader as 'Billy the Quid'.[30]

Lemass enjoyed the life that went with the paper. On the days of big race meetings, office work was over early and a large car was waiting for him at the front door.[31] His new insights into the world of journalism enabled him to make an unusually punishing series of attacks on Seán MacBride's embryo Irish News Agency — the 'fake news agency', as he called it[32] — as well as representations about the need for additional supplies of newsprint. 'Since I shed my ministerial responsibilities,' he informed the Dáil equably, 'I acquired some new sources of information.'[33]

William Sweetman, the editor of the *Irish Press*, was a strong editor, and in general they treated each other with a certain wary respect.[34] Lemass's decisiveness was as apparent as ever, and he had little time for board meetings.[35] There were times, however, when even his legendary forcefulness had to take second place to the complex demands of the institution and its personnel. On one occasion his desire to abolish the newspaper's practice of referring to former military men by their titles — he had a particular aversion to 'General' Mulcahy — foundered when he realised that the ruling would place him in an embarrassing position in relation to Major Vivion de Valera. In a rare confidence to his editor he once told him that he felt his own strength as a politician and as a manager was that he had a perfect memory for detail and for figures and that he was strictly honest, in that he kept every promise he ever made. What he was proudest of was that in any controversy he was involved in there was never any dispute about the facts.

Lemass's greatest achievement during his time at the *Irish Press*, however, was the launch of the *Sunday Press* in September 1949. This was an enterprise he made peculiarly his own, even to the extent of encouraging resolutions at party meetings calling for its establishment.[36] The editor of the new paper, Matt Feehan, had an army background and was a good organiser but had absolutely no newspaper experience. Lemass's own journalistic aptitudes, sharpened by his experiences at the *Irish Press*, led him to take a keen interest in every aspect of the paper's planning and development. Tomás Ó Faoláin, who as Terry O'Sullivan later became famous for his 'Dubliner's Diary' in the *Evening Press*, was one of Lemass's protégés and was sent out of Dublin by him to do the dummy run for a 'country page' for the Sunday paper. When he returned, his journalistic efforts were assessed by Lemass, not by Feehan.[37]

Lemass showed considerable business acumen in the preparations for the launch, working behind the scenes with Liam Pedlar, the circulation manager, on a reorganisation of the critical distribution network, planned on the basis of Ordnance Survey maps so that there would be no blunders or overlapping. The existing newspapers were putting pressure on wholesale and retail outlets in an attempt to scuttle the new paper; Lemass retaliated by creating a whole new network of wholesalers, many of them shop-keepers with party connections who had never been in the newspaper business before. 'We will knock the stuffing out of the *Independent*,' he told his assembled sales force in Dublin, and indeed to some extent he succeeded. But ironically, the circulation war that developed had the effect of extending the *Sunday Independent's* circulation into areas in which it had not previously sold substantially, so that the *Sunday Press's* rise was not accompanied by a proportionate fall in its rival's circulation.

THE OPPOSITION BENCHES

In the Dáil during this period Lemass revelled in opposition, quick on his feet and giving full rein to a sense of humour that had necessarily been hidden in government. He was criticising the wheeling and dealing that had led up to the formation of the inter-party Government when he was interrupted by a heckler from the opposition benches who wanted to know whether the manoeuvres he was criticising had been contemporaneous with an attempt by the Fianna Fáil Minister for Justice to enlist the support of the leader of the National Labour Party, James Everett. 'Just about that time,' he replied cheerfully.[38]

He was more frank than other former ministers about his policy mistakes of the past. In the process he underlined his disappointment at the way in which industry had failed to respond to tariff protection. 'The problem I was trying to solve [in the Industrial Efficiency and Prices Bill] was that of finding some method by which sanctions could be applied to manufacturers enjoying protection but not acting fairly by the community which did not involve the withdrawal of protection entirely, the stoppage of work in the industry and the disemployment of its workers.'[39]

The wounds left by the Department of Finance plainly smarted. When he pressed the minister, Paddy McGilligan, to introduce a milder tax regime for companies that held their hands on the distribution of profits and in relation to depreciation allowances, he won the vocal support of the Government backbencher Maurice Dockrell but encountered, behind McGilligan, the shadow of J. J. McElligott. 'It is a matter on which I have had strong personal views for a long time,' Lemass mused. 'I found equal difficulty in persuading the Minister's predecessor.'[40]

He went even further in an admission of what he saw as his own failure by arguing that the pre-war machinery for price control 'was not only ineffective, but it was on a wrong basis, because it was connected with profits and not with efficiency.'[41] He was also self-critical in relation to his own labour legislation and its failure, as he now saw it, to provide adequate machinery for conciliation.

He was even more explicit about his role in Aer Lingus's purchase of Vickers Viking aircraft, although it had been less an error of judgment than a way out of a dangerous cul-de-sac. The Aer Lingus board and their technical advisers had been strongly opposed to the idea and indeed had been proved correct when the high maintenance costs for the aircraft made them 'completely uneconomic'.[42] Lemass, however, had insisted on their purchase, because he had been told by the British side that if the aircraft were not purchased the 1946 Air Agreement with Britain would be terminated. Not for the first or last time, Lemass had to duck below the parapet in the face of superior firepower.

He made no bones about his view that the External Relations Act, which the new Dáil repealed, could and should have been repealed earlier. There was at least an implicit difference of opinion here with de Valera, who held strongly that the Crown had an important role to play in any eventual resolution of the partition issue. Lemass made a strong speech at Rathfarnham, even before the Government had made its intentions clear, expressing his regret that Fianna Fáil were not in office so that they could repeal the Act.[43] Again his views evoked disagreement within the party. His principal objective, however, was probably less the creation of controversy than a desire to prevent Fianna Fáil from rashly making a pre-election commitment to restore the Act, and in this he was undoubtedly successful.

His utterances on partition itself remained infrequent and strongly traditional, although he was criticised at the 1951 ardfheis for the supposed crime of fraternising with visiting Northern ministers.[44] Throughout the 1948–54 period, in fact, the Fianna Fáil line on partition hardened visibly, which can be seen as a natural reaction to the way in which Clann na Poblachta's more militant and radical republicanism was eating into Fianna Fáil's core vote. It was also a response to the creation of the all-party Anti-Partition League in 1949, on which Lemass was named as a Fianna Fáil substitute for de Valera.[45] There was only an occasional, and very brief, display of deep-seated political emotions, such as during the debate on the Republic of Ireland Bill in 1949.[46]

He was only rarely caught off balance. His extraordinary memory for detail generally served him well, but he was wrong-footed by Seán MacBride on the question whether the envisaged American aid for Ireland would come in the form of grants or of loans. Lemass insisted that grants had been envisaged, but he had not retained copies of departmental papers that would have kept him au fait with the details of the exchanges between the American and Irish governments. MacBride, with access to the files, was able to contradict Lemass and force him back into a cautious holding position. It was a rare example of Lemass on a sticky wicket.[47] When he left office again in 1954 he took with him copies of some Government papers, notably on trade talks with Britain, which he thought might be useful for a defence of his position; in the event, they were not necessary.[48]

Government ministers learned to fear Lemass's quickness of tongue. On one occasion he became embroiled in a series of exchanges with

Seán Mac Eoin about a Government decision, taken in the aftermath of a fatal fire in a Dublin shop, to ban all fireworks. The decision was so extensive that it banned, among other things, the sale of caps for toy guns. Lemass and Mac Eoin had been in arms together thirty years earlier in opposition to British rule; during the Civil War they had taken up arms against each other. Now, improbably, these two former revolutionaries were locking horns in the Dáil over the dangers supposedly caused by cap-pistols. Lemass won the exchange hands down with a withering final remark: 'Was the Minister ever a boy?'[49]

He was evidently delighted at the rapidity with which the inexperience of the new Government had begun to manifest itself in unprepared statements by ministers, some of which had to be explained away by Costello as personal opinions, because they obviously conflicted with Government policy. On one such occasion he asked, with deceptive mildness, whether the Taoiseach would 'arrange to have some signal given, such as the flying of a flag over Government Buildings, whenever a Minister is speaking in a manner in which he is expected to be taken seriously?'[50]

Later he advanced a unique analysis of a rash of contradictory ministerial utterances, arguing that the primary responsibility of the Taoiseach was to keep his team together and to ensure that, whatever their internal differences, they said the same thing in public. 'It may be', he added with a delighted sense of discovery, 'that the conflicting statements which have appeared in the press have come from men who are agreed in secret but who are speaking in different voices in public for the purposes of deception.'[51]

He was careful to mend a fence or two with the trade union movement, agreeing in early 1949 to a proposal (which he had declined to accept as minister) to become a patron of the James Larkin Fund and subscribing five pounds.[52] Fianna Fáil's trade union connection in fact remained strong right up to the late fifties. It had its foundation in the nineteen-twenties republicanism of some of the early trade union leaders, notably Thomas Foran, Thomas Kennedy, and William O'Brien. Dan Desmond, a Cork trade unionist (and father of Barry Desmond of the Labour Party) was a founder-member of Fianna Fáil in his native city and only broke with them when they introduced the Wages Standstill Order in 1939. Thomas Kennedy's son, Fintan, later became a member of Seanad Éireann on the labour panel but was slow to join the Labour Party. After the split in the trade union movement Norton's links with the unions in the ITUC, which included the English unions, led many of the unions in the rival CIU to respond warmly to overtures from Fianna Fáil. As a minister, Lemass always showed himself attuned to the working patterns of his trade union interlocutors, generally scheduling meetings with them in the evening so as to allow them to have a pint after finishing work.[53]

One key participant in this process was Billy McMullen, general president of the ITGWU in 1949–50. He had supported the Trade Union Bill, 1941, at the ITGWU annual conference that year and was a particularly vocal supporter of Lemass's view that workers should be organised in Irish unions wherever possible. There was even a belief in journalistic circles that Lemass had actively encouraged the formation of the Guild of Irish Journalists, a breakaway from the National Union of Journalists in the late forties. There is no direct evidence of this, but Lemass's links with McMullen suggest at least a circumstantial connection. McMullen, whose pro-Fianna Fáil stance was well known, was elected to the Seanad on the labour panel in the 1951 election but was forced to forfeit his seat in September 1952 in unusual circumstances. An employer in Bailieborough with whom the union was in dispute had managed to make him personally liable for losses incurred during the strike, and McMullen, who on principle refused to pay, was declared a bankrupt. The debt was discharged in time to allow him to stand as a candidate in the ensuing Seanad by-election in February 1952, when he was elected unopposed. He resigned from the Seanad in September 1953 when Lemass appointed him to the board of CIE.

McMullen's significance in all of this is that he was a prime mover in the attempt to set up the Guild of Irish Journalists. The guild, in its first press statement on 22 March 1949, asked bluntly: 'Why should Irish journalists be controlled from London?' McMullen attended one of its early meetings in 31 North Frederick Street to promise the fledgling organisation the support of both the CIU and the ITGWU and to assure them: 'If anyone does anything against you we will not delay in dealing with them.'[54] Office-holders of the guild included Liam Skinner, a devotee and later biographer of Lemass; Noel Hartnett, later a Clann na Poblachta TD; Peadar O'Curry, later editor of the *Irish Catholic;* and the broadcasters Micheál O'Hehir and Mitchell Cogley.

For the time being, however, it was business as usual for Lemass. The belief that Fianna Fáil would rapidly and inevitably be returned to power meant that no serious thought was given within the party, or by Lemass himself, to the development of new policies.[55] The old ones, developed over sixteen years in government, were more than adequate in their view, and the main business of opposition was to oppose.

If opposition meant giving some hostages to fortune, this was a problem that could be addressed later. This was especially evident in Lemass's re-action to the Government's proposal to establish the Industrial Development Authority, which he not only opposed but promised to abolish when back in office. This commitment gave one of the members of the new authority, Kevin McCourt, quite a few sleepless nights: he had three children and a mortgage and did not look forward to a suddenly jobless future. Many years later he mentioned this to Lemass, with whom he had built up a friendly working relationship in his period as secretary of the Federation of Irish Industry. Lemass chided him gently: had he not realised that there were certain things that politicians had to say? He would not have done such a thing to McCourt, or indeed to Beddy, he maintained — but he might have made an exception for Luke Duffy, the senator and secretary of the Labour Party, who had also been appointed to the authority.[56]

Much has been made of Lemass's reversal of policy on this issue when he returned to power, but it had already been signalled while he was still in opposition, when he suggested that the problem was less the existence of the IDA than its inactivity.

> It is true that no impediment to industrial development is being created by the Department or the Industrial Development Authority, acting in conjunction with it, except perhaps a certain difficulty in getting expeditious decisions, but there is certainly no stimulus forthcoming either.[57]

On a range of other issues, notably tariffs and foreign investment, his views were unmistakably evolving. On tariffs he was to a certain extent in a cleft stick. His considered view now was that they were less a standard instrument of policy than something to which Governments would have recourse only in an emergency. Given the extent of the existing tariff regime and the slowness with which it was being eroded under his own management, this shift of perspective is certainly noteworthy. To an extent it was opportunist, in that a Government dominated by Fine Gael was not going to reduce the tariff regime dramatically (although for different reasons from those advanced by Fianna Fáil). His initial advice to the Government that the promoters of new industries would continue to require from the Government assurances of protection were notably qualified.

> It is, I admit, true that many industries do not require protection now. Probably in the circumstances that will exist for some years ahead, protection of the kind given before the war will not be necessary in many cases, but no person will undertake to finance a substantial long-term industrial project unless he has some assurance that if international economic conditions change, and if the economic circumstances that existed before the war reappear, he will get the assurance of protection from the Government.[58]

Shortly afterwards he suggested that even some new industries could do without protection[59] and that the extension or reintroduction of protection on a large scale would only be necessitated by a doomsday scenario — 'the economic conditions that existed before the war.' Later, again in charge of the highly oiled machine of the Department of Industry and Commerce in 1951 and in the difficult balance of payments situation that then pertained, his enthusiasm for reviewing sanctions evidently cooled or was constrained by political or practical difficulties, although the conditions could not by any stretch of the imagination have been compared to those existing in the thirties.

On external investment questions his defence of the Control of Manufactures Acts was made in terms that implied a substantial reassessment of policy. The original legislation, he now argued, had been designed primarily 'to prevent industrial development here taking the form of the establishment of branch companies by *English* concerns,' which 'of course would disappear if, at any time, the tariff which caused them to come into being was removed.' (Emphasis added.)[60]

As on the question of tariffs, however, his tendency to suggest changes in established policy was more in evidence in his early period in opposition. Specifically, he made the intriguing suggestion that the arguments that applied to British capital did not necessarily apply to capital from other sources.

> It is quite clear that the particular circumstances which make us hesitant about encouraging the investment of British capital in this country, because of the political influences or other influences that capital might bring with it, do not necessarily apply to capital from other countries. It is, I think, desirable that we should have, so far as we can ensure it, the direction of Irish industrial development in the hands of boards which meet in this country and which have a majority of Irish persons on them; but I see no reason why we should not make it known through the European Recovery Programme administration that we are interested in this plan they have for the encouragement of American businessmen to invest in industrial development in Europe in order to expand output and avail of that device, if it can be done, to secure the creation here of many of those new industries of which we are in need and which, obviously, require a very heavy capital investment.[61]

In other words, British investment was undesirable for political rather than economic reasons. And the central thrust of the Control of Manufactures Acts, the national control of industrial investment decisions and policies, was now modified by the classic escape clause: 'so far as we can ensure it.' In that industries established by capitalists from other countries behind the Irish tariff wall would be subject to an identical array of constraints and temptations, there is no obvious basis for this attempt at differentiation beyond the lingering suspicion, no doubt coloured by the experience of the war years, that British promises were especially unreliable.

The possibility remains that the shift in policy may have been motivated less by any objective view about the trustworthiness or otherwise of British capitalists and more by a recognition that if traditional policy was to be

altered, Fianna Fáil's traditional value system was more politically recon-
cilable with an opening to the west than with one to the east. A central
and related question — the degree to which any investors, particularly in
capital-intensive projects, would cede control over their own resources
to Irish nationals — was fudged but certainly appeared less difficult of
resolution when illuminated not by the baleful glare of sterling but by the
munificent glow of the dollar economy. In one speech in 1949 Lemass
made a somewhat elliptical defence of Fianna Fáil policies when he noted
that we could always have got far more substantial industrial development
'if we had been prepared to proceed through foreign capital and under
foreign direction.'[62] This defence, which raised a number of important
questions, was not advanced with anything like confidence and was in
effect an acknowledgment that Fianna Fáil policies were primarily nationalist rather than economic in origin and for that reason had major costs
in the area of employment.

Lemass's speeches during this period in opposition provide evidence of
an ideological gradient between the 1948 and 1951 elections. In 1948
Fianna Fáil's loss of office was accompanied by rather more truculent
statements about the banking system and its effect on industrial development and more positive noises about the need for state intervention in
certain sectors.

The 1949–51 period, when Fianna Fáil appetites for a return to power
were being whetted by the perceived weaknesses and internal disagreements
of the inter-party Government, saw the emergence of a more conservative
rhetoric. Speaking on the estimates for the Department of the Taoiseach in
the summer of 1948, for example, Lemass made no bones about his view
that 'those who direct the policy of the Irish banks are, in the main, people
who have not absorbed any new ideas since long before Lord Keynes
revolutionised economic thought by his writings ... They were based on
rigid mid-Victorian principles.'[63] During the same debate he insisted that
protected or monopoly industries would have to be satisfied with lower
returns on capital, that they would have to be subject to 'permanent
machinery for the supervision of profits and general efficiency,' and that
there could never be a total reliance on private enterprise, 'because there are
many industries which will not be established because of exceptional
difficulties or high capital costs.'[64] Much more, indeed, would be needed
than the financial plans proposed by Beveridge or Keynes if Ireland was ever
to have full employment.[65]

A matter of months later his view of state intervention was considerably
less positive: he would have no objection to it 'where it was quite clear that
private enterprise was ineffective.'[66] By 1950, criticising the Government's
declared intention to finance its programmes at the expense of private
investment, he argued that this would force the country into a position

in which all private enterprise would cease and in which any new development in industry and agriculture would inevitably have to proceed under state auspices. Somewhat to the surprise of Government deputies, he continued:

> I have said already that the Government, in ignorance, are leading the country into a form of cockeyed Socialism, and I, for one, believe that more beneficial results will be secured if the Government goes avowedly for a Socialist policy, controlling all forms of economic activity, controlling all investment and taking all the responsibility for the economic consequences of its acts.
> *Mr. Hickey:* Do you believe all that rubbish?
> *Mr. Lemass:* I do. I, as a rule, do not say here what I do not believe.[67]

Lemass's declaration that the country would do better under an unalloyed form of socialism conflicted sharply with his repeated assertions that industrial development outside the state sector would 'come more quickly and more effectively and over a wider field if it is promoted by private enterprise and initiative.'[68] Frustration at his removal from the levers of power, even the memory of frustrations experienced while he held them, as well as scorn for a Government without a clear sense of purpose and direction, may all have played a part. Little more than a week after his 'socialist' outburst, as it turned out, he was to mend his hand, qualifying this statement or at least hinting that it had been made tongue in cheek. There was, he said, a 'weakness' in the political situation in Ireland, in that

> the large body of conservative opinion among our people has no means of expressing itself in the current Dáil. Those who might be regarded as the spokesmen for that body of opinion are — under pressure of political needs — momentarily silent. This is a weakness which is bound to have undesirable consequences on the development of national policy ... The absence of representation of that opinion means that the country was marching rapidly towards the left [and] those who wanted a change had no check whatever.[69]

The idea that conservative Ireland was without its spokesmen in the Dáil in 1950 appears, even at this remove, somewhat far-fetched, but it is difficult to avoid the impression that Lemass's attack on Fine Gael for being under the thumb of the Labour Party and Clann na Poblachta was not entirely devoid of sympathy for Cosgrave's party. It also plainly reflected both an attempt at articulating the mood of the day and his own personal belief that in politics it is difficult to give leadership in the absence of some kind of consensus.

THE RETURN TO POWER

In 1951 the Government collapsed, and a general election was called for 30 May. On the day the Dáil was dissolved Lemass was summoned to the Fianna Fáil head office in Mount Street to take part in an election strategy meeting. For the previous three years his life had been quite different. He had been not only an exceptionally able and effective backbencher, free from the responsibilities of office, but had had more time with his family. In addition he had been managing director of the *Irish Press* group and because of this financially better off than he had ever been in his life. As he drove rapidly down Harcourt Street, he reminisced many years later, he paused for a moment and asked himself: 'Am I mad to be giving up all this, and going back to the hassle, low pay, long hours and all the rest of it?'[70]

Lemass asserted during the 1951 election campaign that Fianna Fáil had 'learned much in opposition.'[71] Little else supported this statement. On the same occasion on which he discerned Fianna Fáil's learning curve he announced proudly that essentially they were going to the electorate with their 1948 programme unchanged. The chief burden of his own speeches was criticism of the concept and practice of coalition government. The Fianna Fáil policies he advanced were a rehash of existing ones. He was not above resurrecting the red scare of previous elections in an attempt to de-stabilise James Everett in Wicklow,[72] or even predicting a possible outbreak of World War III,[73] but he also had his eye firmly fixed on the main chance, notably the possibility of obtaining Marshall Aid funds for Ireland.[74]

It was a lack-lustre election, and the result was indecisive. The main loser was Clann na Poblachta, and Fianna Fáil, although it gained only one seat and was five short of an absolute majority, was able to form a minority Government with the support of a number of independent deputies, including Noel Browne, who was later to join Fianna Fáil. Although Fianna Fáil had previous experience of working minority Governments (and were to have it again under Lemass himself), the 1944 option of a quick dash to the country did not present itself and probably would not have been taken even if it had.

For Lemass personally, going back into Government was something of a mixed blessing; he had been enjoying his period at the *Irish Press* so much that his summons back to Merrion Street, he later confessed, was a personal disappointment.[75] This surprising admission was due less to the political disappointments of the previous three years than to the expected difficulties ahead.

> During that period after the 1951 election when it was not certain how the Independents were going to vote, I made no personal effort to influence any of them as to how they were going to vote because I realised that whoever got their support and became the Government

was going to have a very difficult time. It was not our most successful period in office, as you know. We felt hamstrung by the insecure position in the Dáil and we had not really got down to clearing our minds on post-war development.[76]

He told one correspondent: 'The position cannot be satisfactory no matter what happens.'[77] His forebodings must have been accentuated by the growing problems with the Taoiseach's health. De Valera's eyesight had been causing him increasing difficulties, and he was forced to spend considerable periods in the Netherlands for specialist attention.

Among the nettles Lemass had to grasp was that of the IDA, and he grasped it early and firmly a month after resuming office. Although he had opposed its establishment, he reminded the Dáil, he had 'always recognised that there would be some advantage in having a body outside the Civil Service with powers and resources to promote the creation here of new industries … of a kind that do not exist now or are not likely to be brought into being by private initiative.'[78]

The chairman of the authority, J. P. Beddy, added to the undoubted pressure on Lemass by making a presentation of the authority's case personally to him, and Lemass relented. The fact that Beddy had gone to the IDA from the department itself undoubtedly helped, and indeed he and Lemass maintained a personally friendly and ideologically close relationship until Beddy's retirement.[79] On a trade visit to the United States with Lemass, Beddy once asked for the minister's advice on how he should fill out the section on 'occupation' on his disembarkation form; possibly he thought that to describe himself as chairman of the IDA would not greatly illuminate the US immigration authorities. 'Plumber,' suggested Lemass succinctly.[80]

STANDING IN FOR THE CHIEF

Lemass's attention had to be divided between his departmental responsibilities and his role as stand-in for de Valera during the latter's four-and-a-half month absence for eye treatment. Nor was his own health especially robust: for a period in 1952 Aiken had to deputise for him as Minister for Industry and Commerce.[81] De Valera was not even able to be present for the twenty-fifth anniversary celebration of the founding of Fianna Fáil in October 1951, and in his absence Lemass had not only to chair Government meetings but to engage in the tricky series of negotiations on Fianna Fáil's Health Bill.

The gulf that had opened up between the Catholic hierarchy and the previous Government was difficult to bridge. In de Valera's absence in Utrecht, Lemass and Ryan were in charge of negotiations for the Government and — in the bishops' view — ready to comply with the episcopal agenda.[82] In de Valera's continuing and unforeseen absence — 'I hate to be a lame duck like this,' he confided to Lemass, 'but of course I can't help it'[83] — the situation deteriorated, and Lemass was engaged in frosty negotiations with the hierarchy. The bishops had decided at their October meeting that the White Paper was not satisfactory[84] and plainly believed that the commitment to a process of consultation had not been fully honoured. The Archbishop of Dublin, John Charles McQuaid, wrote to the Primate, Cardinal d'Alton, about a meeting he had with Lemass, at which one of the chief points at issue had been the proposed extension of ministerial powers over medical schools.

> On Friday again I saw Mr. Lemass and went over the Mother and Child position. While stating that it was very hard to take back what had been promised in print, he assured me that he would see what he could do. I could get no explanation of the failure to consult beforehand, but I think that the error is now very clearly felt.[85]

Lemass knew that agreement would not be easy to reach and wrote to de Valera to keep him informed. De Valera's response was to the point:

> I agree that the great danger ahead is the White Paper. I have for years been afraid of the health service, not because of the ecclesiastical implications, but of the difficulty of getting a workable rather than a comprehensive scheme. The whole thing is so complex once you envisage providing a full service. As far as the Church side is concerned, Dr. Ryan ought to be able through his preliminary conversations to find out exactly what are the snags that must be avoided.[86]

McQuaid, equally guarded, wrote to Lemass to put the Government on notice that matters were not proceeding satisfactorily, and Lemass forwarded the letter to de Valera, who urged him to reply to the effect that 'the Government before reaching any final decisions on the Health Bill will give the fullest consideration to the objections which you have brought to their notice.'[87] He also urged that 'every member of the Government should first acquaint himself with the traditional position taken up by the Church in Church versus State disputes,' and added:

> Were I at home, and able to consult with the Minister, I would suggest that each particular proposal of ours to which objection was made be taken up with the Archbishop, and that he be asked to make a draft with the qualifications which would satisfy him. This draft could then be examined from our point of view, and amended if necessary, until an agreed text was arrived at. That was more or less what happened in regard to the corresponding articles of the Constitution.

The controversy rumbled on until after de Valera's return, and the Taoiseach himself was personally involved in the highly charged exchanges in April 1953 that almost resulted in a public challenge to the Government by the hierarchy, before the matter was eventually resolved.

As far as his responsibilities in the Department of Industry and Commerce were concerned, Lemass had to cope with the consequences of a deteriorating economic situation, the most obvious sign of which was a sharp rise in the balance of payments deficit. The evidence was unmistakable. We could not, he warned, expect to maintain the standard of living represented by a 60 per cent increase in the volume of imports while exports were still below their pre-war levels.[88] Since the war, all western European countries had increased their production of foodstuffs by up to 22 per cent: only in Ireland and Austria — which was still occupied by foreign armies — had the production of food actually decreased,[89] and there was an 'extraordinary inflexibility' in agricultural production.[90] 'There is no use', he added, 'in blaming all our difficulties on international conditions.'[91]

In industry the situation was even starker. As Fianna Fáil returned to office, only 17.9 per cent of the Republic's economically active population were engaged in industry — a figure lower than that for Portugal and Iceland at the same period and almost out of sight of that obtaining in Northern Ireland (39.7 per cent) and the remainder of the UK (46.2 per cent). Not all of this could be comfortably blamed on three years of coalition misrule; and the worsening balance of payments situation was to become an effective block to radical action to cure it.

Identifying the problem was easier than recommending a solution. Strengthening the tariff regime plainly would not help. The need to increase production and efficiency was paramount. 'Where an industry had problems due to rising prices causing sales to contract the remedy would have to be sought first in revised methods of working which would get costs down, and not by trying to bolster up high costs by higher protection,' Lemass told the Federation of Irish Manufacturers.[92] Whatever he was thinking of in private — and he suggested many years later that he had been thinking of ending protection as early as 1952 — there was little evidence that he was prepared to go further in public than to suggest that it no longer needed to be extended to new industries on the same basis. One of his principal civil servants summed it up:

> Between 1951 and 1954 he loosened up on ownership policy, but gingerly. At the same time he began to encourage exports; and he was coming to the conclusion that one of the keys to progress was technical know-how which could be imported from abroad. The Irish Management Institute was established in 1952 — this was a key development, and one in which Leydon was involved. The Institute for Public Administration was the equivalent of the IMI, but in the public sector.[93]

There were, however, two other elements to his strategy. One of them was his attempt to harness national, and specifically religious, ideology to the shafts of the cart he was steering along the rutted road of industrial development. The other was Fianna Fáil's rediscovery ('discovery' is probably too strong a word) of the need to industrialise the western parts of the country, leading to a renewed emphasis on decentralisation and indeed to a modification of Lemass's earlier and somewhat dismissive attitude towards the Gaeltacht.

In early 1952 in particular he articulated, in an exceptionally distilled form, a vision of the Ireland of the future that, for once, blended his own and de Valera's ideas in a powerful cocktail. With industrial development, he noted, had come industrial strife and 'the danger of class warfare which was one of the gravest problems of our day and a certain destroyer of civilisation as we knew it.' There was a need for the recognition that workers and management had a common interest, in which workers could recognise

> that their factory had become for them not merely a place in which to earn a living, but a stabilising force around which they could develop satisfactory lives ... That sense of common interest ... could be more readily developed in small towns than in the less personal, more materialistic atmosphere of a large city. It was the strongest of practical arguments in favour of industrial decentralisation ... In this country we should be able — with our deep religious sense and our acceptance of Christian teaching, and because our entry into industrial organisation had been so delayed — to produce a better kind of industrial organisation than had developed elsewhere, and maybe show some more powerful nations a way out of their social problems.[94]

This use of inclusive rhetoric was — shorn of its religious overtones — to be a recurring theme of his period as Taoiseach, especially during the difficult industrial relations period of 1964–65. It was accompanied now by a fresh directing of energy towards the west in general and the Gaeltacht in particular. For Lemass the potential gain in output would have been enhanced by the foreseeable electoral popularity of the strategy. The Undeveloped Areas Act[95] was completed and passed and put under the wing of the young parliamentary secretary Jack Lynch, who was entitled to attend Government meetings at which questions of western development were being discussed and who was to be given an office in the Department of Industry and Commerce. This was not, however, to be simply a hand-out: 'the West was expected to repay the nation for the exceptional measures which were being undertaken for its development by a wholehearted effort to expand its contribution to the pool of national wealth.'[96]

Although important in themselves, initiatives like these were secondary to the main task of getting the economy moving again. This was an area in which Lemass was not short of advice. Along with the IDA he had inherited from his predecessor the report known as the IBEC Report, compiled between June 1951 and June 1952 by the American IBEC Technical Services Corporation. The report's authors noted the paradox that Ireland was 'progressing best in the field where it carries the greatest handicaps, and least in the one in which it has, seemingly, the greatest natural advantages.'[97] It came down strongly against protection and mirrored conventional wisdom in its support for agricultural expansion. It also pointed with particular emphasis to the low levels of productivity in industry. In one of its more sweeping statements it drew a picture of political culture that was as powerful a critique of de Valera's vision as it was of Costello's Government, which had commissioned it.

> Paradoxically, along with this actively voiced ambition for economic betterment, there runs an undercurrent of pessimism or lack of confidence in the prospects of achieving the pronounced aim. The talk is of economic expansion, but the action of government, business and labour alike is too often along the lines of consolidating present positions rather than of accepting the hazards inherent in changed practices upon which expansion depends. There are few evidences of boldness or assurance in economic behaviour to give substance to expressed economic aims. In fact, the declarations of expansive purpose are frequently qualified by expressions of a conflicting, anti-materialist philosophy, or an asceticism that opposes material aspirations to spiritual goals, and hence writes down the former as unworthy.[98]

Although he had considerable reservations about the American-inspired predilection for freer trade embodied in the report,[99] Lemass took to heart at least some of its analysis, quoting part of it, without attribution, almost verbatim in a speech to the Dublin Chamber of Commerce in October 1952. The response of the business community was less wholehearted, but Lemass offered them little comfort. He rejected their suggestions that the country's economic needs might best be discussed by a commission that would sit in private, arguing that there would be 'little public confidence' in such a response.[100]

The British Empire, or at least its representative in Dublin, took a keen interest in what Lemass was up to. Its ambassador, W. C. Hankinson, in a despatch that typically blended analysis with condescension, noted 'a marked expansion in State-aided or sponsored enterprise.' It went on:

> National pride and strategic considerations have probably been the main if silent inspiration. For it is clear that there must be an early limit to the industrial expansion of a country with a population of less than 3 million and a relatively low standard of living, unless it has highly specialised products to offer on the world market at highly

competitive rates. On neither of these counts does the Irish Republic qualify as yet.[101]

The expansion to which the British diplomats were drawing London's attention was indeed forceful. Bord na Móna had been established in 1946, and further development was put in train after Lemass returned to power. Irish Steel — in an industry whose growth benefited hugely from the memory of the supply difficulties encountered during the war — was soaking up investment, no doubt to the chagrin of the Department of Finance, which had vetoed Lemass's proposal to acquire it when it was first broached in 1947.[102] Even the ranks of Tuscany could not, at this stage, forbear to cheer. The *Irish Times,* one of Lemass's fiercest critics on occasion, suggested that 'if Mr. de Valera is the architect of modern Ireland, then Mr. Lemass is indisputably the engineer, the contractor, and the foreman, rolled into one.'[103]

The Shannon Free Airport Development Company, however, was (with Irish Steel) one of the enterprises closest to Lemass's heart. His vision of Ireland linked, through Shannon, to the United States and the rest of the world was a powerful and compelling one and prompted some of his most imaginative decisions.

In July 1945, for instance, there were considerable differences of opinion about the likely future of transatlantic air travel; in particular, it was unclear whether it would be based on the flying-boat or the ordinary long-haul aeroplane. R. C. Ferguson in the Department of Industry and Commerce, who had made a study of the options, went to see Lemass and told him that the Americans probably did know but wouldn't say; the British probably didn't know. His advice was to wait for a year before committing the department either to a new runway at Rineanna or to a flying-boat dock. Lemass thought for a moment and then said: 'Build both — then we can't lose.' The supplementary estimate for the runway went through on the nod at the end of a busy day: Lemass found a gap in the Dáil business and seized his chance. The flying-boat dock was built but never drained; it is still there.[104]

Shannon's success was based in part on a close relationship between Lemass and Brendan O'Regan.[105] In 1942 O'Regan had been working in the Falls Hotel in Ennistimon, where the visitors would have included senior civil servants and other Dublin notables. Through these connections he was invited to Dublin in the winter of 1942 to become involved in the management of the Stephen's Green Club. The airport manager in Foynes knew that there was an intention to set up a restaurant there and contacted T. J. O'Driscoll to suggest that he look at 'a young man from Sixmilebridge.' The young man was Brendan O'Regan, later to become chairman of Bord Fáilte after O'Driscoll had become director-general of that body. The idea had originally come from de Valera, who had seen the

Imperial Airways set-up at Foynes and had come to the not unsurprising conclusion that Ireland should do something similar on its own account. When land-based transatlantic air services were moved to Rineanna, O'Regan was for a time running both the original establishment at Foynes and the new one on the other side of the Shannon. Lemass used to joke afterwards that when he brought TDs down by air to see the developments at Shannon he always instructed the pilot to fly directly over the Foynes establishment so that it would be invisible to those inside the plane, thus avoiding the possibility that they would ask awkward questions about two buildings apparently fulfilling the same function on different sides of the Shannon.

There was no board between O'Regan and the civil service; and Ferguson in Industry and Commerce, who oversaw the drafting of the contract, thought it would never get through Finance, because of the provision that allocated O'Regan a specific share of the profits of the organisation. But Finance, in the end, did not demur.

The importance of Shannon for Lemass was that it was 'a development which would prevent us from being cut off from the rest of the world.'[106] His desire to be part of that larger world was emphatically underlined in the autumn of 1953 when he visited Canada and the United States to preside at the formal opening of the offices of the Irish Export Promotion Board, later Córas Tráchtála. The Department of Finance apparently thought that his visit was not really necessary,[107] but this was hardly enough to dissuade him. His mission was threefold: to make a case for American aid; to explore possibilities for developing exports to North America; and, equally importantly, to develop avenues for North American investment. Ireland, he pointedly told a New York audience, would now permit a 'limited investment' of external capital in order to increase the production capacity of industry. The country offered American investors everything they could desire: a good geographical location, a plentiful supply of labour, freedom to repatriate profits, and safety from political upheaval.[108] The Control of Manufactures Acts were not so much as mentioned, and there can be little doubt that this was the point at which Lemass's support for an export-driven industrial policy became positive and not merely hortatory. 'I've just written a policy for the party,' he cheerfully informed the chairman and chief executive of Córas Tráchtála, T. J. O'Driscoll, in New York.[109] If American capital took up the offer it would undoubtedly create problems; but they were problems that were easier to solve than those caused by an investment famine.

It was a visit that was also notable for the emphasis Lemass placed on partition. This may in part have been expected of him, given his stature and the expectations of Irish America, and he played the part with a will. There were, however, increasing, though subtle, differences of emphasis between him and de Valera on the issue; in particular, hints that American help on partition would evoke a positive response from Ireland were set in an internationalist framework that de Valera would have been slow to adopt.

> So long as Ireland is divided and governed in a manner which is contrary to the wishes of the vast majority of its people, their first aim will continue to be the winning of their freedom. It is only when that cause of internal weakness has been removed that Ireland will be free to consider how it can play a more effective part in promoting international co-operation ... To a far greater extent than ever before the fate of the world rests in American hands, and we for our part would not wish it differently.[110]

This lightly coded message concealed a disagreement between de Valera and Lemass that had, if anything, been gathering momentum over the years. In effect there had been a role reversal: Lemass, who as a young firebrand had proposed unsuccessfully to Fianna Fáil in 1931 that Ireland withdraw from the League of Nations when they assumed power, was now a nascent internationalist; his party leader, whose rise to international stature had been enhanced by his presidency of the pre-war League of Nations, had become disillusioned by his international experiences and was erecting emotional barriers against further supranational experimentation. Opening the Dáil debate on Ireland's application to join the United Nations in 1946, de Valera had damned the concept with faint praise. 'In the circumstances, although it is impossible to be enthusiastic, I think we have a duty as a member of the world community to do our share.'[111] From then on he occupied a no-man's land between disillusion and apathy. He told the Council of Europe in 1949:

> For seven and three-quarter centuries we have fought to preserve our own national being and prevent it from being destroyed, submerged or absorbed by a larger political entity. It must be obvious that it would be extremely difficult now to induce our people to reverse suddenly the whole current of their thought and history, and voluntarily to give up or seriously endanger their identity, towards the preservation of which such glorious devotion has been shown and such sacrifice endured.[112]

He derived a certain grim satisfaction, he told one British diplomat, from 'scoring off European federalists' by telling them that Ireland had only recently managed to extract itself from a much smaller combine; and his antipathy towards federalists was increased by his realisation that most of them found the issue of Irish partition 'irrelevant'.[113] On the eve of Lemass's departure to North America he was, in private, even more lugubrious. 'Mention of the United Nations', a British embassy official in Dublin reported, 'led Mr. de Valera to remark that he was no longer much interested in the Republic's becoming a member of the United Nations. He thought indeed that had she been admitted years ago she would probably have walked out before now.'[114]

When Lemass met the US Secretary of State, John Foster Dulles, he raised only one question: Ireland's application for membership of the United Nations.[115] When he met Eisenhower on 1 October he was more forthcoming, and the brief discussion ranged widely over economic policies, trade, and tariffs.[116] The most successful outcome of Lemass's visit, however, was one he was not destined to enjoy: an agreement under the US scheme for post-war aid to Europe. A new agreement was in fact prepared and passed by Congress and entered into force on 16 February 1955. Lemass, by then returned to the opposition benches, was forced to watch his successors spend the money. It would indeed have been exceptionally useful in the latter half of the 1951–54 Government's term of office.

Whatever plans Lemass may have had for kick-starting the economy again during this period were additionally frustrated, however, not only by the Government's reliance on the independent deputies but by a deepening recession and a balance of payments crisis, which led the Minister for Finance, Seán MacEntee, to introduce in 1952 the most stringent budget since the war — a decision for which he was warmly praised, as he handed over the reins of office to his successor in 1954, by no less an authority than T. K. Whitaker.[117] The budget had a seismic effect within Fianna Fáil. A number of people left the party in disgust, but some of the Dublin membership instead transferred their allegiance to the Dublin South-Central constituency, in the belief that Lemass represented the authentic voice of Fianna Fáil, which would, in time, win out.[118]

The circumstances surrounding the Government debates on that budget and its accompanying fiscal strategy have been depicted as a battle between MacEntee and Lemass, which MacEntee won,[119] and in a sense this is true. It needs to be qualified, however, in the light of the fact that Lemass too was warning insistently about the exhaustion of the country's financial reserves throughout 1951 and 1952[120] and pounding away at the need to increase production. The industrial recovery that followed the 1952 depression prompted a Lemass counter-attack, which focused on the need for renewed capital investment and, in particular, the creation of a national development fund that would oversee the inauguration of a large number of infrastructural projects at a cost of some £10 million.[121] MacEntee and Finance were by now on the retreat, as de Valera sided — somewhat guardedly — with Lemass. Frustrated by his enforced stay in Utrecht, the Taoiseach wrote encouragingly to the Tánaiste:

> The Balance of Payments position may turn out as I remember you told me you believed it would. The reaction to a possible £11 million is satisfactory. Finance appears to think we shall be down on the Budget. You are more optimistic, I know.[122]

It was too late. The recovery in employment had been sectoral in a way that disadvantaged traditional Fianna Fáil supporters, notably in the building trade, which had been heavily affected by the cut-backs in public expenditure, and the national development fund never got off the ground. In early 1954 it was announced that four of the five industrial alcohol factories would cease production when their stocks were exhausted,[123] and Fianna Fáil lost two by-elections in March. But even as an election hove into sight, Lemass was not inclined to trim his sails. If anything, he let his feelings show in a number of terse speeches that were not conspicuous for their desire to win friends and influence people.

In November 1953 he warned that the Government intended to review industrial efficiency and the current effects of protective tariffs; it was clear that he was not referring to their supposed beneficial effects.[124] He criticised farmers for 'relying on State aid and political agitation,'[125] the 'large merchant class' who were interested only in importing goods,[126] and industrialists who used protection as a cover for 'unduly high production costs.'[127] And he argued that 'a far more extensive development of Irish industry can be secured by means of private business enterprise than by any system of socialised industry.'[128] This did not mean that he had ceased to be an interventionist: it was simply a question of which form of intervention he believed to be most effective. His preferred policy in this area, however, was that industry should put its own house in order voluntarily. He was warning that the Government was being pressed to take more powers to knock heads together and that the operation of industry was no longer, and never again would be, the exclusive concern of its owners.

Further action on the industrial policy front was precluded by the 1954 election, which became unavoidable after de Valera's options were closed off by the loss of two by-elections, in Cork and Louth, in March 1954. The election was called for May; Fianna Fáil lost, and returned to opposition for the second time in six years.

THE ORGANISATION MAN

Lemass went into opposition unaware of one honour paid to him by the new Government: he was one of the few opposition politicians in 1954–57 to have his speeches filed by the Government Information Bureau. If he had known, his traditionally wolfish smile would have flickered for no longer than a moment; there were more urgent matters on the agenda. The lessons of 1948–51 had finally been learnt. Next time around, Fianna Fáil needed both policies and organisation to win back office. Lemass was given the job of providing the former and, despite internal opposition, increasingly arrogated to himself the latter.

Reappointed a joint honorary secretary of the party, he fell to his multifarious tasks with an energy he was rarely, if ever, to replicate. He was a combination of organiser, pacifier, strategist, and one-man research bureau. The first thing to attract his attention internally was the party's central organisation. In June 1954 he proposed the establishment of an Executive Committee, which would consist of the party leader, five deputies nominated by the leader, and five TDs elected by the parliamentary party who had not previously held ministerial office.[129] This tightly structured model did not survive the suspicions of some of the party's senior members, who succeeded in securing membership for all former ministers who had not otherwise been appointed; but the principle of election by the parliamentary party remained.

Later in the year Lemass was allocated an annual payment of £500 in expenses as director of organisation[130] (£7,850 in 1997 terms), by which time the work of reorganisation had been well established throughout the country. He hand-picked an Organisation Committee, whose membership by 1957 comprised Kevin Boland, Stephen Ennis, Charles Haughey, Kieran Kenny, Noel Lemass, Brian Lenihan, Thomas O'Connor, Alec O'Shea, and Eoin Ryan.[131] He instituted a ten-shilling (50p) registration fee for each cumann and ordained that the party be reorganised locally on the basis of one cumann for every 2,500 to 3,000 electors.[132] By the end of 1955 the number of registered cumainn had reached 1,787, a figure that had not been exceeded for twenty years and was not to be exceeded again for as long as Lemass remained active in politics.

The party's two handbooks, *Bealach Bua* and *Córas Bua,* had also been prepared and distributed to the faithful.[133] Lemass's attention to detail is evident. He advised cumann members to go out in pairs to check the electoral register, marking their cards carefully.

> It is important that the canvassers should make clear that this visit has no other purpose. Subscriptions should not be elicited or accepted. Voters, even if obviously sympathetic, should not be invited to become Cumann members unless they suggest it on their own initiative ... Canvassers should make a note of the trend of public opinion on such matters as prices, taxes and employment, and particularly of comments bearing on the activities and policies of Fianna Fáil, or other parties, and report to their Cumann ... Cumann reports are to be forwarded to the Comhairle Dáilcheantair and the Head Office.[134]

He was prepared to say in public what he said in private. Fianna Fáil, he warned, had tended to become 'too much of an election machine' and was not fully living up to its responsibilities as a national organisation. Even in respect of its election campaign it was less efficient in some constituencies than it should have been.[135] He did not mind stepping on toes when it was necessary, and some toes were more inviting than others. In 1957, for instance, he shoehorned the young Brian Lenihan — who had stood unsuccessfully in Longford-Westmeath in 1954 — into the Roscommon constituency, which Gerry Boland had represented since 1923 and which had not returned two Fianna Fáil TDs since 1948. The patriarch was finally to be dethroned by Lenihan in 1961.

As his history within the party shows, Lemass was not always universally popular with his fellow-TDs, but the Fianna Fáil rank and file always had a high regard for him. On the occasions on which he stood for election to the 'Committee of Fifteen' (elected as part of the National Executive by the delegates to the ardfheis) he was generally among the first three and was the first elected on three occasions.[136]

His tasks involved defusing potentially embarrassing conflicts, and the names of the younger Fianna Fáil deputies who were to figure largely in his own Government and the subsequent history of the party begin to appear. On one occasion he had to persuade George Colley not to resign as a cumann secretary and even, apparently, from the entire organisation after Colley had written to him to complain that a relative of one of the candidates in Dublin North-East 'had some time ago attempted by bribery to have this particular candidate elected to a public position.' By remaining in his position, he told Lemass, he would be 'condoning bribery and corruption in public life.'[137] The absence of a reply in the file, coupled with Colley's decision not to resign, indicates that this was one of the occasions on which Lemass typically preferred to sort out matters informally.

Charles Haughey, Brian Lenihan and Eoin Ryan, along with Kevin Boland, were all involved at various levels in the intensive reorganisation of the party that he inaugurated and that was accompanied by a patent spirit of renewal. Haughey, for instance, told Lemass in his ebullient report as secretary of the Dublin North-East Dáilcheantar that 'the self-seeker will soon see that Fianna Fáil is an organisation of service and not a ladder for his ambition and he will soon steal away.'[138]

Lemass developed a renewed and unexpected interest in agriculture. This was in marked contrast, if not in direct opposition, to his views of some three years earlier, when he had stated categorically that 'the expansion of the heavier industries, which gave employment to adult male workers, was essential if we are to develop in this country the variety of occupations which we need to check emigration.'[139] He was now arguing that

> in recent years ... I was forced to the conclusion that the future growth of industry was not likely to be very extensive, so long as agricultural productivity problems remained unsolved. The key to future industrial expansion lies in agricultural policy, in the maximum development of agriculture. If the Report of the Commission [on Emigration] does no more than bring about a realisation of that

situation by Irish people and by their legislators, it will have been worth all the time spent in its preparation. Taking the emphasis off industrial expansion and putting it on agriculture may not be a very welcome idea in Irish towns, which look to the establishment of a factory as the answer to all their problems, or to urban employed workers who may visualise themselves being drafted to agricultural work. The point is that industrial progress must stop in any case unless agricultural progress begins.[140]

The context makes clear the reason for this fresh emphasis. It was spurred by the report of the Commission on Emigration and Other Population Problems, chaired by J. P. Beddy, which had been set up by the inter-party Government in April 1948. The commission reported in March 1954, and the report was published in July 1954. It included a minority report by the Bishop of Cork, Dr Cornelius Lucey, in which he charged that 'the neglect of agriculture for industry in recent decades is not only socially and morally indefensible but demographically unjustifiable as well.'[141]

Emigration was the acid test of Government policies for Lemass, and the inability of many Governments with which he was associated to effect any more than a temporary reduction was a permanent reminder of an uncompleted task. His frustration was not in any way alleviated by the surprising information, garnered as the result of private studies by Fianna Fáil, that up to half of those who were emigrating were doing so because they wanted to rather than because they were economically obliged to. And his concern about and sensitivity to this issue in particular was reinforced by the occasionally sentimental treatment of the problem, which he regarded as part of the panoply of stage-Irishry to which he was implacably opposed. Many years later, at a social get-together between politicians and journalists after a Council of Europe meeting in Strasbourg in 1966, he reacted frostily to the song 'Lough Swilly' — whose theme is emigration from Donegal — sung by Michael Mills, then political correspondent of the *Irish Press*. Meeting Mills the following morning, he described it to him as a 'dirge'.[142]

The strength of Lemass's emotional commitment to the ending of emigration is indeed one of the few factors that can readily explain the way in which he wavered between a total commitment to industry and a more traditional reliance on agricultural expansion. The latter policy had of course the additional advantage of being more in tune with traditional Fianna Fáil policy and of assuaging his critics, particularly inside the party.

His establishment of Comh-Chomhairle Átha Cliath within Fianna Fáil was designed both to offset the perceived weakening of support in the capital and to provide an intellectual stimulus to the business of policy formation. This particular group became a public foil for the private arguments on policy matters within the parliamentary party while Lemass was in opposition. Lemass's close friends Dave McIlvenna and Joseph Griffin were involved in much of the planning for the organisation, and its inaugural meeting in January 1955 was the occasion for a typically Lemassian overview of the country and its economic problems.

Could we direct savings to home industry? Were our social services inadequate, or were they overstraining the economy? Had the system of proportional representation justified itself? Adopting the interrogative mode to soften the potentially controversial nature of his remarks, he went on to look back over the previous twenty-five years of the country's economic progress — all but six of which had been under Fianna Fáil Governments — and to express his disappointment that economic development still seemed to require a great deal of Government stimulus. He identified five reasons why this should be so, including early political opposition to Fianna Fáil, the effect of history on Irish self-confidence and initiative, the lack of sympathy among business leaders as a class with the national struggle, and the attitude of banks and investors in general.

Less expected was his view that Fianna Fáil policy was, in one important respect, now counterproductive. 'It might be that part of the answer lay in the restrictions which were, for good reason, placed on the participation of foreign capital in Irish industrial expansion, when the industrial drive was first launched. It was now an open question whether these restrictions needed to be retained any longer, in their present form.'[143]

For all its qualifications, this statement plainly represented the opening shots in a campaign aimed at modification of the Control of Manufactures Acts. His change of policy, in common with that policy's original elaboration, was innocent of any detailed rationale, and indeed none seems to have been demanded: the discussion after the early meetings of the Comh-Chomhairle was not, he thought, 'of a very high standard.'[144] He was plainly influenced, however, by figures relating to outward investment flows. In 1953 the external investments of commercial banks had increased by £7.4 million and private investment abroad by £5.1 million, while the external holdings of the Central Bank had increased by £5.2 million.[145]

One significant omission from the speech was any substantial reference to the tariff policy. It was still part of received wisdom in the party that this policy had contributed in an essential way to the party's electoral growth and continuing popularity, and it might have been difficult to address this issue without running the risk of exciting too many contrary opinions.

The tone of the criticisms from within the party can be gauged from an exchange between Lemass and MacEntee on fiscal strategy that had taken place in the context of devising the party's approach to the coalition Government's budget in 1955. Fianna Fáil had actually decided not to vote against the budget proposals,[146] and Lemass subsequently sent a lengthy memorandum on budgetary policy to Seán MacEntee, whose pungent annotations[147] made their disagreements abundantly clear. MacEntee's star may have been in decline, but within the parliamentary party he was still a doughty opponent.

Lemass argued that Fianna Fáil should not hesitate to propose increased expenditure where the advantages more than counterbalanced the disadvantages; MacEntee saw this as 'politically a Godsend to Fine Gael.' Lemass praised income and inheritance taxes; MacEntee viewed them as 'fettering all ambition, and energy, and enterprise' and argued for their reduction. Lemass supported the concept of PAYE; MacEntee saw it as inflationary. Lemass suggested that the party should positively consider having a budget deficit as long as it was not a substantial one; MacEntee commented sardonically, 'Many a mickle makes a muckle.'

MacEntee in particular queried Lemass's use of the term 'full employment', which he considered had not been defined. His point was perhaps stronger than he knew. Although Lemass realised the political pulling power of the term, he was slow to define it and, when he did so, was careful to give himself plenty of room within which to manoeuvre. At the 1946 ardfheis he had argued that full employment itself meant that 'between 5% and 10% of the work force might be unemployed at any one time.'[148] This figure, which he used on the rare occasions that he used any figure at all, seems to have its origin in Colin Clark's book *The Conditions of Economic Progress,* an excerpt from which Lemass included with his 1940 memoradum to the Government on the controversial question of family allowances. 'At a time when the economic system is working at full pressure,' Clark had written, 'there generally remains somewhere between 5 and 10 per cent unemployed due to occupational maldistribution.'[149] By March 1957, in the middle of a general election campaign, even the 10 per cent figure had become unacceptable: 'one thing the nation cannot afford is to have 10% of the nation's productive capacity unemployed.'[150] In general, however, Lemass's enthusiasm for new ideas and plans was tempered by a political canniness that prevented him offering too many hostages to fortune in the shape of precise figures or targets.

The Clery's Ballroom speech

Lemass was to deliver his famous 'Clery's Ballroom speech' on full employment on 1 October 1955 but took the precaution of submitting it first, in the form of a memorandum, to the parliamentary party. The party was wary. From the context it appears that what most concerned them was an attack on the role of the banking system and an implication that native resources might not, after all, be sufficient to finance the industrial expansion that was necessary. The latter point in particular cut to the root of Fianna Fáil policy as it had existed since the nineteen-twenties. Eventually, after due consideration, the party decided 'that Mr. Lemass could speak in public in general terms on proposals set out in his memorandum, but that reference to the Central Bank should be omitted; it could be pointed out, however, that our resources are ample to finance agricultural and industrial development.'[151]

When the party — no doubt still strongly influenced by MacEntee — gave its heavily qualified approval for his endeavours, Lemass went ahead with his speech. His target was 100,000 new jobs in five years. The mechanics of his scheme were the result of some creative borrowing: he had heard of the 1954 Vanoni Plan for post-war reconstruction in Italy, had got a copy of it from the Italian embassy, and had done his best to adapt it to Irish conditions, with help from C. S. Andrews.[152]

In retrospect, it is easy to identify the problems inherent in this approach, particularly the simplistic assumption of a positive and dynamic relationship between increased production and increased employment and services. In fact, and especially as technological development accelerates, there can be an inverse relationship between productivity and employment. This apparent blind spot is all the more remarkable in the light of a comment Lemass made five years earlier in the Dáil, during an exchange of views about the proposed Industrial Development Authority. Free of collective Government responsibility at that time, more particularly in relation to agricultural policy, Lemass had argued passionately for the case of industry as the key to the future.

> If we are ever going to build up a national economy that can withstand the storms that are bound to arise in international trade, it has to be through industrial development. We spend a lot of time here discussing agriculture and the problems of agriculture. Nobody will deny the importance of agriculture to the nation now or in the future but, if we are ever going to end unemployment, it will not be through an expansion of agricultural employment alone; it will be through an expansion of industrial activity.[153]

Pressed on the question of the likely trend in agricultural employment, he agreed:

> Employment in agriculture could diminish even with considerable expansion in agricultural output.[154]

The question why he appeared to accept a link between increased productivity and increased unemployment in agriculture but assumed the opposite for industry five years later needs further analysis. The most likely explanation, however, is that at the beginning of the fifties the potential for increased mechanisation in agriculture, with concomitant employment losses, was more clearly foreseen, whereas the assumption in relation to industry — where technological development was not experiencing any quantum leaps — was that increased productivity would not of itself be enough to satisfy growing market demands and that increased employment would inevitably ensue as the domestic or export market expanded, even if not necessarily on a strictly proportional basis.

These arguments, however, were for the future. In the short term, the speech plainly aroused considerable controversy within Fianna Fáil. Inside a month he was replying to criticisms of it at a specially organised meeting in his own constituency.[155] No public criticisms had been made by any party member, so that they can be identified only by reading between the lines of his second speech.

Firstly he replied to suggestions from within the party that he had neglected agriculture and that he had been unclear about state investment. He defended himself in particular against the charge that his readiness to throw old ideas overboard was an admission of past inadequacies. It was not that Fianna Fáil had failed: it was simply that 'the original Fianna Fáil plan has not proved to be comprehensive enough to end unemployment and emigration and … has now to be extended.' In a later series of speeches he inserted into the public record the comments about the banking system that had been excised by the party from his Clery's Ballroom speech.

In the same month as the Clery's Ballroom speech he was hinting that if changed circumstances necessitated a breach in the parity relationship with sterling it would be considered, but the main problem lay with 'the attitude of mind of those who control capital.'[156] Increases in bank charges were 'a decision taken by bankers, solely in the interests of bankers,'[157] and 'there also existed among the people at home who controlled these things an unnatural preference for investment abroad.'[158] Such investment, he urged, should be made the subject of a special capital gains tax.[159] The banks, he alleged, had a low level of interest in national progress,[160] and the free outward movement of people from the country could not be checked unless the free outward movement of capital was checked first.[161]

If this was an attempt at a diversionary tactic, it failed, and his strong and positive stance was not, it appears, enough to satisfy his critics. By January of the following year he was returning to the fray, again at a Comh-Chomhairle meeting, with a 'Plan for National Recovery' in which he attempted — without, it must be said, much evident hope of success — to meet objections by some of his colleagues to his proposed methods of financing the programme. Everybody who was not unemployed, he argued, should play their part by reducing their personal consumption by about 5 per cent — voluntarily, by saving, or involuntarily, through tax — to make the resources available.[162] He was necessarily silent on the administrative mechanisms that might be devised to separate the voluntary sheep from the involuntary goats. In fact the speech appears to have been mainly a holding operation designed to protect the central elements of his plan against the withering attacks being directed at it from inside; he described it himself as reflecting 'ideas that are now being discussed within the party rather than a finalised programme.'[163] Only a couple of days earlier he had given to the parliamentary party an outline of 'certain short term proposals involving Government expenditure and retrenchment which he felt were required to deal with the grave immediate problem of unemployment.'[164]

His speech was also, however, calculated to mend his hand in relation to certain elements of the plans recently announced by Costello's Government, which had been accompanied by specific proposals for both industry and agriculture.[165] His recommendations for the improvement of the agricultural sector addressed an issue that had been conspicuous by its absence from his Clery's Ballroom speech; and his espousal of tax-free profits for exports, while it echoed speeches he had made as far back as 1948, was also an attempt to trump Costello's proposals in the same area.

The target of 100,000 jobs became a millstone around Lemass's neck — although it was substantially modified in his January 1956 speech — for the simple reason that it was rapidly reinterpreted as a political promise. That his enemies should do so was to be expected; but the positive side of such a development was that, inasmuch as it also attracted the enthusiastic adherence of the party faithful, it helped mightily in the psychological process of rebuilding morale.

Nothing, however, annoys a political party more than when another party tries to steal its clothes. Lemass's successor in Industry and Commerce, William Norton, visited the United States on a promotional tour early in 1956 and spoke about foreign investment in terms that closely mirrored Lemass's 1953 invitation to American industrialists. Lemass, however, was clearly unwilling to give carte blanche to his rival and riposted with a critical speech that bore evidence of tortured logic. Conscious of his 1953 speech, he indicated that foreign investment might be of assistance in some areas and even emphasised the fact that 'in present circumstances, agriculture and industry cannot generate new capital in sufficient volume to give the national economy the buoyancy it should have.'[166] Political considerations, however, now came to the fore, and he charged that the coalition were 'pushing the idea to the ridiculous extent of giving preference to foreigners over Irish enterprises with propositions of equal merit.'[167] Foreign capital was not the answer if it meant 'the *uncontrolled* transfer of profits to foreign shareholders' (emphasis added),[168] and foreign capital was desirable only where there were 'exceptional' technical or marketing problems that Irish industry could not solve for itself in the present stage of its development.[169]

In private the following year, and while still in opposition, he had abandoned all the qualifications with the exception of the one limiting foreign investment to firms geared for export. He wrote to Pádraic O'Halpin:

> I am now of the opinion that, in regard to future industrial expansion, we must start thinking in terms of attracting into this country large

external firms to establish export factories here, and frame our tax and other laws to encourage and facilitate this result. I cannot say the effort will succeed but I would prefer to make it before planning further state activity in the industrial field.[170]

In other speeches during this period the political factor in general, and his dislike for Norton in particular, bulked less large. Indeed he was not going out of his way to court powerful interests. While arguing against the total repeal of the Control of Manufactures Acts, he suggested that there might be a case for amending them.[171] Industrialists, he warned, had to cease thinking of tariffs as props to lean on and consider them instead as a form of aid given to them conditionally by the community.[172] Unless they shifted their emphasis from protection to efficient low-cost production there would be no prospect of an export trade or of creating the 15,000 jobs that were needed in non-agricultural occupations. 'There is a danger', he added acidly, 'that the Federation of Irish Manufacturers will become nothing more than a pressure group for the preservation of protection.'[173]

His view of intervention was now increasingly focused on the need to promote competition as an aid to efficiency, rather on the need to prevent it as an aid to employment. His experience, he revealed, had shown him how dangerous it was to the ordinary citizen when businessmen got the taste of easy profit. 'If an agreement exists between traders who should be in competition, it was an actual or potential menace to the public welfare.'[174] Protection was now patently failing to provide jobs; it was also, as he admitted by implication, operating to prevent competition.

These were the signs and portents of a new Lemass policy, but it represented such a radical break with the old one that it was to take several years, and a return to government, before its lineaments could be fully discerned. As it happened, things were already moving in that direction. Norton himself was suggesting a merger of the IDA, Industrial Credit Corporation, and An Foras Tionscal.[175] The ICC itself was recommending further amendments of the Control of Manufactures Acts, on the grounds that they were now largely superfluous,[176] and Córas Tráchtála was pushing the idea of tax concessions for investments of American origin.[177] Ironically, in all these initiatives the Department of Industry and Commerce was the most cautious and hesitant. Just as Lemass had developed a personal loyalty to many of the new captains of industry, such as it was, his department had developed an institutional one, which was to be sorely buffeted by the change of policy in the late nineteen-fifties and early sixties.

APERTURA AL NORTE

All this, however, was still in the future. Lemass's most striking policy initiative during this period was not in the area of economic policy but in relation to partition, and it took place in private. It was not an issue that, either as a minister between 1932 and 1948 or in opposition from 1948 to 1951, he had referred to in other than somewhat perfunctory and unremarkable terms. To do otherwise would patently have meant exploring an area that his party leader had made peculiarly his own. In 1954–57, however, he was to address this topic with unwonted enthusiasm. The fact that de Valera could not continue at the helm for ever was becoming increasingly evident, and this may partly explain this new staking out of the territory. It may also explain why Lemass's public speeches on some occasions re-stated traditional Fianna Fáil policy in particularly uncompromising terms. Throughout the 1948–57 period, in fact, the Fianna Fáil line on partition hardened visibly and can be seen as a natural reaction to the way in which Clann na Poblachta's more militant and radical republicanism was eating into the larger party's core vote. It was also in line with the creation of the all-party Anti-Partition League in 1949, in which Lemass had been named as Fianna Fáil substitute for de Valera.

Lemass made a number of uncompromising speeches on partition, which in a sense marked a final flourish of the old rhetoric. One of the starkest was to a Trinity College audience in January 1953, when he argued that the division of the country was absurd, that Ireland was historically the home of the Irish race and that, under 'a deep crust of prejudice and misunderstanding,' unionists were as Irish as we were. Partition had arisen out of British trickery; and no state could allow a disgruntled minority to vote itself out. The British politicians who had engineered it were thinking only of British interests and British policy and were happy to portray the Irish as 'a sort of European mob who get in each other's hair and cut each other's throats.'[178]

There was, however, an unspoken rationale for the strong tone of this speech. Ernest Blythe had been suggesting, in a series of letters to the *Irish Press,* that the Irish language was the cement of nationality and that until the undoing of the Anglicisation of the past century had been achieved it would be useless to seek an incentive to the ending of partition. Without attacking Blythe directly, Lemass was to use his TCD speech to re-state his party's traditional agenda forcefully and in a context that made clear his belief in the essential primacy of the political over the linguistic. Parenthetically it indicated a view that laying too much emphasis on the revival of Irish might be counterproductive in the whole partition debate.[179]

When, at the beginning of June 1954, Fianna Fáil was again consigned to opposition, the immediate effect was, as it had been in 1948, a hardening of the rhetoric. Feeling about partition, Lemass told a Dublin audience, was stronger than ever before: this was due to the renewed evidence of a desire to suppress national sentiment in the north-east 'and to the recent successes of other peoples, such as the Egyptians, in bringing an end to similar circumstances affecting their territories.'[180]

References to the 'national territory' were being increasingly replaced — or at least substantially amplified — by references to the unity of Irish people. Side by side with this was a new and growing emphasis on the economic rather than the constitutional aspects of partition. The rationale Lemass advanced for ending partition was now less frequently the undoing of an ancient wrong and more regularly something that made good economic sense. 'They had to find a way of ending partition so that the two sections of the Irish people could work in unison to end the economic and social problems persisting in both the twenty-six and the Six Counties.'[181] And again, 95,000 unemployed and 60,000 emigrants a year were not good arguments for the ending of partition: Fianna Fáil should not allow its faith in national unity to be weakened by the present economic depression but had to prove that it could be justified by practical results before they could carry conviction in the Six Counties.[182]

These public attitudes were being accompanied by a striking private re-evaluation of political priorities, which took place for Lemass between his Trinity and Helsinki speeches. Fianna Fáil had already established a standing committee on anti-partition matters and in January 1952 had written to units of the party looking for suggestions on partition policy. Responses were relatively few and slow to materialise. Matt Feehan, founding editor of the *Sunday Press* under Vivion de Valera, suggested bluntly that 'it is now apparent that the anti-Partition campaign has failed.'[183] One Dublin cumann proposed a campaign of civil disobedience in one or two areas of Northern Ireland with nationalist majorities contiguous to the border, 'to be controlled and directed by the Irish government' and associated with the non-payment of rents, non-recognition of Northern courts, and the involvement of the Irish army 'if necessary'.[184]

Lemass in effect was in charge of the standing committee's deliberations, and on 6 April 1955 he sent a remarkable document to de Valera, representing a draft of the committee's proposed final report. Its preamble was unexceptionable, stating the aim to 'induce in all sections of the Irish people the desire to restore the political unity of the country' and to 'secure throughout the world sympathy and support for the ending of partition.'[185] The body of the document, however, enumerated a number of policy steps that, in the amount of detail and in the political direction they embodied, involved substantial departures from existing priorities.

The first policy objective was 'to maintain and strengthen, wherever possible, all links with the Six County majority, especially economic and cultural links, to encourage contacts between the people of both areas in every field, and to demonstrate that widespread goodwill for the Six County majority can be fostered by such contacts.' The steps involved were spelled out: they included the elimination of impediments to the free movement of goods, persons and traffic and the establishment of joint authorities for transport, electricity, safety at sea, drainage programmes, civil defence, and tourism. On the political plane, the recommendations were equally specific:

— to keep constantly in mind, in relation to all aspects of twenty-six county internal policy and administration, the prospect of the termination of Partition and so to direct them as to avoid or minimise the practical problems that may arise when Partition is ended ...

— to urge on the people of the twenty-six counties the desirability of giving to the Six-County majority of such assurances as to their political and religious rights in a United Ireland as may reasonably be required, and as to the maintenance of local autonomy in respect of such matters as may be desired by them.

Finally, the committee recommended two organisational steps. The first, somewhat ambitiously, foresaw the establishment of a permanent council 'representative of all sections of Six County opinion and of all major parties in the twenty-six counties, to advise the Government on all matters relating to partition and to the conduct of international activities for its termination.' The second called for the establishment of an information service in the North 'to eliminate misunderstanding among the majority there and to promote the growth of goodwill for the Movement to restore Unity.'[186]

The significance of this document can be perceived principally in one of its most positive themes and two striking omissions. Its positive — if unrealistic — attitude to the Northern majority, coming in the wake of five years of anti-partition propaganda, certainly broke new ground. Its omission of any specific reference to Britain's role in the North is dramatic. And the absence of any reference whatever to the political and other problems experienced by the Northern nationalist minority is little short of astonishing.

De Valera's political antennae immediately sensed danger, particularly on the last point, and his response was immediate. He wrote to Lemass within twenty-four hours of receiving the draft report:

While a great deal of it does not seem open to serious objection, some of the steps are not so, and are of more than doubtful value. They would certainly give rise to very serious controversy and would possibly make confusion worse confounded amongst the Nationalists of the Six Counties. It seems to me that there are two things in question which must not be confused: (*a*) a party programme which can be published; (*b*) a carefully considered scheme in accordance with which conduct must be governed and action directed if the desired end is to be reached. This to be effective may have to be kept as a private norm. Publicity might in fact defeat the purpose of the scheme.[187]

De Valera's suggestion was that the report should be considered by the party's Central Committee and that decisions should be taken there before sending it to the National Executive. In effect, the report seems to have been shelved. Lemass's enthusiasm appears to have subsided at this point, but, in a parting shot, he pointed to the need to end the 'immorality and absurdity' of partition so that 'the two sections of the Irish people could work in unison to end the economic and social problems persisting in both the 26 and the Six Counties.'[188]

The report, though not destined to become party policy, nevertheless marks a decisive point in the evolution of Lemass's strategy on the North. From here on, references to the immorality of partition were to be infrequent, while references to the economic advantages of unity were to become commonplace. He maintained, however, the aspect of de Valera's policy that saw getting international support as essential. This was evident the following year, when he told an interparliamentary meeting in Helsinki that Ireland was suffering from 'an invasion of her territorial integrity and sovereignty, and from external interference in her affairs.'

> We do not ask for much more from Britain than that she will leave us alone to work on these problems, that she will accept and declare her acceptance of our right to territorial unity, to exercise our sovereignty over the whole of the national territory. We ask her to cease interference in our affairs, to cease fostering dissension among our people, so that we will have a fair chance of ending the evil consequences of her past aggression.[189]

The tradition in the Oireachtas is for the leader of the opposition to lead interparliamentary delegations. The fact that Lemass was in effect a substitute for the 73-year-old de Valera on this occasion may help to explain the tone of the speech, although there is no reason to suppose that he disagreed at any important level with its sentiments. The other evidence available from this period, however, suggests growing conviction on his part that this particular mode of expressing anti-partition policy was counterproductive.

His views about the political immorality of partition were acquiring an added dimension as he realised the size of the mountain to be climbed. This changing perspective was being marked to an ever-increasing extent by a new emphasis on communal reconciliation and 'breaking down the barriers of prejudice, suspicion and bigotry between the two sections of the people. Some said there was not such a way, but that attitude was a denial of Irish nationality, an admission of the rightness of the propaganda of the partitionists, and must be rejected.'[190]

Some of the seeds germinating in Lemass's shelved 1955 report were to sprout in another part of the forest. He made a speech in 1956 to the Belfast Newman Society, which was a *tour d'horizon* of a whole range of economic issues as they affected development north and south and veered towards the heterodox in its assertion that closer economic co-operation between the two parts of Ireland was desirable, irrespective of political considerations.[191] It was the most unambiguous statement yet of his desire to separate the political and economic aspects of partition, of his explicit belief that if the latter aspects were tackled with vigour the former would be easier of attainment, and perhaps of an implicit belief that for too long the political cart had been put before the economic horse. He emphasised the greater freedom enjoyed by Dublin in matters of economic policy and seized the opportunity offered by a recent conference of the all-Ireland trade union movement (which had taken place in Belfast) to identify areas of common concern where progress might be made.

The recrudescence of the IRA border campaign on 12 December 1956, with ten simultaneous attacks on British army and RUC establishments, threatened to cause serious problems within the Fianna Fáil parliamentary party. The atmosphere was particularly tense after the unsuccessful IRA raid on the RUC barracks at Brookeborough, County Fermanagh, on New Year's Day 1957, in which Fergal O'Hanlon and Seán South died. South's funeral in Limerick on 5 January 1957 was a massive affair, with the whole-hearted participation of a number of clergy and a vast crowd of sympathisers.

De Valera called a meeting of the parliamentary party for 15 January, evidently with the purpose of holding the line. The meeting, after a long discussion on the North, finally agreed unanimously:

> There can be no armed force here except under the control and direction of the Government. The meeting also considered the feasibility of the use of force by any future government as a means of solving the Partition problem and while no definite decision was taken, the views expressed indicated that the employment of force at any time in the foreseeable future would be undesirable and likely to be futile.[192]

The tensions underlying this agreement are evident in the statement that 'no definite decision' was taken on any use of force by a future Government. They were even more evident at the meeting. According to one participant, at a critical juncture one TD suggested that peaceful methods had failed. Lemass, in a quite untypical display of emotion, erupted. The problem with peaceful methods, he told the meeting with all the emphasis at his command, was that they had not been tried. Every time there was the prospect of some advance in North-South relations, the IRA surfaced to blow it out of the water.[193]

Lemass's intervention, both in its form and in its timing, undoubtedly helped de Valera significantly in his task of stiffening the resolve of the parliamentary party at a difficult time. Equally importantly, it laid down a marker for at least part of the policy he was to adopt as Taoiseach. For the time being, however, the whole area of Northern policy was one that was approached extremely gingerly by Fianna Fáil, not only because of de Valera's advancing years and failing health but because of the continuance of the IRA campaign, which was not finally abandoned until 1962.

THE ECONOMIC PROGRAMME

As the North retreated into the background again and the inter-party Government began to wind down, the economy again assumed pride of place. One new factor in the whole equation was the reunification of the trade union movement, which was to take place formally on 12 January 1956, and it was one to which Lemass, given his own background, could not remain insensible. At the end of 1955 the provisional United Trade Union Movement made its own bid for recognition as part of the social partnership with a document *Planning for Full Employment*, prepared for a special delegate meeting on 3 December 1956.

The title alone might have been especially designed to appeal to Lemass's proclivities. In the event, his response — possibly conditioned by the imminence of the general election — was curiously indecisive and even contradictory. In a speech commenting on the document six weeks later he scattered praise and criticism alike. He welcomed the unions' support for the idea that the state should run a budget surplus for capital programmes but criticised them for their silence on taxation, on restrictive practices, on wages, and on productivity, which had 'created doubts about the bona fides of the whole production.' If their attitude was, as he alleged, 'vague and ambiguous,' his own was equally ambiguous in at least one respect: in spite of the doubts he had voiced about the bona fides of 'the whole production' he for his part was 'prepared to accept the good faith of the men who prepared it.'[194]

This speech, however, marks in a particularly forceful way the fact that Lemass had at last broken loose from the political fetters that had been placed on him within the parliamentary party by MacEntee and others. It was to all intents and purposes a mini-manifesto. It promised amendments of the Control of Manufactures Acts; the abolition of the coalition Government's import levies; gearing industry for export, 'even to the extent of leaving the home market temporarily short of supplies'; the provision of £60 million in new capital investment, 'the majority from current income' (i.e. with the balance to be found from borrowing); the amalgamation of smaller industrial concerns; the introduction of the joint industrial councils whose virtues he had been preaching since 1947; and dragging all farms up to the level of the most profitable. It would be a hard, tough road, but 'the world does not owe us a livelihood on our terms.'

The inter-party Government brought down the price of tea five days before the 1957 election, but to no avail: the electorate swung to Fianna Fáil, which won exactly half the seats in the Dáil. This in effect gave them a working majority, as the four Sinn Féin candidates who had been elected were precluded by their own party policy from taking their seats. De Valera, at seventy-five, had in effect formed his first majority Government since 1944, and Fianna Fáil, although they were not to know it, were emerging from the political wilderness for a second sixteen-year term.

Éamon de Valera's last Government was, in all respects but one, an ideological carbon copy of the one he had formed some six years earlier. The difference was MacEntee's departure from Finance to Health, at Lemass's insistence.[195] Lemass is also thought to have been the moving force behind Jim Ryan's elevation to the seat vacated by MacEntee.[196] Ryan had for years been one of his closest friends in a party in which he had few enough people to match this description. Gerry Boland had been replaced by his son Kevin, but although this was evidently a generational shift it hardly represented an ideological one. Neil Blaney and Jack Lynch were the only other representatives of the younger generation: Blaney, at forty, was the stripling of the group, twelve years younger than Lynch and the only one of Lemass's ginger group to be rewarded with ministerial office at this time.

While Lemass waited for de Valera to make up his mind, there was plenty of work to do. The core of his project was to be the Programme for Economic Expansion, a blend of the ideas he had been canvassing in speeches before the 1957 election and those articulated by a group of public servants under the chairmanship of T. K. Whitaker, Secretary of the Department of Finance.

Whitaker had been appointed secretary in May 1956 by Gerard Sweetman of Fine Gael, coincidentally three days after reading a paper to the Statistical and Social Inquiry Society in which he recommended that increases in national output be devoted to industrial plants and factories, that savings be increased and used as productively as possible, and that decreasing taxes and adopting a more liberal attitude towards profit-making would enhance the possibility of achieving these objectives. Whitaker's career in the public service had been little short of meteoric. He took first place in the clerical officer examination in 1934, first place again in the executive officer examination in 1935, and became an assistant inspector of taxes in 1937 and an administrative officer in 1938. In twenty-two years he had gone from the bottom of the ladder to the top.

His exceptional ability was noted by the British, who described him in 1963 as 'brilliantly able, but with a quiet and unassuming but pleasant manner.'[197] His work in Finance had included a period as personal adviser on monetary policy to Frank Aiken when the latter was Minister for Finance in 1945.[198] This evidently did not stand against him, and he was preferred over the claims of Sarsfield Hogan, who had also had a model career in Finance, and more seniority. Two explanations were current at the time for Hogan's failure to achieve promotion. The more malicious suggested that it was related to the recent exploits of his son Paul, who had taken one of the Hugh Lane paintings from the National Gallery in London to draw public attention to Ireland's claim to the Lane Bequest. The more orthodox, and more likely, explanation was that Hogan's undisguised passion for rugby had contributed to a somewhat distant relationship to the worlds of economics and high finance.

The idea of preparing a major plan for economic development was not, of course, new. Lemass's efforts of almost a decade earlier had run into the sand or been sabotaged by the electoral defeats of Fianna Fáil. A later attempt was made by Seán MacBride, who returned insistently to the theme throughout 1956, eventually preparing, at Costello's request, a detailed memorandum on the need for a ten-year plan that was presented to the Government in November 1956. Whitaker, who had been heartened by Lemass's speech of January 1957, began work on his own document in the same month.[199] It was almost a year before he brought it to his new minister, James Ryan. Entitled 'Has Ireland a Future?' it listed twenty-one proposals for change and posed a central psychological question that echoed a familiar theme of Lemass's: 'The Irish people ... are falling into a mood of despondency. After thirty five years of native government can it be, they are asking, that economic independence achieved with such sacrifice must wither away?'[200]

The economic indicators were certainly gloomy. Between 1955 and 1957 Ireland was the only country in the western world where the total volume of goods consumed had actually fallen. Between 1955 and 1958 two out of every five workers in the building industry lost their jobs. In 1957 unemployment had reached a record 78,000, and 54,000 men and women had emigrated.[201]

De Valera endorsed Whitaker's memorandum, claiming afterwards that it merely represented another articulation of what he and Fianna Fáil had been arguing for since 1926.[202] Whitaker, at least, was under no such illusion.

> I must say it was a very pleasant surprise when the Fianna Fáil government, committed so much to self-sufficiency and protection, abandoned it all so readily. There is no doubt that Lemass was the great moving dynamic spirit in all of this. There was grudging acquiescence, or recognition granted, that without Lemass's drive and also probably without de Valera's benevolent blessing, change would not have come about nearly as quickly.[203]

Lemass's delight at this development was unrestrained, and he remarked to his Government colleagues: 'I told you all these things. I put these ideas before you.'[204]

Now that the ball had been firmly placed in his hands at last, he was quick to run with it. The document Whitaker was authorised to prepare,

'Economic Development', was produced at speed and was delivered to the Government on 29 May 1958. Charles Murray of the Department of Finance was charged with drawing up a White Paper based on Whitaker's document, supervised by a four-member Government subcommittee headed by Lemass on 22 July. The membership of the committee was significant not only in that it excluded MacEntee, now Tánaiste and Minister for Health, but because it included, as well as James Ryan and Paddy Smith (Agriculture), Erskine Childers, whose department (Lands) was hardly central to its deliberations but who was becoming, and was to remain, a listening-post for de Valera.

The White Paper, entitled *Programme for Economic Expansion,* was published on 11 November 1958, eleven days before Whitaker's study, which was to become known (because of the colour of its cover) as the 'Grey Book'.

The differences between the two documents betrayed their different parentage. Where Whitaker had argued for intensive cattle production as the foundation of agricultural prosperity, the White Paper preferred not to abandon completely Fianna Fáil's traditional predilection for tillage. Another Fianna Fáil policy, the radical decentralisation of industry, ensured the omission of Whitaker's proposal for establishing new industries at or near large urban centres, despite Lemass's own doubts about his party's policy. Whitaker had proposed abandoning some agricultural price supports; the White Paper was not so specific.

There were differing opinions about the wisdom of establishing a nitrogenous fertiliser factory, and the argument rumbled on for years. As early as 1954 Lemass had promised that a new fertiliser factory 'would confer great benefits on a wide area of the midlands.'[205] While he was out of office the plans went into cold storage, but the disagreements were to persist into Lemass's years as Taoiseach. Whitaker thought that Ireland should exploit the worldwide slump in fertiliser prices; the Government called for the construction of a plant in Ireland and, on Lemass's proposal, authorised advance planning for a factory to be built at Blackwater Bog, County Offaly, four months before the publication of the White Paper.[206]

The White Paper indicated the Government's commitment to creating a statutory exports corporation, Córas Tráchtála. Most significantly of all, it indicated a hard-edged political commitment to a 2 per cent annual growth in GNP over each of the succeeding five years, whereas Whitaker's document was studiously vague about targets. It is not difficult to see, particularly in this final area of difference, the expression of Lemass's belief in the power of specific targets and ideals to motivate people at all levels.

Lemass and Ryan joined forces to support the idea that *Economic Development* should go out under Whitaker's name and overrrode MacEntee's objection. At least two factors were operating here. One of these was the political one: the fact that Whitaker had been appointed by Sweetman might be expected to draw the teeth of any Fine Gael attack. The point was made, somewhat decorously, by Lemass in the context of the growing convergence of economic policies between the two main parties.

> Publication as an anonymous government publication would give it political aspects which we did not want ... The association with the name of a non-political civil servant would help to get its acceptance over political boundaries ... It was a deliberate decision, part of our effort to get economic development away from party political tags.[207]

The other factor was, quite simply, the fruit of experience. Fianna Fáil, who had come into office in 1932 as suspicious of the civil service as they were of their political opponents, had come full circle. Jim Ryan suggested that 'the civil service never gets the credit it deserves.'[208]

Commentators generally were slow to pick up the significance of either document. The *Irish Press* bestowed praise in the sort of language that would have been expected from that source, but not until after the publication of the Grey Book;[209] the *Irish Independent* ignored it, and the *Irish Times* decided that it contained 'nothing basically new.'[210]

They were not alone. Neither Dáil nor Seanad discussed either document in any structured way. The Fianna Fáil parliamentary party's response was desultory, to say the least. That this was so was partly, no doubt, related to the fact that few parliamentarians, inside or outside Fianna Fáil, were interested in economic policy at the macro level. Lemass evidently did not feel that it was in his interests to encourage discussion on such issues in any case, although he took care to keep the party informed in a suitably opaque way. In January 1958 he made a 'general statement' to the parliamentary party on the prospects for further industrial expansion but declared that, because of the confidential nature of many industrial proposals being considered by his department at that time, he was unable to go into further detail on the matter.[211]

The first discussion by the parliamentary party took place in December 1958. Lemass himself was not present, and the discussion centred, astonishingly, on arterial drainage. A special session planned for January 1959 to discuss the document was never held; and the agricultural chapter, which appears to have been the only section to receive any detailed consideration, did not exercise the minds of the parliamentarians until March.[212] A decade later, John Healy of the *Irish Times* was to suggest that it was 'a myth to even think of a huddle of Fianna Fáil deputies solemnly considering the implications of the Whitaker Grey Paper ... The poor whores, most of them still don't know what GNP means and "indices" looks like a dirty word.'[213]

Lemass's own analysis was more complimentary to his colleagues, as might be expected.

The debate was more in the country than in the Dáil. There was no desire to have a Dáil debate on the fundamentals of planning because Opposition politicians did not want to contribute to the support of a Government document, and besides Government is always pressed for time in the Dáil.[214]

No matter how pressed they are for time in the Dáil, Governments can find time for anything they want to debate. Reading between the lines of Lemass's comment, it is easy to see not only pleasure at the fact that the Whitaker ploy had worked but a strong managerial style on the part of the politician who had made this topic peculiarly his own: Lemass was not going to allow his bone to be taken away from him.

He also started prodding public opinion in a closely packed series of speeches that served notice that change was on the way. He noted in February 1959 that there had been 'inhibitions and limitations' associated with what he described as the 'first stage of our industrial development programme, when under the stimulus of tariff protection production was expanding to meet home market needs only.'[215] It was as close as he came in public at this time to a *mea culpa*. Not that tariffs were being completely discounted: on one occasion towards the end of Lemass's period of office as minister he told a deputation from the clothing industry, led by Colm Barnes of Glen Abbey, that a particular import restriction they were asking for could not be granted because, under the terms of the 1938 Anglo-Irish Trade Agreement, the British government would have to be notified, and might object. To Barnes's surprise, the restriction was applied almost immediately. When he met Lemass some time later at a social function he enquired mildly how this had been possible. Lemass smiled enigmatically and replied succinctly: 'Necessity knows no law.'[216]

He was also beginning to take important public, as distinct from private, initiatives on Northern policy. In 1958 Lionel Booth TD proposed at a parliamentary party meeting that steps be taken 'to initiate discussions at a high level between the Government and Stormont to promote co-operation and close liaison between the two governments and all their departments, and to lay the foundation for maximum joint planning of agriculture and industry.'[217] De Valera warned that this was a matter 'on which we should move very carefully' and noted that there had been no response to previous offers.

Booth's suggestion was withdrawn from the parliamentary party as a result of de Valera's intervention, but Lemass was not so easily put off. Later the same month, in a speech to the Irish Association in Belfast, he drew attention to the 'remarkable' fact that recent economic agreements between North and South had been negotiated 'without any serious conflict with national sentiment or any pre-requirements of recognition or concessions of a political character.' He added:

A cold objective appraisal of the Irish economic scene must condemn the existing division of the country as a very considerable and unnecessary burden on its economic and social progress. Not the least part of that burden derives from the fact that the controversies to which it gives rise divert public attention from economic realities and prevent the development of a comprehensive policy for the improvement of conditions.[218]

A year later he returned to the same theme, outlining one of the basic elements of what would be his Northern policy:

The economic problems of the North East and the rest of the country had the same characteristics and would respond to the same remedies. By emphasising that, they could hope to break through the barriers of suspicion and distrust that divided our people. The approach to partition should be a positive one, emphasising not so much anti-partition as the securing of unity for their people. We have not yet pushed our national development to the point where it cannot be undone. If we do that, the other national problems, including the restoration of unity, will become far less intractable.[219]

DE VALERA: THE LAST ACT

Lemass's impatience by now was palpable. He began to organise weekly off-the-record briefing sessions with the political correspondents of the national newspapers; de Valera's retirement was among the subjects that frequently came up for mention.[220] He was a regular source of leaks — as was James Dillon, another leader-in-waiting — to Hector Legge, the editor of the *Sunday Independent*.[221] One outsider to witness Lemass's impatience was Margaret MacEntee, wife of his long-time Government opponent, who nevertheless fulfilled the role of occasional confidante to Lemass and indeed possibly to other Fianna Fáil ministers.[222] In one of a number of typically acerbic marginalia scribbled on his copy of Brian Farrell's ground-breaking work on Lemass, the old war-horse referred in passing to 'Lemass's tirade to Margaret against Dev.'[223] The personal closeness of the two political antagonists is underlined by the fact that Margaret could readily share this confidence with her husband, evidently without any feeling of disloyalty. MacEntee's reference is undated, and it is unclear whether it referred to a disagreement on policy matters or to the question of de Valera's retirement; either way, it indicated that the legendary Lemass self-composure could occasionally slip.

Another recipient of this otherwise deeply buried sense of impatience was the veteran republican Aodhagán O'Rahilly, who was particularly close to Frank Aiken and whose relationship with Lemass hinged in part on his involvement with Todd Andrews and Bord na Móna. O'Rahilly, who had carved out a highly successful business career for himself and was not directly involved in politics, recognised that he could say things to de Valera that others might have hesitated to express, and offered to go and put this point of view directly to de Valera. Lemass, somewhat surprised, agreed with this suggestion, and O'Rahilly subsequently put it into operation, although without evident success.[224]

If Lemass's impatience was becoming increasingly apparent, there was one other area in which he and de Valera were more evidently in agreement, even if they addressed the problem with slightly differing agendas. This was the question of proportional representation, which had been on Lemass's own agenda since at least 1955, when he made clear his preference for the 'straight' vote.[225] The question of electoral reform was becoming of increasing relevance to Fianna Fáil, as two defeats in the space of seven years indicated to them that their hold on the electorate under the present system, even with de Valera at the helm, was an increasingly shaky one.[226]

The parliamentary party subsequently set up a subcommittee on PR, and when its report was presented to the full parliamentary party in October 1958 it was Lemass who introduced the discussion, intimating that the committee had recommended 'reversion' (sic) to the single-member constituency and the straight vote. This evidence qualifies Farrell's suggestion that by 1959 'Lemass's energies were to be diverted from economic issues to de Valera's crusade against proportional representation.'[227] Farrell himself reports that Lemass shared what he describes as de Valera's preference for the alternative vote in single-seat constituencies, although it is not clear how such powerful support for this variation on PR should have failed to secure the agreement of the Government as a whole if Taoiseach and Tánaiste both favoured it. Lemass was also to return to the theme, with considerable emphasis, as Taoiseach, when, the evidence suggests, he had modified his position, preferring the alternative vote in single-member constituencies.

Lemass's most considered attempt to deal with the question of proportional representation in a public forum was his radio broadcast in June 1959, shortly before the referendum.[228] His argument, framed in somewhat populist terms, suggested a scenario in which there were three boys competing for the prize of an apple. 'In the case of one of the boys, if it was decided to award the prize, say, to the one who did best in an exam, do you think it would be fair to keep it from him because the two others failed to qualify?' This parable had an unusual origin. The previous month the editor of *Dublin Opinion,* C. E. Kelly, had published a full-page cartoon showing a teacher in front of a blackboard with three apples drawn on it and three boys of differing sizes standing beside it. Headlined 'The School Only Just Around the Corner',[229] the caption recorded the master as saying: 'Three boys, three apples ... Under PR each boy gets an apple ... Under the "straight vote" the biggest boy gets the lot.'[230]

Kelly had been director of broadcasting at Radio Éireann, a fact that caused no small amount of displeasure to Fianna Fáil, some of whose deputies even alleged in the Dáil that *Dublin Opinion* was being produced on Government time. At one stage Kelly found himself transferred out of Radio Éireann completely and to a less attractive job — Director of Savings — by a Fianna Fáil Government that would have been unaware of the fact that while he was satirising them he was usually voting for them as well.[231]

That Government's sensitivity to even the most innocuous forms of satire was evidenced in a particularly dramatic form by Lemass, who was shown the cartoon on the steps of Leinster House and — or so Kelly later told family and friends — tore it across on the spot, performing a little dance of rage as he did so. His first riposte was to arrange for the publication of a convoluted and unfunny cartoon in the following week's *Sunday Press*; his second was the broadcast, another ham-fisted attempt to match Kelly's gentle humour.

Lemass's detailed arguments against PR were sketchy enough, and in private he admitted to Brian Lenihan that he was well aware that the public's fondness for PR was rooted in the fact that it was a system that gave them the best of all possible worlds. He was also slow to underestimate what he described to Lenihan as 'the innate conservatism of the Irish people,' and, because he was certain that de Valera would be elected to the Park, he personally devised the slogan 'Vote yes and de Valera.'[232]

Lemass contended in his broadcast that the case where no candidate received a majority over all the others combined was not likely to happen very often and in practically all cases would make no difference anyway. He warned against emulating the experience of newly created states, suggesting that dissatisfaction with PR had even led some electorates 'to accept and even to welcome dictatorship.' He carefully avoided identifying any of these countries, just as he declined to pinpoint the 'great democracies' (presumably because they would necessarily have included Britain) that had stuck to the straight vote system and in which 'continuous progress had been recorded and democratic principles had never been seriously or successfully challenged.'

An objection to PR that he could not publicly voice was his growing conviction that one of the principal deleterious effects of PR on economic progress — which he tended to equate with Fianna Fáil's continuance in power — was that it inhibited the potential involvement in political life by the sort of business and industrial leader who shared his views and, by the same token, reduced the pool of political talent from which any Taoiseach chose his ministers.[233] To say this during the campaign would have been in effect a criticism of his Government and parliamentary party colleagues.

One of his more surprising arguments, both in his radio broadcast and in a speech in Cork during the campaign, was that 'under PR virtual immunity from the penalty of personal defeat tends to make some party leaders less responsive to public opinion.'[234] His own party leader, although by no means assured of victory in the presidential election then under way, had for most of the preceding quarter of a century, and despite physical handicaps that would have daunted a lesser man, frequently provided compelling evidence that the opposite might equally be true.

As de Valera contemplated moving to the Park, Lemass too was tidying up. Only six months earlier he had been confronted, in a peculiarly symbolic way, with a minor administrative and political decision that encapsulated some of the changes that were, however belatedly, taking place. At a conference in the Department of Industry and Commerce he was asked to approve the sketch of a mural to be presented on behalf of the Government to the ILO building in Geneva. His legendary attentiveness to detail did not let him down, and two changes were ordered. The first was the removal of a commercial device — that of Shell — from a lorry in the drawing. The second was a ministerial direction that 'the thatched cottage should go out altogether or be replaced by a more modern type house.'[235]

The two critical questions facing Lemass were, when would de Valera go, and would Lemass be the automatic choice to succeed him? At the same time there was what appears, at least on the face of it, as a certain ambivalence in Lemass's relationship to ultimate power. His growing impatience with de Valera was not always accompanied — if we are to believe his own words — by an overt desire to assume de Valera's responsibilities. He told his final press conference as Taoiseach in 1966 that he had never wanted to be Taoiseach and had not wanted de Valera to retire in 1959.[236] Certainly, as the heir apparent, it would have been impolitic of him to urge de Valera to leave the stage, even if this was his private opinion. He made no secret of his own belief, much later, that both Adenauer and de Gaulle had held on for too long.[237] There are also the circumstances in which he made this statement to be considered: he had just weathered a stormy interlude at the parliamentary party, when Seán MacEntee had accused him of leaving the party in the lurch, and the subtext of his message was that he, like de Valera before him, was strong enough to resist the importunings of those who were begging them to stay.

At the same time it is difficult to entirely discount his 1966 remarks or to assume that they — and his 1959 suggestion to Valera — were simply routine genuflections, part of a political liturgy that nobody was really intended to take seriously. He had inhabited the offices of the Department of Industry and Power in Kildare Street for so long that they fitted him like a glove, and Brendan O'Regan, among others, noted that a pall descended on the same offices with his departure.[238] Tadhg Ó Cearbhaill, who had worked with him for many years, suggested in an obituary notice that 'he would have been far happier to have been left in charge of the Department of Industry and Commerce.' There is, after all, something comforting in the role of Tánaiste, particularly as Lemass experienced it in the latter part of his tenure of that office. His power was substantial and growing but always qualified by the knowledge that to a considerable degree the main political responsibility rested with the Chief, whose electoral magnetism was still palpable and who was the only person who had ever succeeded in changing Lemass's mind on any significant issue. Lemass, for all his frustrations, still felt generally comfortable in the shadow of the older man, as he might have felt comfortable in the shadow of his brother Noel had he survived the Civil War.

The conventional political wisdom is that a retiring leader — especially of a party in power — should afford his successor two clear years in which to read himself into the part before tackling a general election. Had de Valera won an overall majority in 1948 he could conceivably have retired in 1950, but this option was not open to him. Nor was it possible in 1954–57, given the shakiness of his control over the Dáil. Political impracticalities, therefore, combined with his continuing sense of indispensability to deny his lieutenant supreme political power until he was fifty-nine — almost ten years older than de Valera had been when he first became Taoiseach, twenty-seven years earlier. All in all, Lemass's relationship with his leader evidently reflected, even in complete political maturity, a sense of living in a no-man's-land between loyalty and impatience, an ambiguity that was finally resolved only by de Valera's decision. It is perhaps significant that this decision was not taken under pressure from Lemass: the decisive intervention was by Oscar Traynor.[239]

De Valera's holding on to power, if one wanted to take a positive view of it, could be said to have cleared the way for Lemass in that it ruled out the older members of the party as potential successors. Gerry Boland, only three years younger than de Valera himself, was no longer in government. MacEntee was a decade older than Lemass, and Ryan was eight years older. In the words of a later Fianna Fáil Taoiseach, 'Dev set it up for Lemass. He made him Tánaiste, neutralised opposition. I'm sure he talked to the old guard as well.'[240]

De Valera may well have used whatever influence he had, but that influence, though great, was now waning, and there is evidence that the impressive display of party unity that enveloped Lemass's eventual election as leader was prefaced by political dyspepsia of a kind that will surprise only those who believe everything they read in the papers. Although undoubtedly popular, Lemass had made critics as well as friends within the party in a ministerial career spanning more than two decades. The degree of power he had exercised during the war years had not been forgotten, along with his unwillingness to show favouritism on party lines during that difficult period. The type of industrial development he espoused was seen in some quarters as representing a diminution — as indeed it was — of the traditional Fianna Fáil doctrine of self-sufficiency, closely associated with Aiken and Boland. In addition, he was widely known to speak little or no Irish, a fact that continued to have an influence in the election of Fianna Fáil party leaders for a number of years afterwards.

The considered view of the British embassy at the time was that there was a conflict between Lemass and Aiken that was potentially so deep and so divisive that Jim Ryan would be chosen as a compromise candidate.[241] This view, although exaggerated, and conditioned by traditional British hostility towards Aiken, whom they regarded as having been pro-German during the war, was not completely wide of the mark. Aiken had a certain following among the old guard and was on occasion used by them as a means of access to de Valera in ways that bypassed the Government.

De Valera announced his decision to retire as Taoiseach and as president of Fianna Fáil at a party meeting on 15 January 1959. The guessing game would soon be over, and in the meantime all the players had to put their money on the table. As events unfolded rapidly, the British embassy kept London informed.

> In my letter of 3 December I reported that there was quite a chance that Dr Ryan, the Minister for Finance, might find himself Taoiseach as a compromise candidate. This was indeed the general view held at the time and it came to us as some surprise, when Mr de Valera's candidature [for the presidency] was announced, that all sources were quite confident that Mr Lemass would succeed him. The struggle was, of course, primarily between Mr Lemass and Mr Aiken, and I was interested to be told the other evening that what finally tipped the scales was that Dr Ryan made it plain that he would not take the job of Taoiseach and would himself support Mr Lemass. I report this with all reserve as no more than cocktail party gossip, but my source is a reliable business man with political connexions and it seems to make sense. Some additional weight is added to it by the enclosed cartoon from Dublin Opinion in which you see Mr Lemass being pulled back into bed by Dr Ryan — the inwardness of which I had not appreciated until the conversation which I now report.

By June 1959 all was over bar the shouting — or almost all. But de Valera had at long last been persuaded to resign, although he held on to the reins of power to the end: 'I'm not President yet,' he reminded one official who asked him, in advance of the election result, about making arrangements for his resignation.[242] Nothing was left to chance: some IRA internees were released from the Curragh on 11 March, and the budget on 15 April reduced income tax from 7s 6d (37½p) to 7s (35p) in the pound.

After the hurlyburly of de Valera's narrow election victory and the defeat of the constitutional referendum on PR, the parliamentary party and the National Executive met in rapid succession to determine the leadership. When MacEntee proposed Lemass as leader, the *Irish Press* loyally reported that 'there was a spontaneous outburst of applause and cheering which drowned his concluding remarks,' and some considerable time elapsed before Frank Aiken formally seconded the proposal. A few discontented backbencher voices were raised in the ensuing discussion, but no opposition.[243] In short order the National Executive met to ratify the decision, and Lemass, on Deputy Paddy Burke's nomination, became president of the party and a trustee. He was now leader of Fianna Fáil; the following day he would be Taoiseach.

Part 2

6

Politics

'A breath of fresh air'

Seán Lemass was elected Taoiseach by the Dáil on 23 June 1959 and served continuously for almost seven-and-a-half years. The fact that most of his tenure was in the nineteen-sixties added to the sense of excitement, of a different age dawning, in which the remote and somewhat forbidding figure of de Valera would be replaced by someone who might not be particularly affable but was unmistakably more in tune with the times.

He was at heart an optimist, and his desire to convey his sense of optimism and self-confidence to a people he felt needed it was palpable — and had been since he returned to office in 1957. In 1957, he told one businessman, the missing ingredient had been confidence: 'everywhere I went I spoke about it, and it became infectious.'[1] In his first speech to the Dáil as Taoiseach he called for 'an upsurge in patriotism,'[2] as if it were patently in short supply. It underlined one of the constants in his political philosophy, going back at least as far as his 1929 memorandum to the party on economic policy, one that acted as a subtext to many of his statements as Taoiseach: nationalism and idealism, and the eradication of the 'slave spirit',[3] were the best guarantees of economic prosperity.

The belief that a watershed had been reached was confirmed by tangible changes throughout society as a whole, and not only in politics. Four months after Lemass's election as Taoiseach, James Dillon succeeded Richard Mulcahy as leader of Fine Gael. Five months after that again Brendan Corish succeeded William Norton as Labour Party leader. Politics, peopled with new faces, became interesting again.

From the very start there were strong indications that things were going to be different. Overtures to the North, particularly on social and economic issues, were at first rebuffed by unionists but reawakened interest in the partition issue nationally and internationally. The First Programme for Economic Expansion performed even better than expected under a revivified Department of Finance, and Lemass's eyes were set firmly on Europe. Fianna Fáil, however, suffered substantially in the first election they fought without de Valera, in 1961, and Lemass only just managed to hold on to power with the aid of independents. Despite this, it was a solid enough Government for four years.

The last IRA internees were released from the Curragh in April 1961, and just under a year later the armed campaign waged intermittently since 1956 was itself abandoned. Brookeborough was succeeded as Northern prime minister by Terence O'Neill in March 1963: three months later Ian Paisley led one of his first protest marches. In January 1965 O'Neill invited Lemass to the historic meeting at Stormont.

These were among the multiplicity of signposts to the future, although the route maps were still sketchy. The new Irish Congress of Trade Unions, which had been formed in the dying days of the de Valera Government, held its inaugural conference in Dublin in September 1959. Trade union unity gave Lemass a new opportunity to embark on national bargaining on wages policy — but it also gave the unions, and the public service unions in particular, a new sense of their industrial strength, which was to usher in unparalleled unrest in 1964 and 1965 and wage settlements that ran quickly out of control.

Ireland's reaching out to the wider world was measured in practical and symbolic terms. In July 1960 an Irish battalion left for the former Belgian Congo as part of a UN peace-keeping operation. Nor was this just a matter of showing the flag: within four months the coffins of nine of them were coming home. At the United Nations itself Frederick Boland was elected president of the General Assembly. In a development that related strongly to Lemass's own personal scale of priorities, Aer Lingus inaugurated its first jet aircraft service to the United States in December 1960. President Kennedy was to make a historic visit to Ireland in 1963, and Lemass returned to the United States at his invitation in October the same year, just before Kennedy's assassination.

In August 1961 Ireland applied for full membership of the EEC, and for some fifteen months, until de Gaulle vetoed the British application, this was at the forefront of Lemass's economic and foreign policy. The First Programme for Economic Expansion, which he had inaugurated in 1958, was succeeded in August 1963, after de Gaulle's veto, by the first part of the Second Programme. It was not to be as successful; the second part did not in fact appear until July 1965, by which time economic targets generally were slipping, emigration was creeping up again, and the country's economic progress was beginning to falter.

The intersections of British and Irish politics became more numerous. When Britain elected Harold Wilson to Downing Street in October 1964 there were high hopes in Ireland for progress, not only on partition but on economic matters as well. Despite a good personal relationship between Wilson and Lemass, the hiccups in the British economy forced changes that had dramatic downstream effects on Ireland.

The media and the Irish language were battlegrounds, which often overlapped. Telefís Éireann, the new national television service, broadcast for the first time on New Year's Eve, 1961; six months later Gay Byrne presented the first edition of the 'Late Late Show'. The Commission on the Revival of the Irish Language, which had been established in 1958, finally reported in 1963, and some eighteen months later the Government published its response in a White Paper. Television was under pressure to play its part in the revival; so were the schools, and Irish became a party political issue when Fine Gael proposed that Irish no longer be a compulsory part of the educational system.

Lemass's second election, in April 1965, saw Fianna Fáil win exactly half the seats in the Dáil. Lemass's programme for the period between the election and his eventual retirement did not betray much tiredness. He had to deal, in short order, with the growing economic difficulties caused by the British import surcharge and with increasing restiveness on the part of the trade union movement and farmers. He also had to oversee de Valera's campaign for re-election as President in the summer of 1966.

He had only qualified success in each of these areas; and the narrowness of de Valera's eventual victory may also have affected his intended personal timetable. The Anglo-Irish Free Trade Area Agreement of December 1965, on the other hand, not only undid the worst effects of the protectionist policies adopted by the Wilson government late in 1964 but marked in a formal way the end of the protectionist economic philosophy that had guided Lemass and Fianna Fáil since the nineteen-twenties and had been progressively whittled away since the late fifties.

When Lemass resigned, in November 1966, the election of Jack Lynch as his successor was accompanied by infighting and political manoeuvring of a type Fianna Fáil had never witnessed before. Lemass had built a bridge between de Valera and the future, but it was to an uncertain future.

De Valera, even before he handed over to his successor, once told a young TD with whom he shared a constituency that Lemass's taking of power would be 'a breath of fresh air'.[4] The agenda Lemass set himself at the beginning of this era would have taxed a younger and a fitter man, but there was an initial period in which, to his surprise, the recurring sensation was one of frustration. Liam St John Devlin remembers hearing from T. J. Barrington of the Institute of Public Administration at the time that Lemass 'expressed the futility of his role as Taoiseach. He didn't have executive responsibilities, he had a clear desk and few staff. It didn't accord with his style, which was pro-active.'[5] The fact that he was now dependent, to at least some extent, on other people's timetables called for a change of focus that he at first found unwelcome.

Lemass was used to action within his own domain, but the Department of the Taoiseach had not got a domain. It was the office of the chairman; it was a department that was only tangentially concerned with policy and devoted primarily to the machinery of government. Its secretary (and therefore secretary to the Government) was for the first year or so Maurice Moynihan, who had acted in this capacity for de Valera and who was later to become Governor of the Central Bank. He was succeeded in January 1961 by Nicholas Nolan — known, not entirely charitably, by some of his colleagues as 'meticulous Nicholas' — who personified an attention to detail that was the hallmark of a particular kind of public servant. (He once had a batch of official stationery reprinted because there were too few strings on the harp.)

Lemass, however, soon found that the Taoiseach's necessary attention to strategy and to governmental co-ordination was to keep him as busy as he wanted to be. Correspondence and memorandums that reached him were generally despatched with replies or decisions within two days, and often on the day they arrived. Although he kept strict office hours — often going home for lunch and a brief nap — his work rate was bred in the bone. On the administrative side he soon had the help of a civil servant who had served under him in Industry and Commerce, Tadhg Ó Cearbhaill, who was to become intimately involved with policy management in Government Buildings on a wide range of issues, not least industrial relations. Ó Cearbhaill was to finish his administrative career as secretary of the Department of Labour.

The new Taoiseach also activated — or, more properly, reactivated — the 'Committee of Secretaries'. This group, comprising the secretaries of four key departments — Finance, External Affairs, Agriculture, and Industry and Commerce — was to play a pivotal role in the years ahead not only in relation to foreign trade, EFTA and the EEC but also in relation to Northern Ireland policy. It had been set up as an initiative of the previous Government in October 1956[6] and played a central role in the development of strategic thinking on international organisations. The committee was chaired by Whitaker and reported to a committee of the ministers concerned, which was itself chaired by Lemass when he was Minister for Industry and Commerce in 1957–59; he retained its chair after becoming Taoiseach. On a whole range of important issues this committee acted as a powerful instrument for the co-ordination and occasionally the elaboration of Government policy. The fact that the Secretary of the Department of the Taoiseach was not a member may seem anomalous, but it fitted in with that official's administrative role as he interpreted it.

His civil servants had to get used to his style, which was so brisk that it affected severely the more leisurely presentations. Con Cremin was an early casualty of Lemass's style in this respect, as he later told Paddy Hillery:

> Once Lemass asked [Cremin] for a briefing on a UN matter, and Cremin began with one side of the story. As soon as he had finished,

Lemass said, 'Right,' and a decision was given before the other side had been heard. Cremin had to vary his technique after that to make sure that both sides were presented.[7]

Lemass focused on two immediate objectives. One was picking his first Government; the second was defining his national priorities. In the first instance he felt bound by loyalty and tradition to make as few changes as possible before he had achieved his own electoral mandate: 'I really only felt myself to be Taoiseach in my own right when Fianna Fáil won the 1961 General Election.'[8]

Three who had served with him in de Valera's original 1932 government were retained. One of them, MacEntee, was given additional responsibility in the combined ministries of Health and Social Welfare — hardly an allocation that reflected any serious doubt about his capabilities. A second, Frank Aiken, was retained in the Department of External Affairs. The third was James Ryan in Finance.

Lemass's relationship with Aiken was problematic, characterised by a sense of reserve at best. Other observers were more blunt: according to Brian Lenihan, Lemass 'regarded Aiken as a fool' and was delighted to see him disappear over the horizon in the direction of the United Nations for three months every year.[9] This opinion, perhaps conditioned by the younger man's impatience with the old guard — Lenihan was eventually to become Minister for Foreign Affairs himself and always evinced a keen interest in this policy area — was almost certainly overblown. A more measured assessment, by Conor Cruise O'Brien, suggests that Aiken and Lemass 'were not on particularly good terms,' because 'they had been rivals for a long time, and Dev wasn't going to lay hands on either of them.'[10] On Northern Ireland, according to O'Brien, Lemass's view was 'consistent with Aiken's, but Lemass's was from a pragmatic point of view, while Aiken's was more idealistic.'[11]

Lemass was for the most part content to let Aiken engage in policy-making at the United Nations to his heart's content, as long as it did not impinge too closely on matters domestic. Lemass's attitude to the United States, on the other hand, did not intersect with Aiken's at all points. Cruise O'Brien's view was that the non-aligned UN policy was essentially Aiken's creation and that its evolution over time was influenced not only by Lemass's greater openness to the United States but by internal departmental dynamics.

> I suggested to [Aiken] that the acid test would be the issue of Red China. If we were seen to vote in favour of discussing the question it would indicate clearly that we were not in the pocket of the United States and the United Kingdom. He agreed with this, but it gave rise to great tensions within the department, not least from Boland, our then UN ambassador, and Kennedy. Boland had an inside track to

Lemass and was convincing Lemass that Aiken was messing up our relationship with the US and Britain for some incomprehensible reason and ought to be stopped. I had a definite sense that Aiken was in difficulties on this — not because of the Spellman thing[12] — and indeed Lemass would have taken this line, not because of clerical pressure but because it was sensitive within the cabinet from the point of view of our business interests, as it were.[13]

The situation changed to a certain extent after 1961, when Kennedy succeeded Eisenhower. Aiken in any case found the Democratic administration more congenial[14] and envisaged mending fences with them. It was hardly a coincidence that in his 1962 ardfheis address Lemass saluted the United States as the guardian of the 'free world', coupling this sentiment with a strong denunciation of the communist bloc.

Lemass interested himself only tangentially in UN matters, and they were rarely discussed at Government meetings. One of the few occasions on which this happened was early in 1961, when MacEntee made a spirited but unsuccessful attempt to torpedo Aiken's nuclear non-proliferation initiative, arguing that 'nuclear weapons have come to stay and … platitudes will not prevent their development.'[15] Lemass, for his part, was prepared to pull the British lion's tail over Southern Rhodesia (Zimbabwe), but not too hard.[16] His only UN speech, in 1963, was essentially the Iveagh House draft.[17]

MANAGING THE GOVERNMENT

Lemass's first Government was very much a 'steady-as-you-go' administration and exemplified one of his own core values, revealed with typical conciseness in a post-retirement interview some ten years later: 'It is far more important to retain goodwill and harmony than to seek a more effective distribution of responsibility.'[18] Three of the youngest ministers — Lynch, Blaney, and Boland — had received their first Government positions from de Valera in 1957. With hindsight, it can certainly be described as betraying a caution that few people would have associated with Lemass; but the next general election, Lemass's first as Taoiseach and Fianna Fáil's first without de Valera, was looming over him. He was plainly unwilling to disturb a political formula at a time when doing so would have exposed him to unacceptable levels of risk. His most radical Government-making was to be postponed until 1965, less than two years before his retirement.

With the departure of de Valera and of Seán Ormonde, who had been Minister for Posts and Telegraphs in de Valera's last government and who retired for health reasons, against Lemass's wishes, the new Taoiseach had room for only two new Government appointments. One was Michael Hilliard, the parliamentary secretary from County Meath, who became Minister for Posts and Telegraphs; the other was the selection of Paddy

Hillery as Minister for Education. His choice of Hillery may have been motivated partly by geographical considerations, given that Hillery represented the same constituency as the departing Chief, but it evidently had a greater significance, in that Hillery, who had earlier turned down an invitation from de Valera to join the Government, was unable to resist Lemass's more forceful approach. He later described the occasion:

> When Dev retired and the parliamentary party was meeting to choose a successor, Maeve and I were on holidays at Portmarnock, and I was to play that morning. It was assumed that it would be Lemass, and I didn't think I'd bother going in, but my first round was washed out and I went in. The meeting was over quickly, but then Mick Hilliard grabbed me, told me not to leave, and held on to me. When I was taken in by Mick Hilliard to Lemass he said: 'I want you in the Cabinet ... you're not escaping this time.' No specific post was mentioned. Dev had asked me earlier and I had declined; medicine was too important, and I was busy at it. I explained as much to Lemass too, but he brushed it aside.[19]

The other appointment Lemass would have regarded as of particular significance was the move of Jack Lynch from Education to Industry and Commerce, Lemass's old stamping ground. When Lynch had received his first appointment as Parliamentary Secretary to the Government and to the Minister for Lands in June 1951 he had been given specific responsibility for the Undeveloped Areas Act and an office in the Kildare Street building where Lemass ruled like a benevolent despot. On that occasion he was shown in to Lemass's office, where he saw the minister confronting a pile of files more than a foot high. Lemass gestured towards the files and told him: 'If you don't make up your mind, nothing will happen. You may make a mistake, but you may do some good too. Go off and make up your own mind.' Now, a decade later, and just before he took over as Taoiseach, he called Lynch in to the same office and told him: 'I want you to sit at this desk. I won't be looking over your shoulder.'[20]

No significant changes were made at the level of parliamentary secretary. Lemass's one new appointment at this level, that of his son-in-law Charles Haughey, was not made until the following year, after a well-documented hiccup in which his original choice for the post, Seán Flanagan, was displaced as a result of party pressure in favour of the Dublin deputy.[21] Thereafter, Lemass made sure that the practice of allowing the party in effect to determine the allocation of parliamentary secretaryships — a practice that was also followed elsewhere, certainly in the Labour Party, at the same time — was abrogated in favour of the Taoiseach's discretion.

With his Government in place, Lemass's other tasks now fell to be tackled. Three of them were in the key policy areas of the economy, the North, and social policy. Three were structural: the regeneration of the Fianna Fáil party; tackling the administrative side of decision-making, and in particular the complex web of relations between the public and the state-sponsored sectors; and the question of constitutional as well as institutional reform.

If the direction of economic policy was now in much more confident and self-assertive hands, so also was policy on the North. Two factors are particularly relevant here: Lemass's own views on the North as they had been elaborated over four decades in public life, and the precise nature of the policy he had inherited.

He had, of course, inherited not only policies but personnel; his desire not to replicate de Valera's management style was not matched by any evident desire to indulge in radical Government-making. As Farrell has pointed out, Lemass was more ready than de Valera to press for a decision but was at the same time careful not to permit adverse votes on topics of significance to his own programmes.[22] It was not all plain sailing, however. Lemass was 'quite often at loggerheads' with some members of his Government, particularly where he found an overemphasis on agricultural and rural policies, and was 'anxious for a more modern approach to the creation of wealth.'[23]

There was at least one physical change in the organisation of Government meetings, which in itself spoke volumes: Lemass changed the shape of the table from rectangular to oval. When he had done so he told one of his civil servants that he was 'able to see who was saying no to me.'[24] In one respect at least he had no difficulty in identifying the critics: the place immediately opposite Lemass at the oval table was generally occupied by MacEntee, who as Tánaiste between 1959 and 1965 was as adept at opposing plans brought to the Government by other ministers as Lemass was supportive of them. One of his colleagues noted: 'Lemass was always prepared to get things done rather than to be "famous for being famous". In Government everything was crisp; he had no patience with waffle.'[25] Confrontations tended to be smoothed out by Ryan, while Lemass sat tight.

This was not to say that his management of the Government was un-informed by subtlety. As will be seen, his handling of some issues — notably the Hillery initiative on comprehensive schools — provided evidence of willingness to take an occasional short-cut. The O'Malley 'free education' initiative was a more complex matter and spawned at least one imitation: Micheál Ó Móráin's later decision, which was also not cleared with the Government in advance, to decentralise a section of the Department of Lands to Castlebar, in his own constituency.[26]

In contrast to de Valera's fondness for lengthy discussions, Lemass's organisation of the business could be startlingly brisk. One of the regular Government meetings in 1965 — admittedly on 24 August — lasted for no more than three-quarters of an hour. He was conscious too of the need for regeneration and renewal, and in some respects consciously planned for it. When he appointed Brian Lenihan as Parliamentary Secretary to the Minister for Justice in October 1961 he asked the newcomer specifically to read himself into the politics of European integration, as he would have need of a minister who was informed in this area.[27]

Before 1961, possibly the only Government change to merit attention was that of Erskine Childers, who had received his first appointment as Minister for Lands from de Valera in 1957. Lemass regarded Childers as a lightweight and as a 'landlord's man' who had 'no time for the peasants, for the small farmers,'[28] and demoted him first to Posts and Telegraphs and then, after the 1961 election, to Transport and Power. This was a particularly noticeable demotion, given that the ESB and Bord na Móna were in effect sovereign in relation to power and that transport was under the day-to-day control of CIE. Childers felt, probably correctly, that it was a job fit only for a parliamentary secretary;[29] nonetheless he continued to serve in all Lemass's Governments, although Lemass would have been aware that he was a frequent visitor to de Valera in Áras an Uachtaráin and probably suspected that one of Childers's extraministerial functions was to act as a conduit to the Park for political information.[30]

His leadership role within the parliamentary party was, while in no way as overarching as that of his predecessor, generally recognised. He frequently introduced discussion on departmental matters himself in the absence of the relevant ministers, even on recondite or complex policy questions.[31] He always made a point of briefing the party fully and in advance on controversial matters that were about to be raised in the Dáil by opposition deputies. He would also — though he was an infrequent contributor to general discussions — encourage, by his body language, the younger members of the parliamentary party to intervene, to the occasional discomfiture of their elders. 'Sometimes you'd get the impression that, at cabinet as much as at parliamentary party meetings, he'd be encouraging the younger members to have a go, to stir things up a bit.'[32] He was less successful in his attempts to encourage the rank and file of the parliamentary party generally to participate in policy committees, which he plainly envisaged as a way of keeping ministers up to the mark. Only in a few areas — such as foreign affairs, where young men like Lenihan and Michael O'Kennedy were active — did such committees have any noticeable effect.

At the party's National Executive the tenor of meetings also changed. One participant recalled a significant difference in the way in which letters of resignation were dealt with. Such letters were often, as Lemass realised, submitted out of a sense of pique or as part of an attempt to pressure the Executive into taking a particular action. De Valera's response was not infrequently one of alarm or, at the very least, concern: a member of the Executive would on occasion be despatched to interview the fractious chairman of the comhairle dáilcheantair or cumann, as the occasion demanded, in an attempt to inveigle him back into the fold. Lemass's response to the first such letter he received as president of the party was to propose that the resignation be noted with regret and that the meeting pass on to the next business — a tactic that miraculously stemmed the flow of threatening and disgruntled letters.[33]

There is little doubt that the party responded positively to the new order. Members who had assisted Lemass in the 1954–57 reorganisation — notably Charles Haughey, Brian Lenihan, and Eoin Ryan — were key allies in this process, and the first two were shortly to assume full ministerial rank. The electoral results, however, were not at first encouraging, despite the fact that the omens were extraordinarily good.

Maintaining Fianna Fáil's electoral dominance in the post-Dev era was high on Lemass's personal scale of priorities. Ideally the change from PR to the 'straight vote', as advocated in the 1959 referendum, would have staved off electoral defeat for Fianna Fáil into some indeterminate future. But that proposal had been defeated by the electorate, and although Lemass would for some time harbour hopes that the question could be reopened, the party had to rapidly come to a decision about an alternative. There was in addition a constitutional urgency, as the twelve-year limit set by the Constitution for the revision of constituencies had expired, and one of the new Government's first tasks was to rush through the Oireachtas a new Act to give effect to a revision based on changes in population that had taken place since 1947, when the last revision had taken place.

The new Act was a more open attempt than any Fianna Fáil had made before to maximise the value of their electoral support. It adhered on a national basis to the constitutional requirement that the total number of deputies not exceed 1 per 20,000 inhabitants, but only just: the national average proposed was 1 to 20,100. There were, however, considerable, and calculated, local variations. In the four western counties of Donegal, Galway, Mayo, and Kerry, where the population had been declining but where Fianna Fáil's electoral strength was disproportionately strong, the ratio was one deputy to 17,758. In Dublin, where the reverse was the case, the ratio was 1 to 22,753.[34] This was challenged in the courts by Dr John O'Donovan, a university professor and Labour politician, and declared unconstitutional by the High Court; Fianna Fáil had to go back to the drawing-board.

Lemass took personal charge of the new Bill, and his memorandum, drafted in his familiar blue scrawl on small sheets of paper, became the basis for the revision, which juggled the numbers of three and four-seat constituencies in Fianna Fáil's favour while maintaining the 'tolerance' (the variation on either side of the 20,000 population optimum specified in the Constitution) within legally safer limits. He also altered his own constituency, hiving off parts of Ballyfermot to Dublin South-West, where his son, Noel, was a TD.[35]

He made an attempt to defuse political opposition by making the allocation of an additional seat in the south-east a matter for a free vote, and he indicated as much in private discussions with William Norton and Liam Cosgrave (then acting as Fine Gael chief whip) in late 1959, but this suggestion was brusquely rejected by his own parliamentary party, and he had to write to the other parties in November withdrawing it. The climb-down must have caused him some chagrin, as he had been party leader for less than six months. The new Bill was then successfully submitted to the Supreme Court for a decision before it was signed into law by the President, thus ruling out the possibility of a subsequent constitutional challenge.

Lemass's first attempt to win a Dáil majority on his own account had the wind behind it in some respects. The Labour Party had decided at its annual conference in 1957, in the bitter aftermath of the collapse of the second inter-party Government, that it would remain in opposition until it succeeded in obtaining an overall majority. The electorate responded accordingly: only 29 per cent of Labour Party transfers went to Fine Gael candidates in by-elections between 1957 and 1961.[36] The party's new leader, Brendan Corish, faithfully reflected the no-coalition mood in the party; the most he was prepared to consider was the possibility of supporting a minority administration without participation in the Government. Between 1961 and 1965 the transfer patterns between the Labour Party and Fine Gael began to improve, but the party leadership — and indeed some TDs, such as James Tully, who were rarely accused of being ideological revolutionaries — were notably hard-line on this issue, arguing that the principal political onus was on Fianna Fáil and Fine Gael to merge their separate identities in one large conservative grouping. The evidence they had to go on was slight — the increase in the Labour Party's share of the vote from 8.7 per cent in 1957 to 11.6 per cent in 1961 — but was plainly enough to convince them that they were on the right road. The anti-coalition view, therefore, was maintained and if anything reinforced in the period up to the 1965 election, even though it was accompanied by a studied unwillingness to say what the Labour Party would do if it held the balance of power. It was a view that played into Fianna Fáil's hands.

The first Irish Gallup poll took place in July 1961, indicating that 76 per cent of respondents approved of membership of the EEC, with 7 per cent opposed and 17 per cent undecided; equally significantly, support for membership was particularly high among the better-educated respondents.[37] For a politician with as keen a nose as Lemass had, the prospect of going to the country on a platform with which three-quarters of the electorate were in apparent agreement was to all intents and purposes irresistible, and he informed the Dáil on 2 August that there would be an election between the middle of September and October. In the same speech he used an aeronautical metaphor to reinforce his view of the significance of the occasion:

> The country is, I think, like an aeroplane at the take-off stage. It has become airborne; that is the stage of maximum risk and any failure of power could lead to a crash. It will be a long time yet before we can throttle back to level flight.[38]

The theme of Ireland's application for EEC membership formed a major part of his approach to the general election campaign in October that year, so much so that it formed in effect part of the mandate he received as a result of that contest, even though it was a far more inadequate mandate than, in the circumstances, he had a right to expect. One of the reasons undoubtedly was the ESB strike, which began on 21 August following the rejection of a Labour Court award by the workers concerned. The threat to power supplies forced the unprecedented recall of the Dáil and Seanad by telegram on 1 September to pass the Electricity (Temporary Provisions) Act, and it was only in the face of this threat by the Government to invoke legislative *force majeure,* aided by a parallel series of negotiations that had seen the initial six pence an hour award increased by stages to ten pence, that the workers called off the strike at midnight on 7 September.

Not even the successful resolution of a critical industrial relations problem, combined with the promotion of a policy that three-quarters of the electorate agreed with, was enough to ensure success. There was a general air of lassitude, despite the fact that the three major parties had new leaders. The election campaign was described as one of the dullest on record, and Lemass addressed only fifteen meetings.[39] Extreme caution was the order of the day as the party and its leader tiptoed into the post-Dev era with considerable apprehension.

Lemass himself intervened to persuade a number of older deputies, such as Mark Killilea in Galway, to remain in the fray, even though they had intimated a willingness to retire, and was chided by 'Backbencher' (John Healy), whose campaign to radicalise political journalism had just been inaugurated in the pages of the *Sunday Review,* for his unwillingness to swing the axe more vigorously. The Killilea ploy backfired, and the older man was defeated, but elsewhere it seemed to be more successful, seeing the re-election of such stalwarts as Martin Corry (first elected June 1927), Oscar Traynor (born 1885), Tom McEllistrim (born 1894), Gerald Boland (born 1885), Dan Breen (born 1894), Michael Hilliard in Meath, and another Old IRA man, Gerald Bartley, who had first been elected in 1932.

It is significant that, apart from Traynor, the older men tended to be elected in rural constituencies. In the cities, less likely to be impressed by genealogy, the news for Fianna Fáil was not good and indeed suggested that Lemass's legendary pulling power in urban areas was vulnerable. His party's representation in Cork city went from three seats to two; in Dublin, despite an increase in the number of seats from thirty to thirty-four, Fianna Fáil failed to gain even one of the additional seats, and Fine Gael gained three. In the circumstances, the fact that the Labour Party's representation in the capital remained a solitary seat — that of Michael Mullen — was scant enough consolation.

Fianna Fáil's apprehension about fighting an election without de Valera had been fully justified. Their first election in four decades without the Chief saw a slide in their vote — from 48.3 to 43.8 per cent — that was only just short of forcing them out of office, and a decline from 78 to 70 seats in the Dáil. Things might have been even worse but for three factors: the eclipse of the four abstentionist Sinn Féin TDs from 1957, which was worth a substantial bonus in certain areas (5 per cent and an extra seat in Cavan-Monaghan, for instance); the revision of the constituencies carried out before the election in 1961; and the Labour Party's no-coalition stance. These facts ensured that Fianna Fáil collected a bonus in seats that was the highest since 1943. It was also politically vital: the majority of six bequeathed to Lemass by de Valera had been transformed into a minority of two, and the outcome would have been much more problematic without this bonus. Lemass was elected Taoiseach on 11 October by an uncomfortably narrow margin of 72 to 68, with three opposition deputies abstaining.

Lemass was used to minority Governments, although he did not relish them. His experience in 1961–65 was, however, more positive on all counts than that of the minority Government of 1951–54. He was also dealing with Government material of a different calibre from that which he had inherited from his predecessor. The old guard was a minority in the 1961 Government, being represented principally by MacEntee (born 1889), Ryan (born 1891), Aiken, and to a lesser extent Smith.

From the point of view of making necessary changes this was evidently an advance; but at least some members of the party saw a potential drawback. One of them, Ruairí Brugha, went so far as to issue what he felt was a necessary warning to Lemass about his Government, specifically because so many of them did not share Lemass's background. Lemass replied simply that he had to take geographical considerations into account when appointing them, and that after that all he could do was kick them hard if they didn't perform.[40]

Some of Lemass's more significant changes were not in the area of politics but of law. In December 1961 the Government made two simultaneous appointments. One was the appointment of Cearbhall Ó Dálaigh (who had been a member of the Supreme Court since 1953) as Chief

Justice; the other was the appointment of Brian Walsh to the Supreme Court. Lemass had a brief chat with each of them on their appointment and indicated openly to them that he would like the Supreme Court to be 'more like the United States Supreme Court' — in other words, that it would prove flexible and creative in its interpretation of the Constitution.[41] Walsh believed that Lemass's view was a personal one, shared by no more than one or two other members of the Government. Perhaps for this reason, among others, Lemass told Walsh that he wouldn't bring the subject up again. Then again, he didn't need to. As Walsh put it: 'I think the horse was chosen for the course. He probably felt he was talking to someone who had much the same views. I certainly was very much influenced by the American experience. I had studied it to a very considerable extent and kept myself familiar with it all through my career.'

Ó Dálaigh and Walsh were, in the latter's view, actively involved in 'giving life to a constitution which, in the early days perhaps, had been regarded as an ornament rather than something of actual practical utility,' but not all the decisions would have necessarily pleased the Government, and the whole process of amending the Constitution by way of the Supreme Court was a long and circuitous one at the best of times and indeed one not guaranteed to produce the desired outcome, especially as the court could only decide law on the basis of the cases that reached it.

Lemass was less successful in bringing about administrative change. His views on the nature of Government departments and on the role of state-sponsored organisations and the proper relationship between them embody a number of insights: the twin dangers of institutional ossification and human frailty; the primacy of clearly delineated Government policies; and the need also for clarity in the allocation of departmental and extra-departmental responsibilities.[42]

This need for institutional reform was one of his earliest priorities. He had considered it in a lecture to the Institute of Public Administration even before his election as Taoiseach, in 1958, and was to return to it in several addresses in 1961 and 1962. Without even attempting to read between the lines it is possible to see in these speeches his felt need to give state companies more freedom than had traditionally been accorded to Government departments, together with his concern that this freedom could be misused, that unproductive empire-building could take the place of developmental initiatives. He also wanted the departments of state to rethink their role and to see themselves more as development corporations — although he was careful to emphasise that this implied a new spirit in which they should operate rather than reform of a structural kind. He was possibly up against greater obstacles than he knew, as the fact that this item tended thereafter to slip off his agenda also indicates.

THE LAST HURDLE

In politics, however, it was business as usual, and Fine Gael and the Labour Party provided a usual tempting array of targets. Lemass was careful not to let victory go to his head. In December 1963 he had occasion to warn Charles Haughey, then Minister for Justice, about too facile a characterisation of their political opponents. Haughey had sent his father-in-law a memorandum on electoral tactics with which the older man was not entirely in agreement. Lemass's reply gave a strong sense of his own political strategy.

> The presentation of Fine Gael as a 'right-wing conservative party' implies that they have a definite political philosophy — and one which many people would probably consider as respectable. I think this would flatter them. Their outstanding characteristic is irresponsibility. This is the feeling about them that I have found to be most prevalent. As the art of political propaganda is to say what most of the people are thinking, this would seem to be the right line for us ... You describe Labour as the party of protest and discontented elements. I agree. It is their political effectiveness and not their aims that should be the subject of their criticism ... Our political propaganda must, however, always strive to sound the positive note. It may be true that people find it easier to be 'against' than 'for' and we must use this attitude as much as possible, but this should not be inconsistent with the maintenance of the image of Fianna Fáil as the party which is planning for the future, which has definite aims and a known policy, the displacement of which from office would be the prelude to a period of economic recession.[43]

Elsewhere, and in public, he described Fine Gael's main ambition as aspiring to be 'some sort of an alternative stop-gap government to Fianna Fáil.' On the other hand, he even admitted to a 'tinge of sympathy' for the Labour Party, who were 'aspiring to the heights but seem to lack the nerve for the journey.'[44]

The sense of self-confidence here is palpable. During this first full period in office, according to one academic observer, Lemass now 'exuded power.'[45] This, allied to his customary decisiveness, was most clearly shown in his approach to wages policy in 1964 and the not unrelated wrangle with his Minister for Agriculture, Paddy Smith, culminating in the latter's resignation.

1964 dawned in a particularly problematic way for Lemass and his Government. They were facing two critical by-elections, in Cork and in Kildare. In Cork they were fighting to retain their seat; in Kildare the tussle was over the vacancy caused by the death of Lemass's old adversary William Norton. The loss of the Cork seat would have seriously weakened Lemass's position in the Dáil, and during the first two weeks of January he actively encouraged negotiations between employers and unions on the basis for a ninth-round wage agreement. Events now began to follow each other at breakneck speed and in an order that suggested strongly that they were politically connected. It was announced on 14 January that the ICTU had accepted a formula for the ninth round, and the FUE accepted it the following day. The formula provided for increases not exceeding 12 per cent, which were not to be reviewed for two-and-a-half years — in other words, safely after the presumed date for the next general election.

On 19 January 1964 Lemass announced that there would be a general election if Fianna Fáil were defeated in the two by-elections. This had the presumably intended effect of concentrating minds wonderfully, but it was still not quite enough. The poll was scheduled for 19 February. Ten days before, Neil Blaney, who was director of elections, rang Lemass to tell him that things were looking bad and that Kildare, where a contentious ESB wage claim was making things particularly difficult, would almost certainly be lost. Lemass asked bluntly: 'What are you going to do about it?' Blaney requested, and received, permission to dragoon anyone, including ministers, into the front line as he saw fit. Before Blaney left his office, Lemass asked him: 'What's wrong?' and Blaney told him: 'There's been no Seán Lemass since you became Taoiseach.'[46]

The elections, which were held on 19 February, saw Fianna Fáil hold its Cork seat with a record vote and snatch Kildare from Norton's son.[47] It was a rare electoral feather in Lemass's cap, but the price was a high one.

Despite the by-election victories, the wage settlement added critical momentum to another move by Paddy Smith, who was a persistent critic in the Government of what he regarded as Lemass's unduly soft approach to organised labour. This disagreement reached its climax in late 1964, when Smith finally decided, after several earlier threats, to resign in protest against what he described as the 'tyranny'[48] of the trade union movement — an implied criticism of Lemass for concluding agreements with the tyrants. On the morning of the day he resigned, Smith stopped on his way from Cavan to Dublin at a Garda barracks in Meath, from which he telephoned the head of the Government Information Bureau, Pádraig Ó hAnracháin, to say that he was coming up to town to resign. Ó hAnracháin immediately rang Lemass at home to give him this information. There was a brief pause before the gravelly voice replied: 'Ring me back when there's better news.'[49]

While he was dealing with brush fires like that caused by Smith's resignation, Lemass also had an eye for the larger picture and was actively considering ways in which a more substantial safety net could be devised for his own and future Fianna Fáil Governments. The 1959 defeat on PR had not completely extinguished the spark of hope that some form of constitutional revision other than that which had been rejected by the people might ultimately prove acceptable. He had obviously been thinking about this for some time when he wrote to the Attorney-General, Aindrias Ó Caoimh, late in 1964, enclosing a memorandum for a scheme that he believed might be enacted without the need for a constitutional amendment. Lemass's scheme involved the transfer of the 'unused' votes in each constituency (in a three-seat constituency with a quota of 10,001, he argued, there would be almost 10,000 'ineffective' votes) to a national constituency, which would be filled from a list.[50] Ó Caoimh dismissed the idea virtually out of hand, arguing that it would be extremely vulnerable to constitutional challenge.[51]

The autumn of 1964, however, proved the apogee of Lemass's progress in the political and economic field, and the countdown to the 1965 general election began in effect after the British general election in October. Although political relations between the two countries improved with dramatic speed in the wake of the Labour Party victory in Britain — the return of the 1916 GPO flag and of Roger Casement's remains marked this in a particularly symbolic way — the new British trade policy caused Lemass serious problems.

The Wilson government, pleading a balance of payments problem, published a White Paper on the economic situation in October 1964, announcing a 15 per cent surcharge on all manufactured or semi-manufactured imports. Irish exports to Britain were seriously affected. Lemass, reacting immediately in the Dáil, described it as 'a real body-blow' as well as a violation of the 1938 Anglo-Irish Trade Agreement, which it probably was.[52] But *force majeure* was the operative factor now, and when Lemass and Lynch went to London early in November for talks with Wilson and other British ministers it was without any evident hope of success. Lemass himself was not well — so much so that he decided not to attend one ministerial meeting, assuming, correctly, that no breach in the British stone wall would be forthcoming.[53] The only positive outcome was a decision to begin talks at official level on the possibility of an Anglo-Irish free trade agreement, and the first of these took place the following month.

Domestic political indicators were also discouraging. At a by-election in East Galway in December following the death of the Clann na Talmhan leader, Michael Donnellan TD, the late deputy's son, John, stood as a Fine Gael candidate and won the seat, more than doubling the Fine Gael first-preference vote.

In all the circumstances, the sudden rapprochement between Dublin and Stormont as a result of the Lemass-O'Neill visits early in 1965, and the fact that the worsening economic situation — particularly on the incomes policy and balance of payments fronts — was not yet publicly visible, created a situation in which the prospect of an election suddenly began to look enticing. The temptation to go to the country would if anything have been enhanced by discussions that had been taking place within the Department of Finance on economic policy, involving Whitaker, S. F. Murray and C. H. Murray from the department and a cross-section of experts including

Louden Ryan, Patrick Lynch, Brendan Menton, and Professor Charles Carter. The non-departmental voices were concerned, but not too much so: Whitaker, on the other hand, could see the writing on the wall, warning in particular that a repetition of the 1964 wage agreement would be 'disastrous' and urging that the next agreement 'should be held at bay as long as possible.'[54]

Lemass was hedging his own political bets. He declared resoundingly in February 1965 that there was no desire in the Dáil for an election and that it would only create problems for the future. In private he was more sanguine. As he told an interviewer after the election,

> a situation was developing which was so diminishing the effectiveness of the government that this was the only course to take. I hadn't much doubt about the outcome. Mr Dillon and others said in the Dáil that we hoped to lose. But this is nonsense. That would have been letting down my own Party, colleagues and everything else to an exceptional degree. I saw that unless we could get a renewal of authority from the people, we'd be far less effective as a government and that the longer we held off on the issue the more ineffectual we'd become. So I did not regard this as a gamble in any sense, but the right thing to do.[55]

Back in the public arena, he continued to be upbeat. The idea that the economy was in such a bad way as to necessitate official widespread price control was 'an absurd proposition' (he was to legislate for just such an eventuality in September, after winning the election).[56] Elsewhere, however, the political omens were more promising. In February the British government reduced its import levy from 15 per cent to 10 per cent, and Jack Lynch announced a review of trade union legislation in relation to the 1961 Educational Company case, which had restricted traditional picketing rights.[57] The following day Casement's remains returned to Dublin, and Lemass, after welcoming them home, departed to Rome for the highly visible conferring of the red hat on Cardinal William Conway.

On the Dáil front, Fine Gael was seething with disagreements about Declan Costello's draft of his 'Just Society' policy. The Labour Party had again declared against coalition. The death of Dan Desmond TD in Cork and the selection of his widow, Eileen, as the Labour Party's by-election candidate now presented Lemass with an opportunity that he found difficult to refuse. In three of the previous five by-elections the deceased TD's widow had been returned and in a fourth the deceased TD's son. When Lemass declared that Eileen Desmond's election would precipitate a dissolution of the Dáil[58] it was the shortest-odds political bet he had taken in years. He was not even perturbed when he was telephoned by Kevin McCourt, the director-general of RTE, who told him that because of an industrial dispute there would be no television during part of the campaign.

This, Lemass remarked to an astonished McCourt, was the best news he had had in years.[59] Desmond won, and Lemass asked the President to dissolve the Dáil before she had even taken her seat, and fought the general election under the slogan 'Let Lemass lead on'.

He attacked Fine Gael vigorously on the economy — particularly on their contention, which was more accurate than he cared to admit, that things were getting out of control, particularly in relation to the balance of payments. He revelled in portraying Labour as a party 'tied up by antiquated ideas and out of place notions about the world in which we have to live and work' and as 'an ineffectual group of well-meaning men who would like to do some good but have no very clear notions how to go about it.'[60] Fianna Fáil increased its vote from 43.8 per cent (in 1961) to 47.7 per cent, winning seventy-two seats, exactly half the total.

The election was more vigorously fought than the one in 1961, with Lemass harping particularly on Fine Gael's promise to restrict credit in order to deal with the crisis and on the Labour Party's inability to break with its no-coalition strategy. A number of the older deputies had been at last prevailed on to step aside. They did not include Seán MacEntee, who resisted Lemass's suggestion and, reminded of his age, replied tartly: 'You're no chicken yourself.'[61] MacEntee's obduracy was rewarded by two Fianna Fáil seats in his constituency — the first such victory since it was created in 1948 — and a bitter defeat for Noel Browne, who was running for the National Progressive Democrats after failing to secure the Fianna Fáil nomination in 1961.

An unexpected element of light relief was provided in mid-campaign when Terence de Vere White, the literary editor of the *Irish Times,* wrote an editorial that was published on the morning of 1 April, asking why Lemass had pledged to introduce prohibition if returned to office and pleading: 'May we at this late hour beseech Mr Lemass to reconsider his decision, face the charge of pusillanimity, and cancel unequivocally his promise?'[62] Despite the fact that the article was festooned with references to the date, Lemass or his officials reacted before seeing the joke, and the Government Information Bureau issued a statement quoting the Taoiseach as saying that 'the *Irish Times,* which seems to have passed under the control of a group of crypto-reds, supporting left-wing elements in the Labour Party, has now, for the first time, introduced the Communist tactic of attributing to its political opponents statements which they never made.' Shortly afterwards Lemass was apprised of the joke and was offered the opportunity of withdrawing his statement. Possibly realising that the resultant publicity wouldn't do him any harm in the long run, he decided to let the statement stand. The *Irish Times* published it in full on its front page the following morning, accompanied by a photograph of a jovial Lemass sipping a glass of stout. Beside the photograph were two reports of election speeches, in which Proinsias

Mac Aonghusa and Garrett Cooney, vice-chairman of the Labour Party and chairman of the Central Branch of Fine Gael, respectively, were quoted as alleging that the same newspaper had now irretrievably sold its soul to Fianna Fáil.[63]

Lemass's last rally, held at the GPO, was notable less for its upbeat prediction that Ireland would be in the Common Market by 1972 than for its sombre reference to an unfinished agenda linked to an invocation of the first battle in which he had ever participated.

> Those who fought in the Rising visualised freedom ... not as an end in itself, but as an opportunity of wiping out the squalor, decay, depression and ignorance which external rule had signified in Ireland. This is the spirit of Fianna Fáil. We have not yet fulfilled these great duties.[64]

A call to arms, or a confession of at least partial failure after nine years of continuous Fianna Fáil rule, seven of them under his stewardship? The judgment depends on the perspective of the listener, but even those most committed to Lemass's party could not fail to notice its dogged, exasperated tone.

Fianna Fáil's showing in Dublin under Lemass was particularly encouraging. Its vote went up to 48.2 per cent, the highest since 1944 and a figure that was not to be exceeded until Jack Lynch's landslide in 1977; two additional seats were filched back from Fine Gael in the capital, and another one in Cork city, where the Fianna Fáil vote went up by just over 5 per cent. Plainly the effects of the ninth-round wage increase had not yet been dissipated, despite the inroads it was beginning to make into the economic infrastructure. At one campaign speech in Meath, Lemass made no bones about it: Fianna Fáil was the party that had put a pound a week in the working man's pocket, and no other party or parties could promise or deliver as much.[65]

The overall result of the election was not exactly comfortable, and it could easily have been better. Fianna Fáil lost seats in Dublin North-East and in Mayo by handfuls of votes, a seat in Mayo by fourteen votes, and seats in Carlow-Kilkenny and Waterford by slightly larger margins. It was, nonetheless, a lot more comfortable than governing with a minority that varied between three and four seats, and Lemass formed what was to be his last Government.

It also represented a substantial gain on the 1961 result, even though the objective circumstances were in some respects less favourable. One important political element was different in 1965, however: this was the fact that, as a result of the 1961 election, Fianna Fáil had won two elections in a row for the first time since 1944. The electoral volatility that had been inaugurated in 1948 appeared to have subsided. Lemass was no longer the new and untried face on the poster. And the ill-starred (as it turned out) eighth-round wage increase of 12 per cent had been concluded, with its implication for many workers of a psychologically important additional pound in the weekly wage packet.

By now, however, Lemass was feeling his age and the cumulative effects of smoking a pound of strong pipe tobacco every week. Even before 1965, the year of his sixteenth successive election battle, he confessed to an intense dislike of the old forms of electioneering: torchlight processions, brass bands, and hours of oratory from creaky platforms at gale-swept crossroads. 'I wish to God I hadn't to go through with this,' he told one reporter after the Dáil had been dissolved. 'It would be nice to get some disease that can be cured so that I could stay out of it and get some sympathetic votes at the same time.'[66]

This was an election that also saw the introduction to the electoral process — at least by Fianna Fáil — of marketing techniques, which plainly fascinated Lemass as well as amused him. A year later he publicly reflected on this, tongue in cheek, noting that Harold Wilson had told him that he owed his own political success to his ability to project the image of a family doctor.

> At the beginning of a recent general election here, the public relations experts who were assisting my political party had to select a photograph of myself for reproduction on posters and so forth. I wished to have one chosen which might, with some touching up, depict me as a dynamic, keen-eyed and determined sort of person, and project a general image of competence and efficiency. I found that our public relations people would have none of this and were determined to present a photograph which was supposed to depict me as benign and good-humoured — almost placid in fact. It was the idea of these experts that the public, in selecting their political representatives, prefer those who look most human to those who look most competent. I suppose this does credit to the good sense of the ordinary voter. In most walks of life, and not only in politics, is humanity valued more highly than efficiency.[67]

By now, 'efficiency' was shouldering at least some of those with a more avuncular mien out of the way. Aiken and Lemass himself were the last surviving members of de Valera's 1932 government still in office. By now, however, Lemass was only twenty months away from his own retirement, and the job of radically reshaping a Government, a party and a policy would remain unfinished in certain important respects. He spoke about all of this not long after the election, when he suggested that it had 'marked a new stage in Irish political development.' Specifically, he made no bones about his belief that the 'younger men, now acquiring greater responsibilities, are in many respects far better equipped personally for the duties of political leadership than were those who carried them in the period which is now ending.'[68]

He still had time, however, for two more political initiatives. One was the revision of his predecessor's Constitution; the other was the overhaul of the public service. He had already taken somewhat unorthodox steps to achieve the first objective by appointing reforming judges to the Supreme Court. Now, coming towards the end of his career, Lemass decided to increase the pressure. In a carefully worded speech in Limerick in March 1966 he identified a number of constitutional areas in particular that needed attention: the way in which the working of the Dáil impeded the expeditious disposal of business; new ideas about the organisation of government; the structure of Government departments; and the soundness of administrative methods.[69]

Lemass's original idea was that it would be a mixed committee — that it would include non-elected experts as well as members of the Oireachtas. In negotiations with the leaders of Fine Gael and the Labour Party, however, he had to modify his ideas in order to get agreement, and Jack Lynch was concerned about a possible overlap with the work of the Devlin Committee. Brendan Corish was opposed to non-members of the Oireachtas being included, and Liam Cosgrave insisted that membership should in no sense bind those who served on it, or their parties, to any proposed action or recommendation.[70]

Lemass managed to incorporate in the eventual press release the suggestion that the committee's membership would be 'initially' confined to Oireachtas members; but in fact it was never broadened. Nor, so far as can be ascertained, did it ever set up a proposed subcommittee on legal matters, which would — or so the Attorney-General suggested — have included Dónal Barrington, Matt Russell, Liam Hamilton, John Kelly, Gerald Goldberg, Brian Walsh, and John Kenny.

Lemass ran George Colley's name past both Lynch and Aiken for their approval as chairman of the committee and told Colley that 'we should select the younger members of the party for the committee, and in this way ... emphasise that our main concern is to adapt the rules and practices of government to the country's future needs.' This led directly to the appointment of the all-party informal committee on the Constitution under Colley's chairmanship in August 1966. It had no Northern representative, a fact that evoked a bitter comment from the leader of the Nationalist Party in Northern Ireland, Eddie McAteer.[71] The question of electoral reform was clearly being left on the back burner: in his March speech Lemass took care not to specify any issues that might prove controversial, and in his various suggestions about subjects for the agenda sent to the Attorney-General and to Colley while he was still Taoiseach he did not include divorce. The

Irish Press did its best to mark everyone's cards: 'There can, of course, be no question of tampering with the democratic and Christian nature of the document.'[72]

Late 1966 saw action on the second initiative, designed to run side by side with the committee on the Constitution: the Public Services Organisation Review Group (later commonly called 'Green Devlin', from the colour of its report), which had as its remit the examination in particular of the huge web of state-sponsored bodies that had grown up over the years, not least under Lemass's tutelage, the relationship between them and Government departments, and the implications of rapid social and economic change for administrative and political decision-making systems.[73] As one of his closest collaborators put it,

> doubts about the ability of departments to operate as development corporations in certain areas led him to set up boards and other bodies and give them executive functions: the inevitable fragmentation arising from a succession of such decisions was one of the reasons for the Devlin review of the organisation of the public services, which was set up a matter of weeks before his retirement in 1966.[74]

Lemass's 1961 injunction to departments to think of themselves as development corporations had an undesirable effect in at least one sense, as far as the state-sponsored companies were concerned. Given that some of them had made mistakes — as Lemass himself foresaw was inevitable — it encouraged some departments to attempt to reassert a degree of control over some of their operations that those whom Lemass had originally put in charge of them, at any rate, believed to be the negation of his original concept.[75] Equally, some of the state bodies interpreted his encouraging remarks as a licence to expand, and the financial basis for such expansion — much of it under Lemass's successor — was not always sound, which in turn prompted fresh departmental irredentism.

The situation was complicated in addition by a growing disparity in culture between the administrative leadership in both sectors. While the state-sponsored bodies were being given their head, central administration remained highly compartmentalised. In 1966, just before he retired, Lemass returned once more to this theme and chose Liam St John Devlin, an energetic young Corkman who had been plucked from the Cork Harbour Board by Lemass's Department of Industry and Commerce to oversee a reorganisation of Irish Shipping, and asked him to head a new committee to look into the public service as a whole. When Devlin and Thekla Beere, who had been appointed Secretary of Industry and Commerce during Lemass's last reign there, interviewed secretaries of departments in 1967, 'it was apparent that some Secretaries had never met their colleagues either on a business or on a social basis. In general they were not encouraged to meet in committee, and this isolation strengthened the autonomy of departments.'[76]

Lemass's last intervention on the topic, in an interview in 1968, instanced in particular his failure to gain acceptance for the idea of the interchangeability of senior officers between departments and between the civil service and the state boards. He admitted that

> this idea never got off the ground. Even Ministers who supported it in theory were reluctant to apply it in practice when it meant passing over 'the next in line' for promotion or involved the risk of discontent among their officers. I suppose I was really trying to change human nature, and that the idea is in practice unworkable.[77]

Lemass had not been able to finish the agenda himself, but he had certainly left a full list of items for his successor.

Any momentum he might have achieved in his final period of office was now increasingly vulnerable to rumours of his impending retirement, rumours that he did little to quell and in some cases instigated. When he spoke at Jim Ryan's retirement in 1965 he noted that this was a prospect he would have to face himself, and 'that might not be too far off.'[78] He told at least four ministers — Lynch, Colley, Haughey, and Hillery — that he believed them to have leadership potential; Hillery rejected the suggestion,[79] as initially did Lynch. There were times, he confessed early in 1966, when he felt

> frustrated and exhausted, and where the prospect of walking out and leaving the whole thing behind me is terribly attractive. A president of one of the South American states did this, didn't he? He took a boat for Europe and left everything behind him. I can understand this very well indeed.[80]

On 4 October 1966 the *Irish Times* announced confidently that Lemass was 'certain to retire within 8–9 months.'[81] It was not to know how much closer the date would actually be.

7

The Economy

'A very broadminded gentleman with a world-wide conception'

In his first press conference as Taoiseach, Lemass signalled his intention of establishing a Development Branch in the Department of Finance. The contrast with his predecessor could not have been more marked. In 1958 de Valera met a delegation from the International Monetary Fund, which Ireland had joined the previous year. T. K. Whitaker, who shepherded the delegation in to see the ageing Taoiseach, recalled:

> When I took them in to see Dev they were treated to a version of the St Patrick's Day 1943 speech. I tried, without much success, to introduce the development note. After we left, Merwin, the United States member of the IMF group, noted carefully: 'He's a strange man, your prime minister.'[1]

De Valera, conscious of the impact that any reduction in tariffs would have on employment, was lukewarm at best about the prospect of opening up the economy.[2] For Lemass, on the other hand, it was a question of economic life or death. His objective was the early integration of the economy into an international trading bloc that would provide it with an export market for agricultural and industrial production and stimulate investment. The difficulty was to achieve both of these objectives without opening the door to free trade so rapidly that the resulting draught would extinguish the still fitful flame of industrial employment. At the same time he hoped to harness the energies of the recently reunited trade union movement, but in a manner that would not unleash wage inflation and undermine competitiveness.

What he was doing, in a sense, was redefining nationalism. Although it still had an irreducible geographical aspect, its principal components were now human and economic: uniting people, and building a new society. The times too were propitious. International trading conditions, of key significance for a small and increasingly open economy, were improving, and 'the terrible and inevitable cycle of boom and slump, so murderous between the wars, became a succession of mild fluctuations.'[3] The European market was stabilising and growing as the unemployed were transformed into consumers: throughout the nineteen-sixties, Europe averaged only $1\frac{1}{2}$ per cent of its labour force out of work.

Reflecting these changed international circumstances and in large part assisted by them, the Irish economy was to grow at an unprecedented rate. The apparently optimistic targets of the First Programme were not only achieved but exceeded, as growth averaged an unprecedented 4 per cent per year and emigration, Lemass's greatest bugbear, shrank satisfactorily from a high of 44,427 in 1961 to a satisfying figure of 12,226 in 1963.[4]

His attempt to open up the economy had four distinct phases, some of them strongly influenced by external factors over which he had no control. The first phase lasted from the time he took power until the French veto on Britain's EEC application in January 1963. The second extended from then until the import surcharge imposed by the Labour Party government in Britain in October 1964. The third took him up to the successful conclusion of the Anglo-Irish Free Trade Area Agreement in December 1965. The fourth and final phase took him into an economic endgame up to his retirement in November 1966, which was marked — in spite of the relief afforded by the 1965 agreement with Britain — by a rapidly worsening balance of payments problem and industrial and farmer unrest. There had been brief honeymoons with the trade union movement early in 1964 and with the farmers later the same year, but both organisations rapidly broke the silken fetters with which he had attempted to bind them, and the fragility of the mechanisms set up to encourage a consensus on economic policy became ever more apparent.

PHASE 1: NEW HORIZONS

The new Fianna Fáil Government in 1957 had inherited, and supported, its predecessor's application to join the emerging European Free Trade Area (EFTA). In July 1958 Lemass secured the passing of the Industrial Development (Encouragement of External Investment) Act, which removed many of the remaining restrictions imposed by the Control of Manufactures Acts. In late 1958, however, the prospect of joining EFTA (with suitable safeguards, of course) evaporated with the French veto on Britain's involvement. Lemass reacted with 'disappointment, concern and dismay'[5] as Europe split down the middle: Britain and six other countries in EFTA, France and five more in the Common Market.

He was faced with Hobson's choice. EFTA membership would remove such special access as Ireland had for its industrial goods to the British market, without any corresponding or balancing gains for Irish agriculture. If he abandoned Britain and aimed at the Common Market (always assuming that this was an option, which in reality it was not) the huge volume of Irish trade with Britain would immediately be sacrificed to the

Common Market's external tariff system, without any very real expectation that German or French consumers would rapidly take the place of their British counterparts.

The economic relationship between the two countries had always been, as far as Ireland was concerned, part life-jacket, part straitjacket. As Lemass strove to refocus the economy, the dependent aspects of this relationship were becoming increasingly irksome, but the relationship itself could not be too hastily jettisoned or radically altered without imposing politically and economically unacceptable domestic costs, especially in relation to employment.

The only realistic option in the short term was to intensify the trading relationship with Britain while maintaining a diplomatic level of interest in both EFTA and the Common Market. In the short term, EFTA — despite its disadvantages — had to be given priority, if only because it would smooth the path of negotiations with Britain. Whichever option would finally be adopted, one problem remained the same: how to calculate the maximum extent to which Ireland's claim for derogations could be advanced, without running the risk of being fobbed off with associate status on the basis of its own protestations of unreadiness.

Less than a month after Lemass had become Taoiseach, in July 1959, the Government decided to explore the possibility of a new bilateral trade agreement with Britain. The British, however, had two problems: one was their new association with the other EFTA countries; the other was their long-standing structure of preferences for Commonwealth imports. When Lemass met Reginald Maudling, the Chancellor of the Exchequer, in July the British response involved renewed suggestions that Ireland should bite the bullet and join EFTA; the soft terms accorded to Portugal were at least part of the bait.

Lemass called a meeting of senior officials in October to indicate his own view, which was that Ireland should play hard to get and should not consider joining EFTA except under pressure from Britain to that end. It was not entirely clear to him why Britain was anxious that Ireland should join, and he believed that Ireland's interests were primarily to seek maximum advantage in the British market: the markets in the other EFTA countries were of marginal importance. For the time being, therefore, he suggested doing nothing, simply taking soundings in London to assess the British motives.[6] This rapidly assumed some urgency.[7]

There were, however, serious internal disagreements between Finance and Industry and Commerce about the wisdom of these tactics, and Lemass's new policy met doughty opposition from his former department. In December 1959 he told the Dáil: 'We must face up to the fact of having to reduce our protective measures at some time not too far ahead.' On the same occasion he outlined the country's strategic economic problems as he saw them:

> Neither the European Common Market nor the European Free Trade
> Area offers us prospects for increasing our agricultural trade ... Our
> principal trading customer, Britain, is in the EFTA, and this precludes
> us from considering the possibility of joining the Common Market,
> with its obligation to maintain common external tariffs against
> non-members ... It is in these circumstances that the Government
> have initiated trade negotiations with Britain.[8]

His negative assessment of the implications of the Common Market's
agricultural policy was, to say the least, surprising, even at this early
juncture. Probably he thought that any foreseeable benefits would be more
than cancelled out by the adverse consequences for agricultural exports
to Britain.

The disagreements between Finance and Industry and Commerce
found expression in a remarkable correspondence between October 1959
and January 1960, which embodied a vigorous rerun of the classic
arguments in the controversy of protection versus free trade. Whitaker, who
describes this period as 'the dark night of the soul when the acceptance in
principle by Industry and Commerce of the importance of foreign trade
began to wane,' believed that some of the civil servants involved were
against it in principle and that others were 'apprehensive of the employment
effects.'[9]

The correspondence had some of the aspects of a battle by proxy.
The letters were 'semi-official; they would have been seen by Lemass: he
knew we were writing to each other.'[10] What emerges with striking clarity
from the documents is the strength of feeling within the Department of
Industry and Commerce, which was arguing in October 1959 that the main
protected industries, employing some 65,000 workers, were so sensitive that
tariffs would have to be maintained to protect them for at least a decade.

Whitaker pressed hard for change, arguing in a memorandum for 'the
need for systematic tariff reductions here as one of the ways of ensuring
improvement in industrial efficiency and expansion of exports.' He added:

> Only formal 'free trade' arrangements with Britain, or a group includ-
> ing Britain, can provide the necessary drive and discipline on the
> industrial side as well as some prospect of gain on the agricultural side.
> One could not contemplate, without grave disquiet, the possibility of
> our remaining in what I have described as 'unprogressive isolation'.[11]

J. C. B. MacCarthy, Secretary of the Department of Industry and
Commerce, hit back sharply. The suggested reductions in tariffs would, he
argued, 'immediately hit industries providing a very large percentage of our
industrial employment.'[12] Whitaker promptly characterised this attitude as
'diehard',[13] and the tone became distinctly sharper. MacCarthy replied to

another Whitaker salvo: 'I hope that your memorandum was provocative rather than doctrinaire, based on a somewhat idealistic approach not backed by anything more than faith in the operation of the economic laws which are expounded. Tariff reduction and free trade are easy in the abstract, difficult in practice.'[14] Whitaker's reply, which began with a reference to the impending season of good will, might have been designed to pour oil on the troubled waters but only succeeded in setting it alight. 'We both of us know people who are more Catholic than the Pope,' he observed. 'Should Industry and Commerce not guard against being more protectionist than the Federation of Irish Industry?'[15]

Tadhg Ó Cearbhaill, a civil servant who worked in the senior echelons of Lemass's administration both in Kildare Street and in the Department of the Taoiseach, was prepared to see several sides to the argument:

> Industry and Commerce would have felt an obligation to a lot of those people who set up industry and did so on encouragement and the word of Industry and Commerce and also because they got protection. I don't think there was any question that they were obstructing the advent of free trade, but they definitely felt an obligation to those already in industry. Thus they argued their views strongly.[16]

Whitaker was actually fighting on two fronts. While engaging MacCarthy with one hand, he was fending off J. J. McElligott with the other. The former Secretary of the Department of Finance, now ensconced in the Central Bank, was complaining to Whitaker that 'instead of dismantling our tariff wall we seem to be constantly adding to it,' adducing as evidence a number of additional tariffs that had been applied to expensive consumer goods.[17] Whitaker was unrepentant. Noting that German economic expansion had not been inconsistent with a markedly illiberal regime in relation to agricultural imports, he made his position clear:

> My own fears in regard to high tariffs are concerned more with the effects of high protection on economic progress in the context of Free Trade than with their effect on consumers as such (paragraph 99 of the White Paper). So far as the consumer is concerned I find it hard to reconcile a strong sympathy for purchasers of refrigerators, motor cars and cameras with the general philosophy that consumer spending in this country tends to be excessive ... In fact one could ask if, in the case of motor cars, the rates are sufficiently high having regard to the contribution that motor cars make to our trade deficit and the way they help to accentuate the difficulties of our public transport system.[18]

The dominance of Lemass and Finance in the argument was underlined by the successful conclusion of trade negotiations with London on 13 April 1960, which produced a modest loosening of the protectionist regime in return for commitments by Britain favouring Irish agricultural exports. The previous day, as it happens, Whitaker had been in touch with Maurice Moynihan about the text of answers that had been prepared for Lemass in connection with an interview with the *Guardian*. What is striking about his observations is the degree to which they underline his conviction that Ireland's need was not for capital as such.

> I do not think it sound to suggest that Irish capital resources are drawn into Britain and ... I think it inappropriate to imply that it is an insufficiency of investment resources which limits the rate of industrial expansion here ... There has been no net reduction since the war in the availability of capital for Irish enterprises ... Indeed, over the period sales [of extern stocks and shares] have exceeded purchases by some £17 million ... In effect, enterprise is scarcer than capital.[19]

In five years' time there was to be a dramatic change in that position, but for the time being the new trading arrangements with Britain were confidently put forward as the blueprint for the future.

When Lemass spoke at Shannon in June about Ireland's need to internationalise its economy, British officials envisaged that 'Lemass may now have no choice but to join EFTA if Éire is not to be left outside European groupings altogether.'[20] In fact Lemass was in the process of hedging his bets. In public he adopted a positive but cautious attitude to international organisations; in private he was expressing an increased sense of urgency about the need for industrial change.

His Government's attitude was expressed in classic form in two memorandums — the first from Whitaker — to the OEEC Committee on Trade Problems early in 1960.[21] These memorandums, in a series outlining Ireland's case for accession to the proposed free trade grouping of seventeen states, laid considerable emphasis on the special circumstances governing the Irish economy, coupled with a plea that it would be unfair to exclude Ireland from any international grouping because of these. It argued in effect for an appropriate transition period before the country could assume the obligations of full membership in any multinational organisation and offered a firm purpose of amendment in relation to protection: 'It is government policy in future in the case of new industries to confine the grant of tariff protection to cases in which it is clear that the industries will, after a short initial period, be able to survive without protection.'

The most striking paragraph in this document, however, is one that painted a picture of the history of Irish industrial development policy that those responsible for that policy, notably Éamon de Valera and Lemass himself, might have had difficulty in recognising.

> It has always been recognised in Ireland that the home market for many types of goods is too small to support industry on a scale that would

give adequate employment and enable goods to be produced at prices comparable with those of the mass-production industries of Britain and the continent. For that reason it has been the constant aim of Irish governments to encourage manufacturers to find markets abroad.

Acceptance of this fetching portrait of economic policy involves a notably flexible interpretation of the words 'always' and 'constant'. It is difficult to date Irish commitment to exports, other than the traditional agricultural exports to Britain or exports to other countries on a reciprocal basis, to any date earlier than 1945, fifteen years earlier. Equally, the recognition of the inability of the home market on its own to support the industrial base necessary to reduce unemployment — although Lemass had been arguing this case since before the war — had not become political orthodoxy until the publication of the First Economic Programme. When it did so it was in a slightly different context, as the Government was arguing somewhat disingenuously that the opportunity to develop exports now arose primarily because of the virtual satisfaction of the domestic market. In some areas, as already noted, the domestic market's needs had been virtually satisfied since before the war.

Lemass, far from being tempted by the prospect of joining EFTA, as Britain supposed (plainly the smokescreen he had thrown up had to this extent been successful), had now come to realise that the Common Market represented a far bigger prize. As one former civil servant who was intimately involved in the negotiations recalled later:

> In the end we were not that enthusiastic as there was a feeling within government at the time that the whole concept of Europe would come right in the end and it was within a much larger unified EEC that we wanted to be associated. Lemass was very much of that view. Policy was directed with that in mind.[22]

When Lemass met Macmillan in London in July 1960 he put most of his cards on the table and told him that Ireland was considering going ahead, regardless of the attitude that Britain took. British officials were relatively sympathetic to Lemass's needs. While arguing that the opportunity existed for altering the terms of trade between the two countries to some extent in Britain's favour, they could see the benefit of coming to some agreement that would stimulate economic activity in the Republic, not least because they believed that hard times proved a fertile breeding ground for terrorism.[23] It is worth noting also at this point the British belief that Ireland 'intend to move the emphasis in their development plans more on to agri-culture.'[24] This assessment, undoubtedly grounded in *Economic Development,* was rapidly becoming out of date.

In May 1961 the Government formally decided not to join EFTA. In the same month the Minister for Finance, Jim Ryan, hinted broadly that the

EEC was now the preferred option. On 31 June the Government issued its White Paper about the EEC, and a week later it was announced that Lemass would lead a delegation to London in mid-July, not to negotiate but 'to facilitate a general exchange of views.'[25] At the end of these discussions, Lemass announced frankly, 'the position now is that if Britain decides to apply for membership, we will apply too.'[26]

The pace of events accelerated. At the end of July, Britain's decision to apply was announced, to be followed within twenty-four hours by the announcement of the Irish Government's decision.

Both before and after the formal application, Lemass made the EEC the constant topic of his speeches. His harping on this theme was not because there was any serious political opposition to the decision. The level of support was, if anything, embarrassingly high: all organised political and social groups were unusually supportive, even the Labour Party, which was to oppose the 1972 referendum on membership. The organised trade union movement was broadly in favour, as were the Federated Union of Employers and the Federation of Irish Industry, both of which had overcome their initial hesitancy about the removal of protection. The writing was on the wall for the last remnants of the Control of Manufactures Acts, despite the fact that Lemass still continued to portray the need for foreign firms as 'not so much a financial need, as for the introduction of skills in management and production in which we are still deficient.'[27] His speech on this particular occasion — a factory opening — was greeted with rare enthusiasm by the foreign industrialist involved, Dr M. Schottenhamel, who wrote later to the Taoiseach to praise him as 'a very broadminded gentleman with a world-wide conception.'[28]

Lemass could not resist the occasional bit of hands-on activity, not least in connection with projects involving his old department, Industry and Commerce, and particularly where the new production skills of which he had spoken were at issue. The Potez experiment was a prime example of this, and it was driven at least in part by his passion for aviation. Henri Potez was a French manufacturer of light aircraft, who came to Lemass with a proposal to set up a plant just outside Dublin. He was a former Resistance fighter and a man of great personal charm, who convinced Lemass that the small executive aircraft was the thing of the future: the sky taxi. When Lemass was convinced, he pressed the button on it.

The project got off the ground in May 1961, when a memorandum from Lemass to the Government suggested an endorsement of the Potez plan and argued that it would provide initial employment for a thousand people, rising eventually to double that number.[29] The problem was the money: Potez was looking for a combination of grants and loans amounting to some £2 million, whereas under normal criteria no more than £250,000 would be allocated to any one new project.

The Department of Finance could hardly wait to get its teeth into the proposal, but, undeterred by this opposition, and equally uninfluenced by an invitation from Potez to visit the Paris Air Show (which he declined), Lemass pushed ahead. Despite a second, furious memorandum from the Department of Finance, the Government agreed to a grant and loan package of almost £2 million.[30] Many years later — long after the Potez enterprise had foundered, with substantial losses — when Lemass was asked why he had taken such a risk when an equivalent investment in smaller enterprises might have produced more lasting employment, he replied simply: 'You have to go for the big ones.'[31]

Taoisigh generally get their way; but on one other project — a proposal by an Asian businessman to establish a large liner as a floating conference centre in Dublin Bay — Lemass's initial enthusiasm eventually evaporated in the face of a powerful combined assault from Whitaker and Dr Thekla Beere in Industry and Commerce.[32] By 1966 the Government was forced to agree to withdraw all further assistance to Potez 'unless there is legal entitlement thereto,' and the IDA was instructed to inform Potez that no further state assistance would be recommended.[33]

THE EEC AND NATO

Lemass's enthusiasm for particular projects did not interfere with the central policy objective: Common Market membership. The EEC suggested in October 1961 that the Government should present its case in Brussels the following January, and officials went ahead with some urgency on the preparation of the necessary documents. Frank Biggar, the Irish ambassador in Brussels, strongly advised the Government to emphasise its willingness to accept the political implications of membership as a counterweight to the perceived difficulties posed by the country's less developed economic status. The problem with the draft he was sent arose

> from a failure to emphasise sufficiently at the outset our appreciation of the fact that the EEC despite its title, is first and foremost a political concept and not merely an economic organisation with a few political ideas as an afterthought.[34]

This brought up the question of NATO membership in a particularly forceful way. As Ireland was not a member of NATO, anything Lemass said on the subject was bound to be of interest to the existing EEC member-states, all of whom were also members of NATO. There was also, however, a serious potential disadvantage involved in airing the topic, in that any increase in the doubts expressed about the nature and extent of Ireland's commitment to the concept of European defence ran the risk of raising a number of important European eyebrows. Lemass had to steer a canny middle course.

He had told the Oxford Union in a speech in October 1959 that as far as NATO membership was concerned, 'a matter so momentous for the future of all Ireland should be determined by a parliament representing all Ireland' and that 'the removal of Partition would make possible a fresh approach to consideration of the place of a reunited Ireland in the scheme of Western defence.'[35] This was a straightforward replication of de Valera's policy, but it was followed within two months by another speech that provided evidence that a 'fresh approach' was already in the making. In this speech Lemass linked Ireland's commitment to the United Nations with a repetition of his rejection of ideological neutrality but also with a verbal formula on NATO that studiously avoided mentioning partition. Lemass habitually used language with great care and with exceptional clarity and precision. It is evident, therefore, that his lapse into vagueness on this occasion was far from accidental.

> We do not accept ... that it is only through a regional military alliance that this country can make a useful contribution to the defence of these principles. We do not consider ourselves to be in any default of our obligations to the free world by reason of our not joining NATO, *apart altogether from difficulties which certain provisions of the NATO agreement present to us in our existing circumstances,* and the relative insignificance of any military contribution which we could make. [Emphasis added.][36]

In a series of speeches and press conferences thereafter, Lemass made clear his support for the aims of NATO, and in completely unambiguous terms. Ireland, he said on more than one occasion, was on the side of the democratic western nations in any conflict, real or potential, with the eastern bloc. It was an area in which his personal views about communism, and the political exigencies of the world of international affairs in which he was manoeuvring, coincided neatly. In December 1960, before the Irish EEC application, he stated baldly: 'There is no neutrality and we are not neutral.'[37]

Not just because of the permanent aura of ambiguity about NATO, Fianna Fáil's enthusiasm for the European venture was in some respects muted, not least among Lemass's Government colleagues.[38] To counter any hesitancy, Lemass embarked on a flanking manoeuvre, making his 1961 ardfheis the platform for a public endorsement of his policy by the party faithful. He secured the adoption of a motion expressing 'approval of the manner in which the government is handling the negotiations for Ireland's entry into the EEC and on its approach to international affairs in general.'[39] He told the ardfheis:

> Membership of the Common Market is open to those nations which accept the political aims which inspired it. A movement to political

confederation in some form, is indeed a natural and logical development of economic integration. Henceforth our national aims must
conform to the emergence, in a political as well as in an economic
sense, of a union of Western European States, not as a vague prospect
of the distant future but as a living reality of our own times.[40]

This statement, if it had been made in the nineteen-nineties, would
appear little more than a bland truism; in the circumstances of the early
sixties, on the other hand, it carried far more weight. It was a finely calculated exercise in political revisionism, and one designed to take over the
high ground at that. One of its two key revisionist sentiments is to be found
in the approval of the concept of confederation — a concept long rejected
by de Valera. The other, potentially more explosive, was the declaration that
'our national aims' were no longer pre-eminent in themselves but now had
to conform to external criteria.

It is difficult to overestimate the degree to which this global framework,
even more than the economic policy that underpinned it, constituted a
reversal of the policies that Lemass and his predecessor had enthusiastically
endorsed. In the circumstances it was a brilliant finesse, enhanced by his
accompanying suggestion that one of the primary national aims — the abolition of partition — would be facilitated by the internationalisation of the
economy. He was writing a scenario in which his economic and political
objectives were deliberately linked; the final abandonment of the national
aim of self-sufficiency would deliver the political aim of unity.

His ardfheis speech, in particular, evoked a warm welcome from the
American Under-Secretary of State, George Tyler, who told the Irish
ambassador in Washington, T. J. Kiernan, that it had removed 'any feeling
that we are to be seen in the same position as any other country, such as
Sweden, Switzerland, Austria.'[41]

Lemass followed this up by orchestrating, or at least indicating prior
approval for, a remarkable speech delivered by the Minister for Lands,
Micheál Ó Móráin, at a party function in Mayo in February 1962.
Ó Móráin argued that 'neutrality [between communism and freedom] is not
a policy to which we would even wish to appear committed.'[42] Noting that
the 'profits and advantages' of EEC membership brought with them
'responsibilities and commitments,' he went on: 'We have a full part to play
... and to this end it may be necessary for us to share any political decisions
for the common good.' The speech created a storm of controversy.
Ó Móráin, who had not been led to expect any such response, was besieged
by journalists looking for amplification of his remarks and telephoned
Lemass in a state of considerable anxiety. Lemass's unhelpful advice was to
'hold a press conference'![43] Ó Móráin, uncharacteristically, went to ground.

Inside as well as outside Fianna Fáil, the temperature increased
perceptibly. In the Dáil Noel Browne and Jack McQuillan, the only

parliamentary members of the tiny National Progressive Democrats party, scented blood. Lemass told them that Ó Móráin's speech — 'but not the interpretation placed upon it in certain newspapers' — was in accordance with Government policy.[44] This was not destined to be the end of the affair.

Lemass's positive 1961–62 noises on NATO, indeed, had the dual function of reassuring the EEC powers and at the same time 'tweaking' the potential American interest in the Northern problem.[45] His creative flexibility on the issue of NATO arose from the fact that — as he had come to realise but as many of his questioners were slower to find out — there is nothing in the treaty that compromises the Irish position on Northern Ireland. The key section refers primarily to the need for participating states to consult each other 'when, in the opinion of any them, the territorial integrity, political independence or security of the Parties is threatened'[46] — which is quite a different thing.

In Europe, Lemass's noises were being noted with approval by senior Commission officials, by one of the commissioners, Dr Sicco Mansholt, and by the Dutch Minister for Foreign Affairs, Henri Spaak.[47] Whitaker for his part was more conscious of the possible dissonance arising from the reaction in the Dáil and warned against the possible growth of 'the impression that we would not join any defence arrangement that included Great Britain.'[48]

Jack McQuillan TD put it up to Lemass in the Dáil in March 1962. Either the NATO treaty involved recognition of partition or it didn't, he suggested. If it didn't — as Lemass was now saying, despite having said precisely the opposite ten years earlier — both the Taoiseach and his predecessor had been talking through their hats.[49] Lemass, after disingenuously remarking that he could not understand why McQuillan and others kept 'harping on this question of NATO' and accusing them of trying to cause embarrassment for Ireland in the EEC negotiations, finally bit the bullet.

> I confess I never read the text of the North Atlantic Treaty until it became necessary for me to do so when certain questions were addressed to me in the Dáil relating to its provisions. I had no occasion to study it earlier. When I did read it, however, and came across this article which had been interpreted over the years as implying that accession to the Treaty would involve some implication in relation to partition, some undertaking to do nothing about Partition, I began to ask myself was it wise in the national interest that we should persist in forcing that interpretation on the Treaty article.[50]

He stopped well short of pointing out that John A. Costello had been one of the principal architects of the misunderstanding he was now abandoning, no doubt because it would have meant also admitting that de Valera was the other.

Few shifts of national policy in the field of partition or of international affairs can have been enunciated with so little fanfare — or finessed so expertly. Keatinge suggests that in his 1962 reply Lemass 'argued that the existence of partition was *no longer* in itself a reason for refusing to join the North Atlantic Treaty Organisation.' (Emphasis added.)[51] It was not that it was 'no longer' a reason for the refusal to join: Lemass's statement was, on the face of it, an admission that it never had been.

By July 1962 the weakness of the anti-NATO argument was implicitly recognised, and the anti-NATO stance itself all but abandoned, when Lemass told the *New York Times* that 'we are prepared to go into this integrated Europe without any reservations as to how far this will take us in the field of foreign policy and defence.'[52] He made similarly reassuring noises in private meetings with British ministers in London in 1963.[53]

Throughout 1962, enthusiasm for EEC entry became more palpable, especially after the formal presentation of Ireland's case by Lemass in Brussels in January. In an hour-long private discussion there the previous evening Lemass told Desmond Fisher, then London editor of the *Irish Press,* that he accepted that there were political implications that might not have universal support. Neutrality, he said, had only a limited life. He was certain that we would have to give it up eventually if we joined, but he felt that Irish people would accept as a Christian nation that we could not be seen to be neutral in the fight against communism. Fisher later recalled:

> He predicted great changes in Ireland before the end of the century — contraception and divorce being legalised and materialism becoming widespread because of growing prosperity. Back in 1962 these predictions seemed, at least to me, to be a bit daring. Up to a point, he welcomed changed social *mores,* but I felt that he was a bit pessimistic about a future in which some of the good qualities of the Irish people would be lost or diminished. It was the first intimation I had got that there was a human being behind what appeared on the surface to be a politico-economic machine.[54]

Lemass followed this with a tour of European capitals, during which he advocated Ireland's case with his customary forcefulness. His priority was to ensure the acceptability of Ireland's application for full membership; haggling about transitional arrangements could wait until later. One of his meetings was with the French Minister for Finance, Valéry Giscard d'Estaing, who, according to one account, was surprised to hear from Lemass that both Irish industry and agriculture were now well placed to take on the challenge of Common Market membership. Towards the end of the discussion Giscard d'Estaing apparently suggested to Lemass that, whatever about the strengths of the Irish economy — about which he had plainly been misled in the past — there was a possibility that Ireland would need some sort of assistance for the *décollage.* Lemass replied confidently: 'I don't know what that is, but you can take it that we don't need any of it in Ireland.'[55]

The political difficulties unconnected with NATO now began to loom larger on the horizon. Chief among them were the potential fate of the British application. Those familiar with de Gaulle's thoughts on the matter, first published in 1959, would not have needed a crystal ball. Since 1940, de Gaulle wrote, he had been convinced of the need to create a new organisation of those states bordering the Rhine, the Alps, and the Pyrenees, and to make of it a world power that could, if necessary, also become the arbiter between the Soviet and the Anglo-Saxon camps. 'Now that France is on its feet,' he added triumphantly, 'I will hasten to achieve these objectives.'[56] The top levels of the EEC were not unaware of this, or of the symbiotic economic relationship between Ireland and Britain.

A month after Lemass's presentation, Fisher returned to Brussels for an on-the-record interview with Walter Hallstein, president of the EEC Commission, and asked him how the processing of the Irish application was going.

> He opened a drawer on the left-hand side of his desk and pointed to a fat folder inside. 'That's the Irish application,' he said. 'I have not even opened it.' I asked him why. 'There's no need to,' he replied. 'If the UK goes in, you go also; if not, you too will stay out. Britain can possibly come in without Ireland but Ireland cannot come in without Britain.'

Fisher reported as much to the *Irish Press,* but his article was never published. He was later told by the paper's managing director, Vivion de Valera, that it had been suppressed in order not to shock the Irish public. Ironically, the Government was aware of it: Fisher gave a carbon copy to his friend Valentin Iremonger, who was then attached to the Irish embassy in London, where it went onto the official file.

Lemass warned the 1962 Fianna Fáil ardfheis in graphic terms of the perils facing Ireland if it did not join. 'The alternative course would condemn us in perpetuity to a position of economic inferiority, leave us a beggar among the nations, seeking to maintain a dying economy on the crumbs of charity from our wealthy neighbours.'[57] George Colley even asked the parliamentary party to consider the possibility that Fianna Fáil should formally adhere to one of the political groupings in the European Parliament; Lemass, evidently anxious not to raise hares at this stage that could not easily be run to ground, told the party that the time was not yet opportune, and the motion was withdrawn.[58]

PHASE 2: BACK TO THE DRAWING-BOARD

On 1 January 1963 the first 10 per cent slice was taken off the protective tariff regime. Two weeks later, however, de Gaulle vetoed the British application for membership of the EEC, presenting the Irish Government with a fait accompli. Lemass put the best possible face on it, reassuring the parliamentary party at its meeting on 30 January and telling the Dáil a few days later that the suspension of negotiations 'should be viewed as a temporary setback and not as a final breach.'[59]

Public composure on this issue was not, however, matched in private, and Lemass wrote to the secretary of his department early in February urging that the provisions of the EFTA agreement relating to the accession of new members be re-examined.[60] He suggested the tactic of making an informal approach to the EFTA secretariat, of which he knew the British government would instantly be informed; the rumoured interest of the Danes in increased opportunities for agricultural products within EFTA, he thought, might be a convenient peg on which to hang the Irish initiative. Two days later the Committee of Secretaries advised against such a move, and the business of getting the economic lifeboat ready was abandoned, at least for the time being.

In the circumstances, Lemass's suggestion that membership of EFTA was the alternative approach now open to the Government was difficult to understand, given the serious disadvantages for agriculture in particular attendant on such a move. The more likely rationale for the suggestion was threefold: firstly, to indicate clearly that internationalisation of the economy, in whatever form, was not an option but a necessity; secondly, to remind industrialists that the necessary work of adjustment and reorganisation could not be postponed; and, thirdly, to smooth the path for subsequent negotiations with Britain aimed at further improving the terms of trade between the two countries as an end in itself.

Negotiations with Britain were further down the line; for the moment the main emphasis was on internal reorganisation. One of the chief instruments designed for this purpose was the Committee on Industrial Organisation, a tripartite body involving the Government, employers, and trade union representation (the union representation was omitted from the initial formula for membership but included after protests). The very fact that the committee was created at all came as the result of a decisive intervention by Lemass. Louden Ryan, who served in a number of capacities in the Department of Finance while Lemass was Taoiseach, had, with C. H. Murray, been pressing Jim Murphy in the Department of Industry and Commerce to do something to encourage industry to adapt for free trade but got a 'polite brush-off'.

> Ken Whitaker raised the issue with Lemass. I think it was probably Lemass's suggestion that I should air the issue in an article in the *Irish Banking Review*. Certainly, I think that the setting up of the CIO soon after that was his decision.[61]

In a very short time the committee put together a series of twenty-six sectoral reports covering the whole range of industry, revealing 'a bleak picture of an industrial sector beset by shoddy design, poor marketing, and short production runs.'[62] The 1963 veto intensified rather than slackened this process. An Bord Bainne and Córas Tráchtála were strengthened; the 1962 budget had already provided additional help for the adaptation of industry to meet EEC conditions, including a doubling of tax allowances on industrial plant, buildings and equipment and the introduction of other incentives to help with re-equipment, production, and marketing.

THE UNIONS: APERTURA A SINISTRA

At this point the convergence of Lemass's macro-economic strategy and his micro-economic policy becomes clearer. The fact that he was stalled on the macro level, while it was undoubtedly a disappointment, also gave him a breathing-space within which to attempt to rectify some of the problems he had identified. And the reunification of the trade union movement that had taken place in 1959 gave him an opportunity that had not existed for more than two decades to knit unions and employers together into a new framework that would help him to achieve industrial progress without — he hoped — industrial conflict.

This framework depended in turn on a strategy that had formed the basis of Lemass's praxis since his earliest days in Industry and Commerce: the identification — and where necessary the consolidation — of key negotiating partners, whose primary characteristic was their ability to speak authoritatively on behalf of particular sectors of economic activity and their capacity to deliver their membership behind agreed targets and programmes. Ideologically, this could perhaps be described as corporatist or semi-corporatist in approach; but it was more essentially a management technique, as can be seen from Lemass's undoubted belief that the Government was the place where all key decisions were ultimately made and where political responsibility resided.

His approach to the unions, in particular, had at first been upbeat. At his first meeting with the ICTU, in September 1959, his warnings about the need to keep incomes in check were softened by his revelation that the Government was contemplating a scheme to provide retirement pensions and by his praise of the role of the state-sponsored enterprises. Generally, he told the delegation, he was 'always in favour of promoting a State enterprise if there was a reasonable prospect of success — success in this case being represented by a smaller return on capital than would normally satisfy a private concern.'[63] Six weeks later he told the Dublin Chamber of Commerce that competitive costs were not inconsistent with higher wages, and argued: 'We have too many employers whose attitude to efficiency and cost control is limited to turning long faces to their workers when they propose wage increases.'[64]

It was not long, however, before this somewhat gung-ho attitude to development had been displaced by concern about the emerging gap between wages and productivity, expressed largely in the eighth-round pay increases in 1961, which fed through into an emerging balance of payments problem. Lemass described the haphazard way in which the eighth round had taken place as 'most disturbing' and warned that, especially in the light of the Government's level of involvement in the employment market, 'the feasibility of the Government's maintaining their passive role in the future must now come into question.'[65]

Matching action to words, in February the Government issued a White Paper entitled *Closing the Gap,* which called for wage restraint; the ICTU retaliated by withdrawing from the bipartite National Employer-Labour Conference. From early 1963 on, therefore, Lemass's attention was turned, with a growing sense of urgency, towards the solution of this problem. In March 1963 he prepared a note on arrangements for increasing wages and salaries for discussion at meetings with both the FUE and the ICTU, in which he urged that 'wages and salaries should, in each alternate year, be adjusted upward at an average rate slightly less than the realised growth of national production' — the idea behind the differential being to provide a margin 'for social insurance benefits or other desirable social objects.'[66] He suggested a two-year period for a national pay agreement and was even prepared, he told the delegations, to consider the possibility of legislation to enforce national agreements made between employers and unions, in circumstances in which the negotiating parties were finding it difficult to deliver their members' commitment to implement what had been decided.

In private, as he was telling Jack Lynch at the same time, his view was that 'one of the main weaknesses in our present situation is the lack of cohesion and authority in the Trade Union movement.' He added:

> I have often considered the desirability of amending our Trade Union legislation to require a Trade Union of workers, as a condition of enjoying the protection of the Trade Union Acts, to be affiliated to the Congress of Trade Unions (or approved by them in some manner), the Congress having the power to withdraw affiliation in any case, subject perhaps to some system of appeal. I do not suggest that the Irish Congress of Trade Unions would welcome such legislation at this time and would probably object to its enactment, but I do not see how they could refuse to operate it.[67]

Lemass's harking back to the unachieved aim of the 1941 trade union legislation was fruitless on this occasion — Industry and Commerce advised strongly against the proposed course of action — but it was an objective to which he returned later. In the meantime he was so keen to achieve progress on this front that he was prepared to keep the FUE, initially at any rate, at some distance from the process of reviewing trade union legislation that Lynch and the ICTU had inaugurated. And he took pains, in the first address ever made by a Taoiseach to a conference of the ITGWU, to praise the change in the attitude of the unions 'from a defensive aloofness to positive participation.'[68]

His desire to incorporate the unions in the business of national planning was stimulated ostensibly by the process, then in train, of preparing the Second Programme for Economic Development. The institutional mechanism created by Lemass in 1963 for this process was the National Industrial Economic Council, chaired by Whitaker, which was welcomed by the unions as a 'bold and imaginative approach.'[69] This was in spite of the fact that Lemass plainly saw one of its main functions as the elaboration of a stable incomes policy and instructed it to 'have regard to the level and trend of incomes, from whatever source.'[70]

Even at this stage, however, there were signs, unacknowledged in public, that the optimism of 1960–62 had been built on somewhat shaky foundations and that the French veto had failed to act as a brake on the surge in expectations that had been deliberately created to help secure public acceptance for the EEC application. Wage increases had led to import increases, and wholesale prices for domestic products had risen significantly faster than those for comparable imports.[71] In other words, domestic products were becoming less, rather than more, competitive. This trend was mirrored by that for wages: between 1960 and 1961 unit wage costs rose by 8 per cent and in the period 1960–64 by 17 per cent; the increase in Britain over the 1960–64 period was 7 per cent.[72]

The emerging picture, therefore, was one of diminishing competitiveness; increasing consumption, which was not being matched by productivity and which was fuelled by larger wage increases than were justifiable in the circumstances; the direction of much of that consumption towards imports; and a major contribution by the Government in directing much investment into the social sector, especially from 1964 onwards, as younger ministers in spending departments began to get the bit between their teeth.

All this was compounded by an accelerating drift from the land, which, combined with the slow-down in emigration, began to produce an employment problem that was looking increasingly unmanageable on the basis of any realistic projection for national growth. In the decade to 1961 the farm population had fallen by almost 400,000.[73] The largest subcategory after farmers themselves, that of sons and daughters working on the farm, had fallen by 39.8 per cent. Emigration was falling rapidly — it had been more than 44,000 in 1961 and was to fall to just over 12,000 by 1964 — and the pressure on the labour market from both factors was building up inexorably.

If this were not enough, the Central Statistics Office decided to change the basis for compiling the unemployment statistics between the time when

the economic statistics were created for the 1962 budget and the formulation of the Second Programme. The Government was unaware
of this change, although Lemass had himself been pressing Jim Ryan and,
through him, the CSO for changes in the calculation of the live register
that would exclude people who 'could not, because of age, infirmity, or
lack of interest in work, be really regarded as wage-earners involuntarily
unemployed.'[74] The change envisaged by the CSO, however, had the effect
of worsening rather than improving the unemployment figures. The fact
that it had been made did not emerge until the ICTU asked for labour
force statistics during 1963. Before providing the statistics the CSO
notified the Government of the effect of the changes, prompting Tadhg
Ó Cearbhaill to warn the Secretary to the Government of the import of
the new calculations.

Essentially, they meant that instead of an increase in employment aver-
aging 0.7 per cent per year in the two previous years, total employment had
actually fallen. The task facing the Government was now to find 87,000
new jobs between 1963 and 1970 instead of, as had previously been
thought, 78,000 between 1960 and 1970. In other words, new jobs were now
required at a rate of some 15,000 a year, almost twice the projected seven to
eight thousand. Not only was the hill ahead turning into a mountain but
the slope already climbed was beginning to look less impressive.

No matter how the figures were calculated, the Taoiseach was warned,
they showed a continuous decrease in total employment going back as far as
1951, only a modest proportion of which could be laid at the door of the
second inter-party Government.[75] Dr M. D. McCarthy, the head of the CSO,
was diplomatically invited to consider whether there were other possible
ways of looking at the figures; but, after a somewhat guarded exchange of
views, the matter was allowed to drop. Lemass referred to this problem in a
somewhat aggrieved tone in the budget debate, when he expressed his
disbelief in the labour force statistics that indicated that 19,000 relatives of
farmers had left full-time farming in 1962 and that in the previous year the
number of relatives who assisted farmers had increased by 5,000.
'Something seems to have gone seriously wrong with some of our national
statistics,' he commented.[76]

It was going to be a difficult year for other reasons too. Restoring price
and income stability had to be given precedence, and the mechanism
chosen — the $2\frac{1}{2}$ per cent turnover tax, introduced in the budget on
23 April — proved to be one of the most unpopular and controversial of
Lemass's fiscal initiatives. The second and committee stages of the Finance
Bill were passed by a margin of only one vote, and one particular deputy
who voted for the tax, Joe Leneghan from County Mayo, earned the sobriquet 'Turnover Tax Joe', which was to stick with him for the remainder of
his relatively brief parliamentary career.

Signs of the Government's unpopularity were immediately evident. In May, in a by-election in Dublin North-West, where Fianna Fáil had taken three of the five seats in 1961, its candidate secured only 33.4 per cent of the first-preference votes.

Lemass's speech on this budget was noteworthy in particular for what has been described as his *apertura a sinistra* — his suggestion, in effect, that national policy should move to the political left. It embodied an extraordinary 139-word sentence in which he expressed sentiments that his Labour Party opponents, at least, would have had difficulty in disagreeing with. On one level it was plainly an attempt to repair the damage caused by *Closing the Gap*. Its deeper significance, however, was probably in its attempt to identify and encapsulate a social mood that, in his opinion, was likely to be electorally significant in the future.

> I believe that the time has come when national policy should take a shift to the left. By this I mean, first, more positive measures than have heretofore been attempted involving Government initiative to ensure the effective translation of the benefits of economic progress into the improvement of social conditions and specifically an equitable wage structure, wider educational opportunities, the extension of the health services and of our systems of protection against the hazards of old age, illness, and unemployment; secondly, more direct Government intervention when necessary to keep the national economy on an even keel while maintaining the pace of our economic advance; thirdly, the maintenance of State investment activity at the highest possible level having regard to available resources; and fourthly, the more detailed planning of our economic activities so as to ensure the flow of resources in the directions where prospects are best, if necessary, diverting them from sectors where prospects are poorest.[77]

This, as one perceptive commentator pointed out, might also have been designed to take the sting out of the turnover tax measure.[78] It was also part of a strategy to reharness public good will for the necessary disciplines of economic development by holding out a prospect of the social benefits obtainable at the end of the process, as can be seen from the timing of the publishing of the draft outline of the Second Programme for Economic Expansion shortly afterwards, on 22 August.

It was certainly warmly welcomed by the trade unions, who for the most part opted to ignore other sections of his speech that might have been more difficult to digest. A similar motive could be ascribed to the decision to require banks, in accordance with the recommendations of the Commission on Taxation, to make returns of the deposits they held. The turnover tax, for its part, caused considerable unease within the Fianna Fáil parliamentary party — unease that Lemass quelled by telling the TDs bluntly that the choice was between maintaining the tax and cutting expenditure.[79]

None of this reassurance, however, even when combined with the national mood of self-congratulation that accompanied President Kennedy's visit to Ireland in June 1963 and Lemass's return visit to the United States in October, was enough to offset the precariousness of his Dáil position, which was underlined when he narrowly won a vote of confidence on 30 October. At this stage, despite public reiterations of confidence in the status of Ireland's application for full EEC membership, he was acknowledging that he intended to explore the possibility of making some arrangements with the EEC in respect of trading until such time as it should become possible to resume negotiations on the application for full membership.[80]

The following year, 1964, was to see critical developments in which politics re-established its primacy over economics. This was the year in which the ninth-round national wage agreement was concluded, at a figure of 12 per cent. The nature of the agreement was, at the time, unique, in that it was the first national wage agreement as such: before this, unions and employers had come together to hammer out a recommended figure, which was then applied industry by industry. In 1964, however, the objective was to secure a national agreement into which all the member-unions of the ICTU would in effect be tied. Also of significance was the growing power of the public sector unions — whose membership at the time included many low-paid workers — and the direct participation in the talks by the Government, as an employer, alongside the FUE. It is evident that at this stage Lemass saw his principal hope for economic development and non-inflationary expansion, in a context in which the EEC had banged the door shut, as based on a wages truce with the unions.

The settlement figure, though it was intended to cover a period of two-and-a-half years, was psychologically high and was conditioned by a number of factors. One, as already noted, was the imminence of a critical pair of by-elections. The ninth round was agreed in January; the election was held in February, just after a warning by Lemass that defeat in either by-election would cause a general election. Another was the undoubted and growing strength of the united trade union movement.

Lemass, who was personally involved in suggesting the final figure, may also have been unduly optimistic about the possible date of accession to the EEC — an eventuality that, had it come earlier, would have cast even such a generous wage settlement in quite a different light. After his death a contemporary, Frederick Boland of the Department of External Affairs, suggested that Lemass had actually lacked negotiating skills. 'He would accept a breaking point sooner than was necessary,' he said. 'Whether or not he knew of this trait in his character, it often puzzled me why one so confident in other things disliked the crunch in negotiations.'[81] Another criticism came from a more surprising source: Dan Breen, who said, while Lemass was still alive, that his former Taoiseach 'hadn't the strength of leadership. He was a great man, and most excellent as a Minister, but not as a leader. He couldn't keep the control that old Dev got. Dev could be very cruel, very hard. He was heartless when he had to be, but he succeeded.'[82]

Whether he shrank from confrontation or simply miscalculated, Lemass has to bear substantial personal responsibility for the outcome of the ninth-round agreement. The idea that any strongly organised group of workers would claim less, or be satisfied with less, than the full 12 per cent was, as might have been expected, a largely pious aspiration. The overall figure might, at a pinch, have been justified by a very optimistic projection for national growth. What was less predictable — and in the event it proved to be an unfounded hope — was whether the agreement would last for the full thirty months, a time span previously unhoped for and six months longer even than the interval proposed by Lemass himself in his 1963 note to the unions and employers.

In 1965, while he referred with some anxiety to a 'revolution of rising expectations,' in what was in effect a final retreat from his 1935 position (that workers' pay could not be 'determined by the laws of supply and demand'), he commented: 'In regard to personal incomes, we have to rely upon the explanation of the dangers and the growth of understanding of the serious effects upon the levels of prices and employment of further pressures.'[83] Later, still relatively unrepentant, he observed:

> For a first agreement, I think that the National Wage Agreement negotiated in 1964 was expressed for too long a term. It was probably asking too much of trade unionists to sit with their arms folded for two and a half years. Looking back, it's easy to be wise and see that it was inevitable that some of them would be thinking in terms of ways of getting around the obligations of that agreement. I think the ideal system would be an annual review and adjustment of wages in proportion to the growth of the economy, but this would have to be a very limited adjustment. In Britain they're striving to get a three and a half per cent increase every year. In France they went down to one per cent every three months, which is probably a bit too rapid.[84]

In fact the length of the proposed agreement was not the primary cause of the problem. There were two related difficulties. One of them was contained in clause 3 of the agreement, which provided for the possibility of additional negotiation to correct anomalies arising from the agreement itself. Innocent enough in itself, this proved explosive when combined with another element of the agreement — the 'floor' or minimum payment for all workers, no matter how low-paid, which was designed to offset the traditional bonus to higher-paid workers arising from across-the-board percentage increases.

The 'floor' was extremely popular electorally, as Lemass knew it would be; but it disturbed a whole series of wage differentials. A procession of unions took place through the arbitration channels with 'status' claims as the more powerful wage-earners sought, with some success, to restore their traditional margins. It was this nexus, combined with the cumulative effects of tariff reductions in 1963 and 1964, rather than the time span of the agreement or even the percentage adopted, that fuelled the resultant erosion of the competitiveness of Irish-produced goods and an increasing balance of payments problem. By 1965 the NIEC was warning that if exports ceased to be competitive, 'the resultant decline in *direct* employment could be about 30,000 workers.' (Emphasis in original.)[85]

THE FARMERS: NO LONGER 'FINE GAELERS ON TRACTORS'

Meanwhile, and in contrast with the economic and political turbulence of the previous year, the remainder of 1964 was set fair: the so-called 'farmers' budget', introduced in April, caused little controversy, not least because of its evident objective of levelling the playing field between agriculture and industry in the wake of the ninth round; and there were friendly trade talks between Lemass and the French Minister for Foreign Affairs, Couve de Murville.

The 1964 budget was in fact an important stage in a long process of rapprochement between Fianna Fáil and organised farmers, which was punctuated by bitter wrangles and worse, culminating in the historic sit-down by the National Farmers' Association outside the offices of the Minister for Agriculture, Charles Haughey, in the late autumn of 1966.[86] It fell to Lemass to oversee this process at a critical stage in its development, and his urban persona did not make the task any easier. Part of the problem, however, was unrelated to his real or imagined difficulties in coming to terms with the needs of farmers. They went further back, into the nineteen-forties and fifties, when the original alliances that had been forged between Fianna Fáil and the smaller farmers in particular were being fractured by hard times, by the increasing perception of Fianna Fáil as a party driven by industrial policy under Lemass's stewardship of Industry and Commerce, and by the political expression of the growing sense of disenchantment that ensued. James Ryan, no enemy of the farmers, put it with brutal frankness as late as 1958, not long after the nascent NFA had passed a vote of no confidence in Government policy:

> I can recollect three or four Farmers' Unions in the last forty years; they all began by telling us they were non political and non sectarian but they all ended where they belonged, in the ranks of Fine Gael.[87]

Lemass as Taoiseach was as ecumenical, at least in public, as anyone of his background could have been expected to be. Despite the increasing volume of complaints coming from his Minister for Agriculture, Paddy Smith, he continued to maintain the importance — even the primacy — of agriculture in a whole series of public speeches. He told the Dáil in 1960 that the Government 'have never treated, and do not now treat, the interests of manufacturing industry as the predominant consideration in their approach to the question of association with either of the European trading groups, or in their trading policy generally, in the sense of having failed to attach due importance to agricultural interests.'[88] In August 1962 he was declaring that the general body of taxpayers would willingly support measures to improve agricultural productivity and that 'the problem of the small farm areas is one which has to be resolved before all our aims of national development are secured.'[89] In late 1963 he told a television interviewer that he was 'wrong in assuming that the small farming unit, as we understand it in Ireland, is necessarily uneconomic ... Not all the experts in the field would agree that the small farm of 40 to 45 acres is not capable of returning a reasonable livelihood to its owner.'[90]

On a policy level, this deceptively mild statement was potentially explosive. A quarter of all farm holdings at the time were in the 10–30 acre category, and of course there were also many farms even smaller than 10 acres. Some of Lemass's other suggestions would have caused considerable alarm within Fianna Fáil had they been more widely published. At a meeting with Father James McDyer and others associated with western development in July 1963, Lemass suggested baldly that if pilot areas were to be selected for special development, as the deputation suggested, the dole should be suspended in the same localities. McDyer was quick to object to this, but Lemass stuck to his point: he wanted to change the 'present system under which, in effect, the lazy farmer gets the dole and the industrious farmer disqualifies himself by his work.'[91]

On the political level, Lemass had to balance his impatience with farmers against his need to identify an organisation that could speak authoritatively for them at the negotiating table. The only serious candidate for this role was the NFA, and Lemass, despite his privately expressed opinion that 'we will get no credit from the NFA whatever we do,'[92] went to considerable lengths to build them up, including making funds available to them to travel to international conferences[93] and eventually, early in 1964, extending official recognition to them.[94] This final step may, as Gary Murphy argues, have been partly influenced by the need to bring the Kilkenny rates strike of the previous year to an end,[95] but it would probably have occurred sooner or later even without this stimulus.

Lemass told Seán Healy, who had been Secretary of Macra na Feirme from 1948 to 1955 and later a leadership figure in the IFA (as the NFA had become), that he was impressed by the way in which the NFA marshalled their arguments and their case; he was also intrigued and encouraged by the links that had grown up between the association and the Ulster Farmers' Union. Dealing with representative organisations that could deliver their membership behind agreements was at the core of Lemass's political style. At one meeting with the NFA he specifically brought up his experience as Minister for Industry and Commerce in handling a number of rival organisations in the retail trade. 'I examined them for what they were worth, and came to the conclusion that the most representative was RGDATA. Whenever I wanted information I went to them — in a sense I made them.'[96]

The extent to which he had personally been responsible for moving the NFA onto centre stage as one of the social partners must have been especially galling to Lemass later on when, barely two years after the Kilkenny rates strike, with its implied challenge to the authority of the state (Lemass himself described it at the time as 'the road to anarchy'[97]), the farmers mounted their spectacular sit-in in Merrion Street. Nor can it be coincidental that Lemass's famous, and fully premeditated, comment on the proper role he envisaged for RTE in relation to public policy was related to, and enunciated in, the opening stages of the latter controversy.

In 1964, however, all this was in the future, and there were grounds for supposing that the organised farmers were now perceived by Lemass and Fianna Fáil, in Murphy's lapidary description, as 'a troublesome but essentially apolitical grouping, [whereas] ten years earlier they would have regarded them simply as Fine Gaelers on tractors.'[98]

There was still a degree of mutual incomprehension on agricultural matters, although Rickard Deasy, then leader of the NFA, maintained very good personal relations with Lemass and admired many of his policies. In a verdict delivered many years later he expressed his belief that Lemass had

> absolutely no ideas of his own about agriculture — only the self-serving bull that he had been fed by small time gombeen types (but loyal Party supporters) who therefore had to be heeded — people who owned hole-in-the-wall meat factories etc. And don't forget that Avonmore was at that time not even a dream in anyone's eye; nor were any other of the great dairy co-ops who are now household names not only at home but in many important export markets. At one of our first working meetings he asked me what was the single most important factor in getting Agriculture going. I was not expecting this, but replied: 'farmers' confidence in the future is the key' — meaning that once there is a general feeling of confidence, farmers will respond, with improvements right through the whole production system. His answer is still stamped on my mind: 'But people tell me that if we had a subsidy on fertilisers, it would start things going.' Whether he had been fed this by a dumb civil servant, or an over talkative small fertiliser manufacturer, it was still rubbish. Producing more and better grass

is only sensible if you have planned the extra stock to turn it into milk or meat, and laid on some kind of marketing arrangements, so that the production of a comparatively small surplus, does not result in collapsing the prices. If he had ever been made Minister for Agriculture, then he had the mental agility to master the job. As it was, he had all the wrong people around him. The kind of people who enabled him to make such a success at the time of the semi-states just were not heard or listened to in Agriculture.[99]

Seán Healy shared Deasy's perception that Lemass did not generally bring himself up to date on agricultural issues and, when these were raised in any detail, referred the farmers straight away to the Minister for Agriculture. Deasy was certainly accurate in criticising Lemass's simple faith in fertilisers. It was driven essentially by two things: the enthusiasm of J. B. Hynes, a civil servant in Industry and Commerce during Lemass's tenure there, and Lemass's own conviction, born of his wartime experience, that fertiliser was a strategic material and that Ireland should never again be dependent for supply on outside sources. There was the additional advantage that it offered the prospect — or at least it did when the project was first mooted — of reducing the cost of farm inputs and therefore making agriculture more competitive.

The birth of this enterprise was, however, accompanied by long and protracted labour pains. The Departments of Finance and Agriculture were opposed to the idea. It was first planned for an unspecified site somewhere in the midlands, as Lemass personally announced during the 1951 election campaign. This would have made a certain amount of sense from the point of view of transport economics — most of the poor land being in the west of the country — but the election of Michael Deering for Fine Gael at a by-election in the Wicklow constituency in June 1953 prompted a change of site,[100] subsequently justified on the grounds of the local availability of the raw material.

The problem was that as the project came to maturity there was a worldwide glut in the phosphate industry, and prices sank to a record low, to remain there for many years. As Finance pointed out with increasing asperity, there was little prospect of such a factory ever achieving financial viability, which indeed proved to be the case. Lemass, however, had given an informal commitment to Hynes and one of his colleagues while in Industry and Commerce that if they could counteract the opposition of the other two departments he would go ahead and establish the enterprise, and put them in charge of it.[101]

When he became Taoiseach he was in a powerful position to protect the project, and he did so. Hynes was given to writing to him privately in an attempt, eventually successful, to derail the powerful objections coming from Whitaker, who was convinced that this 'would have been one of the few occasions on which we could be happy that we were becoming a dumping ground for other countries' cheap nitrogen-based fertiliser, of which there was a glut.'[102] An academic economist put it more strongly: 'In the interests of perhaps 1000 people gainfully employed [the fertiliser industry was] protected to the detriment of more than 500,000 people gainfully employed in agriculture.'[103]

The farmers' leader, however, was not being entirely fair either to Lemass or to the Department of Agriculture in some other respects. The department had commissioned from the American expert Joseph Knapp a study of the options facing agriculture, and when his report was published, early in 1964, it laid particular stress on the value of co-operative effort in farming. This struck a chord with Lemass, who made at least three major speeches on the topic during the year,[104] stressing the need for education in co-operative principles and for practical research. Correspondence between his departmental secretary, Nioclás Ó Nualláin, and J. C. Nagle in Agriculture provided further evidence of his desire to keep up the pressure. Nagle, for his part, percipiently remarked that in the department's view farmers saw co-operation too much in terms of engineering and services and too little in terms of the application of the principles involved to farming practices generally.[105]

Lemass must have sensed that his words were falling on deaf ears. As early as March he warned farmers against making threats, and suggested, not entirely light-heartedly, that 'some [NFA members] must have an inkling that, unless the Bog of Allen turns into gold, they were more often than not day-dreaming instead of preparing practical plans.'[106] For all their unwillingness to take Lemass's hints, the farmers were at least temporarily happy and were particularly enthusiastic about his pro-EEC policy.

Not even the retention by Fine Gael of its seat in Roscommon at a by-election there in July 1964 — their candidate was Joan Burke, widow of the deceased TD — caused much of a ripple in the placid political scene. On the adjournment of the Dáil in the same month, Lemass spoke at length on the Second Programme, which was published in full the following day. In speeches throughout this period he continued to warn industry of the need to prepare for free trade and of the folly of expecting a reintroduction of protection. Even the Department of Industry and Commerce was being dragged reluctantly back on board. Official files for the period show that Lemass remained intimately involved both in examining proposals by foreign industrialists and in scanning objections by their Irish counterparts.[107]

The Control of Manufactures Acts had by this stage been to all intents and purposes eviscerated. A booklet prepared by the IDA assured intending investors that non-nationals could hold a majority of the capital, or even all the capital, in an increasingly wide range of companies, not by any means restricted to those producing solely for export.[108] In October the Government approved the text of a Bill further amending the Acts.[109]

There were already signs that the 1964 national wage agreement might be unravelling, but Lemass contented himself with a warning shot: 'It is not the function of government to relieve men of the trouble of living or to spare them from work and thought, but so to arrange the general environment that their work will be more productive of economic and social benefit to themselves.'[110] It was a measure of the distance he had travelled since 1932 when, in the first flush of ministerial power, he had declared resoundingly his acceptance of the principle that 'if people are to be enabled to provide for themselves and their dependants only by being given the opportunity to work, then, undoubtedly, we accept it, as a direct obligation on the Government, to see that work is provided.'[111]

PHASE 3: UPHILL TO DOWNING STREET

The even tenor of 1964 was sharply disturbed by the British election in October. Harold Wilson, almost immediately on bringing his Labour Party government into office, discerned a serious balance of payments problem and imposed a levy of 15 per cent on all imports. This affected Ireland to an inordinate degree, given the extent to which Irish export trade was geared towards Britain. The British were not unsympathetic to the cries of protest but also saw in Ireland's difficulty England's opportunity. 'It would be preferable from all points of view if the Irish could be induced to join EFTA,' one high-level briefing document noted in December 1964.[112] And among the benefits of such a development, as perceived by the British (echoing a comment they had made in 1960), was that it would 'help to soften the grievances about Partition ... and diminish support for terrorist activities.'

January 1965 saw Lemass's visit to O'Neill, which certainly softened the psychological blow of the British import surcharge, even though it may have done little to cushion its economic effects. The 1965 election campaign, which followed shortly afterwards, was fought largely on the issue of the economy.

The published statistics had already indicated that there were serious slippages in key economic indicators, and Fine Gael's election campaign, which to some extent marginalised its emerging 'Just Society' programme, was focused to a considerable extent on the party's plans to control credit. Lemass seized on this with alacrity, warning that the main opposition party had given no indication of how they proposed to exercise such control and that their accession to power would be the signal for a flight of capital.[113] In a radio interview he was even more specific:

> People everywhere are very sensitive about government control of, or interference with, the banks. If deposits should be transferred in any

degree, bank loans and overdrafts would have to be called in. This could spark off a trade slump and widespread unemployment. Probably the Fine Gael people did not think of this very practical consideration, and it shows the risks of giving government power to people who have so little understanding of the consequences of their proposals.[114]

His reaction to Fine Gael's proposal for a Department of Economic Affairs (later adopted, in all but name, by his successor, though destined to be short-lived) underlined this belief. It was, he said, 'the type of impractical idea which could appeal only to people who have no knowledge or understanding of the functioning of the Government.' He added, just in case there should be any doubt about the matter:

> In relation to national economic development, which must be planned and executed on a broad scale and embrace the work of every State Department, the only member of the Government who can accomplish the necessary co-ordination of activities, and possess the necessary authority to keep all Ministers working in line with general Government policy, is the Taoiseach.[115]

Back in office after the election on 7 April, however, Lemass had to face the problems he claimed Fine Gael were unable to solve — and to solve them by measures very similar in some respects to those Fine Gael had advocated. Almost immediately, the Government took one decision that was to have a critical effect on the progress of the negotiations with Britain: an agreement to consider, in principle, participation in EFTA at the end of a five-year period following the creation of a free trade area between the two countries.[116] Lemass kept the idea alive: he held out the prospect of EFTA membership as late as January 1966, in a speech to the Council of Europe.[117]

In the meantime, however, more pressing concerns had to be faced. Jim Ryan, the Minister for Finance, warned the Government in July that the economic situation was more difficult than any experienced since 1955–56.

> The balance of payments is currently running at an annual rate of at least £50 million. The net external assets of the banking system and departmental funds have shown a substantial fall, reflecting the enlarged trade deficit and a reduction in the net capital inflow. There has been a slowing down in the rate of growth of industrial production. Personal consumption has tended to rise at a faster rate than in 1964. Prices have continued to increase ... Non-agricultural incomes have gone up by several percentage points more than 12 per cent ... At the same time, considerable dissatisfaction appears to exist among workers about comparative levels of remuneration and conditions of employment.[118]

Whitaker took advantage of a private meeting with Lemass at which he was reporting on the progress of the Anglo-Irish negotiations to present him with 'a personal view of the present economic situation ... in language not suitable for a public speech.'[119] His analysis was stark.

> The economic situation is more serious than we have been admitting officially. We have deliberately not been too pessimistic in public for fear of undermining confidence and also in the hope that as the months went by things would show a sufficient turn for the better. This hope is not being realised — indeed, it was not soundly based — and we now have to increase the corrective measures. We should also, without being alarmist, be more forthright about the nature and extent of our problems. We would be deluding ourselves if we continued to make reassuring comments about their temporary nature, by high-lighting the cattle shortfall and the British surcharge. There is a basic difficulty of a more lasting character and it is time we did something effective about it.

He warned specifically against the danger that departments or agencies might 'wriggle their way out of a control intended to reduce the balance of payments gap by looking for money from foreign sources'; declared that 'the amount of time and effort devoted to reducing public capital expenditure has borne only miserable fruit'; argued that people had to be asked to be 'content with their present degree of comfort unless they want themselves or their neighbours to be put out of employment'; and stressed the need to 'dispel the present phoney atmosphere in which this department is still being pressed for money for newly thought up schemes and employers and unions are currently considering an interim increase in preparation for a tenth round next year.'

Whitaker's exasperation may have been fuelled in part by Lemass's somewhat cavalier public dismissal of the balance of payments problem only three months earlier as 'merely a book-keeping exercise.'[120] Ironically, his own department was not immune to the possibilities of foreign borrowing, sometimes from the unlikeliest of sources. During the summer it caused discreet enquiries to be made through the Irish ambassador about the possibility that the Vatican might place some of its portfolio of investments in Ireland. The ambassador, after making extensive enquiries with highly placed but anonymous Vatican bankers, warned the Government in a report seen by Lemass in August that Vatican investment policies were governed by two prime criteria — security and profitability — and that, on the first of these criteria alone, Ireland's link with sterling and the consequent risks to any investment in the wake of a British devaluation was enough to make any such investment highly unlikely.[121]

The workers' dissatisfaction that Ryan had drawn attention to was spreading. Industrial relations was an issue very much on Lemass's mind, and he returned to the theme with increasing frequency. The calm that had at first succeeded the ninth-round pay agreement was being increasingly ruffled by industrial disputes: strike pay accounted for 26.2 per cent of ITGWU expenditure in 1965, more than twice the percentage of the previous year.[122] A strike by members of the Irish Telephonists' Association evoked sympathetic meetings and demonstrations by thousands of workers from other unions; some of the striking trade unionists found themselves in jail for breaches of the law and went on hunger strike, which only ended after a compromise was negotiated by the Attorney-General. This was the general climate in which Lemass asked Hillery — who had succeeded Lynch in Industry and Commerce after the election — if he would arrange

> a general conference of workers and employers to consider in a comprehensive way the possibilities of introducing a new era in industrial relations ... in which it may be possible to get the principles which should govern industrial relations defined and accepted. I have in mind something like a 'code of good conduct' which would have moral rather than legal compulsion to support it.[123]

Hillery was not enthusiastic, and the suggested initiative never got off the ground.

By now the successful conclusion of an Anglo-Irish agreement was virtually the only option left and one whose achievement would depend heavily on the new relationship established between the Lemass and Wilson governments. It was a relationship that was plainly coming rapidly closer. The log-jam — particularly over Irish exports of synthetic fibres to Britain — was broken finally at a meeting in London in July 1965 at which the remaining problems relating to cattle and sheep exports and butter were also considered. Lemass argued for some concessions, not only on grounds of equity but for what he described pointedly as 'presentational' reasons. Wilson, for his part, alluded delicately to his own political agenda when he suggested that 'it might be a good thing if the Taoiseach, in any comment on the proposed agreement, were to make a statement regarding the consideration by Ireland of the possibility of joining EFTA.'[124]

The President of the Board of Trade, Douglas Jay, was strongly opposed to an agreement on the terms envisaged. The fact that he was in effect overruled shows the relative primacy of political considerations and, in particular, the way in which the growing rapport between the two leaders was operating to the advantage of the Irish negotiators. It also acted to further Lemass's personal objective of creating a fundamentally new economic relationship between North and South.

One draft clause put forward by the British during the negotiations suggested that Ireland might reduce some of its tariffs at a more rapid rate than the agreement stipulated. Lemass disliked this clause but saw that it

contained the seeds of something more significant, as he told Lynch following a private meeting he had with Wilson during the discussions.

> I told the Prime Minister that this clause would be embarrassing for us
> as it stood, because of the implied moral obligation it carried, but that
> it might provide for the possibility of this more rapid reduction or
> elimination of tariffs for bona-fide Six-County products without an
> obligation to give similar treatment to British products. I pointed out
> to Mr Wilson the political purpose which I had in mind, and the
> possibility of Six-County political objections. He gave the appearance
> of being not unsympathetic to the suggestion and assured me that it
> would be considered.[125]

It was considered, and with considerable sympathy, not least by the
Commonwealth Secretary, Arthur Bottomley, who advised his colleagues
privately:

> We have been much helped by Mr Lemass's public statements that after
> the conclusion of a Free Trade Agreement with the United Kingdom,
> the Irish Republic could consider joining EFTA. Mr Lemass hopes
> that if the Republic's tariffs against the United Kingdom are lowered,
> Irish industry will be forced to be efficient and improve their exports
> to all destinations … The disappearance of old leaders in the Republic
> and the increased prosperity there have introduced a new realism into
> Irish politics. There is a readiness to put less emphasis on the question
> of partition and [by] the growing middle class and the business leaders
> to accept the economic interdependence of the Republic and Britain.
> [This] could place our political relationship with the Republic on a
> better footing than ever in the past … Although the Irish are being
> very demanding, a breakdown would lead to a revulsion in opinion …
> Subject to our approval in each instance, the Irish may reduce their
> tariffs in favour of Northern Ireland on particular items.[126]

Discussions took place on the proposed agreement during the autumn.
Northern ministers became increasingly alarmed, and the Stormont
Department of Agriculture in particular was fearful of the possibly deleterious effect on them of concessions to Dublin on farm products. The
series of meetings that had succeeded the Lemass-O'Neill rapprochement
were, however, bearing some fruit. At one of the meetings in London to
discuss these issues, Whitaker had the private satisfaction of being able to
introduce the Northern delegation to the British officials when they
arrived; the British had never met them before.[127]

The significance of the agreement was certainly not underestimated on
the Irish side. Lemass took the precaution of securing the Government's
agreement, at its meeting on 10 December 1965, to give his delegation

18. Lemass in 1953

19. This caricature of a saturnine Lemass appeared in the Sunday Express *in the 1950s.*

20. One of the first photographs of Lemass as Taoiseach, taken in November 1959. Left to right: a young Garret FitzGerald; John Leydon; Lemass; Professor C.F. Carter; Colm Barnes

21. *Lemass speaking at the opening of the Alcock and Brown memorial in County Galway in 1962*

22. *On the golf course.* Left to right: *Sammy Lyons; Dave McIlvenna; Harry Bradshaw; Lemass; John Dunne. Lyons and McIlvenna were two of Lemass's closest friends.*

23. Addressing the National Press Club in Washington in 1963

24. *Kathleen Lemass*

25. *At the opening of the new American Embassy in 1964.* Left to right: *Dr Dunne, Archbishop of Nara; Seán MacEntee; Mrs McCloud, wife of the former US Ambassador; Lemass; Mrs McCluskey, wife of the then US Ambassador*

26. *At Downing Street for the talks that led to the Anglo-Irish Free Trade Area Agreement of 1965.* Left to right: *Harold Wilson; Charles J. Haughey; Jack Lynch; Lemass*

27. *With Terence O'Neill at Stormont, January 1965*

28. Lemass's funeral cortège at Dean's Grange cemetery

29. At the graveside: Maureen and Charles J. Haughey. On the right, Brendan Corish, leader of the Labour Party

plenipotentiary powers.[128] This may not have been an empty formula: Bottomley recorded his belief that although Lemass wished to sign an agreement, 'it was not certain all his colleagues did.'[129] When the agreement was signed, on 14 December, it received a universally good press, even from Stormont,[130] reconciled since 1963 to the advantages involved in receiving special treatment by Dublin. It was subsequently approved by the Dáil without a division[131] and was, Lemass said, 'by far the most important trade agreement we have concluded.'[132]

It was certainly not without its risks. According to one calculation, even in 1966 the tariffs and export incentives were the equivalent of a 19 per cent devaluation of the Irish currency in relation to sterling,[133] and dismantling the protective wall could have had serious adverse consequences. Whitaker recalls that Lemass was particularly worried about the possible effect of removing the last 10 per cent, as projected in the agreement, and he had to reassure him that the probability of a British-Irish devaluation in advance of EEC membership would afford both countries a measure of economic protection.[134]

As one contemporary historian has noted, 'the economic war initiated by de Valera against England in the 1930s was finally brought to a close by the man who had been his deputy leader for 15 years.'[135] This is perhaps an overstatement, but there was a germ of political truth in it. There were, nonetheless, a few straws in the wind. Sensitivities in relation to the North remained, despite the trend noted so approvingly by Bottomley. 'Throughout this document [the Anglo-Irish Agreement],' Lemass told the secretary of his department, 'I wish to have the term Britain used instead of United Kingdom. In some cases it may be desirable to substitute, in the interests of clarity, the term Britain and/or Northern Ireland.'[136]

Lemass put the potential Irish commitment to EFTA into context for his domestic audience when he told a reporter just before leaving for London that 'it will only be an interim agreement; membership of the EEC is still the aim.'[137] Despite this apparent bluntness, Lemass continued to keep the door open and referred in positive if guarded terms to EFTA at his press conference in Dublin following the signing of the Anglo-Irish Agreement, in the Dáil debate on the agreement, and in a later speech to the Council of Europe. This prompted the Department of External Affairs to prepare and circulate a document summarising the Irish position on the issue, in which it argued that

> the best course in present circumstances seems to be to defer any move towards EFTA until it is seen whether expectations in relation to the EEC are likely to be realised. If events turn out otherwise, we shall, as a result of the implementation of the Free Trade Area Agreement, be better placed in a few years time to make the adjustments which would be necessitated by accession to EFTA.[138]

PHASE 4: ENDGAME

The season of good will created by the Anglo-Irish agreement was not to last for long. The harsh realities of the domestic political agenda were pushing talk of treaties and international negotiations onto the sidelines. As the Government itself had to admit, money incomes had risen in the aggregate by 20 per cent in two years, as against a rise of $6\frac{1}{2}$ per cent in the volume of national production.[139] This expression of the Government's concern about the pace of income increases was not in fact published, although it was prepared as an official response to the NIEC report on the economic situation in 1965 and its projection for incomes in 1966.

The reason it was not published was because of a *démarche* by Whitaker, who recognised that, even though it might accord with his own priorities, it would in all probability be inflammatory in the context of debates on economic policy that were due to take place both in the Dáil and in the ICTU. What would have aroused most comment had it been published was the Government's intention that the aggregate increase in money incomes in 1966 should not exceed 3 per cent, and its intention of imposing additional taxes to avoid a cut in the level of Government services.[140] In the event, additional taxes of some £$12\frac{1}{2}$ million were imposed in the budget in March but in such an expertly tailored fashion that it evoked little serious public disagreement or concern.

The problems, however, remained, and if anything became worse, particularly on the industrial relations front. In the Dáil in January 1966, Lemass hinted openly at the desirability of a new tripartite framework, in which the Government would also be involved.[141] In February he met representatives of both the FUE and the ICTU for discussions on incomes policy and managed to broker a resumption of negotiations between the two bodies, which had broken down in December 1965. In the same month the Government faced a gap in funds available for the public capital programme of £11 million.[142] No doubt impelled by this ominous shortage of capital, Lemass suggested to Lynch that a capital gains tax might be imposed on a limited basis, i.e. only on gains arising from investments that had been made abroad. He admitted that it might not produce much revenue but suggested that it would have at least some beneficial effect and would in addition help to provide some knowledge of how such a tax operated. He had, he reminded Lynch, made such a suggestion while in opposition. But Lynch, in government, was no more prepared to accept the proposal than Fine Gael had been.[143]

Strikes broke out with increasing frequency, including disputes involving dockers and confectionery workers. Whitaker was warning against acceptance of the 'extreme socialist notion', fostered by the unions, that everybody should be paid the same. In trade union propaganda, he argued, a condemnation of excessive differences between incomes is really aimed at spreading a sense of inequity about differences as such … I think it important to avoid being trapped by trade union manoeuvring into becoming guilt-conscious about differences in income. Most socialists don't expect everyone to be paid the same; and neither Pope John nor any other Pope (so far as I am aware) considered that equality of human dignity depended on equality of incomes![144]

There is little doubt that as the year wore on Lemass's sense of disillusion increased. The leaders of 1916, he told an audience at the King's Inns,

would be surprised and disappointed to find that patriotism, in its finest sense, appears today to have so little influence on individual and sectional behaviour, and the extent to which self-interest is so often pursued in a manner which implies disregard for the national damage it can do.[145]

At two high-profile party meetings within a month he returned to his theme. At a Comh-Chomhairle Átha Cliath meeting he spoke with evident feeling about the 'antiquated conceptions and outmoded ideas' that governed industrial relations generally.[146] At the second he referred to the gains and losses of his own protectionist policy in language that echoed with faint praise for its achievements and dwelt with some asperity on its disappointments.

Protection has served its purpose in ensuring the creation and development of an industrial arm which helps to give a better balance to our economy. We had to pay a fairly high price for the benefits it gave the country, and part of that price was the atmosphere of complacency and inertia it generated in our industrial organisation.[147]

On the eve of yet another ESB strike he spoke out with particular force against people who, he said, engaged in law-breaking as a method of voicing their complaints.[148] The nation, he implied, was beginning to feel intimidated by its difficulties and was beginning to indulge in self-pity. At the IMI conference in Killarney in April industrial disputes and national wage agreements were the main topics on his agenda, and he reflected wistfully on the disclosure by economists that there were 'human factors which influence economic growth and behaviour which are not capable of precise measurement, and whose existence and force can sometimes be detected only by their effects.'[149] Even in the course of a cautiously upbeat address to the Junior Chambers of Commerce in Galway he had to admit that the rise in industrial employment was faltering — from 8,500 in 1964 to 3,600 in 1965, with a forecast of 2,400 in 1966 — and speculated almost wistfully whether some methods could be devised, or procedures established, by which industrial disputes could be settled more frequently without stoppage of production.[150]

In May the Government rescinded an earlier decision to increase the subsidy to CIE. Public service recruitment was virtually frozen, although without any public announcement of the change in policy. The tempo of Government meetings increased: between the first meeting of the present Government on 27 April 1965 and Lemass's final meeting as Taoiseach on 8 November 1966 it met on no fewer than ninety-six occasions, an average of almost six meetings a month.

The Labour Court did not make matters easier by suggesting pay guidelines that the Government privately thought excessive: on the basis of Finance calculations, the £1 increase the ICTU was looking for represented an annualised increase of $7\frac{1}{2}$ per cent, whereas the Government was attempting to hold the line at 3 per cent.[151] The £1 increase, for all that it was official ICTU policy, became the floor demand for many groups of workers rather than the optimum.

When Hillery suggested to Lemass that it might be a good idea if a new Department of Labour were to be created to cope with the growing problems in this area,[152] Lemass not only did so, in July 1966, but, in much the same way that de Valera had made him Minister for Supplies after he had suggested the creation of the new department in 1939, handed the responsibility to the man who had given him the idea. After his appointment Hillery went away on holidays, leaving instructions that no direct telephone line from the Taoiseach was to be installed in his new office. When he returned, not only had a direct line been installed but each of his Government colleagues had been given a similar facility.[153]

Hillery's account of his dealings with Lemass while in the Department of Labour provide an insight into some of the inevitable tensions. For one thing, Lemass did not allow the fact that he had created a new department and its structures to stand in his way if he felt that ministerial intervention was required. He would push Hillery on the phone to intervene, only retreating when Hillery made clear his conviction that direct intervention would be unwise. The minister's reasons were clear in his own mind: 'Once you get the Government in, the unions can't lose.'[154] Hillery detected in Lemass, once he had become Taoiseach, a sensitivity to a wider range of interests than when he was in charge in Kildare Street, and the unions were undoubtedly one of the most important of these. He also interpreted Lemass's pressure on industrial relations issues as essentially his way of testing whether his minister really believed in the stand he had taken.

Trade union matters remained extremely sensitive, and Lemass often took a close personal interest in them. When George Colley succeeded Hillery as Minister for Industry and Commerce in July 1966 he inherited the usual folder full of invitations that had been accepted in principle by his predecessor. One was to an industrial enterprise that had a record of unwillingness to recognise unions' negotiating status. Colley refused to go, and the possibility then arose that Hillery, as the minister on whose behalf the invitation had originally been accepted, should go instead. Lemass personally ensured that Hillery would not go, because he recognised that for the new Minister for Labour to make this his first official function would seriously undermine his credibility with the trade union movement generally.

While they were anxious for a continuing flow of American investment, Lemass and his Government did not take too kindly to some American practices in relation to trade unions. One recognition issue surfaced (but was not solved under Lemass) in relation to the Irish subsidiary of General Electric, which had been set up in the Shannon industrial zone. Lemass was so unhappy about the shamrockery implicit in the name chosen by the company for its Irish subsidiary — 'Emerald Isle' — that he succeeded in having it referred to only as the 'EI Company', a designation that stuck. And, where employers were concerned, he made it clear that there were certain lengths to which he was not prepared to go. E. C. Bewley, the chairman of W. and R. Jacob, who had written to him in 1966 to complain about 'communistic influence' in the trade union movement, was told briefly that there was no 'complete solution of the problems created by irresponsible trade union behaviour, outside of dictatorship.'[155]

On 13 July the Government, at whatever cost in loss of face, moved to rectify the situation, announcing a series of anti-inflationary measures: hire purchase was to be subject to tighter controls, Government expenditure was to be cut back, bank credit restricted, and special market development grants made available for exports. Later a Control of Prices Bill was introduced, usefully for the Government during a national newspaper strike.[156] Significantly, it was moved in the Dáil not by the new Minister for Industry and Commerce, Paddy Hillery, but by Lemass himself, together with the estimate for his own department. The picture he painted was a bleak one, softened only slightly by a much more upbeat speech by Hillery the following day in which he described this sudden reversion to statutory price control as 'not a change but a digression from normal government policy.'[157]

Lemass was grim.[158] Imports were rising, exports falling. The balance of trade would worsen, from £31.4 million to at least £50 million. The rate of growth had fallen below that for 1964. External reserves had fallen by £33½ million, compared with an increase in the previous year. The national wage agreement was under threat. If the measures being taken by the Government were not enough they would have to be reviewed and intensified. In fact the impact of the Bill was considerably softened, and its operation rendered more successful, by Hillery's acceptance of an amendment from Frank

Cluskey, the Labour TD, that had the effect of warning manufacturers and retailers six months in advance of any decision to impose an order under the Act.

Out of public view, the reverberations inside the Government were intensifying. Donogh O'Malley, now Minister for Health, was objecting to what he described as 'smart-aleck' misrepresentations of his spending plans by the Department of Finance and appealing directly to Lemass for support. Neil Blaney equally was spending money on road development that Finance thought the country could ill afford.[159] Finance's anxiety about departmental spending was colliding headlong with the desire of energetic younger ministers to make their mark.

Four months later Lemass announced his retirement. It is difficult to avoid the impression that the 'political considerations' that, he told his final press conference, had governed his decision included the realisation that his successor needed time to put the economy back on a sound footing, and perhaps an acceptance of the fact that he himself no longer had the energy or the health to undertake such a demanding task. By late 1966 the targets of the Second Programme were already under intensive review. A memorandum from the Department of Finance to the Government pointed out, for example, that whereas employment had been forecast to rise by 1.1 per cent to 1970, in the first three years of the programme it had actually fallen by 0.3 per cent annually; the outflow from agriculture (3.2 per cent annually) had been far higher than expected. The target for the increase in employment over the period of the programme was 81,000: the likely outcome was 2,000.[160] Finance proposed, and the Government agreed, that all aims and targets in the programme were now in need of a realistic review. By the following year many of them had in practice been tacitly abandoned, such was the political difficulty of establishing any reasonable public relationship between the original projections and the expected outcomes.

As might have been expected, Lemass put most of the blame for the decline that accompanied his final years in office on the broad shoulders of the Wilson government. What was undeniable, however, was that this alone could not explain all the economic indicators. The bright hopes of the early sixties were already being dimmed, at least in the gloom cast by the national accounts.

The positive atmosphere that Lemass himself had done so much to create and sustain was, however, still very much in evidence and is, even today, regarded as an intrinsic part of his legacy. Paradoxically, it was to impede, until some time later, the development of a general acceptance of the seriousness of the economic situation. Emigration, which had reached a low point of some 12,000 in 1963, had more than doubled to 25,000 in 1964, more than the 1962 figure, even before the British import levy had bitten. Lemass's apparent success in knitting employers and labour into the

$2\frac{1}{2}$-year 1964 wage agreement had been undermined by the working out of the agreement in practice, and indeed some of the dissatisfaction at that agreement was traceable to the Government's failure to tackle the problem of incomes other than wages as the later stages of the Lemass era became associated, unfairly as far as he personally was concerned, with financial speculation, rapacious property development, and other unsavoury business trends and practices.

The problems of agriculture seemed intractable. In the decade to 1970 the balance of the work force between agriculture and industry changed less than in almost any other country in Europe.[161] And the quarrels in the Government were intensifying as the spoils to be divided dwindled. The public, on the other hand, were still not fully in the picture. It was as good a time to leave as any.

8

Northern Ireland
Two steps forward, one step back

The policy on Northern Ireland that Seán Lemass inherited from
Éamon de Valera had the merit of simplicity, and the disadvantage
of failure. It was not really a policy on Northern Ireland as such but
a policy on partition. Its simplicity lay in de Valera's belief that the British
had engineered the problem, that they could therefore re-engineer it, and
that a solution was inevitable. Its failure was a failure to recognise — with
only rare and fleeting exceptions — that the fissile combination of
Northern unionism and Southern irredentism could not be defused only by
actions taken by another government in another country. It also fatally
underestimated the degree to which Britain continued to view Northern
Ireland as its 'jugular vein'.[1]

The Second World War, de Valera thought, would provide the lever
that would budge the British rock. The fact that Britain would not move
in 1940 when Germany was at its throat should have given him some
inkling of the vacuity of this policy. By 1944, when his lieutenant, Seán
MacEntee, was holding out the prospect (in private) that British movement
on partition would release 'the entire manpower and resources of Éire'
to the Allied cause, it was still too little and in any case too late to offset
the obvious commotion that would be caused by any attempt to coerce
the unionists.[2]

Part of Lemass's inheritance was also a failed, last-ditch and secret initiative by de Valera, who was now, in Frank Aiken's words, 'at the end of his
career and deeply anxious to find some line of advance before he left
office.'[3] In public de Valera was expressing a rare willingness to meet
Northern politicians; in private he was offering to rejoin the British
Commonwealth as a *quid pro quo* for the ending of partition — but only if
the British first invited him. In spite of the fact that the Irish initiative was
regarded by one British official as a reversal of policy,[4] it ultimately served
only to reinforce the same official's view of the validity of Lord Rugby's
assertion that 'Irish rapprochement is a unilateral process in which you
advance while he [de Valera] stays put.'

The IRA border campaign, launched in 1956, was still spluttering on, reinforcing the sense of siege that had by now become the hallmark of the Northern majority and in particular of its elderly Prime Minister, Lord Brookeborough. Despite this there was a new openness by the British towards the prospect of some sort of development. Lemass might have been surprised had he known how open British policy was becoming. A memorandum prepared by the Commonwealth Relations Office for Lord Lansdowne as early as 1957, of which neither he nor de Valera can have been aware, observed:

> There are obvious arguments against the maintenance of two political systems in a country of some four million people which geographically is one unit, and which for many centuries was one unit historically and politically. But the division between North and South already had deep roots when self-government for Ireland first became an active issue. The situation is one that, without a real desire on both sides to reach agreement, will be most difficult to remedy. It may be that through increased co-operation between the two governments in administrative matters lies the best hope of some better understanding between them in the future.[5]

The British ambassador, Sir Alexander Clutterbuck, who was coming to the end of his posting, had a number of private conversations with Lemass shortly after the latter's election in which the new Taoiseach was, by the standards of his time and certainly by those of his predecessor, refreshingly unguarded. Clutterbuck was evidently sufficiently impressed to record these conversations in an unusually detailed memorandum, which presents a vivid pen-picture by a professional observer of Lemass in his first months in office.[6] He reported that Lemass had 'no sympathy with the campaign for the restoration of the Irish language' but that he would remain cautious on this and other issues with de Valera watching from the Park and many of the old guard still in office. He was much taken with Lemass's 'moderate' approach to the partition problem and with his statement that he sympathised with Brookeborough's problems because 'they were the same as his own, only in reverse.'

But the most substantial policy innovation, Clutterbuck perceived, was a confession of past failure and a strong hint that the new policies would be different.

> Mr Lemass said quite frankly to me that he fully realised on looking back that a great number of mistakes had been made by the government here in relation to the North; these he would work to rectify. It was a totally wrong conception, for instance, that this country should seek to bring pressure on the North, whether direct or through Britain

or the United Nations. Any such pressure would be self-defeating, as it would only serve to harden opinion in the North, instead of bringing the day of reunion nearer.

Lemass's reported statement that using Britain or any other country to bring pressure on Northern Ireland was a 'totally wrong conception' is one of the most surprising to emerge from this interview — surprising because only a month earlier he had said the exact opposite in a conversation recorded by Sir Gilbert Laithwaite, when he 'reverted to the earlier Irish suggestion that the United Kingdom government should for their part make some declaration about the ultimate desirability of uniting the people of Ireland.'[7]

Was his statement to Clutterbuck taken up wrongly? The fact that both before and after his conversation with Clutterbuck he appears to have preferred de Valera's approach lends weight to this suggestion; but Clutterbuck was a skilful observer and unlikely to have got things wrong. In this context Lemass's declaration at his first press conference that he wanted to end negative anti-partition rhetoric and substitute a desire for the restoration of national unity already had a different tinge to it.

At this stage he was being quite cautious in public, although a modern historian's contention that Lemass 'on the whole ... preferred to say nothing at all about Northern Ireland'[8] is, as will be seen, very wide of the mark.

Even these tentative remarks evoked a positive private response north of the border. Jack Sayers, the editor of the *Belfast Telegraph,* commented:

> I believe that Lemass is reaching out towards better relations, and that we should be as encouraging as we can. As you know, the question of recognition governs everything. If in time Lemass could say something helpful on this point, then we should have no hesitation in urging all the co-operation that may be feasible. We should do this, I think, in the face of the fairly general attitude that Northern Ireland should have nothing to do with the South if it can be avoided ... He has begun something that, properly fostered, may lead to a definite improvement in relationships of all kinds, and that indeed is what we seek.[9]

Lemass's new policy was positive to a degree that was, at the very least, an implied criticism of his predecessor's immobilism. Over the next five years the succession of Dublin initiatives and Stormont responses resembled nothing as much as a tennis game in which lengthy baseline rallies were punctuated by frenzied sessions at the net, while the players looked for unforced errors by their opponents. The high points in this process were Lemass's initial overtures embodied in his speeches at Oxford in October 1959 and at the Fianna Fáil ardfheis the following month; his Tralee speech in early 1963 and the controversy engendered by his speeches in the United

States later that year; and his exchange of visits with Terence O'Neill in early 1965. At a less public level he was to take a number of important initiatives in relation to cross-border trade.

The initial mode was the baseline rally, complicated by the fact that manoeuvring was already taking place within the Unionist Party as Brookeborough approached the end of his twenty-year tenure as Prime Minister. The initial unionist response was wary in the extreme: it was safer to believe that the leopard had not changed his spots. Lemass's eirenicism, therefore, was countered with the traditional charge — notably from Brian Faulkner, whose ambition to succeed Brookeborough was patent — that no progress could be made until Dublin 'recognised' Northern Ireland.[10] The same issue was to bedevil relations until long after Lemass left office, although one of the major effects of his policy was to defuse it as a problem in the Republic.

Brookeborough, surprisingly, was less dismissive, saying early in August that he did not rule out co-operative efforts for mutual practical advantage.[11] By the end of the month, however, the IRA — underlining Lemass's critique at the parliamentary party two years earlier — had carried out another attack at Rosslea, County Fermanagh, which succeeded in raising unionist and British hackles as never before. No-one, Brookeborough now averred, would be impressed by Lemass after what had happened at Rosslea. 'In our view the situation will not be met by telling miscreants to behave themselves ... More drastic action is needed.'[12] Within a week he had refused an invitation to debate the question of Northern Ireland with Lemass at the Oxford Union, because the Taoiseach was 'head of a government which has failed to deal effectively with terrorist operations from republican territory.'[13]

Coincidentally, and almost as Brookeborough was speaking, Lemass was having a private meeting with the British chargé d'affaires in Dublin, Gurth Kimber, at which the British concerns about border security were being aired. Lemass told Kimber that a central thrust of his policy was to diminish public support for IRA actions, in spite of the fact that he knew that unionist coolness towards his initiatives might even intensify support for republicans. He told Kimber in addition that it would be unrealistic to assume that there would not be attempts to stage further incidents, 'as organisations of that character must try to show some activity to keep in existence.' He rejected Kimber's suggestion that sentences on captured IRA men in the Republic had been too mild, commenting that 'our legal advisers had doubted whether they had evidence that would have secured convictions at all, if the men had been defended.'[14]

The imminence of the Northern election ensured that the Unionists kept a high profile. Brian Faulkner again returned to the fray, drawing attention to a large meeting in Tralee by IRA sympathisers at which inflammatory speeches had been made,[15] and Brookeborough himself attacked the Republic's alleged softness on terrorism in a speech at Southport,[16] a part of the United Kingdom whose voters must have been relatively unacquainted with this phenomenon.

Lemass's objectives were outlined in his speech in Dáil Éireann in July 1959 on the estimate for his department, in his Oxford speech in October, and in his speech to the Fianna Fáil ardfheis the following month. These were planned to be the ingredients of a concentrated initiative on Northern policy, whose objectives were chiefly the following:

(1) to move the political and intellectual argument away from purely territorial criteria and base it increasingly on economic and social considerations, and to this end to create a free trade area involving the whole country;

(2) to increase economic and social co-operation between the two parts of the country;

(3) to institute an effective dialogue with the Northern majority;

(4) to engineer appropriate changes in attitudes and legislation in the Republic, including marginalising or neutralising the appeal the IRA still had for young men and women;

(5) to create an atmosphere of international good will for the proposed reunification of Ireland; and

(6) to reassure Northern nationalists that their interests were in safe hands.

Not all these objectives were, or are, immediately compatible, and there were continual tensions in particular between points 3 and 5 and between 3 and 6. Nor is it possible to assume that a politician of Lemass's experience and skill could have been unaware of the tensions involved, or that he could have failed to predict some of the reactions to his more traditional utterances. These, while they undoubtedly risked slowing progress and raising unionist hackles in the North, had two positive functions. They reassured those members of his own party and others who may at first have been suspicious of his initiatives, and they protected him against the accusation that he was trying to achieve unity by stealth. He consistently maintained that his motives were not hidden, but for all his sense of urgency on the economic and political front he was playing a long game on the constitutional issue, and it is in this context that his sometimes provocative interventions can best be interpreted.

In his first Dáil speech on the estimate for the Department of the Taoiseach, in July 1959, Lemass combined the agenda of Pearse (although without mentioning him) with an explicit invocation of Connolly and the latter's statement that 'Ireland without her people means nothing to us.' He did not hold out the prospect of unity in any timetabled sense but set his sights more modestly on the creation of 'a climate of opinion ... in which the realisation of that national aim will be achieved in harmony and agreement.'

This phrase marks a significant subliminal break with the de Valera era, in that his predecessor's policy, while it never excluded the possibility of harmony and agreement, seemed to expect it as a by-product of unity rather than setting out to create it as a means to that end. It was a policy that tended to assume, at best, a grudging, suspicious and tentative attitude by unionists, under *force majeure,* to new constitutional arrangements decided on between London and Dublin. De Valera did, it is true, make occasional overtures to unionism, but given his ranking in unionist demonology such invitations were never to be taken seriously. The irony was that, although Lemass's ultimate objectives in relation to Northern Ireland differed not a whit from de Valera's, the changing temper of the times, his own tactical sense, and the election of Terence O'Neill, ultimately combined to create a completely new situation.

Lemass's July 1959 speech plainly prefigured the post-1969 Lynch era. It also, and conveniently, left unaddressed one central political issue, which is still a live one today: if the objective of Government policy is unity by consent, where are the dividing lines between invitation, persuasion, and coercion?

This question would remain unanswered, and indeed unasked. In the meantime Lemass's economic agenda was emphasised. Noting that steps were in train to set up a new Anglo-Irish committee on trade matters, he suggested a similar initiative between Dublin and Belfast. 'The fact that we have that hope of eventual unity is not, I suggest, a reason why people in the north should refuse to consider even now possibilities of concerting activities for the practical advantages that may result.'[17] These included adjustments in trading arrangements (a euphemism for reducing Dublin's tariff barriers) as well as possible initiatives in tourism promotion and cross-channel shipping.

His speech to the Oxford Union was in October. The organisers had originally hoped to have de Valera debate with Brookeborough; in the event, Lemass was faced with an up-and-coming 28-year-old Tory barrister, evidently well briefed by British government sources, Patrick Mayhew. Lemass repeated his assurances that unity should not exclude the maintenance of a Northern parliament in an agreed form, and underlined statements by Southern Protestants about the generous treatment of minorities in the Republic. He explicitly looked for an encouraging statement from the British government about their willingness to support moves towards unity, but only in terms that King George V had used in 1925. In an attempt to redefine the terminology of the debate he referred to unionists as the 'minority'. He did not, however, describe them as unionists but, throughout his speech, as 'partitionists'. It was not the most ecumenical note he struck.

On other matters he was more persuasive. 'Quite apart from any views one may hold about the reunification of Ireland,' he asked, 'is it not common sense that the two existing communities in our small island should seek every opportunity of working together in practical matters for their mutual and common good?'[18] The relegation of the central aspiration of nationalism to the status of a subordinate one was plainly designed to woo rather than to challenge.

Unionist politicians reacted with hostility,[19] but in the British civil service, and particularly those parts of it that had been charged with overseeing trade matters between Ireland and Britain, ears were pricked.

Lemass's first ardfheis speech, in November 1959, fired in effect the third gun in his salvo, and had three key ingredients. One of them was designed to satisfy the undoubted expectations of his domestic and patriotic audience and to reassure any who might have doubted his republican credentials; the other two were intended more to appeal to at least some unionist palates.

The first was an assertion that his policy, and any developments that might flow from it, were part of the seamless garment that had been woven by his predecessor. This was buttressed by his explicit endorsement of the concept of Irish unity and the 'true line of Irish Republican tradition from Wolfe Tone.'[20] The second was the offer to Brookeborough of 'unconditional' discussions on matters of mutual interest and advantage. The third was the extent to which he formally recognised the existence of partition. 'We make no secret that our aim is to bring partition to an end,' he said, 'but we recognise that it exists.'[21] At this remove in time it is easy to underestimate the political frisson that would have been caused by a Fianna Fáil Taoiseach's decision to include the two words 'partition' and 'recognise' in the same sentence. It was plainly a closely calculated gambit, and, to a large extent, it came off.

His public vision of the future shape of a united Ireland was clear: he was willing to consider, even as an 'ultimate' solution of the whole problem, an arrangement that would keep the government and parliament of Northern Ireland in operation, with safeguards for the ordinary rights of the nationalist population there, in a context in which the rights currently exercised by Westminster would be transferred to Dublin.[22] In the circumstances it was an extraordinarily specific and public commitment. It was not, however, unique; nor did it represent a conversion by Fianna Fáil to the insights of the inter-party Government, as the *Irish Times* mistakenly thought when it declared that Lemass had 'bravely adopted Mr MacBride's principle of federation.'[23]

Its Fianna Fáil lineage was in fact impeccable. It replicated the ideas on constitutional solutions to the Northern problem agreed by the united Republican government in 1921 and advanced later by de Valera in his

Evening Standard interview in 1938, which had aroused such fierce hostility among unionists. It was to be advanced again by de Valera as late as 1966 in a controversial speech during his presidential re-election campaign. In effect it envisaged the creation of a united but federal Ireland and finessed the complicated constitutional questions of the composition and powers of the Dublin and Belfast parliaments, or the relationship between them, in any such arrangement. For this very reason it was a proposal that might not have secured the universal approval of Fianna Fáil members had they considered its implications in any detail and one that would undoubtedly have been coolly received by Northern nationalists. It was a position to which Lemass adhered consistently throughout his period as Taoiseach, despite reservations expressed by Aiken. It was central to his attempt to woo Northern unionists, or at least to explore the possibility that some of them might be more reasonable than others.

Whether Lemass's — and de Valera's — approach on this question was entirely altruistic or motivated solely by concern for the susceptibilities of Northern unionists is another matter entirely. W. T. Cosgrave certainly had his suspicions from an early date and confided to a British diplomat as early as 1940 that 'he himself [Cosgrave] did not agree with Mr de Valera's idea of a separate parliament from the North. He would prefer to have only one parliament. It occurred to him that Mr de Valera was nervous of the access of strength which would come to the Fine Gael party from the North.'[24]

It is certainly noteworthy that the downgrading and virtual abandonment of the federal policy dates principally from the breakdown of the power-sharing Northern Ireland Executive in 1972. No Government since then has made it part of its policy, and only Sinn Féin maintains it, in a highly modified form, as a constitutional objective. Lemass was therefore the last Taoiseach to make support for a Stormont parliament an explicit part of his policy towards Northern Ireland.

The IRA campaign on the border was, of course, still a serious political problem, and it was raised by Unionist politicians with the British Home Secretary, R. A. Butler, when he visited Belfast in December 1959. Essentially they wanted the British to retaliate by imposing sanctions on imports from the Republic. Butler demurred, but his own view of Lemass was peppered with disdainful negatives. 'I do not think', he told a Belfast audience, 'the disposition of the Head of Government there is other than to discourage it, but I do not think they realise how serious it is.'

Lemass replied in a speech in Castlebar that was flagged loyally by the *Irish Press* as a 'reply' to Butler but which in fact went through a series of historical contortions. Enlisting all the republican deities in a litany designed — without any subsequent signs of success — to reassure simultaneously both his audience and his unionist critics, he declared that 'the Republican tradition is against seeking to solve that internal Irish problem by means of violence.' Enlisting Tone, Davis, Pearse and Casement as unlikely defenders of this proposition, he went on:

> We have perhaps been too mealy-mouthed in this situation and have allowed the true Republican doctrine to be distorted and mis-represented, and some people to be confused regarding it ... Any course of action which tends to raise and strengthen these barriers [of hostility and distrust] ... means also breaking faith with those great national leaders of the past who so constantly declared their rejection of such methods.[25]

The most positive thing that can be said about this speech is that his argument suffered from compression — in particular his implicit claim that while armed insurrection against Britain of a kind that the named leaders (and Lemass himself) had engaged in was acceptable, 'seeking to solve that internal Irish problem by means of violence' (i.e. post-1923 IRA activity) was not. Such fine distinctions were, at any rate, lost on his audiences.

THE 'SIX COUNTIES'

In private, however, Lemass was attempting to shift the de Valera goalposts ever so slightly, in a way plainly calculated at least to offset one of the traditional unionist sources of criticism: the very public reiteration of the territorial claim involved in the constant use of the term 'Six Counties' to refer to Northern Ireland. This had been standard practice for many years in political and administrative circles in Dublin. A 1953 note on official practice stated that 'when it is necessary to make it clear that the reference is to the area of the Twenty-Six Counties, for example, in statistical and similar returns, either the expression "Ireland (exclusive of the Six Counties)" or the word "Ireland" with an asterisk and a footnote reading "exclusive of the Six Counties" is used instead.'[26]

This formula had a number of attractions for traditional nationalists. It conveyed the general irredentist thrust of national policy with admirable economy. It also plainly irked the Northern majority, who responded both by hijacking the Constitution's official description of the state as Éire, using it so contemptuously that Dublin's political establishment eventually all but abandoned it, and by referring continuously to the Republic as the 'Free State', long after the latter entity had ceased to exist in 1937.

Lemass's first ardfheis speech deftly finessed the question of terminology. References in his speech were unambiguously to the 'Constitution of Northern Ireland' and to the 'government and parliament of Northern Ireland'.[27] In private his views were expressed more pointedly, notably when the *Irish Press* reprinted parts of an interview he had given to the *Guardian* in May 1960 but, in accordance with the *Press's* invariable practice, changed 'Northern Ireland' (which he had used throughout the interview) to 'the

Six Counties'. Lemass wrote to the *Press's* managing director, Vivion de Valera — Éamon de Valera's son and also a Fianna Fáil TD — in a letter 'not intended as conveying a complaint but for the purpose of letting you know my views in this regard.'

> I used the term 'Government of Northern Ireland' very deliberately and have, indeed, resorted to it with increasing frequency in Dáil statements. In my view the practice of substituting alternative statements like 'Belfast Government', 'Stormont Government', 'Belfast authorities' has been the outcome of woolly thinking on the Partition issue. As you know our proposals for the political organisation of a united Ireland have, since 1921, involved the continuation of a parliament in Belfast with subordinate powers. If these proposals had been accepted at that time or since some name for the subordinate northern Parliament and Government would have had to be accepted, and it seems clear that the united Dáil of 1921 would not have dissented to the retention of the name 'Government of Northern Ireland' which is, indeed, nearly as good as any other. Our continued reluctance to use this title, in the conditions now prevailing, seems to me to serve no national purpose and it is of course advanced in the North as evidence that our proposals in this regard are not seriously meant, or are only a trap.[28]

The *Irish Times* and *Irish Independent,* presumably as the result of an off-the-record briefing, drew attention to the new policy, suggesting that the use of a 'changed terminology' had now been informally communicated to the media.[29] This attracted the attention of the parliamentary bloodhounds Noel Browne and Jack McQuillan, who questioned the Taoiseach about it in the Dáil. No final decision, he told them, had been taken by the Government on the name of Northern Ireland or to giving 'formal or official recognition to the Government of Northern Ireland.'[30] The initiative, however, discreet as it was, had also ruffled important feathers that had to be smoothed; and Michael McInerney, a senior *Irish Times* journalist who enjoyed Lemass's confidence to a certain extent, reported that

> the informal agreement among Ministers that the term Six Counties would be dropped in favour of the description Northern Ireland for the North's regime has been quietly resisted and is unlikely to be revived. Its only result was to create uneasiness among the Nationalists of the North that this was a form of recognition, while the result from the North was an agreed form of jeering at the Republic.[31]

Archival records suggest, however, that this was more a form of press management used by Lemass to pacify some members of his own party than a decision to abandon the policy. In 1961 his department secretary was telling enquirers: 'It is this Department's frequent, but not invariable, practice to use the expression "Northern Ireland" as a name for the geographical area comprising the Six Counties.'[32]

The device of stating that no final decision had been taken managed to satisfy both sides and showed how Lemass's aptitude for terminological subtlety had been honed by a long association with his predecessor. The policy on terminology was, however, relatively slow in securing universal acceptance. Three years later Garrett FitzGerald wrote to the *Sunday Press* to complain that they had changed his terminology without his consent and quoting Lemass's 1961 Dáil statement.[33] Intradepartmental usage showed a wide variation in practice for a number of years thereafter, as did speeches by various ministers.

The advance had been a small but a significant one; it also served to show the extreme sensitivity of the territory into which Lemass was now marching. One of the areas where the advance was slowest — apart from the *Irish Press* — was RTE. In January 1965 George Colley felt sufficiently annoyed by the station's continuing use of the 'Six Counties' appellation that he asked Lemass to issue an instruction to RTE to stop.[34] In March 1966 Jack Lynch wanted to incorporate the term 'Northern Ireland' into a statutory order relating to preferential tariffs for Northern goods, but Lemass, somewhat surprisingly, hedged on this and, while noting that the invariable practice of his own department was to refer to the area as 'Northern Ireland', was apparently unwilling to tread too firmly on Aiken's toes by making his personal policy an official and general one.[35]

The reverberations caused within Fianna Fáil by Lemass's attempt to defuse the recognition issue were probably responsible for his decision to reassure doubters in his speech to the 1962 ardfheis. This speech included a restatement of Fianna Fáil policy that was considerably less nuanced than his first ardfheis speech the previous year. Fianna Fáil, he asserted, had never accepted that a minority had the right to vote itself out of the nation; the right of the Irish nation to exercise sovereignty over the whole of the 'national territory' was unchallengeable; and there was nobody in Ireland or in Britain who did not know in his heart of hearts that Irish unity would eventually be restored.[36]

These reverberations died away. There were also, but less overtly, signs of changing attitudes in the North. In the summer of 1963 the former secretary to the Stormont cabinet, Sir Robert Grandison, while on holiday in the Republic, met Hugh McCann of the Department of External Affairs at his own request to discuss North-South relations. Grandison thought that traditional unionist insistence on constitutional recognition was 'utterly unrealistic' but marked McCann's cards about the danger attending any unionist politician who went too far ahead of grass-roots opinion; if O'Neill tried to go too fast, he said, he might be 'shot out on his ear.'[37]

Lemass's most considered expression of his views about the vexed question of 'recognition' of Stormont and the role of a future Northern parliament is to be found in a letter he wrote to Ernest Blythe in 1962. He found himself in 'some measure of agreement' with the view of his old Civil War opponent on the Northern problem, he wrote.

> The religious basis of the division amongst our people is, I believe, being more widely understood by everyone who is giving it serious consideration, and the need, because of it, of maintaining a separate parliament in the North-east, with powers equivalent to those now exercised at Stormont, has I think been generally agreed ... I have never been fully able to understand what is meant by 'recognising the legitimacy of the Northern Government.' If this expression is intended to convey that they represent the majority in the Six-County area, this is no difficulty. If it means that the Northern Government is seen as having a permanent future, within an all-Ireland Constitution, this is not a difficulty either. If it means a judgment on their historical origins, this is a different matter. It seems to me that when Brookeborough speaks of recognition this is what he has in mind — acceptance of the two-nations theory, or at least a confession that, because of the religious division, partition was the only right and practicable solution of the problem.[38]

This formulation of the problem is notable for two reasons. The first is its explicit linking of the need for a continuing Northern parliament to his perception that the roots of the problem were essentially related to 'religious division'. The second is his supposition that any such assembly, even within a united Ireland, would have powers 'equivalent to those now exercised at Stormont.' It is doubtful, to say the least, whether either of these viewpoints would be echoed by any of Lemass's more recent successors in office.

The question of recognition, although it continued to be used intermittently as a stick by unionists, particularly in Stormont, with which to beat the nationalist minority — it enabled them, for instance, to torpedo the 'Orange and Green' talks in 1963 — began to lose much of its irritant qualities. The British government even came to the conclusion that Aiken, of whom they continued to harbour deep suspicions, had 'shown a notable change of attitude to the Partition problem and is adopting a more philosophical attitude to it.'[39]

Mainstream unionism, as might be expected, was unimpressed by Lemass's initial overtures. Brookeborough warned the Standing Committee of the Unionist Party in April 1960 that 'the hand of friendship, and this brotherly embrace from Éire, would very quickly turn into a bear's hug.'[40] He repeated the same message, in one guise or another, at least four times in the next two months.[41] Undeterred, Lemass pressed ahead privately with the other central plank of his policy: the dismantling of the tariff wall between North and South, which he, among others, had been instrumental in erecting.

Brookeborough responded with initial hostility to Lemass's proposals for closer trade links, but his and his cabinet's opposition to such links has to be considered in context. Political factors were especially pertinent. Stormont ministers were hypersensitive to what they perceived as attempts by Dublin to drive a wedge between Northern Ireland and the rest of the United Kingdom and were therefore determined to resist all such attempts, even if their objective effect would have been to benefit the Northern economy. They concluded, in the immediate aftermath of Lemass's election, that the proposal for a limited free trade area between the Republic and Northern Ireland could not be supported, specifically 'on political grounds.'[42]

These political convictions held firm even against continued pressure from Northern industrialists, who had witnessed a progressive deterioration in the balance of trade between the North and its closest available market. Equally, given the deep doubts about British solidarity that frequently coloured Stormont's perception of the issues, London's attempts to nudge Unionist politicians towards some form of accommodation with Dublin can only have increased their sense of embattled isolation. One of the most striking of these attempts was the memorandum sent to Stormont by the Home Office early in 1960, which, though unsuccessful in its plea for a change of heart, was remarkably explicit about the political view from London.

> There are political as well as economic arguments for going such distance as we can in reply to Mr Lemass. With the end of Mr de Valera's lengthy dominance of the Irish political scene, and the emergence of Mr Lemass, himself a business man, at the head of a more business-like administration, the political atmosphere in the South is changing. The metamorphosis will be neither rapid nor dramatic. But already there have been signs that the Dublin government are anxious to move away from the negative attitudes of earlier administrations.[43]

The process of chipping away at unionist intransigence, by both Lemass and London, was aided by unilateral action on the part of Northern businessmen, who, impatient with the speed of progress, increasingly took matters into their own hands. Furniture manufacturers took the first initiative, and early in 1961 a group of them made a private visit to Dublin, where they met Lemass's successor in the Department of Industry and Commerce, Jack Lynch, to urge concessions for their products.[44] They told him that Brookeborough had been unwilling to endorse their initiative publicly but had privately wished them good luck. The Northern premier also, with misgivings that can be imagined, helped to rein in Unionist backbenchers who were hostile to the initiative and were threatening to criticise it publicly.

The contrast with what had happened in 1932 is striking. Then, Northern manufacturers and politicians alike were united in their hostility to the tariff regime being organised by Lemass and de Valera, predicting that it would ruin important sectors of the Northern economy. Three decades later most Unionist politicians were greeting proposals to modify the tariff wall with undisguised alarm, while their fellow-unionists in industry were trekking to Dublin to look for concessions. Brookeborough, trying to square the circle, told the Stormont cabinet that 'the government would find it difficult to stand in the way of these developments ... but ... for political and constitutional reasons, they should refuse to be drawn into direct negotiations with the Republican authorities.' It would be rather difficult, he added, for the Northern Ireland government to sustain an attitude of being wholly against something that could be of benefit to the commercial community. Other members of his government were less constrained and in the ensuing discussion loudly lamented their inability to actually prevent the extension by Dublin of trade concessions to their fellow-unionists.[45]

Towards the end of the year relations at some levels were evidently softening. The head of the Government Information Bureau, Pádraig Ó hAnracháin, a confidant of Lemass's, gave a private lunch at the Dublin Airport restaurant in December to four Unionist notables: I. G. Hawthorn MP, the Unionist whip; Joseph Morgan MP; William Douglas, the secretary-general of the Unionist Council; and James Baillie.[46] It was certainly a sign of the times that the four were en route to a public discussion of the Northern issue in Tullow.

Ironically, Lemass was not having things all his own way in Dublin, or at least not initially. There was a war of attrition between his department and his old stamping ground Industry and Commerce, where the department secretary, J. C. B. MacCarthy, seemed to be having great difficulty in abandoning the corpus of protection that had been so painstakingly assembled over so many years. Within the Government, Paddy Smith, the Minister for Agriculture, opposed it strenuously but unavailingly,[47] finding himself, not for the first or last time, in a minority. The argument in effect was only marginally about economic advantages and disadvantages and much more substantially about seizing a political moment and giving added impetus to an initiative whose ultimate speed and direction were still impossible to predict.

The Northern minority

Lemass may have softened the approach to Britain and embarked on important initiatives in relation to unionists, but the Northern minority was, as so often, fairly far down the queue. The brutal fact was that the nationalists, partly because they had no political power, did not figure very largely in the immediate calculations of a leader for whom executive power was the primary language of political communication. 'Provided we were not to appear to make an issue of the matter,' he said not long after assuming office, 'the British would hardly object to our mentioning to them the preoccupations of the Nationalist representatives in the Six Counties.'[48] Nationalists were not disregarded, but in some sense they were not fully central to his strategy, even though he was broadly sympathetic to their situation. He told his old adversary Ernest Blythe, who had written to him privately in 1962 to praise his initiatives:

> I think it is much too easy to find fault with the attitude of the Northern Nationalists. It would be expecting far too much of human nature not to expect them to express their resentment of their second-class status, and their desire to end it in the only way which at present seems possible by destroying the authority whose policy it is to sustain it. If the Northern Government had ever shown any disposition to want to treat them otherwise the position might have developed differently.[49]

It is certainly significant, on the other hand, that apart from his first ardfheis speech in November 1959, Lemass's references to the need to provide for the protection of nationalists' rights, in a united Ireland that would retain a Northern Ireland parliament, were few and far between. His relationship with the Northern minority in general, and the Nationalist Party in particular, was characterised by a cautious willingness to help, tempered by a firm determination to remain in the driving-seat. He knew as much — or as little — about the realities of life on the ground for members of the northern minority as most of the Republic's politicians of his era.

In addition, Dublin's seeming lack of involvement in the day-to-day grievances of the minority was in fact founded on a political and ideological position. Hitherto, as an official memorandum in the Department of External Affairs noted in 1962, official policy had tended to concentrate entirely on the ending of partition, and this had meant 'that generally we have not been prepared to envisage attacking individual grievances of the Nationalist inhabitants of the North, as this would seem to imply acquiescence in the overall political status quo.'[50]

According to Conor Cruise O'Brien, who worked in Iveagh House at the time, Aiken had been expressing the view that it would be wise to reduce the emphasis on Ireland's 'right' to unity and put more emphasis on the forms of discrimination that existed within Northern Ireland. He had also sent Cruise O'Brien to make contact with the Nationalists and urge them to make contact with the Unionists, 'which didn't go down well, as you may imagine.'[51] It is far from certain that this political brinkmanship would have excited much enthusiasm among the self-same Nationalists had they ever been consulted about it.

Nationalists would have envisaged themselves as having a much more central role than Dublin had allocated to them. The human realities of living under unionism were by and large unknown to members of the Dublin Government. Representatives of the Nationalist Party had not even been invited to the presidential inauguration of Seán T. O'Kelly in 1945 until they wrote to the Government in Dublin to complain.[52] The Costello Government rejected in 1956 the suggestion that Northern Ireland elected representatives should address the Dáil; the suggestion had come from Eddie McAteer, who had sought the right for all Stormont MPs, although it was tacitly acknowledged that only Nationalists would have availed of it. The inter-party Government's policy was privately endorsed by the Fianna Fáil parliamentary party.[53]

Few ministers, even, would have been fully aware of the degree to which that Government, and Fianna Fáil especially, were held in Messiah-like reverence for decades by nationalists in the North. From the early nineteen-thirties in particular it was the practice for crowds to gather outside the offices of the *Derry Journal* in Shipquay Street on the night when the votes in the Republic's elections were being counted. After each result reached the newspaper office by telephone it was relayed to the waiting crowd, who greeted the news of each Fianna Fáil seat won with a storm of cheers.[54]

Similarly the strength, and thrust, of Northern nationalist opinion often came as a surprise to Dublin politicians. Lemass noted after his retirement that when as Taoiseach he had met nationalists in the North he had formed the impression that 'for them the day Partition ended would be the day they would get their foot on the throat of the Orangeman across the road.'[55]

Contacts between the Nationalist Party and the Government were maintained, however, and evoked from Lemass an expression of willingness to receive deputations from the party 'at all suitable times.'[56] This was in essence a replication of part of de Valera's policy. It is also clear, however, that the question of the Northern nationalist minority had been on the back burner for some time. An internal Department of External Affairs memorandum of 20 February 1960 sought authorisation for a resumption of visits to the North by department staff. Noting that it had been four-and-a-half years since the last visit, it suggested that 'another visit seems to be called for, if only to show the Six-County people that we are still with them.'[57]

The 'Six-County people' were undeniably in need of reassurance. They would have been even more concerned had they been aware of a letter Lemass received from Erskine Childers quite early in 1961, which reported:

Discrimination is decreasing, although it still exists. We hear of the local authorities who show discrimination in the allocation of houses, but there are quite a number who are not guilty of this practice, about whom we hear nothing. Discrimination in industry varies enormously. Some of the new English and American industries permit no discrimination whatsoever.[58]

The sense of isolation experienced by the Northern minority helps to explain the strength of the response when, in 1961, Nationalist members of the Stormont parliament were invited to state receptions in Dublin for Cardinal Agagianian and for Prince Rainier and Princess Grace of Monaco. On each occasion Lemass singled out the leaders of the group and made a point of presenting them to the guests of honour — a gesture that, according to McAteer, gave 'untold strength' to the representatives of the Northern minority.[59]

The Nationalist Party soon decided to turn up the volume. Cahir Healy wrote to Lemass in February and March 1962 urging him to take action on the general question of discrimination. Lemass passed the letters to Aiken with a request for appropriate briefing material. Aiken's reply, on 29 March 1962, is a two-page apologia for Government policy up to that date, which, although it referred to the need for 'direct negotiations with Britain and Belfast,' laid particular and virtually exclusive emphasis on the role of the British government. 'Over the years,' he told Lemass, 'I have taken every opportunity to urge the British authorities to improve the position, particularly in the matter of gerrymandering of constituencies which I regard as fundamental in the whole matter.'[60] He drew attention to the possibly negative implications of a policy that was focused too much on the United Nations, even though a 'fair volume of support' could be mustered behind a General Assembly resolution on partition. 'The votes in favour', he warned, 'could well include countries whose support might be more harmful than otherwise, and we might even find quite a number of countries whose attitude is of importance to us either abstaining or voting against us.'[61]

Lemass's reply to Healy trod gingerly over the slippery ground. Although he assured him that the Government was 'very well aware of the discrimination from which the nationalists in the Six Counties suffer in various respects,' he went on to suggest, in terms that veered dangerously towards self-incrimination, that 'it would help us to have reliable, up-to-date knowledge of discrimination within the Six-County area.'[62] He urged Healy to organise, with his colleagues, the collection of this detailed information for sending to him personally. Healy responded with enthusiasm and much material, but the planned document was never published, although a bulky typescript found its way into the capacious departmental files.

In 1962 some signs of a thaw in internal Northern Ireland relationships came with the inauguration of the 'Orange and Green' talks between the leader of the Nationalist Party, Eddie McAteer, and Sir George Clark,

Grand Master of the Orange Order.[63] These were to founder the following year on the vexed question of 'recognition' of Stormont, but Lemass did what he could to help. He ordered Government departments in Dublin to assist the Nationalist parliamentarians by providing them with background information on legislative proposals in Northern Ireland and, where necessary, by arranging meetings with department officials. The Government Information Bureau, for its part, was instructed to send them automatically copies of White Papers and other relevant documents.[64]

The talks were accompanied by a series of parallel discussions between McAteer and officials of the Department of External Affairs and Aiken, in the course of which a number of departmental memorandums on the electoral system, public employment, housing and the Mater Hospital were prepared as the basis for Dublin's contribution to the talks. The intention at first had been that the full memorandum should be given to McAteer at a meeting he had with Aiken on 11 September 1962, but Lemass, who had a prior discussion with Aiken on the matter, gave instructions that McAteer not be given anything in writing.[65]

THE O'NEILL FACTOR

The marginalisation — to put it no more strongly — that characterised relations between Dublin and the Nationalist minority was if anything intensified by the election of Terence O'Neill as Prime Minister of Northern Ireland on 25 March 1963. O'Neill had been Minister of Finance since 1956, and his election was viewed in Dublin and in London as a decisive break with the two-decade rule of his predecessor. O'Neill had been educated largely in England. Brought up away from the bitterness and animosities of Northern Ireland, he was less a prisoner of these than he might otherwise have been. On the other hand, the very same factors left him fatally ill-prepared for the task of understanding the nature, and managing the power, of bedrock unionism.

He plainly regarded himself as a reforming Prime Minister. In his first major speech he told unionists that the challenge was 'literally to transform the face of Ulster.' He commissioned an economic plan for the province, recognised the ICTU, and spoke openly of 'building bridges in the community.'[66] The period was typified by a spirit of optimism, which probably led all the main participants to overestimate their own strength and in some instances to turn a deaf ear to certain inconvenient messages coming from the other side of the fence, until they could no longer be ignored.

Coincidentally, the inauguration of the O'Neill era saw the emergence of a new kind of nationalism in the North, a nationalism that would not be regarded as exceptional today but that, in the shadow of de Valera, was initially a unique phenomenon. This kind of nationalism, which owed its origins in part to the new generation of Northern Catholics who had benefited from the 1944 Butler Education Act, created the National Unity movement, whose first aim was to have a 'United Ireland brought about by the consent of the people of Northern Ireland.' Its secretary, Michael McKeown, a teacher and journalist, and its chairman, James Scott, quickly launched initiatives aimed not only at Northern nationalist opinion but also at the Dublin Government. They invited the Taoiseach to their dinner on St Patrick's Day in 1963. Lemass did not go but sent George Colley, which at the very least was a straw in the wind.

Lemass's positive view of the new movement was not shared elsewhere in Dublin. An External Affairs official warned that it was guilty of the ultimate heresy, in that it 'aims at achieving a united Ireland by the consent of the people of Northern Ireland. This, in effect, is an endorsement of the constitutional position of Northern Ireland as set out in Section 1 of the Ireland Act, 1949 … This position has not, of course, been accepted by our government.'[67]

Lemass even advised Colley to approach 'selected private persons' to raise funds for the movement's magazine, *New Nation,* because a public grant would require a Dáil vote.[68] Aiken was by no means as enthusiastic and considerably less helpful. Six months later, when Hillery asked him for advice on the same topic, Aiken warned that the Taoiseach had informed Colley 'that it would be undesirable to consider an allocation of public funds for this purpose'[69] and carefully omitted to mention Lemass's much more positive private suggestion about fund-raising. Lemass was certainly more open to National Unity's financial needs than he was to those of the Nationalist Party: an appeal to him from Healy for funding for elections in the same year was politely ignored.[70]

O'Neill's early period in office, and the emergence of a new spirit among Northern Catholics, created an atmosphere that Lemass used as a springboard for a further initiative. The occasion he chose was a function in Tralee in July 1963 to commemorate the fortieth year in Dáil Éireann of Deputy Thomas McEllistrim. The timing was a direct response to O'Neill's early initiatives; the venue was no less significant. Kerry generally had been a hotbed of militant republicanism for many years, and in fact Lemass had in the nineteen-thirties failed in an attempt to get Dunlop to establish its projected Irish manufacturing centre there — an attempt influenced strongly by the sense of political alienation then evident in the county. Tralee itself was a venue for republican meetings, one of which was pointed to by Brian Faulkner, early in Lemass's period as Taoiseach, as an example of how little the Government were doing to combat the IRA and its sympathisers.[71] Nor was McEllistrim himself indifferent to the political sensibilities of many of his constituents.

The 'spiritual damage' that had been done by the Civil War, Lemass told his audience — a trifle optimistically — had now been finally and completely healed; partition was the problem.[72] Neatly deflecting the issue of recognition, he set out positively to reassure unionists, whom he described, in a telling piece of verbal sleight of hand, as 'the religious minority in the North' and 'the dissentient minority'. He did so in two ways: by telling them that he accepted the genuineness of their fears and by formally recognising 'that the Government and Parliament there exist with the support of the majority in the Six-County area — artificial though that area is.' Carefully placing the blame for partition on external causes — divisions within the British coalition government of the day — he went on to argue for 'an extension of useful contacts at every level of activity.'

McAteer greeted Lemass's speech as 'a lucid restatement of the National-ists' goal,'[73] but reaction elsewhere was more muted. Brian Faulkner thought it represented nothing new, and the *Belfast Telegraph,* which reported his views, editorialised on the same day that the speech represented something of a riddle but was perhaps 'a move towards educating opinion in the Republic in the democratic practice of agreement to differ.'[74] The Belfast *News Letter* was more forthright, describing it as a 'backward step',[75] but the Westminster Unionist MPs were more positive, notably Henry Clark and William Orr, who said that it was 'couched in a language that showed a change of spirit we warmly welcome.'[76] The Stormont MP Phelim O'Neill, later to incur political displeasure because of his refusal to join the Orange Order, was also notably supportive. In Dublin the *Irish Independent* thought there was 'nothing startlingly new' in the speech,[77] whereas the *Irish Times* thought it 'a note of sanity and hope.'[78] Terence O'Neill, who evidently waited for some time to take the temperature of his supporters before making his own position clear, gave it a moderate welcome some six weeks later.[79]

The effect of the Tralee speech on Northern political and public opin-ion was probably overestimated in the Republic. Certainly the Northern Ireland cabinet minutes for that period, generally speaking, are noteworthy less for any hostility to the Republic than for their general lack of concern or interest in what was happening anywhere south of Newry. Lemass, on the other hand, followed words with action, instructing all Government departments, through his Assistant Secretary, Tadhg Ó Cearbhaill, to draw up lists of possible areas for co-operation with Northern Ireland.[80]

THE AMERICAN CONNECTION

Any actual or potential thaw in North-South relations as a result of the Tralee speech was seriously impeded by developments in Irish-American relations and more specifically by a number of speeches made by Lemass in the United States later in the year. The American president, John F. Kennedy, was extremely conscious of the political advantage accruing to him from his Irish background and in 1956 had unsuccessfully co-sponsored a Senate resolution urging self-determination for the people of Ireland and urging that the Republic of Ireland 'should embrace the entire territory of Ireland, unless a clear majority of all the people, in a free plebiscite, declared to the contrary.'[81] His experiences as a young man in London, however, had also made him a strong political ally of the British government, and his accession to office tempered his earlier enthusiasm.

In his political calculations — and Lemass, by his own account, found Kennedy a somewhat cold and calculating politician — the British alliance came first, and he was unwilling to jeopardise it for as long as he could sustain Irish-American political support without going overboard on the territorial issue. The Irish ambassador to Washington, Dr T. J. Kiernan, had first-hand evidence of this when he delicately brought up the national issue in a discussion with Kennedy.

> I thought it better to begin with the hard part and said that while we did not expect him to express views in any public statement concerning partition, the subject would, he could expect, arise in his conversations with President de Valera and the Taoiseach and Minister. The President looked as if another headache had struck him and asked me was he expected to say anything in public. I repeated that we were not asking for this but only that we hoped for his continued goodwill towards the solution of the reunification of the country. He said he would study the dossier.[82]

Terence O'Neill, looking over Lemass's shoulder, made a vigorous but unsuccessful attempt to get the American president to include Northern Ireland in his itinerary: the Giant's Causeway was suggested as a suitably neutral venue.[83] He followed this with a personal visit to the White House (although he did not get to meet the President). His renewed invitation to Kennedy to visit the Giant's Causeway was declined 'for tactical reasons.'[84] Undeterred, he took the matter up again after Kennedy's assassination, arriving in Washington in 1964 to seek audience with Lyndon Johnson 'on St. Patrick's day, of all things.'[85]

Larry O'Brien, who had accompanied Kennedy to Ireland the previous year, expressed concern to the President, but by then McGeorge Bundy, another former Kennedy official, had 'incautiously' committed the White House to receiving the Northern Ireland premier. 'If you simply speak of President Kennedy's warm feeling towards him,' Bundy told Johnson, 'the job is done.'[86] A brief off-the-record meeting ensued, and O'Neill, on his return to Belfast, expressed his thanks to Johnson in a letter that betrayed his total unawareness of the gathering storm. 'As relations between the North of Ireland and the South of Ireland improve,' he told Johnson, 'I do so hope that the Irish question can be removed from American politics as it has been from English politics for the past 40 years.'[87]

The Kennedy visit to Ireland was a political and public relations success for both leaders, not least because the thorny subject of the North was submerged in an ocean of sentiment, and Lemass was invited to pay a visit to Washington in return in October 1963. In contrast to the soft-edged approach that had characterised Kennedy's visit to Ireland, Lemass's American speeches were notable for a cutting edge that suggests that he had decided to capitalise on the reaction to his Tralee speech but without directly involving the American President. Lemass had actually signalled in advance of leaving Ireland that he wanted to discuss partition with Kennedy (among other topics), but the subject was not raised at all. The main concerns of the meetings were trade (on the Irish side) and international affairs (on the American side). What surprised American officials most was that Lemass did not come as a supplicant: the proposal that was activated at the Kennedy-Lemass meetings for an American-funded fishery research vessel originated on the American side.[88]

What most annoyed the Northern Ireland Prime Minister about Lemass's speeches in America was the political recidivism he perceived in Lemass's address to the National Press Club on 16 October, when he called on the British government to issue a statement that it would welcome an opportunity to end partition whenever Irishmen wanted to get rid of it.[89] O'Neill's public expressions of alarm may have been to some extent contrived and were undoubtedly prompted less by the content of Lemass's speeches — with which he would hardly have been unfamiliar — than by the audience to which they were addressed. Anti-partition rhetoric in Dublin, Cork and Monaghan could for the most part be safely ignored by unionist politicians unless it suited them to make an issue of it; but the political impact of the rhetoric increased in direct proportion to the speaker's distance from Dublin and Belfast, especially if the intervening space included the North Atlantic. Lemass repeated this call in his address to the United Nations the following day, recording in addition his belief, undoubtedly inflammatory as far as unionists were concerned, that 'the circumstances of partition were also under review in Britain.'[90] At Boston College he rejected — citing Lincoln as his exemplar — 'the claim of a minority to vote itself out of the nation.'[91]

These American speeches, and their call for renewed British involvement, amounted to a public repudiation of his privately expressed view, just after his election as Taoiseach, that Dublin should seek to bring pressure on the North, whether directly or through Britain or the United Nations. There is some evidence, however, that Lemass's flirtation with the idea of leaving Britain out of the equation had been short-lived. Thereafter, his belief that a British statement would help in the process of securing Irish unity, though less frequently and more cautiously expressed than similar sentiments by his predecessors or successors, remained part of his political armoury.

Lemass's political acumen is the essential key to his nuanced stance on this issue. He was not going to ask for something if there was a high probability that it would be publicly refused: this was a tactic that was guaranteed to produce political embarrassment. Knowing, as he did, that Kennedy was not going to get himself embroiled in the Irish question at this level, Lemass disarmingly told one of his questioners at the National Press Club, who had asked him specifically whether the President would be bringing his influence to bear on the matter, that 'the problem was one for the Irish to solve, and I doubt that outside pressure could help.'[92] The same motivation helps to explain his reluctance to raise the matter with Kennedy: he knew that he would not get an open display of support on the issue.

The same political factors operated, paradoxically, to support a different set of tactics in relation to Britain. While an American refusal to get involved would be politically counterproductive, a British refusal to do so would at worst be politically neutral at home and might even enhance his domestic political credentials.

Some Irish people, however, were not impressed. One of them, J. J. Horgan, wrote to Lemass in the immediate aftermath of his American speeches to acquaint him with the response of a Northern business acquaintance who was also a friend of O'Neill's. The unnamed Northerner had just met O'Neill and found him 'astonished at the change of front.' It was a response, plainly, that provided evidence that wishful thinking could take place on either side of the border. Horgan added his own, typically pungent, view:

> To appeal to the British is ... merely an aggravation and a waste of time and purpose. Their attitude is clear and has not changed for forty-three years. Read the much abused Act of 1920 which in effect told us to go away and settle our differences ourselves, and actually provided the means of uniting Ireland. The simple fact is that no British government could or would prevent the ending of partition if Irishmen were agreed, but also no British Government can or will drive NI out of the UK. So long as we keep picking at the partition sore so long will it remain septic. Co-operation is not really possible if our real object is to undermine and destroy the status quo. The only way to end partition is to forget about it and work with the North for the prosperity of Ireland.[93]

This critique, it should be noted, represented only one end of a fairly broad spectrum. While Lemass's American remarks would have evoked general approval in the Republic, there were, at the very least, straws in the wind to indicate that some of the items omitted from his agenda had not escaped attention. The *Irish Catholic* unblushingly drew attention to some deficiencies in the Taoiseach's raiment and in particular to a statement that amounted in its view to 'an unfortunate suggestion that Irishmen do not want to get rid of partition just yet.'

> The contrast between the brief reference to partition in his speech before the United Nations Organisation and the total length of his discourse is a striking one. It is as if he were looking to the ends of the earth for causes to champion while being strangely reluctant to speak out boldly there about glaring injustices suffered by the country in whose name he spoke. [It is] strange that he made no reference to the presence of British troops in the Six Counties.[94]

Any prospect, however faint, that Lemass's visit might have significantly altered American policy was dashed by Kennedy's assassination. By early 1964, George Reedy, a hold-over from the Kennedy administration, advised Pierre Salinger to be cautious in framing statements of US policy for the new President. 'I would doubt whether the President would have any feelings on this one. This is strictly a "family affair" and while I personally would have some strong views on the matter I would hesitate to ascriibe them to a man named Johnson.'[95] As late as 1965, White House officials were bravely resisting the temptation to get involved, even in the week of the Lemass–O'Neill meetings, which they interpreted as justifying even greater caution on the matter.[96]

Lemass was unabashed when he was asked, on his return from the United States, whether O'Neill was not entitled to be disappointed at the tone of his remarks there. 'Sure. Did I not want to have discussions with the ultimate aim of ending partition?'[97] Some six weeks after the Taoiseach's return, Lionel Booth, the Fianna Fáil deputy for Dún Laoghaire-Rathdown — the 'Bible belt', as the constituency was sometimes known in sectarian small-talk — visited Belfast to defend his party leader. It was not Lemass's intention, he told an evidently disbelieving Northern audience, 'to get Britain to throw you people into our laps.'[98] Lemass's former adversary Ernest Blythe, on the other hand, almost glowed with approval. 'Although some ignoramuses to the westward complained, and Captain O'Neill complained in the North, it can be said that the Taoiseach succeeded reasonably well in keeping to the middle of the road.'[99]

By then, however, the damage had been done, and relations between North and South entered a renewed Cold War. In his address to the Fianna Fáil ardfheis in November 1963 Lemass barely mentioned Northern Ireland, giving it less space in his address than he devoted to an encomium on Irish.[100] He was not prepared, however, to allow the British government to close the book, and the chill was accentuated early in 1964 when he told a Fianna Fáil convention in Arklow that it was 'only a matter of time before British leaders would make — as I have urged on them — a clear political expression that they had no desire to maintain the partition of Ireland.'[101] His speech evoked another tart response from O'Neill.

The period from the end of 1963 to late 1964, therefore, was marked by a resumption of the old coolness and little evident contact between Dublin and Northern politicians of any hue. O'Neill, undoubtedly conscious of the danger of burning his political boats, did little to foster intracommunity relations in Northern Ireland that was not merely cosmetic and much that tended in the opposite direction. What was seen as an increasingly hard line emanating from the Republic would in turn have facilitated, and perhaps even encouraged, two key Stormont decisions in 1964: the siting of the new city at Craigavon, and the Lockwood imbroglio that resulted in the awarding of the North's new university to Coleraine instead of to Derry. Two factors probably influenced these decisions more than any others. One was the increasing restiveness of Northern nationalists, symbolised by the Divis Flats riots in 1964 over the flying of the Tricolour; this helped to propel Ian Paisley onto a wider political stage and reduced O'Neill's already limited room for manoeuvre. The second, probably more marginal, factor was the imminence of yet another Westminster election, although the destination of the Westminster seats was never seriously in doubt. To court nationalist good will on either Craigavon or Coleraine would have exposed O'Neill's flank dangerously within the Unionist Party at any time; with Paisley threatening, and on the eve of a general election, it would have been seriously destabilising.

THE LEMASS-O'NEILL MEETINGS

The British general election, when it was finally held on 15 October 1964, returned a Labour Party government, which immediately posed a new set of potential problems for the Stormont government. The somewhat languid attitude of the previous Tory administrations to the Irish problem generally (the most helpful suggestion made to Irish officials by the Commonwealth Secretary, Duncan Sandys, in 1963 was the hope that they would be able to 'muddle through'[102]) had been replaced by a noticeably more active stance by Labour Party politicians.

Lemass had in fact met Wilson privately in London a month before his Arklow speech, on 16 March 1964. Their discussion provided evidence for Wilson's openness towards the idea of encouraging co-operation between Stormont and Dublin, particularly in relation to a number of key areas suggested by Lemass: transport, electricity, and eventually nuclear power. Lemass made it clear that his suggestions were being made 'without prejudice to the political position of either side,' and Wilson, for his part, observed cannily that he had rejected a suggestion that he should visit Northern Ireland before the election, as this would not win him any seats 'and I might lose my own.'[103] He went so far as to say that he would be quite happy to receive a delegation from the Nationalist Party if he became Prime Minister.

The furore created within the Northern minority, and to a more limited extent in the Republic, by the Craigavon and Coleraine decisions, coupled with the fact that the new Wilson government was bound to take a closer interest in what was happening in its own political back yard, evidently suggested to O'Neill towards the end of 1964 that he should mend his hand. As before, he faced a dilemma: something had to be done, but if it seriously threatened to alter the balance of power or the balance of economic advantage accruing to the majority within Northern Ireland it would present him with political problems that could rapidly get out of control. In the circumstances, inviting Lemass to visit him at Stormont was a calculated risk. He could be reasonably sure that Lemass would agree not to raise any constitutional or political issues; this was his envisaged insurance against a potential unionist backlash. At the same time the dramatic nature of the gesture created the possibility of winning back some ground among the nationalist population, or at least drawing the teeth of its opposition to his government's deservedly unpopular decisions.

The O'Neill initiative might still not have been successful if it had not been for the relationship that had built up over the previous years between a number of key people on both sides of the border, notably between T. K. Whitaker, Secretary of the Department of Finance, and O'Neill himself. Whitaker was the leading official in the Irish delegations to World Bank and IMF meetings, at which O'Neill himself was generally present as part of the UK delegation, together with his private secretary, Jim Malley.[104] The relationship went back as far as 1957 at least. One of the World Bank vice-presidents, William Iliffe, was a native of Tyrone and had become friendly with Whitaker, who was from Rostrevor, County Down. At a World Bank meeting in Paris in 1958, Iliffe put Whitaker and O'Neill sitting beside each other. Over this period, relations between delegates from the Republic and those from Northern Ireland were becoming increasingly cordial.

Malley travelled to Dublin on 3 January 1965 with the invitation and went first to Whitaker's office. Whitaker suggested that he pay a visit to the National Gallery while he himself brought the invitation to the Taoiseach.

> The quickness of Lemass's response was notable. I had to remind him it might be well to have a word with Frank Aiken. 'I suppose so,' he said. He rang Aiken straight away. Aiken was a bit taken aback but fairly quickly agreed.[105]

This was followed by a brief chapter of errors, as a result of which O'Neill very nearly never received Lemass's acceptance. The acceptance letter, written by Whitaker, was placed inside an envelope and then given to a secretary to be placed inside another envelope to be posted to O'Neill's private secretary, Jim Malley.[106] The outside envelope was addressed to *The Private Secretary to the Prime Minister, Stormont Castle, Dublin 4*. Not surprisingly, it had not arrived at this strange address a week later. It eventually arrived two days before the meeting took place (in its absence, the final arrangements had been made by telephone), adorned with a scrawled suggestion from a percipient Dublin postal official, *Try Belfast, Ireland*.[107] Lemass apparently told two other ministers (apart from Frank Aiken) in advance, but, in spite of leaks to the press, nothing was published. Those in the know did not include Jack Lynch, who, quite coincidentally, had been asked to visit his opposite number in Northern Ireland at about the same time and thought it wise to check with Lemass first. 'Do nothing about that until you hear from me,' was Lemass's cryptic instruction.[108]

The meeting eventually took place on 14 January. Lemass and Whitaker were met at the customs post outside Newry by Malley, who travelled with them up to Belfast. Malley, who had never met Lemass before, thought him 'a most extraordinary man': the small talk in the car was about poker, and Lemass confessed to a fellow-feeling for the Unionist cabinet minister Brian Maginnis, 'because he played poker too.' Ken Bloomfield, head of the Northern Ireland civil service, remarked later that Lemass, whom he had not previously met, struck him as 'burly, leonine and rather gruff, like some veteran French politician of the left.'[109] For conciseness, it was as good a pen-picture as you could get.

The well-documented minutiae of the meeting include the famous vignette of the Taoiseach and Prime Minister, standing side by side at the palatial Stormont urinals, speculating about which of them would suffer most from the political fall-out. If Lemass held the better hand — as he undoubtedly did — he was too polite to show it. Although O'Neill had taken the initiative in issuing the invitation, the fact that Lemass did the travelling showed his willingness to appear the suitor in the relationship and to take the greater initial risk.

O'Neill's gamble was, however, the greater one, and one he eventually lost. He deliberately played down the 'recognition' issue when asked about it after his return visit to Dublin.

> I don't want to create any trouble for Mr Lemass in Dublin but my own feeling is that the statement issued in Dublin — describing me as the visiting Prime Minister of Northern Ireland — is good enough for me. Lawyers scribbling on bits of paper might argue endlessly about it.[110]

This was in marked contrast to his attitude four years later. By then he was under intense political pressure and claimed that the invitation to Lemass had been 'an initiative to clothe our constitutional status with a new moral authority' and that when Lemass's car drove through the gates of Stormont 'the grandiose and empty claims of Éire's constitution were exposed for the vanity they are.'[111] Lemass, by now in retirement, forbore to comment. In fact his own main political success was in carving out new territory between the language of recognition and the provocations of unvarnished irredentism.

The content and context of the two meetings — O'Neill came to Dublin on 9 February, driving his own car — were significant in that they not only spelt out areas for co-operation but presaged areas of difficulty. O'Neill informed London in advance, but only Ivan Neill, the Minister of Finance, among his own cabinet ministers, and the Governor of Northern Ireland, Lord Erskine.[112] The only other person given advance notice was Sir George Clark, Grand Master of the Orange Order.[113] Lemass's shopping-list was specific: the abolition of barriers to tourism; the facilitation of educational exchanges; sharing health facilities where urgent and necessary; trade matters; the joint development of nuclear power 'where this proves economic'; joint agricultural research projects; reciprocal practising rights for lawyers; and the joint administration of certain charities.[114]

The fly in the ointment was industrial promotion. Lemass suggested the elimination of wasteful counter-bidding; the Northern officials 'doubted if this risk could be altogether eliminated.'[115] At the same meeting, Northern officials expressed a reservation about trade initiatives, observing that trade was not within the powers of the Northern Ireland government. O'Neill also exhibited a certain nervousness when the Dublin side suggested recipro-cal exchanges of industrial trainees: this impinged on the sensitive area of Northern Ireland employment practices.

Although the agenda for each meeting included some political matters — industrial promotion was plainly political, as was trade — they did not include items that might have raised specifically unionist hackles. The final text of the joint statement issued after the meeting of 14 January, however, was 'essentially the Stormont draft';[116] the Dublin side also agreed that it should be on Stormont letter-heading, and signed. The omission of any reference to the continuing complaints of the Northern minority was particularly marked, but this was a 'political' matter, which, as the final communiqué noted, was off the agenda.

Lemass had not only been prepared to shelve the question of dis-crimination against the Northern minority but had come dangerously close to the *bête noire* of republican politicians, 'recognition' of the Stormont administration. Perhaps luckily for him, more than four decades of partition had bred a certain insensitivity among all but the most dedicated Southern nationalists to the plight of their Northern compatriots. Eddie McAteer was unhappy about this but kept his concerns loyally to himself. Only his brother Hugh, a former chief of staff of the IRA and a republican election candidate in the North, was sufficiently enraged to break ranks; he described Lemass's visit to Stormont as 'the greatest betrayal of all.'[117] His, however, was a lone voice, and any republican doubts that existed would have been dramatically lessened by the welcome extended to the talks by the British Foreign Secretary, Patrick Gordon Walker.

> I reject the suggestion that the British government is maintaining partition and I feel certain that any problems in this connection are best settled by the Irish people themselves. For 700 years Britain has made the mistake of trying unsuccessfully to run the affairs of Ireland, and that mistake must not be repeated.[118]

Walker's remarks appear to have been made in an off-the-cuff manner at a political meeting but were pointedly welcomed by Fianna Fáil politicians in general and by Lemass in particular. It did, as it happened, mirror a view of Ireland by the new Labour Party government that was as positive as anything Lemass could have hoped for, and he went to some lengths to welcome it in his Dún Laoghaire speech a few days later.

There were times indeed when the British reaction nearly went over the top. The Secretary of State for Commonwealth Affairs, Arthur Bottomley, had to be dissuaded by the British ambassador in Dublin, Sir Geofroy Tory, from making a statement welcoming the Lemass–O'Neill talks, 'because it might make it appear that the get-together had been inspired by London, which would detract from the significance of the meeting.'[119] Bottomley took the point and subsequently managed to prevent Harold Wilson from making exactly the same mistake.[120] This did not prevent the British Prime Minister from ruffling diplomatic feathers when he spoke at a St Patrick's Day dinner at the Irish embassy in London and suggested cheerfully that the next North–South meeting should take place in London.[121]

The Government now agreed to the creation of a ministerial committee chaired by the Taoiseach.[122] Lemass's agenda generally was adopted, with the exception of the suggestions about promoting participation in sport on an all-Ireland basis and the creation of an all-Ireland charities board, which were deleted after being considered by the ministerial committee.[123] This committee was shadowed by a committee of departmental secretaries comprising T. K. Whitaker (Finance), Thekla Beere (Industry and Commerce), J. C. B. MacCarthy (Industry and Commerce), Hugh McCann (External Affairs), J. C. Nagle (Agriculture), and T. O'Brien (Lands). The two committees swung into action with Lemass's full weight behind them, and a flurry of North–South meetings between officials and ministers took place. Among the participants was Donogh O'Malley, now Minister for Health, who met his counterpart, W. J. Morgan, in Belfast on 3 June and — no doubt delighted to upstage his colleagues — became the first Dáil minister to enter the Stormont parliamentary chamber.

There were, as might have been expected, a few glitches, and the sensitivities were mostly on the Dublin side. George Colley and Frank Aiken both objected to the use of terms such as 'Republic of Ireland', 'Irish Republic', and 'the Republic' — 'Ireland' was the only term to be approved. Industry and Commerce officials, on the other hand, were prone to foot-dragging on the question of tariff reduction, and Agriculture was also hostile to making concessions: Whitaker had to rap MacCarthy over the knuckles on this issue later in the year, noting that 'we shall have to improve on our previous record in the matter of tariff concessions.'[124] It was not the first or the last time that Lemass as Taoiseach found himself on the opposite side of the fence from the stewards of his old department.

In his first Dáil comments on the meeting, Lemass's main concern was to make a pre-emptive strike against the accusation that he had afforded 'recognition' to the Northern government. He did this partly by relying on the pre-Treaty acceptance by the original Dáil of the continued existence of a Northern parliament and by moving the goalposts from 'recognition' to 'approval', with a subtlety of which his predecessor might have approved, however much he might have been alarmed by its content.

> As regards the suggestion that my visit to Belfast involved recognition of the present constitutional status of the Northern Ireland Government, *if by recognition is meant approval,* I did not regard it as implying this, nor should it be so considered ... For my own part I would regard as an honourable solution of this national problem, an arrangement on the lines of that put forward on behalf of Dáil Éireann prior to the Treaty negotiations of 1921 and repeated on many occasions since involving, subject to safeguards, the confirmation of the position of the Northern Ireland legislature with its existing powers within an all-Ireland constitution, for so long as the people of the north eastern counties might desire it. [Emphasis added.][125]

The drafting of this part of his statement involved subtle but substantial differences of emphasis between Lemass and some of his advisers. His initial wording had a somewhat stronger reference to the powers of a Stormont parliament under a united Ireland constitution, and this was toned down at Whitaker's suggestion. On the other hand, the passage emphasised above evoked concern on the part of both Frank Aiken and Hugh McCann, the former at least most carefully tuned in to the possible implications for de Valera's traditional policy; but this concern was explicitly discounted by Lemass.[126] The new formulation, for all that it involved a discreet shift from one form of ambiguity to another, was plainly one to which O'Neill was not going to take exception.

Although it appeared to have been written out of the initial script, the Nationalist Party now moved back into the frame. Lemass met McAteer in

Dublin on 21 January 1965 for a general review of the Nationalist Party's position and options in the new situation that had been created. In his discussions Lemass focused on four main areas: the ideological basis for political action, party organisation, acceptance of the role of official opposition at Stormont, and arrangements for continuing co-operation.[127]

On the first issue, Lemass wanted the Nationalist Party to issue a statement that would replicate his own repeated view that Irish unity could be achieved on the basis of the continued existence of Stormont with its present powers. He argued with McAteer that too much and uncritical support from the South for Northern nationalists actually reinforced unionist opinion and that in order to reassure the unionists there was a continuing need for a Northern parliament.

This view was actually as unpopular with Aiken as it was with the Nationalists. Aiken was concerned that Lemass might stray too far into the murky swamp of federalism. 'We might well be faced', he warned, 'with a demand for three parliaments and for equal representation of the Six Counties and the 26 Counties in the all Ireland Parliament. An all Ireland Constitution of this kind with a built-in veto would render normal government impossible — as happened in the recent tragic case of Cyprus.'[128]

Lemass and Aiken shared a somewhat pessimistic view of the quality of Nationalist Party organisation at the local level and agreed that its reinforcement should be a priority for that party. 'As an immediate field of action,' Aiken suggested helpfully, each local club 'might concentrate on securing social justice in such matters as housing, employment at Government and local authority level, etc. where this may be denied at present.' This advice, though no doubt well meant, evoked incredulity among Northern nationalists, who wondered how precisely they were supposed to inaugurate such a policy in the light of the political realities with which they were faced.[129] On the other hand, suggestions that perceived organisational weaknesses in the Northern minority could best be remedied by an extension of the legendary Fianna Fáil party machine across the border were firmly rejected. The Southern correspondent of the *Belfast Telegraph* told his readers that 'people at the top of Fianna Fáil, and particularly Mr Lemass, would not favour any action of this kind, which could conceivably be regarded as a kind of Southern interference in the North's affairs.'[130]

Lemass proposed setting up a system of consultation with the Nationalists on any practical proposals affecting Northern commercial interests arising in future discussions on economic issues with Northern Ireland ministers. This, Aiken thought, would be 'useful'. In a coda, however, he struck a note that, in essence, underlined the long view taken by successive Dublin administrations of the Northern problem and of the role of the nationalist minority within that problem. He warned Lemass, in words that would undoubtedly have had an inflammatory effect on McAteer and his colleagues had they been made aware of them: 'I doubt whether such consultations should become any more formalised than those which take place from time to time with representatives of the Nationalist group. Naturally no Government wishes another Government with which it is negotiating to be in regular formal consultation with its own Opposition in parliament.'[131]

Increasingly, however, the tenuous relationship between Fianna Fáil and the Northern nationalists was in danger of becoming a dialogue of the deaf. McAteer and the Nationalist Party had for some time been convinced that the Republic's failure to move decisively on the question of unity had kept the republican physical force ethos alive in the North, undermining the party's somewhat desultory attempts to garner electoral support. Their suspicions had been enhanced by Fianna Fáil's unsuccessful attempt to scrap PR in tandem with the presidential election of 1959, which struck them as yet another example of how out of touch the Dublin political establishment had become. De Valera's strategy on this issue was seen in effect as a gross betrayal of all that the nationalists had been arguing for in relation to their own electoral system and gave the unionists yet another stick with which to beat the hapless Northern minority.

In February 1965, however, the Nationalist Party agreed, at Lemass's urging and despite their misgivings, to accept the role of official opposition at Stormont. The lack of generosity in the unionist response took the bloom off the initiative, and, while Lemass pursued his policy of ministerial contacts at every possible level, the political representatives of the Northern minority remained to some extent sidelined.

The intense dialogue between Dublin and Stormont following the O'Neill-Lemass meetings — intense at any rate relative to the stasis of the previous four decades — succeeded in the end only in arousing a deepening sense of misgiving. Domestic politics began, on both sides of the border, to reassert themselves. In the Republic the 1965 general election was fought by Lemass at least partly on the positive factors generated by his Northern visit, but not even this gave him the absolute majority he wanted — indeed the closeness of the result suggests that without the Northern issue he might have been forced into yet another minority Government. Fianna Fáil won exactly half the seats, seventy-two, which in the circumstances of the time was a working majority, even though they still had to rely on the support or abstention of a number of independent deputies.

THE 1966 COMMEMORATION AND THE AFTERMATH

In the North too the effects of the visit, to the extent that they were positive, were wearing off. In the general election held on 25 November 1965, Unionist MPs were returned in their customary numbers but with majorities that were in many cases reduced, either by slightly reinvigorated political nationalism or — far more significantly — by suspicious loyalism. Then, in April 1966, came the fiftieth anniversary of the 1916 Rising.

The planned ceremonies coincided with the high point of de Valera's campaign for re-election to the presidency against Tom O'Higgins of Fine Gael. From the start it was evident that Fianna Fáil were determined to exploit the occasion for maximum political advantage. No Government ministers made speeches: that public role was reserved for the subliminally campaigning de Valera. No opposition politicians were invited onto the reviewing stand for the march-past of troops at the GPO; they were well aware what was happening but decided that it would be unseemly to make a fuss about it.[132] They possibly derived some sort of grim satisfaction as they realised later that a complete sheaf of invitations had unaccountably gone missing, so that some ministers — Neil Blaney among them — were also forced to watch proceedings from the crowd.[133]

Lemass acted to minimise the twin dangers of raw irredentism and potential revisionism. He politely rejected Kathleen Clarke's claim to a place on the committee organising the celebrations, aware of the unrepentant nature of her republicanism. He explained the Commemoration Committee's decision not to issue an invitation to the ceremonies to Bulmer Hobson, the veteran republican who had opposed the Rising, in a typically laconic phrase: 'He wasn't here for the fighting.'[134] Not that he always got things his own way: he failed to persuade Jack Lynch that the pensions of former IRA men relating to their service in 1916 should be doubled.[135]

There was a heightened sense of anticipation about the proceedings — of foreboding even. An astonishing speech by Jim Ryan, now in semi-retirement in the Seanad, argued that 'a government speaking for the majority of the people in these 26 counties had a right to demand a plebiscite of the people of all Ireland, and if this was denied, would further have a right to use force if they thought this course a wise one.'[136] He hardly softened the impact of his remarks by adding that it was not the moral issue that he questioned but the wisdom of seeking a solution through force.

Southern republicans decided to organise 'freedom trains' to take supporters to demonstrations in the North. CIE, after consulting Lemass, declined to take bookings for these trains, citing a supposed shortage of rolling-stock, and then announced that all North-bound rail traffic would be suspended for more than twenty-four hours. The *Irish Times* helpfully pointed out that 'intending gunmen and demonstrators' would still be able to travel north before and after the standstill period.[137]

Northern politicians were on the *qui vive*. An emollient speech by O'Neill endorsing the movement towards Christian unity nonetheless warned that there could be no compromises on the constitutional position or on the maintenance of 'British living standards'.[138] Brian Faulkner, speaking to the Apprentice Boys, was less circumspect: there could be no celebration of an 'act of sedition', and the Apprentice Boys would be well advised to lock the gates against it.[139] Ian Paisley offered a public prayer of thanks for the 'failure' of 1916 and because Ulster was still free from Papal tyranny.[140] An Ulster Constitution Defence Committee warned 'all disloyal and disruptive people … that the loyalists of Ulster have no intention of standing idly by.'[141]

The dominant atmosphere in the Republic, however, was of solid self-congratulation, mixed with not a little triumphalism, notably evidenced by a huge pageant in the Phoenix Park, starring Micheál Mac Liammóir. The official files of the Commemoration Committee also show the virtual abandonment, by Lemass and all the other participants, of the description 'Northern Ireland' and a reversion to 'Six Counties' terminology.[142]

Tension increased towards the end of the week, with sporadic but small republican demonstrations in different parts of the North. By the standard of what was to follow it was small beer: at the biggest demonstration, in Belfast, skirmishes took place, but only six people were arrested.[143] De Valera spoke on several occasions, all but one of them non–controversial. What set things alight was his Parthian declaration, at the conclusion of the week's commemorations, that the British government could solve matters by simply transferring to Dublin the powers over Northern Ireland currently exercised by Westminster, allowing Northern Ireland to retain its local autonomy. With an optimism hard to credit even for the time, he declared: 'Not so much remains to be done.'[144] O'Neill was not slow to respond: the two states, he declared, were now 'poles apart'.[145] It was no less than the truth.

Lemass's role in all this was driven not just by party considerations but by his unique relationship with de Valera. Not long after becoming Taoiseach he had replied to a congratulatory message on his sixtieth birthday from his former party leader: 'You are a wonderful man, and surely as tough as teak.'[146] He would have been more aware than most of the threat posed to the elderly president by Tom O'Higgins's candidature, and he was concerned to minimise all dissentient voices that might have detracted from the party's central objective. He had personally acted to persuade de Valera to run again — a recommendation that echoed his urging him forty years earlier to establish Fianna Fáil against what appeared to be all the odds.

Although nobody in Fianna Fáil would have dared to question de Valera's second candidacy, it patently failed to ignite the party faithful as his first campaign had in 1959. Early in the campaign Fianna Fáil members and supporters were invited to a meeting in the Mansion House. Lemass opened the proceedings with a statesmanlike speech in which he said that in coming generations they would be able to boast that they had voted for de Valera, in the same way that he remembered in his youth old men being able to say that they had voted for Parnell. Charles Haughey and George

Colley spoke in much the same tone but without being able to evince much in the way of spontaneous enthusiasm from the assembly. Then Seán MacEntee got up to speak. His speech, laced with attacks on the 'Bantry Band', raised the spectre of Tim Healy, the Bantry-born Parnellite who, with an eye for the main chance, had switched allegiances so often and so successfully that he had ended up as Governor-General of the Free State. As MacEntee spoke the crowd cheered: this was what they had come to hear. Through it all Lemass sat with a wry expression on his face, as much as to say, 'What is the point of doing anything with such incorrigible people?'[147]

The prospect of a defeat, to all those inside what has been tellingly described as the Fianna Fáil moral community, was daunting. For Lemass it would in addition have had a personal dimension of incalculable proportions. All other considerations were therefore to be put aside, including the foreseeable effect of the celebrations on unionist opinion.

It is debatable how much of the chill was due to de Valera's speech. The sentiments he uttered, after all, were those that went back to his *Evening Standard* interview in 1938 and, even further, to the stance adopted by the republican government in 1921. They had been echoed on several occasions, albeit in a more muted form, by Lemass himself, and were plainly a statement of established Government policy. They could hardly have surprised the more sophisticated segments of his Northern audience.

A more considered verdict suggests that the internal dynamics of Northern politics were at least as responsible. O'Neill himself told Conor Cruise O'Brien many years later that what had really destabilised him was not so much de Valera's speech as the reaction to the commemoration by Northern nationalists, and in particular the renewed widespread display of the Tricolour.[148] If O'Neill had moved against such displays, as he was entitled to do under the controversial Flags and Emblems Act, he would have exposed the paper-thin nature of his reaching-out to the nationalist community; by failing to move against them he delivered himself into the hands of his growing band of critics in the Unionist Party and effectively sealed his own fate. He was in a no-win situation.

Attempting to restore some lost ground, he went on the offensive in October, charging that the existence of articles 2 and 3 of the Constitution of Ireland were 'a major irritant' in relations between North and South.[149] Lemass, questioned on this in the Dáil, stuck to his original line in favour of practical co-operation without sacrifice of principle, but added: 'We do not recognise that the partition of the country is a just or durable arrangement and could not therefore consider any constitutional change or other step which would imply an abandonment of that position.'[150] The hopes raised by the meetings of 1965 had been dashed or had been shown to be, in many important respects, illusory.

In an eerie echo of his predecessor's last-ditch attempt to secure a fresh British initiative on the matter, Lemass sought to persuade Harold Wilson, at a specially requested meeting in July 1965, to declare that the British government had no interest in maintaining partition 'when Irishmen want to get rid of it.' Arthur Bottomley, the Commonwealth Secretary, urged caution and an attitude of 'benevolent detachment' on his Prime Minister, and the fuse spluttered out.[151] From now on the domestic political agenda, combined with Lemass's increasing ill-health, precluded any possibility of another Northern initiative.

Lemass has been claimed by some writers as the political leader who inaugurated the era of revisionism on the North. It is inescapable that political revisionism would have taken place in any case, whether or not Lemass inaugurated or assisted it. His continually and bluntly repeated views about the essential and inevitable character of national unity, however, make it to all intents and purposes impossible for revisionists to claim him as a pioneer without ignoring or distorting significant portions of the historical record. His personal credo was expressed with precision little more than a year after his election as Taoiseach:

> First and foremost we wish to see the re-unification of Ireland restored. By every test Ireland is one nation with a fundamental right to have its essential unity expressed in its political institutions. The unit for self-determination is the whole country and we do not accept that a minority has the right to vote itself out of the nation on the ground that it is in disagreement with the majority on a major policy issue. We cannot and will not depart from that position. We hope that in time a climate of opportunity will be created in which the realisation of our national aim will be achieved in harmony and agreement. To that end it is our policy to develop closer and more neighbourly relations with Northern Ireland and to promote economic co-operation for the mutual benefit of both parts of the country.[152]

There is no evidence whatever that he ever materially departed from this position, although at different times and in different places he may have chosen to emphasise one element of it rather than another. At the same time his reordering of national priorities on the North was revisionist to the extent that it gave the principle of consent a new significance that it had not hitherto possessed. It was not a new principle: de Valera himself had enunciated it when he said, many years previously, that the best way to end partition would be to create in the Republic a society that unionists would want to join. It was, however, the cornerstone of Lemass's strategy in a way in which it had never been for de Valera or for Aiken. The full definition of that principle, and the exploration of the practical and policy consequences flowing from it, were another day's work, to be carried out in blood, sweat and tears and which is still far from complete. What flowed from this apparently modest initiative acted, in the end, not only to accelerate the processes of change that were already taking place within Northern Ireland but eventually to destabilise Fianna Fáil itself under Lemass's successor.

McAteer and his colleagues, although they did not disclose this in public at the time, had already become substantially disillusioned with Terence O'Neill at the time of the Lemass–O'Neill meetings in 1965 and were fearful that his new policy was simply another element in a confidence trick they had already deconstructed for themselves. Many years later, moreover, McAteer recorded his final view of the Lemass era with a sense of disillusion and even betrayal.

> In my role as leader of the Nationalist people, I made many trips to Dublin, some publicised, some private, for talks and consultations with Dublin ministers. I got hospitality but little real support. There was less than enthusiasm to get involved. The Unionists, not knowing that, again missed the chance to woo us. When I returned home after my post-O'Neill talk with the Taoiseach I was more worried than ever. I got neither the encouragement nor understanding of our position that I expected. Lemass said that it appeared to him that Catholics in the North were just as intractable as the Protestants. It was hardly the reaction I expected from a Taoiseach with his Republican background to the representative of the oppressed Irish minority in the six counties. The Taoiseach expressed the opinion that industrial progress in the twenty-six counties would help to bring the Unionists towards a united Ireland. I did not share his optimism and was surprised to hear such a naive opinion from a man who had been born into revolution. I came away with the conviction that as far as Seán Lemass was concerned, the Northern Irish were very much on their own.[153]

The judgment was harsh and not by any means deserved. When Lemass died McAteer had hinted that he and the former Taoiseach had not always seen eye to eye but added: 'There was good national fire in him. This was good medicine for a people held so long in bondage.'[154]

What is inescapable, however, is that the relationship between Dublin and political nationalism in the North, which had begun with an inbuilt sense of distance and reserve, was ending in an atmosphere little short of open hostility. Three years later, officials in the Department of External Affairs were to warn Lemass's successor, Jack Lynch, against formalising exclusive relations with the Nationalist Party, because of secret information they had just received about the impending formation of the SDLP.[155]

9

Culture, Church, and State

The nineteen-sixties in Ireland, as in many other countries, were socially turbulent years. The spread of television heightened public consciousness about social change. Subjects that were previously all but taboo were treated by the new medium with openness and even irreverence; to be anti-clerical did not involve the same social and political risks as hitherto; and as the level of education rose inexorably it was accompanied by a sense of impatience at traditional ways of doing things and a desire to throw off constraints that were seen as outworn or unduly restrictive. Ireland under Seán Lemass became a sort of supercharged stereotype, and journalists and documentary-makers from all over the English-speaking world descended on us to chronicle our supposed escape from the Dark Ages. Lemass received the ultimate accolade in this process — a cover story in *Time* — on 12 July 1963.

There was, particularly in the urban areas, a growing educated Catholic middle class that took its loyalty to the church and to at least some of its teachings with increasingly large pinches of salt. One of the first pieces of detailed sociological research in Dublin, carried out at the behest of a far-sighted if conservative Archbishop McQuaid, revealed that while traditional loyalty to the Catholic Church and its teachings was still very strong there was an inverse correlation between loyalty and the level of educational attainment of the respondents.[1]

This was one of the challenges facing Fianna Fáil under Lemass, although it took some time for it to become apparent. He undoubtedly sensed the tide of change that was lapping at the foundations of traditionalism generally: his problem was how to harness it without allowing it to undermine the political and party base that was, in his view, absolutely essential to guarantee economic and social progress. It was a problem that was all the more pressing because Fianna Fáil was a party that had built its electoral base on a powerful and self-sustaining definition of Irish tradition. Its flirtation with modernisation dated from the late nineteen-fifties at the very earliest and was still far from being a full-blooded romance. None of his policy objectives were capable of achievement if the party failed to deliver the electoral goods; this demanded close attention to its workings at Government, parliamentary party and National Executive level.

Lemass's 1963 'move to the left' budget speech was more than just an aside. His political sense had told him that, just as emigration was declining sharply, a new breed of voter was in the offing, one that would not be satisfied with traditional nostrums, was increasingly conscious of international trends, and was all too ready to make disparaging comparisons between the social standards pertaining in Ireland and those of other countries. The growth of the welfare state in Northern Ireland since the war must also have been a consideration;[2] the gap in social provision between the Republic and the North could not be allowed to expand and should if anything be reduced to vanishing point.

Considerations like these prompted Lemass to develop a new policy on social matters, even as the capacity of the economy to finance such a policy became more and more questionable.

Religious conservatism reached its high-water mark at around the beginning of the decade. In September 1960 the Archbishop of Cashel and Emly, Dr Thomas Morris, issued instructions that all dances in his diocese were to end by 1 a.m. and that there should be no dances at all on Saturday nights.[3] By 1967 he and the other bishops had virtually thrown in the towel, at least in this area. Television in particular was what exercised the clerical mind. In 1961 the *Catholic Truth Quarterly* told its readers a cautionary tale about a woman who had given birth in a taxi on the way to the hospital, 'because she just couldn't tear herself away from her favourite programme,' and warned:

> Where people had to go out of their homes to see movies, television can bring all the pagan propaganda into the family circle — with even more disastrous results. This is the big weapon in the anti-Christian forces today. More souls may be taken away from Christ through the gospel of pleasure they absorb through TV, than if the anti-Christ would start an open bloody persecution in our country.[4]

For all its lurid imagery, the sentiments of this publication were well in tune with contemporary mainstream Catholic thought. Only six years earlier Pope Pius XII had declared:

> The painful picture of the evil and disturbing power of the cinema is at present before our minds. But it is impossible not to be horrified at the thought that through the medium of television it may be possible for that atmosphere poisoned by materialism, fatuity and hedonism, which is too often breathed in so many cinemas, to penetrate within the very walls of the home.[5]

The bishops as a group were similarly concerned, recording in private their apprehension of the 'danger of the harm to the moral sense of the country through imported programmes,' although they expressed some support for the standard of programmes made by the BBC.[6]

It was 1964, however, before Lemass found time to put his thoughts into a formal structure. That structure indicated his strategic thinking at a time when public support for the Government's stated economic objectives was plainly on the wane, or at the very least was being adversely affected by industrial unrest and jockeying for position in the labour market. In the interim, additionally, social policy was coming under increasing strain. In Dublin in 1962 only 1,035 local authority houses were under construction; the waiting-list was 9,000. In 1963 four people were killed when decaying tenement houses collapsed in Bolton Street and Fenian Street. The new social radicalism of Sinn Féin, which was later to find a vehicle in organ-isations such as the Dublin Housing Action Committee, was also plainly beginning to irk the Government.

In Lemass's view, the prospect of improved social benefits was something that could focus public attention and support in a way that purely economic objectives might not. In August 1964 he took an initiative, aimed principally at the Department of Social Welfare, that spelt out the possibilities as well as acknowledging the risks. He suggested drafting a 'Programme for Social Development', which, 'linked in some clear way to economic growth, could help to promote understanding of the links between them.'[7] The risks, as he was well aware, were that social targets would be interpreted as political promises and would have to be delivered, no matter what they cost. His own view was that they should be dangled before the public like a carrot, to revivify interest in the flagging Second Programme.

Education and health were excluded. Policy decisions and spending priorities in education were already under consideration by the Investment in Education team, which was to report in 1965; a similar study was being undertaken in relation to the activities of the Department of Health. As it happened, there had already been stirrings in the undergrowth of the policy community on this issue. In August Whitaker had written to W. A. Honohan, Secretary of the Department of Social Welfare, suggesting the setting up of an interdepartmental committee aided by qualified people who were not civil servants to consider possible changes to social welfare services 'as the objectives of the Second Programme were achieved.'[8] Despite the understandable caveat, this was a notable shift in emphasis from his position of some seven years earlier, when he had gone on record to his minister to castigate unproductive investment and to argue that 'a slowing down in housing and other forms of social investment must be faced from now on because of the virtual satisfaction of needs over wide areas.'[9] Lemass's initia-tive had taken place before Honohan replied, and Whitaker had already secured Lemass's agreement to a proposal that 'we should first try to find a rational basis for policy, postponing until later the question of the extent to which specific commitments to improve and extend the social services should be published.'

Honohan and his minister, Kevin Boland, were deeply suspicious of this invasion of their territory and inaugurated a delaying action in a lengthy correspondence that eventually persuaded Lemass to abandon his initiative for the time being. He told Boland that he would not press for further action 'in view of your strong feelings in the matter.'[10]

Lemass regarded this as a temporary reverse rather than a defeat. In the 1965 budget debate he returned to the fray with a suggestion that we would 'have to consider the implications of steadily rising national wealth, steadily rising living standards for our people, and to think about the social problems which in this situation will be generated for us.'[11] During the election campaign, in a speech that underlined the importance of manpower policy, housing, and education, he noted that 'it might be possible to draw up a Social Development Programme not dissimilar to and linked with the Economic Development Programme, although this would not be easy.'[12] He was more than a little influenced by the action of Wilson's government in Britain in deciding to harness an economic development programme to social objectives.[13]

Six weeks later the Minister for Finance, Jack Lynch, responded in a letter that bore all the hallmarks of Whitaker's style and that noted the various initiatives currently under way in social welfare, housing, education, and physical planning. Lynch warned that it would be 'wasteful and dangerous to prepare programmes for the various sectors in isolation' and suggested that Dr M. D. McCarthy of the Central Statistics Office might be asked to look at the overall problem of co-ordination involved.[14]

The Government finally agreed in August to prepare a social development programme on the basis of a memorandum from the Department of Finance.[15] Lynch simultaneously secured approval for projected developments in the Economic Research Institute, soon to become the National Economic and Social Research Institute in accordance with the recommendations of Dr Henning Friis, a UN adviser on secondment to the Institute of Public Administration. A year later, the day before Lemass's resignation, Lynch secured from the Government the money necessary for the new organisation's enlarged responsibilities.[16] The latter proposal was particularly noteworthy for its suggestion, evidently designed with Lemass's priorities in mind, that priority be given in the work load of the new institution to studies that would help 'to identify important obstacles to economic development related to popular attitudes and behaviour patterns; as well, in relation to incomes policy, the research should cover the income expectations of persons at work, their attitudes to the organisation of industry and the influence of various incentives on increased output and productivity.'[17]

EDUCATION AND THE HILLERY AND O'MALLEY PLANS

There is evidence that Lemass may have considered this progress rather too leisurely, or that at the very least he allowed himself to be used to force open one particular social policy door, that of education. As noted earlier, Lemass's first successful Dáil election campaign, in 1924, was remarkable for a pledge that, in its acknowledgment of the opportunity costs of remaining in full-time education, was politically and economically far-sighted. In subsequent years his immersion in industrial policy precluded any detailed consideration of education, except so far as it impinged on the needs of industrial society. Indeed there is some evidence that he at first thought of industrial education and general education as being in competition with each other, rather than complementary aspects of the same question.

It was not until some time after he became Taoiseach that Lemass sensed that the electorate as a whole was ready and willing to carry the cost of improved educational services. Those who were to co-operate with him in this enterprise — Patrick Hillery, George Colley, and Donogh O'Malley — were temperamentally and politically very different, but each helped to slot a key piece of the educational jigsaw into place, and Lemass's approach to the question of educational change over the period provides a textbook example of his management style. It also shows that Hillery played a larger role than is realised and that he may have been unfairly overshadowed by O'Malley's more expansive political style.

Hillery was at first a reluctant minister but once in office realised — not least as the result of the work of a committee of inspectors under Dr Duggan, the deputy chief inspector[18] — that there were a large number of gaps in the provision of education. The proposals he made for remedying the situation were continually turned down by the Department of Finance. After a number of such rebuffs Hillery decided to bring the matter directly to the Government, and his department prepared a lengthy memo that was sent directly to the Taoiseach on 9 January 1963.[19] The plan was for a pilot scheme of comprehensive post-primary education related specifically to small-farm areas, to be considered, in the first instance, by the Government's Committee on Small Farms. The memorandum suggested Ballaghaderreen, County Roscommon, as the site for a possible senior-cycle school and a number of others for pilot junior-cycle schools, including Castlecomer, County Kilkenny, where the diocesan authorities — presumably the Catholic bishop, Dr Peter Birch — were said to be keen.

Hillery wrote to Lemass:

> I would like you to regard the suggestions as the archetype of a system of post-primary education which should apply to the whole country ... It will be expensive but it is necessary, and probably inevitable, so I

think this government should commit itself to doing it. Certain 'vested interests' in education would be annoyed at the introduction of such a school on a national basis but in this particular area the interests have not provided for the children and cannot therefore object to State action. Once a beginning is made the general application of this system to the whole country would follow slowly with time.[20]

Hillery's original intention, foreshadowing O'Malley, was that entry to post-primary education should be free, but he later noted that he found the policy difficult to implement at that time because of 'the accepted assumption of a very limited role for the State in education, the department of Finance's fear of cost and its penny-pinching attitude, and the Church's proprietary attitude to the running of education.'[21]

The meeting of the Committee on Small Farms took place two days later, but its outcome had been determined in advance. On Lemass's instructions, the detailed memo was not in fact shown to the ministers involved,[22] and the proposal was withdrawn from the committee and sent to a smaller, ad hoc committee comprising Ryan (the Minister for Finance), Hillery, and Lemass himself. According to Hillery,

> when I told Lemass about it he said: 'You'll never get that through the Government.' There were a number of reasons. The obvious one was money: it was like signing a blank cheque in a way, and indeed it turned out very expensive in the end. And at cabinet, if any fellow was getting more money someone else was getting less. So he took it to that meeting of himself, myself, and Ryan. Ryan was very helpful. In retrospect I think Ken Whitaker probably was too.[23]

Within days, Lemass had made his own position clear and had marked his minister's cards on the appropriate strategy to be adopted. Suggesting that the scheme be adopted on a pilot basis for western counties, he commented:

> I am in agreement with your general idea of providing one system of post-primary education. It seems to be the answer to our problem, although I have as yet no idea of its cost or of the practical problems in bringing it into operation. Until it has been formally adopted and publicly announced, it is to be expected that there will continue to be some confusion in the public mind ... You will need to come to this meeting with the nature of the decisions you require very clear in your mind, both in respect of the Western development and the subsequent extension of the new system of post-primary schools into all areas. If you could send me, in advance, a draft of the decisions as you wish to have them recorded, it would be helpful, although I should be surprised if the Minister for Finance would find himself in a position to reach finality on them at our first meeting.[24]

Hillery went to the meeting, as he told Lemass's department in advance, looking for authorisation for three initiatives: (1) approaching the solution through a system based on comprehensive courses and, wherever necessary, comprehensive schools providing a common three-year cycle with subsequent streaming; (2) as a first step, the creation of a pilot scheme as outlined in his initial memo; and (3) authority to 'consult with the Bishop concerned in each case.'[25] On the potentially difficult question of cost, Hillery suggested that a 400-pupil comprehensive school could be built for about £90,000 (£974,000 in 1996 values) and that buses for each school would cost about £2,500 each (£30,000 in 1996 values) but that 'the amount of building which a scheme of comprehensive education would entail in areas which are already reasonably provided for in the matter of secondary and vocational education would be comparatively small.'[26]

When the scheme had been agreed with Lemass and Ryan, Hillery suggested that it would perhaps now be appropriate to bring it back to the Government. Lemass's response was swift: 'Hold a press conference!'[27] The Hillery scheme for comprehensive schools was announced on 20 May 1963.

Although it never became a blueprint for educational change throughout the country, it was an important forerunner of the community school concept, which eventually secured substantial public and ecclesiastical acceptance as the post-primary system expanded dramatically in the nineteen-sixties and seventies. Just as significantly, the episode indicates Lemass's willingness — and ability — to successfully finesse Government procedures when he felt that important proposals risked becoming bogged down in ministerial rivalries and suspicions.

The reasons for the expansion at post-primary level were many and included a reduction in the level of emigration as well as heightened parental aspirations for their children. In June 1964 Lemass told the Dáil that he considered that the proportion of the nation's resources being devoted to education was still insufficient. His Government's education policy, he said, would be 'settled in the tradition of Tone.' And he added, somewhat ominously for those who had ears to hear, that 'it might be better if in our establishments, and in UCD in particular, Wolfe Tone's conception of the Irish nation was better understood and better respected.'[28]

In March 1965 Lemass had already indicated that 'the overhaul of the nation's education system, including a considerable extension and improvement of facilities for secondary, vocational and higher education, is now about to be undertaken.'[29] In the same year the report *Investment in Education* was published, the work of a gifted group of experts including Professor Paddy Lynch and W. J. Hyland, a statistician who had been seconded from his work with the United Nations for this project and who eventually returned permanently to the Department of Education.

This study made only one concrete recommendation, and a management one at that — the creation of a Development Branch within the Department of Education — but it pinpointed two problems in the educational system. One was the preponderance of small rural primary schools; the other was the dangerously haphazard provision of post-primary education, which in many parts of the country had been left largely to private interests, and to the poor and uncoordinated nature of such provision as existed.

The report was manna for George Colley, the newly appointed and energetic young Minister for Education, who had reason to believe that the Taoiseach was now in favour of educational initiatives and who moved initially to rationalise the situation at the primary level by amalgamating a number of the smaller schools.

There were two main potential obstacles to the implementation of such a policy: the INTO and the Catholic hierarchy. Opinion within the INTO was divided but was swayed in the direction of change by the likely positive effect that amalgamation would have on promotional prospects for teachers. Other possible objections were answered, at least in part, by a Government commitment to providing a school transport service to bring children to the new or enlarged centralised schools. Not all the Catholic clergy were happy, however, seeing in the dismantling of this network of small country schools — many of them one and two-teacher schools — a threat to the survival of rural society. The Bishop of Galway, Dr Michael Browne, took up the cudgels on their behalf and on behalf of a number of unorganised parents who were disturbed at the proposals.[30] Colley, who belonged to the radical republican tradition within Fianna Fáil and did not particularly shrink from confrontations with the hierarchy, defended his corner vigorously. He also kept Lemass informed privately that he was engaged in a flanking manoeuvre with the Catholic primate, Cardinal Conway, with whom he had discussed the matter some time previously and who 'agreed in principle with the policy and, in fact, suggested an area in his own diocese where it might be carried out.'[31]

Lemass fully approved of Colley's strategy, suggesting that the policy arguments would be seen to be convincing by all reasonable people, but added: 'I do not have the impression, however, that the case for larger schools has as yet been sufficiently publicised and I assume that you have it in mind to make a few speeches on early and suitable occasions to get it more widely understood.'[32] This in turn underlined a central aspect of Lemass's political method. Policy-making within the Government was one thing: its promulgation in ways that would secure public acceptance was just as important. Charles Haughey, as Minister for Agriculture, was reminded on at least one occasion to make a series of speeches designed specifically to secure public appreciation of and support for the details of agricultural policy.[33]

The controversy surrounding this initiative rumbled on but was quickly overshadowed by the introduction of 'free post-primary education' during Donogh O'Malley's tenure as Minister for Education. O'Malley was a mercurial character of enormous energy and ability who had been first appointed by Lemass as one of his key parliamentary secretaries in 1961. He also — in a conspicuous break with general Fianna Fáil tradition — sought out and used media contacts with a rare sense of application and self-interest. In July 1966, during Lemass's last year in office and as part of a Government reshuffle caused by the creation of the new Department of Labour, O'Malley succeeded Colley in Education. It was an appointment that 'terrified the party at the time,'[34] and with reason. Some nine years earlier Lemass had taken part in a three-man mission to discipline the tearaway young TD. The others were de Valera himself and Gerald Boland, and they had been instructed by the parliamentary party to see O'Malley and 'finally warn him that if he is again seen under the influence of drink he will be expelled from the party.'[35] When, much later, Lemass appointed O'Malley to full ministerial rank he again warned him to stay off drink; the injunction was not always obeyed.[36]

O'Malley's interest in education had been noted by Lemass at a parliamentary party meeting as early as 1960, when the Governing Body of UCD was engaged in radical expansion plans and was simultaneously embroiled in a dispute, prompted in part by the then auditor of the college's Literary and Historical Society, about the legality of a considerable number of academic appointments. A College Visitor — John Kenny, a lecturer in the college's law department and later a distinguished member of the judiciary — had been appointed to investigate the rumoured illegalities. O'Malley was impatient and put down a motion for the parliamentary party urging that action be taken against the 'UCD junta'. Lemass counselled caution until the Government examination of the matter had been concluded, and O'Malley withdrew his motion,[37] but he had plainly made his mark. He received his first junior ministerial appointment in October 1961 and became Minister for Health after the 1965 election.

O'Malley was hesitant at first about his new responsibilities. A particularly well-informed contemporary observer noted:

> Everyone except Mr O'Malley was sure that there must be big plans for education and he came very glumly into the Dáil on the morning after his new appointment. Mr Lemass had suggested he should come in and listen to his speech. For half an hour, during which the new minister became more and more bored, Mr Lemass ranged over the economic field with his usual panache. Eventually he got around to education, and Mr O'Malley's face brightened. Education was to be given priority. There was great empathy between the two men. They

both had extremely fertile minds and they understood each other's little idiosyncrasies.[38]

Their relationship was a casually friendly one, with the younger man often trying, and rarely succeeding, to slip one past his mentor. As O'Malley, in his incarnation as Minister for Health, would rush into Lemass's office with yet another scheme for approval, Lemass would look at him in mock puzzlement and enquire: 'But, Donogh, where would you get the money?' Later O'Malley would confide to a friend: 'What would you do with a hoor like that?'[39]

On 10 September 1966 O'Malley announced to a meeting of the National Union of Journalists in Dún Laoghaire that he proposed 'to introduce a scheme whereby up to the completion of the Intermediate Certificate course, the opportunity for free post-primary education will be available to all families.'[40] It was — as it was intended to be — a sensation. The speech was on a Saturday and garnered suitably dramatic publicity in the media on the Sunday and Monday. The preliminaries to the speech, however, subsequently became a matter of controversy in their own right.

O'Malley had met Lemass on 7 September to discuss his ideas on the development of free post-primary education. Just before the meeting he sent around to Lemass's office a copy of a memorandum outlining various options in some detail and indicating that his speech would involve 'a general reference — *without going into details* — to some of the matters referred to in this Memorandum should you so approve.' (Emphasis added.)[41] His letter made a strong political case for an initiative, arguing that Fine Gael were 'evidently panicking at the fact that in their publication *The Just Society* they have no proposals whatsoever on education.'

On Monday 12 September, Whitaker exploded. Observing that O'Malley had left the Department of Health 'gravely insolvent' on his departure, he brought all his heavy weaponry to bear on this perceived affront to Government and administrative procedures.

> It is astonishing that a major change in educational policy should be announced by the Minister for Education at a weekend seminar of the National Union of Journalists. This 'free schooling' policy has not been the subject of any submission to the Department of Finance, has not been approved by the Government, has certainly not been examined from the financial (whatever about the educational) aspect, and therefore should have received no advance publicity, particularly of the specific and definite type involved in Mr O'Malley's statement ... If substantial commitments are to be announced by individual Ministers without the consent of the Department of Finance or the approval of the government, we shall have a situation which is the negation of planning. It will become increasingly futile to be drawing up 5 or 7

year programmes, and even the financial and economic policy of the Government in the short-term will be seen to bear no relation to what the country can afford.

O'Malley was at pains afterwards to indicate to a variety of sources, not least to journalists, that he had acted in good faith. He told Haughey directly that he had shown Lemass the speech in advance and that Lemass changed it to make it less definite.[42] Kevin Boland understood that Lemass had warned O'Malley that if the Government came down against him he would have to withdraw it.[43]

The documentary evidence, however, confirms only that O'Malley showed Lemass a memorandum on the basis of which he proposed to make his speech, rather than the text of his actual remarks. The implication is that Lemass did not in fact connive at the specific nature of O'Malley's proposals but that O'Malley, in his desire to make the people an offer in terms the Government could not refuse to honour, recklessly converted Lemass's general approval into backing for a scheme so specific that if it were not to be implemented, political convulsions would ensue. He may even have reinserted into his speech some of the specifics that Lemass had wanted excluded.

What is undeniable is that from this point onwards Lemass watched O'Malley exceptionally closely. He wrote to him on 12 September reminding him forcefully that all normal procedures would have to be followed and full Government approval secured. O'Malley replied two days later, his contrition qualified by a somewhat disingenuous attempt at self-justification.

> My speech on Saturday was made in the light of our discussion last week, when we went in detail through the Memorandum I had prepared as the basis for the speech I told you I was going to make. It was my understanding that I had your agreement to my outlining these lines of action, particularly in view of the fact that Fine Gael were planning to announce a comprehensive educational policy this week … If I was under a misapprehension in believing that I had your support for my announcement, I must apologise. I would hope, however, that what I have said will persuade you that I was right in making it and that you will give me your full support in getting my plans approved by the Government.[44]

On 21 September Jack Lynch, the Minister for Finance, who had been away at the time, brought up O'Malley's unauthorised speech with Lemass, who wrote again to O'Malley to convey Lynch's 'grave concern' about the speech and to warn him that 'any new proposals, *even* in the area of education, must be framed with strict regard to financial possibilities and in such a way as to provide for their gradual implementation so as to avoid a considerable addition to the Estimate total in any one year.' (Emphasis added.)[45] Further evidence that Lemass was extremely unwilling to allow any more scope to his overenthusiastic minister is contained in exchanges in which Lemass insisted that he should personally see and approve in advance any draft answers to Dáil questions on the scheme addressed to O'Malley; and in fact he amended some of them to remove a repetition of the specificity that O'Malley had sought to include.[46]

O'Malley was not above trying to enlist the Taoiseach's support sub-sequently. Once, when Lynch brought up the matter, O'Malley immediately tried to involve Lemass, beginning 'The Taoiseach ...' Before he could get any further Lemass cut in: 'Don't involve me in this. This is a row between you and the Minister for Finance.'[47] Less than a month before Lemass resigned, moreover, he wrote to O'Malley to criticise his latest memorandum, which O'Malley wanted approved by the Government as a matter of urgency, because he needed to be able to go on television and announce the details.

> It is very improbable that other Ministers are likely to agree readily to proposals which would involve an addition to the Education Votes of £3 million in 1968, and would therefore make impracticable any size-able improvement in other Government services, such as Health and Social welfare, in that year without substantial tax increases. You should therefore consider what it may be possible to achieve in the next few years in the post-primary education sphere at a lower cost.[48]

The Department of Finance was even more scathing.

> If the proposals of the Minister for Education are to be approved, there will be no alternative to the imposition of new taxation; this may have serious economic reactions. To describe this scheme as 'free' is mis-leading. The scheme really means that many parents at present paying moderate school fees voluntarily will have to pay an equal or greater amount compulsorily in the form of additional taxation.[49]

The scheme eventually went into operation after a series of decisions by Jack Lynch's first Government and in a context in which at least some of the hoped-for social gains were in effect nullified or at the very least postponed. Another of its negative effects, whether expected by Lemass or not — and it is doubtful in the extreme that he would have welcomed it had he anticipated it — was to dramatically change the balance of advantage between vocational and privately run secondary schools. At the time the scheme was introduced, and for some time thereafter, vocational schools were not permitted to take students to Leaving Certificate level. Parents, naturally, chose the avenue that offered advancement for their children, not one that offered only a dead end at Group or Intermediate Certificate level. The result was to delineate the second-class status of vocational education in an unmistakable way.

Nor was the scheme as it was introduced supplemented by any measures to subsidise the poorer pupils, for whom the opportunity cost of post-compulsory second-level education — even if the fees were abolished — was in many cases insurmountable. In this way Lemass and Hillery's aim of a single system of second-level education was to be frustrated for a considerable time, in many areas and for many pupils, by a daring initiative that it had been hoped would have had precisely the opposite effect. An editorial verdict on this initiative, delivered as part of an obituary tribute, noted that 'both men politically gambled on announcing post-primary education in the fashion that they did [and] both men won.'[50] In some respects it was a Pyrrhic victory; but O'Malley's initiative, at the very least, ignited a desire for educational expansion among the electorate as a whole that became unquenchable.

THE IRISH LANGUAGE

The policy on Irish that de Valera bequeathed to Lemass had its own idiosyncrasies. The older man actually saw the revival of Irish as a more urgent task than that of ending partition, because of the way in which the language was under siege from other influences, and attempted to reconcile the increasing use of English with the national aim of reviving Irish by adopting a consciously bilingual policy. 'In this,' his biographers suggested, 'he was more realistic than those whose aim was to make Irish the sole language spoken in the country. He himself would have Irish and English as the two languages, with Irish as the home language, while English remained the language which gave most ready access to the outside world.'[51]

There were actually many tensions within the revival movement. Some enthusiasts argued for the complete replacement of English by Irish. De Valera's suggestion that Irish would be the language of the home and English the language of international communication was an attempt to articulate a functional bilingualism that did not really cut much ice either in political or sociolinguistic terms but that found its most significant expression in the Constitution of 1937. Lemass was to nudge Fianna Fáil's policy towards a more defensible and realistic expression of the same ideal, although he remained sensitive to criticism and was occasionally prepared — as in the election campaign of 1961 — to mount a rousing defence of traditional methods.

Before he became Taoiseach, Lemass spoke about Irish infrequently and used it even less. Those Fine Gael deputies who were Irish-speakers, and some who were not, harped on his well-known inability to speak it. At one point Richard Mulcahy's near-obsession with the language tempted him to turn an obviously well-meant remark from Lemass into an attack on his linguistic competence. After Lemass had expressed the view that Mulcahy would be a positive force for Irish in his role after the 1948 election, the new Minister for Education snapped: 'Cén saghas Gaeilge atá ag an teachta?' Lemass, evidently nettled, replied:

> That is not the point. Deputy Mulcahy will be honest enough to admit that there are many people who are not as fluent in Irish as he is but who are nevertheless sincere in their desire to promote the revival of Irish through the schools; and I think there are many people who are as fluent as he is who are not.[52]

Much later, another leader of Fine Gael, James Dillon, was driven to remark that Lemass — by then Taoiseach — 'couldn't bid a dog good day in Irish.'[53]

The record shows that when Lemass spoke about Irish at all it was more than likely to be in the context of party politicking, and his most colourful speeches on the topic were made during the 1948–51 and 1954–57 inter-party Governments. During the 1948 election campaign he went so far as to imply that those who were opposed to Irish were following the instructions of 'the campaign to destroy Christian democracy in this country … those who have the instructions of the international organisation to destroy the faith of our people in democracy, to win them away from their allegiance to the Constitution.'[54]

By 1951 he was declaring that the restoration of Irish was 'second only to national unity,'[55] and this was a theme to which he returned frequently during the second inter-party Government.[56] These speeches, largely made in opposition, were somewhat perfunctory in their argument and on occasion no more than declaratory. If they failed to revive Irish, he told a Cork audience extravagantly, 'they would leave the whole cause of Irish freedom in jeopardy.'

What was even more significant in the long term was his reference to the teaching — rather than to the speaking — of Irish as the core element in that policy. He could not, indeed, have endorsed any policy that required everyone to speak Irish, for, like many other politicians in all parties, he did not speak it himself with any facility and used it very rarely. According to Charles Haughey, he 'forced himself to learn to read passages in Irish,'[57] but compulsion, whether from within or from without, was not notably successful. In 1956–57 he was ill with phlebitis and was inactive for some months. He sent a note to T. K. Whitaker: 'Dev wants me to brush up my Irish — please send me some books on economics and finance.'[58]

Professor Al Cohan, who interviewed Lemass in 1968 for his book *The Irish Political Elite,* formed the impression that Lemass had no interest in the language at all[59] and suggested that most of the Irish-language enthusiasts in Fianna Fáil were older men who had rural backgrounds. It was certainly true that Lemass's interest in Irish, such as it was, was not that of a devotee and was for the most part distant and cousinly. He was also needled by the persistent and vociferous campaigns and controversies generated by those in whose nationalist agenda Irish held a more central place than it evidently had in his. As he once remarked, 'enthusiasts often vex me; but then, only enthusiasts get things going.'[60]

Those who did not share the traditional Fianna Fáil view of such matters were continuously alert to the possibility of Lemass-led change and probably embarrassed him politically with their praise. The *Irish Times,* for example, welcomed one of his speeches as evidence that he was 'departing from the de Valera practice of introducing his remarks with a genuflection to the Irish language.'[61] As Taoiseach he could hardly avoid it on occasion but plainly was mightily uncomfortable with it. He did, unusually, speak in Irish on television as part of his campaign to garner support for the White Paper in 1965, when he delivered himself of the weighty opinion 'go raibh súil aige go léifidh oiread daoine agus is féidir an Páipéar Bán ar fad, go mór mór daoine a raibh páistí scoile acu.' More significantly, he used the same occasion to suggest that television audiences 'are not attracted by party harangues, and Fianna Fáil intends to avoid them.'[62]

His most extensive public utterance in Irish was a carefully scripted one, when he read the lesson at the consecration of Bishop Thomas Russell in Waterford on 19 December 1965. Towards the end of his period as Taoiseach he was actively looking for new political formulations that would remove the language from the area of political controversy altogether. When he came to propose Jack Lynch as his replacement in the Dáil in November 1966, it was in 'his usual atrocious Irish.'[63]

To the extent that he referred to the language at all as Taoiseach it was almost always in the context of an extended syllogism: language reinforced nationalism; nationalism reinforced language; both together reinforced national self-esteem; and national self-esteem drove economic development. He initially saw the task of reviving Irish as primarily a technical matter, which is why he (and other politicians, inside and outside Fianna Fáil) concentrated on the schools as the locus of policy. He reacted somewhat defensively to increasingly publicised suggestions that the preponderance of Irish, particularly in the primary school curriculum, was disadvantaging children in other areas.[64] In one of his post-retirement interviews with Michael Mills he espoused de Valera's bilingual policy almost word for word but was far more realistic about the obstacles and specifically rejected the suggestion that the task could be achieved in two generations.

> We have to examine again and again the effectiveness of the methods being used to promote the widespread use of the language. The belief that it can be achieved mainly through the schools is still the basis of policy, but the methods of teaching in the schools have to be revised because we have a lot of young people coming out of school, quite fluent in Irish but losing that fluency very quickly. Examination of teaching methods has been and continues to go on and I do not think we have yet devised the method that promises any certainty of success.[65]

If the right technical response could be found, the language could be saved; in the meantime, the existing methods, inefficient and all as they had turned out to be, had to be defended. In the same interview he admitted that it was a 'fallacy' that enthusiasm for the language was growing — but did so as part of his defence of compulsory Irish in schools.

It was, in effect, one of the few areas in which he was still prepared to defend compulsion. The no-nonsense, no-exceptions philosophy of the war years and the draconian attempts to discipline industry embodied in the draft 1947 industrial efficiency legislation had long since given way in other areas to the emollient assurance that 'we in Fianna Fáil do not believe in methods of compulsion. Compulsory tillage, the regulation of wages, undue control of private business — none of these forms any part of our plans.'[66] Plainly, as far as Irish was concerned, the political costs of abandoning compulsion were so gigantic — and so readily imaginable — that such a prospect did not even appear on the political agenda.

It is worth noting, on the other hand, that Lemass's expressed views about the importance of the educational system to the revival movement were not implemented in practical policy terms; indeed, the opposite tended to be the case. The abolition of the primary teacher preparatory colleges, for example, which took place under Patrick Hillery's stewardship in the Department of Education, certainly made a dent in the culture of education through Irish that had existed up to then at primary level. At the post-primary level, Donogh O'Malley's 'free education' scheme led to a massive influx of children to the post-primary system and probably accelerated the trend towards the virtual extinction of the 'A' schools, in which all subjects were taught through Irish.

Any suspicions or doubts Lemass might have entertained about the wisdom, let alone the efficacy, of the policy were dramatically sidelined by Fine Gael's decision, in the run-up to the 1961 election, to promise the end of 'compulsory Irish'. This prompted two responses from Lemass, one private, the other public.

In private he suddenly began to apply pressure to the Commission on the Revival of the Irish Language, under its chairman, Rev. Tomás Ó Fiaich, which had been established in July 1958 but had been making only leisurely progress towards a final report and conclusions. Prior to the Fine Gael initiative there had been little evident sense of impatience on Lemass's side either. 'Considerations of urgency', he told Ó Fiaich in May 1961, 'should not be allowed to interfere in any way with the formulation by the Commission of their considered recommendations.'[67] The election took place on 4 October 1961, and almost immediately Lemass told Ó Fiaich of his concern at the inability of the commission to submit its report as early as he had expected.[68] Typically, he facilitated the new object-ive by giving the commission a full-time secretary for the first time.[69]

His public response was elaborated during the 1961 election campaign and re-ignited political embers that apparently had to all intents and purposes become extinct. Fine Gael announced its policy on 12 September 1961 and received a magisterial pat on the back from an *Irish Times* editorial headed 'Sense at last'.[70] Within a week Lemass counter-attacked in a speech in which he charged that Fine Gael were apparently soliciting support for a 'policy of retreat'. In fact his speech used a vigorous attack on Fine Gael's policy as a smokescreen for a careful reformulation of his party's own policy. The aim was neither the replacement of English by Irish nor even the re-establishment of Irish as a universal medium of communication but 'to bring the language into common use in the daily life of the nation.' He added pugnaciously:

> I want no misunderstanding of Fianna Fáil's aim ... We are not pre-pared to lower our target by even a fraction. I believe, vehemently, in the beneficial force of nationalism. It is the most dynamic element in the whole Irish situation, the motive which inspires people to unite and work for the nation's advancement. I do not believe that we can build our country by abandoning any of the characteristics of our nationhood. A policy of retreat in this respect would herald the defeat of all our national purposes. The people of the world will respect us only to the extent that we respect ourselves, our history, our traditions, our culture and our language. If Ireland is going into the EC it is all the more important that we should preserve and develop every characteristic and value which distinguishes us from other nations. The movement of the Irish people which brought us so far on the road to independent nationhood was never inspired by materialistic motives alone. If it had been, it would have failed, and we in our day will fail also unless we recognise and utilise the spiritual forces which activate both men and nations. Of these, nationalism, the desire to see the advancement of one's own country, is very potent, and it is by harnessing that force behind a comprehensive plan, which embraces not only economic affairs but also every aspect of national endeavour, that we can make this country's future secure.[71]

He rejected the argument about the supposedly malign effects of com-pulsory Irish by pointing out that the number of pupils who had failed the Leaving Certificate because they had failed in English was twice the number who had done so because of failure in Irish. 'Is it suggested that these figures support a case for taking English out of the examination?'[72] And he did his best to sow dissension in the Fine Gael ranks by charging that Richard Mulcahy and Ernest Blythe had shared Fianna Fáil's common national purpose, while their successors had made Irish an election issue for the first time in history. One of the staunchest proponents of the revival,

Aindrias Ó Muimhneacháin, a former president of Conradh na Gaeilge and the presenter of a series of Irish-language educational programmes on Radio Éireann, wrote to Lemass to thank him for this expression of a 'virile national pietas'.[73]

The vigour of Lemass's attack had two sources of energy. One was the gift of an issue that clearly marked off Fianna Fáil from Fine Gael and even provided a bit of domestic knock-about relief from the earnest agenda that he had consciously set himself for the election: Ireland's bid for membership of the EEC. The other, undoubtedly, was a real sense of threat. Fine Gael would not have proposed such a policy, nor would Lemass have reacted to it so forcefully, if each had not been aware of the potential electoral attractiveness of the idea.

The commission eventually published its report in July 1963, and it immediately became the focus for renewed campaigns by Irish-language organisations of every hue. Dónall Ó Móráin of Gael-Linn and a number of other enthusiasts organised a 'Let the Language Live' campaign, which secured 270,000 signatures but patently failed to impress the Taoiseach. Lemass told Ó Fiaich privately: 'If the 270,000 started speaking Irish immediately, there'd be no problem.'[74] He reinforced this in his speech on the Taoiseach's estimate in the Dáil in 1964, when he suggested, with an understandable sense of impatience, that 'if there were one million people interested in Irish in a real personal sense, and not as signatories of resolutions, the Government would hardly need a programme.'[75]

He was also, however, in the process of taking out insurance. Early in the year he had set in train an effort to promote Irish in the state and state-sponsored sector, observing that 'some of them are very lax in this respect.' He asked each of them to report on what they were doing in relation to Irish and ordered that 'this communication should issue from this Department rather than the Department of Education as I wish to stress the national policy rather than the education aspect.'[76] The lack of follow-through on this initiative, unusual given Lemass's management style, suggests that it may have had its origin with de Valera.

The drafting of the Government's response to the White Paper took almost eighteen months. As it proceeded, Lemass tested a number of propositions in his speech at the Fianna Fáil ardfheis in November 1964. The first was unexceptional: there was no body of individuals in the country more capable of generating the necessary enthusiasm for the revival than were to be found in the ranks of Fianna Fáil.[77] What gave rise to sudden concern, however, was his suggestion that the time was ripe for a 'redefinition' of the national aim — a phrase that was probably enough to arouse suspicion all by itself. Those who were temperamentally inclined to be suspicious were given additional food for thought by Lemass's view that this redefined aim would be 'to make the Irish language again a normal method of communication throughout our national community' and 'to set objectives which are reasonable and realisable, and which the ordinary man-in-the street will recognise as such.'

This shift of perspective was underlined by two further phrases. One suggested that Irish would continue to have a 'primacy of respect'. Most frightening of all was Lemass's typically frank admission that 'in practice English will remain the general vernacular.'[78] This set off alarm bells in a number of quarters — some more significant than others. Aindrias Ó Muimhneacháin told Lemass that he was 'worried, perplexed and gravely perturbed' by the tone of his ardfheis comments.[79] Rev. Martin Brennan described his speech as a 'sentence of death for the language,'[80] and similar sentiments were uttered by a number of other correspondents. More significantly, and more politically, Dr Ó Fiaich wrote to Lemass as spokesman for the joint committee of voluntary language organisations asking him to 'clarify' his remarks.[81]

Lemass rapidly embarked on a damage limitation exercise in a number of letters to his critics, but without abandoning his ardfheis position. His reply to Brennan in particular depended on a sophisticated exegesis of his speech that might have been expected to appeal to a Jesuit. 'I did not say that there is any aim of *keeping* English as the general vernacular, nor is this our aim. There was no intention of fixing any boundary to our progress in relation to the language.' (Emphasis added.)[82] To another correspondent he was more forthright: 'If the targets set appear to be impracticable or if there is public argument now about the rate of progress which it may be possible to maintain it will end up in futility. The government must define and set in motion the process, leaving for later the question of how far it may be possible to go.'[83]

These missives — written without the assistance of the Department of Education, to which he normally referred all questions relating to Irish for draft replies — had the desired effect. Brennan was 'greatly relieved' by his assurances,[84] and Ó Fiaich 'warmly welcomed' them.[85] The origin of many of the phrases he used, moreover, can readily be traced to the White Paper — then being drafted but not to appear until January 1965 — which talked about the need to 'restore Irish as a general medium of communication' and stated that 'objectives will be set which are reasonable and realisable but which fix no boundary to progress.'[86] The resemblances were hardly coincidental and indicate that Lemass as Taoiseach was putting his own stamp on the White Paper.

The process of drafting the White Paper was itself interesting. The drafting was entrusted to the Department of Finance, rather than the Department of the Gaeltacht or Department of Education. Also of significance is the fact that one of the senior officials involved suspected that drafts of the White Paper were circulated not only to the relevant Government departments but also to Áras an Uachtaráin.[87] By the time drafts reached the

Government, and perhaps because they had already received the ultimate imprimatur from the Park, few changes of any significance remained to be made, but one at least is worth noting: the decision to delete the description of the historical status of Irish as the 'principal language' of the country in paragraph 7 of the White Paper and replace it with the softer phrase 'language in general use'.[88]

The controversy Lemass had stirred up, however, plainly demanded more public reassurance, and he consciously embarked on this in a speech in January 1965. Its timing — just after his visit to Terence O'Neill and after the publication of the White Paper — ensured maximum publicity for his accusation that none of the opposition parties had commented on the White Paper, although he indicated that he would welcome their support. He also came out, in a carefully qualified way, on the vexed question of compulsion, in a context that plainly was designed to appeal to the middle ground.

> There are, of course, a few people who are so concentrated on this one national aim that they urge compulsions of the most rigorous kind for its achievement, and appear willing to sacrifice democratic freedom and even some fundamental human rights to this end. We do not share this attitude, and indeed it is our conviction that, while strong Government leadership is essential, the restoration of the Irish language requires, more than anything else, the building up of enthusiasm for its wider use, and reliance in the main on patriotism and voluntary effort.[89]

If this was a hint that traditional 'compulsory Irish' was at risk, he retreated from it with extraordinary rapidity. In May 1965, in sharp contrast to his Dún Laoghaire speech in January, he told an American journalist that it was intended not only to maintain but to extend the policy on Irish as a requirement for job applicants in the public service — a policy that in practice was increasingly being sidelined: 'If a student does not want to learn Irish, he must give up any idea of public employment.'[90] Two years later, free of the cares of office, he had again modified his position considerably, admittedly in relation to the special needs of Northern Ireland: 'It would be completely unrealistic to say to the man in the Post Office in Belfast "no job in the post office without Irish."'[91]

The controversy stirred up by his 1964 ardfheis and subsequent speeches showed that the more keen-eyed among the enthusiasts for the language had spotted or guessed at this policy shift and were apprehensive about it. Political considerations, however, continued to engender a tension between Lemass's private views and his need to support certain aspects of public policy.

Although he had been a strong proponent of economic development in the west, the degree to which this might be combined with development programmes for Irish in Gaeltacht areas never seemed to leap to the forefront of his attention. Ruairí Brugha, the Dublin Fianna Fáil deputy and son of Cathal Brugha, whose support for Irish was sophisticated and carefully focused, once approached Lemass in an attempt to persuade him that the revival of Irish would come from the cities or it would not come at all. As far as the Gaeltacht industries would help, Brugha believed, it was essential that only the best people should be selected in order to ensure success. Lemass objected: 'I can't very well appoint all the managers of Gaeltacht industries myself — I have to get civil servants to do that.' Brugha, undaunted, argued that the civil servants might not be appointing the right sort of people, because they might not really know the problem. Lemass agreed that this was possible but implied that there was little he could do about it.[92]

A Consultative Council on Irish was set up by the Government early in 1965,[93] with Dr Ó Fiaich, the former chairman of the commission, at its head. Almost immediately it focused on that area of Government policy that was, to those enthusiastic about the revival, the least satisfactory because the most public: the new television service. The polite but firm language of its complaints underlined its belief that any recognition that had been given to Irish by the television service had been 'conceded only after intense effort on the part of the language organisations' and drew attention to 'the number and variety of television programmes in which the national aim of restoring Irish was either held up to ridicule or attacked in such an un-balanced fashion as to leave viewers with the overall impression that the revival should be abandoned.'[94]

It was an accusation that was probably unfair to Lemass personally. There is certainly little doubt that he saw the new service as one of the technical methods that was needed if the language revival was to succeed. In addition, by appointing Ernest Blythe to the first authority he achieved a singular combination of purposes: nullifying possible Fine Gael criticism of the authority's composition and ensuring that nobody could question his *bona fides* in relation to the Government's commitment to using Telefís Éireann in helping to restore Irish as the everyday language of the people.[95] It was a commitment that was only marginally qualified by Lemass's own view, expressed in a letter to Maurice Moynihan, that the Irish content of Telefís Éireann should be made subject to the station's primary objective of providing entertainment, information, and news, and that the station's function should be to revive the language 'by promoting the love of it rather than by pushing it down the public's neck.'[96]

The significance of this modest objective can be more clearly appreciated in the light of the fact that it was written in the knowledge that the Commission on the Restoration of the Language had already (on 20 March 1959) submitted an interim report recommending that Irish be used in the control and administration of the service, that the majority of children's programmes be in Irish, and that anyone who had been employed because no suitable Irish-speaker was available should be taken on only for a temporary period. Probably only a minority of appointments to the two authorities that were created during Lemass's period of office as Taoiseach were made by him personally, and the degree of pressure that must have been exercised by powerful lobby groups on members of the Government generally was exemplified in the membership of the second authority, which included Phyllis Uí Cheallaigh, Ruairí Brugha, and Dónall Ó Móráin. Uí Cheallaigh and Ó Móráin in particular made the Irish-language issue a constant refrain.

TELEFÍS ÉIREANN

Lemass's involvement in the new television service, however, went far beyond the question of the revival of Irish. Its first phase was during the formative period, when Government policy was being framed; its second was during the period of office of the first and second RTE Authorities, as Government and broadcasters, in a series of range-finding exercises, tested each other on the limits and competence of the new service.

The debate about the shape the television service would take was in the form of a lengthy argument, carried out directly or through intermediaries, between Lemass and the secretary of the Department of Posts and Telegraphs, Leon Ó Broin.[97] It was an argument that was eventually won, somewhat to his surprise, by Ó Broin, after Lemass became Taoiseach and reversed the position he had vigorously espoused for a number of years as Minister for Industry and Commerce.

Lemass had a record of favouring the involvement of private interests in broadcasting that went back as far as 1934. In that year Irish Hospitals' Trust, alarmed by the passing of the Betting and Lotteries Act in England, where the Hospitals' Trust was then selling between four and five million tickets a year, had put forward to him a scheme under which the trust would build a new radio facility, which it would transfer to the Government but which it would operate. It would provide advertising time for 'enterprises of national importance', and would broadcast 'instrumental and vocal items of a light and popular character, and the more tuneful and unobjectionable dance music apart from the type known as "hot jazz" or crooners.' It would also form 'at least one orchestra of such a high class as to build up Irish prestige throughout Europe.'[98]

Lemass had forwarded this scheme to the Government with his enthusiastic endorsement, but the Department of Posts and Telegraphs poured cold water on the idea, suggesting that it was 'impracticable under international regulations'[99] and suggesting as a compromise that the Hospitals' Trust might be offered an hour on the Athlone transmitter. This episode is notable for being the antecedent of the Hospitals' Trust sponsored programme, which was broadcast on Radio Éireann for many years; even more significantly, it bore a striking similarity to the proposed scheme for a privately financed television service in the nineteen-fifties, which was also strongly supported by the Hospitals' Trust, and provides prima facie evidence of the extent to which the trust was a driving force in the unsuccessful move for privatisation.

The idea of a television service had been mooted in the early fifties and was strongly resisted by the Department of Finance, which believed it would inevitably be a drain on the public purse. It argued in August 1957, for example, that 'arrangements to provide a national television service should not be made until the demand for more essential amenities (particularly housing) has been largely satisfied.'[100] This statement, however, can be usefully contrasted with the memorandum from its author's superior, T. K. Whitaker, a mere four months later in which Whitaker argued that 'a slowing down in housing and other forms of social investment must be faced from now on because of the virtual satisfaction of needs over wide areas.' Plainly Finance could play into either goal as the occasion demanded.

In October 1957 the Government decided to establish a television service 'as early as practicable … under public control … So far as possible, the service should be provided without cost to the Exchequer.'[101] A Government subcommittee was set up, dominated by Lemass.

The committee's first — and most controversial — fruit was the announcement by Neil Blaney in November 1957 that the Government was now prepared to license a commercial company to provide the necessary service, but under public supervision. This decision in effect reversed the one taken only two months previously to reject two commercial proposals then on the table. One of these was from Charles Michelson, a Romanian expatriate living in Paris; the other was from the American McLendon company. Both had their attractions for Lemass: the Michelson proposal had the powerful support of Joe McGrath's Hospitals' Trust, among others; the McLendon proposal offered the possibility of substantial American investment and also had potential for encouraging American tourism. Under pressure from Lemass, in December 1957 the Government subcommittee reopened consideration of these proposals.

There were other important differences between Lemass and Ó Broin. Lemass wanted the Department of Posts and Telegraphs to choose the successful applicant; Ó Broin, wary of the possibility of political interference or bias, wanted the choice made by a powerful television authority. A proposal by Seán MacEntee in February 1958 for the establishment of a Television Commission saved Ó Broin, for the time being; but the commission, when it reported in May 1959, favoured the private option. Given Lemass's record, it was therefore on the face of it extraordinary that, in one of his first acts as Taoiseach, he presided over a Government meeting on 31 July 1959 that threw out the Television Commission's recommendation and decided to establish the new television service under a public statutory authority.

Ó Broin described this in his autobiography as 'an extraordinary *volte face*'.[102] This was hardly an understatement. Lemass's change of heart, however, may not have been as substantial as Savage and others suggest. A perceptive contemporary observer reported, without quoting Lemass directly as his source, that he 'never wanted Telefís Éireann to be set up as a State body, but his colleagues outvoted him.'[103] But why would the new Taoiseach have been faced down so rapidly by all his colleagues on an issue on which he had made his own views plain for many years? To understand what happened it is necessary not only to look at the membership of that Government, their ages and political backgrounds but at a key memorandum they received from Ó Broin in May 1969, while de Valera was still Taoiseach.

This memorandum was ostensibly a response to the interim report of the Commission on the Revival of the Irish Language, which had argued strongly for more Irish in the broadcasting services. It subtly combined criticism of some of the commission's more unreasonable demands with a pious appeal to the known cultural proclivities of the Government.[104] A programme contractor given the responsibility envisaged by the Television Commission, Ó Broin argued, would be motivated solely by the prospect of private profit and would by definition ignore 'national objectives' — including that most important objective of all, the revival of Irish. 'If television is to be used positively for national objectives, the proper procedure in the Minister's view is that the Television Authority should itself operate the programmes — that is, *all* the programmes.' (Emphasis in original.) This was plainly the crucial argument, for this Government and its immediate successor.

Lemass did not entirely close the door on the private interests involved, even after the decision had been taken. Michelson wrote to him again, pleading for a private meeting and adjusting the terms of his original proposal to provide 'all funds' for the operation of the television service of 'superlative quality', in return for access to the commercial radio wavelengths he coveted.[105] Lemass did not turn him down out of hand and gave him a definitive refusal only a month later, after Michael Hilliard had expressed the strongest possible opposition to any projected meeting, because it 'could give rise to embarrassing rumour and speculation.'[106] He also made it clear to his minister that he would not like to see the door entirely shut.

> It might be interesting to suggest to him [Michelson] that proposals regarding international sound broadcasting, having no relationships with television, could be received without commitment on our part. If the granting of a concession for such a service is possible under international law, as he asserts, and could be very profitable, as appears to be agreed, I do not think we should refuse to consider it.[107]

After his retirement Lemass spoke frankly about his doubts. Not long after his appointment as Taoiseach, he told an interviewer, he had still been of the opinion that Telefís Éireann should be set up not as a 'semi-state' body but as a new entity under the control of 'one of the private groups who were seeking the service,' such as Gael-Linn or a second Irish group that was also interested. He also supported the idea of creating a second channel to provide competition for Telefís Éireann.[108] The eventual choice of the state-sponsored model was taken 'not without some hesitation,' because the Government were 'for a time uncertain as to the desirability of entrusting it to an authority outside the Government, relying only on directive principles set out in legislation and on the power of the Government to appoint the members of the authority, to ensure that the direction of the service would be consistently in harmony with the highest and most enduring purposes of our nation.'[109]

The new medium represented a considerable challenge for Lemass, as well as for other politicians. He had over the years developed a broadly commonsense attitude to the print media, which encouraged him in the belief that threatening them, suing them or responding intemperately to provocation was rarely advisable. Unfair press criticism was for the most part just another cross politicians had to bear, not least because libel juries, he suspected, would rarely be on their side and would expect politicians to have thicker skins.

On a purely personal and technical level his attitude to the new medium mirrored his ease with the older one. He was virtually unaffected by stage fright and was never hypnotised by the camera. Michael Johnston, an RTE producer who worked with him on a number of party political broadcasts, noted that 'Lemass was a natural television broadcaster. Not only did he not use the autocue himself, he told his ministers not to use it, as it wasn't necessary. Some of them could have done with it. He had a homespun, direct manner, which went down very well on the box — much better than on radio.'[110]

The political and institutional aspects of the new service were, however, a different matter. It is worth while remembering, as part of the context within which the attitude of Lemass and his Government to Telefís Éireann is being considered, that the Government was in effect taking two steps in one. In the first place it was authorising the creation of a new medium — and one that was thought to have a significant, though unquantifiable, impact on public and political opinion. At the same time it was removing this untried new medium from the safe hands of the Department of Posts and Telegraphs. Additionally, it could be expected that the Fianna Fáil organisation at local level, conscious of Lemass's own interventionist style in the past and hypersensitive to any real or perceived slight to their Government's achievements, would bring substantial direct and indirect pressure to bear on Lemass and his ministers to rectify any supposed transgressions.

Even where the print media were concerned Lemass could occasionally be prickly. He supported MacEntee in his successful libel action against Proinsias Mac Aonghusa in 1964, although he warned his touchy minister about the implications of his ideas for a special system of tribunals for journalists who criticised public men.[111] He even explored the possibility of suing the *Irish Times* for a column by Myles na gCopaleen alleging that he was guilty of jobbery and corruption[112] and once tried to prevent the publication of an article in *Business and Finance* about dynastic families in the Dáil (which mentioned his son Noel) by threatening to withdraw permission for the magazine to publish an interview it had carried out with him for the same issue.[113]

His unease about television was manifested in a number of ways.[114] He incorporated many of his own views in his speech for the opening night and in a script he prepared for the Minister for Posts and Telegraphs to be delivered to the inaugural meeting of the television authority, which was sent to Hilliard with a covering note to the effect that any changes Hilliard planned to make should be notified to him directly.[115] He was particularly conscious of the question of the national image.

> Because the image of themselves which is offered by a national tele-
> vision service can influence the people of any nation to aspire to a better
> life, the pretext of objectivity should not be allowed to excuse the
> undue representation of our faults. What you should aim to present is a
> picture of Ireland and the Irish as we would like to have it, although
> our hopes and aims may well be helped by the objective presentation
> of facts in association with constructive comment.[116]

His assessment of the power of the new medium — one widely shared by his contemporaries — was equally evident in the care with which he drafted the passage on the North, rewriting Moynihan's draft to exclude any explicit reference to 'the force issue'.

> Our broadcasting services, reaching across the present border, can help
> to promote that sense of common nationality and understanding
> which will in time bring about the spiritual reunification of our
> people. The natural and traditional unity of Ireland should be accepted
> as a matter of course and as a fact on which special emphasis is not
> required. The programmes which are suited to the needs and tastes of
> one part of the nation will appeal equally to the other. Care must be
> taken, at all times, to avoid presentations which could cause offence to
> any section. The national aim is to bring about a solution of the par-
> tition problem by promoting a general desire amongst the people to
> remove the obstacles of misunderstanding and outworn prejudices, and

to seek, by general agreement, the road to reunification, and this aim must inspire the conduct of the national broadcasting services.[117]

In the circumstances it was to be expected that during the early years of the new service there would be an element of mutual suspicion in the relationship between the Government and the new authority. Boundaries would be established by trial and error, or by private negotiation. Sometimes there were long-range artillery exchanges; sometimes the conflict was confined to sniper fire. Lemass and some of his ministers found it difficult to come to terms with the new broadcasting structures, which they themselves had instituted but which neglected to provide any channels through which ministers might communicate with the station when they felt that important considerations of national policy were involved. In the circumstances the Taoiseach's direct interventions were few and far between, but his Minister for Posts and Telegraphs and other close associates were more frequently involved in discussions about the station and its supposed impertinences.

At first Lemass was prepared to allow the new service room to breathe, politically speaking. When an *Irish Times* interview with the Director-General of Telefís Éireann, Ed Roth, in November 1960 aroused the ire of one correspondent, Lemass expressed his agreement with Roth's thesis that the station 'would not be a political organ of the government of the day.'[118] As Telefís Éireann became more assertive and independent-minded, however, Lemass's interventions followed a readily recognisable pattern. He rarely responded to third-party criticisms of the station, many of which reached his desk, other than by passing them on to the Minister for Posts and Telegraphs, Michael Hilliard, or getting Hilliard's officials to draft a suitably bland reply. 'There is, under the law,' one such reply noted, 'no power of interference with [Telefís Éireann's] programme arrangements given to any Minister.'[119] His own direct interventions, which were considerably less frequent than those of members of the Government in later years, were never directed at any supposed party bias in Telefís Éireann but at what he perceived as a lack of balance in certain programmes dealing with economic issues. Emigration in particular was a topic that cut him to the quick.

His unwillingness to give the station a blank cheque was marked by a number of differences of opinion with its officials on programming matters throughout his early period as Taoiseach. His consciousness of the importance of the medium was signalled as early as October 1961, when he secured an apology from Roth for a report that had misrepresented some aspects of his Dáil election as Taoiseach.[120] The following February his political antennae picked up an advertisement on Telefís Éireann offering jobs for young Irishwomen in London hotels, which, he told Hilliard, were 'a very definite encouragement to emigration and must be a considerable embarrassment to hotel proprietors and others who have difficulty in retaining staffs.'[121]

In May he was considerably irked by the publicity given by Telefís Éireann reporters to the expulsion from the Dáil of Deputy Seán Dunne. He took the matter up with the head of the Government Information Bureau, Pádraig Ó hAnracháin, urging him to raise it with the station's news editor, because 'everyone realised ... that it was staged for personal publicity purposes ... had no other significance ... and the discipline of the Dáil was undermined.'[122]

He was an avid consumer of Telefís Éireann's news and current affairs output. His viewing habits may be deduced from the fact that he declined a suggestion to arrange for the reception of BBC and ITV in his Dáil office, 'to avoid the erection of an unsightly aerial on Leinster House.'[123] It is perhaps not too fanciful to suggest that it would also have been politic to avoid rumours that the Taoiseach was watching foreign stations. Members of his family remember the entire family watching the wedding of Grace Kelly and Prince Rainier at their home in Palmerston Road; in later years his home viewing centred on news broadcasts. Interruptions of these bulletins by family members were one of the few things that could ruffle his normally placid demeanour.

Ó hAnracháin, who had served de Valera as head of the Government Information Bureau and was to continue in a cognate role with Jack Lynch and Charles Haughey, shared Lemass's views about the appropriate role for Telefís Éireann in the work of national development. The current affairs programme 'Broadsheet' attracted considerable attention from both men. 'If a Minister cannot put the official point of view regarding topics ventilated in Broadsheet, who can?' Lemass asked Ó hAnracháin. He went on to suggest that Telefís Éireann should be supplied with lists of specific ministers who would deal with the topics of the day.[124] Ironically, one of the contributors to this programme, who voted for Fianna Fáil in the 1961 general election and was later to become Taoiseach in a coalition Government, was Garret FitzGerald.

In September 1962 Lemass complained again to Ó hAnracháin about the general tone of 'Broadsheet', which, he thought, was becoming increasingly 'a medium for the uncritical presentation of the views of persons associated with various rumps and crank projects.' This evoked an enthusiastic response from the latter, advocating a total reorganisation of the station and the establishment of a 'Minister of Information'![125] Ó hAnracháin told Lemass that he had discussed the matter with Roth, who had accepted his criticisms. The fact that no personnel or programme changes were made at the station, however, suggests that the primary object of the admission was to deflect criticism.

The radical proposal for a Minister for Information was not acted on, but a close watch was being kept. In January 1963 Lemass took umbrage at the general tenor of a programme on emigration, which was 'thoroughly bad and depressing, and represented exactly the approach to serious national problems that Telefís Éireann should not adopt.' The station, he said, should 'take the whine out of their voice.'[126] He even went so far as to sketch out a series of 'challenging questions' about emigration that he said should be addressed by programme makers to a wide range of interest groups — shopkeepers, trade unions, farmers and bankers.[127] Hilliard was deputed to mark the station's cards in the matter, and did so.

Television was of course under scrutiny by other powerful interests as well. In 1962 Lemass had a private meeting with two of the Catholic archbishops, Dr McQuaid of Dublin and Dr Morris of Cashel, who took the extraordinary step of identifying three named individuals working in television and complained about their supposedly subversive influence. The people concerned were Jack White, former features editor of the *Irish Times* and now controller of programmes at Telefís Éireann; Proinsias Mac Aonghusa, an old foe of Seán MacEntee; and Shelah Richards, a producer. Lemass asked the head of the GIB, Pádraig Ó hAnracháin, for his private views on the people concerned. Ó hAnracháin responded with the unguarded and somewhat salty candour of a close political associate; his comments also provide a rare insight into the political culture within which television was struggling to find its authentic voice.

> [White] has no great firm beliefs about anything in particular and certainly gives me the impression of having no national outlook in the broadest sense of the term and has no loyalties. He … would think of Ireland as a place where those, like himself, who are 'liberal' on outlook must suffer as best they may. My impression of Mac Aonghusa is that he is a complete opportunist, a very slick operator with considerable talent … Of the three mentioned he is undoubtedly the most undesirable generally and I would go so far as to say capable of doing the greater amount of damage. I do not think there is anything that Mac Aonghusa would not exploit to his own advantage. Regarding Miss Richards I know that her selection as the producer of the 'Recollection' series was the subject of divisive comment within and without T.E. It is incredible that a Catholic was not chosen for this. Miss Richards herself could most charitably be described as a non-Catholic … Certainly a change of producer from this particular type of programme seems essential in addition to some such appointment as you mention. [Lemass's letter to Ó hAnracháin does not survive.] Perhaps the appointment of Fr Dunne to the R.E. staff on a consultancy basis, for which he would be paid a retainer, would suffice. This would leave the way open for the appointment of consultants representing other faiths should such a need arise or should they be requested. It is amazing indeed that such a rare crew as those mentioned — and some others — could get such a toe-hold in

T.E. in so short a time. Their activities are, undoubtedly, menacing and, I believe, the root cause of much of the present troubles in T.E.[128]

The episcopal initiative, as it happened, fell on relatively stony ground. A Catholic religious adviser was in fact appointed, but it was not Father Dunn — who had been given specific training by Dr McQuaid in the hope that he would be chosen to fulfil this function — but Father Romuald Dodd, a Dominican chosen by Telefís Éireann itself.

Father Dunne's disappointment was to the eventual benefit of television in other ways. He went on to head the Catholic Communications Institute, of whose Council Seán Lemass and the author were simultaneously members in the late sixties. He also established the gifted 'Radharc' documentary team, whose work confidently explored new territory for the medium in Ireland. He was a loyal but critical member of the church, and his later books *No Tigers in the Hierarchy* and *No Vipers in the Vatican* set headlines in clerical forthrightness. Father Dodd, for his part, fulfilled an extremely delicate and important role during the formative years of Irish television with tact, patience, and an unfailing sense of humour.

During this period the first chairman of the Broadcasting Authority, Éamonn Andrews, was frequently in the firing-line. Replying to an obviously testy complaint from Lemass in late 1963, he confessed on behalf of the authority that there had been an 'imbalance' in a programme on the turnover tax to which Lemass had objected. Given Lemass's precarious situation in the Dáil and the jitters within the Fianna Fáil parliamentary party engendered by this particular measure, it was a topic on which Lemass was more than usually sensitive. He plainly thought of the authority as having a hands-on role and expected it to exercise it when necessary. 'You asked me', Andrews added, 'about the Authority's functioning in the area of programmes. I want to repeat my assertion that the Authority consistently contributes criticism and proposals in connection with programmes either seen or projected.'[129]

This was evidently the programme mistakenly identified in *Sit Down and Be Counted* as having been broadcast in 1964.[130] According to this account, the Director-General, Kevin McCourt (a former member of the board of the IDA in the nineteen-fifties), told Lemass that if he insisted on a 'make-good' programme he would 'call the Authority into emergency session immediately.' McCourt, however, had no authority to call the authority into session and did not threaten to do so. He did have a meeting with Lemass, and refused to back down, warning him that the reasons for the sudden appearance of a 'make-good' programme would inevitably leak out and that the press would make a meal of it. McCourt was then asked to get Andrews to meet Lemass, which he did. At the end of a forty-minute discussion — most of which was apparently about English League football, in which

Lemass was keenly interested — Lemass told Andrews to tell McCourt that although he was still angry about the coverage given to protesters against the tax, McCourt had probably been right. 'If he was to take instructions from every Tom, Dick and Harry, he'd go mad.'[131]

As late as 1964 Lemass was still expressing a public lack of conviction about the wisdom of allowing Telefís Éireann to maintain and develop its sense of autonomy in relation to the Government. The arrangement for the governance of Telefís Éireann, he told Michael McInerney of the *Irish Times,* 'was still regarded as experimental in some degree but no change is at present contemplated.'[132] If he had thought that this shot across the bows of unruly broadcasters would have the desired effect, he was destined to be continually disappointed.

Matters of central economic policy and direction evoked the strongest response from Lemass. The Second Programme for Economic Expansion provided a case in point. It was not greeted by the public or the media with anything like the unqualified enthusiasm with which its predecessor had been welcomed, and when Telefís Éireann broadcast a special discussion about it in July 1964, Lemass took particular exception to comments by the economist Dr Frances Ruane of Trinity College, which he categorised as 'misleading, shallow and unconstructive.' He instructed the secretary of his department in unambiguous terms:

> I wish to have the Radio Éireann Authority approached to enquire what arrangements they have in mind to enable these criticisms and misrepresentations to be corrected. Their function in this matter should be primarily to support the Programme rather than to facilitate criticism, and certainly criticism must not be allowed to go un-answered. If there is any resistance on the part of the Authority, let me know and I will deal with it.[133]

Kevin McCourt argued in defence that the programme had been '90% favourable' and counselled against arranging a rebuttal programme, because 'if he [Lemass] were to call for it, it would be all over Radio Éireann and outside that Government pressure had been put on him [McCourt].'[134] The matter was eventually smoothed over at a lunch between Andrews and the Secretary of the Department of the Taoiseach.

A similar controversy arose later in relation to a programme, which Lemass thought very negative, on the economics of importing disassembled cars into Ireland and assembling them here; again a 'make-good' pro-gramme was suggested but was never prepared.[135]

Whereas current affairs programmes on economic issues provoked occasional flash-points, the question of Irish became more of a running sore. Gunnar Rugheimer's version of events indicates the extent to which this was the case.

Two of the people on the Authority, Phyllis O'Kelly and Ernest Blythe, were completely unreasonable on this issue, and there was considerable acrimony about it. I got hell from these two. They wanted to operate on the basis of a belief that everybody spoke Irish, and that the appropriate thing to do would be to sprinkle Irish throughout the programming: this was complete rubbish. Instead of this we had Buntús Cainte. After the 1964 Commission on the Restoration of the Irish Language, Éamonn thought that for the Authority to throw responsibility for Irish onto RTE in this way was unreasonable and unfair; this is why he resigned.[136]

Whereas these interventions were in private, there were also occasional public rows between the Lemass administration and RTE (as Telefís Éireann had now become). One of the best-documented was the 1966 controversy involving the then Minister for Agriculture, Charles Haughey, and the 'Division' programme. The issue was whether the programme, which was pushing the boat of political journalism on television out into largely uncharted waters, was to be a forum for politicians alone or whether non-elected experts and others could also participate. After a disagreement between the whips of the various political parties about what had actually been agreed between them, Fianna Fáil boycotted the programme, which went ahead without them.

Lemass's speech about RTE's role in the formulation and defence of national policy, when it was finally and formally expressed in the Dáil in late 1966, was made in this very specific context. It was during the row between Charles Haughey and the National Farmers' Association, at a time when Lemass and others felt that the farmers were mounting a direct challenge to the Government's authority; it was also dangerously close to Lemass's impending, though not yet announced, retirement. Lemass had two years earlier expressed in the Dáil his view that the farmers' rates strike then in progress was setting the country on the road to anarchy. Their 1966 protest was not calculated to make him revise his position, and his response, though measured and defensible in legal and political terms, betrayed a certain testiness, which would have been exacerbated by his own knowledge of his intended retirement and the difficulties the farmers' protest created for him as he tried to control the timetable leading up to the succession.

Asked by Brendan Corish whether he had made suggestions to the authorities at RTE 'following which news items were changed or deleted,' Lemass pointedly declined to answer these specific questions and declared that he was prepared to stand over any actions any of his ministers had taken.[137] Moreover, he emphasised,

Radio Telefís Éireann was set up by legislation as an instrument of public policy and as such is responsible to the Government. The

Government have over-all responsibility for its conduct and especially the obligation to ensure that its programmes do not offend against the public interest or conflict with national policy as defined in legislation. To this extent the Government reject the view that RTE should be, either generally or in regard to its current affairs and news pro- grammes, completely independent of Government supervision. As a public institution supported by public funds and operating under statute, it has the duty, while maintaining impartiality between political parties, to present programmes which inform the public regarding current affairs, to sustain public respect for the institutions of Government and, where appropriate, to assist public understanding of the policies enshrined in legislation enacted by the Oireachtas. The Government will take such action by way of making representations or otherwise as may be necessary to ensure that Radio Telefís Éireann does not deviate from the due performance of this duty ... There is, I think, a very special obligation on Government to ensure that the decision to entrust this responsibility to an independent authority does not conflict with the public interest.[138]

The subtext of his answer was clear, as he no doubt intended it to be. Anything that had been done in the past in relation to RTE was justified, and the process would be repeated if it were thought to be necessary. There was, in effect, a grey area between the Government's view that RTE could not be 'completely independent of Government supervision,' which was, in the strictly legal sense, true, and the broadcasters' view that this was tantamount to expecting RTE to be, in the paraphrase of one critic, 'an instrument of Government'.[139] In the event, the 'Seven Days' programme devoted a week's programming to issues connected with freedom in broad- casting and roped in an impressive display of international authorities, including Grace Wyndham Goldie and Walter Cronkite, to help them make their point. Pearse Kelly, the Head of News, resigned for unspecified reasons, and the Dublin print media warned that a sharp watch should be kept for Government interference.

There are two ways of looking at the relationship between Lemass and RTE. From the perspective of the nineteen-nineties his interventions — or at least those recorded in the archives — could be portrayed as overbearing or unduly sensitive. Given the context in which they were made, however, it is also possible that, by the standards required of him from within his own party, his interventions were less lethal than might have been expected. The fact that he saw little difficulty in committing them to paper in most cases is indeed firm evidence that he believed himself to be acting in the national rather than in any narrow party interest. It might also have been evidence of arrogance, but that was not generally his style. Much later, the difficult and tension-filled days of the late sixties and early seventies showed that these exchanges had indeed been little more than skirmishes. The big battles were still to come.

CHURCH AND STATE

If Lemass was concerned about television's propensity — as he saw it — to impede the Government's attempts to get the economy onto a sound footing, he was certainly as liberal on a range of other issues as many broadcasters. For the most part, however, he confined his liberal sentiments to the sphere of private negotiations, and with good reason: on two separate issues he had to accept that he was powerless to act and to withdraw as gracefully as possible rather than commit himself politically to a battle he knew he could not win.

Both in public and in private his attitude to religion was never supine, sometimes combative, and on occasion deeply sceptical. He was frequently asked in interviews about the power of the Catholic Church and for the most part contented himself with remarking that in his view the Catholic laity were in general somewhat in advance of their clergy and would respond positively to enlightened church leadership.

> The Irish Catholic hierarchy is probably the least inclined to change, but the lay leaders among Catholics, and the public at large, are in advance of their Church in this respect. They would accept new dogma, if decided on by the Vatican Council, without demurring, I think.[140]

On another occasion at about the same time he noted:

> There is certainly no active interference in politics by the Catholic Church. One time, before the Irish government was formed, communities in need of leaders frequently sought from parish priests advice on all matters, and this forced them into political attitudes. The broad concepts of policy which have been laid down in encyclicals do in fact inspire the policies of Irish governments, but this is because we agree with them.[141]

The first part of the latter statement was, given his experience as a negotiator for the absent de Valera with the bishops in 1952, somewhat economical with the historical truth. The second part reflects his undoubted admiration for Pope John XXIII; at one point, according to a report at the time of his death in the *Irish Times,* he instructed his ministers to keep a copy of the latter's encyclical *Mater et Magistra* on their desks for guidance.

It is certainly true that he saw the need to consult bishops when he felt their interests were involved, just as he did not always feel the need to take their advice. He was also prepared to clash with them, publicly or privately, when he felt it was necessary to do so. His well-publicised row with Bishop Michael Browne of Galway following the publication of the Report of the Committee on Vocational Organisation in 1943, which he believed slighted the work of his department, was a case in point. Nor did he suffer in any way electorally because of this. An equally significant but more private controversy in the same year saw him lock horns with Dr McQuaid, who had been appointed to head the new Commission on Youth Unemployment. McQuaid suffered from a confusion of roles and was unwilling to take certain administrative steps in relation to the other Christian denominations, because he felt that it would compromise his position as Catholic Archbishop of Dublin. Lemass refused to back down, and McQuaid appealed to de Valera, who in effect supported his minister and facilitated a compromise in order to allow McQuaid not to lose face.[142]

As far as the public was concerned, Lemass was an orthodox Catholic politician — never more so than in his address at the Patrician Year ceremonies in 1961. He was asked to speak by McQuaid on 'The Church in the Modern World' and originally had the idea of dealing with social policy.[143] This suggestion, however, encountered significant opposition — not from McQuaid but from his own colleagues in the Department of Foreign Affairs and Department of Justice and from his Tánaiste — and the title was eventually changed to the more innocuous 'St Patrick in Our Times'. The speech, which was largely drafted by the secretary of the Department of External Affairs and to which Lemass made few changes, was notable principally for the assumptions it embodied, not least its unmistakable inference that Irishness and Catholicism were synonymous. *Ut Christiani et Romani sitis,* as he told his delighted audience: 'whatever the future, this is the faith by which we shall live. On this rock we shall continue to stand.'

Had he paused for a moment to think of the implications of such phrases for his emerging Northern policy he might well have hesitated, but the immediately pre-conciliar era in which he was speaking was kind to him. This was partly because Northern unionists would not seriously have expected him to say anything else and therefore saw no need to comment adversely on it, and partly because his Catholic audience (incredible as it may now seem, no invitations were sent to the leaders of any other Christian denomination) were suffused with an intoxicating mixture of religious fervour and national pride. A visiting English bishop put it concisely: 'The Taoiseach has stolen the show.'[144]

The first issue in this area that Lemass had to face as Taoiseach was that of the proposed restructuring of the National Library. Its Director, Dr Richard Hayes, conceived the idea in 1960 that a renovated National Library might make common cause with the library of the nearby Trinity College, which was undergoing a considerable expansion as Catholic students entered its courses in increasing numbers. Lemass evidently thought this an excellent idea and gave it his support, writing to McQuaid to discuss the 'tentative suggestions' that had been made in this regard.[145] Lemass and McQuaid met on 4 May, but McQuaid's views, as recorded by Maurice Moynihan, emphasised that in the view of the hierarchy 'the chief university institution in a mainly Catholic community should manifestly be a Catholic institution.' On 9 May Lemass wrote to the Provost of Trinity College, Dr A. J. McConnell, to tell him that 'my examination of the proposal has revealed such substantial difficulties that the particular scheme of Dr Hayes must be regarded as impracticable.' McQuaid wrote to Cardinal d'Alton with evident satisfaction: 'I am glad to report that today I saw the Taoiseach, and that the proposal to conjoin Trinity College Dublin's new library and the National Library will not be heard of again.'[146] The country's loss, as it happened, was Trinity's gain: the university subsequently got substantial public funding for its new library.

The second issue arose early in 1965 when Lemass — partly no doubt as an aspect of his policy in relation to Northern Ireland — decided to explore the possibility of changing the Constitution to alter or remove the absolute prohibition on divorce legislation. He asked Brian Lenihan to explore the matter in private with the relevant authorities. Lenihan did so and returned with the unambiguous message from Monsignor Gerard Sheehy, chancellor of the Archdiocese of Dublin, that 'there would be violent opposition from the hierarchy to any proposal to allow divorce in the State.' Sheehy, according to Lenihan, made it plain that he spoke not only for himself but for 'others', which Lenihan took to mean McQuaid. 'In view of the above,' Lenihan noted, 'there would not appear to be much point in pushing the matter any further.' The proposal was rapidly shelved.[147]

It is tempting, but ahistorical, to regard these incidents as evidence that Lemass was either clericalist or ready to accept ecclesiastical diktats meekly. The more persuasive explanation is that he recognised the realities of ecclesiastical power in the temporal sphere when he saw them and was disinclined to engage in gesture politics, much less to commit his Government publicly to battles he knew could not be won.

He was certainly unimpressed by ecclesiastical ideas that were manifestly unworkable. When he went to Rome in 1965 for the conferring of the red hat on Cardinal Conway he had a private audience with Pope Paul VI, during which the Pope suggested a shopping-list of items for him to bring back to Dublin. One of them was the establishment of a broadcasting station in Ireland that would beam Catholic programmes abroad, especially to Britain. Lemass ran this idea past Hugh McCann, the Secretary of the Department of External Affairs, who in turn submitted it to Leon Ó Broin in Posts and Telegraphs. Lemass's old adversary had little difficulty in rubbishing the scheme. The bishops weren't interested, he told McCann, and in any case 'I have always felt that the proper answer for suggestions for a Catholic station is that we have one already in Radio Éireann.'[148]

Lemass was, however, attentive to the complex triangular relationship between Dublin, London, and the Vatican, not least in the matter of diplomatic representation. When Frank Aiken wrote to him in early 1966 to express his concern at the possibility of the Pro-Nuncio in Britain being raised to full ambassadorial rank and therefore accredited to the queen as monarch of, inter alia, Northern Ireland, his response was immediate. He told Aiken that he had already discussed the matter with Archbishop McQuaid and promised to discuss it further with Cardinal Conway at 'an early opportunity'.[149]

By 1966 his attitude to the still controversial question of censorship was unclouded by any fear of what the Catholic Church might say or do; he was happy to support Brian Lenihan's reforming Bill in the Government, although he tartly asked Lenihan — quoting the example of *Fanny Hill* — whether books that had first been published more than twenty years ago could still be banned if necessary.[150]

In private life Lemass attended Mass regularly and went to midnight Mass every Christmas, very inconspicuously, in a small chapel attached to a convent in Leeson Street.[151] At a deeper level, however, and seen by only a few close friends, there was a strong vein of agnosticism, part of which went back to the ecclesiastical condemnations of Sinn Féin during the Civil War. During his internment in Ballykinlar in 1920 he had offended some of the more devout Northern republicans by his refusal to go to Mass and had provided evidence of a scepticism that was to remain with him for most if not all of his adult life. He told Colm Barnes, with whom he had close dealings over many years as Minister for Industry and Commerce and as Taoiseach, that he never thought to any extent about the hereafter, regarding it as 'purely speculative'.[152]

Sometimes it went even deeper. At the funeral of Jack O'Brien, an old associate whom he had appointed to the Irish Tourist Authority and who died comparatively young, Lemass — who was out of office at the time — arrived late and met his former private secretary at the gate of the cemetery. As they walked together towards the grave, Lemass ventilated his emotion in a typically terse but withering comment: 'This is all nonsense. When it's over, it's over.'[153]

The dark side of Lemass's spiritual journey, if this is what it was, could also be enlivened by a certain gallows humour. He was to survive his old friend and comrade James Ryan, who died in 1970, but at the funeral found the traditional words of comfort uttered at such gatherings not entirely to his liking. When someone, noting that Ryan had died quietly in his sleep, observed sententiously that it was 'a good way to go,' Lemass, by now outside the church and puffing with evident relief on his pipe, observed sardonically: 'As long as it's not tonight.' His own time, in fact, was close enough.

10

Resignation and Succession

'The time to go is before they start criticising you'

T he Government dining-room during Lemass's later years as Taoiseach
was rarely crowded. Many of the younger ministers in particular
would be out at official engagements or lunching in town, and
Hillery and Lemass often found themselves there on their own. At one of
these lunches Lemass told Hillery: 'I'll have to think of my successor.'
Hillery's response was to suggest that, while there was some criticism of his
ministers, there was none of himself. Lemass replied: 'The time to go is
before they start criticising you.'[1]

Lemass's health had never been better than average. His old associate
Todd Andrews remarked, with tantalising obliqueness, that 'his service as an
IRA man involved him in much physical and psychological hardship.'[2] Even
in the nineteen-thirties the records of the parliamentary party show him
absent because of illness. In subsequent years phlebitis and gall-bladder
problems slowed him down from time to time. He took little exercise, apart
from golf. His diet, if the fare available in the Dáil restaurant in the sixties is
any guide, would have been well freighted with carbohydrates.

Although he never took alcohol to any extent, he was a prodigiously
heavy smoker, consuming approximately a pound of strong pipe tobacco
every week.[3] P. J. Carroll, the manufacturers, decided at one point to cease
production of his particular brand, but they took the precaution of informing him in advance. Only half in jest, Lemass sent them a message warning
them that he would close them down if they deprived him of his supply.
Chastened, they made up enough of his brand in vacuum-sealed tins to last
him for several lifetimes before they finally ended its production.

On the other hand, he took his health problems lightly. When during
his last term in Industry and Commerce he called in Brendan O'Regan to
ask him to become chairman of Bord Fáilte, O'Regan at first demurred,
partly for the reason that he had recently been ill with stomach problems.
Lemass was unsympathetic. 'I had that too,' he said. 'Got over it.' He then
told O'Regan that if he hadn't accepted the job in three days he would offer
it to someone else.[4]

On another occasion when he was lunching with Paddy Hillery in the Government dining-room he suddenly became unwell, and his cheeks became suffused with a dark flush. He passed it off lightly, telling Hillery it was because of an allergy — 'I'm allergic to work.'[5] He found the stairs up to the Government and Fianna Fáil rooms in the Dáil extension increasingly difficult and at one point sent a memorandum to the Department of Finance asking, with an evident sense of urgency, when the planned lift would be provided.[6]

At one political function in the Shelbourne Hotel, Dublin, accompanied by Brian Lenihan, he became suddenly faint and had to spend some time sitting in a chair before recovering.[7] At a social function in the Gresham Hotel he became so unwell that he collapsed and a doctor had to be called. He was put to bed in one of the hotel's suites, with strict instructions to refrain from any activity that might make him unwell. Not long afterwards, visitors to the invalid found him sitting up innocently in bed, his hands empty, in a room that reeked of pipe smoke.[8]

In addition to all this, by 1966 he had been continuously in Government for nine years. He had never been able to find much time for his family, except during his periods in opposition, more especially in 1948–51, when he was less actively involved in party reorganisation than in 1954–57. Both he and his wife were well into their sixties, and retirement was a reality that had to be faced sooner or later. The options facing him on a political level were narrowing rapidly. If he decided to stay in office he would have been unlikely to call a general election before 1968 or 1969 at the earliest, unless provoked into doing so by some factor outside his control. After that election he would have to continue in office for at least another year before handing over to a successor. He told Paddy Hillery, long before his resignation was announced, that his preference was to give his successor two years in office before the following general election, and this corresponds to conventional political wisdom.[9] The optimum dates for his resignation therefore would be 1967 or 1970. By 1970 he would be nearing seventy-one, in even poorer health, and not in as strong a position to attract additional income to supplement his pension. He was particularly anxious about making provision for his wife, whom he confidently, and accurately, expected would outlive him; and this question, though undoubtedly not the main factor in his decision, certainly weighed heavily with him.

There was always the possibility of course that if he held on to office he might lose the general election in 1969 or 1970, which would involve the unpalatable prospect of leaving office and leadership as a defeated Taoiseach. He had already been dropping hints, to his colleagues and further afield. In 1963 he had jokingly forecast that by 1970 he would have retired from active politics.[10] In April 1965, at Jim Ryan's retirement, he noted that the situation might come to himself too, 'and that might not be too far off.'[11]

At the end of 1966 his Government was facing two by-elections, the loss of either of which would create an uncomfortable degree of political instability and make a resignation even more problematic. The economy was beginning to stutter, and an argument could easily be made for the proposition that a younger and more energetic man would be better equipped to put it back on the rails. Even though he regretted that time would not stand still for him, 'so that I could go on indefinitely,' he told his final press conference that 'the 1916 celebrations marked the end of a chapter: as one of the generation, this marked the end of the road for me.'[12] This in effect was what made it 1966 rather than 1967.

The strain of office, and of poor health, was making him discernibly testy. When the National Union of Journalists protested in 1966 about his remarks in the Dáil on the relationship between Telefís Éireann and the Government, he wrote to the Minister for Posts and Telegraphs, Joe Brennan, suggesting that he ask the authority 'what action they propose to take to reject the unwarranted assumption of authority by this trade union.'[13] He urged the Attorney-General to strengthen the law about picketing outside Leinster House,[14] and his suggestions were later embodied in part in the controversial Criminal Justice Bill. He sent the Attorney-General a long list of proposed changes for expediting Dáil procedures. And, while emphasising the importance of democracy, he specifically rejected the idea that 'we have to suffer in silence unreasonable behaviour by any individual or action which is detrimental to the national interest.'[15]

Parliamentary party and National Executive minutes for the period make it clear that the temper of the party was becoming frayed by the increasing tempo and severity of Government cut-backs, and also that well before his retirement Lemass made a conscious attempt to prepare both organisations for a change in leadership, in a manner that suggests that the general timing of his decision was certainly fully premeditated, although the precise date may have been influenced by other circumstances.

The old guard was still nipping at his heels or, if they were afraid to tackle him head on, at the heels of some of his ministers. Paddy Smith was more keen than others to stir the pot, and he put down a motion at the parliamentary party meeting in November 1965 recording his conviction 'that it is undignified that members of the Government should entertain lavishly the writer of the weekly article in the *Irish Times* known as Backbencher.'[16] John Healy, who wrote the Backbencher column, cheekily disclosed Smith's concern in his column some weeks later. In Smith's absence, Seán MacEntee found himself able to move the motion, which was discussed without a vote being taken. By February 1966 anxiety was being expressed within the party — not for the first time — about leaks to the press, and Lemass had to stave off suggestions that a special committee be set up to look into the matter. It would be more appropriate, he said soothingly, that the whips should talk privately to those suspected of this nefarious practice.[17] In de Valera's time, Todd Andrews commented, 'it would be impossible to organise cabals in either the cabinet or the party, but they were certainly organised in Seán Lemass's time.'[18]

In March Lemass had to intervene at the parliamentary party to defend, 'in the interests of the economy,' the cuts that had been made in payment to FCA members.[19] This was a relatively minor issue, but he had to intervene again in May, when cuts in the housing programme were discussed. There was, he pointed out, an increased demand for capital at a time when internal sources of capital investment were not expanding and access to external sources was proving a problem 'because of the policies of foreign governments.'[20] Whitaker's 1960 assurance that what was missing was not capital but enterprise was by now only a memory.

In June he had to reply to Smith, who returned to the fray with an assertion that the proposed Department of Labour was merely 'a gimmick'. Although Smith had long since been written off as a political force, it is easy to underestimate the destabilising effect of interventions like these within a parliamentary party, especially if other factors are contributing to a heightened level of political anxiety. The extent of the pressure on public finances may be gauged by the Government's willingness to agree, in August 1966, to a scheme for additional weekly sweepstakes organised by Irish Hospitals' Trust. These would have raised an estimated £2 million (£21 million in 1996 values) for the Department of Health. The idea was apparently broached by Donogh O'Malley, the Minister for Health, rather than by the Hospitals' Trust and was agreed in detail subsequently, despite the Department of Justice's objections that 'a substantial profit for the promoters can be wholly concealed.'[21]

What is more surprising than any of this is that Lemass was forced to back down on an important policy and political issue: the timing of the local elections. When Paddy Burke proposed at the parliamentary party meeting on 9 March 1966 that these be postponed, Lemass argued strongly against any such decision. The National Executive had already decided not to postpone the elections, he pointed out; it would damage the image of the party; it would be unpopular with prospective candidates; they should not run away from their responsibilities; and there was 'no guarantee that the political situation would be better next year.'[22]

Two weeks later a vote was held on the issue; fifty-one members of the parliamentary party voted for postponement and only six against.[23] Lemass's record would not lead one to suspect that he had changed his mind or his vote in the interim, and the result could not be portrayed as anything other than a defeat. His view of his leadership responsibilities in the Government was clear: 'Do as I say or get another Taoiseach,'[24] but on this occasion he had to swallow his disappointment.

If he had not by then been so close to his own retirement it is doubtful that he could have ignored such a development at the heart of his power base. A more benign interpretation suggests that the critics of the original decision were in effect right: the grass-roots feeling (which later proved accurate) was that Fianna Fáil would suffer heavily at the local elections, and, given the choice of pain now or pain later, the entirely reasonable thing to do was to opt for the latter.

In September, at two co-ordinated meetings within a week, one of the parliamentary party, the other of the National Executive, he went to considerable lengths to address the party's organisational problems. At the parliamentary party meeting on 21 September he returned to a familiar theme: the need for confidence — confidence in the party, and confidence in their plans. The party had to be strengthened at all levels; the continuity of administration and fulfilment of the national aims remained vital; and the national collection should be doubled.

As it happened, his own fund-raising efforts during his later years had been substantial. He had overseen the setting up of a fund-raising committee with John Reihill, of the coal importing family, as chairman. It used to meet regularly in the Shelbourne Hotel, and Lemass was 'not slow to suggest companies he thought could afford a contribution.'[25] Todd Andrews suggested that this committee was the forerunner of the controversial Taca organisation, which was set up after Lemass left office but while he was still in the Dáil, and commented on the 'symbiotic relationship' between Reihill and Lemass, although it was 'impossible to imagine two men more different in character or motivation.'[26]

The September meeting of the parliamentary party was the one at which he finally broached the question of his retirement, and he observed that the increasing tempo of press references to this 'were not maliciously inspired.' He would have to retire sooner or later, he noted, and would do it at an opportune time, but the timing of the decision itself would be important. At the National Executive meeting on 26 September he again castigated the 'very unhealthy' financial situation of the party and drew attention to what he described as a 'closed shop mentality' in certain urban cumainn, which was preventing people from becoming members of the party and so leading to organisational weakness.[27]

He had certainly been thinking actively about the succession. In his series of post-retirement interviews with Michael Mills, political correspondent of the Irish Press, he said he had 'encouraged every member of the Government to think that when I retired each would be involved in the party selection of a Taoiseach.'[28] It was, however, a situation in which some members of the Government were more equal than others. He had specifically approached both Hillery and Lynch: both had said they were not interested.[29] He may well have been acting on the hunch of those party advisers who had told him during the run-up to the 1965 election that 'the public, in selecting their political representatives, prefer those who look most human to those who look most competent.'[30] For the time being, however, neither of these two reassuring public faces was available.

At the very least, his prior approach to Hillery and Lynch suggests a hierarchy of choice on his part and implies that the Colley-Haughey conflict that ensued was not his preferred option at that stage. Hillery was in fact a greater threat to any ambition on Haughey's part: he was only two-and-a-half years older than him and had been in the Dáil six years longer. The refusal by both to be leadership candidates — and it is difficult to see that either of them would have been defeated had he entered the lists at an early stage — also says something about morale within the party at that time and the perceived difficulties of managing it.

Lemass certainly told Colley early on that he should think about himself in the context of the party leadership and should 'go out and make Republican speeches.'[31] Colley's version of events, recounted by him to the journalist Bruce Arnold on various occasions in the late sixties and noted by him at the time, is intrinsically coherent and credible as far as it goes, for all that it largely reflects Colley's perspective. Haughey too was certainly in the frame: the fact that their candidacies were announced virtually simultaneously — Colley's was in effect first — indicated that both had been preparing for this eventuality.

Outside the party rooms the political temperature was increasing dramatically. The National Farmers' Association, on whose behalf Haughey had eventually secured belated — but evidently unsatisfactory — income increases from the Government, were on the war path and mounted a large protest, involving a march to Dublin and a permanent picket outside the offices of the minister. Within the party the initial response was one of some derision; because of the inclement weather, some TDs were given to referring to the NFA as the 'Nine Frozen Arses'.[32] Later the party and Government closed ranks in solidarity, and a potentially dangerous and unmanageable confrontation developed. Haughey told the parliamentary party that although the nature and scope of the protest was partly related to the struggle for leadership between the NFA and the ICMSA, 'a responsible organisation could not and should not be allowed to usurp the functions of government.' Paddy Smith, back on side for once, declared that the NFA 'should not be let destroy Fianna Fáil.'[33]

But events had started to move, and they did so rapidly. Even though the information emerged in a somewhat ragged and uncoordinated fashion, there was also evidence of Lemass's desire to remain in the driving-seat. His widow later recalled: 'We had discussed the issue and one day he came home and told me that he had retired. By that time I was happy that he had done so, as he was getting on, the workload was heavy and he had had a couple of blackouts.'[34]

Michael Mills was intimately involved and ran a story in the early editions of the *Evening Press* saying that Lemass was going to resign.

> I was contacted by a backroom person. I was told I could run the story, and told it was from the horse's mouth. He was going for medical reasons, but I was to avoid saying this. All hell broke loose. The story was denied. The *Irish Press* people were very worried. Joe Walsh rang Leinster House at 3 p.m. and there was no news. He said the paper would have to publish a retraction. The pressure was on me. I said 'wait until 6 o'clock.' Just before 6 p.m. I was in the little 'box room' in Leinster House when the door opened and there was a message from Fianna Fáil offices to say that there would be a special meeting of the Fianna Fáil party on the following Monday, and I knew it was OK. Lemass had been suffering from growing hoarseness; we assumed it was cancer.[35]

Even today the timing of the leak, and of the subsequent confirmation of Lemass's decision, is difficult to explain with any certainty. Colley and Haughey in fact were both out of the country. Colley had earlier asked Lemass, before leaving for the United States on a trade mission, whether he was likely to retire before the ardfheis. At that stage, Lemass said later, he thought it unlikely — but then he changed his mind.[36]

Some senior Government members, however, were perturbed at the choice being offered to the party and knocked on Hillery's door, where they got the same answer that Lemass had received.[37]

> He started the race between Charlie and George, but some of the older ministers came to me and said they didn't like the choice being offered. Jack said no first, too. The party persuaded Jack Lynch: I saw a deputation outside his door; it included Ó Ceallaigh from Clare.[38]

Without any special insight into the circumstances in which the final decision about the timing was taken, the most likely explanation for Lemass's admitted change of mind was suggested by Aiken, who was in New York. When he heard that Colley was being summoned home his reaction was that 'Lemass was losing control of the situation, and that the canvassing was getting out of hand.'[39] Haughey and Colley, according to one account, 'had teams openly canvassing for the job.'[40]

Another factor cannot be ruled out, and it relates to the tense political situation involving the farmers. The NFA was engaged in its sit-down out-side Government Buildings, and Haughey had refused to meet them under duress. There was complete deadlock on the issue, and the NFA protest was becoming the focus of nationwide media attention that was becoming extremely damaging for the Government.

The timing of Lemass's decision, even if it was not explicitly intended to remove the NFA from the front pages of the newspapers, had precisely this effect. Better again, it opened the way for Lemass, now caretaker Taoiseach, to broker a compromise between the NFA and Haughey, which he did without delay. But if Lemass now hoped that the outcome would be a straight fight between Colley and Haughey (a fight that Haughey would certainly have won), he was not in a position to ensure it.

Todd Andrews and others subsequently blamed Lemass for the lack of smoothness in the handling of the succession. Andrews, writing seventeen years later, gives a verdict that is critical to the point of acidity.

> When Lemass came to retire, he made no effort to provide for the suc-
> cession, as prudence and commonsense would have demanded. The
> result has been years of dissension and near ruin for the Fianna Fáil
> party. As a Taoiseach, Seán Lemass had not been very successful. Hope
> deferred had made the heart sick.[41]

Lemass himself had argued that 'the most damaging thing you could do with a party is to give the impression amongst the members that everything is cut and dried behind closed doors and that they have no choice or say in the matter at all.'[42] The more likely explanation, however, was that the situation was now to all intents and purposes unmanageable: Donogh O'Malley, for example, was negotiating with both sides.

The prospect of a two-horse race finally disappeared when Kevin Boland put forward Neil Blaney's name. Blaney's candidacy was inspired largely by a belief, which he himself shared with Boland, that the race between Colley and Haughey was a media creation. The three-way contest was dangerously unpredictable, and the only certainty at that stage was that neither Colley nor Haughey would withdraw in favour of Blaney.

Blaney, though he was by no means certain of winning, had one advantage that was difficult to counter: his ministerial experience was the same as Lynch's — more than nine years — whereas Haughey had been in the Government for only five years and Colley for less than eighteen months. Lynch had been in the Dáil for nine years longer than Haughey; but Haughey, like Lynch, had one great advantage over Colley: electability. Lynch had amassed an astonishing 12,800 votes in Cork at the previous election; Haughey, in Dublin North-East, had secured only three hundred fewer, more than twice as many as Colley, his constituency colleague, who was not elected until the ninth count.

There was also the matter of the candidates' ages. Blaney was only just forty-four; Haughey was just forty-one, Colley a bare month younger. The election of any one of the three would have put the other two out of contention for the future. Lynch, however, was eight years older than Colley and Haughey, a factor that gave each of them room to manoeuvre.

Frank Aiken had been for some time virtually managing Colley's campaign, not least by appointing actual or potential Colley supporters to the politically insignificant but financially advantageous Council of Europe in Strasbourg. Initially he thought that the younger crop of deputies who had come into Fianna Fáil after the 1965 election would ensure Colley's victory, and he had to be disabused of this notion by a percipient political journalist.[43] He now realised that Colley's candidature was imperilled by the timing of Lemass's decision, and he wrote to the Taoiseach from New York, where he was attending the United Nations, to say that he was 'very distressed' and to express the hope that Lemass could still be persuaded to carry on for another two years. He had already discussed the matter with Colley, and added:

> As I see it, George would be the most acceptable to the party, but he could do with another few years of experience. He would also need time and opportunity to become better known to the country ... I appeal to you to change your mind. Both the country and Fianna Fáil need you.[44]

Despite his relative inexperience, Colley believed he had other reasons to hope for success. He told Bruce Arnold that he had earlier discussed the leadership issue with Lynch and had urged him to stand, to avoid 'the party being taken over by elements which would damage its image in the country.' What gave him grounds for hope was that Lynch, who at that point had decided against standing, had responded to his suggestion by offering to support him. This factor, while it did not by any means guarantee success, was a significant encouragement.

By 31 October, therefore, a plainly optimistic Colley had returned from America, cutting short his visit (to the consternation of the IDA), and Haughey was back from London. Haughey received a rousing welcome at Dublin Airport, where supporters carried banners proclaiming 'Charlie is our darling' but at which, the *Irish Times* noted with unsuccessfully feigned surprise, 'no farmers were present.'[45] The same paper's political correspondent, in his analysis of the succession, stated without qualification that Lemass had already announced to close associates that he favoured Colley but that the position had changed the previous Wednesday, when Lemass and the party had come out in support of Haughey in his continuing entanglement with the NFA. Lemass's doctors, the same journalist wrote, had advised him that he could not carry any longer the enormous burden of office without grave danger to his health. Many years later his son-in-law put it more simply: 'The pipe killed him.'[46]

Lemass saw both Haughey and Colley on 1 November, without promising either of them his support but equally evidently favouring a contest. It is difficult to accept that Lemass would have favoured Colley: his knowledge of the feeling within the parliamentary party — let alone Aiken's letter — would have left him in little doubt about the weakness of Colley's position;

indeed it is doubtful if anything short of a laying-on of hands by Lemass would have altered Colley's chances, and it was in any case far from certain that Lemass could do for any leadership candidate what de Valera had done for him.

Following Blaney's candidacy a group of Fianna Fáil TDs from Cork and elsewhere started to mount a 'draft Jack Lynch' campaign, from which Lynch at first remained aloof. The *Irish Times,* despite reporting that Haughey was 'far and away the strongest candidate,' observed editorially that 'it is possible that the lot may fall on neither Mr Haughey nor Mr Colley.'[47]

By 3 November a tide had started to flow in favour of Lynch, although Aiken returned the following day and publicly announced his support for Colley. The versions offered by three of the main participants many years later throw some light on the detail of what happened and have a high degree of consistency, despite the passage of time. They also confirm that the critical intervention was by Lemass himself, when, realising that the situation was rapidly getting out of hand, he made a direct second approach to Lynch to ask him to reconsider his earlier decision not to stand. Lynch was already under pressure to reconsider from other elements in the party, but Lemass's intervention was decisive.

First Kevin Boland:

> There were rumours that Lemass was going to resign. I didn't believe them. Childers rang me: apparently he fancied himself. He knew nothing normally, but he told me that one parliamentary secretary was canvassing for Charlie and another for Colley. Aiken was away at the UN. There was no way, in my view, that the party would accept Colley or Haughey. I contacted Aiken, by telegram or by phone — I think by phone — to ask him about the rumours. He said there was nothing to worry about and that he would be looking into it when he got home. What I didn't know was that he was basically pro-Colley: he was the person who nominated all the FF members of the Council of Europe and that made a ready-made team for Colley. Gibbons was one of them; I don't remember the others. Aiken was anti-Haughey — hated him like poison. He was anti-Haughey's father, who had let him down by joining the Free State Army. Both Haughey and Colley were too young, and they were both from Dublin.
>
> Blaney came into my office — we were the two organisers of the party — and he said: 'There's nobody left only you or me.' I said, 'That means you.' My only mental reservation was that he knew no Irish. I simply didn't want to be Taoiseach, for the simple reason that I didn't want to have to make hypocritical speeches in the Dáil about people who had died. A Taoiseach could express sympathy, but it

should be up to the leader of the opposition to make speeches about people (on that side). Blaney would have won, but it would have been very divisive.

We told Michael Mills. That brought Lemass into action. He was right in his belief that Lynch was acceptable. He said: 'What kind of people have I got when one man has to get his wife's permission to run and the other has to get his wife's permission to withdraw?' [Lynch and Colley, respectively.] After we got Lynch to agree we still weren't sure that he was serious about it, and Paudge Brennan and myself pursued him to Waterford, where there was a by-election on — everyone thought it was in connection with the by-election that we were there — to make sure for ourselves.[48]

Blaney's version confirms and to some extent amplifies Boland's.

At the time the succession was decided, Jack Lynch regarded me as his confidant. He came into my room after the order of business and discussed his dilemma — principally caused by the fact that Máirín was unwilling to allow him to run. He went out to Garville Avenue [Lynch's home] to attempt to get her to change her mind, and came back before question time: there had been no change in her attitude.

After question time he went out to Garville Avenue again. On the stroke of five o'clock it emerged that Máirín had agreed. Jack told Lemass; Lemass rang me and I went down to his office to see him. When I went in he was walking the floor and invited me to sit down.

'You know Jack is going ... What are you doing?'

I asked him: 'What are George and Charlie doing?'

'Charlie's no problem.'

'What about George?'

'George is going out to get Mary to allow him to withdraw ...'[49]

Haughey's version is much the same.

Lemass told me he was going to ask Lynch to go. When he asked me to withdraw I said I would and he said: 'I'm glad someone can give me a straight answer around here.'[50]

According to Colley's later version of what happened, Lemass sent for him after he had got Lynch's agreement to stand. He told him that Lynch was in the race, that Blaney had withdrawn, and that Haughey had indicated that he would withdraw in favour of Lynch. When he asked Colley what his intentions were, Colley told him he wanted to talk things over first with Lynch — understandably, in the light of the earlier assurances he believed he had received from that quarter. He phoned Lynch, and they agreed to meet the following day, but was then astonished to hear on his car radio a report suggesting that Lynch would be elected unanimously and that all the other candidates had withdrawn.

The same bulletin was heard by Paddy Lalor, also in his car. He drove straight to Colley's house and advised him not to withdraw. Colley rang RTE to correct the report and told a somewhat unhappy Lynch the following morning that an election would be best for the party. Haughey and Blaney were in all probability equally unhappy, if not even more so: they would both have stayed in if they had known there was going to be a vote, but they could not go back on their undertakings to Lemass.

On 8 November, the day before the vote, Lemass had engineered a breakthrough with the farmers to allow Haughey and the NFA to meet again without either side losing face. As far as Haughey was concerned, of course, this was now irrelevant, at least to his leadership chances: he had withdrawn and could not re-enter the lists.

The following day the parliamentary party met to make the decision. Lemass opened the proceedings by saying he wanted no sympathetic speeches to be made and hoped the decision could be made without any long speeches. He was to be disappointed. The *Irish Times* reported that Smith and MacEntee both spoke in favour of Colley,[51] but it is not at all certain that MacEntee supported Colley; the main burden of his speech was an extended, and typically waspish, reproach to his party leader. The only reference to his speech in the minutes of the meeting was to the effect that he was 'appalled by the Taoiseach's decision to leave at this juncture in our history,' and that he could not have chosen a worse time to do so.'[52] No other official record remains of MacEntee's speech beyond this brief phrase, but if it resembled even to the slightest degree the notes he prepared for it and left with his personal papers it was a most extraordinary performance.

De Valera, his notes began, had got the Fianna Fáil organisation under way forty years ago.

> Today, however, the organisation which did so much is at its lowest ebb, and in the minds of the general public appears to be riven apart … Responsibility for this situation in my view rests mainly on the Taoiseach … The devious course which he has pursued, not only in relation to his leadership and on the succession, but to other questions as well, have confounded the members of our organisation so that none of them knows where we stand on any issue … I have no knowledge of the circumstances which have moved the Taoiseach to seek to relinquish his responsibilities as head of the Government and leader of Fianna Fáil … It is astonishing and unjustifiable that the Taoiseach, at this precise moment should propose, by resigning, to wash his hands of responsibility for the country's affairs … Only reasons of the utmost gravity, on the borderline, so to speak between life and death, can

justify such a step on the part of a leader ... Is he so weary, so unnerved, that he baulks at the task which he will leave to his successor? ... Now he is proposing to let us all down ... Mr de Valera left Lemass a great heritage in Fianna Fáil, and he squandered it. Sometimes in recent years it seemed as if it were being dealt with like a personal possession ... The State was tottering towards anarchy.[53]

If Lemass resigned now, MacEntee's notes continued, it would be the equivalent of 'deserting in the face of the enemy.' He should stay until the end of 1968.

The force of MacEntee's argument, such as it was, was weakened by an appeal to the images of de Gaulle, Franco and Salazar — two of them dictators — as prototypes to be followed. And his spirited denial, in his own papers, of Brian Farrell's suggestion that this amounted to a 'personal attack' on his Taoiseach rings hollow. At the very least he was expressing the deep anger of disappointment, if not personal hostility. Only seven months earlier he had inscribed a copy of his little book *Episode at Easter* to Lemass 'with warmest good wishes.'[54]

Most members of the parliamentary party heard him out in stunned silence — astonished as much by the timing and manner of Lemass's going as by the ferocity of MacEntee's speech. Dicky Gogan TD immediately protested against the tenor of MacEntee's remarks, and then Lynch was proposed and seconded by Tommy McEllistrim TD and Eugene Kilbride TD, respectively. Aiken spoke 'at some length' to express his support for Colley. He objected to the manner in which Lynch had been selected and expressed his detestation of the 'tyranny of consensus'. He was supported by Bobby Molloy, who called for strong leadership rather than a *'via media'* leader. Seán Flanagan tried without success for an immediate vote to end the 'acrimonious debate', and Paddy Smith supported Colley in terms that are not recorded but can readily be imagined.

Kevin Boland then intervened to contradict part of Aiken's speech, indicating that he had telephoned Aiken in New York but that Aiken had declined to go forward (this implies, although without much clarity, that he asked Aiken to stand). The newspapers, Boland alleged, had been dictating candidates to them, and he had no love for a leader 'who lusted for power, or the methods adopted to further his candidature.'

At this point MacEntee indicated that he would be supporting Lynch. Lynch's victory, by now a certainty, was established by 59 votes to Colley's 19. Later, MacEntee came to Lemass to shake his hand and to express his regret for any personal slight he might have taken from his remarks. Lemass, who had once described his colleague in the Dáil as 'the minor poet', is supposed to have commented equably: 'Typical MacEntee: always said the wrong thing, did the right thing!'[55] And his verdict on Lynch, before the tumultuous days of 1969–71, was that he was 'if anything a tougher individual than I am.'[56]

At his final press conference Lemass maintained stoutly that his resignation had been for political rather than for personal reasons and that his 'general health' was 'quite good'. It was certainly true that political considerations were primary: his privately declared desire to give his successor two clear years in office was the principal one. His comment on his own health, however, was carefully understated: none of the journalists picked up the careful qualification in the reference to his 'general' health.

On 10 November, at 10:33 a.m., Lemass stood up in the Dáil chamber and announced, with his customary penchant for brevity: 'I have resigned.'

THE LAP OF HONOUR

No sooner had he resigned than the business invitations began to flow. He joined the board of McDonagh and Boland, with which there was a Haughey connection — and indeed a McDonagh connection, through his sister-in-law Moll (McDonagh) Lemass — as early as 15 November,[57] and by the end of December 1966, when he joined the board of Unidare, he was already a director of seven other companies.

His association with the McGrath family was reflected in his directorship of Waterford Glass; Dermot Ryan, an admirer for many years, invited him to join Ryan's Tourist Holdings; James H. North and Company, the auctioneers, gave him, as well as a directorship, a small office on the top floor of the firm's building in Dame Street; and other directorships included Electrical Industries of Ireland and United Breweries.[58] Subsequent directorships included the Bateman organisation (January 1967), from which he was to resign in 1968 following a takeover; Irish Security Services (1970); Cement-Roadstone (1970); Wavin Pipes; and John D. Carroll Catering Ltd.

The rapidity with which he acquired these directorships is indicative of a certain anxiety on his part, if not for himself then at least for his wife. One businessman who asked him after his retirement why he had accepted directorships of companies that were relatively small, and so shortly after his retirement, was told: 'I was afraid no-one else would ask me.'[59] The self-deprecatory tone did not entirely hide the combination of anxiety and modesty that attended this last career move. Later, at an informal post-retirement meeting in the Irish Management Institute, he was in a more ebullient mood when he was asked why he had taken so many directorships. In the first place, he replied, he wanted some reason to get up in the morning, and secondly, he could use the money.[60] Bobby Molloy, however, who as a young TD shared a small office and a fraction of a secretary in Leinster House with the former Taoiseach, remembers the endless stream of letters Lemass patiently dictated turning down offers of other directorships.[61]

'None of us', Lemass had remarked presciently at the outset of his period as Taoiseach, 'came into politics for the sake of its precarious rewards.'[62] In fact after his resignation he lost some of his savings when he invested them, somewhat unwisely, on the basis of an old friendship, and this loss made him feel to some extent insecure.[63] Todd Andrews's judgment on this aspect of his life was bleak and may have been conditioned to some extent by the known coolness between Lemass and Aiken, with whom Andrews had a special relationship.

> He came to office a poor man, and was a poor man when he left it, but in his later years he accepted the ability to make money as a criterion of success in others.[64]

Lemass announced in January 1969 that he would not contest the forthcoming general election,[65] but he had not been politically inactive in the interim. Much of his energies had gone into the work of the all-party Committee on the Constitution, which he joined immediately after his resignation, taking the place of Don Davern, who had become a parliamentary secretary in the ensuing reshuffle. It was an interesting committee, in that the Fianna Fáil membership for the most part comprised young parliamentarians who had been hand-picked by Lemass. It was also an informal committee, which meant that the Dáil parties would not be bound by its findings. This in itself prompted an easy-going atmosphere, in which a useful amount of work was done, although it devoted an inordinate amount of space in its final report to the sensitivities of politicians about media criticism.

The Lemass of the committee was, to the surprise of some of its members, a dramatically different man from the Lemass of the Department of Industry and Commerce or the Taoiseach's office. The clipped, laconic style and sense of personal reserve and distance had been replaced by an unbuttoned affability. 'Often, before committee meetings, he would be extremely relaxed, chatting and reminiscing. There would be times when George Colley, as chairman, would have to suggest mildly to him that perhaps it would be a good idea for business to start.'[66] He even treated members of the committee to a disquisition on his current reading.

> On one of these occasions he revealed that he had been reading a history of the Egyptian dynasties. As we wondered what this was in aid of, he remarked that every couple of hundred years or so one of the great Egyptian rulers had built a pyramid or some great monument of that kind. What — he wondered out loud — had been happening in between? The answer he gave was that there was 'probably a crowd of politicians trying to make the damn thing work.' It was plain that he regarded himself as one of the 'crowd of politicians' rather than a Pharaoh.[67]

Lemass was almost certainly the unnamed source for suggestions in articles by Michael McInerney, political correspondent of the *Irish Times,* about his own agenda in setting up the committee. One of his ideas, apparently, had been to set up a committee of electors as part of a new system of presidential election. McInerney suggests that Lemass backed away from this idea in the wake of de Valera's exceptionally narrow victory in 1966.

It also included a number of critical issues in trade union law. One of them related to article 40.6.1, under which two landmark cases had been heard. In the first, in 1947, the National Union of Railwaymen had defeated one of the provisions of the Trade Union Act, 1941, setting up a tribunal that could give particular unions the sole right to organise workers of any particular class. In a later case, involving the Educational Company of Ireland Ltd in 1962, the same constitutional provision had been successfully invoked to prevent picketing intended to force workers to join a union. The NUR case in particular had acted to frustrate Lemass's plans (although the Bill was actually shepherded through the Dáil by MacEntee) to weld trade unionists into a coherent body with which the Government could negotiate in the confidence that agreements arrived at would be adhered to.

In the wake of the Educational Company decision in 1962 Lemass had personally inaugurated discussions with the ICTU to see what kind of law could be passed to meet the situation that had arisen. The ICTU was slow to take up his offer to prepare draft legislation to suit their own interests, but a working party under the chairmanship of the Attorney-General did produce a scheme for a Bill that was subsequently sent to the ICTU and the Federated Union of Employers. It was never introduced in the Dáil and was still hanging fire when the Committee on the Constitution met some four years and a general election later. When the committee came to discuss it the only consensus it could achieve was that 'it would be very difficult to draft a constitutional amendment to cover the [Educational Company] point without going into a degree of detail in regard to trade union activities which would be inappropriate in the text of a Constitution.'[68]

According to T. F. O'Higgins, the senior Fine Gael member of the committee, he and Lemass virtually ran the committee as leaders of their respective groups. When it came to the question of electoral reform, Lemass's view was that 'with the kind of system we had there would always be a problem in persuading people of the right calibre to stand, so that they would be available for Cabinet.'[69] One option, however, had been ruled out: when the 'straight vote' was being discussed, Lemass was blunt: 'The people have decided that. It's as dead as the dodo.'[70] O'Higgins came to the conclusion that Lemass now favoured the alternative vote in single-seat constituencies, which later became known as the Norton Amendment and as such was narrowly defeated in Jack Lynch's Government. The approach finally adopted by the committee was to eschew a recommendation; but the order in which they listed their recommendations was a lightly coded guide to their preferences.

Lemass also supported the recommendation on divorce that emerged from the committee's deliberations. This recommendation, largely drafted by the committee's secretary, J. C. Holloway, was a peculiar attempt at compromise, which envisaged the possibility of allowing divorce but only to those citizens whose religion did not forbid it. The legal and administrative complications such a solution would have brought in its train were not difficult to identify, and while O'Kennedy — a barrister — opposed it, Lemass supported it, 'probably on the grounds that any change was better than no change.'[71] Another possible reason for supporting it would have been that the subject would at long last be placed on the public agenda in an unambiguous way, and indeed the negative reaction to the particular solution that was proposed did inspire a detailed public debate, although the relevant section of the Constitution was not to be changed until 1995.

Free from the responsibilities of office, Lemass was still sanguine, believing that the problem of the North would be solved, if it could be solved, through negotiations between the principal centres of political power. In private he had already been heard to refer unflatteringly to some Nationalist politicians as 'old women',[72] and in a speech at Queen's University in October 1967 he made a similar point in a more oblique way, blaming politicians of all parties for their unwillingness to look beyond religious labels.[73] And he remained sceptical — to put it no more strongly — about the efficacy of the political representatives of the Northern minority.

Nationalist politicians were quick to respond. Eddie McAteer at first contented himself with describing the former Taoiseach's remarks as unfortunate.[74] Gerry Fitt went one better by drawing attention to the fact that Lemass was now a director of a Northern company and had been met in Belfast by Robin Kinahan, a businessman and former Unionist lord mayor of the city.[75] McAteer, perhaps unwilling to be outflanked on this issue, returned to the fray a few days later, charging that Lemass had not got his facts right and was ingratiating himself with the Unionists by tarring everyone with the same brush.[76]

Lemass underestimated, at least at first, the impact of the nascent civil rights movement. Commenting on the early rumblings of the movement during an interval in a board meeting in 1968, he expressed his belief that 'two or three wet days will finish things.'[77]

One other reported episode with a bearing on Northern policy is, on the face of it, inexplicable. In January 1978 Lemass's daughter, Peggy Lemass-O'Brien, wrote to the press to comment on remarks by the journalist John Healy and by Paddy Harte TD of Fine Gael in separate reviews of Kevin Boland's book Up Dev. Her father, she said, viewed the EEC as the 'strongest single instrument which could help persuade the British to withdraw from Ireland.' This sentiment was unexceptional, and indeed is supported by many of the policies Lemass adopted during his political career. Two other recollections, however, gave rise to controversy. One was a prediction, which she said her father had made on the day Jack Lynch was elected in 1966, that the nationalists in the North were at the limit of their endurance. Lemass had added, according to this account: 'They will rise up in 1969; there will be no end to the bloodshed and it will continue in various forms until the British withdraw.'[78] The other was that

> in an effort to copperfasten that idea, he paid a visit to leaders of each of the six EEC countries and told them that when we came to conduct our negotiations we would insist that if at some later date Britain's application was accepted, that the Six would have to ensure the departure of British troops from Irish soil before we could accept partnership with her in the EEC. Both Adenauer and de Gaulle promised enthusiastic support for this stance, as did the other leaders of the Six.

The problem about this statement is that, if it was made in 1966, it predated other statements in 1967 and 1968 that provide evidence of a rather different thinking on these issues. Nor did Lemass express such sentiments, or anything remotely resembling them, in his lengthy series of interviews with Michael Mills published early in 1969. When it was reported in 1978 the media immediately raised the matter with Lynch, who had accompanied Lemass on many of his visits to Continental capitals. Lynch, although he carefully noted that he was not aware of any private discussions Lemass might have had either with his own family or with European leaders, said he had never heard the then Taoiseach making the departure of British troops a condition of EEC membership.[79] On the other hand, Lemass's public position had hardened perceptibly by late 1969, a year in which he made a point of publicly criticising discrimination against Northern nationalists, which existed 'to a degree evident nowhere else in the world.'[80] It is certainly possible that in private discussions with both de Gaulle and Adenauer the role of perfidious Albion might have been discussed; the leaders of both countries had their own reasons for suspecting British motives and for offering private support for the Irish position on partition to the extent that it brought further pressure to bear on Britain.

Lemass had regular monthly lunches with Brian Lenihan at the Intercontinental (now Jury's) Hotel in Ballsbridge. One of these meetings took place in the immediate aftermath of the first phase of the arms crisis, when his son-in-law, Charles Haughey, was dismissed from the Government by Jack Lynch, together with Neil Blaney, and when Kevin Boland resigned. According to Lenihan, Lemass was considerably distressed by this turn of events but expressed the view that if people's motives for what they had done had not been unworthy he was to some extent reassured.[81] What is less well known is that Lemass and Lynch had a meeting at which the matter was discussed.[82] Lemass's advice to his successor on that occasion could have been predicted fairly closely by anyone familiar with his record: 'You're the Taoiseach: do what you have to do.'[83]

It would not, in any case, have been Lemass's style to make public statements that would create political embarrassment for his successor. His somewhat slighting reference to Northern politicians — nationalist as well as unionist — during his Belfast visit in 1967 was a notable exception to this general rule. He preferred, for the most part, to contribute his remaining political energies to the European movement, which was by then largely uncontroversial.

After his retirement Lemass's view of the United Nations and of Europe, and of Ireland's role in relation to both, was thoughtful and oriented towards the future. He knew that the small European states no longer held the position they had for a few years at the end of the fifties and believed that one of the disadvantages of the Hammarskjöld era had been that the world was led to expect too much of the organisation and then became disappointed. On the vexed question of Irish adherence to the American line he argued in a later interview — it is hard to imagine that his tongue was not at least partly in his cheek — that 'we've usually found the United States to be prepared to take the line that we ourselves are taking.'[84]

His commitment to the EEC not only remained strong but, if anything, became stronger. 'If political unification of Western Europe is ever brought about,' he argued, 'and we participate in it, as we should, then that means that we must participate in all respects and this would include a European defence system wherever it may be required.' He even went so far as to envisage that it would be possible 'to preserve a lively interest in the development of national cultures ... and at the same time to be tuned into the idea of integrating all the peoples of Western Europe into one State. That State, which would be a very powerful state in the economic sense, as well as multi-cultural, should develop a commitment to the improvement of the lot of mankind all over the world.'[85]

Four decades earlier, in his memorandum on economic policy for the party, the young Lemass had held out the social and economic cohesion of the United States and the pan-European ideals of the then French Minister for Foreign Affairs, Aristide Briand, as valuable and important ideals and objectives. He was now, in a sense, back to the point from which he had started.

His resignation as Taoiseach gave him more free time than he had ever had to spend, especially with his family. His children recall that his life with Kathleen was a tranquil one: they would even find him on occasion, when they turned up at his home in Rathfarnham, wielding the vacuum-cleaner.

He was able to go horse-racing again, not only in Ireland but abroad; trips to Longchamps were occasionally on the agenda. It was a pleasure he had largely denied himself as Taoiseach, because he felt it was inconsistent with the dignity of the office. He even had a part share in a somewhat erratically performing racehorse with the fish merchant Frank Hardy. It was named 'Credibility' and was trained by Michael Collins at the Curragh. In June 1969 he won £531 when he drew a 100 to 1 outsider in the sweepstake on the Irish Sweeps Derby.

He never expected special treatment. He was a keen follower of the Irish rugby team and always received complimentary tickets for internationals from the IRFU but never complained about the fact that these were high up in the stands, although the effort involved for him in climbing up the steep concrete steps was considerable.

By now his health was steadily disimproving, although he minimised the discomfort he was experiencing. He attended a rugby international in Lansdowne Road in February 1971, and the effort involved in climbing to his seat made him feel unwell enough to go to his doctor, Bryan Alton, the following Monday for a check-up. 'You have five minutes,' he told Alton. Later, referring to the imminent collapse of one of his lungs, he told his family cheerfully: 'The bird can fly on one wing.' Alton insisted that he enter the Mater Hospital for further investigation of his condition; he was never to leave it.

His health declined slowly and inexorably during his last stay in hospital. As always, he insisted on minimising his medication: he wanted to remain conscious and in control of his faculties at all times. He continued to have visitors. One was the young Seán Sherwin, who saw him just before leaving on his honeymoon. Sherwin expressed concern about articles 2 and 3 of the Constitution, which had been increasingly discussed in the context of constitutional revision since the publication of the committee's report in 1967. 'They're not as important as they're made out to be,' Lemass commented enigmatically.[86] Another visitor was Brian Lenihan, who went into the hospital on the Saturday before Lemass died. Lemass, he said, knew already that he was going to die. Sitting in a chair in his dressing-gown, he did a series of quick permutations on that day's races, covering every race on the card, and then sent Lenihan out to a bookie's shop on the corner to place the bet. 'There wasn't a tenner in it,' Lenihan said. 'He did it just for the fun of it.'[87]

His family got a strong sense from him that he wanted to cease treatment that was not only increasingly inconvenient but was reducing him to the status of a helpless invalid. He also insisted that there should be no pomp and circumstance associated with his funeral,[88] and that he did not want to be buried in the Republican plot in Glasnevin.

He died in the early hours of 11 May 1971. His death certificate described him as a company director and gave the cause of death as pyopneumothorax — in effect, his lungs had finally collapsed. Although no announcement had been made about the route, crowds emerged to watch the hearse as it brought his body from the Mater Hospital back to Churchtown. In Camden Street, in the heart of his old constituency, the crowds were immense, and even Todd Andrews, whose own view of Lemass was sometimes jaundiced, was driven to admit: 'Fair play to him: he was a Dub.'[89]

All the national papers, and almost all political leaders, were generous in their tributes. The *Irish Times* said he had 'left his country a better, healthier and richer nation than he found it.' Its rival, the *Irish Independent,* noted that he had 'left his mark on this country and it is a better place to live in for what he did.'[90] Michael Mills, in the *Irish Press's* tribute, scattered the adjectives like rose petals: 'He could be gruff, charming, incisive, intuitive, astute and pragmatic, but he could never be bitter or malicious.'[91] Two of his contemporaries, C. S. Andrews and Seán MacEntee, contributed their appreciations. MacEntee's was, if anything, the kinder: despite the 'strong bias in favour of the worker and organised labour' that he perceived in his old colleague he was a man who had been 'as cynically realistic as an Elizabethan' and who, had he not gone into politics, would have been the Henry Ford of Ireland, or a great scientist.

In the Dáil, Brendan Corish, leader of the Labour Party, offered an almost wistful adieu. 'If he had been Taoiseach at an earlier age, it might have been a somewhat different Ireland ... It might have been a somewhat different Parliament.'[92] Liam Cosgrave referred to him in warmer tones than any Fine Gael figure had ever used about a Fianna Fáil Taoiseach and certainly in far warmer phrases than that employed by his later coalition Government to mark de Valera's passing. He saluted in particular Lemass's 'lack of any kind of pretentiousness' and the 'immense contribution he made to social and economic improvement.'[93] In a sense he was repaying the compliment paid by Lemass as Taoiseach to the memory of his own father, W. T. Cosgrave, when he died in 1965. On that occasion Lemass had asked the Dáil to accept a 'departure from parliamentary precedent' in order to mark Cosgrave's work and influence. He paid a particular tribute to 'the grace with which he handed over responsibility when the people so willed' and the 'dignity with which he carried out his duties as leader of the opposition.' These, Lemass observed, in words probably never before uttered by one Civil War veteran about another, were 'the elements of a legacy which we in Ireland, and indeed people who value freedom and democracy everywhere, will forever cherish.'[94]

Tomás Mac Giolla, the president of the Gardiner Street wing of the recently sundered Sinn Féin, rejected the popular mood in dramatic fashion. Lemass, he said, would be remembered as the man who opened the floodgates to foreign speculators, signed the new Act of Union with Britain, opened the way to federal talks with O'Neill, began the move to place Ireland under EEC control, split the trade union movement, and always backed capital and big business. Taking their cue from Mac Giolla's hostile remarks, Sinn Féin members later hung derogatory banners along part of Lemass's funeral route through Stillorgan. Even allowing for political hyperbole, Mac Giolla's broadside would have struck few people as appropriate in the circumstances.

Lemass's will, when it was probated six years later, certainly underlined the fact that he had not made money out of politics, or out of anything else. It left everything to his widow. His estate was £43,586 — an almost identical figure, as it turned out, to that left by his brother Frank, the former general manager of CIE. In 1996 terms it would amount to £350,900 — smaller than the estate of most substantial farmers and roughly equivalent to that of a well-insured senior civil servant. His comfortable but by no means ostentatious bungalow in Rathfarnham would have accounted for part of that total. It was a modest enough finale for a man who was, at heart, essentially modest himself.

11

Conclusion

The Politics of Change and the Paradox of Progress

History is always to some extent what we make it, an attempt by the present generation to take possession of the past and to use it as a way of helping us to understand the modern world, and even as a route map to the future. The paradox is that research into verifiable historical facts, of which there is a virtually infinite number, often increases ambiguity rather than certainty, as explanations once confidently advanced fall victim to fresh revelations and new hypotheses. This can also be true of biography, especially if biographical study is driven by the belief that the actions of men and women necessarily form part of a seamless, emotionally and intellectually coherent mesh of motives and circumstances.

Allied to this is the need, more often felt than openly expressed, to encapsulate complex historical events and phenomena in the persona of one particular individual or to use one particular leader to buttress a wider ideological analysis. Seán Lemass's pivotal position in Irish history, on the cusp of the post-revolutionary period, makes him a particularly valuable prize to be fought over. The apparent accessibility of his career, on the other hand — in contrast to the ambiguities of de Valera and the unachieved promise of Collins — also operates to conceal an enigma that can never be entirely explained in terms of his own motivation and record and that demands a fuller understanding of the social and political environment within which he operated.

In Lemass's case analysis is further complicated by the fact that for thirty-three years — a generation, in fact — he operated in the shadow of de Valera, who was seventeen years older than him; to be the 'Benjamin' of the Fianna Fáil governments, as de Valera described him, was to embody a special role and place in governments that were themselves characterised, certainly in the thirties, by exceptional youthfulness, combativeness, and vigour.

The temperamental and psychological contrasts between Lemass and de Valera, while undoubtedly real and significant, sometimes act as too convenient a peg on which to hang an examination of their differences. The

348

sheer physical contrast, in 1959, between the ailing and almost blind Taoiseach and his forceful, crisp heir-apparent has always been seductive for analysts, especially those who used each man as an exemplar of his generation. At one level this produces stereotypes such as those contained in the 1963 assessment by *Time,* contrasting de Valera, 'the aloof, magnetic revolutionary with a martyr's face and a mystic's mind ... doggedly indifferent to the country's plight' with the 'reticent, pragmatic planner ... more Gallic than Gaelic ... of a belated industrial revolution.'[1]

It was too much to expect that such a chiaroscuro portrait would long survive Lemass's departure from power; and a contemporary generation of historians, more radical and revisionist than those of an older school, have argued that Lemass represented the 'humane, social-democratic face of Fianna Fáil's modernising mission.'[2] In their view it was also a face that masked an attempt to persuade organised workers and the socially marginalised that it was Fianna Fáil, rather than any Irish variant of socialism, that offered the best hope for authentic social and economic progress. An even more critical version of this analysis suggests that a neo-corporatist approach, of which Lemass was the exemplar, was actively encouraged by a union leadership anxious to outflank its own militants and secure significant power in the general area of economic management.[3]

On a more subliminal level, partition and Northern Ireland policy generally became another kind of battleground. Lemass's quick and imaginative response to the invitation from Terence O'Neill for a meeting in 1965 certainly caught the imagination of an electorate for which the whole partition issue had for decades been steadily diminishing in interest and relevance. It was easy too to contrast the speed with which Lemass swung into action on this issue with the immobilism of his predecessor, and even to assume that the differences in tactics signified a difference also in strategy and even in objectives. This would, however, be in some respects unfair to de Valera, in that he too had made attempts to open up channels of communication with the political representatives of the Northern majority, right up to the point of his own retirement in 1959.

Lemass's early invitations to Brookeborough, although never made directly, met the same fate as de Valera's initiatives. What brought about the thaw in the end was not only the personality differences between the two men (Lemass, after all, would have been in unionist eyes as much a 1916 activist as de Valera) but a complex and evolving political situation. Nor did Lemass first invite O'Neill to Dublin: had he done so, O'Neill would almost certainly have refused, and it would have made it far less likely that O'Neill would have invited Lemass north. In the end Dublin had to wait for Belfast to make the first move. O'Neill, in issuing the invitation, took a greater risk than Lemass did in accepting it, but Lemass's articulation of the principle of consent, in its own way, opened up a Pandora's box of issues that still influence national and international policy-making. There was, indeed still is, a tension between Lemass's refocusing on the need to secure unity by agreement and his stoutly expressed conviction that no minority had the right to vote themselves out of the nation.

There is another paradox in his attitude to the North, and it relates to the grounds on which he attacked political immobilism there. In 1969, as the civil rights movement was gathering momentum, he criticised Northern politicians of all parties because they found it 'easier to rely on the religious affiliation of constituents rather than refer ... to serious economic and social problems.'[4] He saw no contradiction, on the other hand, between criticising religion as the basis for political loyalty in the North and promulgating nationalism as the binding agent for political activity in the Republic. It was almost as if he were advocating, for the solution of the North's political problems, the emergence of the class politics that he so often decried as obsolete in the Republic.

If many people thought Lemass was different from de Valera, perhaps it was in part because they wanted him to be different. As the older man receded into the shadows, Lemass and his legacy would be claimed as a national asset, and not only by his own party, who were happy to accept the rationalisations for policy changes that he so expertly articulated for them. The fact that an economist who voted for Lemass in 1961 could become Taoiseach in a Government led by Fine Gael in 1981 is a small but significant indicator of the way in which Irish politics might have developed in different circumstances. If there was one sense above all in which Lemass towered above not only many of his political opponents but also many of his contemporaries in Fianna Fáil it was in his conscious and programmatic conclusion that raking over the embers of the Civil War was not only politically sterile but nationally counterproductive.

T. P. Kilfeather, who as a political journalist probably knew Lemass as well as anyone outside politics, expressed his astonishment, in an article written on Lemass's death, that the former Taoiseach had so rarely referred to history in his speeches. In the speech in Belfast just mentioned, Lemass had gone even further, arguing that Ireland's outlook for the future would have to be that history did not matter — or at least that there was no problem from history that could not be resolved. Towards the end of his career Lemass had gone even further in an attempt to neutralise the malign aspects of history when he publicly expressed contrition for questioning the motives of men who had joined the British army, at least before 1916: 'It must, in their honour, and in fairness to their memory, be said that they were motivated by the highest purpose.'[5] As his successors in office were to find out, history could not be neutralised so readily.

Politics and history, however, are not about what might have been but about what was. This is the context in which a biographer has to attempt to explain Lemass's changes of direction and pace over half a century of direct involvement in public life, from the rooftop of the GPO in 1916 to the surrender of his seal of office as Taoiseach in November 1966. The young man who believed first in the need for armed rebellion to effect political change modulated into a politician who could hardly wait to get his hands on the control levers of a democratically constituted state. That politician in a hurry developed in turn into a senior minister and Taoiseach whose early views on the efficacy of governmental power evolved into a recognition that social and economic change was not the prerogative of politicians alone but of a whole range of institutions that could rarely be bullied and only occasionally seduced.

What he came to recognise too was that the motivation that had driven him and most of the men and women of his generation — and not only in his party — for half a century or more was weakening, that the nationalism and idealism that he shared not only with them but with key public servants such as T. K. Whitaker was becoming lethally vulnerable to the claims of special interests and the industrially powerful on both sides of the negotiating table. Almost his last act as Taoiseach was to charge the newly established Economic and Social Research Institute with the task of carrying out research into the motivations of peoples' economic behaviour and choices. It was almost as if he recognised that what had driven him was no longer driving the majority of his fellow-citizens; and the search for a restored sense of national motivation and purpose was paramount.

The paradox was that the sectional interests that he felt were in danger of running out of control were partly the product of the revolution he had engendered. That was not only a revolution in economic activity but also a revolution in confidence. In the nineteen-fifties, when nothing seemed to be going right, for Fianna Fáil or for inter-party Governments, he had at first preached the need for productivity: it was, for him, a more acceptable platform than that of retrenchment, from which most of his colleagues spoke. In his last term as Minister for Industry and Commerce in 1957–59 he sidelined many of the abstractions of economics in favour of an overt appeal to self-esteem and public confidence. Even as he was about to leave office he was castigating 'the old slave spirit'[6] as something that had to be eradicated from the collective Irish psyche. The rhetoric of economic self-sufficiency gave way not only to a new international perspective focused on Europe but to a powerful ideal of psychological and imaginative self-sufficiency. Although he intended this to drive economic progress, it also acted to generate unreal expectations and economic conflict, whose full dimensions were becoming apparent only as he retired.

Lemass's own political and economic ideas evolved from the *dirigisme* of the early years, at least up to 1948, and the anxiety to plug the gaps in economic development by the development and growth of the state companies, to the managerialist approach of the sixties. It does not admit of any one-dimensional explanation, or even consistency, beyond his overriding need to find the best recipe for economic progress. It would plainly be ahistorical to put it all down to a grand design, driven by a rootless and cynical desire to exploit those political and social trends that offered the best prospect of electoral success at a given time, from the nationalist populism of the thirties to the febrile acquisitiveness of the sixties. It would be simplistic to explain it all in terms of personal psychology, as an example of the route march of an individual brought face to face with political and economic problems less susceptible of easy or radical answers than he at first suspected. It would be tempting, but ultimately unrewarding, to portray Lemass as the man thrown up by a bourgeois-dominated political and economic system whose historic role was to copperfasten the political and economic position of privileged groups in society: at the very least this would be to deny him the autonomy of thought and action that he plainly regarded as central to his own philosophy.

That autonomy was, however, necessarily limited, both by the social and economic circumstances in which he operated and by the political realities he had to face. One of the central factors here was the emergence and development of Fianna Fáil and of his role within it. The study of this phenomenon, however, has been hampered by a number of factors, chief among which has been the quite extraordinary reticence of the first wave of Fianna Fáil politicians about the nature and extent of the divergences on social and economic issues that, of necessity, marked a group of people characterised accurately as 'politicians by accident'.[7] The public archives hold papers from Seán MacEntee and C. S. Andrews, as well as those of Frank Aiken, which will be released towards the end of 1997. They also contain papers from many opponents of Fianna Fáil, such as Desmond FitzGerald, Richard Mulcahy, and Ernest Blythe. With the exception of the MacEntee papers, however, little is available that might throw light on the internal disagreements of these warrior politicians. Their natural tendency to close ranks against the outside world was also case-hardened by the embattled frame of mind in which Fianna Fáil took office in 1932 as a minority government.

Lemass himself, in opposition in 1948, referred publicly to the intensity of their disagreements but was understandably silent about the issues involved, preferring to contrast the public unity of the 1932–48 Fianna Fáil government with the Hydra-like aspect of its successor. Brian Farrell sees the Lemass-MacEntee tension as a central one, as it undoubtedly was. Tim Pat Coogan, in his biography of Éamon de Valera, tends to see the political tension as subsisting more between his subject and Lemass. But the archival records themselves are very telegrammatic as guides to the strains within such a group of strong-minded people, and not even the release of the records of the Fianna Fáil parliamentary party and National Executive, admirable in themselves, are enough to complete a tantalisingly sketchy picture.

All that can be said with any certainty is that any view of the history of Fianna Fáil, and of Lemass's place within that history, that is presented principally as a Lemass-MacEntee conflict or a Lemass-de Valera conflict is reductionist in the extreme. If Lemass can be taken fairly to represent a strongly interventionist and even statist centre of influence within early Fianna Fáil governments, and MacEntee the orthodox, 'sound money' approach so ably represented in public administration by the towering presence of J. J. McElligott, this by no means exhausts the range of opinions present. There were the undoubtedly quirky financial and other ideas of Frank Aiken, who was Minister for Finance himself for a period. There were also at least two divergent currents of opinion on the optimum direction for economic development, which pitted Gerald Boland and Oscar Traynor, who favoured a decentralised industry based primarily on natural resources, against Lemass, who evinced a predilection for manufacturing industry — based if necessary on imported raw materials — and for industrial concentration. There was the powerful agricultural presence within the parliamentary party and the Government, which could rely on de Valera's support whenever proposals for industrial development held out the prospect of even more rapid rural depopulation than was already taking place. And above all was the figure of de Valera himself, whose preferred technique for party management seemed to be to allow the protagonists to talk themselves into a state of near-exhaustion.

It was a battleground on which Lemass lost at least as many battles as he won. On the other hand it is arguable that de Valera's role in this was critical in a way that is different from what it is generally supposed to have been. He may have acted on occasion to frustrate and delay Lemass's plans and proposals, as the historical record plainly indicates; but Lemass could not have won the battles he did, or become as powerful as he did — much less de Valera's actual successor — without at least the implicit support, on a number of key issues, of his party leader. That support in turn would not have been forthcoming if de Valera had not believed Lemass to be basically sound, especially on the national issue, which had become for him the touchstone of fidelity to the authentic national tradition.

A central factor equally was Lemass's early acceptance, as the heady rush of revolution turned into the grinding business of politics, that Fianna Fáil was not just a useful vehicle but essentially the only one that offered him a realistic prospect of implementing any of his ideals. This led him to accept a series of compromises and to overlook the implicit conflicts between certain policies, at least for as long as these conflicts had no deleterious electoral consequences.

The early emphasis on protection, for example, while it promoted a policy of national self-sufficiency, could also lead to industrial inefficiency, profiteering, and sluggishness. It ran counter to the — as yet infant — policy of promoting exports, other than agricultural exports to Britain, which of course were in a special category. It also had serious implications for the Government's policy on partition. The political and social emphasis on the need for dispersal of industries had potentially negative effects, not only because it militated against the development of certain kinds of industries, which required a high degree of concentration or immediate access to major urban markets, but because in Gaeltacht areas — to the extent to which it was successful — it would imperil the second Fianna Fáil national aim of retaining and strengthening the Irish language.

The generally unresolved tension between Lemass's perceived need for a high degree of interventionist control in industrial development, and his Government colleagues' wariness about entrusting him with the powers he sought, ran the risk of creating a situation in which Lemass was mandated with the task of implementing an industrial policy and achieving certain objectives but shorn of many of the powers he deemed essential for success.

More significantly, the short-run successes of the new Fianna Fáil Government in stimulating economic activity, which were in some cases equally the product of external factors, masked the horrendous effects of the economic war with Britain (of which they were also in part a product) and tended to be credited exclusively to that party's policies, with the result that it became progressively more difficult to modify or abandon them when their usefulness could legitimately be queried. The same successes also produced political dividends for the government in the form of increased votes and seats, an elixir that few governments have ever been able to resist quaffing, while rarely pausing to read closely the small print on the label.

From 1938 onwards the record shows that Lemass was searching actively for new policy instruments to replace those of protection and restrictions on foreign investment that characterised Fianna Fáil's initial policies. The outbreak of war in 1939 and the electoral volatility that followed, however, substantially impeded his attempts to secure a broader base within the party for the review of these key policies. This process of policy review was itself impeded by the belief that the first inter-party Government was a historical and political aberration and the concomitant comforting but unsubstantiated belief that the electorate's decision had been unrelated to policy inadequacies.

Lemass's partial escape from politics into the congenial atmosphere of the *Irish Press*, while undoubtedly an enhancement to journalism, further postponed the vitally necessary task. It was not until 1954 that some basic tenets began to be questioned, and it was only in 1958 that the results of that questioning began to be incorporated in policy measures. 'The post-war period', Lemass said after his retirement, with noticeable understatement, 'was very difficult; it was hard to get coherent economic and social policies, criticism being generally of impracticality rather than of undesirability. The task of preparing the First Programme produced a change of approach within the Government. By that stage the emphasis was being increasingly given to economics.' He might have said, was being switched from politics to economics.

That switch was itself made possible by the ascendancy he had achieved within the party: it was the political return on the ideological and administrative compromises he had accepted. This is the common lot of politicians, even — perhaps especially — the most successful ones. The word most frequently used to describe Lemass, especially since 1959, has been 'pragmatic'. The problem with this word, of course, is that it begs a few important questions. It allowed those politically opposed to him to praise some of his policies without having to emulate his loyalty to Fianna Fáil. It allowed those within Fianna Fáil to accept radical policy reversals on the basis of Lemass's own soothing but misleading assurances that he was merely discarding one set of policies, not because they had failed but because they had achieved their objectives. And it allowed debate on the partition issue to explore new territory that had been closed off for years, with consequences that are still with us today.

By the time Lemass became Taoiseach, in 1959, he had come to realise that his options were at once narrower and broader than they had been. Narrower, because any government's capacity to influence the growth and development of a small open economy was in fact much more limited than traditional thinking (particularly within Fianna Fáil) had supposed it to be. Broader, because the world — or at least Europe — was now the stage for development, and the fixation on our nearest neighbour could be abandoned or at least radically modified. In his approach to decision-making in these crucial areas, Lemass differed profoundly — and not only in style — from his predecessor.

In the course of this refocusing of national objectives, Lemass tacitly abandoned at least one of his predecessor's core values: the belief that a high degree of control, both of economic and social policy, was not only necessary but possible for a small island nation. This was a strategy involving a greater degree of risk than de Valera was ever prepared to envisage, but in a sense it was not the gamble that Lemass's opponents assumed it to be but Hobson's choice. In two spheres in particular it was to have effects that were incalculable: the opening of the economy to foreign capital to a degree hitherto unimaginable, and the opening up of the partition debate within a framework that recognised for the first time the central role of unionism, just as that power was being challenged, as never before, from within.

He was not unaware of the dangers this posed, not just for politics in general but for Fianna Fáil in particular. 'There are new men coming into the party because of an intellectual choice, and not just because their fathers were in it,' he observed after his retirement. 'This is going to present an increasing problem of party management. At the moment the unity of Fianna Fáil is sound. I have never been able to pinpoint an individual who might become a source of Party weakness. But this could happen in the future.'[8]

His intuitive identification of party management as the problem of the future was prophetic. Many years later Pádraig Ó hAnracháin[9] contrasted Lemass's style with that of his successor. When Lemass accepted Paddy Smith's resignation, he pointed out, Charles Haughey had been appointed Minister for Agriculture within two hours. When Neil Blaney made a speech in Letterkenny at which he had implicitly challenged Lynch's Northern policy, Ó hAnracháin met the Taoiseach as he arrived for work and asked him what he was going to do about his troublesome minister. 'Has he said something?' Lynch asked mildly.

The contrast was perhaps not quite all that Ó hAnracháin made it out to be. Lemass had, by some accounts, a drawerful of resignations from Smith — according to some accounts seventeen in all — none of which had been accepted. It was with the utmost difficulty that he told MacEntee, then seventy-six, on the eve of the 1965 election that he did not contemplate appointing him again to ministerial office. He was slow to change his Government even in 1961, when he had an electoral mandate. He was conscious of the fact that he did not embody the sort of magnetism that had made de Valera such a formidable party manager and may even have found the fractiousness of the parliamentary party towards the end of his term of office a tiring distraction from the business of running the country.

Jack Lynch rode out a more turbulent period in politics than Lemass had ever had to face. The nature of that turbulence had something to do, in the end, with the timing of his departure and with the choice of his successor. Charles Haughey's succession, however, had already been pencilled in by November 1966, and the timing of Lynch's departure was probably only marginally affected by events within the party. He was, after all, bowing to traditional political wisdom in allowing his successor a two-year run to the following general election.

This is not to say that Lemass was less successful than Lynch: that comparison would be invidious, in any case, in a book devoted primarily to the former. He was certainly more successful than Lynch in managing the succession, however tartly Todd Andrews and others may have commented on his apparent failure in this area. And the convulsions that subsequently racked the party had less to do with Lemass's alleged failure in this particular — as Andrews saw it — than with a whole series of externally fuelled political tensions that affected Fianna Fáil more visibly but affected all parties deeply.

The conventional wisdom is that Lemass came to power too late. It might be more accurate to say that by the time he reached it it was a different kind of power and exercised in a society of a complexity his predecessor had never had to try to understand. He opened up the country to change but was too frail, at the end of the day, to ride the whirlwind. The economy might have progressed even faster had he been able to escape earlier from the trammels of the policies he had so passionately believed in and enthusiastically implemented. If de Gaulle had not vetoed Britain's Common Market application in 1963, Lemass's vision would have been considerably closer to achievement by the time he left office; but luck plays a powerful role in politics, and Lemass's hand after 1963 was always short a few vital cards. One of his most specific economic contributions — the development and growth of the state sector — could be described by his critics as empire-building, but it was at one and the same time a Houdini-like escape from the policy limitations imposed on him by his more conservative Government colleagues and a policy that engendered, at the heart of one of the most conservative electorates in Europe, an affection for public enterprise (for good and, sometimes, for ill) that has left a permanent mark on Irish economic development.

His other abiding legacy is probably more psychological than economic but none the worse for that: the growth of a spirit of national self-confidence, which is thankfully still with us and in times he would have longed to see.

Appendix 1

Seán Lemass: Election Results 1924–65

	Seats	Lemass	Nearest rival	Vote as multiple of quota
1924 (Mar.)*	1	13,639	15,884	0.84
1924 (Nov.)	1	17,297	16,340	1.06
1927 (June)	7	8,522	8,183	1.29
1927 (Sep.)	7	11,240	9,400	1.65
1932	7	10,426	7,381	1.51
1933	7	14,716	7,596	1.94
1937	7	15,969	5,941	2.24
1938	7	14,151	6,877	2.06
1943	7	16,399	4,971	2.47
1944	7	15,385	4,322	2.50
1948†	5	13,274	4,931	1.79
1951	5	10,759	5,684	1.55
1954	5	7,753	7,474	1.32
1957	5	8,136	4,607	1.53
1961	5	10,211	7,007	1.91
1965	5	12,400	7,098	2.08

*Dublin South City. The 1924 elections were both by-elections.
†Dublin South-Central.

Source: Brian Walker (ed.), *Parliamentary Election Results in Ireland, 1918–1992,* Dublin: Royal Irish Academy 1994.

Appendix 2

Seán Lemass: Public Sector Income 1927-71

	Dáil allowance	Ministerial salary	Ministerial pension(s)	Military pension	Dáil pension	Total	Adjusted for consumer price index (1996)
	£	£	£	£	£	£	£
1927	360						13,280
1932		1,000		99		1,099	45,188
1937		1,700		99		1,799	68,313
1947		2,125		99		2,224	46,765
1948	624		500	99		1,223	24,905
1951		2,125		99		2,224	41,255
1954	624		500	150		1,274	30,176
1957		2,125		150		2,275	33,032
1960	1,000	3,000		167		4,167	57,675
1964	1,500	3,300		200		5,000	59,072
1966 (Oct.)	1,500	3,300		240		5,040	55,051
1966 (Nov.)	1,500	—	2,211	282		3,993	43,615
1968	2,500	—	2,211	282		4,993	50,481
1969 (June)	2,500	—	2,211	282		4,993	46,999
1969 (July)	—	—	3,610	310	1,667	5,587	52,560
1971	—	—	3,610	340	1,667	5,617	44,848

Note: All figures are rounded. Private income (directorships etc.) not ascertained.

Notes

Abbreviations

ADA	Armagh Diocesan Archives
CBP	Colm Barnes papers
FA	Franciscan Archives, Killiney
FF	Fianna Fáil Archives
ICA	Department of Industry and Commerce Archives
JFK	John F. Kennedy Library, Boston
LBJ	Lyndon Baines Johnson Memorial Library, Austin, Texas
LP	Lemass family papers
MA	Military Archives, Dublin
NA	National Archives, Dublin
NLI	National Library of Ireland
OHP	O'Halpin papers, UCD
PRO	Public Records Office, London
PRONI	Public Records Office, Northern Ireland
UCD	UCD Archives

Chapter 1 (p. 3–20)

1. Leo Flanagan interview.
2. Lee (1973), 149.
3. The league, established by the anti-Parnellite John O'Brien, was founded in 1898 and had a brief period of success before coming under the control of the Irish Party in 1902; Lee (1979), 122.
4. *Freeman's Journal,* 16 June 1899.
5. Interview with Lemass by Kees van Hoek, *Irish Times,* 17 Feb. 1971. An earlier date, 1820, is given in the obituary of Lemass published in *Éire-Ireland* (Bulletin of the Department of Foreign Affairs), no. 837, 18 June 1971.
6. Interview with Lemass by Brother Paul, *The Word,* Jan. 1966.
7. Lemass to Michael J. Lennon, 20 July 1959, LP.
8. The history of the Lemass family is drawn in part from an article by M. J. Lennon in *Father Mathew Record,* Apr. 1961.
9. O'Brien (1982), 35.
10. Daly (1984), 215.
11. Information from Moll Lemass (widow of Frank Lemass), 1 Mar. 1995.
12. Maureen Haughey interview.
13. This section is partly based on Skinner (1961), chap. 13.
14. Skinner (1961), 71.

15. Regina Roche, *The Children of the Abbey* (1798), quoted in Dillon (1909), 77.
16. Dillon (1909), 77.
17. Daly (1984), 239.
18. O'Brien (1982), 45.
19. Ibid., 40.
20. Ibid., 107.
21. Ibid., 110.
22. Information from Moll Lemass (widow of Frank Lemass), 27 Feb. 1995.
23. *Irish Times,* 14 June 1965.
24. O'Connor interview.
25. O'Doherty interview.
26. *The Word,* Jan. 1966.
27. *The Ionian,* New Rochelle, New York, 8 Oct. 1953; report of Lemass's speech at the conferring on him of an honorary doctorate.
28. Profile in *Sunday Review,* 15 July 1959.
29. This information has been extracted variously from the school records and the school's handbook for 1915, where he is erroneously referred to in the examination section as 'John T. Lemass'.
30. Brian Inglis in Cruise O'Brien (1960), 115.
31. Leo Flanagan interview.
32. Clery (1919), 131.
33. Daly (1984), 110.
34. Kearns (1994), 176, 192.
35. Mills, *Irish Press,* 20 Jan. 1969.
36. Obituary of Lemass, *Irish Press,* 12 May 1971.
37. Skinner (1961), 170.
38. *Irish Times,* 17 Feb. 1951.
39. Seán Lemass, interview with Brother Paul in *The Word,* Jan. 1966.
40. Ibid.
41. Seán Lemass, speech to Law Students' Debating Society, 18 Feb. 1966 (duplicated), CBP.
42. Skinner (1961), 170.
43. Seán Lemass, interview with Michael Mills, *Irish Press,* 20 Jan. 1969.
44. Unless otherwise indicated, details in this section are taken from 'I remember 1916' by Seán Lemass, *Studies,* spring 1966, 7–9.
45. Seán Lemass, interview with Michael Mills, *Irish Press,* 20 Jan. 1969.
46. Ibid.
47. Ibid.
48. FA, 1527/2: memoir of the War of Independence and the Civil War by Oscar Traynor. Later, and quite coincidentally, the Hanlons became close friends of Lemass.
49. O'Rahilly interview.
50. Seán Lemass, interview with Michael Mills, *Irish Press,* 20 Jan. 1969.
51. Ibid.
52. Ibid.
53. Skinner (1961), 173; letter from Robert Pringle, who was released from Richmond Barracks with Lemass, *Irish Times,* 8 May 1964.
54. Quoted in O'Brien (1982), 267.
55. Ibid.
56. Seán Lemass, speech to Law Students' Debating Society, 18 Feb. 1966.
57. Skinner (1961), 174.

58. Mills, *Irish Press,* 21 Jan. 1969.
59. Interview with Seán Lemass, 10 Dec. 1943, in connection with the Sinn Féin funds case, NA, 2B/82/116.
60. Mills, *Irish Press,* 21 Jan. 1969.
61. O'Doherty interview.
62. Sweetman interview.
63. Skinner (1961), 74.
64. Mills, *Irish Press,* 21 Jan. 1969.
65. O'Rahilly interview.
66. Skinner (1961), 175.
67. Ibid., 176.
68. Ibid.
69. Interview with Kees van Hoek, *Times Pictorial,* 4 Apr. 1953.
70. Richard Brinsley Sheridan, *The Works of Richard Brinsley Sheridan,* London: Ward Lock Bowden 1891, 64.
71. Ibid., 64.
72. Ibid., l–li.
73. *Evening Mail,* 12 Jan. 1920.
74. The programme for this event is in the possession of the O'Connor family.
75. Memoir by Oscar Traynor, FA, 1527/2.
76. Major Fitzpatrick to John T. Lemass, 10 Dec. 1920, LP.
77. Andrews papers, P91/135, UCD.
78. O'Doherty interview.
79. Family source.
80. Skinner (1961), 177.
81. O'Malley (1936), 207.
82. Skinner (1971), 179.
83. Letter from Eoin Duffy, Old IRA, to Colm Barnes, 16 Sep. 1982, CBP.
84. Browne (1981), 278.
85. *Irish Press,* 12 May 1971.
86. Autograph book in the possession of Mr O'Rourke's daughter, Máire O'Carroll.
87. Frank Carney's autograph book is in the possession of his nephew, Dr James Montague, Ederny, Co. Fermanagh.
88. Letter to author from Máire O'Carroll, 28 Nov. 1994.

Chapter 2 (p. 21–63)

1. Lemass in conversation with Colm Barnes, CBP.
2. Ibid.
3. The recollection of Mrs Richard Mulcahy—Jim Ryan's sister—as told to her son, Dr Risteard Mulcahy (conversation between Dr Mulcahy and the author, 15 May 1995).
4. Garvin (1996), 58–9.
5. Mills, *Irish Press,* 22 Jan. 1969.
6. Report of Garda Commissioner on security situation to government, 1931, NA, 96/6/31.
7. Andrews (1979), 222.
8. Younger (1970), 319.
9. Skinner (1961), 181.
10. Younger (1970), 333.

11. Boland interview.
12. Ibid.
13. Younger (1970), 347.
14. Skinner (1961), 182.
15. Information from Jim Fleming, Co. Laois, 4 June 1993.
16. *Irish Press,* 23 Mar. 1948.
17. NA, Department of Industry and Commerce, R312/67, letter from Lemass to Joseph Fleming, 11 Mar. 1959.
18. Mills, *Irish Press,* 22 Jan. 1969.
19. Andrews (1979), 259–60.
20. MA, lot 115.
21. See for example Col. D. Neligan to command intelligence officer, Dublin Command, 8 Oct. 1923, on interrogation and treatment of prisoners, MA, A/14/726.
22. Recollection of Joe O'Brien, former internee in Hare Park and the first councillor elected for Fianna Fáil in Limerick, as recounted by Mick Herbert, former Fianna Fáil TD, in conversation with the author, Dublin, 31 Aug. 1993.
23. Tim McGloughlin, grandson of Alf Mac Lochlainn, in conversation with the author, 6 May 1993.
24. Mills, *Irish Press,* 22 Jan. 1969.
25. Ibid.
26. Skinner (1961), 186.
27. O'Sullivan (1994), 21.
28. Kit Fox, Skerries, in conversation with the author, 12 Apr. 1995.
29. Skinner (1961), 187.
30. McCague (1994), 50.
31. *Irish Independent,* 25 Apr. 1924.
32. *Dáil Debates,* vol. 113, col. 452–4, 24 Nov. 1948. The reference is to the ambush by Free State forces during the IRA action in Enniscorthy in which O'Brien was killed.
33. *Dáil Debates,* vol. 208, 4 Mar. 1964; see also 'Backbencher', *Western People,* 14 Mar. 1964.
34. Typescript article by Prof. Tom Garvin, UCD, Jan. 1994.
35. Author's conversation with Michael Mills, 14 Jan. 1993.
36. Presidential address to 1959 ardfheis; text in NA, D/T S9361 I/64.
37. FF/887, FF/888, and FF/889.
38. Letter to author from Francis McKay, Donegal, 21 Oct. 1994.
39. Andrews (1983).
40. Sinn Féin Standing Committee minutes, 23 June 1924, NA, 2B/82/117. The minutes frequently refer to him as 'Seán T. Lemass'.
41. As told by Tommy Davy to Kevin O'Doherty (O'Doherty interview).
42. Letter from Mary O'Kelly to Kathleen Lemass, 11 May 1971, LP.
43. *Irish Independent,* 3 Mar. 1924.
44. John McCann, a founder-member of Fianna Fáil, on 'Bowman Saturday 8:30', RTE radio, 11 May 1996.
45. *Irish Independent,* 6 Mar. 1924.
46. Ibid., 12 Mar. 1924.
47. Family source.
48. *Irish Independent,* 7 Apr. 1924.
49. Ibid., 15 Apr. 1924.
50. Ibid., 21 Apr. 1924.

51. MA, letter from Kerry No. 1 Brigade, 17 Apr. 1924.
52. Skinner (1961), 185.
53. Quoted in *Irish Independent,* 12 May 1971.
54. O'Sullivan (1994), 25, says that the marriage took place in Westland Row church and that Gertrude O'Dea was bridesmaid. The details above, however, appear in the marriage register for the Church of the Holy Name for the date in question.
55. NLI, LO p 117 (66).
56. NLI, LO p 117 (122).
57. *Irish Times,* 10 Nov. 1924, quoted in Farrell (1991), 11.
58. Carroll (1993), 151.
59. John McCann, RTE radio, 11 May 1996.
60. Sinn Féin Standing Committee minutes, NA, 16 Mar. 1925; UCD, Fitzgerald papers, P80/847.
61. NA, 2B/82/117, Sinn Féin funds case, 1943.
62. Quoted in Murphy (1993), 146.
63. Sinn Féin Standing Committee minutes, NA, 15 Dec. 1924.
64. Ibid., NA, 15 Jan. 1926 (actually 25).
65. Farrell (1991), 12.
66. Sinn Féin Standing Committee minutes, NA, 4 May 1925.
67. His address at the time was Rokeby, Terenure Road. The house has since been demolished.
68. Murphy (1993), 150.
69. Ibid., 180.
70. Lyons (1971), 453.
71. Boland interview.
72. Comhairle na dTeachtaí minutes, 22 June 1925, FA, folder 356.
73. Ibid.
74. Comhairle na dTeachtaí, undated document on 'suggested lines of policy', 1925, FA, folder 357.
75. Comhairle na dTeachtaí minutes, 22 June 1925, FA, folder 356.
76. 30 Oct. 1925, UCD, FitzGerald papers, P80/847.
77. 21 Nov. 1925, UCD, FitzGerald papers, P80/847.
78. Intelligence summary, Jan. 1926, UCD, FitzGerald papers, P80/847.
79. *Irish Press,* 23 Nov. 1933.
80. *Irish Independent,* 19 Nov. 1925.
81. Mac Eoin (1980), 303. Price was to become a member of the IRA Army Council in the nineteen-thirties.
82. 20 Oct. 1925, UCD, FitzGerald papers, P80/847.
83. Army Intelligence, Eastern Command, S/12022, 10 Feb. 1926, quoted in Reynolds (1976), 40.
84. UCD, FitzGerald Papers, P80/875.
85. Comhairle na dTeachtaí minutes, 15 Nov. 1925, FA, folder 356.
86. O'Neill (1970), 240.
87. Comhairle na dTeachtaí minutes, 15 Nov. 1925, FA, folder 356.
88. Ibid.
89. Interview with Lemass in connection with Sinn Féin funds case, 10 Dec. 1943, NA, 2B/82/116. Aiken's letter on expulsion, *Irish Press,* 16 Nov. 1933.
90. Comhairle na dTeachtaí minutes, 28 June 1925, FA, folder 359.
91. *An Phoblacht,* 18 Oct. 1925.
92. Ibid., 16 Oct. 1925.
93. Farrell (1991), 14.

94. Farrell (1991), 14.
95. Murphy (1993), 155.
96. Maureen Haughey interview.
97. MacEntee papers, UCD, P67/443.
98. *An Phoblacht,* 19 Apr. 1926.
99. MacEntee papers, UCD, P67/443.
100. *Sunday Press,* 10 Nov. 1966.
101. John McCann, 'A fighter from his 'teens', *Sunday Press,* 10 Nov. 1966.
102. Raymond Foxall, 'On the Tin Lizzie trail with Seán Lemass', *Sunday Express,* 22 Oct. 1961.
103. McCann, *Sunday Press,* 10 Nov. 1966.
104. Interview by Gerry Moriarty with John Susie, Donegal, *Irish Times,* 1 Dec. 1995.
105. Boland interview.
106. John McCann, RTE radio, 11 May 1996.
107. Carty (1983), 94–7.
108. *Irish Times,* 9 June 1927.
109. Parliamentary party minutes, 22 June 1927, FF/437.
110. Ibid.
111. Gallagher manuscripts, NLI 18,339, 252.
112. Mac Eoin (1980), 303.
113. Ibid., 299.
114. Parliamentary party minutes, 22 June 1927, FF/437.
115. Vincent Browne, 'Lemass: a profile', *Nusight,* Dec. 1969.
116. 'Labour leader's letter—Fianna Fáil and coalition', *Irish Independent,* 23 Aug. 1927.
117. Letter from Duffy to Colm Barnes, 16 Sep. 1982, CBP.
118. Quoted in Farrell (1991), 21.
119. Records of attendance in FF/439.
120. FF/700. For further details of Lemass's organisational activity for the party see Horgan (1996), 36–45.
121. FF/702.
122. Parliamentary party minutes, 29 Nov. 1928, FF/438. The Free State army had in fact been reduced in strength from 50,000 in 1923 to 7,000 in 1927.
123. Ibid., 16 May 1929, FF/438.
124. Ibid., 5 July 1928, FF/438.
125. Ibid., 8 Nov. 1928, FF/438.
126. Ibid., 7 Mar. 1929, FF/438.
127. Ibid., FF/432.
128. General Committee minutes, 4 May 1928, FF/433.
129. Ibid., 6 Mar. 1931, FF/443.
130. Ibid., 16 Jan. 1931, FF/443.
131. *Irish Times,* 14 Sep. 1927.
132. General Committee minutes, 26 Feb. 1931, FF/443.
133. Ibid., 17 Apr. 1931, FF/443.
134. Parliamentary party minutes, 12 Oct. 1927, FF/442. Lemass was also appointed a member of the committees on the ESB, on finance, and on public accounts.
135. Parliamentary party minutes, 18 Oct. 1927, FF/442.
136. Ibid., 27 Apr. 1928, FF/442.
137. Report, 3rd ardfheis, FF 702.

138. *Connacht Tribune,* 10 Mar. 1928, quoted in Reynolds (1976), 186.
139. *Free Press,* Wexford, 23 May 1931, quoted in Reynolds (1976), 186.
140. Parliamentary party minutes, 27 Apr. 1928, FF/442.
141. Gallagher manuscripts, NLI 18,339. All subsequent references to the document are from this source.
142. Rolo (1974), 11.
143. Ibid., 14.
144. Parliamentary party minutes, 16 Nov. 1928, FF/442.
145. *Dáil Debates,* vol. 26, col. 639, 18 Oct. 1928.
146. Ibid., col. 830, 24 Oct. 1928.
147. Family source.
148. Farrell (1991), 26–7.
149. Speech to Belfast Newman Society, *Irish Press,* 12 Dec. 1956.
150. General Committee minutes, 8 May 1931, FF/443.
151. *Dáil Debates,* vol. 22, col. 1615, 21 Mar. 1928.
152. Ibid., col. 2165–9, 30 Mar. 1928.
153. Farrell (1991), 24.
154. *Dáil Debates,* vol. 22, col. 1618, 21 Mar. 1928.
155. Ibid., col. 1434–5, 20 Mar. 1928.
156. Taped interview with Lemass to history of Ireland 1913–39 class, TCD, 9 Jan. 1970, chaired by David Thornley; quoted in Reynolds (1976), 240.
157. *Irish Times,* 7 Sep. 1927, report of election meeting at Kilbeggan. According to press reports, Lemass addressed at least nine meetings in the last fourteen days of the campaign, many of them outside Dublin.
158. *Irish Independent,* 31 Aug. and 7 Sep. 1927.
159. Ibid., 6 Sep. 1927.
160. Ibid., 7 Sep. 1927.
161. *Irish Times* and *Irish Independent,* reports of meetings in Mullingar and Dublin, 7 Sep. and 8 Sep. 1927.
162. Farrell (1991), 22, 128.
163. Lemass in conversation with Colm Barnes, CBP.
164. Quoted in Daly (1992), 93.
165. Farrell (1991), 29.
166. *Dáil Debates,* vol. 36, col. 394, 20 Feb. 1931.
167. Ibid., vol. 23, col. 1435–51, 16 May 1928.
168. Ibid., vol. 24, col. 870–1, 18 July 1928.
169. 24 Mar. 1928.
170. 1 Dec. 1928.
171. O'Doherty interview.
172. Cosgrave interview.
173. *Irish Times,* 11 Jan. 1930. Fianna Fáil had earlier tried to hamper the appointment of a Nuncio, possibly in the knowledge that this new departure by the Vatican was less than popular with the Catholic hierarchy. See Keogh (1995).
174. General Committee minutes, 13 Jan. 1930, FF/443.
175. Meenan (1970), 141.
176. *Irish Times,* 15 Feb. 1932. Lemass's colleague Seán MacEntee was evidently so annoyed by this allegation that he subsequently analysed the first-preference votes in the election and—although he did not indicate how he ascertained the voters' religious allegiance—claimed that 'at least 640,000 Catholic voters' had voted for a change of government, as against 430,000 who had voted for Cosgrave; *Irish Times,* 22 Feb. 1932.

177. Mac Eoin (1980), 33.
178. Speech at Grand Canal Street, Dublin, *Irish Times*, 6 Feb. 1932.
179. Speech in Dublin, *Irish Times*, 10 Feb. 1932, and in Tullamore, *Irish Times*, 15 Feb. 1932.
180. Speech in Tullamore, *Irish Times*, 15 Feb. 1932.
181. Speech in Dublin, *Irish Times*, 3 Feb. 1932. Cardinal MacRory, in a speech the previous October, had spoken of the need to 'rebuild some of [Ireland's] ruined industries.'
182. Speech at Cork, *Irish Times*, 25 Jan. 1942.
183. Speech at Kilkenny, *Irish Times*, 1 Feb. 1932.
184. O'Rahilly interview.
185. *Irish Times*, 16 Feb. 1932.
186. Ibid., 22 Feb. 1932.
187. Ibid., 10 Mar. 1932.
188. Ibid., 11 Mar. 1932.

Chapter 3 (p. 64–96)

1. C. S. Andrews in an interview with Pádraic O'Halpin, 11 Feb. 1977 (OHP).
2. Ó Broin (1982), 145.
3. Campbell (1967), 39.
4. Roche (1979), 233–4.
5. This account of the events leading to Leydon's appointment is from an interview with Leydon by Pádraic O'Halpin in July 1974, OHP.
6. Roche (1982), 235.
7. Roche (1982), 252.
8. O'Halpin interview with John Leydon, July 1974, OHP.
9. See for example *Dáil Debates*, vol. 122, col. 1718, 13 July 1950, for one of Lemass's many rehearsals of this complaint.
10. See Cullen (1993), 42.
11. *Dáil Debates*, vol. 40, col. 881, 4 Nov. 1931.
12. Peters to Dominion Office, 24 Jan. 1934, PRO, DO35/228/1.
13. *Business and Finance*, 2 June 1967.
14. *Irish Press*, 9 Nov. 1933.
15. *Irish Times*, 24 Mar. 1932.
16. Ibid., 26 Mar. 1932.
17. *Irish Press*, 16 Apr. 1932.
18. Ibid., 12 Apr. 1932.
19. Farrell (1991), 50.
20. Ibid., 36, 44, 50.
21. Information from the editor of the memoir, Father Anthony Gaughan, 17 July 1995.
22. Fanning (1978), 218.
23. *Irish Press*, 19 Apr. 1932.
24. Labour TDs occasionally participated in government meetings: for example William Norton and William Davin on 14 Nov. 1932; NA, S6274.
25. He also met the future Prime Minister of Northern Ireland, Lord Brookeborough, but only briefly and formally.
26. Provisional Note on Ireland's Attendance at Commonwealth Conferences, 8 Mar. 1965, NA, DFA96/3/91.
27. Fanning (1978), 248.

28. NA, CAB 18 Mar. 1932; NA, D/T 6230.
29. NA, CAB6/29, 23–24 May 1932; NA, D/T S6230.
30. Daly (1992), 72.
31. *Dáil Debates,* vol. 42, col. 1234, 14 June 1932.
32. Memorandum from J. J. S. G. detailing Peters's views, 6 Dec. 1933; PRO, DO35/243/5.
33. *Dáil Debates,* vol. 50, col. 346–8, 22 Nov. 1933.
34. Daly (1992), passim. Unless otherwise stated, the examples that follow are drawn from Daly's account.
35. Ibid.
36. NA, TID 1207/187, memorandum of meeting prepared by Leydon, 8 Mar. 1933.
37. Memorandum, Department of Industry and Commerce, 23 June 1934, NA, D/T S6613.
38. *Irish Times,* 24 Jan. 1934.
39. Peters to Dominion Office, 24 Jan. 1934, PRO, DO35/228/1.
40. PRO, DO35/227/6.
41. See PRO, DO35/243/5, from which the succeeding references are all drawn.
42. Memorandum from E. J. H., Dominions Office, 7 Dec. 1933, PRO, DO35/243/5.
43. Tennyson to Sir Edward Harding, Colonial Office, 1 Aug. 1934, PRO, DO35/243/5.
44. Sir Horace Wilson, Board of Trade, to Sir. E Harding, Colonial Office, 2 Mar. 1934, PRO, DO35/243/5.
45. Parliamentary party minutes, 6 Apr. 1933, FF/439.
46. Ibid., 11 May, 22 June and 28 Sep. 1933, FF/439.
47. Ibid., 9 Aug. 1933, FF/439.
48. Speech at Tipperary, *Irish Press,* 9 Jan. 1933.
49. *Irish Press,* 12 Jan. 1933.
50. Ibid., 14 Jan. 1933.
51. Ibid.
52. Speech at Carrick-on-Suir, *Irish Press,* 11 Jan. 1933.
53. Speech in Dublin, *Irish Press,* 21 Jan. 1933.
54. *Irish Press,* 24 Jan. 1933.
55. Memorandum, inter-departmental committee, 27 Jan. 1933, PRONI, COM62/1/696.
56. E. E. Brown, Ministry of Commerce, 22 July 1932, PRONI, COM60/B/2/11.
57. Lemass memorandum to government, 14 Nov. 1932, NA, D/T S6274.
58. Notes of conference, 4 Sep. 1933, NA, D/T S6511A.
59. Speech to TCD cumann of Fianna Fáil, *Irish Press,* 4 Nov. 1933.
60. Memorandum from Department of Foreign Affairs, 6 June 1934, NA, D/T S6511A.
61. Meenan (1938), 61.
62. Dennis Kennedy (1988), 189.
63. Meenan (1938), 62.
64. Dennis Kennedy (1988), 189.
65. Speech to Law Students' Debating Society, 18 Feb. 1966 (duplicated), CBP.
66. Michael Mills, *Irish Press,* 24 Jan. 1969.
67. Ó Gráda (1994), 396.
68. Whitaker (1973), 409.

69. Johnson (1989), 40.
70. McCarthy (1977), 135.
71. *Dáil Debates,* 17 May 1935, vol. 56, col. 1284.
72. Ibid., col. 1262–79.
73. *Economist,* 2 Jan. 1937.
74. Quoted in O'Brien (1991), 98.
75. Andrews (1982), 60.
76. De Valera to the parliamentary party, 9 Aug. 1933, FF 439. He possibly meant 'less detrimental'.
77. Speech to Bolton Street Debating Society, *Irish Press,* 22 Jan. 1934.
78. Explanatory memorandum, section 4 (iii), Conditions of Employment Act, 25 June 1934, NA, D/T S6462A.
79. See Jones (1988), 123–33.
80. Daly (1992), 124.
81. Memorandum, Department of Industry and Commerce, Sep. 1933, NA, D/T S6462A.
82. Explanatory memorandum, section 5 (ii), Conditions of Employment Act, 25 June 1934, NA, D/T S6462A.
83. *Dáil Debates,* 17 May 1935, vol. 56, col. 1281–3.
84. NA, D/T S11987.
85. Interview with Patrick Lynch, former chairman of Aer Lingus, 18 Oct. 1994.
86. Farrell (1991), 49–50.
87. Daly (1992), 114.
88. Whitaker interview.
89. Speech to Model Aeronautics Council of Ireland in the Mansion House, Dublin, *Irish Press,* 3 Jan. 1952.
90. Share (1986), 11–25.
91. O'Doherty interview. O'Doherty was a passenger on the flight.
92. Speech to Irish Airline Pilots' Association, Dublin, 11 Nov. 1958, NA, GIS1/215.
93. Cathcart interview.
94. NA, D/T 9715 A and B, and S10160.
95. Curran (1995), 297.
96. *Irish Press,* 20 Jan. 1937.
97. Ibid.
98. Ibid.
99. Skinner (1961), 67.
100. AFL weekly news service, 19 June 1937 (LP).
101. *Irish Press,* 18 June 1937. Summerfield was president of the Society of Irish Motor Traders, a group of businessmen with whom Lemass had long had close links as part of his strategy of establishing a viable motor assembly industry.
102. 9 June 1937.
103. *Irish Press,* 25 June 1937.
104. Speech in Co. Meath, *Irish Press,* 29 June 1939.
105. *Irish Press,* 23 June 1937.
106. Ibid., 24 June 1937.
107. Ibid., 1 July 1937. This formulation was a somewhat less optimistic one than the version he had delivered in Geneva some weeks earlier.
108. Speech at Naas, *Irish Press,* 30 June 1937.
109. Seán Lemass, General Election Report to Fianna Fáil National Executive, 17 June 1938, FF/791.

110. Bowman (1982), 176–8; Fisk (1959), 159–88.
111. Seán Lemass, memorandum to Government re 1938 Trade Agreement, MacEntee papers, UCD, P67/180/5.
112. Quoted in Fisk (1983), 174.
113. PRONI, COM62/1/696.
114. PRO, BT11/2833, quoted in Daly (1992), 163.
115. Lemass to de Valera, 8 Oct. 1938, NA, DFA, 1995 release, Secretary's Office files, S94/39.
116. *Evening Standard,* 17 Oct. 1938.
117. T. G. Jenkins, Board of Trade, London, to Leydon, 22 Nov. 1938, NA, DFA, S94/39.
118. Ó Gráda (1994), 398.
119. Johnson (1989), 29.
120. Dunphy (1995), 147.
121. CKD stands for 'carriage knocked down', i.e. the vehicles were disassembled at the English port of shipment and reassembled after they had arrived in Ireland.
122. Draft review by Kevin Boland of Brian Farrell's *Seán Lemass,* manuscript furnished to the author by Mr Boland.
123. Interviewed by Aindrias Ó Gallchobhair, Radio Éireann, Mar. 1983; transcript in CBP.
124. Leo Flanagan interview.

Chapter 4 (p. 97–134)

1. Interview with Kathleen Lemass by Kerry McCarthy, *Evening Herald,* 21 Nov. 1975.
2. Family source.
3. Maureen Haughey interview.
4. 'Profile' of Kathleen Lemass, 1968, LP.
5. Ibid.
6. O'Connor interview.
7. Mhac an tSaoi interview.
8. Interview with Kathleen Lemass by Kerry McCarthy, *Evening Herald,* 21 Nov. 1975.
9. Occasion recalled by Colm Barnes, Barnes interview.
10. Holloway interview.
11. O'Neill (1970), 453.
12. For example the fee he received for an article based on his speech to the Social Study Conference in 1961, which was subsequently published in a Jesuit magazine in Belgium.
13. Information from Moll Lemass, 21 Feb. 1997.
14. *Irish Press,* 21 Feb. 1949.
15. PRO, PREM8/824.
16. Letter to the author from Pamela Clark, deputy registrar, Royal Archives, 10 Jan. 1995. Farrell (1991), 61, regards this as an 'unlikely story', but the evidence is irrefutable. There is a further reference to the visit in a letter from the king's private secretary, Sir Alexander Hardinge, to Stephenson at the Dominions Office (who would have arranged the visit) on 10 June 1940, which mentions that the Irish ministers 'had written their names in the Book here,' Royal Archives, ibid.

17. PRO, DO35/893/X 11/258, quoted in Bowman (1983), 199.
18. Chamberlain diary, 28 June 1940, C papers, NC2/24A, quoted in Bowman (1983), 230.
19. See Department of Supplies Record of Activities, NA, Department of Industry and Commerce E37/578, passim.
20. Notes of discussion between Pádraic O'Halpin and John Leydon, July 1974, OHP.
21. Reynolds, an accountant and long-time friend of Lemass, was appointed by him to the first board of Aer Lingus and later became general manager of CIE.
22. Keogh (1994), 250.
23. Charles Haughey interview.
24. Interview with Kathleen Lemass by Kerry McCarthy, *Evening Herald,* 21 Nov. 1975.
25. Leo Flanagan interview, from which the information in this section is drawn unless otherwise credited.
26. Ibid.
27. Personal recollection of Colm Barnes, CBP.
28. *The Word,* Feb. 1966.
29. Ryan interview.
30. O'Driscoll interview.
31. Recollections by Bill Murray, CBP.
32. O'Driscoll interview.
33. Farrell (1991), 59.
34. O'Doherty interview, which is also the source of information about incidents in this section that are not otherwise attributed.
35. Private source.
36. O'Doherty interview.
37. Ibid.
38. Ibid.
39. Ibid.
40. Whitaker interview.
41. Note of discussion between John Leydon and Pádraic O'Halpin, July 1974, OHP.
42. O'Doherty interview.
43. Sweetman interview.
44. *Irish Times,* 19 May 1943.
45. Cronin interview. Cronin recalls a conversation with the late Pádraig Ó hAnracháin, head of the Government Information Bureau when Lemass was Taoiseach, in which Ó hAnracháin said that Lemass had disclosed this to him in a private conversation.
46. Kerry McCarthy, interview with Kathleen Lemass, *Evening Herald,* 21 Nov. 1975.
47. Girvin (1989), p, 132–6.
48. 'Appreciation: Gerry Lamb', *Irish Times,* 24 Aug. 1992.
49. Interview with Kathleen Lemass by Kerry McCarthy, *Evening Herald,* 21 Nov. 1975.
50. *Weekly Irish Times,* 23 Aug. 1941.
51. O'Doherty interview.
52. Hobsbawm (1994), 273.
53. *Irish Press,* 13 Feb. 1943.
54. Ó Gráda (1994), 389.

55. Johnson (1989), 27.
56. June 1942, NA, D/T S12882A, from which all subsequent quotations from the document are drawn.
57. Coogan (1993), 630.
58. NA, D/T S13101A; minutes in NA, D/T S13026A.
59. *Irish Press,* 10 Apr. 1943.
60. Girvin (1989), 114.
61. *Irish Times,* 8 May 1944.
62. Ferguson to Secretary, Department of the Taoiseach, 1 Dec. 1942, NA, D/T S11987.
63. *Irish Press,* 9 Feb. 1944.
64. Memorandum from Lemass, described as 'not an official publication' and sent to MacEntee and de Valera on 16 Jan. 1945; MacEntee papers, UCD, P/67/264/3.
65. A second, long-promised Department of Finance memorandum on the issues raised by the White Paper had not materialised as late as Feb. 1947.
66. Lemass memorandum, para. 9, NA, D/T S13101A.
67. NA, D/T S13101A, para. 13.
68. Ibid., para. 23.
69. Interview with John Mageean in *Feature,* Mar. 1946.
70. NA, D/T S13101A.
71. Ibid., para. 30.
72. Ibid., para 36.
73. Ó Gráda (1994), 407–10.
74. NA, D/T S13101A, para. 49.
75. *Irish Press,* 30 Nov. 1944.
76. Ibid., 28 Mar. 1945. This detailed summary of the Cork speech is the only one of his speeches preserved in an extended form in de Valera's papers, FA.
77. *Dáil Debates,* vol. 97, col. 1637, 26 June 1945.
78. T. P. Kilfeather, *Sunday Independent,* 16 May 1971.
79. *Irish Press,* 4 Dec. 1944.
80. Fanning (1978), 366–74.
81. *Dáil Debates,* vol. 97, col. 1557, 26 June 1945.
82. Seán Lemass, memorandum on industrial development for An Taoiseach, Oct. 1945, NA, D/T S11987B.
83. *Dáil Debates,* vol. 97, col. 1578 and 1582, 26 June 1945.
84. Ó Gráda (1994), 399.
85. *Dáil Debates,* vol. 112, col. 1158–9, 21 July 1948.
86. Memorandum to Government, 15 Feb. 1947, NA, D/T S11987B.
87. *Dáil Debates,* vol. 83, col. 1542, 4 June 1941.
88. Ibid., vol. 75, col. 263, 29 Mar. 1939.
89. Emergency Powers (No. 83) Order, 7 May 1941.
90. McCarthy (1977), 235–7.
91. I am indebted to Martin Maguire for insights into this area contained in his current research into the history of the Local Government and Public Services Union.
92. Murphy to R. J. P. Mortished (future chairman of the Labour Court), 1 Feb. 1944, Mortished papers, quoted in O'Shea (1988), 161.
93. O'Shea (1988), 189.
94. McCarthy (1977), 246.
95. Seán Lemass, speech in Dublin, *Irish Press,* 7 June 1943.

96. Seán MacEntee, speech in Dublin, *Irish Press,* 8 June 1943.
97. C. S. Andrews, 'Intimate memory of a comrade in arms: the realist who built modern Ireland', *Irish Press,* 12 May 1971.
98. Andy Pollak, 'Dublin closed doors on Jewish refugees', *Irish Times,* 14–15 Apr. 1995.
99. *Dáil Debates,* vol. 119, col. 1598, 9 Mar. 1950.
100. PRO, PREM11 4326, Apr. 1963.
101. Oration by Mgr Pádraig de Brún, president of UCG, at the conferring of an honorary DEconSc degree on Lemass by the NUI, *Irish Press,* 9 Apr. 1954.
102. *Cork Examiner,* 18 June 1945. Relying on its readers' short memories, the same newspaper reported two days later that Lemass's appointment 'came as no surprise'; *Cork Examiner,* 20 June 1945.
103. *Irish Times,* 18 June 1945.
104. Farrell (1991), 75.
105. Memorandum to Government from Department of Industry and Commerce, 27 Oct. 1933 (approved 31 Oct. 1933); all documents in NA, D/T S6413A.
106. Andrews (1982), 118.
107. Contemporary record by Pádraic O'Halpin of discussion with Andrews on 11 Feb. 1977 (OHP). Otherwise unattributed accounts of Andrews's views and the early operation of Bord na Móna in this section are taken from this record.
108. Woods interview, OHP.
109. Whitaker interview.
110. Memorandum, Ministry of Food, 29 July 1947, PRO, PREM8/824.
111. Rugby to CRO, 15 Sep. 1947, PRO, PREM8/824.
112. *Dáil Debates,* 22 Oct. 1947, vol. 103, col. 726.
113. Ibid., col. 726.
114. Ibid., col. 901.
115. Ibid., col. 907.
116. Ibid., col. 750.
117. Farrell (1991), 78.
118. O'Doherty interview.
119. Letter from Leo Flanagan to author, 13 Oct. 1994.
120. *Irish Press,* 5, 7 and 12 Jan. 1948.
121. Ibid., 31 Jan. and 3 Feb. 1948.
122. Lynch interview.
123. *Irish Press,* 17 Jan. 1949. The speech, as it happens, was delivered not to an urban working-class constituency but in Clonmel, Co. Tipperary.
124. *Irish Press,* 10, 21 and 31 Jan. 1948.
125. Ibid., 31 Jan. and 3 Feb. 1948.
126. Ibid., 29 Jan. 1948.
127. Ibid., 30 Jan. 1948.
128. *Dáil Debates,* vol. 110, col. 66, 4 May 1948.
129. T. P. Kilfeather, *Sunday Independent,* 16 May 1971.
130. Fanning (1978), 393.
131. Alexis FitzGerald (son-in-law of John A. Costello) recounted this anecdote in a radio interview with John Bowman, Sep. 1981; transcript in CBP.
132. Private source.

Chapter 5 (p. 135–186)

1. *Dáil Debates,* vol. 116, col. 932, 14 July 1949.
2. Maffey to DO, 2 Aug. 1946, PRO, DO130/69.
3. Parliamentary party meeting, 26 Feb. 1948, FF/48.
4. Ibid., 10 and 17 May 1950, FF/48.
5. Ibid., 21 June 1950, FF/48.
6. Ibid., 1 Mar. 1950, FF/48.
7. Ibid., 10 and 17 May 1950, FF/440b.
8. A summary of Lemass's public sector income is given in appendix 2.
9. Family source.
10. Charles Haughey interview.
11. Sheila O'Connor interview.
12. Letter from manager, National City Bank, to Lemass, 23 Feb. 1948, LP.
13. *Irish Press,* 26 Feb. 1948.
14. Ibid., 23 Mar. 1948.
15. Farrell (1991), 80.
16. *Dáil Debates,* vol. 114, col. 1555, 23 Mar. 1949.
17. Hillery interview.
18. Kiely interview.
19. Gageby interview.
20. *Irish Press,* 13 Mar. 1949.
21. Speech to Solicitors' Apprentices' Debating Society, *Irish Press,* 24 Nov. 1951.
22. Seán Flanagan interview.
23. See chap. 2, p. 36.
24. *Dáil Debates,* vol. 113, col. 732, 1 Dec. 1948.
25. Sweetman interview.
26. *Dáil Debates,* vol. 110, col. 158, 4 May 1948.
27. *Irish Press,* 1 July 1949.
28. Ibid., 2 July 1949.
29. Ibid., 4 July 1949.
30. Recollection of R. N. Cooke SC (junior to Ernest Wood in this case) in conversation with the author, 29 Mar. 1996.
31. Gageby interview.
32. *Dáil Debates,* vol. 116, col. 910, 14 July 1949.
33. Ibid., vol. 112, col. 1129, 21 July 1948.
34. Gageby interview.
35. Sweetman interview, from which the details that follow are also taken.
36. *Irish Press,* 16 Mar. 1949.
37. Recollection of Michael O'Toole, 6 Jan. 1996. O'Toole's history of his life in journalism, particularly in the Press organisation, *More Kicks Than Pence* (Dublin: Poolbeg 1992), is a valuable addition to the genre.
38. *Dáil Debates,* vol. 123, col. 1295, 23 Nov. 1948.
39. Ibid., vol. 115, col. 2060, 25 May 1948.
40. Ibid., vol. 111, col. 885–8, 10 June 1948.
41. Ibid., vol. 112, col. 1143, 21 July 1948.
42. Ibid., col. 1139, 21 July 1948.
43. See reference in *Dáil Debates,* vol. 116, col. 933, 14 July 1949.
44. *Irish Press,* 25 June 1951.
45. See decision of the party's Central Committee on 2 Feb. 1949, FF/440c.
46. See below.

47. *Dáil Debates,* vol. 112, col. 2014, 1 July 1948.
48. Lemass family papers.
49. *Dáil Debates,* vol. 114, col. 2224, 5 Apr. 1949.
50. Ibid., vol. 113, col. 312, 24 Nov. 1948. The reference was to an unscripted speech by Seán MacBride, Minister for External Affairs.
51. Ibid., vol. 116, col. 1375, 20 July 1949.
52. Lemass to T. Waldron, James Larkin Memorial Fund, 27 Apr. 1949, LP.
53. O'Doherty interview.
54. *Bulletin, Guild of Irish Journalists,* Apr. 1949, ADA 324.
55. The minutes of the parliamentary party for this period provide abundant evidence for this assertion during the period of the first inter-party Government; see especially FF/440A.
56. McCourt interview.
57. *Dáil Debates,* vol. 121, col. 794, 30 May 1950.
58. Ibid., vol. 110, col. 53, 18 Feb. 1948.
59. Ibid., vol. 113, col. 1623, 25 Nov. 1948.
60. Ibid., vol. 116, col. 1382, 23 June 1949, and vol. 112, col. 1131, 21 July 1948.
61. Ibid., vol. 112, col. 1131, 21 July 1948.
62. Ibid., vol. 116, col. 1383, 23 June 1949.
63. Ibid., vol. 112, col. 1356, 22 July 1948.
64. Ibid., col. 1123–4, 21 July 1948.
65. Ibid., vol. 113, col. 1632, 25 Nov. 1948.
66. Ibid., vol. 114, col. 1790, 29 Mar. 1949.
67. Ibid., vol. 120, col. 1785, 4 May 1950.
68. Ibid., vol. 114, col. 1790, 29 Mar. 1949.
69. *Irish Times,* 13 May 1950.
70. Hillery interview.
71. *Irish Press,* 8 May 1951.
72. Ibid., 14 May 1950.
73. Ibid., 28 and 30 May 1950.
74. Ibid., 21 and 25 May 1950.
75. Mills, 27 Jan. 1969.
76. Mills, 27 Jan. 1969. See also *Dáil Debates,* vol. 135, col. 896, 4 Dec. 1952.
77. Lemass to Henry Harrison, 4 June 1951, LP.
78. *Dáil Debates,* vol. 126, col. 1514, 12 July 1951.
79. Girvin (1986), 290.
80. O'Regan interview.
81. Fianna Fáil parliamentary party minutes, 2 May 1952, FF/48.
82. Staunton to d'Alton, 29 May 1951, ADA 104.
83. De Valera to Lemass, 27 Sep. 1952, LP.
84. Whyte (1971), 282.
85. McQuaid to d'Alton, 22 Oct. 1952, ADA 104, folder A.
86. de Valera to Lemass, 9 Nov. 1952, LP. Lemass's letter has not survived.
87. De Valera to Lemass, 9 Nov. 1952, LP.
88. *Irish Press,* 6 Oct. 1951.
89. Ibid., 20 Nov. 1951.
90. Ibid., 18 Jan. 1952.
91. Ibid., 14 Jan. 1952.
92. 12 Feb. 1952, NA, GIS1/212.
93. Ó Cearbhaill interview.

94. Speech at Athlone Sportex Centre, *Irish Press,* 9 Feb. 1952.
95. NA, D/T S14474.
96. Speech at Ballina, *Irish Press,* 29 Jan. 1952.
97. IBEC Report (1952), 13.
98. Ibid., 80.
99. Girvin (1986), 290–2.
100. NA, Industry and Commerce, TIC32682.
101. PRO, DO35/5379, report dated 27 Jan. 1953.
102. Memorandum, Industry and Commerce to Government, 15 Feb. 1947, NA, S11907B; Department of Finance memorandum in same file.
103. *Irish Times,* 25 July 1953.
104. O'Doherty interview.
105. Details in this section, unless otherwise stated, are based on author's interview with Brendan O'Regan, 3 May 1995.
106. O'Regan interview.
107. *Sunday Independent,* 26 Sep. 1953.
108. *Irish Press,* 6 Oct. 1953.
109. O'Driscoll interview.
110. 1 Oct. 1953. Speech in NA, GIS1/213.
111. *Dáil Debates,* vol. 102, col. 1325, 24 July 1946.
112. NA, DFA, Holy See box 1, 14/89, memorandum from International Organisation Section, 15 Mar. 1955.
113. W. C. Hankinson, British ambassador in Dublin, to Sir Percival Leisching, CRO, 2 Jan. 1952, PRO, DO130/112.
114. L. B. Walsh Atkins to CRO, 5 Oct. 1953, describing his meeting with de Valera on 29 Sep., PRO, DO35/5205.
115. Details in memorandum of conversation, 30 Sep. 1953, General Records of Department of State, box no. 3493, and items 718 and 719 in *Foreign Relations of the United States, 1952–54,* vol. 6, part 2, Washington: State Department 1986.
116. NA, DFA, Reports from Washington, J. J. Hearne to Seán Nunan, 22 Oct. 1953.
117. MacEntee papers, UCD, P67/227/1.
118. Cronin interview. Bart Cronin was a member of Dublin South-Central Comhairle Ceantair, 1952–54.
119. Girvin (1986), 294.
120. See for example *Irish Press,* 6 Oct. 1951 and 20 Nov. 1951 and 14 Jan. 1952, and other speeches in GIS1/212, passim.
121. Girvin (1928), 296–7.
122. De Valera to Lemass, 9 Oct. 1952 (LP).
123. PRO, DO35/5290, Report from Dublin, 30 Jan. 1954.
124. 27 Nov. 1953; reference in *Irish Times Annual Review* for 1954.
125. *Irish Press,* 2 Feb. 1954.
126. *Irish Independent,* 17 May 1954. He made no fewer than three speeches on 16 May (just before polling on 18 May): one in Dublin, one in Port Laoise, and one in Westport.
127. *Irish Press,* 26 Jan. 1954.
128. Speech at Kilkenny, 20 Jan. 1954; text in NA, GIS1/213.
129. Parliamentary party minutes, 18 June 1954, FF/440A.
130. Ibid., 17 Aug. 1954, FF/440A.
131. Report to 1957 ardfheis, FF/724.

132. Circular, 2 Oct. 1954, FF/277.
133. Report to 24th Fianna Fáil ardfheis, FF/722.
134. Undated memorandum in Lemass's handwriting, probably the first draft of *Córas Bua* (1955–56), FF/280.
135. Speech to ardfheis, *Irish Independent,* 13 Oct. 1954.
136. See for example reports of 1933, 1934, 1948, 1952, 1957 and 1958 ardfheiseanna, FF/707, 708, 715, 716, 719, and 724.
137. Colley to Lemass, 20 May 1955, FF/277.
138. Haughey to Lemass, constituency report, 13 Jan. 1956, FF/277.
139. Speech to meeting at Smith and Pearson's ironworks, Dublin, 16 Oct. 1951; text in NA, GIS1/212.
140. Speech to Dublin Society of Chartered Accountants, *Irish Press,* 27 Nov. 1954.
141. *Report: Commission on Emigration and other Population Problems,* Dublin: Stationery Office 1954, 335.
142. Mills interview.
143. Full details of the speech are in *Irish Press,* 18 Jan. 1955.
144. FF/280.
145. *Irish Independent,* 2 Feb. 1955.
146. Fianna Fáil parliamentary party minutes, 5 May 1955, FF/440A.
147. MacEntee papers, UCD, P67/468.
148. *Irish Press,* 10 Oct. 1946.
149. Lemass's memorandum to Government, 13 Sep. 1940, NA, S12070.
150. *Irish Press,* 5 Mar. 1957.
151. Fianna Fáil parliamentary party minutes, 7 Sep. 1955, FF/440A. No copy of his original memorandum survives.
152. Information from Joyce Andrews, Mr Andrews's widow.
153. *Dáil Debates,* vol. 119, col. 1603–4, 9 Mar. 1950.
154. Ibid., col. 1604, 9 Mar. 1950.
155. *Irish Press,* 9 Nov. 1955.
156. *Irish Times,* 28 Nov. 1955.
157. Speech to Comh-Chomhairle Átha Cliath, 4 Jan. 1956; report in NA, GIS1/213.
158. *Irish Press,* 3 Feb. 1956.
159. *Irish Times,* 14 Feb. 1956. See part 2 for a reprise of these ideas in 1966.
160. Comh-Chomhairle Átha Cliath speech, *Irish Press,* 3 Jan. 1956.
161. Speech to UCD Literary and Historical Society, *Irish Press,* 2 Feb. 1956.
162. *Irish Times,* 18 Jan. 1957.
163. Ibid.
164. Parliamentary party minutes, 15 Jan. 1957, FF/440A.
165. McCarthy (1990), 30.
166. See Desmond Fisher's analysis of the speech in *The Statist,* 10 Mar. 1956.
167. By-election speech at Abbeyfeale, *Irish Press,* 31 Oct. 1955.
168. *Irish Independent,* 19 Jan. 1956.
169. Ibid.
170. Lemass to Pádraic O'Halpin, 16 Jan. 1957, OHP.
171. *Irish Times,* 14 Feb. 1956.
172. *Irish Press,* 15 Feb. 1957.
173. Ibid., 2 Mar. 1955.
174. Ibid., 25 May 1955.
175. Department of Industry and Commerce, departmental conference 398, 25 Apr. 1955, ICA.

176. Ibid.
177. Department of Industry and Commerce, departmental conference 389, 22 Feb. 1955, ICA.
178. *Irish Times,* 30 Jan. 1953.
179. This probably well-informed analysis of his TCD speech is contained in the report of 27 Jan. 1953 to the Dominion Office from the British embassy in Dublin, PRO, DO35/5290.
180. *Irish Independent,* 20 Sep. 1954.
181. *Irish Press,* 27 Apr. 1955.
182. *Irish Independent,* 11 Feb. 1957.
183. Feehan to general secretary, 20 Jan. 1955, FF/42.
184. FF/42.
185. FF/42, from which all references to this document are drawn.
186. An earlier draft had included a proposal for the establishment of a Minister for National Unity, FF/42.
187. De Valera to Lemass, 7 Apr. 1955, FF/42.
188. Speech to Kevin Barry Cumann, Dublin, *Irish Press,* 27 Apr. 1955.
189. *Irish Press* and *Irish Independent,* 26 Aug. 1955.
190. *Irish Independent,* 13 Dec. 1954.
191. *Irish Press,* 12 Dec. 1956.
192. Fianna Fáil parliamentary party minutes, 15 Jan. 1957, FF/441A.
193. Hillery interview.
194. *Irish Press,* 18 Jan. 1957.
195. Farrell (1991), 95.
196. Lenihan interview.
197. Advisory memorandum for 1963 trade negotiations, PRO, PREM11 4326.
198. Fanning (1978), 392–3.
199. McCarthy (1990), 48.
200. Whitaker memorandum, 12 Dec. 1957, NA, D/T 16066A.
201. Fergal Tobin, *Irish Independent,* 30 Mar. 1996.
202. Coogan (1993), 671.
203. Quoted in McCarthy (1990), 52.
204. Maurice Moynihan, as told to Tim Pat Coogan, in Coogan (1993), 672.
205. *Irish Press,* 5 May 1954.
206. Ibid., 8 Aug. 1958.
207. McCarthy (1990), 57.
208. McCarthy (1990), 56.
209. *Irish Press,* 25 Nov. 1958.
210. *Irish Times,* 12 Nov. 1958. The *Irish Times* caught on to the significance of the Grey Book relatively quickly (see its issue of 26 Nov. 1958). Its initial criticism was to some extent accurate, but what was new was the programmatic expression of the ideas contained in the White Paper and the specificity of the political targets.
211. Parliamentary party minutes, 22 Jan. 1958, FF/441B.
212. Ibid.
213. Quoted in McCarthy (1990), 53.
214. McCarthy (1990), 59.
215. Speech to Federation of Irish Industries, *Irish Press,* 4 Feb. 1959.
216. Barnes interview.
217. Fianna Fáil parliamentary party minutes, 22 Jan. 1958, FF/441A.
218. *Irish Independent,* 11 Feb. 1958.

219. Ibid., 12 Jan. 1959.
220. Account by Michael McInerney, *Irish Times,* 12 May 1971.
221. Burns interview.
222. Mhac an tSaoi interview.
223. MacEntee papers, UCD, P67/788.
224. Lenihan interview.
225. *Irish Press,* 18 Jan. 1955. This preference for the 'straight vote' goes against Farrell's statement, although it is of course possible that Lemass had changed his mind in the interim.
226. The MacEntee papers in UCD offer substantial evidence of the fear within Fianna Fáil that without de Valera the party would enter a period of irrecoverable electoral decline.
227. Farrell (1991), 96.
228. Radio Éireann, 13 June 1959; text in NA, GIS1/215.
229. 'The School Around the Corner' was a popular radio programme, featuring a different school every week.
230. *Dublin Opinion,* May 1959, 55.
231. Information from Frank Kelly (son of C. E. Kelly), Sep. 1996.
232. Lenihan interview.
233. O'Kennedy interview.
234. *Irish Press,* 6 June 1959.
235. Industry and Commerce, departmental conference 560, 1 Dec. 1958, ICA.
236. *Irish Times,* 9 Nov. 1966.
237. Mills interview.
238. O'Regan interview.
239. Boland interview.
240. Charles Haughey interview.
241. G. Kimber, Dublin, to G. W. Chadwick, Commonwealth Relations Office, 3 Dec. 1958, PRO, DO35/7906.
242. Farrell (1991), 97.
243. O'Sullivan (1994), 146.

Chapter 6 (p. 189–212)

1. Recalled by Jim Culliton, *Business and Finance,* 5 Jan. 1978, 7.
2. *Dáil Debates,* vol. 176, col. 140, 23 June 1959.
3. *Business and Finance,* 2 June 1967.
4. Hillery interview. P. J. Hillery was, with de Valera, one of the TDs for the Clare constituency.
5. Communication from Liam St John Devlin to author, Jan. 1997.
6. Murphy (1996), 200.
7. Hillery interview.
8. *Irish Times,* 9 Nov. 1966.
9. Lenihan interview.
10. Cruise O'Brien interview.
11. Ibid.
12. Cardinal Francis Spellman, Archbishop of New York, was a noted Cold War warrior who was critical of Irish policy in this regard.
13. Cruise O'Brien interview.
14. Ibid.
15. MacEntee memorandum to Government, 5 Jan. 1961, NA, D/T 16057 G/61.

16. Secretary, Department of External Affairs, to UN delegation, 2 Nov. 1962, NA, D/T 16057 G/62.
17. 17 Oct. 1963; text in NA, D/T S16057 G/63.
18. Farrell (1991), 101.
19. Hillery interview.
20. Lynch interview.
21. Farrell (1991), 103.
22. Farrell (1971), 55–73.
23. Moynihan interview.
24. Ó Cearbhaill interview.
25. Hillery interview.
26. Transcript of interview between Tim O'Brien (Secretary, Department of Lands, 1951–77) and Colm Barnes, Sep. 1982, CBP. O'Brien died in July 1983.
27. Lenihan interview.
28. O'Brien interview.
29. Ibid.
30. Private source.
31. For example on the Exchange Control Bill (Nov. 1962) and on the National Gallery Bill (Jan. 1963); details in FF 440/C.
32. O'Kennedy interview.
33. Ryan interview.
34. O'Leary (1979), 61.
35. NA, D/T S16232A. Lemass's letters to Cosgrave and Norton were on 12 Nov. 1959.
36. Gallagher (1982), 163.
37. *Irish Press,* 12 July 1961.
38. Ibid., 3 Aug. 1961.
39. O'Leary (1979), 62.
40. Author's conversation with Ruairí Brugha, 8 May 1995.
41. Mr Justice Brian Walsh in Sturgess (1988), 418, from which other information in this passage is also drawn.
42. See entries under Seán Lemass in the bibliography; they have not been separately referenced here.
43. Lemass to Haughey, 20 Dec. 1963, LP.
44. Speech to ardfheis, 19 Nov. 1963; text in NA, D/T RA45/63.
45. Observation of F. S. L. Lyons, as recalled by Kenneth Milne, related to the author by Dr Milne, May 1995.
46. Blaney interview.
47. Patrick Norton later joined Fianna Fáil and was the author of the famous but unsuccessful 'Norton Amendment', proposing single-seat constituencies with the transferable vote as an alternative both to traditional PR and the 'straight vote' favoured by his new party.
48. Smith's letter of resignation was published in the daily press on 7 Oct. 1964.
49. Author's conversation with Ó hAnracháin, 1974.
50. Lemass to Attorney-General, 21 Oct. 1964, LP.
51. Ó Caoimh to Lemass, 12 Nov. 1964, LP.
52. *Irish Press,* 28 Oct. 1964.
53. Lynch interview.
54. Economic consultation in Department of Finance, 27 Nov. 1964, NA, D/T S17872 A/65.

55. *The Word,* Feb. 1966.
56. *Irish Press,* 18 Feb. 1965.
57. Ibid., 23 Feb. 1965.
58. Ibid., 9 Mar. 1965.
59. Author's conversation with Pádraig Ó hAnracháin, 1974.
60. *Irish Press,*27 Mar. 1965.
61. Mills interview.
62. *Irish Times,* 1 Apr. 1965; Gageby interview.
63. Ibid., 2 Apr. 1965.
64. Ibid., 7 Apr. 1965.
65. Personal recollection of Jim O'Donnell, Institute of Public Administration, who attended Lemass's rally in Kells.
66. T. P. Kilfeather, *Sunday Independent,* 16 May 1971.
67. Speech to Institute of Public Relations, Dublin, 29 Apr. 1966 (duplicated), by courtesy of T. J. O'Driscoll.
68. Speech to national convention of Junior Chambers of Commerce, Bray, 1 May 1965, NA, D/T 97/6/173.
69. *Irish Times,* 26 Mar. 1966.
70. See correspondence generally in NA, D/T 97/6/515.
71. *Irish Press,* 6 Sep. 1966.
72. Ibid., 5 Apr. 1966.
73. Lemass's views on these topics generally are to be found in his articles on various aspects of public administration as enumerated in the bibliography; they have not been separately referenced here.
74. Tadhg Ó Cearbhaill, 'Seán Lemass', *Public Affairs/Léargas,* vol. 3, no. 9 (June–July 1971), 3.
75. O'Regan interview.
76. Devlin interview.
77. *Léargas/Public Affairs Review,* no. 12 (Jan.–Feb. 1968).
78. *Irish Times,* 2 Apr. 1965.
79. Hillery interview.
80. *The Word,* Jan.–Feb. 1966.
81. *Irish Times,* 4 Oct. 1966.

Chapter 7 (p. 213–251)

1. Whitaker interview.
2. Ibid.
3. Hobsbawm (1994), 266.
4. NA, D/T S1301 G/95.
5. He recalled his emotions in a later speech to the Council of Europe, *Irish Press,* 25 Jan. 1966.
6. Copy of minutes of the meeting, 17 Oct. 1959, in the possession of T. K. Whitaker. Other references in the following section are to the same interview, unless otherwise stated, and the documents referred to are copies of correspondence, Oct. 1959–Jan. 1960, in Dr Whitaker's possession.
7. Moynihan to Whitaker, 27 Nov. 1959.
8. *Dáil Debates,* vol. 178, col. 1574, 11 Dec. 1959.
9. Whitaker interview.
10. Ibid.
11. Whitaker to Moynihan and other secretaries, 26 Nov. 1959.

12. MacCarthy to Whitaker, 27 Nov. 1969.
13. Whitaker to Murray, Department of Finance, 27 Nov. 1959.
14. MacCarthy to Whitaker, 22 Dec. 1959.
15. Whitaker to MacCarthy, 23 Dec. 1959.
16. Murphy (1996), 113.
17. McElligott to Whitaker, 24 Nov. 1959.
18. Whitaker to McElligott, 24 Nov. 1959.
19. Whitaker to Moynihan, 12 Apr. 1960, NA, D/T S16699.
20. G. L. Pearson, British embassy, Dublin, to H. G. Rogers, CRO, 13 June 1960, PRO, DO35/8395.
21. Text in PRO, DO35/8395. The document quoted is dated 21 May 1960.
22. Quoted in Murphy (1996), 246.
23. 'Economic Relations with the Irish Republic', Memorandum for the Northern Ireland government, Sep. 1960, PRONI CAB4/1115.
24. Ibid.
25. *Irish Press,* 6 July 1961.
26. Ibid., 20 July 1961.
27. Ibid., 29 Oct. 1961.
28. Schottenhamel to Lemass, 4 Nov. 1961, NA, D/T S2850 H/61.
29. Memorandum, Department of Industry and Commerce, 11 May 1961, NA, D/T S17066 A/61.
30. Government minutes, 24 Oct. 1961.
31. Mills interview.
32. Whitaker interview.
33. NA, Government minutes, GC11/58, 15 Mar. 1966.
34. Biggar to Department of External Affairs, 30 Dec. 1961, NA, D/T S16877 X/62; quoted in Murphy (1996), 252.
35. *Irish Press,* 16 Oct. 1959.
36. Speech to Solicitors' Apprentices' Debating Society, *Irish Times,* 2 Dec. 1960.
37. Quoted by Garrett FitzGerald in 'Irish credibility under pressure on European defence and security', *Irish Times,* 9 Mar. 1996.
38. Murphy (1996), 272–3.
39. Report of ardfheis, 16 Jan. 1962, FF/729.
40. Presidential address to ardfheis, 16 Jan. 1962, FF/729.
41. Department of Foreign Affairs, copy in NA, D/T S17246 A/62.
42. Full text of speech in NA, D/T S17246 A/62.
43. Hillery interview.
44. *Dáil Debates,* vol. 193, col. 9, 14 Feb. 1962.
45. Whitaker interview.
46. Quoted in *Dáil Debates,* vol. 193, col. 1316, 8 Mar. 1962.
47. Biggar to Secretary, Department of External Affairs, 14 Feb. and 2 Mar. 1962, NA, D/T S17246 C/62.
48. Meeting of departmental secretaries, 1 Mar. 1962, NA, D/T S17246 C/62.
49. *Dáil Debates,* 8 Mar. 1962, col. 1322.
50. Ibid., col. 1321.
51. Keatinge (1973), 34.
52. Joannon (1991), 87.
53. Record of meeting at Admiralty House, 18 Mar. 1963, PRO, PREM11/4326.
54. Letter from Desmond Fisher to author, 13 Sep. 1994, from which subsequent references to Fisher are also drawn.

55. The anecdote was related by Edward Heath, when Minister at the Board of Trade, to A. J. F. O'Reilly, and is unlikely to be apocryphal; communication from Dr O'Reilly, 14 Feb. 1997.

56. Charles de Gaulle, *Mémoires de Guerre: Le Salut* (Paris: Plon 1959), 179–80. I am indebted to T. K. Whitaker for the quotation and the translation.

57. *Irish Press,* 21 Nov. 1962.

58. Fianna Fáil parliamentary party minutes, 5 Dec. 1962, FF/441/b.

59. *Dáil Debates,* vol. 299, col. 924, 5 Feb. 1963.

60. Lemass to Ó Nualláin, 11 Feb. 1963, NA, S17427 A/63.

61. Louden Ryan to Colm Barnes, 6 Dec. 1981, CBP.

62. Ó Gráda and O'Rourke (1994), 17.

63. Report of meeting, 3 Sep. 1959, NA, D/T S11987 D/95.

64. *Irish Press,* 21 Oct. 1959.

65. Speech to Federated Union of Employers, 27 Feb. 1962; text in NA, D/T S17246 C/63.

66. Note given by Taoiseach to ICTU delegation, 15 Mar. 1963, and report of meeting, NA, D/T S13847 D/63.

67. Lemass to Lynch, 2 Mar. 1963, NA, D/T S13847 D/63.

68. 5 June 1963; text in NA, D/T S13847 D/63.

69. McCarthy (1973), 50.

70. Quoted in Jacobsen (1994), 81.

71. National Industrial and Economic Council (1965), 25.

72. Ibid., 26.

73. E. A. Attwood (head of Department of Farm Management, An Foras Talúntais), 'There are too many farms without sons', *Sunday Press,* 1 Mar. 1964.

74. Lemass to Ryan, 9 July 1960, NA, D/T 97/6/45.

75. Tadhg Ó Cearbhaill to Secretary, Department of the Taoiseach, 12 Sep. 1963, NA, D/T S13101 G/62.

76. *Dáil Debates,* vol. 202, col. 313–14, 24 Apr. 1963.

77. Ibid., col. 305, 24 Apr. 1963.

78. Desmond Fisher, *The Statist,* 28 June 1963.

79. Minutes, Fianna Fáil parliamentary party, 13 Mar. 1963, FF/440B.

80. McCloskey, US ambassador in Dublin, to State Department, 8 Nov. 1963, on the basis of a conversation with Lemass, JFK, CO 125.

81. In conversation with T. P. Kilfeather, *Sunday Independent,* 10 Aug. 1980.

82. Interviewed by Des Rushe, *The Word,* Dec. 1968.

83. *Dáil Debates,*vol. 218, col. 1344–6, 9 Nov. 1965.

84. *The Word,* Feb. 1966.

85. National Industrial and Economic Council (1965), 25.

86. Documents on the degree to which the Government was warned about this protest, and the Department of Justice's views on containing it, are in NA, D/T 97/6/102.

87. Speech in Wexford, 28 Feb. 1958, text in NA, D/T S16405; quoted in Murphy (1996), 162.

88. *Dáil Debates,* vol. 185, col. 560–1, 1 Dec. 1960.

89. Speech at Muintir na Tíre Rural Week, Thurles, 14 Aug. 1962, NA, D/T 17313 A/62.

90. Interview on 'Celtic Challenge', RTE, 2 Dec. 1963; *Irish Press,* 3 Dec. 1963. His interviewer was Donald Dewar, at the time of writing (Jan. 1997) shadow Scottish Secretary in the British Labour Party.

91. Report of meeting, 25 July 1963, between Lemass and a west of Ireland deputation, NA, Department of the Gaeltacht, 1965 release, NI/60.
92. Lemass to Smith, 2 Mar. 1962, NA, D/T S11563 C/62.
93. Healy interview.
94. *Dáil Debates,* vol. 206, col. 1974, 16 Feb. 1964.
95. Murphy (1996), 193–4.
96. Healy interview.
97. *Dáil Debates,* vol. 206, col. 1219, 12 Dec. 1963.
98. Murphy (1996), 198.
99. Letter from Rickard Deasy to author, 9 Aug. 1995.
100. Whitaker interview. Deering lost his seat to Fianna Fáil in the 1957 election.
101. Seán Lemass interview, 18 Aug. 1970, quoted in McLellan (1970), 66.
102. Whitaker interview.
103. Johnson (1989), 30.
104. 20 Jan., 1 Apr. and 18 Aug. 1964; texts in NA, D/T S1206 C/95.
105. Nagle to Ó Nualláin, 20 May 1964, NA, D/T S1206 C/95.
106. *Irish Times,* 10 Mar. 1964.
107. Brian Maye, 'Seeing through a ceasefire in the "economic war" with Britain', *Irish Times,* 2 Jan. 1995.
108. Industrial Development Authority (1964).
109. NA, Government conclusions of 13 Oct. 1964, GC 10/179.
110. *Irish Times,* 4 Sep. 1964.
111. *Dáil Debates,* vol. 41, col. 285. The debate was on a Cumann na nGaedheal motion, which the government accepted.
112. Official Committee on Commercial Policy, memorandum (by Richard Powell), 10 Dec. 1964, PRONI CAB9R/60/12.
113. *Irish Press,* 30 Mar. 1965.
114. Radio Éireann election talk, 2 Apr. 1965, NA, D/T 96/6/666.
115. NA, D/T S17658/95.
116. NA, Government conclusions GC 11/1, 27 Apr. 1965.
117. *Irish Press,* 25 Jan. 1966.
118. Memorandum for Government, Minister for Finance, 6 July 1965, NA, D/T S17872/65, especially 15–16.
119. Whitaker's account of his conversation is in his letter to Tadhg Ó Cearbhaill of 22 Oct. 1965, NA, D/T 17872 C/65.
120. Seán Lemass, press conference, Foreign Press Association, London, 5 Apr. 1965; transcript in NA, D/T 96/3/15.
121. The ambassador's report was read and noted by Lemass on 18 Aug. 1965, NA, D/T S17872 B/65 and NA, DFA 96/3/210.
122. ITGWU annual reports, quoted in Allen (1992), 147.
123. Lemass to Lynch, 5 Jan. 1965, and to Hillery, 17 June 1965; Hillery to Lemass NA, D/T 97/6/216; Lemass to Hillery, 14 Mar. 1966; Hillery to Lemass, 24 Mar. 1966, NA, D/T 97/6/325.
124. Anglo-Irish Trade Discussions, ministerial meeting, London, 26 July 1965, NA, D/T S16674 V/95.
125. Lemass to Jack Lynch, 27 July 1965, NA, S16272 A/65.
126. Memorandum to Cabinet, 8 Dec. 1965, PRO, CAB129/123.
127. Letter to the author from T. K. Whitaker, 14 Feb. 1995.
128. NA, Government conclusions, GC 11/40, 10 Dec. 1965.
129. Memorandum to Cabinet, 8 Dec. 1965, PRO, CAB129/123.
130. NA, D/T S16674 Z/65.

131. Jim Larkin TD, a deputy in Lemass's urban constituency, was the only one to dissent.
132. *Irish Press,* 15 Dec. 1965.
133. Dermot McAleese, *Effective Tariffs and the Structure of Industrial Protection in Ireland* (ESRI paper no. 62), Dublin: Economic and Social Research Institute 1971.
134. Whitaker (1973), 114.
135. Brian Maye, 'Seeing though a ceasefire in the "economic war" with Britain', *Irish Times,* 2 Jan. 1965.
136. Lemass to Ó Nualláin, 16 Dec. 1965, NA, D/T S16674 I/65.
137. *Irish Press,* 13 Dec. 1965.
138. Memorandum dated 4 Apr. 1966, NA, DFA, 1996 release, 355 E 15.
139. Unpublished draft statement prepared for release on behalf of the Government on NIEC (1965), 19 Jan. 1966, NA, D/T S17872 E/65. The reason the statement was not released—at Whitaker's insistence—was because of impending debates both within the ICTU and the Dáil on the economic situation.
140. Ibid., 8–9.
141. *Irish Press,* 26 Jan. 1966.
142. NA, Government minutes, GC 11/52, 18 Feb. 1966.
143. Lemass to Lynch, 4 Apr. 1966; Lynch to Lemass, 14 Apr. 1966, NA, D/T 97/6/533.
144. Whitaker to Ó Cearbhaill, 7 Mar. 1966, NA, D/T 97/6/325.
145. *Irish Press,* 18 Feb. 1966.
146. Ibid., 1 Mar. 1966.
147. Speech to Comh-Chomhairle Chorcaí of Fianna Fáil, *Irish Press,* 25 Mar. 1966.
148. Speech to Irish Countrywomen's Association, *Irish Press,* 28 Apr. 1966.
149. Speech to Irish Management Institute, 21 Apr. 1966; text in NA, D/T 97/6/66.
150. 30 Apr. 1966; text in NA, D/T 96/6/325.
151. Drafts of Government statements on Labour Court guidelines are in NA, D/T 97/6/325.
152. Hillery interview.
153. Ibid.
154. Ibid.
155. 'Lemass warned of union power', *Irish Times,* 1–2 Jan. 1997.
156. The *Cork Examiner* continued to publish.
157. *Dáil Debates,* vol. 217, col. 1206, 14 July 1965.
158. Details in *Dáil Debates,* vol. 217, col. 1071–96, 13 July 1965.
159. See correspondence generally in NA, D/T S17872 C.
160. Department of Finance memorandum, 19 Oct. 1966, NA, D/T 97/6/74.
161. Murphy (1996), 154.

Chapter 8 (p. 252–288)

1. Rugby to CRO, 16 Oct. 1947, PRO, PREM8/824.
2. MacEntee made this offer in a conversation with the Canadian High Commissioner in Ireland, John D. Kearney, who included it in a report to his government in Ottawa, copied in PRO, DO130/43.
3. Aiken in conversation with the British ambassador in Dublin, Sir Alexander Clutterbuck, 3 Mar. 1958. This and other unattributed references in this section are from PRO, DO35/7891.

4. G. Anderson, Dublin, to W. F. le Bailly, CRO, 1 Sep. 1960, PRO, DO35/8033.
5. 16 Oct. 1957, PRO, DO35/7891.
6. Clutterbuck to Lord Home, 20 Aug. 1959, PRO, DO35/5379.
7. Record of conversation with Mr Lemass, 13 July 1959, PRO, DO35/7891.
8. Bardon (1982), 629.
9. Sayers to J. J. Horgan, 22 July 1959, commenting on an interview with Lemass that appeared in the *Belfast Telegraph* of the same date, NA, D/T S9361/I. Horgan, a Cork solicitor and public figure with a Redmondite and Cumann na nGaedheal background, was for many years the anonymous correspondent from the Republic for both the *Belfast Telegraph* and the Commonwealth periodical *The Round Table*. The author is his grandson.
10. *Irish Times,* 2 July 1959.
11. *Irish Independent,* 13 Aug. 1959.
12. Ibid., 31 Aug. 1959.
13. *Irish Press,* 5 Sep. 1969.
14. It was IRA policy at the time not to recognise the courts in either jurisdiction.
15. *Irish Times,* 16 Aug. 1959.
16. Southport, Lancashire; *Irish Times,* 21 Sep. 1959.
17. *Dáil Debates,* vol. 176, col. 1576, 21 July 1959.
18. *Irish Times,* 16 Oct. 1959.
19. *Northern Whig,* 15 Oct. 1959.
20. *Irish Times,* 11 Nov. 1959.
21. Ibid. The Department of External Affairs in a later comment on this statement (17 May 1962) noted carefully that 'this indicates clearly that our recognition is only de facto', NA, D/T S9361/I.
22. *Irish Times,* 11 Nov. 1959.
23. Ibid., 22 June 1960.
24. Maffey to Machtig, 11 July 1940, PRO, DO130/1.
25. *Irish Press,*15 Dec. 1959.
26. NA, D/T S1957 C/61.
27. *Irish Times,* 11 Nov. 1959.
28. Lemass to Vivion de Valera, 14 May 1960, NA, D/T S9361 I/94.
29. *Irish Times,* 23 May 1960; *Irish Independent,* 24 May 1960.
30. *Dáil Debates,* 21 June 1960, vol. 183, col. 1–4.
31. Michael McInerney (political correspondent), *Irish Times,* 28 Sep. 1960. McInerney was wont to remark in the *Irish Times* news room: 'There's nothing much happening: I think I'll ring Lemass.' (Author's personal recollection.)
32. NA, D/T S1957 C/61.
33. NA, D/T S1957 C/95.
34. NA, D/T 96/6/23.
35. Ibid. See also Ronan Fanning, 'Lemass: a prophet with mountains to climb', *Sunday Independent,* 7 Jan. 1996.
36. *Irish Press,* 9 Nov. 1960. For the full text of his 1959 speech see NA, D/T S9361I/64.
37. See James Downey, 'The 1993 state papers: O'Neill reluctant to respond to South's overtures', *Irish Independent,* 1–3 Jan. 1994.
38. Lemass to Blythe, 7 Dec. 1962, NA, D/T S16272 D/62.
39. PRO, PREM11/4326.
40. *Irish Press,* 2 Apr. 1960.

41. See for example *Irish Press,* 5, 18 and 13 May and 9 June 1960.
42. PRONI, CAB4/1097, 9 July 1959.
43. PRONI CAB4/1115, 2 Feb. 1960.
44. Reports of meetings between Minister for Industry and Commerce and Ulster Furniture Representatives, 14 Feb. and 16 Mar. 1961, NA, D/T S16262.
45. PRONI CAB4/1161, 1 June 1961. At the time of writing (Jan. 1995), CAB4/1158, which contains the original memorandum from the Minister of Commerce on the proposed trade concessions, has still not been released.
46. The expense account for the lunch is in NA, D/T S12068 B.
47. NA, D/T S17246 M/62.
48. NA, DFA, Secretary's files, P338/1, 14 Oct. 1959. This was in reference to a controversy involving the claims of the Mater Hospital in Belfast, a Catholic hospital, for improved state funding.
49. Lemass to Blythe, 7 Dec. 1962, NA, D/T S16272 D/62.
50. Quoted in James Downey, 'Taoiseach's North trip caused delight', *Irish Independent,* 1–2 Jan. 1996.
51. Cruise O'Brien interview.
52. Curran interview.
53. See, for example, minutes of Fianna Fáil Central Committee (19 Oct. 1956), which decided to vote against Deputy Jack McQuillan's proposal in this regard, FF/440C.
54. Curran interview.
55. *Business and Finance,* 2 June 1967.
56. NA, DFA, Secretary's files, P273/1, 1 Jan. 1960.
57. Ibid., P338/1, Horan to Cremin, 20 Feb. 1960.
58. Childers to Lemass, 1 Mar. 1961, NA, D/T S16272 C/61.
59. NA, DFA, Secretary's files, P338; memorandum to Secretary of Department of External Affairs from M. Mooney, 3 July 1961.
60. 26 Mar. 1962, NA, DFA, 305/14/341.
61. Ibid.
62. Ibid., Lemass to Healy, 31 Mar. 1962.
63. Department of Foreign Affairs, Secretary's files, P338; Lemass to O'Malley, 6 Feb. 1963.
64. Department of Foreign Affairs, 1995 release; 305/114/343; memorandum from R. Ó Foghlú, 12 July 1962.
65. Department of Foreign Affairs, 305/14/342; internal DFA memorandum, 10 Jan. 1963.
66. Wallace (1970), 87–8.
67. Private secretary, Minister for External Affairs, to private secretary, Minister for Justice, 17 Apr. 1963.
68. Lemass to Colley, 30 July 1964, NA, DFA, 1995 release, 305/14/325.
69. Aiken to Hillery, 26 Jan. 1965.
70. Lemass to Healy, 4 Oct. 1963, NA, S9361 K/62.
71. *Irish Times,* 16 Sep. 1959.
72. 29 July 1963; text in NA, D/T S9361 K/63.
73. *Belfast Telegraph,* 30 July 1963.
74. Ibid.
75. *News Letter,* 30 July 1963.
76. *Irish Times,* 2 Aug. 1963.
77. *Irish Independent,* 30 July 1963.

78. *Irish Times,* 30 July 1963.
79. *Irish Press,*12 Sep. 1963.
80. NA, DFA, 1994 release, P363, 16 Sep. 1963.
81. Kennedy's resolution is noted in a letter to an Irish-American journalist, Thomas McGuigan junior, who wrote to the White House in Jan. 1964 to invoke Johnson's assistance in the cause of Irish unity; LBJ, General, CO 125, FG 105.
82. T. J. Kiernan to McCann, Department of External Affairs, NA, D/T S9361 K/62.
83. K. Cunningham, Stormont, to P. de Zulueta, 24 Apr. 1963, PRO, PREM11/4386.
84. McGeorge Bundy to Johnson, 17 Mar. 1964, LBJ, NSF Ireland file, box 195.
85. Ibid.
86. Ibid.
87. O'Neill to Johnson, 26 Mar. 1964, LBJ, NSF, Ireland file, box 195.
88. Kiernan interview, JFK Oral History Project.
89. *Irish Times,* 17 Oct. 1963.
90. *Irish Press,* 18 Oct. 1963.
91. Speech at Boston College, 20 Oct. 1963; text in NA, D/T S9361K/63.
92. *Irish Independent,* 18 Oct. 1963.
93. Horgan to Lemass, 26 Oct. 1963, NA, D/T S16272 E/63. See also note 9.
94. Editorial, 29 Nov. 1963.
95. George Reedy, n.d. [Feb. 1964], to Andy Hatcher, State Department, LBJ, CO 125, FG 105.
96. McArthur to Murphy, 14 Apr. 1965, LBJ, WHCF subject file—Ireland, box 42.
97. Quoted later in *Irish Times,* 19 Nov. 1964.
98. *Irish Times,* 9 Dec. 1963.
99. Writing as 'Beann Madagáin' in *Inniu,* 1 Nov. 1963.
100. Text in NA, D/T S9361 K/63.
101. *Irish Press,* 13 Apr. 1964.
102. Cremin to McCann, 19 Jan. 1963, NA, D/T S9361 K/63.
103. NA, D/T S9361 K/63.
104. References in this section are drawn from the author's interview with T. K. Whitaker or from Ed Moloney's account, *Irish Times,* 15 Jan. 1985, unless otherwise attributed.
105. Whitaker interview.
106. Details in this section, unless otherwise attributed, are taken from Ed Moloney's account, *Irish Times,* 15 Jan. 1985.
107. Whitaker to Malley, 5 Jan. 1965, NA, DFA, 1994 release, Secretary's files, P363. Most of the references to North-South co-operation during this period are taken from this file and its 1995 successor, unless otherwise indicated.
108. Lynch interview.
109. Bloomfield (1994), 80.
110. Interview with Wesley Boyd, *Irish Times,* 25 Jan. 1965.
111. *Parliament of Northern Ireland,* vol. 71, col. 413–14, 29 Jan. 1969.
112. O'Neill (1972), 280.
113. Gageby interview.
114. Report on visit by T. K. Whitaker, 15 Jan. 1965, NA, DFA, 1994 release, Secretary's files, P363.
115. Memorandum on O'Neill-Lemass meeting, 11 Feb. 1965, NA, DFA, 96/3/16.

116. Note from Hugh McCann, Department of Foreign Affairs, on report on visit by T. K. Whitaker, 15 Jan. 1965, NA, DFA, 1994 release, Secretary's files, P363.
117. *Belfast Telegraph,* 4 Feb. 1965. His speech was at a meeting in TCD.
118. *Irish Times,* 21 Jan. 1965.
119. Note of meeting between Hugh McCann, Department of Foreign Affairs, and Tory, 21 Jan. 1965, NA, DFA, 1994 release, Secretary's files, P363.
120. 21 Jan. 1965, PRO, PREM13/411. The draft was sent to London on 16 Feb.
121. *Irish Times,* 18 Mar. 1965.
122. Whitaker to McCann, 16 Feb. 1965, NA, DFA, 1994 release, Secretary's files, P363.
123. Ó Nualláin to Whitaker, 1 Feb. 1965, NA, D/T S16272 G/65.
124. Whitaker to MacCarthy, 22 Dec. 1965, NA, D/T S16272 J/65.
125. *Dáil Debates,* vol. 214, col. 3 ff, 10 Feb. 1965.
126. Drafts in NA, DFA, 96/3/15.
127. NA, DFA, 1995 release, Secretary's files, P363. Aiken to Lemass, 27 Jan. 1965, contains a detailed account of the discussion.
128. Aiken to Lemass, 27 Jan. 1965, NA, DFA, 1995 release, Secretary's files, P363.
129. Curran interview.
130. *Belfast Telegraph,* 14 Nov. 1960. The newspaper's anonymous contributor was Lemass's correspondent from Cork, J. J. Horgan.
131. Aiken to Lemass, 27 Jan. 1965, NA, DFA, P363.
132. Author's conversation with Tom O'Higgins.
133. *Irish Times,* 12 Apr. 1966.
134. John O'Connor interview.
135. Lemass to Lynch, 31 Jan. 1966; Lynch to Lemass, 14 Feb. 1966, NA, D/T 97/6/161.
136. *Irish Times,* 30 Mar. 1966.
137. Ibid., 15 Apr. 1966.
138. Ibid., 7, 8 and 9 Apr. 1966.
139. Ibid., 12 Apr. 1966.
140. Ibid.
141. Ibid., 7 Apr. 1966.
142. NA, D/T 97/6/161.
143. *Irish Times,* 17 Apr. 1966.
144. Ibid., 18 Apr. 1966.
145. Ibid., 19 Apr. 1966.
146. Lemass to de Valera, 15 July 1959, manuscript letter, FA, 1410/2.
147. Recollection of one of those attending the meeting, Hugh O'Flaherty.
148. Cruise O'Brien interview.
149. *Irish Press,* 20 Oct. 1966.
150. *Dáil Debates,* vol. 224, col. 107, 25 Oct. 1966.
151. Bernard Purcell, 'UK government advised to take "back seat" over unification', *Irish Independent,* 1–2 Jan. 1997.
152. Statement recorded by Lemass for Hessische Rundfunk, 7 Oct. 1960, NA, DFA, 305/14/341.
153. Curran (1979), 37–8.
154. *Irish Times,* 12 May 1971.
155. NA, DFA, 1995 release, P363.

Chapter 9 (p. 289–325)

1. Garvin (1982), 31.
2. Lee (1976).
3. Tobin (1996), 20.
4. Quoted in Savage (1996), 109.
5. Ibid., 110.
6. Minutes of general meeting of the Catholic hierarchy, June 1959, ADA B 6–10.
7. Lemass to Ó Cearbhaill, 14 Aug. 1964, NA, D/T S17678/95.
8. Report of meeting in Department of Finance, 8 Oct. 1964, NA, D/T S17678/95. Further references in this section are to this file unless otherwise noted.
9. Whitaker to Ryan, 12 Dec. 1957, NA, D/T S16066 A. This was the document that originated the 'Economic Development' study.
10. Lemass to Boland, 18 Dec. 1964.
11. Dáil Debates, vol. 215, col. 1298, 13 May 1965.
12. Speech at Port Laoise, 2 Apr. 1965; text in NA, D/T S17678.
13. See statement in response to British decision in NA, D/T S17529A/95.
14. Lynch to Lemass, 26 May 1965, NA, D/T S17678.
15. Government minutes, 31 Aug. 1965, GC 11/22; NA, D/T S17678.
16. Memorandums to Government, Department of Finance, 24 Aug. 1965 and 9 Nov. 1966, NA, D/T S17678.
17. Memorandum to Government, 9 Nov. 1966, 3, NA, D/T S17678.
18. The committee was set up in June 1962. Extracts from its report, which was drafted by Dr Finbar O'Callaghan, inspector, appear in Hyland and Milne (1992), 555–60.
19. NA, D/T S17405 C/63.
20. Hillery to Lemass, 9 Jan. 63, NA, D/T S17405 C/63.
21. Interview with Hillery, quoted in Bonel-Elliott (1962).
22. Lemass to Hillery, 11 Jan. 1963, NA, D/T S17405/C 63.
23. Hillery interview.
24. Lemass to Hillery, 16 Jan. 1963, NA, D/T S17405 /C 63.
25. Mac Gearailt to Ó Cearbhaill, 16 Jan. 1963, NA, D/T S17405/C 63.
26. Ibid.
27. Hillery interview.
28. Irish Times, 1 July 1964.
29. Ibid., 22 Apr. 1965.
30. See Dr Browne's letter attacking George Colley, Irish Independent, 28 Sep. 1965.
31. Colley to Lemass, 24 Sep. 1965, NA, D/T 96/6/355.
32. Lemass to Colley, 25 Sep. 1965, NA, D/T 96/6/355.
33. Lemass to Haughey, 7 Dec. 1964, NA, D/T S17437 E/95.
34. Irish Times, 12 May 1971.
35. Parliamentary party minutes, 10 Apr. 1956, FF/440C.
36. Recollection of John Dillon of a conversation with Lemass when Lemass visited the Oxford Union in 1969. Lemass invited a number of Irish students, among whom were Dillon and William O'Malley Armstrong, a nephew of Donogh O'Malley, to tea with him on that occasion. The remark was made to tease Armstrong. Information to the author from John Dillon, 21 Dec. 1992.
37. Fianna Fáil parliamentary party minutes, 24 Dec. 1960, FF/440B.
38. Michael Mills, Irish Press, 18 June 1959.

39. Private source.
40. Quoted in Farrell (1991), 107.
41. O'Malley to Lemass, 7 Sep. 1966, NA, D/T 96/6/357. Other references in this section are to documents in this file unless otherwise specified.
42. Charles Haughey interview.
43. Boland interview.
44. O'Malley to Lemass, 14 Sep. 1966.
45. Lemass to O'Malley, 22 Sep. 1966.
46. Lemass to O'Malley, 26 Sep. 1966.
47. Charles Haughey interview.
48. Lemass to O'Malley, 17 Oct. 1966, NA, D/T 97/6/638. The Finance memorandum was considered at one of Lynch's first Government meetings as Taoiseach.
49. NA, D/T 97/6/638.
50. *Irish Times,* 12 May 1971.
51. Longford and O'Neill (1970), 479.
52. *Dáil Debates,* vol. 110, col. 57, 4 May 1948.
53. *Irish Times,* 2 July 1964.
54. *Irish Press,* 5 Jan. 1948.
55. Ibid., 23 Oct. 1951.
56. See *Irish Independent,* 13 Dec. 1954 (speech at Cork), *Enniscorthy Guardian,* 26 Mar. 1955 (speech at Wexford), and *Irish Press,* 27 Apr. 1955 (speech in Dublin).
57. Charles Haughey interview.
58. Whitaker interview. Whitaker sent him a book on banking by Sayers and other works on development economics.
59. Communication from Prof. Cohan, 7 June 1996.
60. Interview with Kees van Hoek, *Irish Times,* 17 Feb. 1951.
61. *Irish Times,* 31 Dec. 1963. The speech in question included an exhortation to people to 'speak Irish if you know it.'
62. *Irish Press,* 7 Jan. 1965.
63. John Healy, *Irish Times,* 11 Nov. 1966.
64. See Interview with foreign journalists, 5 Sep. 1962, in NA, D/T S16699 E/62.
65. *Irish Press,* 31 Jan. 1969.
66. *Irish Times,* 1 Mar. 1957. The fact that this was an election speech has an obvious bearing on its content.
67. Lemass to Ó Fiaich, 27 May 1961, NA, D/T S13180 D/61. Dr Ó Fiaich was subsequently president of St Patrick's College, Maynooth, and Archbishop of Armagh and Primate of All Ireland.
68. Lemass to Ó Fiaich, 10 Nov. 1961, NA, D/T S13180 D/61.
69. The appointment of Seán Mac Gearailt, on secondment from the Department of Education (and later Secretary of that Department), was made on 1 Nov. 1961.
70. *Irish Times,* 13 Sep. 1961.
71. Speech in Dublin, 20 Sep. 1961, NA, D/T S13180 D/61.
72. Speech in Arklow, 25 Sep. 1961, NA, D/T S13180 D/61.
73. Speech in Limerick, 30 Sep. 1961, NA, D/T S13180 D/61.
74. Ó Móráin interview.
75. *Irish Times,* 2 July 1964.
76. Lemass to Assistant Secretary, 3 Feb. 1964, NA, D/T S13611 C/95.
77. *Irish Press,* 18 Nov. 1964.

78. Text of ardfheis speech in NA, D/T S13180 D/95. Subsequent references to the controversy arising from this speech are from the same file.
79. Ó Muimhneacháin to Lemass, 18 Nov. 1964.
80. Brennan to Lemass, 25 Nov. 1964.
81. Ó Fiaich to Lemass, 24 Nov. 1964.
82. Lemass to Brennan, 26 Nov. 1964.
83. Lemass to P. Ó Séaghdha, Cork, 25 Nov. 1964.
84. Brennan to Lemass, 27 Nov. 1964.
85. Ó Fiaich to Lemass, 1 Dec. 1964.
86. Government White paper, Jan. 1965, para. 4.
87. Whitaker interview. De Valera's continuing interest in Irish-language policy after his retirement had already been commented on by the British ambassador: see PRO, DO35/7891.
88. NA, Government conclusions GC 10/189, Government meeting of 18 Dec. 1964.
89. Speech to Fianna Fáil meeting in Dún Laoghaire, 26 Jan. 1965; text in NA, D/T S16272/G.
90. Interview with Fleur Cowles of *Harper's Bazaar,* 12 May 1965, NA, D/T 97/6/253.
91. Interview reprinted from *Ógra Fianna Fáil* in *Business and Finance,* 2 June 1967.
92. Author's conversation with Ruairí Brugha, Dublin, 8 May 1995.
93. NA, Government minutes 10/203, meeting of 9 Mar. 1965.
94. Liam de Barra, secretary of the council, to Joseph Brennan, Minister for Posts and Telegraphs, 29 Apr. 1965, copied to the Secretary, Department of the Taoiseach, on the following day, NA, D/T 96/6/439.
95. Speech by Michael Hilliard, Minister for Posts and Telegraphs, at the first meeting of the new authority, 2 June 1960; text in NA, D/T S14996.
96. Lemass to Moynihan, 8 May 1960, NA, D/T S14996.
97. Much of the material in this and the following paragraphs dealing with the eventual establishment of the Radio Éireann Authority is based on Savage (1996) where not otherwise attributed.
98. Submission from Irish Hospitals' Trust, 24 Dec. 1934, NA, D/T S7095.
99. Memorandum, Department of Posts and Telegraphs, 5 Jan. 1935, NA, D/T S7095.
100. Department of Finance memorandum from FitzGerald to Ó Broin, 2 Aug. 1957, quoted in Savage (1996), 81. Whitaker's memorandum to James Ryan—the birth certificate of *Economic Development*—is in NA, D/T S16066 A, 12 Dec. 1957.
101. NA, D/T S1499B, memorandum dated 25 Oct.
102. Ó Broin (1985), 209.
103. Michael Mills, *Irish Press,*18 Jan. 1969.
104. Text in NA, Department of Communications, T007/57, file 2.
105. Michelson to Lemass, 24 Oct. 1959, NA, Department of Communications, T007/57, file 2.
106. Hilliard to Lemass, 3 Nov. 1959, NA, Department of Communications, T007/57, file 2.
107. Lemass to Hilliard, 23 Nov. 1959, NA, Department of Communications, T007/57, file 2.
108. Michael Mills, *Irish Press,* 6 Feb. 1969.
109. Speech at inauguration of Telefís Éireann, 31 Dec. 1961, NA, D/T S14996 E/61.

110. Conversation with the author, 20 June 1996.
111. MacEntee papers, UCD, P67/821/4.
112. NA, D/T S17018/61.
113. Information from Wesley Boyd, writer of the article in question, Jan. 1997.
114. Lemass to Moynihan, 11 Apr. 1960, commenting on Moynihan's draft of speech for opening night, NA, D/T S14996.
115. Lemass to Hilliard, 12 Apr. 1960, NA, D/T S14996D.
116. Lemass's rewriting of Moynihan's original draft, Lemass to Moynihan, 4 May 1960, NA, D/T S14996.
117. Lemass to Moynihan, 4 May 1960, NA, D/T S14996. The word 'spiritual' was omitted by the typist who transcribed Lemass's original handwritten draft, written on 11 Apr., but reinserted by him in ink on the typed version of his memo.
118. 12 Jan. 1961, NA, D/T S14996D.
119. Lemass to Miss Maisie Dooley, 7 Apr. 1964, NA, D/T S14996 F/95.
120. Roth to Lemass, 21 Oct. 1961, NA, S3532 C/63.
121. Lemass to Hilliard, 2 Feb. 1962, NA, S3532 C/63.
122. Lemass to Ó hAnracháin, 4 May 1962, NA, S3532 C/63.
123. NA, D/T S10978/61.
124. Lemass to Ó hAnracháin, 4 May 1962, NA, D/T S3532 C/63; Rugheimer interview.
125. Lemass to Ó hAnracháin, 13 Sep. 1962; Ó hAnracháin to Lemass 15 Sep. 1962, NA, D/T S3532 C/63.
126. Lemass to Ó hAnracháin, 4 Jan. 1963, NA, D/T S3532 C/63. The programme was 'Our Emigrants', transmitted on 3 Jan. 1963.
127. Lemass to Hilliard, 7 Mar. 1963, NA, D/T S3532 C/63.
128. Ó hAnracháin to Lemass, 5 Oct. 1962, LP.
129. Andrews to Lemass, 28 Nov. 63, NA, D/T S3532 C/63.
130. Doolin, Dowling and Quinn (1969), 49.
131. McCourt interview.
132. NA, S16699 F/95, interview for publication in *Irish Times,* 6 Feb. 1964. See also NA, S16748 C.
133. Lemass to Secretary, Department of the Taoiseach, 10 July 1964, NA, D/T S3532 D/95.
134. Secretary, Department of the Taoiseach, to Lemass, 14 July 1964, NA, D/T S3532 D/95.
135. Rugheimer interview. In fact Bean Uí Cheallaigh was on the second authority, not the first.
136. Rugheimer interview.
137. *Dáil Debates,* vol. 224, col. 1048, 12 Oct. 1966.
138. Ibid., col. 1045–6 and 1048, 12 Oct. 1966.
139. This inaccurate paraphrase is in Doolin, Dowling and Quinn (1969), 91.
140. Interview with S. J. Goldsmith of the Jewish Telegraphic Agency, *Catholic Herald,* 28 Aug. 1964.
141. Press conference with American journalists, 9 Sep. 1964, NA, D/T S16699 F/95.
142. Correspondence, including a letter from Lemass to McQuaid of 18 Dec. 1943, in FA, 1440/5.
143. Drafts of speech and correspondence in NA, D/T S1694.
144. Letter from Mgr John Power, Northampton, detailing comments of Bishop Parker of Northampton, NA, D/T S1694.

145. Lemass to McQuaid, 31 Mar. 1960, NA, D/T S13795 B/61, from which other references to the library controversy are also taken.
146. McQuaid to d'Alton, 4 May 1960, ADA B 6–10.
147. Lemass-Lenihan correspondence in NA, D/T 96/6/364.
148. Ó Broin to McCann, 9 Apr. 1965, NA, DFA, 96/2/14.
149. Lemass to Aiken, 5 Apr. 1966, NA, DFA, 278b (i).
150. Lemass-Lenihan correspondence, 1 and 5 Sep. 1966, in NA, D/T 97/6/561.
151. Sheridan interview.
152. Colm Barnes, undated note of conversation with Lemass, CBP.
153. O'Doherty interview.

Chapter 10 (p. 326–347)

1. Hillery interview.
2. *Irish Press,* 19 Nov. 1983.
3. Sheridan interview.
4. O'Regan interview.
5. Hillery interview.
6. Personal communication from Prof. Tom Garvin, UCD, who was a civil servant attached to the department at the time and who dealt with the file.
7. Lenihan interview.
8. Family source.
9. Hillery interview.
10. Interview on 'Celtic Challenge', RTE; see also *Irish Press,* 3 Dec. 1963.
11. *Irish Times,* 2 Apr. 1965.
12. Ibid., 9 Nov. 1966, during his final press conference.
13. Lemass to Brennan, 26 Oct. 1966.
14. Memorandum by Tadhg Ó Cearbhaill in relation to meeting of the Government on 9 Sep. 1965, NA, D/T 97/6/441.
15. Speech to Fianna Fáil function, Limerick, 25 Mar. 1966.
16. Parliamentary party minutes, 1 Dec. 1965, FF/441C.
17. Ibid., 2 Feb. 1966, FF/441C.
18. Andrews (1982), 50.
19. Parliamentary party minutes, 2 Mar. 1966, FF/441C.
20. Ibid., 5 May 1966, FF/441C.
21. Memorandum to Government, 10 Sep. 1966, NA, D/T 97/6/637. The proposed scheme was not in fact implemented.
22. Parliamentary party minutes, 9 Mar. 1966, FF/441C.
23. Ibid., 23 Mar. 1966, FF/441C.
24. Michael Mills, *Irish Press,* 3 Feb. 1969.
25. Barnes interview.
26. Andrews (1982), 76.
27. National Executive minutes, 26 Sep. 1966, FF/346.
28. Michael Mills, *Irish Press,* 31 Jan. 1969.
29. Hillery interview; Lynch interview.
30. Speech to Institute of Public Relations, Dublin, 29 Apr. 1966 (duplicated), by courtesy of T. J. O'Driscoll.
31. Bruce Arnold, 'George Colley, the heir apparent', *Sunday Independent,* 16 Sep. 1979; Arnold papers, NLI.
32. Lenihan interview.
33. Parliamentary party minutes, 26 Oct. 1966, FF/441C.

34. Jacqui Dunne, interview with Kathleen Lemass, *Sunday Independent,* 29 Apr. 1979.
35. Communication from Michael Mills, 22 Jan. 1995.
36. *Irish Times,* 9 Nov. 1966.
37. Hillery interview.
38. Ibid.
39. Bruce Arnold, 'George Colley, the heir apparent', *Sunday Independent,* 16 Sep. 1979.
40. Michael O'Regan, interview with Kevin Boland, *Irish Times,* 12 Mar. 1983.
41. 'Lemass and national progress' (review of Brian Farrell, *Seán Lemass*), *Irish Press,* 19 Nov. 1983.
42. Michael Mills, *Irish Press,* 31 Jan. 1969.
43. Mills interview.
44. Aiken to Lemass, 30 Oct. 1966, LP.
45. *Irish Times,* 1 Nov. 1966.
46. Charles Haughey interview.
47. *Irish Times,* 3 Nov. 1966.
48. Boland interview.
49. Blaney interview.
50. Charles Haughey interview.
51. *Irish Times,* 10 Nov. 1966.
52. Parliamentary party minutes, 9 Nov. 1966, FF/440C, from which all references in this section are drawn unless otherwise attributed.
53. MacEntee Papers, UCD, P67/734.
54. Copy in Sheila O'Connor's family library.
55. Charles Haughey interview.
56. *Business and Finance,* 2 June 1967.
57. *Irish Independent,* 2 Dec. 1966.
58. *Irish Independent,* 30 Dec. 1966.
59. McCourt interview.
60. Contemporary note by Colm Barnes, CBP.
61. Personal communication to author.
62. Speech to ardfheis, 10 Nov. 1959; text in NA, D/T S9361 I/64.
63. Family source.
64. Andrews (1982), 250–1.
65. *Irish Times,* 18 Jan. 1969.
66. O'Kennedy interview.
67. O'Kennedy interview, from which other references to Lemass's role in the committee are also taken unless otherwise indicated.
68. *Committee on the Constitution: Report* (1967), 43.
69. O'Kennedy interview.
70. Recollection of Tom O'Higgins in conversation with the author, 29 Dec. 1995.
71. O'Kennedy interview.
72. Private source.
73. *Irish Times,* 24 Oct. 1967.
74. Ibid., 27 Oct. 1967.
75. *Irish Independent,* 30 Oct. 1967.
76. *Irish Times,* 2 Nov. 1967.
77. Letter from W. H. Murray, a fellow-director, to Colm Barnes, 16 Feb. 1982, CBP.

78. *Irish Press,* 5 Jan. 1978, from which all these quotations from the letter are drawn.
79. Jack Lynch, interview on RTE, 8 Jan. 1978; contemporary summary in CBP.
80. Speech to New Ireland Society, Belfast, *Irish Times,* 24 Oct. 1969.
81. Lenihan interview.
82. O'Sullivan (1994), 192.
83. Private source. (For the purpose of clarification it should be noted that Mr Lynch did not discuss this meeting in his interview with the author.)
84. Michael Mills, *Irish Press,* 31 Jan. 1969.
85. Ibid.
86. Author's conversation with Seán Sherwin, 10 July 1973.
87. Author's conversation with Brian Lenihan, 26 July 1992.
88. Moll Lemass, 24 Feb. 1997.
89. Ibid.
90. *Irish Independent* and *Irish Times,* 12 Apr. 1971.
91. *Irish Press,* 12 Apr. 1971.
92. *Dáil Debates,* vol. 253, col. 1503, 11 May 1971.
93. Ibid., col. 1502, 11 May 1971.
94. Ibid., vol. 218, col. 1838–9, 17 Nov. 1965.

Chapter 11 (p. 348–357)

1. *Time,* 12 July 1963.
2. Bew (1989), 81. In 1987 Lemass said that he thought the 'social-democratic appellation', which he had applied to himself, was 'no longer right' and that political leaders should generally be to the left of their more conservative party rank and file; *Business and Finance,* 2 June 1967.
3. Allen (1992), 166–78.
4. Speech to New Ireland Society, Belfast, *Irish Times,* 24 Oct. 1969.
5. Speech at King's Inns, 18 Feb. 1966 (duplicated), CBP.
6. Interview in *Irish Spotlight,* n.d. [1966], CBP.
7. This is the title of a series of pen-pictures, generally in the heroic mode, of early Fianna Fáil politicians by Liam Skinner (1946). Skinner attributes the phrase to Lemass, as did Jack Lynch in his obituary tribute to Lemass in Dáil Éireann.
8. *Business and Finance,* 2 June 1967.
9. Conversation with the author, 1974.

Sources

Interviews

The date shown is the date on which the interview took place. Less formal interviews and conversations with other individuals, and letters from friends or acquaintances of Seán Lemass, are cited individually in the notes.

Barnes, Colm (10 Jan. 1993). Colm Barnes has been a prominent businessman for many years and has been associated principally with the Glen Abbey textile enterprise.

Barrett, Tommy (4 Sep. 1996). Tommy Barrett worked for the *Irish Press* when Seán Lemass was managing director, from 1948 to 1951.

Blaney, Neil (10 Oct. 1994). Neil Blaney, a former Fianna Fáil TD, Government minister under both de Valera and Lemass and MEP, died in 1995.

Boland, Kevin (24 Nov. 1994). Kevin Boland, a former Fianna Fáil TD and Government minister under both de Valera and Lemass, resigned from Fianna Fáil in 1970.

Brugha, Ruairí (8 May 1995). Ruairí Brugha, son of Cathal Brugha, who died in the Civil War, has been a Fianna Fáil senator and has been active in the party and in business circles for many years.

Cathcart, Rex (8 Jan. 1993). Rex Cathcart was an educationalist who also served for a time with Ulster Television.

Cronin, Bart (31 Oct. 1995). Bart Cronin has held a number of senior information posts in Government departments and as information officer of Aer Lingus.

Cruise O'Brien, Conor (25 Sep. 1995). Conor Cruise O'Brien, a former diplomat, TD, Government minister and senator, is a writer and historian.

Curran, Frank (22 Mar. 1995). Frank Curran is a journalist and a former editor of the *Derry Journal*.

Flanagan, Leo (6 Oct. 1994). Leo Flanagan, Skerries, Co. Dublin, is a businessman and former friend and golfing companion of Seán Lemass.

Flanagan, Seán (2 Oct. 1992). Seán Flanagan was a Fianna Fáil TD and Government minister.

Gageby, Douglas (21 Feb. 1995). Douglas Gageby is a former editor of the *Irish Times*.

Haughey, Charles (24 Oct. 1994). Charles J. Haughey is a former TD, Government minister and Taoiseach.

Haughey, Maureen (1 Oct. 1993). Mrs Haughey is Seán Lemass's eldest daughter.

Healy, Seán (6 Oct. 1995). Seán Healy, Co. Wicklow, is a former leading figure in both Macra na Feirme and the Irish Farmers' Association.

Herbert, Michael (31 Aug. 1993). Michael Herbert is a former Fianna Fáil TD.

Hillery, Patrick (14 Dec. 1994). Dr Hillery is a former Fianna Fáil TD, Government minister, EEC Commissioner and President of Ireland.

Kiely, Ben (2 May 1995). Ben Kiely, a novelist and short story writer, worked as a journalist for the *Irish Press*.

Lemass, Moll (1 Mar. 1995). Moll Lemass (née McDonagh) is the widow of Frank Lemass, brother of Seán Lemass.

Lenihan, Brian (28 Sep. 1993). Brian Lenihan, a former Fianna Fáil TD, Government minister and Tánaiste, died in 1995.

Lynch, Jack (11 Nov. 1992). Jack Lynch is a former Fianna Fáil TD, Government minister and Taoiseach.

Lynch, Patrick (18 Oct. 1994). Patrick Lynch is an economist, a former secretary to the Government, and chairman of Aer Lingus.

McCourt, Kevin (24 Feb. 1997). Kevin McCourt is a businessman, former secretary of the Federation of Irish Industry and director-general of RTE.

Mhac an tSaoi, Máire (14 Sep. 1995). Máire Mhac an tSaoi is a poet, daughter of Seán and Margaret MacEntee.

Moynihan, Maurice (28 Apr. 1992). Maurice Moynihan is a former Secretary to the Government under both de Valera and Lemass and former chairman of the Central Bank.

O'Brien, Peggy Lemass, and Commandant Jack (13 Feb. 1995). Mrs Lemass O'Brien is Seán Lemass's second daughter; her husband is Seán Lemass's former aide-de-camp.

Ó Cearbhaill, Tadhg (19 Oct. 1994). Mr Ó Cearbhaill is a former civil servant in the Departments of Industry and Commerce and Department of the Taoiseach and subsequently Secretary of the Department of Labour.

O'Connor, Sheila (née Lemass) and John O'Connor (18 Sep. 1996). Mrs O'Connor was Seán Lemass's youngest daughter; she died in March 1997. Mr O'Connor is a businessman.

O'Doherty, Kevin (3 Oct. 1995). Kevin O'Doherty was private secretary to Seán Lemass from 1944 to 1946.

O'Driscoll, T. J. (22 Feb. 1995). T. J. O'Driscoll was a civil servant, private secretary to John Leydon from 1934 to 1946, later ambassador to the Netherlands, head of Córas Tráchtála and director-general of Bord Fáilte

O'Kennedy, Michael (22 June 1995). Michael O'Kennedy is a Fianna Fáil TD, former Government minister, EEC Commissioner and senator.

Ó Móráin, Dónall (30 Nov. 1994). Dónall Ó Móráin is director of Gael-Linn and a former chairman of the RTE Authority.

O'Rahilly, Aodhagán (26 June 1995). Aodhagán O'Rahilly is a businessman who was closely associated with C. S. Andrews and others in the development of native industries.

O'Regan, Brendan (26 Apr. 1995). Brendan O'Regan is a former chairman of Shannon Free Airport Development Company and is now involved in business and community development in Co. Clare.

Rugheimer, Gunnar (23 Mar. 1995). Gunnar Rugheimer is a former Controller of Programmes of RTE.

Ryan, Eoin (18 Jan. 1995). Eoin Ryan is a son of James Ryan and was for many years a Fianna Fáil senator and member of the Fianna Fáil National Executive

Sherwin, Seán (5 Mar. 1996). Seán Sherwin is a former Fianna Fáil TD; he now works in the party's head office.

Sweetman, William (19 July 1995). William Sweetman was editor of the *Irish Press* from 1948 to 1951.

Whitaker, T. K. (10 Oct. 1994 and 14 Dec. 1995). T. K. Whitaker is a former Secretary of the Department of Finance and chairman of the Central Bank and the author of *Economic Development* (1958).

Manuscript sources

Lemass family papers
Miscellaneous correspondence, photographs and documents in the possession of Mr
and Mrs John O'Connor and Commandant and Mrs Jack O'Brien.

National Archives, Dublin
Government minutes
Department of the Taoiseach records
Department of Industry and Commerce records
Department of Communications records

Public Records Office, London
Cabinet records
Dominion Office records (especially DO130)

Public Records Office, Northern Ireland
Cabinet papers

Military Archives, Dublin
Miscellaneous papers

National Library of Ireland
Arnold Papers
Gallagher Papers

Department of Industry and Commerce archives
Miscellaneous department records, including some records of departmental conferences, 1951–54 and 1957–59.

UCD Archives
MacEntee Papers
FitzGerald Papers
Andrews Papers

Fianna Fáil Archives
Parliamentary party minutes, 1927–66
National Executive minutes, 1927–66
Election accounts
Organisation Committee minutes, 1954–57
Ardfheis reports, 1927–66

Franciscan Archives, Killiney, Co. Dublin
De Valera Papers

Armagh Diocesan Archives
D'Alton Papers

Colm Barnes papers
Notes of conversations with Seán Lemass and his contemporaries, together with
miscellaneous papers and manuscripts in the possession of Colm Barnes.

Skinner papers
Liam Skinner, 'Man of the Moment' (1961): an unpublished biography of Seán
    Lemass.

O'Halpin papers, UCD
Miscellaneous papers and transcripts, mostly relating to the early years of the state-
    sponsored companies.

Other archival sources

Dublin Metropolitan Archives
Dwight D. Eisenhower Library, Abilene, Kansas
John F. Kennedy Library, Boston
Lyndon Baines Johnson Memorial Library, Austin, Texas
Richard Nixon Library, California

Official publications

Dáil Debates
Seanad Debates
Report of the Committee on the Constitution (Pr. 9817), Dublin: Stationery Office
    1967

Newspapers

Belfast Telegraph
Evening Mail
Irish Independent
Irish Press
Irish Times
Irish Times Pictorial Weekly
News Letter (Belfast)
Northern Whig (Belfast)
Sunday Independent
Sunday Press
Sunday Review
(Some smaller newspapers and journals are referred to individually in footnotes.)

Select bibliography

Aalen, F., 'Health and housing in Dublin c. 1850–1921' in F. Aalen and Kevin
    Whelan (eds.), *Dublin City and County: From Prehistory to Present,* Dublin:
    Geography Publications 1992.
Allen, Kieran, 'Fianna Fáil and the Irish Labour Movement, 1926–82: From
    Populism to Corporatism', PhD thesis, University of Dublin, 1992.
Andrews, C. S., *Dublin Made Me,* Dublin: Mercier Press 1979.
Andrews, C. S., *Man of No Property,* Dublin: Mercier Press 1982.
Andrews, C. S., 'Lemass and national progress', *Irish Press,* 19 Nov. 1983.
Baker, Susan, 'Dependency, Ideology and the Industrial policy of Fianna Fáil in
    Ireland, 1958–72', PhD thesis, European University Institute, 1987.
Bardon, Jonathan, *A History of Ulster,* Belfast, Blackstaff Press 1982.
Bew, Paul, and Patterson, Henry, *Seán Lemass and the Making of Modern Ireland,*
    1945–1966, Dublin: Gill & Macmillan 1982.

Bloomfield, Ken, *Stormont in Crisis: A Memoir,* Belfast, Blackstaff Press 1994.

Boland, Kevin, *Up Dev!,* Rathcoole: n.p. 1978.

Boland, Kevin, *The Rise and Decline of Fianna Fáil,* Cork: Mercier Press 1983.

Bonel-Elliott, Imelda, 'The role of the Duggan Report (1962) in the reform of the Irish education system', *Administration,* vol. 44, no. 3, autumn 1996.

Bowman, John, *De Valera and the Ulster Question, 1917–1973,* Oxford: Clarendon Press 1983.

Breen, Dan, *On Another Man's Wound,* Dublin: Three Candles 1936.

Breen, R., and Whelan, C., 'Social class, class origins and political partisanship in the Republic of Ireland', *European Journal of Political Research,* vol. 26 (1994), 117–33.

Broderick, Eugene, 'Irish Corporatism, 1931–39', MA thesis, University College, Cork, 1991.

Brown, Terence, *Ireland: A Social and Cultural History, 1922–79,* London: Fontana 1981.

Browne, Vincent, 'Lemass: A Profile', *Nusight,* Dec. 1969.

Browne, Vincent (with Michael Farrell), *The Magill Book of Irish Politics,* Dublin: Magill Publications 1981.

Callanan, Brian, 'Shannon Free Airport Development Company, 1957–85', PhD thesis, University of Limerick, 1995.

Campbell, Patrick, *My Life and Easy Times,* London: Blond 1967.

Carroll, Denis, *They Have Fooled You Again: Michael O'Flanagan, 1876–1942: Priest, Republican, Social Critic,* Dublin: Columba Press 1993.

Clery, Arthur, *Dublin Essays,* Dublin: Maunsel 1919.

Coogan, Tim Pat, *De Valera: Long Fellow, Long Shadow,* London: Hutchinson 1993.

Cosgrave, Dillon, *North Dublin City and Environs,* Dublin: Catholic Truth Society 1909.

Cruise O'Brien, Conor (ed.), *The Shaping of Modern Ireland,* London: Routledge and Kegan Paul 1960.

Cullen, Joan, 'Patrick J. Hogan TD, Minister for Agriculture, 1922–32', PhD thesis, Dublin City University, 1993.

Curran, Catherine, The Irish Press and Fianna Fáil', PhD thesis, Dublin City University, 1992.

Curran, Frank, *Countdown to Disaster,* Dublin: Gill & Macmillan 1979.

Daly, Mary E., *Dublin: The Deposed Capital,* Cork: Cork University Press 1984.

Daly, Mary E., *Industrial Development and Irish National Identity,* Dublin: Gill & Macmillan 1992.

Daly, Mary E., 'The economic ideals of Irish nationalism: frugal comfort or lavish austerity?', *Éire-Ireland,* vol. 29, no. 4 (1994), 77–100.

de Paor, Liam, *Divided Ulster,* London: Penguin 1970.

Devlin, Liam St John, 'Green Devlin in Hindsight', paper read to senior Irish and Northern Ireland administrators, Portrush, 29 Mar. 1988 (duplicated).

Doolin, Lelia, Dowling, Jack, and Quinn, Bob, *Sit Down and Be Counted: The Cultural Evolution of a Television Station,* Dublin: Wellington 1969.

Dunphy, Richard, *The Making of Fianna Fáil Power in Ireland, 1923–1948,* Oxford: Clarendon Press 1995.

Fanning, Ronan, *The Irish Department of Finance, 1922–58,* Dublin: Institute of Public Administration 1978.

Fanning, Ronan, *The Four-Leaved Shamrock: Electoral Politics and the National Imagination in Independent Ireland* (O'Donnell Lecture Series), Dublin: University College 1983.

Fanning, Ronan, *Independent Ireland,* Dublin: Helicon 1983.

Fanning, Ronan, 'The genesis of economic development' in John McCarthy (ed.), *Planning Ireland's Future: The Legacy of T. K. Whitaker,* Dublin: Glendale Press 1990.

Farrell, Brian, *Chairman or Chief? The Role of Taoiseach in Irish Government,* Dublin: Gill & Macmillan 1971.

Farrell, Brian, *Seán Lemass,* Dublin: Gill & Macmillan 1991.

Fisk, Robert, *In Time of War: Ireland, Ulster and the Price of Neutrality, 1939–45,* London: Deutsch 1983.

FitzGerald, Garrett, *All in a Life: an Autobiography,* Dublin: Gill & Macmillan 1991.

Foley, C., *Legion of the Rearguard: The IRA and the Modern Irish State,* London: Pluto Press 1992.

Garvin, Tom, 'Change and the political system' in Frank Litton (ed.), *Unequal Achievement,* Dublin: Institute of Public Administration 1982.

Garvin, Tom, *1922: The Birth of Irish Democracy,* Dublin: Gill & Macmillan 1996.

Geary, R., 'Irish economic development since the Treaty', *Studies,* no. 50 (Dec. 1951), 399–418.

Girvin, Brian, 'Protectionism and Economic Development in Independent Ireland, 1922–1960', PhD thesis, University College, Cork, 1986.

Girvin, Brian, *Between Two Worlds: Politics and Economy in Independent Ireland,* Dublin: Gill & Macmillan 1989.

Goldthorpe, J., and Whelan, C. (eds.), *The Development of Industrial Society in Ireland,* Oxford: Oxford University Press for the British Academy 1992.

Gorham, Maurice, *Forty Years of Irish Broadcasting,* Dublin: Talbot Press 1967.

Guiomard, Cathal, *The Irish Disease and How to Cure It: Commonsense Economics for a Competitive World,* Dublin: Oak Tree Press 1995.

Hill, Ronald, and Marsh, Michael, *Modern Irish Democracy: Essays in Honour of Basil Chubb,* Dublin: Irish Academic Press 1993.

Hobsbawm, Eric, *Age of Extremes: The Short Twentieth Century, 1914–1991,* London: Michael Joseph 1994.

Horgan, John, 'Seán Lemass: a man in a hurry' in Philip Hannon and Jackie Gallagher (eds.), *Taking the Long View: Seventy Years of Fianna Fáil,* Dublin: Blackwater Press 1996.

Hyland, Áine, and Milne, Kenneth (eds.), *Irish Educational Documents,* vol. 2, Dublin: CICE 1992.

IBEC Technical Services Corporation, *An Appraisal of Ireland's Industrial Potentials,* New York: IBEC 1952.

Industrial Development Authority, *Ireland, Your Manufacturing Base in Europe,* Dublin: IDA 1964.

Jacobsen, John Kurt, *Chasing Progress in the Irish Republic: Ideology, Democracy and Dependent Development,* Cambridge: Cambridge University Press 1994.

Johnson, David, *The Interwar Economy in Ireland,* Dublin: Economic and Social History Society of Ireland 1989.

Jones, Mary, *These Obstreperous Lassies: A History of the IWWU,* Dublin: Gill & Macmillan 1988.

Kearns, Kevin, *Dublin Tenement Life: an Oral History,* Dublin: Gill & Macmillan 1994.

Keating, Patrick, *The Formulation of Irish Foreign Policy,* Dublin: Institute of Public Administration 1973.

Kennedy, Dennis, *The Widening Gulf: Northern Attitudes to the Independent Irish State, 1919–49,* Belfast, Blackstaff Press 1988.

Kennedy, Kieran, Giblin, Thomas, and McHugh, Deirdre, *Economic Development of Ireland in the Twentieth Century*, London: Routledge 1988.

Kenny, Ivor, *Government and Enterprise in Ireland*, Dublin: Gill & Macmillan 1984.

Keogh, Dermot, *The Vatican, the Bishops and Irish Politics, 1919–39*, Cambridge: Cambridge University Press 1986.

Keogh, Dermot, *Twentieth-Century Ireland: Nation and State*, Dublin: Gill & Macmillan 1994.

Keogh, Dermot, 'Ireland and 'emergency culture' between Civil War and normalcy, 1922–61', *Ireland: A Journal of History and Society*, vol. 1, no. 1 (1995).

Lee, J. J., *The Modernisation of Irish Society, 1848–1918*, Dublin: Gill & Macmillan 1973.

Lee, Joseph, 'Lemass and his two partnerships', *Irish Times*, 19 May 1976.

Lee, J. J., *Ireland, 1945–1970*, Dublin: Gill & Macmillan 1979.

Lee, J. J. (with Gearóid Ó Tuathaigh), *The Age of de Valera*, Dublin: Ward River Press 1982.

Lee, J. J., *Ireland, 1912–1985: Politics and Society*, Cambridge: Cambridge University Press 1989.

Lee, Joseph, 'Party baffles theorists who want voters to punish inconsistency', *Irish Times*, 24 May 1996.

Lemass, Seán, 'Time for action', *World Justice*, vol. 2 (Mar. 1961), 324–30.

Lemass, Seán, 'The organisation behind the Economic Programme', *Administration*, vol. 9, no. 1 (1961), 3–10.

Lemass, Seán, 'The European Economic Community: (1) The task of reorganisation', *Administration*, vol. 10, no. 1 (1962), 3–6.

Lemass, Seán, 'I remember 1916', *Studies*, spring 1966, 7–9.

Longford, Earl of, and O'Neill, T. P., *Éamon de Valera*, London: Hutchinson 1970.

McCague, Eugene, *Arthur Cox, 1891–1965*, Dublin: Gill & Macmillan 1994.

McCarthy, Charles, *The Decade of Upheaval: Irish Trade Unions in the 1960s*, Dublin: Institute of Public Administration 1973.

McCarthy, Charles, *Trade Unions in Ireland, 1894–1960*, Dublin: Institute of Public Administration 1977.

McCarthy, John, 'Ireland's turnaround: Whitaker and the 1958 Plan for Economic Development' in John McCarthy (ed.), *Planning Ireland's Future: The Legacy of T. K. Whitaker*, Dublin: Glendale Press 1990.

Mac Eoin, Uinseann, *Survivors*, Dublin: Argenta Press 1980.

McLellan, Martha Synon, 'Lemass and Economic Development', MSA thesis, Trinity College, Dublin, 1970.

Meenan, James, 'Economic policy and population in Éire: Ireland and the Commonwealth' (Irish paper no. 1), prepared for British Commonwealth Relations Conference, London, 1938.

Meenan, James, *The Irish Economy since 1922*, Liverpool: Liverpool University Press 1970.

Munck, Ronnie, *The Irish Economy: Results and Prospects*, London: Pluto Press 1993.

Murphy, Gary, 'The Politics of Economic Realignment, 1948–1964', PhD thesis, Dublin City University, 1996.

Murphy, J. A., and O'Carroll, J. (eds.), *De Valera and His Times*, Cork: Cork University Press 1983.

National Industrial and Economic Council, *Report on Economic Situation* (Pr. 8552), Dublin: Stationery Office 1965.

Nowlan, Kevin B., and Williams, T. Desmond (eds.), *Ireland in the War Years and After*, Dublin: Gill & Macmillan 1969.

O'Brien, Joseph, *'Dear Dirty Dublin': A City in Distress, 1899–1916,* Berkeley, University of California Press 1982.

Ó Broin, Leon, *No Man's Man: A Biographical Memoir of Joseph Brennan,* Dublin: Institute of Public Administration 1982.

Ó Broin, Leon, *Just Like Yesterday: an Autobiography,* Dublin: Gill & Macmillan 1985.

Ó Cearbhaill, Tadhg, 'Seán Lemass', *Léargas,* vol. 3, no. 9 (June–July 1971).

Ó Cearbhaill, Tadhg, 'The Civil Service in Its Place', Seán Lemass memorial lecture, University of Exeter, 18 Nov. 1982 (duplicated).

Ó Gráda, Cormac, *Ireland: A New Economic History, 1780–1939,* Oxford: Clarendon Press 1994.

Ó Gráda, Cormac, and O'Rourke, Kevin, *Irish Economic Growth, 1945–88,* London: Centre for Economic Policy Research 1994.

O'Hagan, John (ed.), *The Economy of Ireland: Policy and Performance,* Dublin: Irish Management Institute 1987.

O'Leary, Cornelius, *Irish Elections, 1918–1977: Parties, Voters and Proportional Representation,* Dublin: Gill & Macmillan 1979.

O'Malley, Eoin, *Industry and Economic Development: the Challenge for the Latecomer,* Dublin: Gill & Macmillan 1989.

O'Neill, T. P., and Longford, Earl of, *Éamon de Valera,* London: Hutchinson 1970.

O'Shea, Finbarr, 'Government and Trade Unions in Ireland, 1939–46: The Formulation of Trade Union Legislation', MA thesis, University College, Cork, 1988.

O'Sullivan, Michael, *Seán Lemass,* Dublin: Blackwater Press 1994.

Paul, Brother, 'Talking to the Taoiseach', *The Word,* Jan. and Feb. 1966.

Reynolds, Brian, 'The Formation and Development of Fianna Fáil, 1926–1932', PhD thesis, University of Dublin, 1976.

Roche, Desmond, 'John Leydon', *Administration,* vol. 27, no. 3 (1979), 233–54.

Rolo, P., *Britain and the Briand Plan: The Common Market that Never Was,* Keele: University of Keele Press 1974.

Ryan, Raymund, *The Office of Public Works,* Dublin: OPW 1992.

Savage, Robert, *Irish Television: The Political and Social Origins,* Cork, Cork University Press 1996.

Share, Bernard, *The Flight of the 'Iolar': The Aer Lingus Experience, 1936–1986,* Dublin: Gill & Macmillan 1986.

Skinner, Liam, *Politicians by Accident,* Dublin: Metropolitan Publishing 1946.

Sturgess, Gary, and Chubb, Philip, *Judging the World: Law and Politics in the World's Leading Courts,* London: Butterworth 1988.

Tobin, Fergal, *The Best of Decades: Ireland in the 1960s,* Dublin: Gill & Macmillan 1996.

Travers, Pauric, *Éamon de Valera,* Dublin: Historical Association of Ireland 1994.

Walker, Brian (ed.), *Parliamentary Election Results in Ireland, 1918–92,* Dublin: Royal Irish Academy 1992.

Wallace, Martin, *Guns and Drums: Revolution in Ulster,* London: Geoffrey Chapman 1970.

Whitaker, T. K., 'Merits and problems of planning', *Administration,* vol. 12, no. 4 (1964), 282–93.

Whitaker, T. K., 'From protection to free trade: the Irish experience', *Administration,* winter 1973, 405–23.

Whyte, John, *Church and State in Modern Ireland,* Dublin: Gill & Macmillan 1980.

Younger, Calton, *Ireland's Civil War,* London: Fontana 1970.

Index